WORLD HISTORY

THE HUMAN EXPERIENCE

NATIONAL GEOGRAPHIC SOCIETY

Mounir A. Farah
Andrea Berens Karls

GLENCOE

McGraw-Hill

New York, New York   Columbus, Ohio   Mission Hills, California   Peoria, Illinois

About the Authors

The **National Geographic Society**, founded in 1888 for the increase and diffusion of geographic knowledge, is the world's largest nonprofit scientific and educational organization. Since its earliest days, the Society has used sophisticated communication technologies and rich historical and archival resources to convey knowledge to a worldwide membership. The Educational Media Division supports the Society's mission by developing innovative educational programs—ranging from traditional print materials to multimedia programs including CD-ROMs, videodiscs, and software.

Mounir A. Farah, Ph.D. is a research historian and Associate Director of the Middle East Studies Program at the University of Arkansas, Fayetteville. Dr. Farah taught history and social science at New York University and Western Connecticut State University and has lectured at many teachers' conferences and workshops in the United States and abroad. He was a consultant to the Ministry of Education in Jordan and served as Coordinator of Social Studies in the Monroe, Connecticut public schools. Named Outstanding History Scholar-Teacher in New England and a recipient of the Connecticut Social Studies Annual Award, Dr. Farah is a past president of the Connecticut Council for the Social Studies and of the Middle East Outreach Council and a board member of the Arkansas Council for Social Studies. He is a contributing writer to several books and has authored numerous articles and reviews. Dr. Farah also is coauthor of Glencoe's *Global Insights.*

Andrea Berens Karls is an educator and coauthor of Glencoe's *Global Insights.* Educated at Wellesley College and Harvard University, she has taught at both the elementary and secondary levels. Ms. Karls was formerly Program Associate at Global Perspectives in Education, Inc., where she edited and wrote curriculum materials and worked with teachers. She is a member of the National Council for the Social Studies and the American Historical Association.

About the Cover

The temple of Amon-Ra—ancient Egypt's most important god—was the major building in Thebes, a city of Egypt. Between the 1300s B.C. and the 1100s B.C. Egyptian builders constructed the temple at the site of the present-day city of Luxor.

The part of the temple shown is an outer court, decorated with colossal images of the great Egyptian pharaoh Ramses II. A pair of granite obelisks covered with hieroglyphics also graced the outer court. One obelisk (shown in the cover photo) still stands. The other was removed to the Place de la Concorde in Paris, France, in 1831.

Glencoe/McGraw-Hill

A Division of The McGraw-Hill Companies

Copyright © 1997 by The McGraw-Hill Companies, Inc. All rights reserved. Except as permitted under the United States Copyright Act, no part of this publication may be reproduced in a database or retrieval system, without prior written permission from the publisher.

Design and Production: DECODE, Inc.
Cover photograph: Temple of Amon-Ra, Luxor, Egypt; Mark D. Phillips/Photo Researchers, Inc.

Send all inquiries to:
Glencoe/McGraw-Hill, 936 Eastwind Drive, Westerville, Ohio 43081

ISBN 0-02-823219-4 (Student Edition) ISBN 0-02-823387-5 (Teacher's Wraparound Edition)

Printed in the United States of America.
4 5 6 7 8 9 10 071/043 01 00 99 98 97

Academic Consultants

Stephen Chicoine
Author/Lecturer, World Affairs
Vice President
Bechtel Energy Resources Corporation
Houston, Texas

Paula Fredricksen, Ph.D.
Aurelio Professor of Scripture
Boston University
Boston, Massachusetts

Madhulika S. Khandelwal, Ph.D.
Research Historian
Asian/American Center
Queens College
City University of New York
New York City , New York

George Demetrius Knysh, Ph.D.
Associate Professor of Political Studies
University of Manitoba
Winnipeg, Manitoba
Canada

Frances Malino, Ph.D.
Professor of History
Wellesley College
Wellesley, Massachusetts

Ali A. Mazuri, Ph.D.
Professor of History
State University of New York
Binghamton, New York

Jesus Mendez, Ph.D.
Associate Professor of History
Barry University
Miami Shores, Florida

Brendan Nagle, Ph.D.
Associate Professor
University of Southern California
Los Angeles, California

Al Naklowycz, Ph.D.
President, Ukrainian-American Academic
     Association of California
Carmichael, California

Donald Niewyk, Ph.D.
Professor of History
Southern Methodist University
Dallas, Texas

Boniface Obichere, Ph.D.
Professor of History
University of California
Los Angeles, California

Sayyid M. Syeed, Ph.D.
Secretary General
The Islamic Society of North America
Plainfield, Indiana

Frank De Varona
Region 1 Superintendent
Dade County Public Schools
Hialeah, Florida

Teacher Reviewers

Christine Allen
North Salem High School
Salem, Oregon

Mattie Collins
Pine Bluff High School
Pine Bluff, Arkansas

Louis Gallo
West High School
Knoxville, Tennessee

Mark Heinig
Reitz Memorial High School
Evansville, Indiana

Paul Horton
Williamsville East High School
East Amherst, New York

Jim Lloyd
Department Chair, History-Social Science
Bullard High School
Fresno, California

Patti Long
Forrest City High School
Forrest City, Arkansas

Willis M. Overton III
Warren Central High School
Indianapolis, Indiana

TABLE OF CONTENTS

TABLE OF CONTENTS

TABLE OF CONTENTS

TABLE OF CONTENTS

Images *of the* Times

CONNECTIONS To...

Geography

Economics

Science and Technology

The Arts

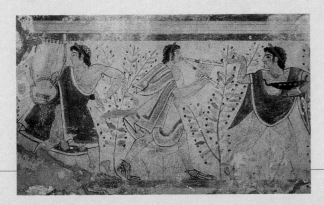

TABLE OF CONTENTS

Footnotes to History

SKILLS

Social Studies Skills

Critical Thinking Skills

Study and Writing Skills

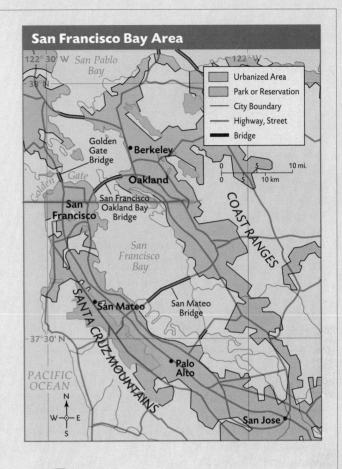

San Francisco Bay Area

Maps

TABLE OF CONTENTS

Babylon c. 500s B.C.

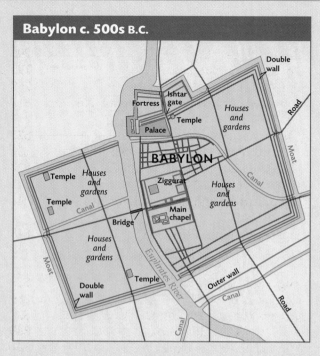

Maps (continued)

The Rise of Moscow

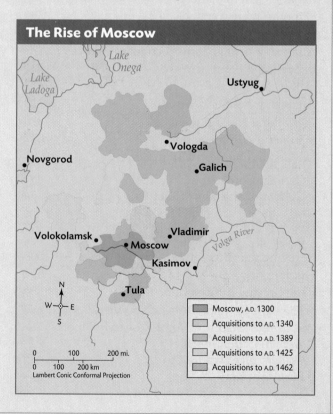

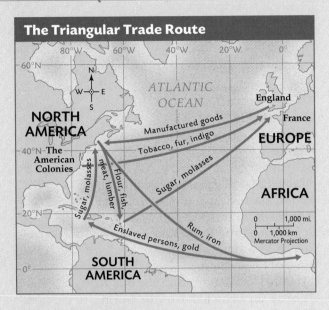

The Triangular Trade Route

The Allies Regain Europe

Population Density of Africa

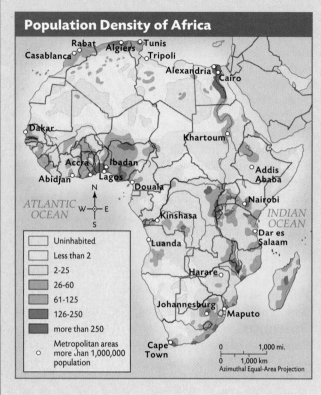

ATLANTIC
OCEAN

INDIAN
OCEAN

Rabat
Casablanca
Algiers
Tunis
Tripoli
Alexandria
Cairo
Dakar
Khartoum
Accra
Ibadan
Abidjan
Lagos
Addis
Ababa
Douala
Nairobi
Kinshasa
Dar es
Salaam
Luanda
Harare
Johannesburg
Maputo
Cape
Town

Uninhabited
Less than 2
2-25
26-60
61-125
126-250
more than 250

o   Metropolitan areas
    more than 1,000,000
    population

0   1,000 mi.
0   1,000 km
Azimuthal Equal-Area Projection

Charts, Graphs, and Diagrams

Maps (continued)

Major Oil Producers in the Middle East

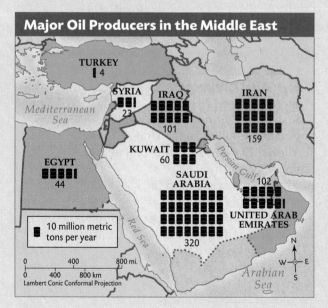

TURKEY
4
SYRIA
23
IRAQ
101
IRAN
159
Mediterranean
Sea
KUWAIT
60
EGYPT
44
SAUDI
ARABIA
320
102
UNITED ARAB
EMIRATES
Persian Gulf
Red Sea
Arabian
Sea

10 million metric
tons per year

0   400   800 mi.
0   400   800 km
Lambert Conic Conformal Projection

Reference Atlas

Atlas Key

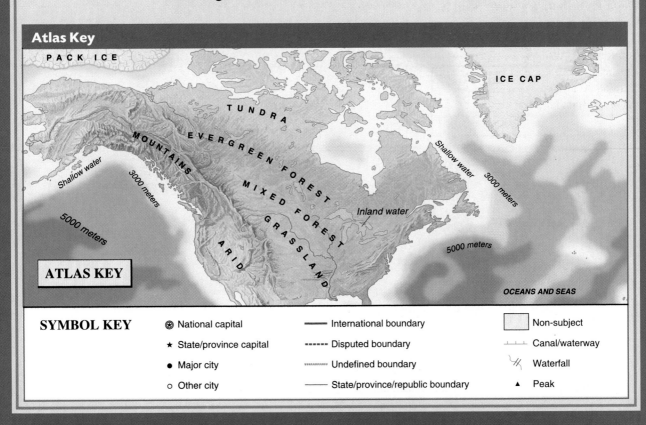

PACK ICE

ICE CAP

TUNDRA

EVERGREEN FOREST

MOUNTAINS

Shallow water

Shallow water

3000 meters

3000 meters

MIXED FOREST

Inland water

5000 meters

GRASSLAND

ARID

5000 meters

ATLAS KEY

OCEANS AND SEAS

SYMBOL KEY

- ⊛ National capital
- ★ State/province capital
- ● Major city
- ○ Other city

- —— International boundary
- ----- Disputed boundary
- .... Undefined boundary
- —— State/province/republic boundary

- ☐ Non-subject
- ⊥⊥ Canal/waterway
- ⅃ Waterfall
- ▲ Peak

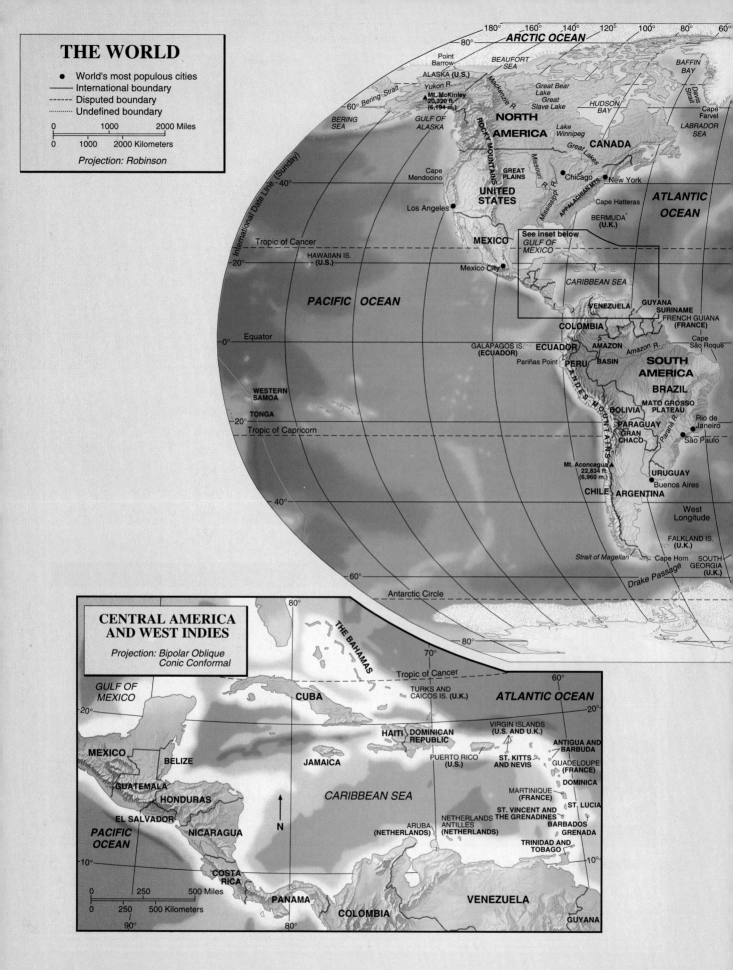

THE WORLD

- ● World's most populous cities
- —— International boundary
- ------ Disputed boundary
- ········· Undefined boundary

0   1000   2000 Miles
0   1000   2000 Kilometers

Projection: Robinson

CENTRAL AMERICA AND WEST INDIES

Projection: Bipolar Oblique Conic Conformal

0   250   500 Miles
0   250   500 Kilometers

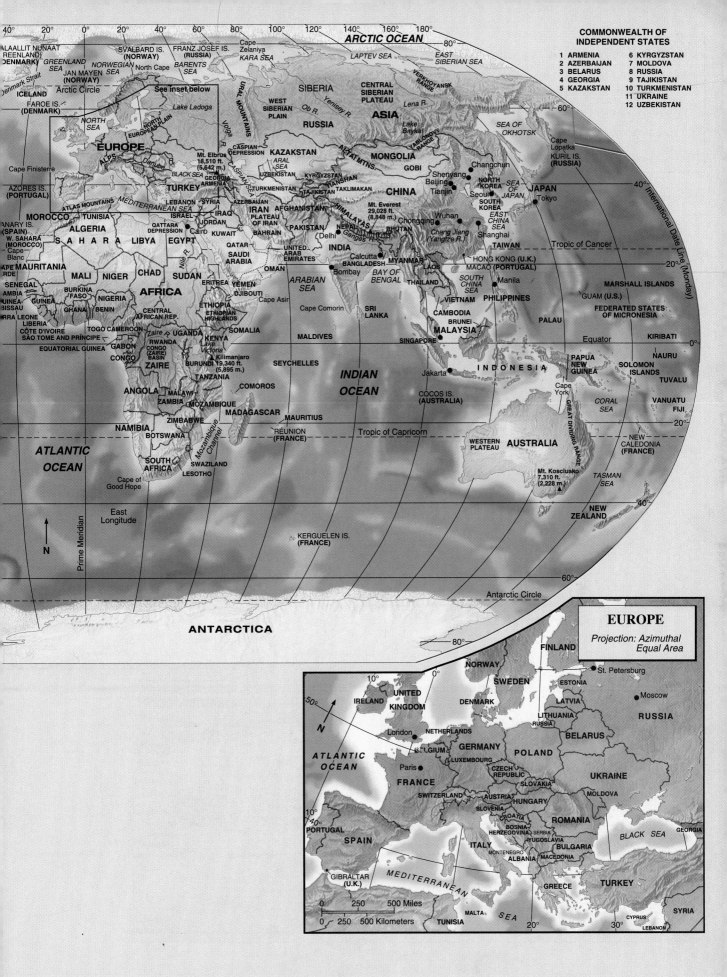

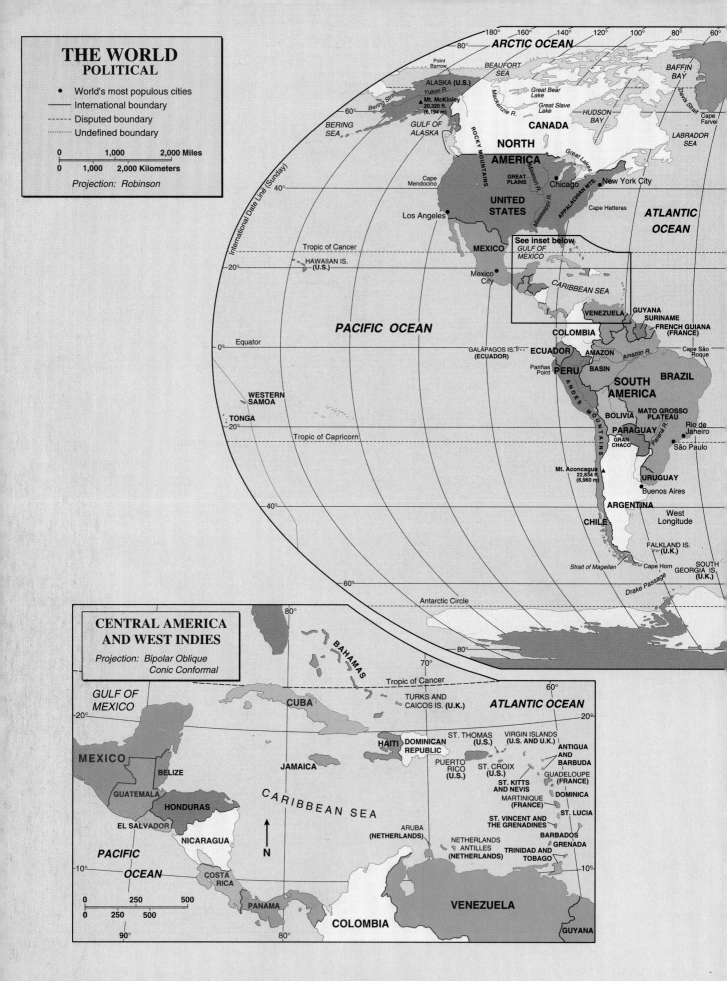

THE WORLD
POLITICAL

- • World's most populous cities
- —— International boundary
- ---- Disputed boundary
- ········ Undefined boundary

0   1,000   2,000 Miles
0   1,000   2,000 Kilometers

Projection: Robinson

ARCTIC OCEAN

Point Barrow

BEAUFORT SEA

BAFFIN BAY

ALASKA (U.S.)
Yukon R.
Mt. McKinley
20,320 ft.
(6,194 m)

Bering Strait

BERING SEA

GULF OF ALASKA

Great Bear Lake

Mackenzie R.

Great Slave Lake

HUDSON BAY

Davis Strait

Cape Farvel

LABRADOR SEA

CANADA

NORTH AMERICA

ROCKY MOUNTAINS

Cape Mendocino

GREAT PLAINS

Missouri R.

Great Lakes

• Chicago

Mississippi R.

APPALACHIAN MTS.

• New York City

UNITED STATES

Cape Hatteras

ATLANTIC OCEAN

Los Angeles •

MEXICO

See inset below
GULF OF MEXICO

Tropic of Cancer

HAWAIIAN IS.
(U.S.)

Mexico City •

CARIBBEAN SEA

PACIFIC OCEAN

Equator

GALÁPAGOS IS.
(ECUADOR)

VENEZUELA

GUYANA
SURINAME
FRENCH GUIANA
(FRANCE)

COLOMBIA

ECUADOR

AMAZON

Amazon R.

Cape São Roque

Pariñas Point

PERU

BASIN

SOUTH AMERICA

BRAZIL

WESTERN SAMOA

ANDES MOUNTAINS

BOLIVIA

MATO GROSSO PLATEAU

TONGA

Tropic of Capricorn

PARAGUAY

GRAN CHACO

Paraná R.

Rio de Janeiro

São Paulo

Mt. Aconcagua
22,834 ft.
(6,960 m)

URUGUAY

Buenos Aires

ARGENTINA

West Longitude

CHILE

FALKLAND IS.
(U.K.)

Strait of Magellan

Cape Horn

SOUTH GEORGIA IS.
(U.K.)

Drake Passage

Antarctic Circle

International Date Line (Sunday)

CENTRAL AMERICA
AND WEST INDIES

*Projection: Bipolar Oblique
Conic Conformal*

GULF OF MEXICO

BAHAMAS

CUBA

TURKS AND CAICOS IS. (U.K.)

Tropic of Cancer

ATLANTIC OCEAN

MEXICO

BELIZE

GUATEMALA

HONDURAS

EL SALVADOR

NICARAGUA

JAMAICA

HAITI

DOMINICAN REPUBLIC

ST. THOMAS (U.S.)

VIRGIN ISLANDS
(U.S. AND U.K.)

PUERTO RICO
(U.S.)

ST. CROIX
(U.S.)

ANTIGUA AND BARBUDA

GUADELOUPE
(FRANCE)

ST. KITTS AND NEVIS

DOMINICA

MARTINIQUE
(FRANCE)

ST. LUCIA

CARIBBEAN SEA

N

ST. VINCENT AND THE GRENADINES

BARBADOS

GRENADA

ARUBA
(NETHERLANDS)

NETHERLANDS ANTILLES
(NETHERLANDS)

TRINIDAD AND TOBAGO

PACIFIC OCEAN

COSTA RICA

PANAMA

0   250   500
0   250   500

VENEZUELA

COLOMBIA

GUYANA

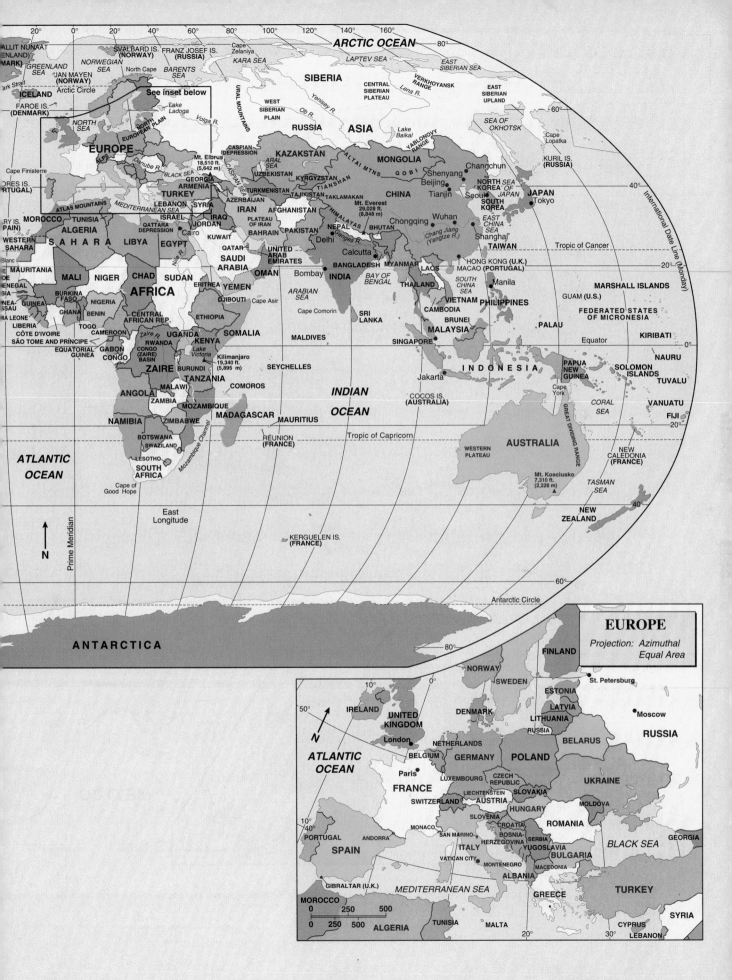

CANADA

MAINE
Moosehead Lake
Bangor
Mt. Washington 6,288 ft. (1,905 m.)
Lake Champlain
Augusta
Lewiston
Portland
Burlington
Montpelier
N.H.
VT.
Concord
Manchester
Utica
Albany
Syracuse
Springfield
Worcester
Boston
MASS.
Hartford
Providence
R.I.
CONN.
New Haven
Yonkers
New York
Newark
N.J.
Trenton
Camden
Philadelphia
Wilmington
Dover
MD.
Baltimore
Annapolis
Washington
D.C.
DELAWARE BAY
DEL.

St. Lawrence River
Lake Superior
Lake Huron
MICHIGAN
Lake Michigan
ADIRONDACK MTNS.
Hudson R.
Lake Ontario
Rochester
Buffalo
Niagara Falls
Lake Erie
Erie
Binghamton
Susquehanna River
Allentown
PENNSYLVANIA
Harrisburg
Pittsburgh
Wheeling

MINNESOTA
Duluth
Red Lake
Lake of the Woods
WISCONSIN
Green Bay
Appleton
Minneapolis
St. Paul
Mississippi River
Rochester
Madison
Milwaukee
Racine
Grand Rapids
Flint
Lansing
Detroit
Ann Arbor
Rockford
Chicago
South Bend
Toledo
Cleveland
Akron
Canton
Youngstown
OHIO
Columbus
Dayton
Parkersburg
WEST VIRGINIA
Charleston
Huntington

Sioux City
IOWA
Cedar Rapids
Dubuque
Davenport
Des Moines
Omaha
Council Bluffs
Lincoln
ILLINOIS
Aurora
Joliet
Gary
Hammond
Fort Wayne
Peoria
CENTRAL LOWLAND
Springfield
Decatur
INDIANA
Muncie
Indianapolis
Cincinnati
Ohio River

Kansas City
Topeka
Lawrence
Kansas City
Independence
Jefferson City
Harry S. Truman Res.
St. Louis
East St. Louis
Evansville
Louisville
Frankfort
Lexington
KENTUCKY
Owensboro
MISSOURI
Springfield
OZARK PLATEAU
Wabash R.
Nashville
Knoxville
PLATEAU
APPALACHIAN MOUNTAINS
Mt. Mitchell 6,684 ft. (2,037 m.)
Charlotte
VIRGINIA
Richmond
Newport News
Roanoke
Norfolk
CHESAPEAKE BAY
Arlington
Roanoke River
ATLANTIC OCEAN
Cape Hatteras
Greensboro
Winston-Salem
Durham
Raleigh
NORTH CAROLINA

Tulsa
R.S. Kerr Res.
ARKANSAS
Fort Smith
Little Rock
North Little Rock
Hot Springs
Pine Bluff
Memphis
Mississippi River
TENNESSEE
Chattanooga
Huntsville
Cumberland River
Tennessee R.
CUMBERLAND
Spartanburg
Greenville
Columbia
SOUTH CAROLINA
Charleston

Lake Eufaula
Lake Texoma
Dallas
Shreveport
LOUISIANA
Toledo Bend Res.
Hattiesburg
MISSISSIPPI
Meridian
Jackson
Birmingham
Tuscaloosa
ALABAMA
Montgomery
Alabama R.
Columbus
Albany
Chattahoochee R.
Atlanta
Augusta
GEORGIA
Macon
Savannah
COASTAL PLAIN

Sam Rayburn Reservoir
Houston
Lake Charles
Lafayette
Baton Rouge
New Orleans
Lake Pontchartrain
Biloxi
Mobile
Pensacola
Greenville
Tallahassee
FLORIDA
Jacksonville

GULF OF MEXICO

N

Orlando
Cape Canaveral
Tampa
St. Petersburg
Lake Okeechobee
Palm Beach
Miami Beach
Miami
Cape Sable
Key West
Straits of Florida

THE BAHAMAS

CUBA

UNITED STATES
⊛ National capital
★ State capital
● Major city
━ International boundary
─ State boundary

0   150   300 Miles
0   150   300 Kilometers

Projection: Albers Equal Area

95° 90° 85° 80° 75° 50° 70° 65°
45°
65°
40°
35°
30°
25°
70°

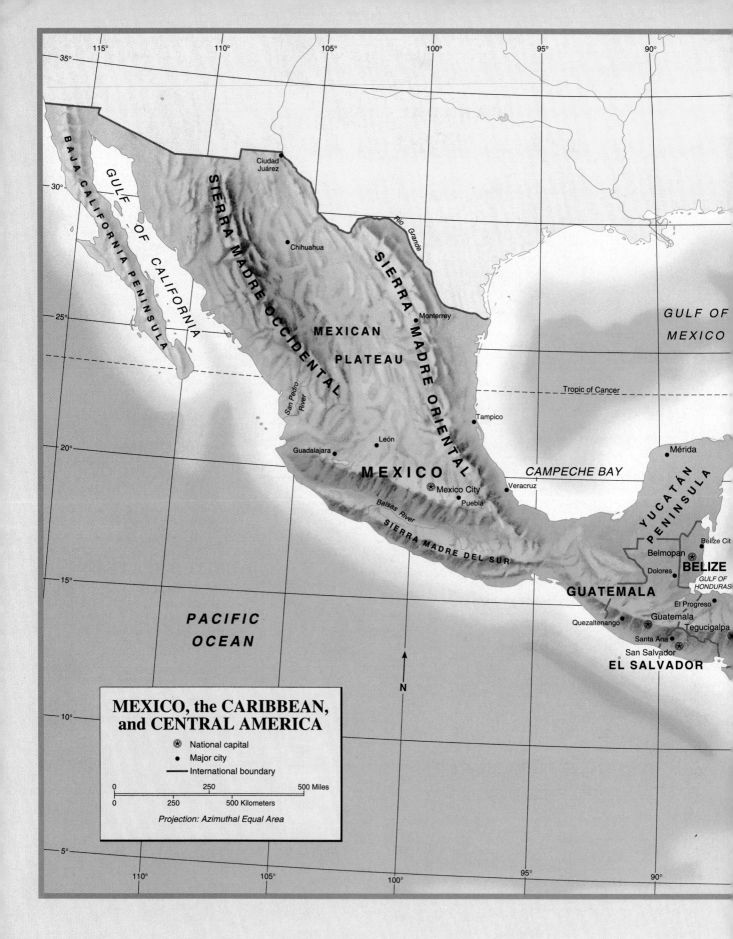

35°

115°   110°   105°   100°   95°   90°

30°

BAJA CALIFORNIA PENINSULA

GULF OF CALIFORNIA

Ciudad Juárez

• Chihuahua

SIERRA MADRE OCCIDENTAL

Rio Grande

SIERRA MADRE ORIENTAL

25°

MEXICAN

PLATEAU

• Monterrey

GULF OF MEXICO

Tropic of Cancer

San Pedro River

• Tampico

20°

• León

Guadalajara •

MEXICO

⊛ Mexico City
• Puebla

Veracruz •

CAMPECHE BAY

• Mérida

YUCATÁN PENINSULA

Balsas River

SIERRA MADRE DEL SUR

Belize Cit •

Belmopan ⊛

Dolores •

BELIZE

GULF OF HONDURAS

15°

GUATEMALA

El Progreso •

*PACIFIC
OCEAN*

Quezaltenango •

Guatemala ⊛
Tegucigalpa •

Santa Ana •
San Salvador ⊛

EL SALVADOR

↑
N

10°

MEXICO, the CARIBBEAN, and CENTRAL AMERICA

⊛ National capital

• Major city

— International boundary

| 0 | 250 | 500 Miles |
| 0 | 250 | 500 Kilometers |

Projection: Azimuthal Equal Area

5°

110°   105°   100°   95°   90°

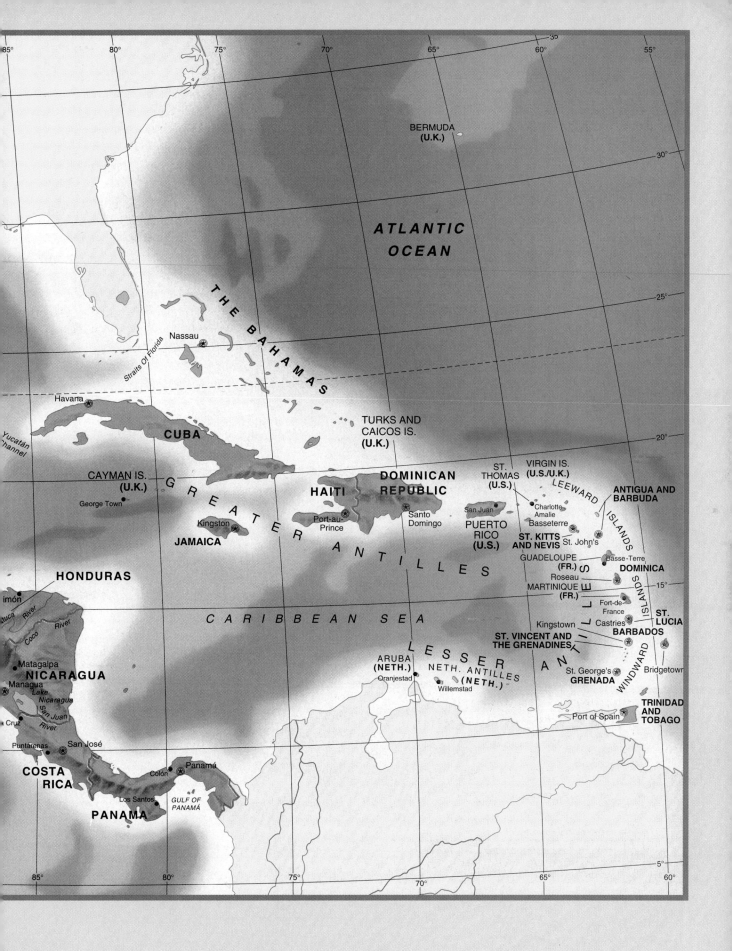

ATLANTIC
OCEAN

35°

30°

BERMUDA
(U.K.)

25°

THE BAHAMAS

Nassau

Straits Of Florida

Havana

CUBA

TURKS AND
CAICOS IS.
(U.K.)

20°

Yucatán
Channel

CAYMAN IS.
(U.K.)

George Town

G R E A T E R

A N T I L L E S

HAITI

DOMINICAN
REPUBLIC

Port-au-
Prince

Santo
Domingo

San Juan

PUERTO
RICO
(U.S.)

ST.
THOMAS
(U.S.)

VIRGIN IS.
(U.S./U.K.)

LEEWARD

ISLANDS

ANTIGUA AND
BARBUDA

Charlotte
Amalie
Basseterre

ST. KITTS
AND NEVIS

St. John's

Kingston

JAMAICA

HONDURAS

imón

tuca

Coco

River

River

CARIBBEAN SEA

GUADELOUPE
(FR.)

Basse-Terre

DOMINICA

Roseau

MARTINIQUE
(FR.)

15°

Fort-de-
France

ST.
LUCIA

Castries

BARBADOS

Kingstown

ST. VINCENT AND
THE GRENADINES

Bridgetown

L E S S E R

A N T I L L E S

W I N D W A R D

I S L A N D S

Matagalpa

NICARAGUA

Managua

Lake
Nicaragua

San Juan

River

Cruz

ARUBA
(NETH.)

Oranjestad

NETH. ANTILLES
(NETH.)

Willemstad

St. George's

GRENADA

TRINIDAD
AND
TOBAGO

Port of Spain

Puntarenas

San José

COSTA
RICA

Colón

Panamá

Los Santos

GULF OF
PANAMÁ

PANAMA

5°

85° 80° 75° 70° 65° 60°

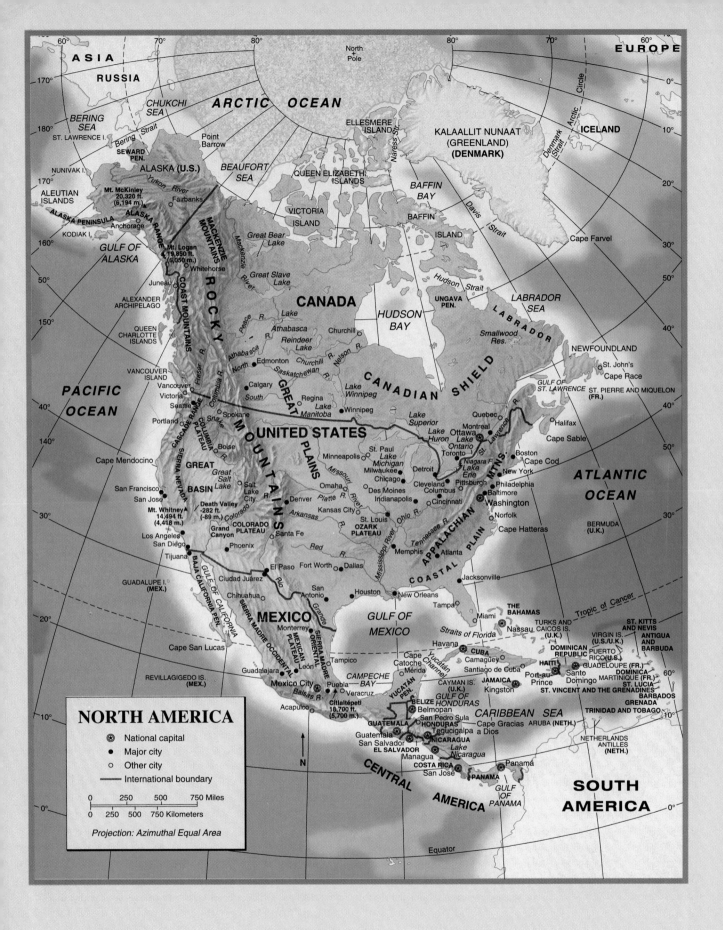

NORTH AMERICA

- ⊛ National capital
- ● Major city
- ○ Other city
- — International boundary

| 0 | 250 | 500 | 750 Miles |
| 0 | 250 | 500 | 750 Kilometers |

Projection: Azimuthal Equal Area

SOUTH AMERICA

⊚ National capital
• Major city
○ Other city
— International boundary

| 0 | 250 | 500 Miles |
| 0 | 250 | 500 Kilometers |

Projection: Azimuthal Equal Area

EUROPE

- ⊛ National capital
- ● Major city
- ○ Other city
- ▬ International boundary
- ▬ Republic boundary
- ┤├ Canal

| 0 | 100 | 200 | 300 Miles |
| 0 | 100 | 200 | 300 Kilometers |

Projection: Azimuthal Equal Area

ICELAND

Reykjavik

Arctic Circle

NORWEGIAN SEA

FAROE IS. (DEN.)

SHETLAND IS. (U.K.)

NORWAY

Trondheim

Goldhöpiggen 8,097 ft. (2,468 m.)

SCANDINAVIAN HIGHLANDS

GULF OF BOTH

SWEDEN

Bergen

Oslo

Åland

Uppsala

Lake Vänem

Stockholm

HIIUMAA SAAREMAA GOTLAND I.

Lake Vättern

ÖLAND I.

BALTIC SEA

Göteborg

Skagerrak

Kattegat

JUTLAND

Copenhagen

DENMARK

Odense

Malmö

BORNHOLM I.

Gdańsk

RUSE

NORTH SEA

OUTER HEBRIDES IS.

Cape Wrath

ORKNEY ISLANDS

SCOTLAND

N

Glasgow

Edinburgh

NORTHERN IRELAND (U.K.)

Belfast

IRELAND

Dublin

Cork

Cape Clear

ISLE OF MAN

IRISH SEA

PENNINE RANGE

Manchester

Leeds

Liverpool

Sheffield

UNITED KINGDOM

ENGLAND

WALES

Cardiff

Birmingham

Bristol

London

St. George's Channel

Kiel Canal

Hamburg

Rostock

Szczecin

POLAND

Bremen

Elbe R.

Berlin

Magdeburg

Poznań

Warsa

Lo

NETHERLANDS

Amsterdam

The Hague

Rotterdam

Mittelland Canal

Hannover

Leipzig

Dresden

Wrocław

ENGLISH Channel

Strait of Dover

GUERNSEY I. (U.K.)

JERSEY I. (U.K.)

BRETON PEN.

Le Havre

Antwerp

BELGIUM

Brussels

Liège

Essen

Dortmund

Cologne

GERMANY

Chemnitz

LUXEMBOURG

Prague

CZECH REPUBLIC

Brno

Ostrava

Kat

SLOVA

ATLANTIC OCEAN

Seine River

Paris

Marne R.

Luxembourg

Frankfurt

Marne-Rhine Canal

Bonn

Nantes

Loire

Stuttgart

Strasbourg

Rhine R.

Danube

Munich

Bratislava

Vienna

Misk

FRANCE

CENTRAL MASSIF

Bordeaux

Lyon

Lausanne

Geneva

Bern

SWITZERLAND

L. Geneva

ALPS

Zürich

Bodensee

LIECHTENSTEIN

Vaduz

Innsbruck

Salzburg

Linz

AUSTRIA

Graz

HUNGARY

Budapest

L. Balaton

Pécs

Tisza

Cape Finisterre

BAY OF BISCAY

CANTABRIAN MTNS.

Bilbao

Garonne R.

Toulouse

Midi Canal

PYRENEES

Mt. Blanc 15,771 ft. (4,807 m.)

Mt. Rosa 12,203 ft. (4,634 m.)

Rhône R.

Milan

PO VALLEY

Po R.

Turin

Genoa

Venice

Bologna

Ljubljana

SLOVENIA

Zagreb

CROATIA

Sava R.

Novi Sa

Belgrade

DINARIC ALPS

PORTUGAL

Porto

Duero River

Valladolid

Zaragoza

Ebro River

Aneto Peak 11,168 ft. (3,404 m.)

Madrid

IBERIAN

Montpellier

Marseille

ANDORRA

Andorra la Vella

GULF OF LION

Nice

Monaco

MONACO

Florence

SAN MARINO

San Marino

APENNINES

ADRIATIC SEA

Split

BOSNIA-HERZEGOVINA

Saraje

MONTENE

Lisbon

Tagus

Setúbal

River

Guadiana

River

PENINSULA

SPAIN

SIERRA MORENA

Seville

Valencia

Murcia

Barcelona

BALEARIC IS. (SP.)

Palma

CORSICA (FR.)

VATICAN CITY

Rome

ITALY

SARDINIA (IT.)

Naples

Bari

MACEDON

Tirane

ALBAN

Cape St. Vincent

Granada

Málaga

Strait of Gibraltar

GIBRALTAR (U.K.)

TYRRHENIAN SEA

Cagliari

MEDITERRANEAN

Strait of Sicily

Palermo

SICILY

Catania

PANTELLERIA (IT.)

MALTA

Valletta

IONIAN SEA

KEFALLINIA

G. OF TARANTO

AFRICA

SEA

40° 60° 30° 20° 10° 70° 0° 10° 20°

30°

50°

40°

30°

Prime Meridian

10° 0° 10° 20

North Cape
30°
40°
70°
50°
BARENTS SEA
Murmansk
KOLA PENINSULA
TIMAN RIDGE
Pechora R.
60°
URAL MOUNTAINS
WHITE SEA
Arkhangel'sk
N. Dvina River
Vychegda River
Mt. Konzhakovskiy 5,147 ft. (1,569 m.)
Kama R.
ASIA
White Sea-Baltic Waterway
FINLAND
Lake Onega
Sukhona River
Perm
Tampere
Lake Saimaa
Lake Ladoga
Volga-Baltic Waterway
Rybinsk Reservoir
Kama River
Ufa
70°
Turku
Espoo
Helsinki
St. Petersburg
Kazan
Kuybyshev Reservoir
50°
GULF OF FINLAND
ESTONIA
Tallinn
Chudskoye Lake
Yaroslavl
Volga River
Nizhniy Novgorod
GULF OF RIGA
LATVIA
Riga
Volga-Baltic Waterway
Moscow
Samara
Orenburg
BALTIC PLAIN
W. Dvina
EUROPEAN PLAIN
River
River
Oka
Tula
RUSSIA
VOLGA UPLAND
Volga River
Ural River
LITHUANIA
Kaunas
Vilnius
Smolensk
CENTRAL RUSSIAN UPLAND
Don
Voronezh
Saratov
KAZAKSTAN
Minsk
Kursk
River
Volgograd Reservoir
BELARUS
Pripet River
Desna R.
DEPRESSION
Kiev
Kremenchug Reservoir
Kharkov
Volgograd
Volga River
UKRAINE
Lugansk
Tsimlyansk Reservoir
Lvov
DNEIPER UPLAND
Dnepropetrovsk
Krivoy Rog
Donetsk
Don River
Astrakhan
CARPATHIAN MTNS.
Dniester R.
Zaporozhye
Rostov
CASPIAN
Delta of the Volga
MOLDOVA
Chisinau
DNIEPER LOWLAND
Kakhovka Res.
CASPIAN SEA
Prut River
Dniep River
SEA OF AZOV
40°
Debrecen
Odessa
CRIMEA
60°
Cluj-Napoca
ROMANIA
Krasnodar
Grozny
Timisoara
Brasov
CAUCASUS MTNS.
WALLACHIA PLAIN
Bucharest
Mt. Elbrus 18,510 ft. (5,642 m.)
Danube River
BLACK SEA
SERBIA
Ruse
Nis
Varna
BULGARIA
Sofia
Plovdiv
Burgas
Skopje
Musala Peak 9,536 ft. (2,926 m.)
Bosporus
PENINSULA
TURKEY
Salonika
Dardanelles
SEA OF MARMARA
BALKAN
Larissa
AEGEAN SEA
ASIA
GREECE
Patras
Athens
Piraeus
PELOPONESE PEN.
RHODES
30°
40°
50°
CRETE (GR.)
Iraklion
30°

60° 70° 80°

10°

Arctic Circle

ARCTIC OCEAN

FRANZ JOSEF ISLANDS

0°

10°

EUROPE

BARENTS SEA

NOVAYA ZEMLYA

Cape Zelaniya

KARA SEA

BALTIC SEA

GULF OF FINLAND

Murmansk

KOLA PENINSULA

WHITE SEA

YAMAL PEN.

GYDAN PENINSULA

50°

(RUSSIA)

Lake Ladoga

Baltic-White Sea Canal

St. Petersburg

Arkhangel'sk

Kara Strait

20°

Lake Onega

Volga-Baltic Waterway

N. Dvina R.

TIMAN RIDGE

Yenisey River

Minsk

VALDAI HILLS

Rybinsk Res.

Vologda

Sukhona R.

Vychegda

River

BELARUS

Lvov

DNIEPER UPLAND

R.

Dnieper

Yaroslovl

NORTHERN HILLS

Pechora

River

U

R

A

L

Ob

Urengoy

WEST

Moscow

Ivanovo

Volga

Kiev

UKRAINE

DNIEPER LOWLAND

Tula

Ryazan'

Nizhniy Novgorod

Kamsk Res.

▲ Mt. Konzhakovskiy 5,147 ft. (1,569 m.)

SIBERIAN

MOLDOVA

Chisinau

River

Dnieper

Voronezh

Volga

Kazan

Izhevsk

R.

Perm

M

O

U

N

T

A

I

N

S

Yekaterinburg

Ob

PLAIN

Odessa

Nikolayev

Krivoy Rog

Kharkov

Kuybyshev Res.

Ul'yanovsk

Kama

R.

Vakh

Dnepropetrovsk

Don

VOLGA UPLAND

Penza

Saratov

Tol'yatti

Samara

Ufa

Chelyabinsk

River

Zaporozh'ye

30°

Donetsk

Lugansk

Mariupol

R.

Rostov

Tsimlyansk Res.

Volgograd Reservoir

Volga

Orenburg

Ural

Tobol

R.

Ishim

Irtysh

River

Omsk

L. Chany

Novosibirsk

Tomsk

Kemerovo

SEA OF AZOV

BLACK SEA

Krasnodar

CAUCASUS

MTS.

Astrakhan

CASPIAN DEPRESSION

K

Y

R

G

Y

Z

TURGAY

PLATEAU

Novosibirsk

Novokuznetsk

Barnaul

40°

▲ Mt. Elbrus 18,510 ft. (5,642 m.)

GEORGIA

Tbilisi

S

T

E

P

P

E

KAZAKSTAN

KAZAKH

Karaganda

UPLAND

Semipalatinsk

▲ Mt. Belukha 14,783 ft. (4,506 m.)

L. Zaysan

ARMENIA

Yerevan

AZERBAIJAN

AZERBAIJAN

Baku

CASPIAN SEA

ARAL SEA

Syr

BETPAK-DALA

DESERT

Lake Balkhash

L. Alakol

USTYURT PLATEAU

PLAINS OF TURAN

Kzyl-Orda

Darya

Ili R.

ASIA

KARA BOGAZ GOL GULF

TURKMENISTAN

UZBEKISTAN

Amu

Almaty

Bishkek

L. Issyk-Kul

KYRGYZSTAN

KARAKUM

DESERT

Ashkhabad

Samarkand

Tashkent

Darya

ALAY MOUNTAINS

Dushanbe

TAJIKISTAN

▲ Communism Pk. 24,590 ft. (7,495 m.)

30°

50° 60° 70° 80°

40°

30°

80° 70° Bering Strait 60° 170°

North Pole

CHUKCHI
SEA

ARCTIC
OCEAN

WRANGEL
ISLAND

CHUKOTSK
PEN.

BERING   SEA

180°

EAST SIBERIAN
SEA

Long Strait

Cape Arkticheski

NEW SIBERIAN
ISLANDS

KOLYMA
RANGE

KORYAK
MTNS.

SEVERNAYA
ZEMLYA

Sannikov Strait

Anadyr R.

170°

Cherskiy

Laptev Strait

KARAGIN
ISLAND

Vil'kitskiy Strait

LAPTEV SEA

KOLYMA
PLAIN

Kolyma

Evensk

KOMANDORSKIY
ISLANDS

TAYMYR
PEN.

SHELIKHOV
GULF

SREDINNY
RA.

BYRRANGA
MTNS.

L. Taymyr

CHERSKIY RANGE

Indigirka

River

▲ Mt. Klyuchevsk
15,584 ft.
(4,750 m.)

160°

A

KAMCHATKA PENINSULA

Noril'sk

VERKHOYANSK RANGE

Verkhoyansk

River

Magadan

Petropavlovsk-
Kamchatskiy

R.

E

Kotuy

Olenёk

Lena

R

SEA OF OKHOTSK

Cape Lopatka

CENTRAL SIBERIAN

S

Markha

River

B

I

Yakutsk

DZHUGDZHUR RA.

R.

Tura Tunguska

Vilyuy R.

LENA PLATEAU

River

Cape Yelizavety

KURIL ISLANDS

150°

Lower

River

Vilyuysk
Reservoir

Aldan

River

SAKHALIN

PLATEAU

R.

ALDAN
MTNS.

Terpeniya Point

Yenisey

Angara

R.

Vitim

STANOVOY RANGE

Uda R.

ISLAND

Tatar

Strait

Krasnoyarsk

Bratsk

River

STANOVOY
UPLAND

Lena

R.

Komsomol'sk

La Pérouse
Strait

Amur

River

SIKHOTE-ALIN RA.

40°

Krasnoyarsk
Reservoir

Bratsk
Reservoir

Lake
Baikal

YABLONOVY RANGE

R.

Khabarovsk

SAYAN
MOUNTAINS

Irkutsk

Ulan-Ude

Chita

Shilka

L. Khanka

140°

ALTAI MTNS.

Vladivostok

ASIA

SEA OF JAPAN

RUSSIA AND
THE EURASIAN REPUBLICS

⊛ National capital

● Major city

○ Other city

—— International boundary

250   500 Miles

250   500 Kilometers

Projection: Two-Point Equidistant

100°   110°   120°   130°   30°

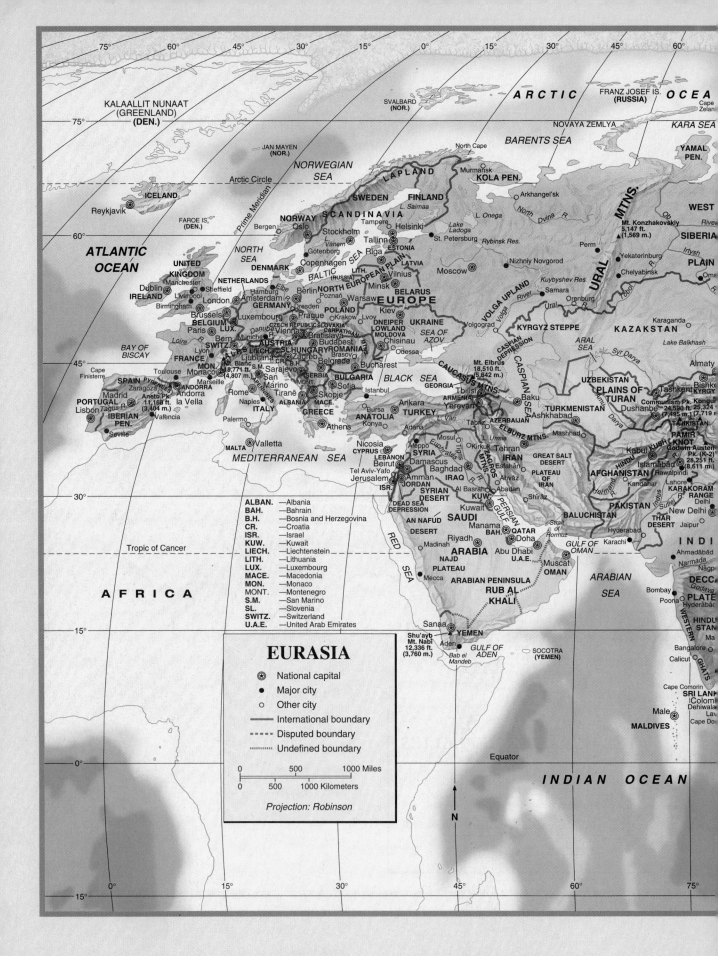

EURASIA

⊛ National capital
● Major city
○ Other city
—— International boundary
---- Disputed boundary
········ Undefined boundary

ALBAN.	—Albania
BAH.	—Bahrain
B.H.	—Bosnia and Herzegovina
CR.	—Croatia
ISR.	—Israel
KUW.	—Kuwait
LIECH.	—Liechtenstein
LITH.	—Lithuania
LUX.	—Luxembourg
MACE.	—Macedonia
MON.	—Monaco
MONT.	—Montenegro
S.M.	—San Marino
SL.	—Slovenia
SWITZ.	—Switzerland
U.A.E.	—United Arab Emirates

0   500   1000 Miles
0   500   1000 Kilometers

Projection: Robinson

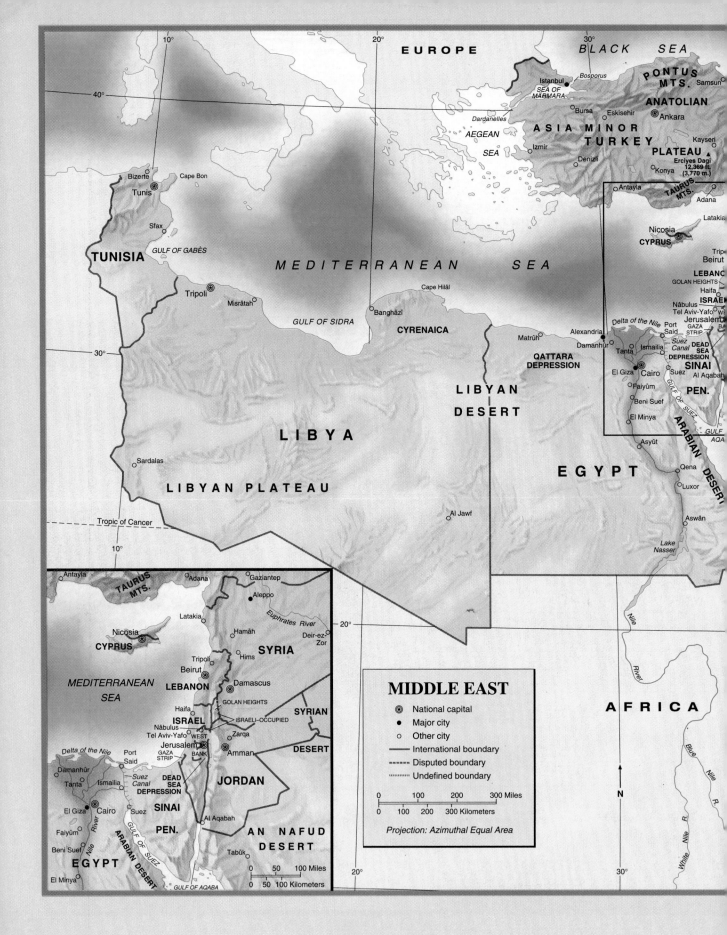

EUROPE

BLACK SEA

PONTUS MTS. Samsun

Istanbul
Bosporus
SEA OF MARMARA
Dardanelles
Bursa
Eskisehir
ANATOLIAN
Ankara
ASIA MINOR
TURKEY
Izmir
AEGEAN SEA
Denizli
PLATEAU
Erciyes Dagi
12,369 ft.
(3,770 m.)
Kayseri
Konya
TAURUS MTS.
Antalya
Adana
Nicosia
CYPRUS
Latakia
Trip
Beirut

Bizerte
Cape Bon
Tunis

MEDITERRANEAN SEA

LEBANC
GOLAN HEIGHTS
Haifa
Nâbulus
Tel Aviv-Yafo wi
ISRAEL
Jerusalem
GAZA
STRIP
BA
DEAD SEA DEPRESSION

Sfax

TUNISIA

GULF OF GABÈS

Cape Hilâl

Delta of the Nile
Port Said
Suez Canal
Alexandria
Damanhûr
Tanta
Ismailia
El Giza Cairo
Faiyûm
Suez SINAI
Al Aqaba
PEN.

Tripoli
Misrâtah

Banghāzī

Matrûh

CYRENAICA

QATTARA DEPRESSION

GULF OF SIDRA

30°

LIBYAN DESERT

Beni Suef
El Minya

GULF OF SUEZ

ARABIAN DESERT

LIBYA

Sardalas

LIBYAN PLATEAU

Asyût

EGYPT

Qena
Luxor

GULF
AQA

Tropic of Cancer

10°

Al Jawf

Aswân

Lake Nasser

20°

Nile River

Antayla
TAURUS MTS.
Adana
Gaziantep
Aleppo
Latakia
Euphrates River
Hamâh
Deir-ez-Zor
Nicosia
CYPRUS
SYRIA
Hims
Tripoli
Beirut
Damascus
LEBANON
MEDITERRANEAN SEA
GOLAN HEIGHTS
Haifa
ISRAELI-OCCUPIED
SYRIAN
Nâbulus
Tel Aviv-Yafo
ISRAEL
WEST
Zarqa
DESERT
Jerusalem
Delta of the Nile
Port Said
GAZA STRIP
BANK
Amman
Damanhûr
Suez Canal
Tanta
Ismailia
DEAD SEA DEPRESSION
JORDAN
El Giza Cairo
Suez
SINAI
Faiyûm
PEN.
Al Aqabah
Beni Suef
AN NAFUD
Nile River
Tabûk
DESERT
EGYPT
ARABIAN DESERT
El Minya
GULF OF SUEZ
GULF OF AQABA

0   50   100 Miles
0   50 100 Kilometers

AFRICA

Nile River

Blue Nile

MIDDLE EAST

◉ National capital
● Major city
○ Other city
— International boundary
---- Disputed boundary
..... Undefined boundary

0   100   200   300 Miles
0   100   200   300 Kilometers

Projection: Azimuthal Equal Area

N

White Nile R.

20°

30°

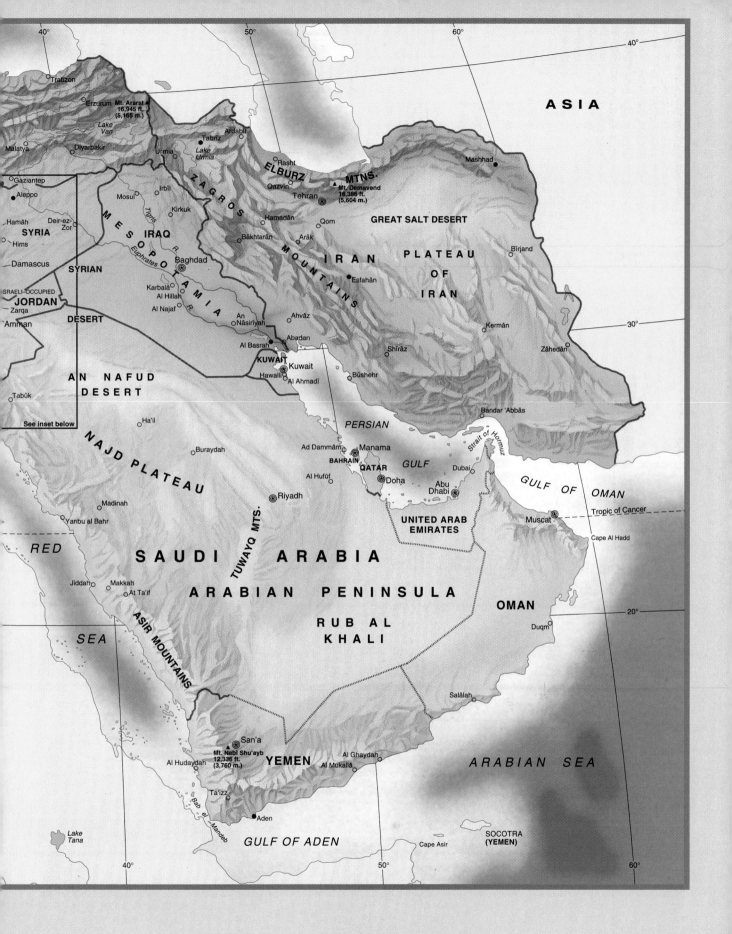

40°

Trabzon

Erzurum Mt. Ararat
16,945 ft.
(5,165 m.)

*Lake
Van*

Malatya

Diyarbakir

Tabriz

Ardabil

*Lake
Urmia*

Urmia

ELBURZ

Rasht

50°

Mashhad

60°

A S I A

40°

Gaziantep

Aleppo

Hamāh   Deir-ez-
Zor
SYRIA
Hims

Damascus

ISRAELI-OCCUPIED

JORDAN
Zarqa

Amman

Mosul

Irbīl

Kirkuk

Tigris R.

IRAQ

Baghdad

Euphrates

Karbalā

Al Hillah

An Najaf

An
Nāsirīyah

Al Basrah

Qazvin

Hamadān

Bākhtarān

M E S O P O T A M I A

Z A G R O S

SYRIAN

DESERT

**AN   NAFUD
DESERT**

See inset below

Tabūk

Ha'il

M O U N T A I N S

Arāk

Ahvāz

Abadan

KUWAIT

Hawalli

Kuwait

Al Ahmadī

Bũshehr

MTNS.
Mt. Demavend
18,386 ft.
(5,604 m.)

Tehran

Qom

Esfahān

Shīrāz

Kermān

GREAT SALT DESERT

**P L A T E A U
O F
I R A N**

I R A N

Birjand

Zāhedān

30°

Buraydah

Madinah

Yanbu al Bahr

N A J D   P L A T E A U

Ad Dammām

Manama

BAHRAIN

Al Hufūf

PERSIAN

Doha

QATAR

Riyadh

RED

Jiddah

Makkah

At Ta'if

SEA

ASIR MOUNTAINS

Bandar 'Abbās

Strait of Hormuz

Dubai

Abu
Dhabi

GULF

**UNITED ARAB
EMIRATES**

GULF OF OMAN

Muscat

Tropic of Cancer

Cape Al Hadd

TUWAYQ MTS.

S A U D I   A R A B I A

A R A B I A N   P E N I N S U L A

**R U B   A L
K H A L I**

OMAN

Duqm

Salālah

20°

San'a

Mt. Nabi Shu'ayb
12,336 ft.
(3,760 m.)

Al Hudaydah

YEMEN

Ta'izz

Al Ghaydah

Al Mukallā

A R A B I A N   S E A

*Lake
Tana*

Bab
el
Mandeb

Aden

GULF OF ADEN

Cape Asir

SOCOTRA
(YEMEN)

40°

50°

60°

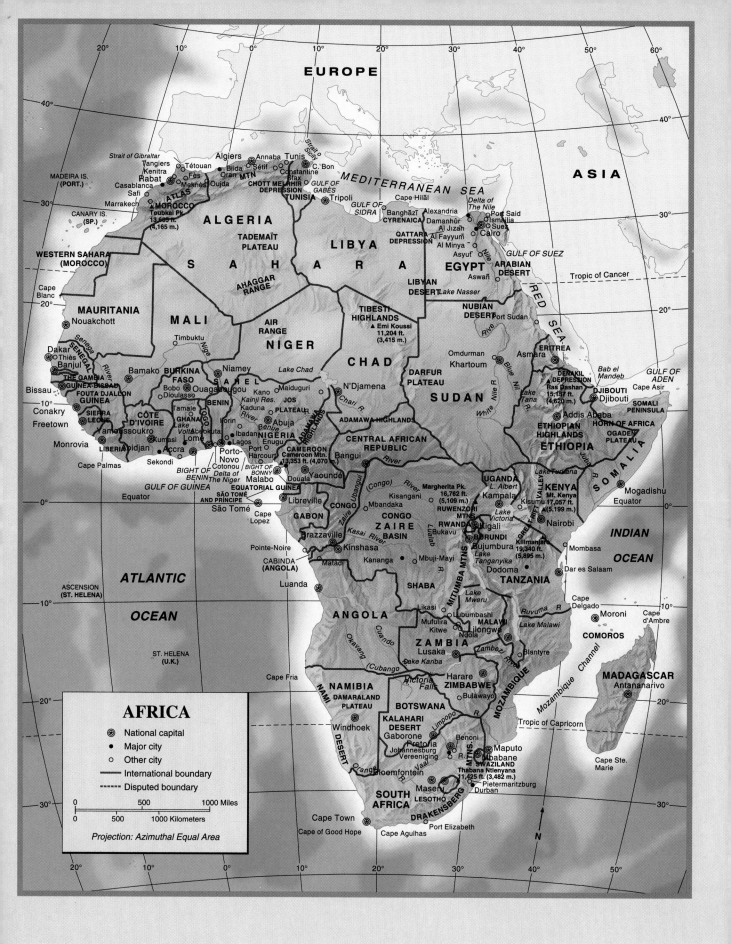

AFRICA

- National capital
- Major city
- Other city
- International boundary
- Disputed boundary

0   500   1000 Miles
0   500   1000 Kilometers

Projection: Azimuthal Equal Area

A20   Reference Atlas

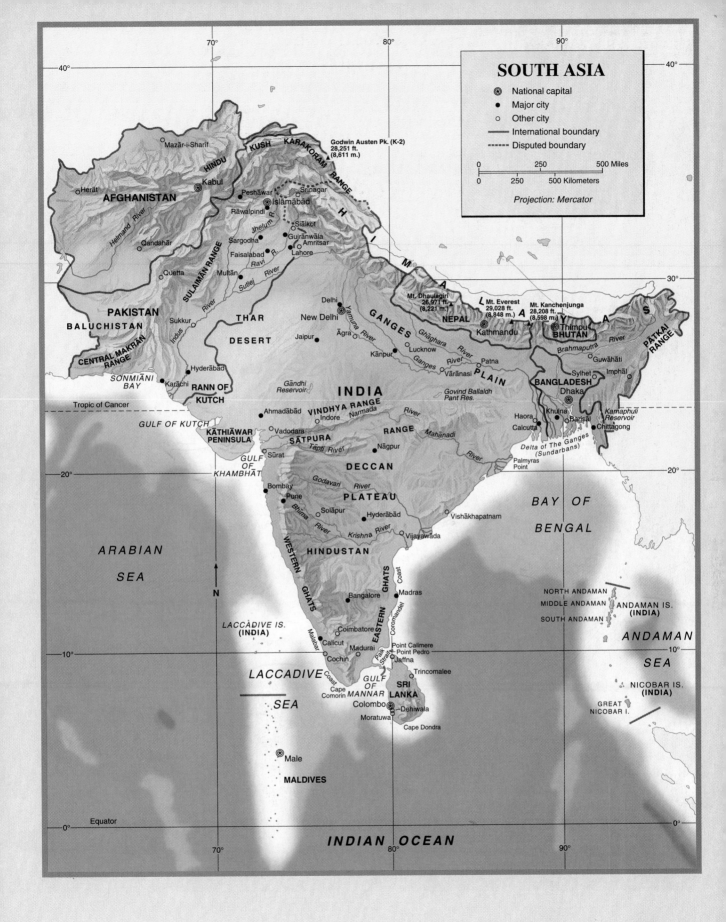

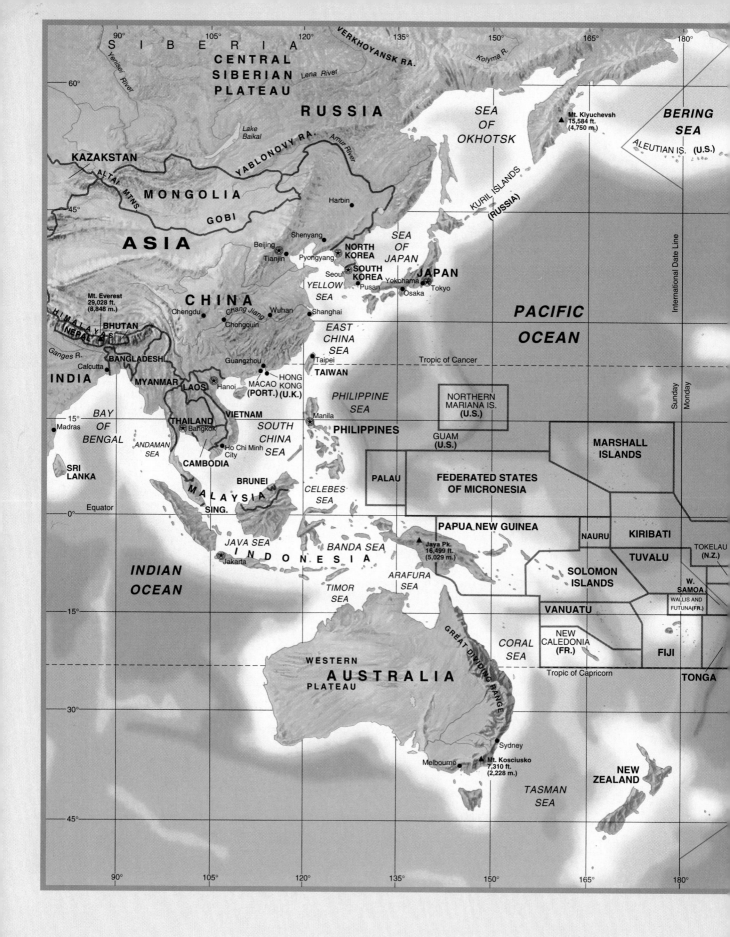

S I B E R I A

CENTRAL SIBERIAN PLATEAU

Yenisei River

Lena River

VERKHOYANSK RA.

Kolyma R.

RUSSIA

SEA OF OKHOTSK

▲ Mt. Klyuchevsh
15,584 ft.
(4,750 m.)

BERING SEA

ALEUTIAN IS. (U.S.)

KAZAKSTAN

ALTAI MTNS

MONGOLIA

GOBI

Lake Baikal

YABLONOVY RA.

Amur River

Harbin

KURIL ISLANDS

(RUSSIA)

International Date Line

ASIA

Beijing

Shenyang

Tianjin

Pyongyang

NORTH KOREA

SEA OF JAPAN

CHINA

Mt. Everest
29,028 ft.
(8,848 m.)

HIMALAYAS

NEPAL

BHUTAN

Chengdu

Chang Jiang

Chongquin

Wuhan

Shanghai

Seoul

SOUTH KOREA

Pusan

JAPAN

Yokohama

Osaka

Tokyo

PACIFIC OCEAN

Sunday Monday

BANGLADESH

Ganges R.

Calcutta

EAST CHINA SEA

INDIA

MYANMAR

LAOS

Hanoi

Guangzhou

MACAO
(PORT.)

HONG KONG
(U.K.)

Taipei

TAIWAN

Tropic of Cancer

Madras

BAY OF BENGAL

THAILAND

Bangkok

VIETNAM

Ho Chi Minh City

SOUTH CHINA SEA

ANDAMAN SEA

CAMBODIA

Manila

PHILIPPINE SEA

PHILIPPINES

NORTHERN MARIANA IS.
(U.S.)

GUAM
(U.S.)

MARSHALL ISLANDS

SRI LANKA

BRUNEI

MALAYSIA

SING.

CELEBES SEA

PALAU

FEDERATED STATES OF MICRONESIA

Equator

JAVA SEA

Jakarta

I N D O N E S I A

BANDA SEA

PAPUA NEW GUINEA

▲ Jaya Pk.
16,499 ft.
(5,029 m.)

NAURU

KIRIBATI

TOKELAU
(N.Z.)

INDIAN OCEAN

TIMOR SEA

ARAFURA SEA

SOLOMON ISLANDS

TUVALU

W. SAMOA

WALLIS AND FUTUNA(FR.)

15°

VANUATU

NEW CALEDONIA
(FR.)

CORAL SEA

FIJI

GREAT DIVIDING RANGE

WESTERN

AUSTRALIA

PLATEAU

Tropic of Capricorn

TONGA

30°

Sydney

Melbourne

▲ Mt. Kosciusko
7,310 ft.
(2,228 m.)

NEW ZEALAND

TASMAN SEA

45°

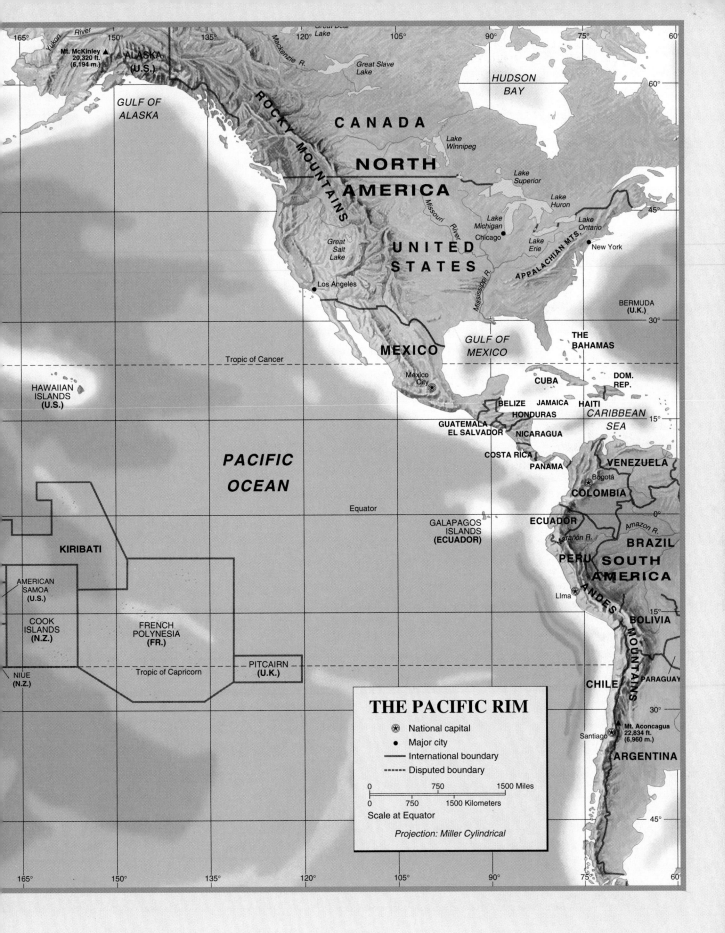

THE PACIFIC RIM

- ⊛ National capital
- ● Major city
- —— International boundary
- ----- Disputed boundary

```
0          750        1500 Miles
0    750   1500 Kilometers
```

Scale at Equator

Projection: Miller Cylindrical

165° 150° 135° 120° 105° 90° 75° 60°

Mt. McKinley
20,320 ft.
(6,194 m.) ▲

ALASKA
(U.S.)

GULF OF
ALASKA

Yukon River

CANADA

NORTH
AMERICA

ROCKY MOUNTAINS

Mackenzie R.

Great Bear
Lake

Great Slave
Lake

HUDSON
BAY

60°

UNITED
STATES

Great
Salt
Lake

Missouri River

Lake Winnipeg

Lake Superior

Lake Michigan

Lake Huron

Chicago ●

Lake Erie

Lake Ontario

APPALACHIAN MTS.

New York ●

45°

Los Angeles ●

Mississippi R.

BERMUDA
(U.K.)

Tropic of Cancer

MEXICO

GULF OF
MEXICO

THE
BAHAMAS

30°

HAWAIIAN
ISLANDS
(U.S.)

Mexico
City ⊛

CUBA

DOM.
REP.

BELIZE

JAMAICA

HAITI

CARIBBEAN
SEA

15°

GUATEMALA
EL SALVADOR

HONDURAS

NICARAGUA

PACIFIC
OCEAN

COSTA RICA

PANAMA

VENEZUELA

Bogotá ⊛

COLOMBIA

Equator

GALAPAGOS
ISLANDS
(ECUADOR)

ECUADOR

Amazon R.

0°

KIRIBATI

Marañón R.

BRAZIL

PERU

SOUTH
AMERICA

AMERICAN
SAMOA
(U.S.)

Lima ⊛

ANDES MOUNTAINS

15°

COOK
ISLANDS
(N.Z.)

FRENCH
POLYNESIA
(FR.)

BOLIVIA

NIUE
(N.Z.)

Tropic of Capricorn

PITCAIRN
(U.K.)

CHILE

PARAGUAY

30°

Mt. Aconcagua
22,834 ft.
(6,960 m.) ▲

Santiago ⊛

ARGENTINA

45°

165° 150° 135° 120° 105° 90° 75° 60°

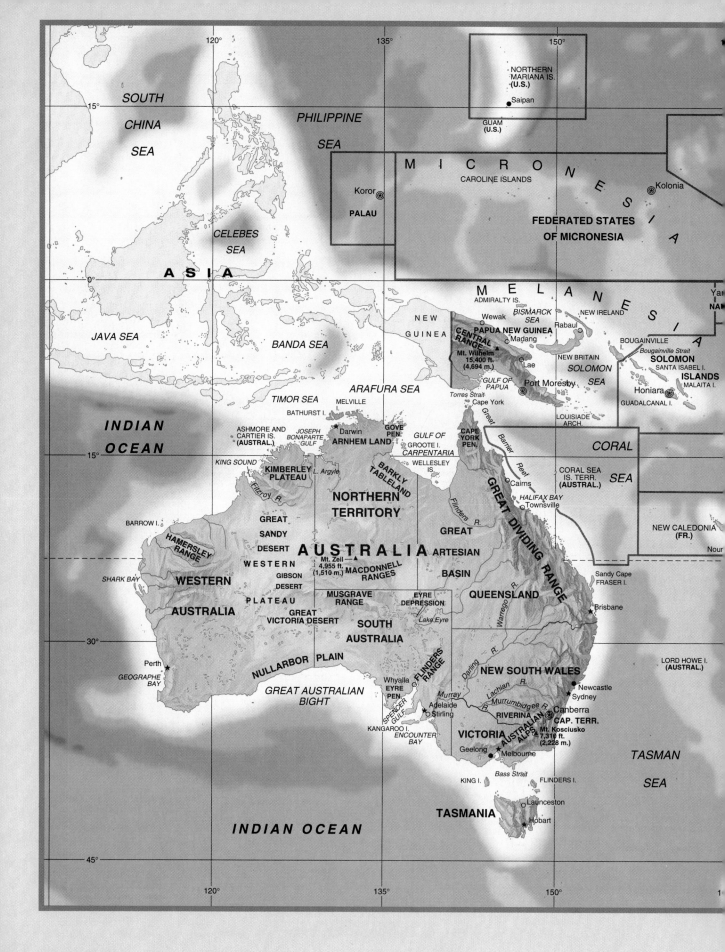

SOUTH

CHINA

SEA

PHILIPPINE

SEA

NORTHERN
MARIANA IS.
(U.S.)
• Saipan

GUAM
(U.S.)

M I C R O N E S I A

CAROLINE ISLANDS

⊛ Kolonia

Koror ⊛

PALAU

FEDERATED STATES
OF MICRONESIA

CELEBES
SEA

A S I A

JAVA SEA

BANDA SEA

NEW
GUINEA

ADMIRALTY IS.

M E L A N E S I A

Wewak
BISMARCK
SEA

NEW IRELAND

PAPUA NEW GUINEA

CENTRAL
RANGE
Mt. Wilhelm
15,400 ft.
(4,694 m.)

• Madang

Rabaul ○

NEW BRITAIN

Lae ○

GULF OF
PAPUA

Port Moresby ⊙

SOLOMON
SEA

BOUGAINVILLE
I.
Bougainville Strait

SOLOMON

SANTA ISABEL I.

ISLANDS

MALAITA I.

Honiara ⊛

GUADALCANAL I.

Yar
NA

INDIAN

OCEAN

TIMOR SEA

MELVILLE
I.

BATHURST I.

ARAFURA SEA

Torres Strait
Cape York

Great

LOUISIADE
ARCH.

ASHMORE AND
CARTIER IS.
(AUSTRAL.)

JOSEPH
BONAPARTE
GULF

★ Darwin

GOVE
PEN.

CAPE
YORK
PEN.

CORAL

SEA

KING SOUND

ARNHEM LAND

GULF OF
CARPENTARIA

GROOTE I.

Barrier

CORAL SEA
IS. TERR.
(AUSTRAL.)

KIMBERLEY
PLATEAU

L. Argyle

WELLESLEY
IS.

Reef

Cairns ○

BARROW I.

Fitzroy R.

BARKLY
TABLELAND

NORTHERN
TERRITORY

Flinders R.

HALIFAX BAY
Townsville ○

HAMERSLEY
RANGE

GREAT

SANDY

DESERT

GREAT

NEW CALEDONIA
(FR.)

Nour

SHARK BAY

WESTERN

GIBSON

DESERT

AUSTRALIA

Mt. Zell
4,955 ft.
(1,510 m.)

MACDONNELL
RANGES

ARTESIAN

Sandy Cape
FRASER I.

WESTERN

AUSTRALIA

PLATEAU

MUSGRAVE
RANGE

GREAT
VICTORIA DESERT

EYRE
DEPRESSION

SOUTH

BASIN

QUEENSLAND

Warrego R.

Brisbane ★

GREAT DIVIDING RANGE

Perth ★

GEOGRAPHE
BAY

NULLARBOR

PLAIN

Lake Eyre

AUSTRALIA

FLINDERS
RANGE

Darling R.

LORD HOWE I.
(AUSTRAL.)

GREAT AUSTRALIAN

BIGHT

Whyalla ○

EYRE
PEN.

Murray
R.

NEW SOUTH WALES

Lachlan R.

Murrumbidgee R.

Newcastle •
Sydney ⊙

SPENCER
GULF

Adelaide ⊙
○ Stirling

RIVERINA

Canberra ⊙
CAP. TERR.

KANGAROO I.

ENCOUNTER
BAY

VICTORIA

AUSTRALIAN
ALPS

Mt. Kosciusko
7,310 ft.
(2,228 m.)

TASMAN

Geelong ●
Melbourne ⊙

SEA

KING I.

Bass Strait

FLINDERS I.

INDIAN OCEAN

TASMANIA

Launceston ○

Hobart ★

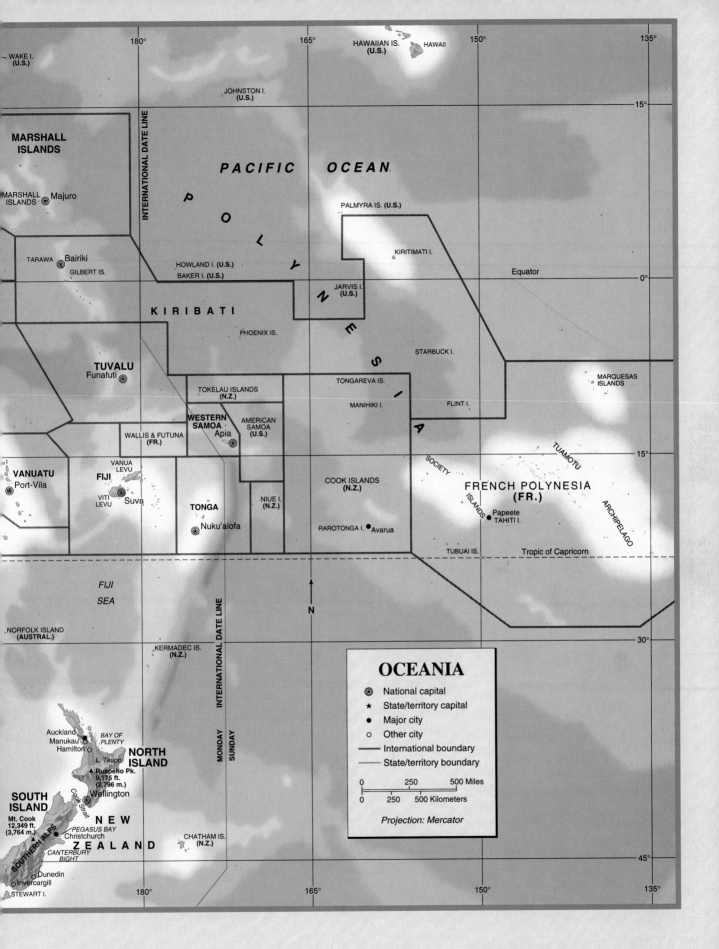

WAKE I.
(U.S.)

HAWAIIAN IS. (U.S.) · HAWAII

JOHNSTON I.
(U.S.)

180°   165°   150°   135°

15°

**MARSHALL
ISLANDS**

PACIFIC   OCEAN

INTERNATIONAL DATE LINE

MARSHALL
ISLANDS · Majuro

P
O
L
Y
N
E
S
I
A

PALMYRA IS. (U.S.)

KIRITIMATI I.

Equator   0°

TARAWA · Bairiki
GILBERT IS.

HOWLAND I. (U.S.)
BAKER I. (U.S.)

JARVIS I.
(U.S.)

K I R I B A T I

PHOENIX IS.

STARBUCK I.

TUVALU
Funafuti

TOKELAU ISLANDS
(N.Z.)

TONGAREVA IS.

MARQUESAS
ISLANDS

MANIHIKI I.

FLINT I.

**WESTERN
SAMOA**
Apia

AMERICAN
SAMOA
(U.S.)

SOCIETY

TUAMOTU

15°

WALLIS & FUTUNA
(FR.)

ISLANDS

**FRENCH POLYNESIA
(FR.)**

ARCHIPELAGO

VANUATU
Port-Vila

VANUA
LEVU

FIJI

VITI
LEVU   Suva

TONGA
Nuku'alofa

NIUE I.
(N.Z.)

**COOK ISLANDS
(N.Z.)**

Papeete
TAHITI I.

RAROTONGA I. ·Avarua

TUBUAI IS.   Tropic of Capricorn

*FIJI

SEA*

INTERNATIONAL DATE LINE

N

NORFOLK ISLAND
(AUSTRAL.)

KERMADEC IS.
(N.Z.)

30°

MONDAY
SUNDAY

OCEANIA

⊛ National capital

★ State/territory capital

● Major city

○ Other city

— International boundary

— State/territory boundary

Auckland
Manukau
Hamilton

BAY OF
PLENTY

**NORTH
ISLAND**

L. Taupo
▲Ruapehu Pk.
9,175 ft.
(2,796 m.)

Wellington

0   250   500 Miles

0   250   500 Kilometers

**SOUTH
ISLAND**

Mt. Cook
12,349 ft.
(3,764 m.)

SOUTHERN ALPS

Cook Strait

PEGASUS BAY
Christchurch

N E W

Projection: Mercator

CHATHAM IS.
(N.Z.)

Z E A L A N D

*CANTERBURY
BIGHT*

45°

○ Dunedin
○ Invercargill
STEWART I.

180°   165°   150°   135°

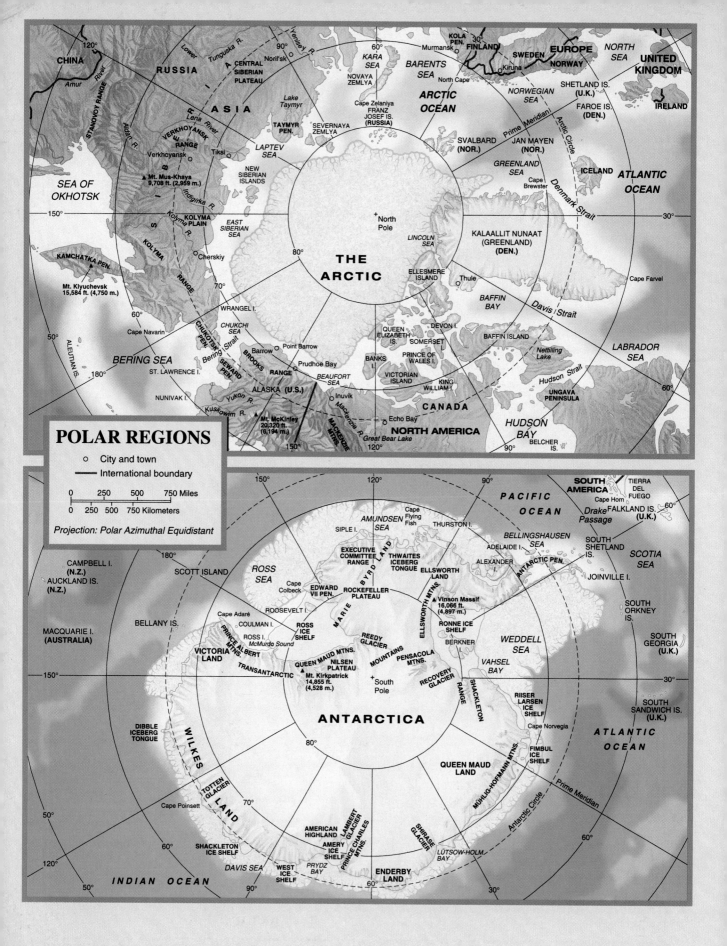

POLAR REGIONS

○ City and town

— International boundary

| 0 | 250 | 500 | 750 Miles |
| 0 | 250 | 500 | 750 Kilometers |

Projection: Polar Azimuthal Equidistant

THE ARCTIC

+ North Pole

CHINA
RUSSIA
ASIA
CENTRAL SIBERIAN PLATEAU
Lower Tunguska R.
Noril'sk
Yenisey R.
KARA SEA
NOVAYA ZEMLYA
Cape Zelaniya
FRANZ JOSEF IS. (RUSSIA)
SEVERNAYA ZEMLYA
BARENTS SEA
KOLA PEN.
Murmansk
North Cape
FINLAND
SWEDEN
Kiruna
NORWAY
EUROPE
NORTH SEA
UNITED KINGDOM
ARCTIC OCEAN
NORWEGIAN SEA
SHETLAND IS. (U.K.)
FAROE IS. (DEN.)
IRELAND
Amur
River
STANOVOY RANGE
Aldan R.
VERKHOYANSK RANGE
Lena River
Lake Taymyr
TAYMYR PEN.
LAPTEV SEA
SVALBARD (NOR.)
Prime Meridian
JAN MAYEN (NOR.)
GREENLAND SEA
Cape Brewster
ICELAND
Arctic Circle
ATLANTIC OCEAN
Verkhoyansk
Tiksi
NEW SIBERIAN ISLANDS
▲ Mt. Mus-Khaya 9,708 ft. (2,959 m.)
Indigirka R.
EAST SIBERIAN SEA
Denmark Strait
SEA OF OKHOTSK
KOLYMA PLAIN
Kolyma R.
150°
80°
LINCOLN SEA
KALAALLIT NUNAAT (GREENLAND) (DEN.)
Cape Farvel
30°
KAMCHATKA PEN.
Mt. Klyuchevsk 15,584 ft. (4,750 m.)
KOLYMA RANGE
Cherskiy
70°
ELLESMERE ISLAND
Thule
BAFFIN BAY
Davis Strait
LABRADOR SEA
WRANGEL I.
60°
CHUKCHI SEA
QUEEN ELIZABETH IS.
DEVON I.
SOMERSET
PRINCE OF WALES I.
Nettilling Lake
BAFFIN ISLAND
50°
CHUKOTSKI PEN.
Cape Navarin
Bering Strait
BROOKS RANGE
Barrow
Point Barrow
Prudhoe Bay
BANKS I.
VICTORIA ISLAND
KING WILLIAM I.
Hudson Strait
UNGAVA PENINSULA
60°
ALEUTIAN IS.
180°
BERING SEA
ST. LAWRENCE I.
SEWARD PEN.
BEAUFORT SEA
Inuvik
Yukon R.
Mackenzie R.
CANADA
NUNIVAK I.
Kuskowim R.
ALASKA (U.S.)
▲ Mt. McKinley 20,320 ft. (6,194 m.)
MACKENZIE MTNS.
Echo Bay
Great Bear Lake
NORTH AMERICA
HUDSON BAY
BELCHER IS.
150°
120°
90°

ANTARCTICA

+ South Pole

CAMPBELL I. (N.Z.)
AUCKLAND IS. (N.Z.)
SCOTT ISLAND
180°
SIPLE I.
AMUNDSEN SEA
Cape Flying Fish
THURSTON I.
PACIFIC OCEAN
SOUTH AMERICA
TIERRA DEL FUEGO
Cape Horn
Drake Passage
FALKLAND IS. (U.K.)
MACQUARIE I. (AUSTRALIA)
BELLANY IS.
ROSS SEA
EXECUTIVE COMMITTEE RANGE
THWAITES ICEBERG TONGUE
ELLSWORTH LAND
BELLINGSHAUSEN SEA
ADELAIDE I.
ALEXANDER I.
ANTARCTIC PEN.
SOUTH SHETLAND IS.
SCOTIA SEA
JOINVILLE I.
Cape Colbeck
EDWARD VII PEN.
ROCKEFELLER PLATEAU
MARIE BYRD LAND
ELLSWORTH MTNS.
▲ Vinson Massif 16,066 ft. (4,897 m.)
RONNE ICE SHELF
BERKNER I.
WEDDELL SEA
SOUTH ORKNEY IS.
ROOSEVELT I.
Cape Adaré
COULMAN I.
ROSS I. McMurdo Sound
ROSS ICE SHELF
REEDY GLACIER
MOUNTAINS
PENSACOLA MTNS.
VAHSEL BAY
SOUTH GEORGIA (U.K.)
PRINCE ALBERT MTNS.
VICTORIA LAND
QUEEN MAUD MTNS.
NILSEN PLATEAU
▲ Mt. Kirkpatrick 14,855 ft. (4,528 m.)
RECOVERY GLACIER
SHACKLETON RANGE
RIISER LARSEN ICE SHELF
Cape Norvegia
SOUTH SANDWICH IS. (U.K.)
150°
TRANSANTARCTIC
FIMBUL ICE SHELF
ATLANTIC OCEAN
30°
DIBBLE ICEBERG TONGUE
WILKES LAND
80°
QUEEN MAUD LAND
MÜHLIG-HOFMANN MTNS.
TOTTEN GLACIER
Cape Poinsett
70°
AMERICAN HIGHLAND
LAMBERT GLACIER
PRINCE CHARLES MTNS.
SHIRASE GLACIER
Prime Meridian
Antarctic Circle
60°
SHACKLETON ICE SHELF
AMERY ICE SHELF
LÜTSOW-HOLM BAY
50°
DAVIS SEA
WEST ICE SHELF
PRYDZ BAY
ENDERBY LAND
90°
INDIAN OCEAN
60°
30°

A26 Reference Atlas

Historical Atlas

AND

World Data Bank

Early Civilizations 3500 B.C –1700s B.C.

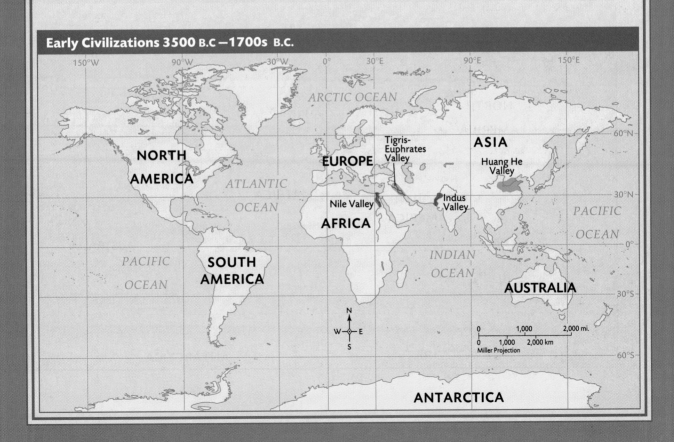

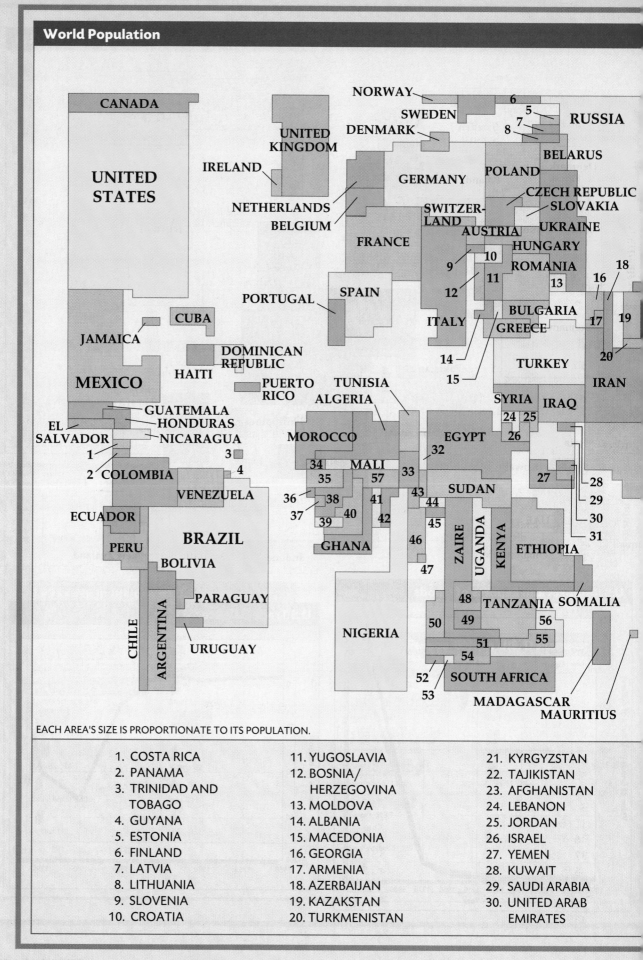

CANADA

UNITED STATES

UNITED KINGDOM

IRELAND

NETHERLANDS

BELGIUM

NORWAY

SWEDEN

DENMARK

GERMANY

SWITZER-LAND

FRANCE

PORTUGAL

SPAIN

ITALY

6

5

7

8

RUSSIA

BELARUS

POLAND

CZECH REPUBLIC

SLOVAKIA

UKRAINE

AUSTRIA

HUNGARY

ROMANIA

9

10

11

12

13

14

15

BULGARIA

GREECE

18

16

17

19

20

JAMAICA

CUBA

DOMINICAN REPUBLIC

HAITI

PUERTO RICO

TUNISIA

ALGERIA

TURKEY

IRAN

MEXICO

GUATEMALA

HONDURAS

NICARAGUA

EL SALVADOR

1

2 COLOMBIA

3

4

VENEZUELA

ECUADOR

PERU

BRAZIL

BOLIVIA

MOROCCO

34

35

36

37

38

39

40

MALI

57

41

42

GHANA

33

43

44

45

46

47

EGYPT

32

SUDAN

ZAIRE

UGANDA

KENYA

SYRIA

24 25

26

IRAQ

27

28

29

30

31

ETHIOPIA

PARAGUAY

CHILE

ARGENTINA

URUGUAY

NIGERIA

48

49

50

51

54

52

53

TANZANIA

56

55

SOMALIA

SOUTH AFRICA

MADAGASCAR

MAURITIUS

EACH AREA'S SIZE IS PROPORTIONATE TO ITS POPULATION.

1. COSTA RICA	11. YUGOSLAVIA	21. KYRGYZSTAN
2. PANAMA	12. BOSNIA/	22. TAJIKISTAN
3. TRINIDAD AND	HERZEGOVINA	23. AFGHANISTAN
TOBAGO	13. MOLDOVA	24. LEBANON
4. GUYANA	14. ALBANIA	25. JORDAN
5. ESTONIA	15. MACEDONIA	26. ISRAEL
6. FINLAND	16. GEORGIA	27. YEMEN
7. LATVIA	17. ARMENIA	28. KUWAIT
8. LITHUANIA	18. AZERBAIJAN	29. SAUDI ARABIA
9. SLOVENIA	19. KAZAKSTAN	30. UNITED ARAB
10. CROATIA	20. TURKMENISTAN	EMIRATES

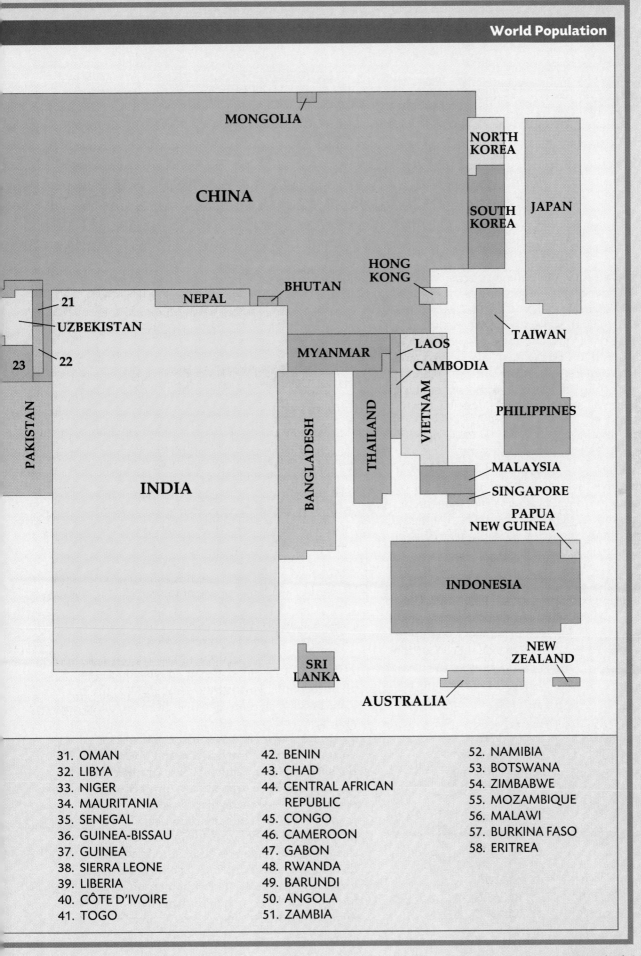

MONGOLIA

CHINA

NORTH
KOREA

SOUTH
KOREA

JAPAN

HONG
KONG

TAIWAN

21

UZBEKISTAN

NEPAL

BHUTAN

23

22

LAOS

CAMBODIA

PAKISTAN

MYANMAR

PHILIPPINES

BANGLADESH

THAILAND

VIETNAM

INDIA

MALAYSIA

SINGAPORE

PAPUA
NEW GUINEA

INDONESIA

NEW
ZEALAND

SRI
LANKA

AUSTRALIA

31. OMAN	42. BENIN	52. NAMIBIA
32. LIBYA	43. CHAD	53. BOTSWANA
33. NIGER	44. CENTRAL AFRICAN	54. ZIMBABWE
34. MAURITANIA	REPUBLIC	55. MOZAMBIQUE
35. SENEGAL	45. CONGO	56. MALAWI
36. GUINEA-BISSAU	46. CAMEROON	57. BURKINA FASO
37. GUINEA	47. GABON	58. ERITREA
38. SIERRA LEONE	48. RWANDA	
39. LIBERIA	49. BARUNDI	
40. CÔTE D'IVOIRE	50. ANGOLA	
41. TOGO	51. ZAMBIA	

What Is Geography?

The story of humanity begins with **geography**—the study of the earth in all of its variety. Geography concerns the earth's land, water, and plant and animal life. It also tells you about the people who live on the earth, the places they have created, and how these places differ. The earth is a planet of diverse groups of people. A study of geography can help you see why the people of the earth are so diverse.

The Five Themes of Geography

The study of geography can be organized around five themes: **location**, **place**, **human/environment interaction**, **movement**, and **region**. Geographers use these five themes to study and classify all parts of the earth and its variety of human activity.

Geography and World History

World geography is especially important to the study of world history. Historians use geography to explain connections between the past and the present. They study how places

looked in the past, how places and patterns of human activity have changed over time, and how geographic forces have influenced these changes.

GLOBES AND MAPS

Globes

Photographs from space show the earth in its true form—a great ball spinning around the sun. The only accurate way to draw the earth is as a globe, or a round form. A globe gives a true picture of the earth's size and the shape of the earth's landmasses and bodies of water. Globes also show the true distances and true directions between places.

Maps

A map is a flat drawing of the earth's surface. People use maps to locate places, plot routes, and judge distances. Maps can also display useful information about the world's peoples.

What advantages does a map have over a globe? Unlike a globe, a map allows you to see all areas of the world at the same time. Maps also show much more detail and can be folded and more easily carried.

Maps, however, have their drawbacks. As you can imagine, drawing a round object on a flat surface is very difficult. Cartographers, or mapmakers, have drawn many **projections**, or kinds of maps. Each map projection is a different way of showing the round earth on a flat map. This is because it is impossible to draw a round planet on a flat surface without distorting or misrepresenting some parts of the earth. As a result, each kind of map projection has some distortion. Typical distortions involve distance, direction, shape, and/or area.

Behaim's Globe

The Hemispheres

To determine location, distance, and direction on a map or globe, geographers have developed a network of imaginary lines that crisscross the earth. One of these lines, the **Equator**, circles the earth midway between the **North Pole** and the **South Pole**. It divides the earth into "half spheres," or **hemispheres**. The Northern Hemisphere includes all of the land and water between the Equator and the North Pole. The Southern Hemisphere includes all of the land and water between the Equator and the South Pole.

Another imaginary line running from north to south divides the earth into half spheres in the other direction. This line is called the **Prime Meridian**. Every place east of the Prime Meridian is in the Eastern Hemisphere. Every place west of the Prime Meridian is in the Western Hemisphere.

Latitude and Longitude

The Equator and the Prime Meridian are the starting points for two sets of lines used to find any location. The two sets measure distances north or south of the Equator, and east and west of the Prime Meridian.

One set of lines called **parallels** circle the earth and show **latitude**, which is distance measured in degrees (°) north and south of the Equator at 0° latitude. The letter *N* or *S* following the degree symbol tells you if the location is north or south of the Equator. The North and South Poles are at 90° North (*N*) and South (*S*) latitude.

Two important parallels in between the poles are the **Tropic of Cancer** at 23 1/2°N latitude and the **Tropic of Capricorn** at 23 1/2°S latitude. You can also find the **Arctic Circle** at 66 1/2°N latitude and the **Antarctic Circle** at 66 1/2°S latitude.

The second set of lines called **meridians** run north to south from the North Pole to the South Pole. These lines signify **longitude**, which is distance measured in degrees east (*E*) or west (*W*) of the Prime Meridian at 0° longitude. On the opposite side of the earth is the International Date Line, or the 180° meridian.

The Grid System

Lines of latitude and longitude cross one another in the form of a **grid system**. You can use the grid system to find where places are exactly located on a map or globe. Each place on Earth has an address on the grid. This grid address is the place's **coordinates**—its degrees of latitude and longitude. For example, the coordinates of the city of San Francisco are 38°N latitude and 122°W longitude. This means that San Francisco lies about 38 degrees (°) north of the Equator and 122 degrees (°) west of the Prime Meridian. Where those two lines cross is called the **absolute location** of the city.

Map Symbols

Maps can direct you down the street, across the country, or around the world. There are as many different kinds of maps as there are uses for them. Being

Hemispheres

NORTHERN HEMISPHERE
North Pole
NORTH AMERICA
Equator
SOUTH AMERICA
South Pole
SOUTHERN HEMISPHERE

WESTERN HEMISPHERE   EASTERN HEMISPHERE
North Pole
NORTH AMERICA
EUROPE
AFRICA
SOUTH AMERICA
Prime Meridian
South Pole   ANTARCTICA

NORTHERN HEMISPHERE
North Pole
AFRICA
ASIA
Equator
AUSTRALIA
ANTARCTICA
South Pole
SOUTHERN HEMISPHERE

EASTERN HEMISPHERE   WESTERN HEMISPHERE
North Pole
ASIA
NORTH AMERICA
180°
PACIFIC OCEAN
AUSTRALIA
ANTARCTICA   South Pole

able to read a map begins with learning about its parts.

The **map key** explains the symbols used on the map. On a map of the world, for example, dots mark cities and towns. On a road map, various kinds of lines stand for paved roads, dirt roads, and interstate highways. A pine tree symbol may represent a state park, while an airplane is often the symbol for an airport.

An important first step in reading any map is to find the direction marker. A map has a symbol that tells you where the **cardinal directions**—north, south, east, and west—are positioned. Sometimes all of these directions are shown with a **compass rose**.

A measuring line, often called a **scale bar**, helps you find distance on the map. The map's **scale** tells you what distance on the earth is represented by the measurement on the scale bar. For example, 1 inch on a map may represent 100 miles on the earth. Knowing the scale allows you to visualize how large an area is, as well as to measure distances. Map scales are usually given in both miles and kilometers, a metric measurement of distance.

purpose maps are physical maps and political maps. **Physical maps** show natural features, such as rivers and mountains. **Political maps** show places that people have created, such as cities or the boundaries of countries and states.

Special-Purpose Maps

Special-purpose maps show information on specific topics, such as climate, land use, or vegetation. Human activities, such as exploration routes, territorial expansion, or battle sites, also appear on special purpose maps. Colors and map key symbols are especially important on this type of map.

LANDSAT Maps

LANDSAT maps are made from photographs taken by camera-carrying LANDSAT satellites in space. The cameras record millions of energy waves invisible to the human eye. Computers then change this information into pictures of the earth's surface. With LANDSAT images, scientists can study whole mountain ranges, oceans, and geographic regions. Changes to the earth's environment can also be tracked using the satellite information.

TYPES OF MAPS

Maps of many different kinds are used in this text to help you see the connection between world geography and the history of humanity.

General-Purpose Maps

Maps that show a wide range of general information about an area are called **general-purpose maps**. Two of the most common general

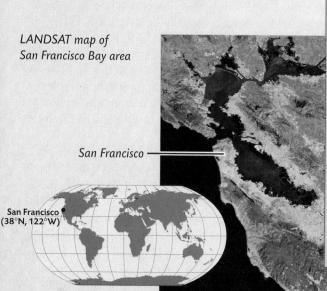

LANDSAT map of
San Francisco Bay area

San Francisco

San Francisco
(38°N, 122°W)

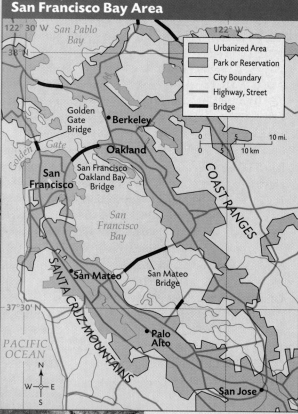

San Francisco Bay Area

- Urbanized Area
- Park or Reservation
- City Boundary
- Highway, Street
- Bridge

122° 30' W   San Pablo Bay
38° N
Golden Gate Bridge
Berkeley
Golden Gate
Oakland
San Francisco
San Francisco Oakland Bay Bridge
San Francisco Bay
122° W
COAST RANGES
0   5   10 mi.
0   5   10 km
SANTA CRUZ MOUNTAINS
San Mateo
San Mateo Bridge
37° 30' N
Palo Alto
PACIFIC OCEAN
San Jose

CONTINENTS

Geographers divide most of the earth's land surface into seven large landmasses called **continents**. The continents are North America, South America, Europe, Africa, Asia, Australia, and Antarctica. Asia is the largest continent in size, and Australia is the smallest.

LANDFORMS

Landforms cover about 30 percent of the surface of the earth. **Landforms**, or the natural features of the earth's surface, include **mountains**, **hills**, **plateaus**, and **plains**. Geographers describe each landform by its **elevation**, or height above sea level, and by its **relief**, or changes in height.

Mountains

Mountains are the highest of the world's landforms. They rise from about 2,000 feet (610 m) to more than 20,000 feet (6,100 m) above sea level. One of the peaks in the Himalaya mountain ranges of central Asia is Mount Everest, the world's highest mountain. It towers 29,028 feet (8,848 m) above sea level. Other mountains, such as the Appalachians in eastern North America, are not as high. Mountains generally have high relief.

Hills, Plateaus, and Plains

Hills are lower than mountains and generally rise from about 500 to 2,000 feet (152 to 610 m) above sea level. They generally have moderate relief.

Plateaus are raised areas of flat or almost flat land. Most plateaus have low relief and vary in elevation from about 300 to 3,000 feet (91 to 914 m) above sea level. The world's largest plateau area is the Tibetan Plateau in central Asia. It covers about 715,000 square miles (1,852,000 sq. km) and has an average altitude of 16,000 feet (4,877 m) above sea level.

Plains are large areas of flat or gently rolling land that generally rise less than 1,000 feet (305 m) above sea level and have low relief. The world's largest plain is the North European Plain, which stretches for more than 1,000 miles (1,609 km) from the western coast of France to the Ural Mountains in Russia.

BODIES OF WATER

About 70 percent of the earth's surface is covered with water. Geographers identify bodies of water by their shapes and sizes. The major types include oceans, seas, bays, gulfs, lakes, and rivers.

Oceans and Seas

The largest bodies of water in the world are the four saltwater **oceans**—the Pacific, the Atlantic, the Indian, and the Arctic. The Pacific Ocean is the largest ocean, covering about 64 million square miles (165,760,000 sq. km)—more than all the land areas of the earth combined.

Seas are smaller bodies of salt water that are usually in part surrounded by land. The world's largest sea is East Asia's South China Sea, with an area of 1,148,500 square miles (2,975,000 sq. km).

Bays and Gulfs

Still smaller bodies of salt water are gulfs and bays. **Bays** are extensions of a sea usually smaller than a gulf. The largest bay in the world measured by shoreline is Hudson Bay, Canada, with a shoreline of 7,623 miles (12,265 km) and an area of 476,000 square miles (1,233,000 sq. km). Measured by area, the Bay of Bengal, in the Indian Ocean and bordering South Asia and part of Southeast Asia, is larger at 839,000 square miles (2,173,000 sq. km).

Lakes and Rivers

Other water features of the earth include lakes and rivers. A **lake** is a body of water completely surrounded by land. The world's largest freshwater lake is Lake Superior, one of the five Great Lakes between the United States and Canada. It has an area of 31,820 square miles (82,414 sq. km). The world's largest inland body of water, however, is the Caspian Sea, often considered a saltwater lake. Lying between Europe and Asia and east of the Caucasus Mountains, the Caspian Sea has a total area of 143,550 square miles (371,795 sq. km).

A **river** is a waterway flowing through land and emptying into another body of water. The world's longest river is the Nile River in Africa, which flows into the Mediterranean Sea from the highlands of Ethiopia. The Nile's length is about 4,160 miles (6,690 km).

GEOGRAPHY HANDBOOK

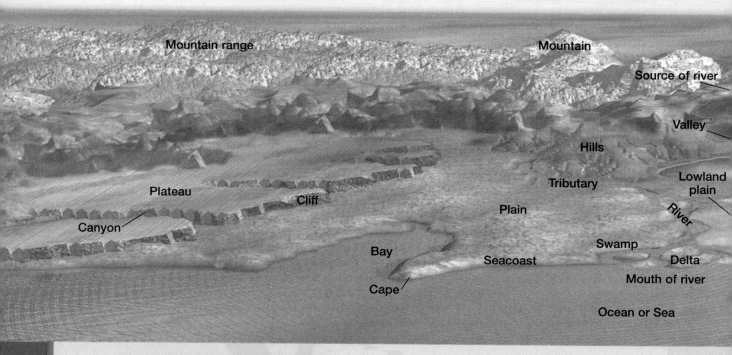

Mountain range
Mountain
Source of river
Valley
Hills
Lowland plain
Tributary
Plateau
Cliff
Plain
River
Canyon
Swamp
Bay
Seacoast
Delta
Cape
Mouth of river
Ocean or Sea

GEOGRAPHIC DICTIONARY

As you read about the world's geography and history, you will discover most of the terms listed and explained below. Many of the terms are pictured in the diagram above. Others you learned earlier in this Geography Handbook.

absolute location–exact location of a place on the earth described by global coordinates

basin–area of land drained by a given river and its branches; area of land surrounded by lands of higher elevations

bay–part of a large body of water that extends into a shoreline

canyon–deep and narrow valley with steep walls

cape–point of land surrounded by a body of water

channel–deep, narrow body of water that connects two larger bodies of water; deep part of a river or other waterway

cliff–steep, high wall of rock, earth, or ice

continent–one of the seven large landmasses on the earth

cultural feature–characteristic that humans have created in a place, such as language, religion, and history

delta–land built up from soil carried downstream by a river and deposited at its mouth

divide–stretch of high land that separates river basins

downstream–direction in which a river or stream flows from its source to its mouth

elevation–height of land above sea level

Equator–imaginary line that runs around the earth halfway between the North and South Poles; used as the starting point to measure degrees of north and south latitude

glacier–large, thick body of slowly moving ice, found in mountains and polar regions

globe–sphere-shaped model of the earth

gulf–part of a large body of water that extends into a shoreline, larger than a bay

harbor–a sheltered place along a shoreline where ships can anchor safely

highland–elevated land area with sloping sides such as a hill, mountain, or plateau hill, smaller than a mountain

island–land area, smaller than a continent, completely surrounded by water

isthmus–narrow stretch of land connecting two larger land areas

lake–a sizable inland body of water

latitude–distance north or south of the Equator, measured in degrees

longitude–distance east or west of the Prime Meridian, measured in degrees

lowland–land, usually level, at a low elevation

map–drawing of all or part of the earth shown on a flat surface

meridian–one of many lines on the global grid

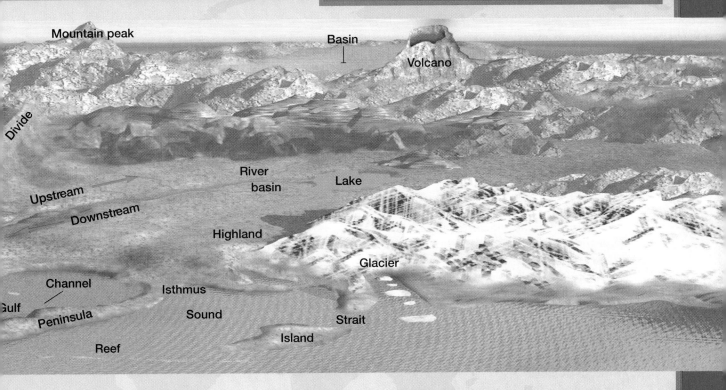

Mountain peak · Basin · Volcano · Divide · River basin · Lake · Upstream · Downstream · Highland · Glacier · Channel · Isthmus · Gulf · Peninsula · Sound · Strait · Reef · Island

running from the North Pole to the South Pole, used to measure degrees of longitude

mesa–area of raised land with steep sides; smaller than a plateau

mountain–land with steep sides that rises sharply from surrounding land; larger and more rugged than a hill

mountain peak–pointed top of a mountain

mountain range–a series of connected mountains

mouth–(of a river) place where a stream or river flows into a larger body of water

ocean–one of the four major bodies of salt water that surrounds a continent

ocean current–stream of either cold or warm water that moves in a definite direction through an ocean

parallel–one of many lines on the global grid that circle the earth north or south of the Equator; used to measure degrees of latitude

peninsula–body of land almost surrounded by water

physical feature–characteristic of a place occurring naturally, such as a landform, body of water, climate pattern, or resource

plain–area of level land, usually at a low elevation

plateau–area of flat or rolling land at a high elevation

Prime Meridian–line of the global grid running from the North Pole to the South Pole at Greenwich, England; used as the starting point for measuring degrees of east and west longitude

relative location–position of a place on the earth in relation to other places

relief–changes in elevation, either few or many, that occur over a given area of land

river–large stream of water that runs through the land

sea–large body of water completely or partly surrounded by land

seacoast–land lying next to a sea or ocean

sea level–average level of an ocean's surface

sound–body of water between a shoreline and one or more islands off the coast

source–(of a river) place where a river or stream begins, often in high lands

strait–narrow stretch of water joining two larger bodies of water

tributary–small river or stream that flows into a large river or stream; a branch of the river

upstream–direction opposite the flow of a river; toward the source of a river or stream

valley–area of low land between hills or mountains

volcano–mountain created as liquid rock or ash are thrown up from inside the earth

CLIMATE

Climate is the usual pattern of weather events that occurs in an area over a long period of time. Climate is determined by distance from the Equator, by location near large bodies of water, and sometimes by positions near mountain ranges

The world's climates can be organized into four major regions: **tropical**, **mid-latitude**, **high latitude**, and **dry**. Some of these regions are determined by their latitude; others are based on the vegetation that grows in them.

Tropical Climates

Tropical climates get their name from the tropics, the areas along the Equator. Temperatures in the tropics change little from season to season. The warm tropical climate region can be separated into two types: tropical rain forest and tropical savanna.

The tropical rain forest climate region is wet in most months, with up to 100 inches (254 cm) of rain a year. In these areas, rain and heat produce lush vegetation and **rain forests**, dense forests that are home to millions of kinds of plant and animal life. The Amazon River basin in South America is the world's largest rain forest area.

The tropical **savanna** climate has two seasons—one wet and one dry. Savannas, or grasslands with few trees, occur in this region. Among the leading tropical savanna climate areas are southern India and eastern Africa.

Mid-Latitude Climates

Mid-latitude, or moderate, climates are found in the middle latitudes of the Northern and Southern Hemispheres. Most of the world's people live in this climate region. The mid-latitude region has a greater variety of climates than other regions. This variety results from the mix of air masses—warm air coming from the tropics and cool air coming from the polar regions. In most places, temperatures change with the seasons.

High Latitude Climates

High latitude, or polar, climate regions lie in the high latitudes of each hemisphere. Climates are cold everywhere in the high latitude regions, some more severe than others.

High latitude climate regions also include highland or mountainous regions even in lower

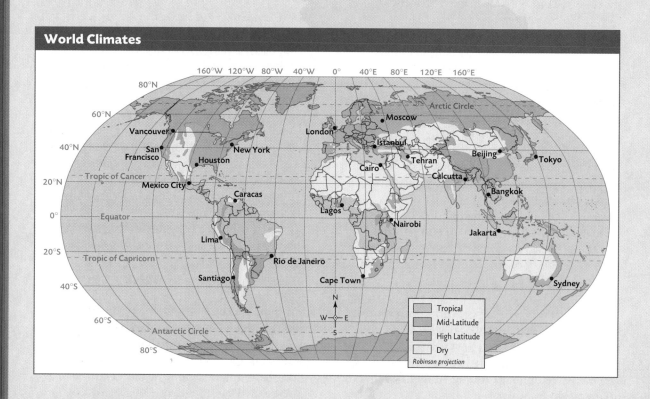

World Climates

World Land Use and Resources

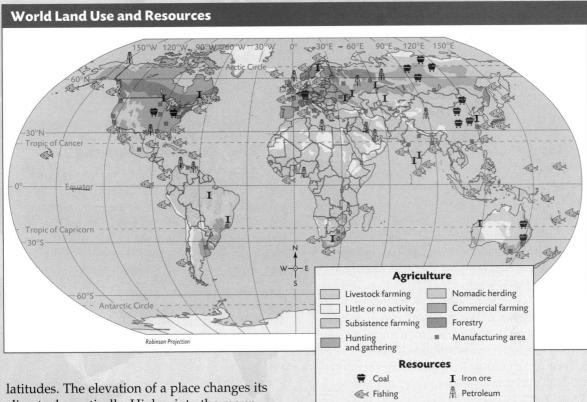

Agriculture

- Livestock farming
- Little or no activity
- Subsistence farming
- Hunting and gathering
- Nomadic herding
- Commercial farming
- Forestry
- Manufacturing area

Resources

- Coal
- Fishing
- Iron ore
- Petroleum

Robinson Projection

latitudes. The elevation of a place changes its climate dramatically. Higher into the mountains, the air becomes thinner. It cannot hold the heat from the sun, so the temperature drops. Even in the tropics, snow covers the peaks of high mountains.

Dry Climates

Dry climate refers to dry or partially dry areas that receive little or no rainfall. Temperatures can be extremely hot during the day and cold at night. Dry climates can also have severely cold winters.

Nearly an eighth of the world's land surface is dry, with a rainfall of less than 10 inches (25 cm) per year. The Sahara in North Africa is the largest desert in the world. The area covered by the Sahara—3,579,000 square miles (9,270,000 sq. km)—is about the size of the United States.

NATURAL RESOURCES

Natural resources refer to anything from the natural environment that people use to meet their needs. Natural resources include fertile soil, clean water, minerals, trees, and energy sources. Human skills and labor are also valuable natural resources.

Renewable Resources

Some natural resources can be replaced as they are used up. These renewable resources can be replaced naturally or grown fairly quickly. Forests, grasslands, plant and animal life, and rich soil all can be renewable resources if people manage them carefully. A lumber company concerned about future growth can replant as many trees as it cuts. Fishing and whaling fleets can limit the number of fish and whales they catch in certain parts of the ocean.

Nonrenewable Resources

Metals and other minerals found in the earth's crust are nonrenewable resources. They cannot be replaced because they were formed over millions of years by geologic forces within the earth.

One important group of nonrenewable resources is fossil fuels—coals, oil, and natural gas. Industries and people depend on these fuels for energy and as raw materials for plastics and other goods. We also use up large amounts of other metals and minerals, such as iron, aluminum, and phosphates. Some of these can be reused, but they cannot be replaced.

ENVIRONMENTAL CHALLENGES

When people use natural resources to make a living, they affect the environment. The unmanaged use of resources is a threat to the environment. Many human activities can cause pollution—putting impure or poisonous substances into the land, water, and air.

Land and Water

Only about 11 percent of the earth's surface has land good enough for farming. Chemicals that farmers use may improve their crops, but some also may damage the land. Pesticides, or chemicals that kill insects, can pollute rivers and groundwater, or water that fills tiny cracks in the rock layers below the earth's surface.

Other human activities also pollute soil and water. Oil spills from tanker ships threaten ocean coastal areas. Illegal dumping of dangerous waste products causes problems. Untreated sewage reaching rivers pollutes lakes and groundwater as well. Salt water can also pollute both soil and groundwater.

Air

Industries and vehicles that burn fossil fuels are the main sources of air pollution. Throughout the world, fumes from cars and other vehicles pollute the air. The chemicals in air pollution can seriously damage people's health.

These chemicals combined with precipitation may fall as acid rain, or rain carrying large amounts of sulfuric acid. Acid rain eats away the surfaces of buildings, kills fish, and can destroy entire forests.

Energy

All of the world nations need safe, dependable sources of energy. Fossil fuels are most often used to generate electricity, heat buildings, run machinery, and power vehicles. Fossil fuels, however, are non-renewable resources. In addition, they contribute to air pollution. So today many countries are trying to discover new ways of using renewable energy sources. Two of these ways are hydroelectric power, the energy generated by falling water, and solar energy, or energy produced by the heat of the sun.

GEOGRAPHY'S IMPACT ON WORLD HISTORY

Geographic factors have shaped the outcome of historical events. Landforms, waterways, climate, and natural resources all have helped or hindered human activities. In many cases, people have learned either to adapt to their environment or to transform it to meet their needs.

Throughout the units of your text, you will discover how geography has shaped the course of events in world history. Here are some examples of the role that geographic factors have played in the story of humanity.

Unit 1 The Rise of Civilizations

Rivers contributed to the rise of many of the world's early civilizations. By 3000 B.C. the Sumerians of the Middle East had set up 12 prosperous city-states in the Tigris-Euphrates River valley. The Fertile Crescent, as the area is often called because of its relatively rich topsoil and its curved shape, was able to support city-state populations ranging from 20,000 to 250,000 people.

Unit 2 Flowering of Civilizations

Landforms and waterways also affected the political relationships of the world's ancient peoples. For example, the rugged landscape of Greece divided the ancient Greeks into separate city-states instead of uniting them into a single nation. Furthermore, closeness to the sea caused the Greek city-states to expand their trade, culture, and sense of civic pride to other parts of the Mediterranean world.

Unit 3 Regional Civilizations

From about A.D. 400 to A.D. 1500, regional civilizations developed at the crossroads of trade between different areas of the world. The city of Makkah (Mecca), in the Middle East's Arabian Peninsula, was a crossroads for caravans from North Africa, Palestine, and the

Persian Gulf. The religion of Islam established a firm base in Makkah, from which it spread to other areas of the Middle East, North Africa, South Asia, and Southeast Asia.

Unit 4 Emergence of the Modern World

The desire to control or to obtain scarce natural resources has encouraged trade and stimulated contact among the world's peoples. At the dawn of the modern era, Asians and Europeans came into contact with one another partly because Europeans wanted Asia's spices and silks. When the Asiatic people known as the Mongols could no longer guarantee safe passage for traders on overland routes, Europeans were forced to consider new water routes to Asia. This opened a new global age that brought the peoples of Europe, Asia, Africa, and the Americas into closer contact with each other.

Unit 5 Age of Revolution

Climate often affects the way a country behaves toward its neighbors. For example, many of Russia's harbors stay frozen during much of the year. In the past, Russia has often gone to war with other countries to capture land for warm water ports. Climate was also one reason why the Russians were able to stop the invasions of French ruler Napoleon Bonaparte in 1812 and the German dictator Adolf Hitler in 1941. The Russians were used to the bitter cold and snow of their country's winter, whereas the invaders were not.

Unit 6 Industry and Nationalism

Exploiting natural resources, such as coal and iron, was an important factor in the growth of the Industrial Revolution. Modern industry started in Great Britain, which had large amounts of coal and iron ore for making steel. Throughout Europe and North America, the rise of factories that turned raw materials into finished goods prompted people eager for employment to move from rural areas to urban centers.

Also, the availability of land and the discovery of minerals in the Americas, Australia, and South Africa caused hundreds of thousands of Europeans to move to these areas in hope of improving their lives. These mass migrations were possible because of improvements in industrial technology and transportation that enabled people to overcome geographic barriers.

Unit 7 World in Conflict

Environmental disasters during the first part of the 1900s affected national economies in various parts of the world. For example, during the 1930s, winds blew away so much of the soil in the Great Plains of central North America that the area became known as the Dust Bowl. Ruined by the drought, many farmers packed up their belongings and headed west. It took many years of normal rainfall and improved farming techniques to transform the Great Plains from a Dust Bowl into productive land once again.

Unit 8 The Contemporary World

As the year 2000 approaches, the world's peoples have become more aware of the growing scarcity of nonrenewable resources. Oil takes millions of years to form, and the earth's supply is limited. Industrialized countries like the United States consume far more oil than they produce and must import large amounts. Many experts believe that the world's fossil fuels will be used up if steps are not taken to limit their consumption and to find alternative sources.

Geography and History Journal

You are about to journey to the past to learn about the people and events that have shaped the world you live in today. Throughout your course of study, keep a record of the events discussed above and any other events in world history that have been affected by geography. When you come to the last unit, you may also want to explore how geography impacts current events or issues: For example, how has geography influenced peacekeeping missions in Bosnia and other parts of the world, or what would happen to Canada geographically if the province of Quebec were to separate and form an independent nation? On a world map locate the places where these historical events have occurred, and identify the units of study in your text in which they are discussed.

Relation to Environment
The ancient Egyptians develop a civilization in northeastern Africa's Nile River Valley.

Bust of infant sun god

Uniformity
Early Chinese dynasties establish and maintain a strong central government in East Asia.

Terra cotta warriors—Qin dynasty

Change
Early modern Europe enjoys a cultural awakening based on ancient Greek and Roman ideas as well as on Christianity and Judaism.

Renaissance musicians

The Gas Factory

Cultural Diffusion
The Industrial Revolution begins in Great Britain and gradually spreads to other parts of the world.

Innovation
New technology transforms many aspects of life in the modern world.

Shuttle lift-off

orld history is a record of the adventures of humankind—both the famous and the ordinary—throughout thousands of years. By studying world history—by gazing across time—you can understand the past and recognize its contribution to the present and the future. World history tells of significant people and events. It also encompasses broad historical themes that happen again and again, providing meaning for events in the past and showing how they affect contemporary life.

World History: The Human Experience introduces 9 key historical themes. Each chapter highlights and develops several of these themes that demonstrate the interconnectedness of ideas and events. These events help organize your study of world history and make connections across time.

Cooperation/Conflict focuses on how people relate to each other throughout history—sometimes in cooperation, working together to accomplish a common goal, at other times in conflict, struggling against one another.

Revolution/Reaction deals with revolution, or the sudden overthrow of long-established ideas and organizations, contrasted with reaction, or the efforts to oppose new ideas and preserve traditional ways.

Change includes political, social, religious, cultural, and economic transformations that influence human activities throughout the centuries.

Diversity/Uniformity focuses on the diversity or variety of world peoples and customs, contrasted with the desire for uniformity or commonality in some societies.

Regionalism/Nationalism deals with a sense of loyalty and belonging, expressed in ties to a region, to a nation, or to the world as a whole—to the global community.

Innovation includes cultural, scientific, and technical breakthroughs that increase knowledge and impact the way people live and think.

Cultural Diffusion focuses on the spread of cultural expressions through a variety of means across nations, regions, and the world.

Movement involves the movement of people throughout history, including patterns of migration, exploration, and colonization as well as imperialism—people in one place on the globe exercising control over people in another place.

Relation to Environment emphasizes human-environment interchange—how people are affected by their environment and, in turn, how they affect that same environment.

Horn player, Benin

Rise of Civilizations

Then & Now

Scholars have divided history into periods according to environmental changes on Earth and cultural developments of mankind. The Paleolithic period or Old Stone Age began about 2 million years ago and lasted until about 12,000 B.C. The earliest evidence of human cultural development was discovered by four teenagers, quite by accident. Jacques Marshal and three young friends entered a cave near Lascaux, France, in 1940 and found the most spectacular cave paintings from Ice Age Europe, created some 17,000 years ago. Cave paintings have been discovered in many parts of the world, but the Lascaux paintings provide the most dramatic and best preserved "snapshots" of early human life yet to be discovered.

A Global Chronology

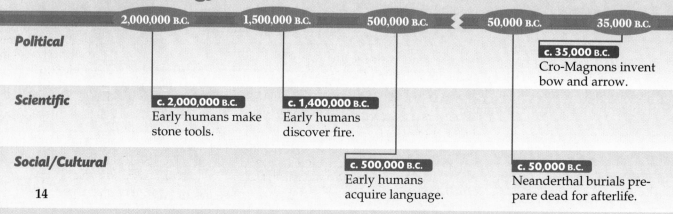

	2,000,000 B.C.	1,500,000 B.C.	500,000 B.C.	50,000 B.C.	35,000 B.C.
Political					c. 35,000 B.C. Cro-Magnons invent bow and arrow.
Scientific	c. 2,000,000 B.C. Early humans make stone tools.	c. 1,400,000 B.C. Early humans discover fire.			
Social/Cultural			c. 500,000 B.C. Early humans acquire language.	c. 50,000 B.C. Neanderthal burials prepare dead for afterlife.	

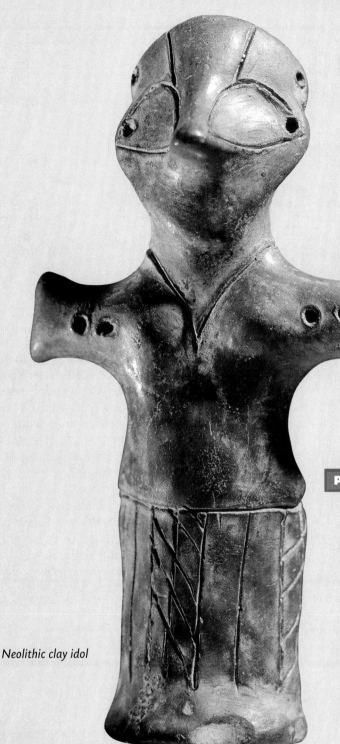

Neolithic clay idol

Portfolio Project

The development of written language is a fascinating study. The earliest writing was a simplified form of drawing objects. The letters of our alphabet have a history going back to these simple drawings. Research the origin of the letters that are your own initials. Write a brief history of the letters you researched. Then create several new alphabet letters using symbols based on modern inventions. Explain the symbols you chose.

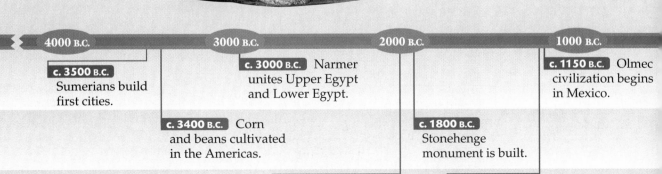

4000 B.C.　　　3000 B.C.　　　2000 B.C.　　　1000 B.C.

c. 3500 B.C. Sumerians build first cities.

c. 3000 B.C. Narmer unites Upper Egypt and Lower Egypt.

c. 1150 B.C. Olmec civilization begins in Mexico.

c. 3400 B.C. Corn and beans cultivated in the Americas.

c. 1800 B.C. Stonehenge monument is built.

c. 2000 B.C. Chinese write on oracle bones.

c. 1200 B.C. Sumerians record *Gilgamesh* epic.

15

The Spread of Ideas

Farming and Civilization

*B*etween 8,000 and 10,000 years ago, a quiet revolution took place. In scattered pockets of the Middle East, Asia, Africa, and the Americas, people learned to cultivate food-producing plants for the first time. As knowledge of farming gradually spread, it dramatically changed human culture. Farming encouraged the growth of permanent communities, which in turn became the seedbeds for the world's first civilizations.

The Middle East
Breadbasket of the Ancient World

Today only sparse vegetation covers the foothills of Iraq's Zagros Mountains. Erosion and overgrazing by sheep and goats have taken their toll. Around 8000 B.C., however, wild wheat known as emmer covered the hills. Experts believe it was here that the world's first farmers may have watched seeds fall to earth and sprout. This observation led these ancient wanderers to plant seeds.

Over time, knowledge of farming spread in a broad arc of fertile land that curved from the Persian Gulf to the Mediterranean Sea. Farmers gradually added other foods to their diets—barley, chickpeas, lentils, figs, apricots, pistachios, walnuts, and more. A hunger for these foods kept people in one place. Hunting and gathering lifestyles changed as people began to develop new ideas and skills. Slowly—very slowly—farming settlements grew into cities. Known by names such as Ur, Babylon, and Jericho, these cities were the centers of Earth's oldest civilizations.

Greek grain storage jar

Foothills of the Zagros Mountains

The Americas
Mexico and Peru: Farming and Diversity

For much of world history, distance separated the Americas from the rest of the world. But the independent invention of farming in the areas of present-day Mexico and Peru created cities as sophisticated as those in other regions. The crops that spurred their growth, however, differed from crops elsewhere. Few of the wild grains found on other continents grew in the Americas. The first farmers in the Americas used the seeds of other plants, especially squash and beans. They also developed two high-yield foods unknown to the rest of the world—potatoes and maize (corn). When distant civilizations made contact, ideas about agriculture accompanied the wide distribution of foods that early peoples had developed and cultivated.

Corn Dance *by Frank Reed Whiteside*

Asia and Africa
Expansion of Earth's Gardens

The farming revolution did not happen just once. It occurred several times in widely separated regions. More than 6,000 years ago, farmers along the upper Huang He in present-day northern China started planting millet. About 5,000 years ago, farmers near the mouth of the Chang Jiang in southern China learned to grow rice. At roughly the same time, farmers along the Nile River in the northern part of Africa harvested their first crops of wheat and barley.

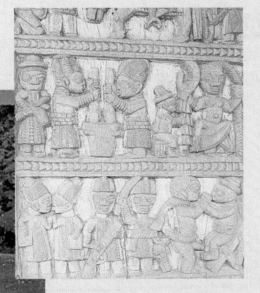

Like the gardens of the Middle East, the gardens of China and northern Africa grew more diverse. By 3000 B.C., farmers cultivated soybeans, bananas, and sugarcane. Supported by the harvests, people had more time to think and dream. Soon they created things that were used by the civilizations of the Middle East—calendars, systems of writing, forms of art and government.

Wood relief of farming activities, Yoruba peoples

LINKING THE IDEAS

1. How do experts think farming probably began?
2. Why is farming considered one of the most important inventions of human history?

Critical Thinking

3. **Cause and Effect** What is the connection between farming and the rise of ancient civilizations?

Prehistory–1000 B.C.

Human Beginnings

Chapter Themes

▶ **Movement** Migrations of prehistoric peoples result in their spread throughout the world. *Section 1*

▶ **Innovation** Early humans produce tools and domesticate animals and crops. *Section 2*

▶ **Change** The earliest civilizations begin with the evolution of farming settlements into the first cities. *Section 3*

S̄toryteller

On the coast of southern Africa, in caves and rock shelters, lived some of the world's first communities of prehistoric people. The region enjoyed a mild climate and abundant food from both the land and the sea. Women gathered supplies, while men made longer journeys inland, hunting for big animals such as antelope, buffalo, and wildebeest. Both men and women searched the coast at each low tide for small sea animals.

The cave dwellers preserved food for times of scarcity by drying leftover meat in smoke from fires. They did not know that more than 70,000 years later scientists and other people exploring the same area would uncover the remains of their long-vanished way of life.

Historical Significance

How did early peoples develop skills that became the basic elements of human ways of life? What developments led to the rise of the world's first civilizations?

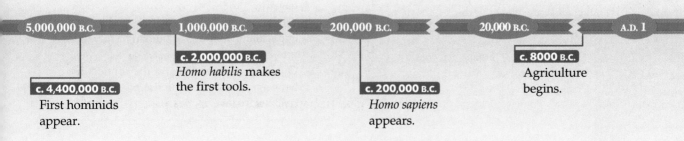

| 5,000,000 B.C. | 1,000,000 B.C. | 200,000 B.C. | 20,000 B.C. | A.D. 1 |

c. 2,000,000 B.C.
Homo habilis makes the first tools.

c. 8000 B.C.
Agriculture begins.

c. 4,400,000 B.C.
First hominids appear.

c. 200,000 B.C.
Homo sapiens appears.

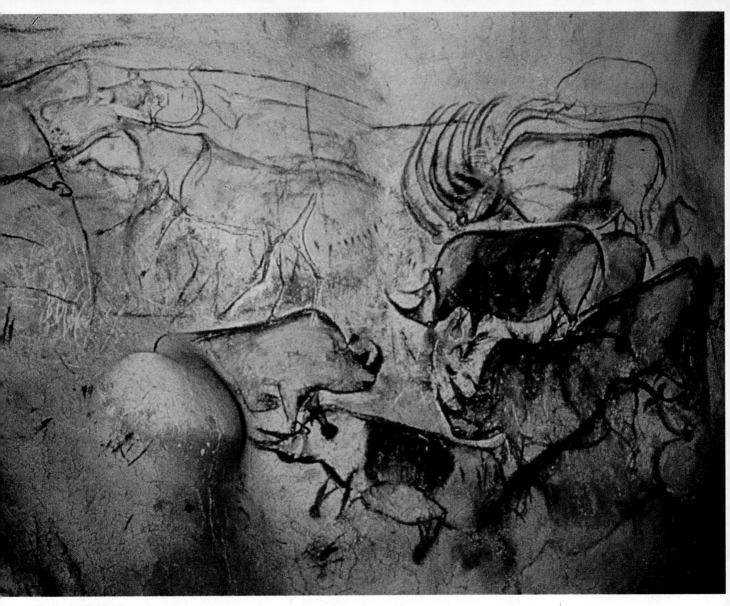

Cro-Magnon cave paintings from Vallon-Pont-d'Arc
near Avignon, France

Your History Journal

Imagine that you and a friend are stranded on a large uninhabited island. You have no tools except a pocket knife. There are many species of small animals, a stream of fresh water, a sandy beach, and a dense forest. You must survive until rescued, perhaps a month later. Write a journal account of your first seven days.

5,000,000 B.C.   3,000,000 B.C.   1,000,000 B.C.

c. 4,400,000 B.C.
Earliest known human ancestor
lives in East Africa.

c. 2,000,000 B.C.
Homo habilis
develops first
stone tools.

c. 1,700,000 B.C.
Homo erectus reaches Asia.

Section 1

Discovery of Early Humans in Africa

Setting the Scene

▶ **Terms to Define**
prehistory, hominid, anthropologist,
paleontologist, archaeologist, artifact,
radiocarbon dating, nomad, culture, technology

▶ **People to Meet**
Gen Suwa, Tim D. White, Donald C. Johanson,
Louis Leakey, Mary Leakey

▶ **Places to Locate**
Aramis, Hadar, Olduvai Gorge

 **Find Out** How have recent archaeological
finds contributed to our understanding of
human origins?

The Storyteller

On the slab lies the shriveled corpse of a
man.… Alongside him lies a long wooden stave with
a fibrous end. Laid out on the slab … are the other
finds—the axe with its elbow-shafting and metal
blade, a stone bead with a strange tassel of twisted
hide thongs, the small dagger … a wooden stick with
holes in it, a scrap of leather, and a nut-sized stone.…
Archaeologist Konrad Spindler's assessment:
'Roughly four thousand years old … [or] even earlier.'

—adapted from *The Man in the Ice*,
Konrad Spindler, 1994

Excavation of an ancient site in Lake Kinneret, Galilee

History tells the story of humankind.
Because historians mostly use written records to gather information
about the past, history is said to begin with the
invention of writing about 5,500 years ago. But the
story of humankind really begins in the time *before*
people developed writing—the period called
prehistory.

Using the best available evidence, scientists
have traced the existence of the first humanlike
creatures back to about 4.4 million years ago in
Africa. Human beings and the humanlike creatures
that preceded them together belong to a group of
beings named hominids (HAH•muh•nuhds). The
scientific study of hominids—their physical features,
development, and behavior—is called anthropology.
Physical anthropologists (AN•thruh•PAH•luh•jihsts)
compare hominid bones and other fossil remains,
looking for changes in such features as brain size
and posture. Anthropologists work closely with
other scientists. Paleontologists (PAY•lee•AHN
•TAH•luh•jihsts), for example, study fossil remains
to determine the characteristics of various prehistoric periods. Archaeologists (AHR•kee•AH•luh
•jihsts) investigate prehistoric life by unearthing
and interpreting the objects left behind by prehistoric people. These artifacts include any objects that
were shaped by human hands—tools, pots, and
beads—as well as other remains of human life, such
as bits of charcoal.

Dating Early Artifacts

As they unearth the remains of prehuman and
human settlements, archaeologists and physical
anthropologists face the additional problem of dating what they find. It is easy to determine the relative sequence in which events happened: More

recent remains are usually found above older ones. The problem lies in assigning a definite age to fossil bones, tools, and other remains.

Among the techniques for determining the age of organic remains is radiocarbon dating. Organic matter includes once-living things like wood artifacts, campfire ashes, bone, and cotton cloth. A very small percentage of the carbon atoms absorbed by every living thing is radioactive. When any living thing dies, it stops absorbing carbon. Then, because radioactive carbon decays at a known rate, archaeologists can measure how much the radioactive carbon in organic remains has decayed and figure out when the animal or plant died.

Radiocarbon dating, however, can be used only for organic matter that is less than 50,000 years old. Researchers have devised other techniques for studying earlier periods. By measuring the rate of decay for chemical elements other than carbon, researchers can date older fossils as far back as 2.6 billion years. These extremely sophisticated methods are not infallible, of course, but they do enable scientists to peer far into the past.

Prehistoric Finds in Africa

On December 17, 1992, a paleontologist from Japan named **Gen Suwa** walked across the rugged desert landscape of Ethiopia in East Africa. At a site called **Aramis**, an object in the ground caught Suwa's eye. It turned out to be one of the oldest hominid teeth ever found—a link to the origins of our human ancestors!

The Oldest Human Ancestor

Over the next two years, Suwa, his colleague **Tim D. White** of the University of California, and a 20-person team uncovered additional remains. They came up with teeth, arm bones, and parts of a skull and jaw that belonged to 17 individuals. Analyzing the fossils, the scientists determined that they were about 4.4 million years old and came from the oldest direct human ancestor known. The small creatures would have weighed about 65 pounds (30 kg) and stood 4 feet (1.2 m) tall. Scientists have yet to determine whether they walked upright.

Discovery of Lucy

About 45 miles (73 km) north, at **Hadar**, two scientists—**Donald C. Johanson** and Tom Gray—in 1974 had uncovered the 3.2 million-year-old skeleton of a hominid nicknamed "Lucy." Lucy received her name from a popular Beatles song of the period,

Visualizing History Mary Leakey, a noted paleoanthropologist, follows a trail of hominid footprints fossilized in volcanic ash. *What are hominids?*

"Lucy in the Sky with Diamonds." Hers was the most nearly complete skeleton of any erect-walking prehuman found up to that time.

Since then, Johanson and his team of researchers have made further discoveries. In 1994 they assembled, from other fossils found at the Hadar site, the first reasonably complete skull of a Lucy-like hominid. The scientists claimed that the skull provided evidence that males and females in this early hominid group were of significantly different sizes. The evidence also indicated that Lucy-like hominids spent some time climbing in trees and could also walk upright.

The earliest known direct evidence of upright walking comes from Kenya, where archaeologists in 1995 discovered a fossilized hominid shin bone about 4 million years old. The shape and size of the bone indicate upright walking.

Human Origins

Scientists disagree about many aspects of the story of human beginnings. As scientists unearth more clues, newer evidence may require them to reinterpret older evidence.

The First Hominids

According to one of the generally accepted theories, the first prehuman hominids, of whom the discoveries in Ethiopia are an example, date back about 4.4 million years. Known as *Australopithecus* (aw•STRAY•loh•PIH•thuh•kuhs), or "southern ape," they stood about 3.5 to 5.0 feet (1.1 to 1.6 m) tall and walked on two legs. They had large faces that jutted out. The brain was small, the nose flat, and the teeth large. The back teeth were suitable for grinding food.

Australopithecus lived in the humid forests of eastern and southern Africa, where they fed on fruits, leaves, and nuts. They probably also ate fish caught in streams and meat from animals killed by lions or other predators. *Australopithecus* were most likely nomads—moving constantly in search of food. They probably had few, if any, possessions and may have shared food with one another. Fossil evidence shows that family groups lived in temporary camps. Perhaps they lived together for protection from large animals. No evidence exists showing that *Australopithecus* made or used tools. They may have used grass stems and twigs as tools and sticks or bones to dig roots, however.

Hominid Groups

Scientists use the Latin word *Homo*, which means "human," to name these hominids and all later human beings as well. Anthropologists today are still not certain whether a direct relationship connected *Australopithecus* and human beings or exactly when hominids became truly human. Scientists divided *Homo*—the genus of humans—into three species that differ somewhat in body structures. These three human or humanlike species arose at different times in prehistory. The earliest of the three was *Homo habilis*, or "person with ability," who lived until about 1.5 million years ago. After *Homo habilis* lived the second type

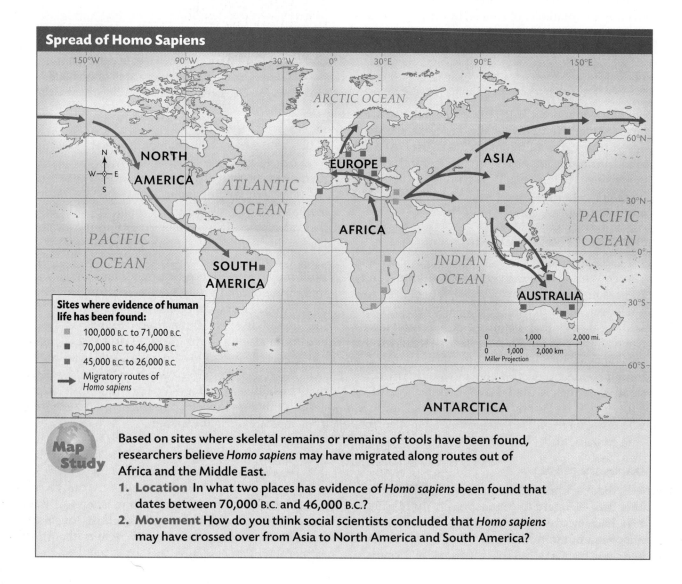

Spread of Homo Sapiens

Sites where evidence of human life has been found:
- 100,000 B.C. to 71,000 B.C.
- 70,000 B.C. to 46,000 B.C.
- 45,000 B.C. to 26,000 B.C.
- Migratory routes of *Homo sapiens*

Map Study

Based on sites where skeletal remains or remains of tools have been found, researchers believe *Homo sapiens* may have migrated along routes out of Africa and the Middle East.

1. **Location** In what two places has evidence of *Homo sapiens* been found that dates between 70,000 B.C. and 46,000 B.C.?
2. **Movement** How do you think social scientists concluded that *Homo sapiens* may have crossed over from Asia to North America and South America?

© Bob Campbell

Hominid Hunter

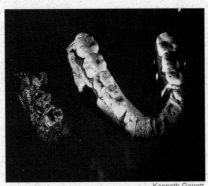

Kenneth Garrett

Meave Leakey, daughter-in-law of famed fossil hunters Mary and Louis Leakey, sifts through the soil near Lake Turkana in northern Kenya, a site in the East African Rift System famous for its treasury of the fossils of early humans. In recent years a wide range of scholars have continued to push back the date for the origin of the earliest humans. Molecular biologists, through the study of human, chimpanzee, and gorilla genes and blood proteins, speculate that hominids, or early humans, originated somewhere between five and seven million years ago. One of a number of scientists influenced by this research, Meave Leakey and her team began exploring for new evidence. They now theorize that a jawbone found near Lake Turkana in 1994 may be 4.1 million years old. Before that discovery there was little evidence of hominids older than 3.6 million years. Some researchers believe that a 5.6 million-year-old jaw fragment (left) discovered in 1967 may be the oldest hominid fossil yet found. ⊕

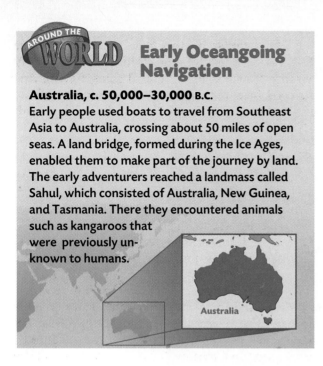

Early Oceangoing Navigation

Australia, c. 50,000–30,000 B.C.
Early people used boats to travel from Southeast Asia to Australia, crossing about 50 miles of open seas. A land bridge, formed during the Ice Ages, enabled them to make part of the journey by land. The early adventurers reached a landmass called Sahul, which consisted of Australia, New Guinea, and Tasmania. There they encountered animals such as kangaroos that were previously unknown to humans.

Australia

of early human—*Homo erectus*, or "person who walks upright"—who was, in turn, followed between 100,000 and 200,000 years ago by *Homo sapiens*, or "person who thinks." All people living today belong to the species *Homo sapiens*.

The Ice Ages

Climatic changes played an important part in the development of early humankind. Between 2 million and 10,000 years ago, Earth experienced four long periods of cold climate, known as the Ice Ages. During each such period, average temperatures in many parts of the world fell to below freezing, and massive glaciers spread out from the Poles, scarring the landforms over which they crept. The northern glaciers covered large portions of Europe, Asia, and North America, and the ice fields of Antarctica stretched over wide regions in the Southern Hemisphere. Only the middle latitudes remained warm enough to support human and animal life. Between glacial periods, Earth's climate warmed overall, and abundant rains brought lush plant growth—until the next glacial period began.

As the sheets of ice formed, the level of the oceans dropped more than 300 feet (90 m). As a result, some areas that are now separated by water were connected then by bridges of land. One such land bridge joined Japan and mainland Korea, another connected Great Britain and Ireland to western Europe, a third led from the Malay Peninsula through the Indonesian islands almost all the way to Australia, and a fourth connected Asia and North America at the Bering Strait.

Early human beings responded to the environmental changes of the Ice Ages in several ways. Some migrated to warmer places. Others found strategies for keeping warm, such as clothing and fire. Those who could not adapt died from starvation or exposure.

Human Culture

Clothing and fire had become part of the culture, or way of life, of prehistoric people. Culture also includes the knowledge a people have, the language they speak, the ways in which they eat and dress, their religious beliefs, and their achievements in art and music.

Toolmaking

One of the earliest aspects of culture that people formed was the use of tools. At first they dug roots and tubers out of the ground with wooden digging sticks. Later, they made crude tools of stone, which enabled them to skin small animals and cut off pieces of meat. Improving their technology—the skills and useful knowledge available to them for collecting material and making the objects necessary for survival—early people began to create specialized tools, such as food choppers, skin scrapers, and spear points.

The Stone Age

The use of stone tools by early people led historians to apply the name Stone Age to the period before writing became established. Scholars divided the Stone Age into three shorter periods, depending on differences in toolmaking techniques. The earliest period, the Paleolithic (PAY•lee•uh•LIH•thihk) or Old Stone Age, began about 2 million years ago with the first toolmaking by *Homo habilis* and lasted until about 12,000 B.C. The Mesolithic (MEH•zuh•LIH•thihk) period or Middle Stone Age is usually dated from 12,000 B.C. to about 8000 B.C. The Neolithic (NEE•uh•LIH•thihk) period or New Stone Age lasted from about 8000 B.C. to 5000 B.C.

Paleolithic Hunter-Gatherers

Archaeologists as yet do not know a great deal about the culture of the early humans called *Homo habilis* and *Homo erectus*. Their knowledge, however, widens as new discoveries are made.

Homo Habilis

Homo habilis lived during the first quarter of the Paleolithic period. It seems probable, however, that these prehistoric people are the oldest hominids known to manufacture tools. They lived in Africa from about 2.5 million to 1.5 million years ago, alongside *Australopithecus*. Their larger brains indicate that they were more physically and mentally advanced. Much of the evidence for *Homo habilis* has come from research by **Louis and Mary Leakey**, and later their son Richard, at **Olduvai** (OHL•duh•VY) **Gorge** and other sites in the eastern part of Africa.

Homo Erectus

Scientists have gathered much more information about *Homo erectus* than about *Homo habilis*. *Homo erectus* first appeared in Africa and lived from 1.6 million years ago to about 250,000 years ago. Their living areas covered a variety of environments from woodlands and grasslands in Africa to forests and plains in Europe and Asia.

Homo erectus at first were mostly food gatherers. Scientists think the females gathered fruits, nuts, and seeds, and the males scavenged for meat—either searching for an animal that had died of natural causes or yelling and waving their arms to frighten carnivores away from a kill. By about 500,000 years ago, however, the males had become hunters, using spears and clubs to kill such small prey as deer, pigs, and rabbits. The females, whose movements were restricted by the constant demands of child care, continued to forage close to home for vegetable food.

Meanwhile, these early humans also had learned how to make fire. This discovery allowed them to keep warm, cook food, and scare away threatening animals. It also enabled them to live in caves. Before, they had protected themselves from the weather by digging shallow pits and covering these with branches. Now, they could drive animals out of caves and use the caves themselves.

Homo erectus by this time not only had fire but also made clothing. Initially they simply wrapped themselves in animal skins, having first scraped hair and tissue off the inner side of the skins. Later, they laced the skins together with strips of leather.

Migrations

Scientists disagree on when prehistoric peoples left Africa and moved to other parts of the world. Some experts believe that *Homo habilis* may have been the earliest to migrate to Europe and Asia; however, clear evidence to support this view is lacking. Scientists do know, however, that *Homo erectus* migrated from their native Africa to Europe and Asia. Skeletal remains found in Java have led anthropologists to conclude that *Homo erectus* reached the Indonesian islands about 1.6 to 1.8 million years ago. *Homo erectus* was clearly well established in China by 460,000 years ago, and the earliest skeletal traces in Europe may also date back around 400,000 years.

Language

Homo erectus may have been talking to each other about 500,000 years ago instead of just making sounds to indicate emotions and directions. Language was one of humanity's greatest achievements. It enabled individuals to work with one another—to organize a hunting group, for example, or to give specific instructions about where to find a spring of fresh water. It allowed individuals to exchange ideas, such as how the world began or what caused animals to migrate across the plains. Individuals could sit around a hearth fire, eat together, and talk about the day's events. They could talk about the best way to fell a tree or build a shelter. Perhaps most significantly, spoken language made it possible for the older generation to pass its culture on to the younger generation, enabling new generations to build upon the knowledge of the past.

SECTION 1 REVIEW

Recall

1. **Define** prehistory, hominid, anthropologist, paleontologist, archaeologist, artifacts, radiocarbon dating, nomad, culture, technology.
2. **Identify** Gen Suwa, Tim D. White, Donald C. Johanson, Louis Leakey, Mary Leakey.
3. **Locate** each of these prehistoric sites and explain their importance: Aramis, Hadar, Olduvai Gorge.

Critical Thinking

4. **Making Comparisons** Compare and contrast the culture of *Homo habilis* and *Homo erectus*. Consider housing, technology, and mobility.

Understanding Themes

5. **Movement** How did changes in climate affect the migration of early peoples from one part of the world to another?

c. 100,000 B.C. Neanderthals spread from Africa into Europe and Asia.

c. 50,000 B.C. Modern humans originate in Africa.

c. 15,000 B.C. World population reaches about 2 million.

Section 2

The Appearance of *Homo Sapiens*

Setting the Scene

▶ **Terms to Define**
 domesticate, deity

▶ **People to Meet**
 Neanderthals, Cro-Magnons

▶ **Places to Locate**
 Neander Valley, Lascaux, Vallon-Pont-d'Arc, Jericho, Çatal Hüyük

Find Out ▶ What were the achievements of the earliest humans?

The Storyteller

The first sign of animal domestication we have discovered, at some of the earliest human settlements, is not of something that pulled a plow, or was eaten; it is the dog. This creature, which willingly chooses a human as the leader of its lifelong pack, was humankind's first friend, it seems, as well as its best. Certain species began to thrive under human care; and humans rearranged their lives to care for the animals that now came to depend on them.

—adapted from *Women's Work: The First 20,000 Years*, Elizabeth Wayland Barber, 1994

Neolithic scraper

Homo erectus discovered, used, and improved upon numerous aspects of culture that are basic to present-day life. These accomplishments occurred extremely slowly, however, taking place over many thousands of years. When *Homo sapiens*, the modern human species, appeared, cultural changes began occurring with much greater frequency and took on greater sophistication. In 1995 archaeologists uncovered in Zaire, Central Africa, a number of 80,000-year-old barbed points and blades. This find indicates that humans made the first sophisticated tools in Africa and at a much earlier date than had been believed.

The Neanderthals

Evidence of early *Homo sapiens* dates back about 200,000 years. The first *Homo sapiens* probably were the **Neanderthals** (nee•AN•duhr•THAWLZ). Anthropologists named them after the **Neander Valley** in Germany where their remains were first discovered in the A.D. 1850s. Fossil evidence indicates that Neanderthal people originated in Africa and began spreading into Europe and Asia about 100,000 years ago.

Neanderthals stood about 5.5 feet (1.7 meters) tall. Their brains were slightly larger than those of modern human beings, and their bodies were stocky, with thick bones and very muscular necks and shoulders. Some scientists today believe that these distinctive physical characteristics enabled Neanderthals to adapt to colder climates.

Technological Skills

Like their predecessors, Neanderthals were nomadic hunter-gatherers who used fire for warmth and for cooking their food, but their toolmaking ability was more sophisticated than that of *Homo erectus*. Neanderthals skillfully crafted stone knives, spear points, and bone tools. Hide-cleaning and food-preparing tools were made of flakes struck from flint or whatever other kind of stone was available. The flakes were delicately shaped by chipping away small pieces from one or more edges of the stone.

Ways of Life

Most Neanderthals lived in small groups of 35 to 50 people. Because they were nomads, Neanderthals did not live in permanent homes. In good weather or warm climates, they lived in open-air camps along the shores of lakes or rivers. In several places, archaeologists have found the remains of Neanderthal shelters built of branches and animal skins. In colder climates, Neanderthals lived together in caves or under the overhangs of cliffs. Heavy clothing made from animal skins must have been worn to fight off the cold.

Culture and Beliefs

The Neanderthals were advanced culturally. They cared for their sick and aged, and may have been the first to practice medicine. A number of Neanderthal fossils shows signs of serious injuries that had completely healed before death. Neanderthals also apparently had a belief in life after death. They covered the bodies of their dead with flowers and buried them in shallow graves with food, tools, and weapons.

Homo Sapiens Sapiens

Most scientists believe that modern humans, or *Homo sapiens sapiens*, originated in Africa about 50,000 years ago. Within 20,000 years, this new group had migrated to almost every continent in the world, including Australia and North America

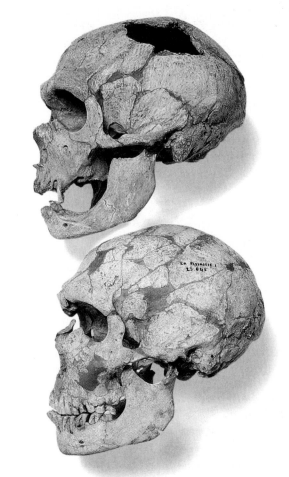

Visualizing History *Homo neanderthalensis* **fossil skulls found in caves in France resemble the original fossil skull from the Neander Valley in Germany. Neanderthals were short, sturdy hunter-gatherers.** *How did Neanderthals adapt to cold weather?*

and South America. Many scientists believe that as *Homo sapiens sapiens* moved slowly from Africa into Europe and Asia, they intermarried with Neanderthals and gradually absorbed them. With the extinction of the Neanderthals, *Homo sapiens sapiens* became the only hominids left on Earth.

The Cro-Magnons

The earliest *Homo sapiens sapiens* in Europe are called **Cro-Magnons**, after the rock shelter in France where their remains were first found in the A.D. 1860s. Since then, a wealth of Cro-Magnon remains have been found in other parts of Europe and in eastern and central Asia. Similar forms of modern humans have been discovered in Russia, China, Southeast Asia, and all over Africa.

The Cro-Magnons were taller but less robust than the Neanderthals. They brought with them improved technology and a more sophisticated

Footnotes to History

The First Razors
Archaeologists have unearthed evidence that prehistoric men were shaving as early as 18,000 B.C. Some Cro-Magnon cave paintings portray beardless men, and early Cro-Magnon grave sites contain sharpened shells that were the first razors. Later, people hammered razors out of bronze, and eventually, out of iron.

culture. Although they still made their living by hunting and gathering, their methods of food gathering were more efficient, and their hunting techniques were more effective than those of earlier groups.

Cro-Magnon Technology

The many advances the Cro-Magnons made in their toolmaking technology transformed human life. Their blades were thinner and had sharper cutting edges than those of the Neanderthals. The Cro-Magnons used bone, antler, and ivory to make new kinds of tools—hammers, hoes, and pincers. Soon they were fishing with bone fishhooks and using bone needles to sew fitted leather clothes.

With the invention of the stone ax, Cro-Magnons could chop down trees and shape them into canoes. Soon they were traveling down rivers and along seacoasts. They even crossed 50 miles (80 kilometers) of open sea to reach Australia.

Cro-Magnon hunters also invented long-distance weapons—the spear-thrower and the bow and arrow. Now they could hunt several animals at once and larger animals, too, such as woolly mammoths and bison. The food supply increased and with it the number of people on Earth. Anthropologists estimate that by 15,000 B.C., the world population of human beings stood at a little more than 2 million.

Social Life

The Cro-Magnons' increased food supply had political and social consequences as well. Because it was not possible for a lone band of Cro-Magnons to carry out a big-game hunt, it became necessary for four or five unrelated bands to cooperate, often for weeks at a time. The cooperating bands probably needed formal rules in order to get along, giving rise in turn to leaders who devised and enforced the rules. The evidence for Cro-Magnon leaders consists of high-status burials. Archaeologists have discovered certain Cro-Magnons buried with ivory daggers, amber beads, and other signs of high rank.

Cro-Magnons at first lived in a variety of temporary structures. Some lived inside cave

Images of the Times

Early Human Technology

Although they are difficult to date precisely, ancient artifacts provide important clues to early human life.

Discovered in France, this bison licking its flank was carved from bone during the Middle Stone Age–12,000–8000 B.C.

A Neolithic scraper, c. 70,000–50,000 B.C., flaked by repeated blows, helped ancient people dig up roots, shape wood, and cut meat.

entrances, while others built huts in forested areas. As better hunting methods developed, Cro-Magnons built more permanent homes. Long houses holding many families were made of stone blocks. There is archaeological evidence that communities of 30 to 100 people lived together.

Cave Paintings

To their technological advances, the Cro-Magnons added accomplished artistry. They created cave paintings like those found at **Lascaux** (la •SKOH) and **Vallon-Pont-d'Arc** (vah•YOHN pohn DAHRK), both in France, as well as those at numerous other cave sites in Spain and Africa. Researchers so far can only speculate on the purpose behind the mysterious wall images. Perhaps the hunting scenes were educational, designed to teach young hunters how to recognize prey. On the other hand, the Cro-Magnon painters may have been reaching out to the spiritual world, creating images meant to have mystical powers that would help the hunters.

Archaeologists have discovered some Cro-Magnon figures sculpted from clay or carved from reindeer antlers. They have also found figures of ivory and bone decorated with animal drawings and abstract designs. Some of these artifacts may well have been used in magic rituals and probably reflect Cro-Magnon beliefs about spirits thought to live in animals, plants, the earth, and the sky.

The Neolithic Revolution

During the Neolithic period and immediately after, humanity made one of its greatest cultural advances. New environments had developed with the end of the last Ice Age, and forests and grasslands appeared in many areas. Over some 5,000 years, people gradually shifted from gathering and hunting food to producing food. Because new agricultural methods led to tremendous changes in peoples' lifestyles, this period is usually called the Neolithic Revolution.

Sumerian cuneiform laid the foundation of writing about 3000 B.C.

REFLECTING ON THE TIMES

1. What clue to early human life does the bison licking its flank provide?
2. How did people store information about the past before writing began?

In a sense, the Mesolithic period was a forerunner of the Neolithic Revolution. Most of the cultural changes of the Mesolithic period came in methods of obtaining food. People domesticated, or tamed for human purposes, the dog and used it to help them hunt small game. They also domesticated the goat to use for meat and milk. Early farmers invented the sickle for cutting wild grains so that they could eat the seeds. Pottery, made from sun-hardened clay, was far more effective for carrying and storing food and water than the pouches of animal skin people had used previously.

The Dawn of Agriculture

The Neolithic Revolution not only took place slowly, but also began at different times in different parts of the world. Archaeologists have found evidence of agriculture in the Middle East dating as far back as 8000 B.C. In contrast, China did not have agriculture until about 5000 B.C.

The crops that Neolithic people domesticated varied from place to place, depending on the varieties of wild plants and on the crops best adapted to the region's climate—wheat and barley in the Middle East, rice in Southeast Asia, and corn in the Americas. Farmers in Africa cultivated bananas and yams, and farmers in South America grew potatoes. Neolithic people also domesticated animals. They used cattle, pigs, and sheep for meat and sometimes milk. Chickens provided eggs as well as meat.

Farming in many ways made life easier. It brought a steady food supply and enabled people to stay longer in one place. However, farmers had to work harder and longer than earlier hunters and gatherers.

Early Humans

	Homo Habilis	Homo Erectus	Homo Sapiens	
Years B.C.	2.5–1.5 million	1.5 million–200,000	200,000–35,000	40,000–8,000
			Neanderthal	Cro-Magnon
TECHNOLOGICAL INNOVATIONS	• Crude stone tools	• Hand axes and other flaked stone tools • Caves used and pits dug • Clothing of animal skins • Fire controlled for warmth, protection, and cooking	• Spear points and hide scrapers • Shelters built or caves improved • Skins laced for clothing	• Knives, chisel, spear-thrower, bow and arrow • Bone tools: needle, fish hook, harpoon • Fish nets, canoes • Sewed leather clothing • Sun-hardened pottery
SOCIAL BEHAVIORS	• Limited speech • Food gathering and scavenging	• Language • Nomadic bands • Hunting-gathering	• Planned burials of dead • Care for disabled members of the community	• Cooperative big-game hunts • Status burials for leaders • Possible magic rituals with cave painting and carved, sculpted artifacts

Chart Study The category "Technological Innovations" describes items found in archaeological digs and dated to a specific period. Interpretation of likely prehistoric social behaviors, however, depends mostly on inferences made by archaeologists and anthropologists. What evidence do researchers have to support the theory that the social behaviors listed above really existed?

The First Villages

Now that they could produce food, many more people survived. Anthropologists estimate that by 4000 B.C. the world population had risen to 90 million. Once they had agriculture, people could also settle in communities instead of wandering as nomads. Soon, agricultural villages of about 200 or so inhabitants began to develop where soil was fertile and water abundant. Archaeologists date one of the earliest such villages—**Jericho**, in the modern Israeli-occupied West Bank—back to 8000 B.C. Another village, **Çatal Hüyük** (CHAH•tuhl hoo•YOOK), in present-day Turkey, dates from 7000 to 6300 B.C.

Çatal Hüyük is the largest Neolithic village that archaeologists have so far discovered. Its people built rectangular, flat-roofed houses of mud bricks placed in wooden frames. Houses of several related families made up a compound with shared walls. People had to walk across roofs. The villagers also painted the interior walls of their windowless houses with vivid scenes of hunting and other activities.

Technological Advances

Neolithic farmers eventually made their agricultural work easier and more productive by inventing the plow and by training oxen to pull it. They also learned how to fertilize their fields with ashes, fish, and manure.

The relatively steady food supply quickened the pace of technological advance. Neolithic villagers invented the loom and began weaving textiles of linen and wool. They invented the wheel and used it for transportation. They found a way to bake clay bricks for construction. They learned how to hammer the metals copper, lead, and gold to make jewelry and weapons. In 1991, for example, the frozen body of a late Neolithic Age man was discovered in the Italian Alps. The 5,000-year-old "Iceman" wore well-made fur and leather clothing and shoes stuffed with grass. He carried a wooden backpack, a copper ax, a bow, and arrows.

The agricultural way of life led to many other changes. People created calendars to measure the

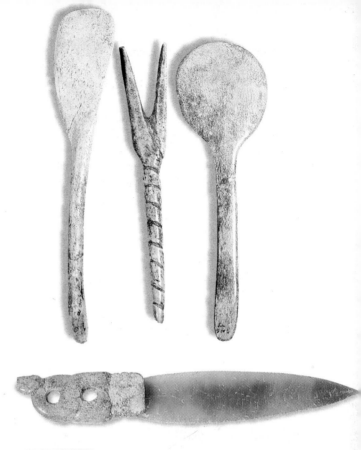

Visualizing History This Neolithic flint knife and these cooking utensils are from Çatal Hüyük. *What evidence tends to show that these people enjoyed art?*

seasons and determine when to plant crops. Because their food supply depended on land ownership, people now cared about such matters as boundary lines and rules of inheritance. Warfare probably came into being as villages competed for land and water.

Neolithic people also believed in many deities, or gods and goddesses. The spirits that supposedly surrounded them throughout nature were transformed into humanlike gods and goddesses with the power to help or hurt people. The people of Çatal Hüyük, for example, set up shrines at which they offered gifts in honor of their deities.

SECTION 2 REVIEW

Recall
1. **Define** domesticate, deity.
2. **Identify** Neanderthals, Cro-Magnons, Neolithic Revolution.
3. **List** the innovations made during the Neolithic period.

Critical Thinking
4. **Evaluating Information**
   Does the use of agriculture by Neolithic peoples deserve to be called a revolution? Give reasons.

Understanding Themes
5. **Innovation** Discuss how technological developments affected the food supplies of early peoples in various parts of the world.

Section 3

Emergence of Civilization

Setting the Scene

▶ **Terms to Define**
civilization, economy, artisan, cultural diffusion, myth

▶ **People to Meet**
the Sumerians

▶ **Places to Locate**
Nile, Tigris-Euphrates, Indus, and Huang River valleys

Find Out What economic, political, and social changes resulted from the rise of cities?

The Storyteller

Archaeological evidence leaves little doubt that women played key roles in every aspect of life in Old Europe. "In the temple workshops … females made and decorated quantities of various pots appropriate to different rites. Next to the altar of the temple stood a vertical loom on which were probably woven the sacred garments…. The most sophisticated creations of Old Europe—the most exquisite vases, sculptures, etc. now extant—were women's work."

—from *The Early Civilizations of Europe*, (Monograph for Indo-European Studies, UCLA, 1980), Marija Gimbutas

Mohenjo-Daro mother goddess

Over thousands of years, some of the early farming villages evolved slowly into complex societies, known as **civilizations**. The people of a civilization lived in a highly organized society with an advanced knowledge of farming, trade, government, art, and science. The word *civilization* comes from the Latin word *civitas*, meaning "city," and most historians equate the rise of civilizations with the rise of cities. Because most city dwellers learned the art of writing, the development of cities also marks the beginning of history.

River Valley Civilizations

As with agriculture, cities formed at different times in different parts of the world. Many of the earliest civilizations, however, had one thing in common: They rose from farming settlements in river valleys like that of the **Nile** River in northeastern Africa. The earliest cities that archaeologists have uncovered so far lie in the valley of the **Tigris and Euphrates** (yoo•FRAYT•eez) Rivers in the Middle East and date back to about 3500 B.C. Cities arose in the **Indus** River valley in South Asia some 1,000 years later. The first urban communities in East Asia appeared about 1500 B.C. in the **Huang He** (HWONG HUH) valley. By about 1000 B.C. cities were flourishing in Europe and in the Americas, and by 750 B.C. in sub-Saharan Africa.

Early river valley civilizations also shared several other basic features. People's labor was specialized, with different men and women doing different jobs. The civilization depended on advanced technology, such as metalworking skills. Each civilization always had some form of government to coordinate large-scale cooperative efforts such as building irrigation systems. The people in each

Behind high baked-brick walls the people of the ancient city of Mohenjo-Daro, near the Indus River in Pakistan, used four-wheeled carts to carry grain to a large granary. *What was the value of surplus food to the development of a civilization?*

civilization also shared a complex system of values and beliefs.

Not all societies formed civilizations, however. Some people continued to live in small agricultural villages, while others lived by hunting and gathering. Some nomadic people built a specialized culture that relied on moving herds of domesticated animals in search of good pasture.

The Economy of a Civilization

The ways in which people use their environment to meet their material needs is known as an economy. The economy of early civilizations depended on their farmers' growing surplus food. With extra food, fewer men and women had to farm and more could earn their living in other ways.

First Irrigation Systems

A major reason that farmers could produce surpluses of grain crops was that early civilizations built massive irrigation systems. Neolithic farmers had relied at first on rainfall to water their crops. Later, farmers transported water to grow the crops by digging ditches from a nearby river to their fields. Then they began building small canals and simple reservoirs.

Farmers also built earthen dikes and dams to control flooding in their valley by the river itself. They could now count on a reasonably steady flow of water and prevent destructive flooding.

Specialization of Labor

As men and women continued to specialize in ways of earning a living, artisans—workers skilled in a craft—became increasingly productive and creative. The longer they worked at one task, such as producing storage vessels, the more they learned about how to handle available materials, such as different types of clay. Gradually they turned out larger quantities of goods and improved the quality of their products.

Jewelry, eating utensils, weapons, and other goods were made by hammering copper, lead, and gold. Later, metalworkers in the early civilizations learned to make alloys, or mixtures of metals. The most important alloy was bronze, a reddish-brown metal made by mixing melted copper and tin. Historians refer to the period that followed the Stone Age as the Bronze Age, when bronze replaced flint and stone as the chief material for weapons and tools.

Bronze, harder than either copper or tin alone, took a sharper cutting edge. Artisans also found it much easier to cast bronze, or shape the liquid metal by pouring it into a mold to harden. Because the copper- and tin-containing ores needed to make bronze were scarce, however, the metal was expensive and therefore used only by kings, priests, and soldiers.

Long-Distance Trade

The search for new sources of copper and tin is an example of the long-distance trade that accompanied the rise of early civilizations. At first farmers and artisans traded within their own communities. They eventually began traveling to nearby areas to exchange goods. After a while merchants, a specialized class of traders, began to handle trade, and expeditions soon were covering longer routes.

Some long-distance trade moved overland by means of animal caravans. Some goods were transported by water. People floated down rivers on rafts. They made boats, propelling them in shallow water with poles and, in deeper water, with paddles and oars. After a time, people learned how to harness the force of the wind, and rivers and seacoasts became filled with sailing ships.

Along with goods, ideas were actively shared. This exchange of goods and ideas when cultures come in contact is known as cultural diffusion. Although early civilizations developed many similar ideas independently, other ideas arose in a few areas and then spread throughout the world by cultural diffusion. When ancient peoples learned about the technology and ideas of different civilizations, the new knowledge stimulated them to improve their own skills and way of life.

Living Together in Cities

Civilizations grew both more prosperous and more complex. Early cities had from 5,000 to 30,000 residents. A population of this size could not function in the same way that a Neolithic village of 200 inhabitants had.

Planning and Leadership

Ancient cities faced several problems unknown in the Neolithic period. Because city residents depended on farmers for their food, they had to make certain that farmers regularly brought their surplus food to city markets. At the same time, farmers could not build dams, dig irrigation ditches, and maintain reservoirs on their own. As civilizations prospered, they drew the envy of nomadic groups, who would repeatedly raid and pillage farms and attack caravans. In short, the first cities needed a way of supervising and protecting agriculture and trade.

The early city dwellers found two solutions to these problems. First, ancient cities organized a group of government officials whose job it was to oversee the collection, storage, and distribution of farming surpluses. These officials also organized and directed the labor force needed for large-scale construction projects, such as irrigation systems and public buildings. Second, ancient cities hired professional soldiers to guard their territory and trade routes.

Army, government officials, and priests belonged to a ruling class often led by a king, although women also held positions of authority. The ruling class justified its power by means of religion. According to ancient beliefs, the land produced food only if the gods and goddesses looked on the people with favor. One of the king's main functions, therefore, was to assist priests in carrying out religious ceremonies to ensure an abundant harvest. The first kings were probably elected, but in time they inherited their positions.

Levels of Social Standing

Archaeological evidence for the position of the ruling class can be found both in the treasures with which they were buried and in the physical layout of the ancient cities. At the city's center was an area that held the most imposing religious and government buildings. Nearby stood the residences of the ruling class. Next to these came the houses of the merchants. Farther out, the shops and dwellings of specific groups of artisans—such as weavers or smiths—were established in special streets or quarters. Farmers, as well as sailors and fishers, lived on the city's outskirts. Archaeological evidence suggests too that slaves, who were probably captured in battle, lived in many parts of the city.

Invention of Writing

Many archaeologists think that writing originated with the records that priests kept of the wheat, cloth, livestock, and other items they received as religious offerings. At first the priests used marks and pictures, called pictograms, to represent products. After a time they used the marks and pictures to represent abstract ideas and, later still, to represent sounds. Priestly records listed the individual men and women who were heads of households, landowners, and merchants. Soon the priests were also recording such information as the king's battle victories, along with legal codes, medical texts, and observations of the stars.

Systems of Values

Among the materials recorded by the priesthoods in early civilizations were **myths**, traditional stories explaining how the world was formed, how people came into being, and what they owed their creator. The priests of **the Sumerians** in the Tigris-Euphrates River valley wrote their myth of creation, for example, on seven clay tablets.

According to the Sumerian story, before creation there were two gods, Apsu the First Father and Tiamat the First Mother. They married and had many children. "But each generation of gods grew taller than its parents … [and] the younger gods could do things their parents had never tried to do." Eventually Apsu's great-grandson Ea made a

magic spell and killed Apsu. Ea's son Marduk killed Tiamat. Then:

> **❝** Marduk turned again to the body of Tiamat.
> He slit her body like a shellfish into two parts.
> Half he raised on high and set it up as sky….
> He marked the places for the stars….
> He planned the days and nights, the months and years.
> From the lower half of Tiamat's body, Marduk made the earth.
> Her bones became its rocks.
> Her blood its rivers and oceans….
> 'We need creatures to serve us,' he said.
> 'I will create man and woman who must learn to plow land to plant, and make the earth bring forth food and drink for us.
> I will make them of clay.'… **❞**
>
> —"Enuma Elish," Sumerian account of creation from *The Seven Tablets of Creation*, date unknown

After relating how the people drained marshes

CONNECTIONS

Geography

First Migration to America

One of the land bridges that formed during the Ice Ages joined Siberia, the easternmost part of Asia, with Alaska, the westernmost part of the Americas. Modern historians have named this land bridge Beringia, after the shallow Bering Strait that covers it today.

Little Diomedes Island, Bering Strait

Approximately 30,000 years ago, groups of Cro-Magnons began crossing Beringia from Asia to the Americas. According to most anthropologists, these groups were nomadic hunting bands who came in search of migrating herds of animals. We do not know whether the migrants crossed all at once or in successive waves.

From the north the migrants gradually moved south into new territory. Anthropologists estimate

that their journey all the way to the southernmost tip of South America took about 600 generations. This equals a rate of migration of about 18 miles (29 kilometers) per generation, over 18,000 years.

About 10,000 years ago, while the migrants were moving south through the Americas, the last Ice Age ended and the glaciers retreated toward the Poles. As the ice sheets melted, large quantities of water poured into the oceans and the sea level rose, covering Beringia and similar land bridges. As a result, the Inuit, or Eskimos, who migrated to North America from Asia about 2,000 years ago, arrived by boat rather than on foot.

MAKING THE CONNECTION

1. Why were the Inuit unable to migrate from Asia to North America by land?
2. Predict the effects on human life today of major changes in global climate, either warmer or colder.

Statue of the god Abu and his consort from the temple at Tel Asmar. *What god was worshiped by the ancient Sumerians as creator of the earth?*

for farmland, built walled cities, learned to make bricks, and built a great temple at the center of their biggest city, the myth continues:

> Daily they sang praises to Marduk,
>   supreme among the gods
>   He who created the vast spaces and fashioned
>   earth and men;
>   He who both creates and destroys; who is god
>   of storms and of light;
>   He who directs justice; a refuge for those in
>   trouble;
>   From whom no evil doer can escape;
>   His wisdom is broad. His heart is wide. His
>   sympathy is warm. 🙶

Creation myths have been found in every civilization. Because these myths vary from place to place, historians often examine them for evidence of a people's customs and values. For example, the seven Sumerian clay tablets could easily imply information about Sumer's values and beliefs. The clay tablets reveal that Marduk, though not the first god, had become—at the time the tablets were recorded—the leading one by supplanting the goddess Tiamat. The Sumerians seemed to believe too that evil should—and would—be punished. Apparently they also thought it was effective to praise and worship Marduk. Of course, the inferences an archaeologist can reasonably make from a myth are often limited and leave many unanswered questions.

SECTION 3 REVIEW

Recall
1. **Define** civilization, economy, artisan, cultural diffusion, myth.
2. **Identify** the Sumerians.
3. **Name** the four river valleys in which the world's earliest civilizations developed.

Where are these river valleys located?

Critical Thinking
4. **Synthesizing Information** Imagine that you rule a city in an early civilization. What instructions would you give to your government officials to

improve the living conditions of your people?

Understanding Themes
5. **Change** How did technological changes of the first civilizations improve toolmaking skills and the transportation of trade goods?

Understanding Map Projections

Greenland appears to be a larger landmass than Australia on some maps, yet Australia actually has a larger land area than Greenland. Have you ever wondered why?

Learning the Skill

When mapmakers attempt to transfer the three-dimensional surface of Earth to a flat surface, some inaccuracies occur. To accomplish this mapmakers use *projections*—an image produced when light from within the globe projects the globe's surface on a flat paper. These projections may stretch or shrink Earth's features, depending on the map's intended use.

Projections create two major kinds of maps. A *conformal map* shows land areas in their true shapes, while distorting their actual size. An *equal-area map* shows land areas in correct proportion to one another, but distorts shapes.

The map on this page is a *Cylindrical Projection (Mercator)*. Imagine wrapping a paper cylinder around the globe. A light from within projects the globe's surface on the paper. The resulting conformal projection makes Alaska appear larger than Mexico. Distortion is greatest near the Poles.

A *Conic Projection* is formed by placing a cone of paper over a lighted globe. This produces a cross between a conformal and an equal-area map. This projection is best to show areas in middle latitudes.

To understand map projections use the following steps:
- Compare the map to a globe.
- Determine the type of projection used.
- Identify the purpose of the projection.

Practicing the Skill

Turn to the map of the world in the Atlas. Compare the sizes and shapes of the features on this map to those on a globe. Based on this comparison, answer the following questions:
1. What is the map's projection?
2. How does the map distort Earth's features?
3. In what way does the map accurately present Earth's features?
4. Why did the mapmaker use this projection?

Applying the Skill

Compare the size of Antarctica as it appears on a map with Antarctica on a globe.

For More Practice

Turn to the Skill Practice in the Chapter Review on page 43 for more practice in understanding map projections.

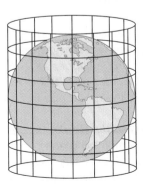

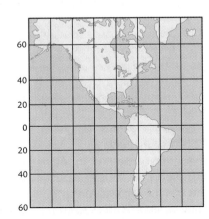

Cylindrical Projection (Mercator): This projection is accurate along the line where the cylinder touches the globe, with great distortions near the Poles.

Sygma

The Iceman

O n September 19, 1991, Helmut and Erika Simon, a German couple hiking near the border between Austria and Italy, wandered slightly off the trail. Suddenly Erika Simon caught sight of a small head and pair of shoulders emerging from the ice. The Simons thought they had stumbled across a discarded doll. In fact, they had found the solitary

prehistoric traveler now known around the world as the Iceman.

At first the Iceman was thought to be 4,000 years old—which would have made the discovery remarkable enough. Scientists later discovered that the Iceman was at least 5,000 years old! In comparison, Tutankhamen, Egypt's boy-king, was born some 2,000 years later.

The Iceman is the oldest body ever retrieved from an Alpine glacier; the next-oldest was only 400 years old. At 10,530 feet (3,210 m),

Overcome by fatigue and cold, a mountaineer (above) lies down to die high in the Alps. Some 5,000 years later, the discovery of his well-preserved body, along with clothes and a copper ax, offers startling clues about how humans greeted the metal age in Europe.

The Iceman (top) emerges from under a melting glacier.

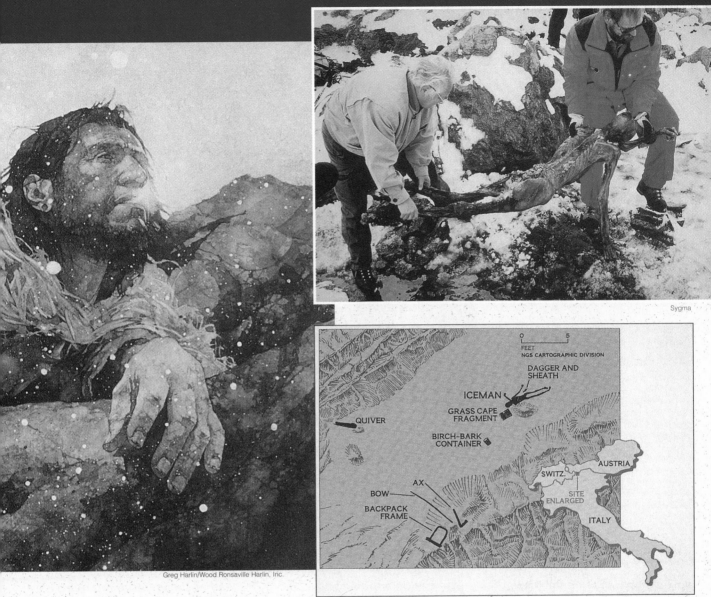

Greg Harlin/Wood Ronsaville Harlin, Inc.

Sygma

FEET
NGS CARTOGRAPHIC DIVISION

DAGGER AND
SHEATH

ICEMAN

GRASS CAPE
FRAGMENT

QUIVER

BIRCH-BARK
CONTAINER

AX

BOW

BACKPACK
FRAME

AUSTRIA

SWITZ.

SITE
ENLARGED

ITALY

NGS Cartographic Division

the site where the Iceman lay is the highest elevation in Europe in which prehistoric human remains have been found. Not even traces of a campfire have ever been discovered at that height.

The body of the Iceman was preserved through sheer luck. Shortly after he died, the rocky hollow where he lay filled with snow. For thousands of years a glacier covered this pocket of snow, only a few yards over the Iceman's head. More commonly, a body caught in a glacier would be crushed and torn by the movement of the ice. Instead, the Iceman was naturally mummified.

In the four days following the discovery, many well-meaning hikers and officials tried to free the Iceman from the glacier. They took turns hacking and prodding around the body with ice axes and ski poles. Unfortunately, they damaged the Iceman and the artifacts found with him—in ways that 5,000 years of glaciation had not. One of the "rescuers" seized a stick to dig with, breaking it in the process; the stick turned out to be part of the hazel-wood-and-larch frame of the Iceman's backpack, a type of ancient artifact never seen before. Workers also snapped off the top

◙ *The local coroner (above) and an assistant remove the corpse from his icy grave.*

◙ *The Iceman was found at an elevation of 10,530 feet (3,210 m) on the Austrian-Italian border. His tools and backpack frame were located near his body.*

Iceman's artifacts photographed by Kenneth Garrett

end of the Iceman's six-foot-long bow. What remained of the Iceman's clothing was torn off, as were parts of his body, and an officer using a jackhammer left a gaping hole in the Iceman's hip. To be sure, none of the salvagers suspected how old the Iceman was.

Not until five days after the discovery did an archaeologist examine the Iceman's body. Basing his estimate on the style of the ax found with the body, the archaeologist guessed that the Iceman was 4,000 years old.

Once officials knew the Iceman's approximate age, a rigorous effort to stabilize his condition began. The mummy was placed in a freezer, where the temperature was kept at a constant 21°F (-6°C) and the humidity at 98 percent—conditions much the same as those of the ice in which he had lain. The Iceman was not removed from the freezer for more than 20 minutes at a time, and then only for the most important scientific research. Part of that research was carbon-dating the Iceman to verify how old he was. Further chemical analysis revealed that the blade of his ax was not bronze, but nearly pure copper. He was, in fact, unique: a mummy from the Copper Age, which lasted in central Europe roughly from 4000 to 2200 B.C. Two different laboratories concluded that he was 5,000 to 5,500 years old.

THE ICEMAN'S DOMAIN was the Alps, stretching from southeast France to the Swiss-German border, and from Austria to northern Italy. Five thousand years ago these mountains were a vast wilderness. In the Copper Age, hardy voyagers trekked these ranges, and the goods they traded traveled even farther. We know from his tools and clothes that the Iceman was one of these rugged mountaineers.

The first half of the Copper Age was an era of climatic warming, when humans penetrated higher than ever into the Alps. The tree line climbed during the warming, game followed the forests, and hunters followed the game. Meadows above the tree line offered the best pastures for sheep, goats, and cattle and contained great green veins of a newly valued metal—which today we call copper. Copper changed the Alpine world forever, leading to the development of major trade routes between isolated valleys. Earlier, wealth was made through cattle or wheat. Copper was not only a form of portable wealth but also a stimulus for the development of specialized occupations. Men became smelters, axmakers, possibly even salesmen. The world's earliest known man-made copper objects—beads, pins,

A fragment of the Iceman's plaited-grass cape (above) was found next to his head.

This stone disk threaded with a leather thong (inset, top right) may have been worn to protect against evil.

The Iceman's copper ax is the oldest ever found in Europe with its bindings and handle intact (inset, bottom right).

A fungus on a string may have been a first-aid kit (inset, above left).

and awls—were made about 8000 B.C. in Turkey and Iran. There is evidence of copper mining in the Balkans by 5000 B.C. From there the technology spread west, reaching the Alps a thousand years later.

copper ax may tell us most. Its yew-wood handle ends in a gnarled joint, where a notch holds the blade. Dark birch gum held the blade firmly in position beneath a tightly wrapped thong of rawhide. It is a ribbed ax, rather than the more primitive flat ax that archaeologists would have expected to find.

Researchers who reconstructed what remained of the Iceman's clothing observed that his garment had been skillfully stitched together with sinew. Cruder repairs had been made, probably by the Iceman himself on his travels. This led researchers to believe that the Iceman had been part of a community, although he was used to fending for himself. Also, tiny pieces of a wheat that grew only at low altitudes, and bits of charcoal from a variety of trees found throughout the Alps were discovered with the Iceman, indicating that he may have come the South Tirol.

Included among the Iceman's possessions were a stick with a tip of antler used to sharpen flint blades; a deerskin quiver that contained 14 arrows; and an unfinished bow. His small flint dagger was similar to those found at other Copper Age sites, but no one had ever seen the kind of delicately woven sheath that held the dagger.

Central Europe's oldest known plow is more than a thousand years younger than the Iceman. Yet Copper Age artists cut images of plows on rocks. Rows of furrows have been found preserved at a major Copper Age religious complex excavated in northwest Italy, though experts believe plowing was ritualistic rather than agricultural.

The Iceman also had tattoo-like marks that might imply something about his spiritual life. Located on normally hidden places—his lower back, behind his knee, and on his ankle—the marks were not for

Kenneth Garrett

The Iceman's head was reconstructed by John Gurche, an anthropologically trained artist. He first sculpted a replica of the skull by using computer images, X rays, and CT scans of the Iceman. Gurche then added clay to duplicate the Iceman's mummified face, complete with smashed nose and lip. Next, he added muscles and fatty tissue, nasal cartilage, and glass eyes. Finally he made a new model of the head with soft urethane, tinted to suggest wind-burned skin. He completed the replica of the Iceman's head by adding human hair.

The work of many researchers over the past 30 years tells us much about life during the Copper Age. Excavations have yielded bones that indicate that by around 5000 B.C. Alpine people had domesticated five animals: dogs, which were originally more important for food than companionship, cattle, sheep, goats, and pigs. Horses and chickens were still unknown in the Alps. Villagers grew wheat and barley and made linen clothes from flax. They had only recently discovered how to milk a cow and how to make cheese and butter. Their sheep may have been used for meat but not yet for wool. Many staple foods of today were still unknown, including potatoes, onions, and oats.

EVENTUALLY, THE ICEMAN'S possessions may tell us more than his body will. Of those possessions, his

show. Perhaps they were meant to confer supernatural power or protection. So might the pair of fungi he carried, each pierced by a leather thong. Archaeologists have never seen anything like this artifact from that period. The fungi contain chemical substances now known to be antibiotic. If the Iceman used them to counteract illness, perhaps they also seemed magical to him.

We may never know what drew the Iceman to the mountain pass where he died. Perhaps he was a shepherd, a trader, or an outcast. But, in the late 20th century, it is our good fortune to have the opportunity to learn from this ambassador of the Copper Age.

Historical Significance

Prehistoric people created the basics of human culture—for example, tools, language, and religious belief. In time, increased food supplies and a diverse labor force led to the rise of cities and civilizations. In ancient times, cities enabled large numbers of people to live together, to cooperate with each other, and to carry out many cultural activities. Today the populations of many cities are more than 100 times that of these first cities. Modern cities serve as complex economic, cultural, and political centers in a world that has become, in many ways, one global civilization.

Using Key Terms

Write the key term that completes each sentence.

a. technology
b. artisan
c. myth
d. civilization
e. nomad
f. economy
g. anthropologist
h. prehistory
i. radiocarbon dating
j. archaeologist
k. artifact
l. cultural diffusion
m. culture

Using Your History Journal

Evaluate your journal account of being stranded on a deserted island. What skills and knowledge, known to early humans but not to you, may have helped you survive?

---

1. The period of time before people developed writing is called _____.
2. Among the techniques used by scientists for determining the age of organic remains is _____.
3. A _____ is a person who uses up the food supply in one place and then moves on to another place.
4. Over thousands of years, some of the early agricultural villages evolved into highly complex societies, known as _____ .
5. _____ includes the knowledge people have, the language they speak, the ways in which they eat and dress, their religious beliefs, and their achievements in art and music.
6. An _____ is a worker who is skilled in a particular craft.
7. The exchange of goods and ideas when different peoples come in contact is known as _____.
8. A scientist known as an _____ unearths and interprets remains left behind by prehistoric people.
9. _____ includes the skills and useful knowledge available to people for collecting materials and making objects necessary for survival.
10. A _____ is a traditional story explaining the origins of the world and civilization.

Reviewing Facts

1. **Name** the four land bridges used by prehistoric people during the Ice Ages.
2. **Locate** the two places in which Cro-Magnons seem to have originated before spreading into other parts of the world.
3. **Explain** why the acquisition of language is one of humanity's greatest achievements.
4. **Describe** how the invention of the spear-thrower and the bow and arrow changed the Cro-Magnons' food supply.
5. **List** two major problems faced by inhabitants of ancient cities that Neolithic village dwellers did not face.
6. **State** what many archaeologists consider to be the relationship between religion and the origin of writing.

Critical Thinking

1. **Apply** How did climatic changes affect the development of humankind?
2. **Analyze** What were the major cultural features of each period in the Stone Age?
3. **Synthesize** How do you think the invention of the stone ax might have changed the culture of

a people who lived along the banks of a navigable river?

4. **Evaluate** What do you think was the most valuable skill that prehistoric people learned during the Paleolithic period? What was the most valuable skill learned during the Neolithic period?

Geography in History

1. **Location** Refer to the map below. What is the relative location of Mesopotamia?
2. **Human/Environment Interaction** Where in this area would ancient peoples have likely begun farming?
3. **Human/Environment Interaction** Why did early farmers build dikes and dams in the river valleys where they raised their crops?

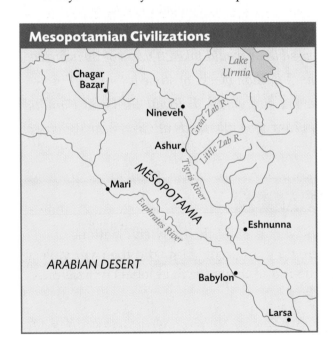

Mesopotamian Civilizations

Understanding Themes

1. **Movement** Describe the migrations of human beings from their place of origin to other parts of the world.
2. **Innovation** How did improvements in tool-making affect the way in which prehistoric people lived?

3. **Change** How did city life differ from village life in early civilizations?

Linking Past and Present

1. Many aspects of human culture are passed down from generation to generation. What cultural achievements of *Homo erectus*—from more than 200,000 years ago—do people still use today?
2. Government officials 5,000 years ago directed the large labor forces needed for large-scale construction projects such as irrigation systems and city walls. They oversaw the collection, storage, and distribution of agricultural surpluses. How do government officials' activities in early civilizations compare with those of government officials in your community?

Skill Practice

Using a small tennis ball, place a dot on each side to represent the North and South Poles. Cut paper strips so that they could completely cover this "globe." (See the example below.)

1. Why are the strips wider at the middle than at the ends?
2. If the strips are laid side-by-side on a flat surface, what pattern do they form?
3. What does this show about the problem of creating an accurate map on a flat surface?
4. The earth is a sphere, but it is somewhat pear-shaped—not a perfect sphere. What additional problem does this create for the cartographer who wants to make a very accurate map of the world?

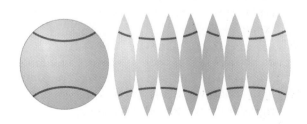

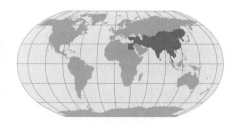

Chapter Themes

▶ **Relation to Environment** The Egyptians learn to control the floodwaters of the Nile River upon which their agriculture relies. *Section 1*

▶ **Cooperation** The peoples of the Fertile Crescent work together to build irrigation systems and cities. *Section 2*

▶ **Cultural Diffusion** Cities in early India develop close trading and cultural ties with the Fertile Crescent area. *Section 3*

▶ **Innovation** Early Chinese civilization excels in metal-casting skills. *Section 4*

The Storyteller

Under the blazing sun, a gigantic stone structure began to take shape on the desert sands of Egypt in northeastern Africa. A hundred thousand men toiled together, building a burial pyramid for Khufu, a king of Egypt about 2500 B.C. Gangs of laborers dragged huge blocks of limestone up winding ramps of dirt and brick to pile layer upon layer of stone. Farmers during the rest of the year, these laborers were compelled to work for the 3 or 4 months during which the annual flooding of the Nile River made farming impossible. It would take 20 years of their forced labor and more than 2 million blocks of stone before the Egyptians completed the massive pyramid. Today, the Great Pyramid built almost 5,000 years ago still stands at Giza, near the city of Cairo.

Historical Significance

In what ways were each of the early civilizations unique? How were they different? How did the river valley civilizations lay the foundations for the global civilization that we know today?

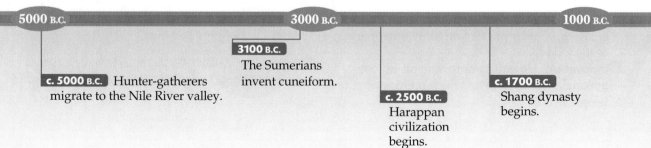

5000 B.C.   3000 B.C.   1000 B.C.

3100 B.C.
The Sumerians invent cuneiform.

c. 5000 B.C. Hunter-gatherers migrate to the Nile River valley.

c. 2500 B.C.
Harappan civilization begins.

c. 1700 B.C.
Shang dynasty begins.

History & Art Fowling scene from a tomb at Thebes along the Nile River, Egypt

Your History Journal

Sumerian scribes studied at special schools called eddubas. *There they learned cuneiform writing. After reading Section 2, write a short creative account of a scribe's day at an* edduba.

c. 3000 B.C.
King Narmer unifies Egypt.

c. 1700s B.C.
The Hyksos invade Egypt.

c. 1480 B.C.
Queen Hatshepsut comes to power.

c. 945 B.C.
Egypt enters long period of foreign rule.

Section 1

The Nile Valley

Setting the Scene

▶ **Terms to Define**
monarchy, dynasty, theocracy, bureaucracy, pharaoh, empire, polytheism, hieroglyphics

▶ **People to Meet**
Narmer, Hatshepsut, Thutmose III, Akhenaton, Ramses II

▶ **Places to Locate**
Nile River valley, Memphis, Thebes

Find Out Why was Egypt called the "gift of the Nile"?

The Storyteller

Live for today; the afterlife will come soon enough! The following message about the brief pleasures of this life demonstrates that Egyptian poets sometimes sang what their wealthy patrons liked to hear:

"The pharaohs, those ancient gods, rest now in their pyramids. The people who built houses; their walls have crumbled, as if they had never been! Listen! Put perfume upon your head, wear fine linen. Make holiday! ... No one who has died has ever returned."

—freely adapted from "Song of the Harper," *Journal of Near Eastern Studies 4*, 1945, translated by Miriam Lichtheim

King Narmer

One of the world's first civilizations developed along the banks of the Nile River in northeastern Africa. The **Nile River valley**'s early inhabitants called their land *Kemet*, meaning "black land," after the dark soil. Later, the ancient Greeks would name the Nile area *Egypt*. Of the four early river valley civilizations, people today probably know the most about the ancient Egyptian civilization. People still marvel at its remains in modern Egypt—especially the enormous Sphinx, the wondrous pyramids, and the mummies buried in lavish tombs.

A River Valley and Its People

Running like a ribbon through great expanses of desert, the Nile River for thousands of years has shaped the lives of the Egyptians. The land of Egypt receives little rainfall, but its people have relied instead on the Nile's predictable yearly floods to bring them water.

At 4,160 miles (6,690 km) in length, the Nile River is the world's longest river. Several sources in the highlands of East Africa feed the Nile. The river then takes a northward route to the Mediterranean Sea. On its course through Egypt the Nile crosses six cataracts, or waterfalls. Because of the cataracts the Nile is not completely navigable until it reaches its last 650 miles (1,040 km). Before emptying into the Mediterranean, the Nile splits into many branches, forming a marshy, fan-shaped delta.

The Gifts of the River

The green Nile Valley contrasts sharply with the vast desert areas that stretch for hundreds of miles on either side. Rich black soil covers the river's banks and the Nile Delta. From late spring through summer, heavy tropical rains in central Africa and melting mountain snow in East Africa add to the Nile's volume. As a result the river overflows its banks and floods the land nearby. The floodwaters recede in late fall, leaving behind thick deposits of silt.

As early as 5000 B.C., nomadic hunter-gatherers of northeastern Africa began to settle by the Nile. They took up a farming life regulated by the river's seasonal rise and fall, growing cereal crops such as wheat and barley. The Nile also provided these Neolithic farmers with ducks and geese in its marshlands and fish in its waters. The early Egyptians harvested papyrus growing wild along the banks of the Nile, using the long, thin reeds to make rope, matting, sandals, baskets, and later on, sheets of paperlike writing material.

Uniting Egypt

Protected from foreign invasion by deserts and cataracts, the early farming villages by the Nile prospered. In time a few strong leaders united villages into small kingdoms, or monarchies, each under the unrestricted rule of its king. The weaker kingdoms eventually gave way to the stronger. By 4000 B.C. ancient Egypt consisted of two large kingdoms: Lower Egypt in the north, in the Nile Delta, and Upper Egypt in the south, in the Nile Valley.

Around 3000 B.C., **Narmer**, also known as Menes (MEE•neez), a king of Upper Egypt, gathered the forces of the south and led them north to invade and conquer Lower Egypt. Narmer set up the first government that ruled all of the country. He governed both Lower Egypt and Upper Egypt from a capital city he had built at **Memphis**, near the border of the two kingdoms.

Narmer's reign marked the beginning of the first Egyptian dynasty, or line of rulers from one family. From 3000 B.C. until 332 B.C., a series of 30 dynasties ruled Egypt. Historians have organized the dynasties into three great periods: the Old Kingdom, the Middle Kingdom, and the New Kingdom.

The Old Kingdom

The Old Kingdom lasted from about 2700 B.C. to 2200 B.C. During the first centuries of the unified kingdom, Upper Egypt and Lower Egypt kept their separate identities as kingdoms. In time, however, Egypt built a strong national government under its kings. It also developed the basic features of its civilization.

CONNECTIONS

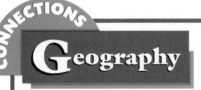

Geography

Stemming the Flood

Ancient Egyptians had to take control of their river environment. Over the years farmers built ditches and canals to carry the floodwaters to basins. There the silt settled and served as fertilizer for planting crops. Machines, such as the shadoof, lifted water to cultivated land. Farmers eventually built dams and reservoirs, making year-round irrigation possible.

Built in the 1960s, the Aswan

High Dam in southeastern Egypt trapped the waters of the Nile in a huge reservoir for later irrigation. When the rising waters of the Nile behind the dam threatened to destroy statues of Ramses II, engineers had to move the statues to higher ground. Today, the dam generates electrical power and protects against flooding. Because the dam prevents the Nile from flowing over the valley land, however, the floodwaters no longer deposit fertile silt annually. Farmers must add expensive chemical fertilizers to their fields. The absence of silt has also increased land erosion along the Nile.

MAKING THE CONNECTION

1. How did the Egyptians gradually manage to control the waters of the Nile?
2. Why might people today object to the building of a dam?

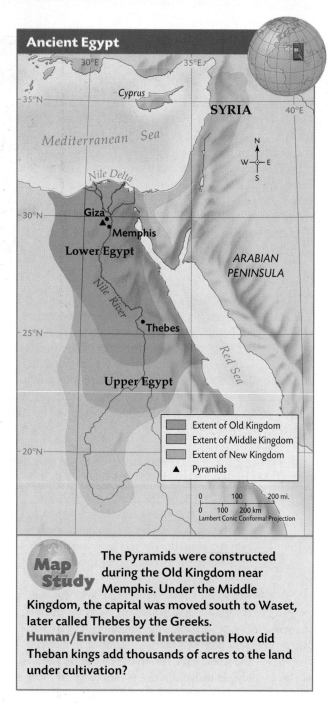

SYRIA

Mediterranean Sea

Nile Delta

Giza

Memphis

Lower Egypt

ARABIAN PENINSULA

Nile River

Thebes

Red Sea

Upper Egypt

Extent of Old Kingdom
Extent of Middle Kingdom
Extent of New Kingdom
▲ Pyramids

0   100   200 mi.
0 100 200 km
Lambert Conic Conformal Projection

Map Study The Pyramids were constructed during the Old Kingdom near Memphis. Under the Middle Kingdom, the capital was moved south to Waset, later called Thebes by the Greeks. **Human/Environment Interaction** How did Theban kings add thousands of acres to the land under cultivation?

The Egyptian Monarchy

The Egyptian people regarded their king as a god who ruled over all Egyptians. Such a government, in which the same person is both the religious leader and the political leader, is called a theocracy. As a god, the king performed many ritual acts believed to benefit the entire kingdom, such as cutting the first ripe grain to ensure a good harvest. As political leader, the king wielded absolute power, issuing commands regarded as the law of the land.

Unable to carry out all official duties himself, the king delegated many responsibilities to a bureaucracy, a group of government officials headed by the king's vizier, or prime minister. Through the vizier and other bureaucrats the king controlled trade and collected taxes. He also indirectly supervised the building of dams, canals, and storehouses for grain—all crucial to survival for an agriculture-based civilization.

The Pyramids: A Lasting Legacy

To honor their god-kings and to provide them with an eternal place of rest, the Egyptians of the Old Kingdom built lasting monuments—the Pyramids. The Step Pyramid was built for King Djoser in the mid-2600s B.C. Overlooking Memphis, it was the first large, all-stone building in the world. Later the Egyptians constructed the three Pyramids at Giza, which stand today as testimony to Egyptian engineering skills. The Great Pyramid, the largest of the three, stands 481 feet (144 m) high. Long, narrow passageways lead to the king's burial chamber deep within the pyramid.

The Egyptians believed that a king's soul continued to guide the kingdom after death. Before entombing a dead king in his pyramid, they first preserved the king's body from decay by a procedure called embalming. Next they wrapped the dried, shrunken body—called a mummy—with long strips of linen and placed it in an elaborate coffin. Only then could the coffin lie in the burial chamber of the pyramid along with the king's clothing, weapons, furniture, and jewelry—personal possessions the king could enjoy in the afterlife.

The Middle Kingdom

Around 2200 B.C., the kings in Memphis began to lose their power as ambitious nobles fought each other for control of Egypt. The stable, ordered world of the Old Kingdom entered a period of upheaval and violence. Then, around 2050 B.C., a new dynasty reunited Egypt and moved the capital south to **Thebes**, a city in Upper Egypt. This new kingdom, known as the Middle Kingdom, would last until after 1800 B.C.

In time Theban kings became as powerful as the rulers of the Old Kingdom and brought unruly local governments under their control. They supported irrigation projects that added thousands of acres to the land already under cultivation. The Theban dynasty seized new territory for Egypt, setting up fortresses along the Nile to capture Nubia (part of modern Sudan) and launching military campaigns against Syria. Theban kings also ordered construction of a canal between the Nile and the Red Sea, and as a result, Egyptian ships traded along the coasts of the Arabian Peninsula and East Africa.

In the 1700s B.C., local leaders began to challenge the kings' power again, shattering the peace and prosperity of the Middle Kingdom. At the same time, Egypt also faced its first serious threat—invasion by the Hyksos (HIHK•SAHS), a people from western Asia. The Hyksos swept across the desert into Egypt with new tools for war—bronze weapons and horse-drawn chariots. So armed, they easily conquered the Egyptians, who fought on foot with copper and stone weapons. The Hyksos established a new dynasty that ruled for about 110 years.

The New Kingdom

The Egyptians despised their Hyksos masters. To overthrow Hyksos rule, the Egyptians learned to use Hyksos weapons and adopted the fighting style of their conquerors. About 1600 B.C. Ahmose (ah•MOH•suh), an Egyptian prince, raised an army and drove the Hyksos out.

Visualizing History This tomb painting from the Valley of the Kings, Deir El Bahri, Egypt, shows Queen Hatshepsut wearing the traditional false beard of the pharaohs. *What does the term "pharaoh" mean?*

Pharaohs Rule an Empire

Ahmose founded a new Egyptian dynasty— the first of the New Kingdom. He and his successors assumed the title pharaoh, an Egyptian word meaning "great house of the king." Ahmose devoted his energies to rebuilding Egypt, restoring abandoned temples, and reopening avenues of trade. The pharaohs who followed him, however, used large armies to realize their dreams of conquest. They pressed farther to the east and into the rest of Africa than had the kings of the Middle Kingdom.

Around 1480 B.C. Queen **Hatshepsut** (hat•SHEHP•soot) came to power in Egypt. She first ruled with her husband and then ruled on behalf of her stepson **Thutmose** (thoot•MOH•suh) **III**, who was too young to govern. Finally she had herself crowned pharaoh. Hatshepsut assumed all the royal trappings of power, including the false beard traditionally worn by Egyptian kings. Hatshepsut carried out an extensive building program, which included a great funeral temple and a tomb built

into the hills of what is now called the Valley of the Kings.

Thutmose III did reclaim the throne at Hatshepsut's death and soon after marched with a large army out of Egypt toward the northeast. He conquered Syria and pushed the Egyptian frontier to the northern part of the Euphrates River. In a short time, Thutmose III had conquered an empire for Egypt, bringing many territories under one ruler.

The Egyptian Empire grew rich from commerce and tribute from the conquered territories. The capital of Thebes, with its palaces, temples, and carved stone obelisks, reflected the wealth won by conquest. No longer isolated from other cultures, Egyptians benefited from cultural diffusion within their empire.

Akhenaton Founds a Religion

A new ruler, Amenhotep (AH•muhn•HOH•TEHP) IV, assumed power about 1370 B.C. Supported by his wife, Nefertiti, Amenhotep broke with the Egyptian tradition of worshiping many

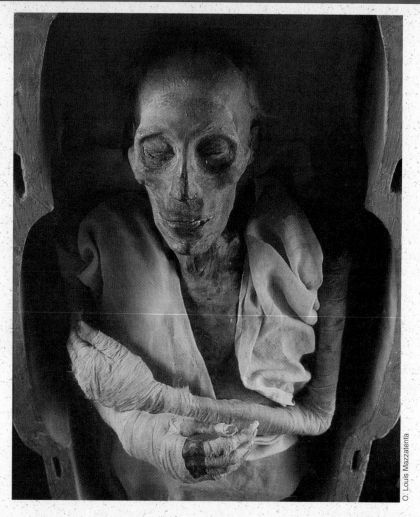

O. Louis Mazzatenta

Ramses the Great

O. Louis Mazzatenta

he mummy of Ramses the Great (above) lies in a display case on the second floor of the Egyptian Museum in Cairo. For many centuries before Ramses was brought to Cairo, the great pharaoh lay in his tomb near Luxor in a richly decorated coffin (left), embellished with symbols of Osiris, god of the afterlife. Ramses was nearly 90 when he died in 1237 B.C. His mummy has remained intact for the last 3,000 years.

Egyptians believed strongly in the afterlife and took great care to preserve the bodies of their pharaohs. Embalmers spent 70 days preparing the corpse of Ramses the Great. First they removed the internal organs and placed them in sacred jars. The heart was sealed in the body because Egyptians believed that it was the source of intellect as well as feeling and was needed in the afterlife. The brain, on the other hand, was thought to be useless and embalmers drew it out through the nose and threw it away. The body was then dried with salt, washed, coated with preserving resins, and wrapped in hundreds of yards of linen. Recent medical tests show that Ramses suffered from arthritis, dental abscesses, gum disease, and poor circulation. ⊕

deities. He declared that Egyptians should worship only Aton, the sun-disk god, as the one supreme deity. Claiming to be Aton's equal, Amenhotep changed his royal name to **Akhenaton** (AHK•NAH•tuhn), which means "spirit of Aton." To stress the break with the past, Akhenaton moved the capital from Thebes to a new city in central Egypt dedicated to Aton.

These controversial changes had an unsettling effect on Egypt. Many of the common people rejected the worship of Aton, a god without human form, and continued to believe in many deities. The priests of the old religion resented their loss of power. At the same time, the army was unhappy about Egypt's loss of territories under Akhenaton's weak rule.

After Akhenaton's death, the priests restored the old religion. They also made Akhenaton's successor, Tutankhamen, move the capital to Memphis. Shortly thereafter, the head of the Egyptian army overthrew the dynasty and created a new one.

Recovery and Decline

During the 1200s B.C. the pharaohs regained some of the territory and prestige that Egypt had lost during the previous century. One of these pharaohs, **Ramses II**, or Ramses the Great, reigned for 67 years. He erected large statues of himself and built many temples and tombs. In A.D. 1995, archaeologists uncovered a vast underground tomb with at least 67 chambers that they believed to be the burial place of 50 of the 52 sons of Ramses II. The find, located near Ramses' own tomb, was hailed as one of the most historically significant discoveries in Egypt in the twentieth century.

In the 1100s B.C., another pharaoh also named Ramses led Egypt into a long and costly war for the control of Syria. Ramses III barely escaped assassination, and after his war, Egypt entered a long period of decline. It eventually split into two kingdoms. Beginning in 945 B.C., Egypt came under control by foreigners—among them the Libyans from the west and the Kushites from the south.

Life in Ancient Egypt

At the height of its glory, ancient Egypt was home to some 5 million persons, most of whom lived in the Nile Valley and the Nile Delta. Even though Egyptian society was divided into classes, ambitious people in the lower classes could improve their social status somewhat.

Levels of Egyptian Society

Royalty, nobles, and priests formed the top of the social order. They controlled religious and political affairs. Members of the wealthy upper class lived in the cities or on estates along the Nile River. There they built large, elaborately decorated homes surrounded by magnificent gardens, pools, and orchards.

Below the upper class in social rank was the middle class. Its members—artisans, scribes, merchants, and tax collectors—carried out the business activities of Egypt. Middle-class homes—mostly in the cities—were comfortable but not elegant.

The majority of Egyptians belonged to the poor lower class. Many were farmers. For the land they farmed, they paid rent to the king—usually a large percentage of their crop. Farmers also worked on building projects for the king, and some members of the lower class served the priests and the nobles. They lived in small villages of simple huts on or near the large estates along the Nile.

Egyptian Families

In the cities and in the upper class the husband, wife, and children made up the family group.

Visualizing History Ramses II holds an offering table—one of many great monuments erected to honor the pharaoh and Queen Nefertari. *What recent discovery yielded more information about the reign of Ramses II?*

Outside the cities, especially among farmers and laborers, a family also included grandparents and other relatives, who took an active part in the life of the household. An Egyptian child was taught great respect for his or her parents, with a son particularly expected to maintain his father's tomb.

The status of Egyptian women changed somewhat as the centuries passed. Literature of the Old Kingdom portrayed women as the property of their husbands and as valued producers of children. Wise men reminded children to cherish their mothers for bearing them, nourishing them, and loving and caring for them. By the time of the empire, documents indicate that women's legal rights had improved. Women could buy, own, and sell property in their own names, testify in court, and start divorce and other legal proceedings. The lives of Hatshepsut and some of the queens of the later pharaohs, like Nefertiti, suggest that privileged women of the royalty could attain prominence.

Worshiping Many Deities

Religion guided every aspect of Egyptian life. Egyptian religion was based on polytheism, or the worship of many deities, except during the controversial rule of Akhenaton. Gods and goddesses were often represented as part human and part animal—Horus, the sky god, had the head of a hawk. The Egyptians in each region worshiped local deities, but rulers and priests promoted the worship of specific gods and goddesses over all of Egypt. These deities included Ra, the sun god, whom the Theban pharaohs joined with their favorite god Amon to make one god, Amon-Ra.

The popular god Osiris, initially the powerful god of the Nile, became the god responsible for the life, death, and rebirth of all living things. The Egyptians worshiped Osiris and his wife, the goddess Isis, as rulers of the realm of the dead. They believed that Osiris determined a person's fate after death.

Because their religion stressed an afterlife, Egyptians devoted much time and wealth to preparing for survival in the next world. At first they believed that only kings and wealthy people could enjoy an afterlife. By the time of the New Kingdom, however, poor people could also hope for eternal life with Osiris's help.

Writing With Pictures

In their earliest writing system, called hieroglyphics, the Egyptians carved picture symbols onto pieces of slate. These picture symbols, or hieroglyphs, stood for objects, ideas, and sounds. For everyday business, however, the Egyptians used a cursive, or flowing, script known as hieratic, which simplified and connected the picture symbols.

Few people in ancient Egypt could read or write. Some Egyptians, though, did prepare at special schools for a career as a scribe in government or commerce. Scribes learned to write hieratic script on paper made from the papyrus reed.

Visualizing History This statue of the falcon god Horus served both as a protector and symbol of the pharaoh, who ruled as the incarnation of Horus, son of the divine king. *Who were Osiris and Isis?*

After the decline of ancient Egypt, hieroglyphs fell from use, and their meaning remained a mystery to the world's scholars for nearly 2,000 years. Then in A.D. 1799 French soldiers in Egypt found a slab of stone dating to the 200s B.C. near the town of Rosetta. The stone was carved with Greek letters and two forms of Egyptian writing. In A.D. 1822 a young French archaeologist named Jean-François Champollion (shahn•pawl•YOHN) figured out how the Greek text on the Rosetta stone matched the Egyptian texts. Using the Greek version, he was able to decipher the Egyptian hieroglyphics.

Some of the oldest writings from the Old Kingdom were carved on the inner walls of the Pyramids. Scribes also copied many prayers and hymns to deities. The Book of the Dead collected texts telling how to reach a happy afterlife, recording more than 200 prayers and magic formulas.

The ancient Egyptians also wrote secular, or nonreligious, works such as collections of proverbs. One vizier gave this advice: "Do not repeat slander; you should not hear it, for it is the result of hot temper. Repeat a matter seen, not what is heard." The Egyptians also enjoyed adventure stories, fairy tales, and love stories:

❝ Now I'll lie down inside
  and act as if I'm sick.
My neighbors will come in to visit,
  and with them my girl.
She'll put the doctors out,
  for she's the one to know my hurt. ❞

–a love poem by a young Egyptian,
date unknown

Achievements in Science

Pyramids, temples, and other monuments bear witness to the architectural and artistic achievement of Egyptian artisans. These works, however,

Stonehenge Religious Site

Salisbury Plain, England, c. 1700 B.C.
Ancient people created a religious monument in southwestern England by dragging huge stones from miles away and arranging them in giant circles. The work probably took hundreds of years to complete. The layout of stones suggests that they were used in ceremonies linked to the rising of the sun on the longest day of the year.

would not have been possible without advances in disciplines such as mathematics. The Egyptians developed a number system that enabled them to calculate area and volume, and they used principles of geometry to survey flooded land.

The Egyptians worked out an accurate 365-day calendar by basing their year not only on the movements of the moon but also on Sirius, the bright Dog Star. Sirius rises annually in the sky just before the Nile's flood begins.

Egyptians also developed medical expertise, having first learned about human anatomy in their practice of embalming. Egyptian doctors wrote directions on papyrus scrolls for using splints, bandages, and compresses when treating fractures, wounds, and diseases. Other ancient civilizations would acquire much of their medical knowledge from the Egyptians.

SECTION I REVIEW

Recall
1. **Define** monarchy, dynasty, theocracy, bureaucracy, pharaoh, empire, polytheism, hieroglyphics.
2. **Identify** Narmer, the Hyksos, Ahmose, Hatshepsut, Thutmose III, Akhenaton, Ramses II.
3. **Explain** how a bureaucracy became part of government in ancient Egypt.

Critical Thinking
4. **Making Comparisons** Compare the reigns of Ahmose, Hatshepsut, and Thutmose III. Which reign do you think contributed most to Egypt? Support your opinion.

Understanding Themes
5. **Relation to Environment** How did geography and climate affect where people lived in ancient Egypt? How did the ancient Egyptians make use of the environment to meet their economic and cultural needs?

The Egyptians

The Valley of the Kings has seen more than its share of visitors. For thousands of years, travelers, warriors, and more recently, archaeologists have descended on this area on the outskirts of what is now Luxor to marvel at the magnificence of ancient Egypt. It was thought that most of what there was to discover had been found after British explorer Howard Carter opened up the tomb of Tutankhamen in 1922.

Then in 1988, plans were made to build a parking lot over the site of Tomb 5, which had been discovered—and looted—years earlier. Wanting to make sure that the parking facility would not seal off anything important, Egyptologist Kent Weeks of the American University of Cairo decided to make one last exploration of the tomb. To his surprise, beyond a few debris-choked rooms, he opened a door that led to the mostly unexcavated tomb of perhaps 50 of the sons of Ramses II, the powerful pharaoh who ruled Egypt from 1279 to 1212 B.C.

Though the tomb was emptied of valuables long ago, archaeologists consider Weeks's discovery a major find. Scientists and researchers hope

Kenneth Garrett

Illustration by C.F. Payne

that artifacts found in the tomb will provide clues about Egyptian civilization during Egypt's last golden age.

For students of Judeo-Christian history, any information on Ramses' oldest son, Amen-hir-khopshef, would be a most important discovery. Ramses was in power when, in retribution for the enslavement of the Israelites, according to the Book of Exodus, the Lord "...smote all the firstborn in the land of Egypt, from the firstborn of Pharaoh that sat on his throne unto the firstborn of the captive that was in the dungeon."

The tomb and pyramids of

ancient Egypt hold many answers: These stone monuments have certainly established the immortality of the pharaohs. But what about the commoners, who vastly outnumbered the royalty? What of the men and women who gave their strength, sweat, and lives to create Egypt's lasting monuments? The widespread fame of the Sphinx and the three Great Pyramids at Giza make it easy to forget that basic questions about Egyptian history have remained unanswered. Only recently have Egyptologists begun to fill in those gaps.

✂

SEVERAL YEARS AGO, archaeologists began to excavate two sites—located about half a mile from the Sphinx—searching for signs of the

 Offerings of food are carved in relief on an official's tomb (left).

Another pyramid nears completion about 2500 B.C. (above). Limestone facing blocks were quarried across the Nile and ferried to the work site. Teams then dragged the blocks to ramps made of rubble that were built around the pyramid during construction. Some experts believe that it took only 10,000 men—far below earlier estimates of up to 100,000—and 25 years to lay 5 million tons of rock. Half lion, half pharaoh, the Sphinx (in the foreground) is carved from an outcropping left unexcavated in a U-shaped quarry.

ordinary people who built the pyramids. Within months they uncovered the remains of many mud-brick buildings, including the oldest bakery yet discovered in Egypt.

This was a significant find. While the pyramids built Egypt by drawing its provinces together in a unified effort, it can be said that bread built the pyramids. For thousands of workers, a loaf of emmer–wheat bread—washed down with beer—was most likely the dietary staple.

At about the time the bakery was discovered, searchers also unearthed a cemetery of 600 graves of workers. Their skeletons revealed years of hard labor: Vertebrae were compressed and damaged from years of carrying heavy loads. Some skeletons were missing fingers and even limbs. A few of the tombs were adorned with mini-pyramids several feet high, made of mud brick. Nothing like these tiny pyramids had been found before. In the past, scholars believed that the pyramid form was invented as the shape for a royal tomb. However, Zahi Hawass, director general of the Giza Pyramids, thinks that the pyramid form actually may have arisen among the common people. He believes that the mini-pyramids evolved from sacred rectangular mounds found in tombs even older than the pharaohs' pyramids.

Life for most ancient Egyptians was hard. Society was built around a preoccupation with the pharaohs' immortality. But perhaps there were spiritual rewards for the common people in this devotion to their pharaohs. Some scholars think that ancient Egyptians believed not so much that the pharaoh was divine,

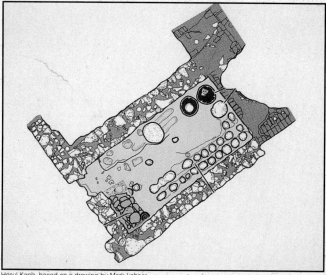

Hosul Kang, based on a drawing by Mark Lehner

Kenneth Garrett

A drawing of an ancient bakery (top) was used to build this replica of an ancient Egyptian bakery near Saqqara, Egypt (bottom).

but that through the pharaoh the divine nature of their society was expressed. Building a pyramid might have been an act of faith much as building a cathedral was in the Middle Ages.

Such recent discoveries about the life of the common people may lead to a new way of seeing ancient Egypt: not only as a brilliant civilization of the elite trickling down to the masses but also as a culture built

from the bottom up—a culture that stood on the daily toil of the workers and the beliefs of ordinary men and women.

Much of the emerging picture of daily life in ancient Egypt is one of arduous toil. The villages were crowded and dirty. Huts were made of thatch and mud brick. Men wore loincloths; women dressed in long sheaths with wide shoulder straps; and children went naked. On wooden sledges workers hauled the giant granite blocks that built the pyramids. Egypt created a vast agricultural empire, yet all the irrigation was done by hand. Farmers filled two heavy jars from the canals, then hung them from a yoke over their shoulders. Oxen dragging wooden plows tilled the fertile soil along the Nile, followed by lines of sowers who sang in cadence as they cast grains of emmer wheat from baskets.

There is much still to be learned and understood about daily life in ancient Egypt. The discovery of the bakery has provided insight into what sustained the masses; the bones in the commoners' graveyard tell us that life was not easy; the mini-pyramids illustrate that art, culture, and faith may have developed up from the average man and woman, rather than down from the royalty. For years Egyptologists have focused on the grandiose—and thereby disregarded most of Egyptian society. Eventually, however, our view of ancient Egyptian culture is broadening to encompass those responsible for creating it.

Kenneth Garrett

Kenneth Garrett

Kenneth Garrett

 A potter was hired to make replicas of the old baking pots. A local worker (top left) heats the tops in a wood fire in preparation for baking.

A kind of wheat known as emmer was supplied by a Californian who collects and grows ancient grains. The wet flour made from the emmer was left outside to collect free-floating native yeast spores and bacteria. (Store–bought yeast was not known to ancient Egyptians.) On baking day, the dough was placed into the pot bottoms and allowed to rise (bottom left). A hole for each pot was dug in the hot coals. The heated pot tops were then placed on the heated bottom halves and were placed in the coals to bake.

Success! For perhaps the first time in more than 4,000 years, a loaf of emmer bread popped out of an Old Kingdom-style pot. Edward Wood (above), who has been baking ancient breads for 50 years, holds up a perfect loaf.

c. 3000 B.C.
Sumerians set up city-states.

c. 2300 B.C.
Akkadian king
Sargon I begins
conquests.

c. 1700 B.C.
Hammurabi develops
code of laws.

Section 2

The Fertile Crescent

Setting the Scene

▶ **Terms to Define**
city-state, cuneiform

▶ **People to Meet**
the Sumerians, Sargon I,
the Akkadians, Hammurabi

▶ **Places to Locate**
Fertile Crescent, Mesopotamia, Tigris and
Euphrates Rivers

ind Out How did Sumer's achievements
enrich the early culture of the Middle East?

The Storyteller

*Sumerians honored the sun god Shamash as a
defender of the weak, giver of life, and even as a
judge of business deals, as in this hymn:*
"The whole of mankind bows to you,
Shamash the universe longs for your light….
As for him who declines a present, but
nevertheless takes the part of the weak,
It is pleasing to Shamash, and he will prolong
his life….
The merchant who practices
trickery as he holds the
balances…
He is disappointed in the matter
of profit and loses his capital.
The honest merchant who holds
the balances and gives good
weight—
Everything is presented to him in
good measure."

*Sumerian
board game*

—from *Babylonian Wisdom
Literature*, W. B. Lambert, in
Readings in Ancient History
(2nd ed.), N. Bailkey

Around 5000 B.C.—at about the same
time as Egyptian nomads moved
into the Nile River valley—groups of
herders started to journey north from the Arabian
Peninsula. Rainfall in the area had declined over
the years, and the lakes and grasslands had begun
to dry up. Other peoples—from the highlands near
present-day Turkey—moved south at this time.
Driven by poor weather, they also fled war and
overpopulation.

Both groups of migrants headed into the cres-
cent-shaped strip of fertile land that stretched from
the Mediterranean Sea to the Persian Gulf, curving
around northern Syria. Called the **Fertile Crescent**,
this region included parts of the modern nations of
Israel, Jordan, Lebanon, Turkey, Syria, and Iraq.

Many of the peoples migrating from the north
and south chose to settle in **Mesopotamia** (MEH
•suh•puh•TAY•mee•uh), the eastern part of the
Fertile Crescent. Located on a low plain lying
between the **Tigris and Euphrates Rivers**, the name
Mesopotamia means "land between the rivers" in the
Greek language. The two rivers begin in the hills of
present-day eastern Turkey and later run parallel to
each other through present-day Iraq on their way to
the Persian Gulf. In this region, the newcomers
built villages and farmed the land.

The Twin Rivers

Beginning with Neolithic farmers, people used
the Tigris and Euphrates Rivers to water their
crops. Unlike the Nile River, however, the twin
rivers did not provide a regular supply of water. In
the summer no rain fell, and the Mesopotamian
plain was dry. As a result, water shortages often
coincided with the fall planting season. By the
spring harvest season, however, the rivers swelled
with rain and melting snow. Clogged with deposits
of silt, the Tigris and Euphrates Rivers often over-
flowed onto the plain. Strong floods sometimes

swept away whole villages and fields. The time of year of such flooding, however, was never predictable, and the water level of the rivers often varied from year to year.

The early Mesopotamian villages cooperated in order to meet the rivers' challenges. Together they first built dams and escape channels to control the seasonal floodwaters and later constructed canals and ditches to bring river water to irrigate their fields. As a result of their determined efforts, Mesopotamian farmers were producing food, especially grain crops, in abundance by 4000 B.C.

The Sumerian Civilization

Around 3500 B.C. a people from either central Asia or Asia Minor—**the Sumerians**—arrived in Mesopotamia. They settled in the lower part of the Tigris-Euphrates river valley, known as Sumer. Sumer became the birthplace of what historians have considered the world's first cities.

The Sumerian City-States

By 3000 B.C. the Sumerians had formed 12 city-states in the Tigris-Euphrates valley, including Ur, Uruk, and Eridu. A typical Sumerian city-state consisted of the city itself and the land surrounding it.

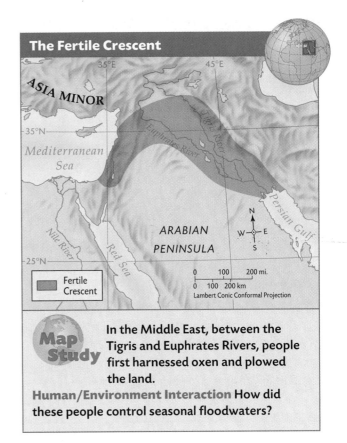

The Fertile Crescent

In the Middle East, between the Tigris and Euphrates Rivers, people first harnessed oxen and plowed the land.

Human/Environment Interaction How did these people control seasonal floodwaters?

The population of each city-state ranged from 20,000 to 250,000.

The people of Sumer shared a common culture, language, and religion. Sumerian city-states also shared some physical features. A ziggurat (ZIH•guh•RAT), or temple, made of sun-dried brick and decorated with colored tile, was built in each city-state. Sumerians built a ziggurat as a series of terraces, with each terrace smaller than the one below. A staircase climbed to a shrine atop the ziggurat. Only priests and priestesses were allowed to enter the shrine, which was dedicated to the city-state's chief deity. In form a ziggurat resembled a pyramid—both being massive stepped or peaked structures—but the feeling and emphasis of the two differed. A pyramid hid an inner tomb reachable only through passageways. A ziggurat raised a shrine to the sky, reached by mounting outer stairs.

Sumerian Government

Each Sumerian city-state usually governed itself independently of the others. In the city-state of Uruk, for example, a council of nobles and an assembly of citizens ran political affairs at first. But later, as city-states faced threats of foreign invaders and began to compete for land and water rights, the citizens of each city-state typically chose a military leader from among themselves. By 2700 B.C. the

Visualizing History A bull-headed lyre from Sumer, c. 2500 B.C. *What was a ziggurat, and how was it built?*

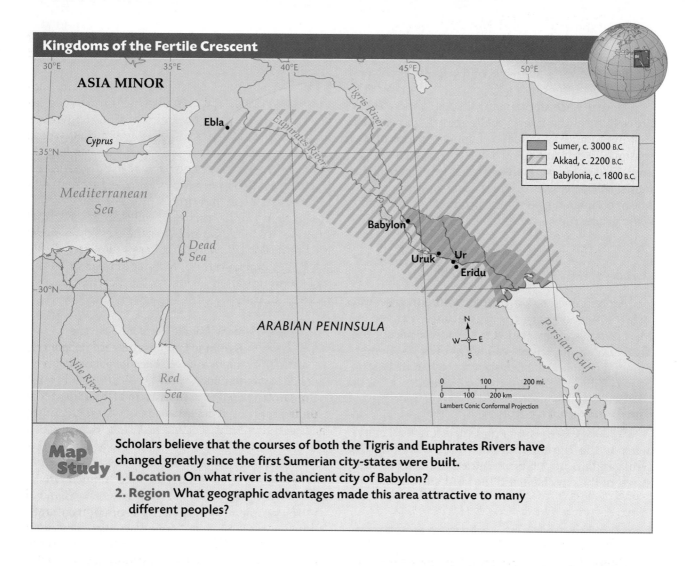

ASIA MINOR

Ebla

Cyprus

Euphrates River

Tigris River

35°N

Mediterranean Sea

Dead Sea

Babylon

Uruk • Ur

Eridu

30°N

ARABIAN PENINSULA

Nile River

Red Sea

Persian Gulf

	Sumer, c. 3000 B.C.
	Akkad, c. 2200 B.C.
	Babylonia, c. 1800 B.C.

N
W — E
S

0   100   200 mi.
0   100   200 km
Lambert Conic Conformal Projection

Map Study

Scholars believe that the courses of both the Tigris and Euphrates Rivers have changed greatly since the first Sumerian city-states were built.

1. **Location** On what river is the ancient city of Babylon?
2. **Region** What geographic advantages made this area attractive to many different peoples?

leaders of several city-states ruled as kings. Soon after, the kingships became hereditary.

A Sumerian king served not only as military leader but as the high priest, who represented the city-state's deity. Thus the governments of the city-states were not only monarchies but theocracies. Because the Sumerians believed that much of the land belonged to a city-state's god or goddess, a king and his priests closely supervised farming. A king also enforced the law and set penalties for law-breakers. Most punishments consisted of fines and did not involve bodily injury or loss of life.

The Roles of Men and Women

Sumerian law extensively regulated family life and outlined the roles of men and women. As the heads of households, men exercised great authority over their wives and children. According to Sumerian law codes, a man could sell his wife or children into slavery if he needed the money to pay a debt. He could also divorce his wife for the slightest cause. For a Sumerian woman, in contrast, the

law codes made divorce much more difficult. Women did enjoy some legal rights, however. Like Egyptian women, they could buy and sell property. They could also operate their own businesses and own and sell their own slaves.

Writing on Clay Tablets

Commerce and trade dominated the Sumerian city-states. The Sumerians developed a system of writing so they could keep accounts and prepare documents. Archaeologists believe that the writing system the Sumerians invented is the oldest in the world, dating to about 3100 B.C. The cuneiform (kyoo•NEE•uh•FAWRM) system began with pictograms—as did Egyptian hieroglyphics—and consisted of hundreds of wedge-shaped markings made by pressing the end of a sharpened reed on wet clay tablets. Then the Sumerians dried or baked the tablets until they were hard. Eventually cuneiform evolved into a script that became—about 2,000 years later—a model for alphabetic systems of writing.

Medical remedies are inscribed on this Sumerian clay tablet—a cuneiform writing tablet that was baked until hard. *How is cuneiform different from alphabetic writing?*

Sumerians wishing to learn cuneiform and become scribes studied for many years at special schools called *eddubas*. As educated professionals, scribes rose to high positions in Sumerian society. They produced business records, lists of historical dates, and literary works.

One of these literary works, the epic poem *Gilgamesh*, was written down before 1800 B.C. Scholars believe that the *Gilgamesh* epic may be the oldest story in the world. The scribes probably based the stories of Gilgamesh, a godlike man who performs heroic deeds, on an actual king of the city-state of Uruk.

Sumer's Many Deities

The Sumerians, like the Egyptians, practiced a polytheistic religion. Each Sumerian deity presided over a specific natural force—rain, moon, air—or over a human activity—plowing or brick making, for example. An, the highest Sumerian deity, was responsible for the seasons. Another important god—Enlil, god of winds and agriculture—created the hoe. Although Sumerians honored all the deities, each city-state claimed as its own one god or goddess, to whom its citizens prayed and offered sacrifices.

The Sumerians pictured their gods and goddesses as unpredictable, selfish beings who had little regard for human beings. The Sumerians believed that if deities became angry, they would cause misfortunes such as floods or famine. To appease their temperamental gods and goddesses, Sumerian priests and priestesses performed religious ceremonies and rituals.

Unlike the Egyptians, the Sumerians felt that humans had little control over their daily lives and could not look forward to a happy life after death. Only a grim underworld, without light or air, awaited them—an afterlife where the dead were only pale shadows.

Sumerian Inventions

Historians credit the Sumerians with numerous technological innovations. The Sumerians developed the wagon wheel, for example, to better transport people and goods, the arch to build sturdier buildings, the potter's wheel to shape containers, and the sundial to keep time. They developed a number system based on 60 and devised a 12-month calendar based on the cycles of the moon. The Sumerian civilization also was the first to make bronze out of copper and tin and to develop a metal plow. They produced an abundance of finely crafted metal work, some of which has been discovered in the Royal Cemetery at Ur. These and other Sumerian achievements have prompted one scholar to observe that "history begins at Sumer."

First Mesopotamian Empires

After a long period of conquest and reconquest, the Sumerian city-states eventually fell to foreign invaders in the 2000s B.C. The invaders of Sumer, like the Egyptians of the New Kingdom, were inspired by dreams of empire.

Footnotes to History

The Umbrella
1400 B.C.—Umbrellas actually originated under the sunny skies of Mesopotamia. Sumerians used palm fronds or feather umbrellas to shield their heads from the harsh rays and scorching heat of the Middle Eastern sun.

Sargon Leads the Akkadians

The first empire builder in Mesopotamia—**Sargon I**—may have been born a herder or a farmer's son. According to legend his mother abandoned him as a baby, setting him out on the Euphrates River in a reed basket. Downstream a farmer irrigating his fields pulled Sargon ashore and raised him as his own.

Sargon's people, **the Akkadians**, were Semites, one of the nomadic groups that had migrated from the Arabian Peninsula to the Fertile Crescent around 5000 B.C. The Akkadians established a kingdom called Akkad (AH•KAHD) in northern Mesopotamia. When Sargon assumed power in Akkad around 2300 B.C., he immediately launched a military campaign of expansion. Sargon's conquests united all of the city-states of Mesopotamia in one empire, which predated the empire of the Egyptian New Kingdom by more than 800 years.

Under Sargon's rule the people of Mesopotamia began to use the Akkadian language instead of Sumerian. But the Akkadians adopted various Sumerian religious and farming practices. After Sargon's death and the successful rule of his grandson, however, the Akkadian Empire disintegrated.

The Kingdom of Ebla

No one really knows how far Sargon's empire extended. Historians do know, however, that Ebla, a kingdom located in what is now northern Syria, fought unsuccessfully against Sargon for control of the Euphrates River trade. When Sargon's grandson captured Ebla, he burned the royal archives. Yet fire did not destroy the thousands of clay tablets stored there. These tablets and other finds from Ebla have convinced historians that highly developed Semitic civilizations prospered in that area of Syria earlier than previously believed.

The overland trade that passed between Egypt and Mesopotamia made Ebla a wealthy and powerful city-state. Ebla controlled a number of neighboring towns, from which it exacted tribute.

The kings of Ebla were elected for seven-year terms. In addition to their political role, they looked

Images of the Times

Mesopotamia

For many centuries, beginning about 4000 B.C., enterprising civilizations rose and fell in the fertile valley of the Tigris and Euphrates Rivers.

The Royal Standard of Ur is an oblong decorated box with panels that represent scenes of war and peace. The war panel celebrates a military victory by the Sumerian city of Ur.

after the welfare of the poor. If the kings failed, they could be removed by a council. After 2000 B.C., Ebla declined and eventually was destroyed by the Amorites, a Semitic people from western Syria.

Hammurabi's Babylonian Empire

Around the same time that they destroyed Ebla, the Amorites also expanded beyond Syria. After the Akkadian Empire disintegrated, the Sumerian civilization had briefly recovered under the leadership of the kings of Ur, but soon it was again in decline. The Amorites poured into Mesopotamia and overran many Sumerian centers, including Babylon. The dynasty that they founded at Babylon later produced a ruler who would dominate Mesopotamia: **Hammurabi**.

Hammurabi used his might to put down other Mesopotamian rulers. He eventually brought the entire region under his control, reorganizing the tax system and ordering local officials to build and repair irrigation canals. Hammurabi organized a strong government and worked to increase the economic prosperity of his people. Under Hammurabi's rule, Babylon became a major trade center. Merchants from as far away as India and China paid gold and silver for the grain and cloth the Babylonians produced.

Hammurabi's Law Code

Historians consider Hammurabi's greatest achievement his effort "to make justice appear in the land." Hammurabi collected laws of the various Mesopotamian city-states and created a law code covering the entire region. When completed, Hammurabi's code consisted of 282 sections dealing with most aspects of daily life. It clearly stated which actions were considered violations and assigned a specific punishment for each. Hammurabi's code penalized wrongdoers more severely than did the old Sumerian laws. Instead of fining violators, it exacted what the Bible later expressed as "an eye for an eye, and a tooth for a tooth." According to the harsh approach of Hammurabi's code:

This goddess, one of many similar preserved relics, along with discovered temple sites, reveals the significance of religion in early Mesopotamian civilizations.

The Kassite stela fragment shows animals that were important to a vigorous agricultural people, the Kassites, who emerged as a dominant force after 2000 B.C.

REFLECTING ON THE TIMES

1. What evidence reveals the importance of religion in Mesopotamian cities?
2. What role might gods and goddesses have in times of war?

King Hammurabi stands in front of the sun god Shamash at the top of the stone slab upon which is inscribed Hammurabi's code of laws. Shamash—the supreme judge—delivers the laws to the king. *Why were Hammurabi's laws carved in stone for public display?*

“ If a builder has built a house for a man and has not made his work sound, so that the house he has made falls down and causes the death of the owner of the house, that builder shall be put to death. If it causes the death of the son of the owner of the house, they shall kill the son of that builder. ”

Other sections of Hammurabi's code covered the property of married women, adoption and inheritance, interest rates on loans, and damage to fields by cattle. Some laws were attempts to protect the less powerful—for example, protecting wives against beatings or neglect by their husbands. The development of written law in Mesopotamia was a major advance toward justice and order. Before this achievement, people who had been offended or cheated often acted on their own and used violence against their opponents. Now, crimes against people or property became the concern of the whole community. Government assumed the responsibility of protecting its citizens in return for their loyalty and service.

Babylonian Society

Historians have been able to infer from Hammurabi's code a threefold division of Babylonian social classes—the kings, priests, and nobles at the top; the artisans, small merchants, scribes, and farmers next; and slaves as the lowest group. His laws varied according to the class of the person offended against, with more severe penalties for assaulting a landowner than for hurting a slave. Most slaves had been captured in war or had failed to pay their debts.

The Babylonians borrowed heavily from Sumerian culture. They used the cuneiform script for their Semitic language and wrote on clay tablets. Babylonian literature was similar to that of Sumer.

Decline and Fall

After Hammurabi's death, the Babylonian Empire declined, and Mesopotamia was again divided into a number of small states. Hammurabi's dynasty finally ended and his empire fell apart when the Hittites, a people from Asia Minor, raided Babylon about 1600 B.C. Babylon, however, would again play a role in Mesopotamian civilization in the 600s B.C. as the capital of a new empire under the Chaldeans.

SECTION 2 REVIEW

Recall
1. **Define** city-state, cuneiform.
2. **Identify** the Sumerians, Gilgamesh, Sargon I, the Akkadians, Hammurabi.
3. **Explain** the purpose of the religious ceremonies and rituals performed by Sumerian priests and priestesses.

Critical Thinking
4. **Making Comparisons** Contrast Hammurabi's code with earlier Sumerian law. Which do you think served justice better? Explain your answer.

Understanding Themes
5. **Cooperation** Identify an economic or cultural achievement of one of the civilizations of the Fertile Crescent region that must have required skillful planning and organization of many people.

Classifying Information

I magine shopping in a store where shoes, rugs, dishes, and books are all mixed together in piles. To find the item you need, you would have to comb through each pile. How frustrating!

Dealing with large quantities of information about a subject likewise can be frustrating. It is easier to understand information if you put it into groups, or classify it.

Learning the Skill

In classifying anything, we put together items with shared characteristics. Department stores group items according to their uses. For example, shoes and boots are in the footwear department, while pots and pans are in the kitchen department.

We can classify written information in the same way.

1. As you read about a topic, look for items that have similar characteristics. List these items in separate columns or on separate notecards.
2. Label these categories with an appropriate heading.
3. Add facts to the categories as you continue reading.
4. Review the groups. If necessary, subdivide the categories into smaller groups or combine categories that overlap.

Once you have classified the material, look for patterns and relationships in the facts. Make comparisons, draw conclusions, and develop questions or hypotheses for further study.

Practicing the Skill

Use the information in the passage below to answer the following questions:

1. The passage describes two groups of children in ancient Egypt. What are these groups?
2. Classify the educational opportunities available to each group.
3. Classify the occupations available to each group.
4. From your classifications, what conclusions can you draw about Egyptian society?

> The royal children ... were privately tutored ... frequently joined by the sons of great noble families.... The most sought-after profession in Egypt was that of scribe.... The most important subjects were reading and writing ... history, literature, geography, [and] ethics. Arithmetic was almost certainly part of the curriculum.... Boys who were to specialize in medicine, law or religious liturgy would perhaps have devoted some of their time to elementary studies in these fields.
>
> Formal education for [a son from] the lower classes ... was not selected for him because he wished to become an artist or goldsmith or a farmer ... he entered a trade because it was his father's work. The sons of artists and craftsmen were apprenticed and went to train at one of the temples or state workshops ... the sons of peasants would have joined their fathers in the field at an early age.
>
> —A. Rosalie David, *The Egyptian Kingdoms*, 1975

Applying the Skill

Find two newspaper or magazine articles about a topic that interests you. Classify the information on notecards or in a chart.

For More Practice

Turn to the Skill Practice in the Chapter Review on page 77 for more practice in classifying information.

c. 2500 B.C.
Settlements develop in the Indus River valley.

c. 2300 B.C. Harappan people trade with Mesopotamia.

c. 1500 B.C.
Indus Valley civilization declines.

Section 3

Early South Asia

Setting the Scene

▶ **Terms to Define**
subcontinent, monsoon

▶ **People to Meet**
the Harappans

▶ **Places to Locate**
Indus River valley, Harappa, Mohenjo-Daro

Find Out How did people of the Indus River valley civilization build cities?

The Storyteller

For a long time, it had been known that the mounds of Mohenjo-Daro and Harappa contained archaeological remains. But neighborhood construction workers actually used the ancient mounds as sources for bricks, until practically none remained above ground. As Sir Alexander Cunningham, the first Director General of the Archaeological Survey records, "Perhaps the best idea of the extent of the ruined brick mounds of Harappa may be formed from the fact that they have more than sufficed to furnish brick ballast for about 100 miles of Lahore and Multan Railway."

—adapted from *Indus Valley Civilization*, Ashim Kumar Ron N.N. Gidwani (Cunningham, 1875), 1982 and *Harappan Civilization*, Gregory Possehl, 1982

Harappan jar lid

A third civilization, larger than both Egypt and Sumer in land area, arose in the **Indus River valley** far to the east, in South Asia. It reached its height at about the time of the Akkadian and Babylonian Empires between about 2500 B.C. and 1500 B.C.

The Subcontinent

Three modern nations—India, Pakistan, and Bangladesh—trace their roots to the Indus Valley civilization. These countries lie on the subcontinent of South Asia, a large, triangular-shaped landmass that juts into the Indian Ocean.

Bounded by Mountains

Natural barriers separate the South Asian subcontinent from the rest of Asia. Water surrounds the landmass on the east and west. To the north rise two lofty mountain ranges—the Himalayas and the Hindu Kush. Throughout history, invaders entering the subcontinent by land have had to cross the few high mountain passes of the Hindu Kush.

Plains sweep across the landscape to the south of the mountains. Across the plains flow three rivers, fed by rain and melting mountain snows. The Indus River drains into the Arabian Sea, and the Ganges (GAN•JEEZ) and Brahmaputra (BRAH•muh•POO•truh) Rivers join and empty into the Bay of Bengal, forming a wide delta. The Ganges-Brahmaputra Delta and the Indus-Ganges plain are formed from soils left by the rivers. Like the Nile Valley and Delta and the Tigris-Euphrates plains, fertile river areas of South Asia have supported vast numbers of people over the ages.

Seasonal Winds

The northern mountains ensure generally warm weather in South Asia. Like a wall, they block blasts of cold air from central Asia. Two seasonal winds called monsoons affect the climate,

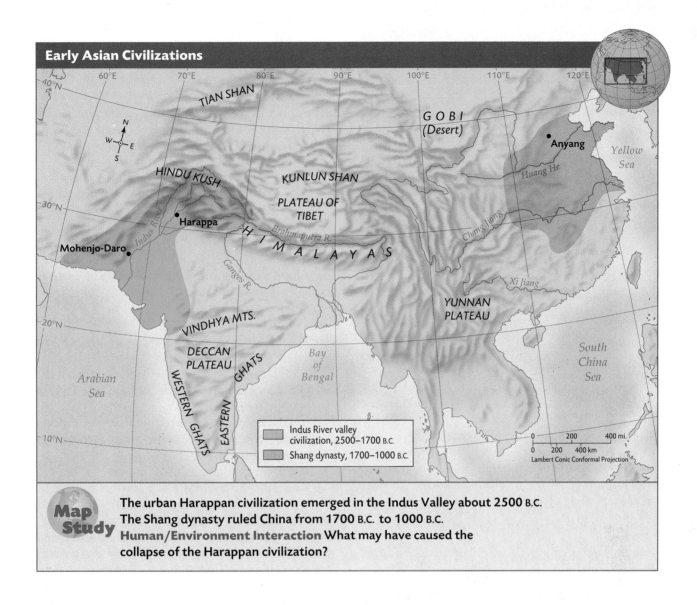

TIAN SHAN

GOBI
(Desert)

Anyang

Yellow
Sea

Huang He

HINDU KUSH

KUNLUN SHAN

PLATEAU OF
TIBET

Harappa

Indus River

Brahmaputra R.

H I M A L A Y A S

Chang Jiang

Mohenjo-Daro

Ganges R.

Xi Jiang

YUNNAN
PLATEAU

VINDHYA MTS.

DECCAN
PLATEAU

GHATS

Bay
of
Bengal

South
China
Sea

Arabian
Sea

WESTERN GHATS

EASTERN

| Indus River valley civilization, 2500–1700 B.C. |
| Shang dynasty, 1700–1000 B.C. |

0   200   400 mi.
0   200   400 km
Lambert Conic Conformal Projection

Map Study

The urban Harappan civilization emerged in the Indus Valley about 2500 B.C.
The Shang dynasty ruled China from 1700 B.C. to 1000 B.C.
Human/Environment Interaction What may have caused the collapse of the Harappan civilization?

however, and shape the pattern of life on the subcontinent.

The northeast, or winter, monsoon blows from November to March; the southwest, or summer, monsoon from June to September. The northeast wind brings dry air from the mountains, and the average winter temperatures of the Indus-Ganges plain remain mild—about 70°F (21°C). By June, temperatures have soared, sometimes exceeding 100°F (38°C), and South Asians welcome the rain-bearing southwest wind blowing off the ocean.

Because of the heavy downpours of the southwest monsoon, the rivers swell rapidly, then widen across the flat plains and rush to the sea. The flooding enriches the soil, but in some years unusually heavy rains drown people and animals and destroy whole villages. In other years the monsoon arrives late or rainfall is light; then crops are poor and people go hungry. The people of the plains are dependent on the monsoons.

The Indus Valley Civilization

Less than a century ago, archaeologists working in the Indus River valley first identified an ancient civilization in South Asia. They dated this early civilization to about 2500 B.C.

Centrally Planned Cities

Archaeologists named the Indus Valley settlements "the Harappan civilization" after one of its major cities, **Harappa** (huh•RA•puh), located in present-day Pakistan. **Mohenjo-Daro** (moh •HEHN•joh DAHR•oh), another important Harappan city, lay nearer the Arabian Sea.

The ruins of Harappa and Mohenjo-Daro are outstanding examples of urban planning. A citadel, or fortress, built on a brick platform overlooked each city—possibly serving as a government and religious center. Below the citadel Harappan engineers skillfully laid out each city in a grid pattern of

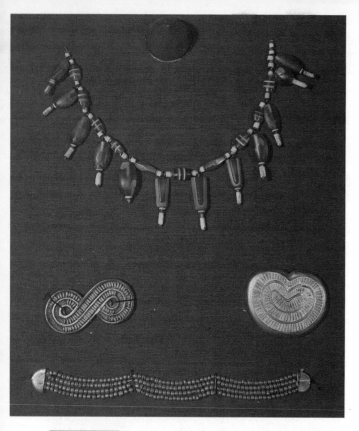

Some fine jewelry crafted by Harappan artisans has survived. **These pieces are now in the National Museum at New Delhi, India.** *Why is less known about Harappan civilization than about Egypt and Mesopotamia?*

grew wheat, barley, rice, and cotton. Farmers planted at the beginning or end of the flood season and relied on the drenched land to provide the necessary water for their crops.

Supported by a food surplus, Harappan city dwellers engaged in industry and commerce. Some artisans worked bronze and copper into tools, while others made silver vessels and gold, shell, and ivory jewelry. The Harappans also mass-produced clay pots, and they spun and wove cotton cloth. Merchants who handled these goods used soapstone seals to identify bundles of merchandise. The discovery by archaeologists of Harappan seals in Mesopotamia indicates that Indus Valley people traded with the people of Mesopotamia as early as 2300 B.C.

Language and Religion

The Harappans inscribed pictograms on the seals they placed on packages of goods. Scientists have yet to decipher these inscriptions—almost the only known examples of the written language of the Harappan civilization. Some believe that the Harappans made their pictograms after adopting the idea of writing from the people of Mesopotamia.

The lack of written records has made it difficult to learn as much about the Harappan civilization as is known about Egypt and Mesopotamia. Artifacts found in the ruins, however, have provided archaeologists with some clues. For example, animal and humanlike figures suggest that the Harappans worshiped gods associated with natural forces.

Collapse of a Civilization

By 1500 B.C. the Harappan civilization had disappeared. Historians have many theories for what caused this collapse. Evidence of floods, for example, suggests possible climate changes. In the Mohenjo-Daro ruins are signs that some of its people may have met a violent end, possibly at the hands of invaders.

straight streets crossing each other at right angles. **The Harappans** used oven-baked bricks to build houses with flat wooden roofs, and some houses rose to several stories and enclosed courtyards. Almost every house had at least one bathroom, with drains and chutes connected to a brick sewer system beneath the streets.

Harappan Life

Most of the Harappan people worked the land. In the fields of the Indus Valley floodplain they

---

SECTION 3 REVIEW

Recall
1. **Define** subcontinent, monsoon.
2. **Identify** the Harappans.
3. **Name** three modern nations of South Asia that trace their roots to the Indus Valley civilization. In what present-day nation were the cities of Harappa and Mohenjo-Daro located?

Critical Thinking
4. **Analyzing Information** What do archaeological clues suggest about the decline and collapse of the Indus Valley civilization?

Understanding Themes
5. **Cultural Diffusion** How might the Indus Valley civilization at Mohenjo-Daro and the civilization at Harappa have been influenced by the Mesopotamian city-states and empires?

2500 B.C.	2000 B.C.	1500 B.C.	1000 B.C.

c. 2500 B.C. Lung-shan culture begins in China.

c. 2000 B.C. Yu founds the legendary Xia dynasty.

c. 1700 B.C. Tang establishes the Shang, the first historical dynasty.

c. 1000s B.C. The Zhou dynasty comes to power.

Section 4

Early China

Setting the Scene

▶**Terms to Define**
  mandate

▶**People to Meet**
  Yu the Great

▶**Places to Locate**
  Huang He valley, Anyang

Find Out What were the major contributions of early Chinese civilization?

The Storyteller

What would the oracle say this time? Tang tried not to lean too far forward to watch as the fortune-teller began to apply red-hot coals to the turtle shell. A man of his station should not appear too anxious: his confidence in divine support should be seen by all. On the shell was inscribed a question known only to him: "Shall I attack before harvest?" So much depended on the answer. There was nothing to do now but wait for the fire to work on the brittle shell covered with scratchings, containing the destiny of China.

—adapted from *Ancient Records of Assyria and Babylon*, Volume 1, edited by Daniel David Luckenbill, 1968

A tortoise shell oracle bone from the Shang Dynasty

Even as the Harappans were meeting their mysterious fate, China's first dynasty had begun to assert its power over another river valley. This fourth river valley civilization has endured to the present day.

For many centuries the Chinese lived in relative isolation from the rest of the world. They called their homeland *Zhong Guo* (JOONG GWAH), or "the Middle Kingdom." To them it was the center of the whole world and the one truly supreme civilization. The lack of outside contacts allowed the Chinese to develop one culture across many regions and a strong sense of national identity as well. As a result, China has the oldest continuous civilization in the world.

China's Geography

China's varied geography has affected its historical development. Mountains make up about one-third of China's area. The Himalayas close off China to the southwest, and on the western border rise the Kunlun Shan and Tian Shan ranges. To the east of the Tian Shan lie the vast desert wastes of the Gobi. These rugged physical features hindered cultural diffusion both into and out of China for many centuries.

On the east, China's coastline touches the Pacific Ocean. Although some Chinese became devoted seafarers, they mostly focused on developing the agriculture of eastern China's fertile river valleys and plains. Unlike the land to the west with its forbidding terrain, the east welcomed life. For centuries large numbers of Chinese have farmed in the region's North China Plain.

Three major rivers drain eastern China: the Huang He (HWONG HUH); the Chang Jiang (CHAHNG JYAHNG), known also as the Yangtze (YANG•SEE); and the Xi Jiang (SHEE JYAHNG), also called the West River. The Huang He flows more than 2,900 miles (4,640 km) from the northern

Oracle bones used to obtain advice about military campaigns were often inscribed with the question and answer and preserved as part of the king's records. *Why were such oracle bones stored by the rulers?*

highlands eastward to the Yellow Sea. On its way it cuts through thick layers of loess (LEHS), a rich yellow soil. The river carries away large amounts of loess, which it deposits farther downstream. The abundance of yellow soil in the Huang's waters gives it its name—Yellow River. The Chinese sometimes call the Huang He "the Great Sorrow" because of the tragedy brought by its floods. However, the silt deposits brought by the flooding river have made the North China Plain a rich agricultural area.

A favorable climate also contributes to successful farming on the North China Plain. Melting snow from the mountains and the monsoon rains between July and October feed the Huang He. Farmers of the region have long depended on the seasonal rhythm of temperature and rainfall.

The Shang Dynasty

Very little is known about the origins of Chinese civilization. In the A.D. 1920s, archaeologists in the Huang He valley uncovered traces of Neolithic life in China. The magnificent painted pots of the Yang-shao (YAHNG•SHOW) culture found by the archaeologists date back to 3000–1500 B.C. Archaeologists have discovered that the Lungshan culture, from about 2500–2000 B.C., used a potter's wheel to make delicate pots and goblets. These and other Neolithic finds dated to earlier than 5000 B.C. make it clear that the **Huang He valley**, like the river valleys of Egypt, the Fertile Crescent, and South Asia, invited settlement from very early times.

Chinese Myths

Over the centuries the Chinese developed many myths to explain their remote past. One myth

tells how the universe was created from the body of a giant named Pan Gu (PAHN GOO), who hatched from an egg. Other legends celebrate the deeds of hero-kings. These larger-than-life rulers included Yao (YOW), a person in the form of a mountain, and Shun, the master of elephants. Another, **Yu the Great**, was a miraculous engineer. According to a myth about Yu:

> 66 When widespread waters swelled to Heaven and serpents and dragons did harm, Yao sent Yu to control the waters and to drive out the serpents and dragons. The waters were controlled and flowed to the east. The serpents and dragons plunged to their places. 99

The myth about Yu—written much later than the first oral tellings—may reflect stories about the attempts of one or many early rulers to channel the floodwaters of the Huang He.

According to tradition, Yu the Great founded China's first dynasty, named Xia (SYAH), around 2000 B.C. Archaeologists, however, have yet to find evidence of the legendary Xia. The first dynasty to be dated from written records in China is the Shang (SHAHNG). The Shang ruled China from about 1700 B.C. to 1000 B.C.

Early Religion

Though the Shang kings were political leaders, they also performed religious duties. As high priests, they could communicate with nature deities on behalf of the people. They prayed, made offerings, and performed sacrifices to gain a good harvest, a change in the weather, or victory in battle. Kings also had special powers for calling upon their ancestors. To do so, they had a priest scratch a question on an animal bone or sometimes on a

(AHN•YAHNG). Their excavations reveal the general layout of Anyang. A palace and temple stood at the center of the city, as in the cities of other early civilizations, and public buildings and homes of government officials circled the royal sanctuary. Beyond the city's center stood various workshops and other homes.

Expansion and Decline

Shang kings at first ruled over a small area in northern China. Later, their armies, equipped with bronze weapons and chariots, conquered more distant territories and finally took over most of the Huang He valley.

The Shang dynasty lacked strong leaders, however, and in time grew weak. Around 1000 B.C., Wu, a ruler of a former Shang territory in the northwest, marshaled his forces and marched on the capital. Wu killed the Shang king and established a new dynasty. Wu's dynasty, known as the Zhou (JOH), ruled China for 800 years.

Many Centuries of Dynasties

From the beginning of its recorded history until the early 1900s, dynasties ruled China. When writing about China's past, Western historians have followed the Chinese practice of dividing Chinese history into periods based on the reigns of these ruling families.

The Chinese believed that their rulers governed according to a principle known as the Mandate of Heaven. If rulers were just and effective, they received a mandate, or authority to rule, from heaven. If rulers did not govern properly—as indicated by poor crops or losses in battle—they lost the mandate to someone else who then started a new dynasty. The principle first appeared during the Zhou dynasty. Indeed the Zhou, as did later rebels, probably found the Mandate of Heaven a convenient way to explain their overthrow of an unpopular dynasty.

tortoise shell. The priest then applied intense heat to the bone. The bone would crack, and the priest would interpret the splintered pattern of cracks as the answer to the king's question. The bones helped the kings to predict the future. The scratchings on the oracle bones, as they are called, are the first known examples of writing in China.

Important Achievements

The priests writing on the oracle bones used a script with many characters. These characters represented objects, ideas, or sounds and were written in vertical columns. To use the script with ease, a writer had to memorize each character. Because only a small percentage of the population could master all the characters, few people in ancient China could read and write.

Not only did the Chinese of the Shang period develop a written script, but they also perfected their metal-casting skills and produced some of the finest bronze objects ever made. These included bronze daggers, figurines, and ritual urns. They built massive ceremonial cauldrons that stood on legs. Bronze fittings adorned hunting chariots, and warriors carried bronze daggers. Artisans also carved beautiful ivory and jade statues. They wove silk into elegantly colored cloth for the upper class and fashioned pottery from kaolin, a fine white clay.

The Chinese built their first cities under the Shang. Archaeologists today have identified seven capital cities, including the city of **Anyang**

SECTION 4 REVIEW

Recall
1. **Define** mandate.
2. **Identify** Yu the Great, Xia dynasty, Shang dynasty, Mandate of Heaven.
3. **Use** the map on page 67 to list the major physical features of China. Explain how these physical features affected the development of Chinese civilization.

Critical Thinking
4. **Making Comparisons** Compare the Mandate of Heaven with the way Egyptian kings justified their rule.

Understanding Themes
5. **Innovation** Explain the basic features of the Chinese writing system as it developed in early times. How widespread was the use of this method of writing in China under the early dynasties?

Bridge to the Past

Literature

from

Gilgamesh

retold by Herbert Mason

*L*ike people today, ancient Sumerians loved adventure tales featuring extraordinary heroes battling the forces of evil. Many Sumerian myths featured a king, Gilgamesh, who lived around 2700 B.C. The earliest known written accounts of Gilgamesh's adventures date from about 1850 B.C., making them the oldest surviving examples of epic poetry. An epic is a long poem recalling the exploits of a legendary hero. Gilgamesh, after the death of his friend Enkidu, searched for the secret of eternal life, which he hoped to share with his departed friend. In the following excerpt, Gilgamesh, hoping to learn how to escape death, listens to a mysterious elderly man, Utnapishtim, recount how he survived a great flood.

*T*here was a city called Shurrupak
          On the bank of the Euphrates.
It was very old, and so many were the gods
Within it. They converged in their complex
    hearts
On the idea of creating a great flood.
There was Anu, their aging and weak-minded
    father,
The military Enlil, his adviser,
Ishtar, the sensation-craving one,
And all the rest. Ea, who was present
At their council, came to my house
And, frightened by the violent winds that filled
    the air,
Echoed all that they were planning and had said.
Man of Shurrupak, he said, tear down your
    house
And build a ship. Abandon your possessions
And the works that you find beautiful and crave,
And save your life instead. Into the ship
Bring the seed of all living creatures.

I was overawed, perplexed,
And finally downcast. I agreed to do
As Ea said, but I protested: What shall I say
To the city, the people, the leaders?

Tell them, Ea said, you have learned that Enlil
The war god despises you and will not
Give you access to the city anymore.
Tell them for this Ea will bring the rains.

This is the way gods think, he laughed. His tone
Of savage irony frightened Gilgamesh
Yet gave him pleasure, being his friend.
They only know how to compete or echo.
But who am I to talk? He sighed as if
Disgusted with himself; I did as he
Commanded me to do. I spoke to them,
And some came out to help me build the ship
Of seven stories, each with nine chambers.
The boat was cube in shape, and sound; it held
The food and wine and precious minerals
And seed of living animals we put
In it. My family then moved inside,
And all who wanted to be with us there:
The game of the field, the goats of the steppe,
The craftsmen of the city came, a navigator
Came. And then Ea ordered me to close
The door. The time of the great rains had come.
O there was ample warning, yes, my friend,
But it was terrifying still. Buildings
Blown by the winds for miles like desert brush.
People clung to branches of trees until
Roots gave way. New possessions, now debris,
Floated on the water with their special
Sterile vacancy. The riverbanks failed
To hold the water back. Even the gods
Cowered like dogs at what they had done.
Ishtar cried out like a woman at the height
Of labor: O how could I have wanted
To do this to my people! They were *hers*,
Notice. Even her sorrow was possessive.
Her spawn that she had killed too soon.
Old gods are terrible to look at when
They weep, all bloated like spoiled fish.
One wonders if they ever understand

Kingdoms and Empires in the Middle East

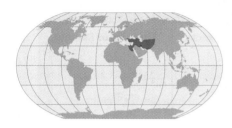

Chapter Themes

▶ **Cultural Diffusion** Aramaean and Phoenician merchants spread ideas throughout the Middle East. *Section 1*

▶ **Innovation** The Israelites contribute to the world the concept of monotheism. *Section 2*

▶ **Conflict** A series of empires—Hittite, then Assyrian, then Chaldean, then Persian—each conquers the previous one. *Section 3*

S*toryteller*

The

Ashurbanipal, the last great Assyrian king, reigned in the mid-600s B.C. The dim rooms were almost still in Ashurbanipal's great palace at Nineveh, the splendid capital of his empire. Men with shoulder-length hair and squared-off beards glided in their tunics and sandals through the vast hallways. But the stone reliefs that decorated the palace walls told a less peaceful story. In intricately carved scenes, the impassive hunter in his chariot lets fly with a volley of arrows into a staggering lion, and the valiant general on the battlefield proudly waves his sword above the defeated enemy legions. Ashurbanipal followed a long line of ruthless Assyrian conquerors who boasted of their military exploits and cruelty.

Historical Significance

How did traders, religious thinkers, and empire builders shape the development of the ancient Middle East? How have their achievements influenced cultural and religious life today?

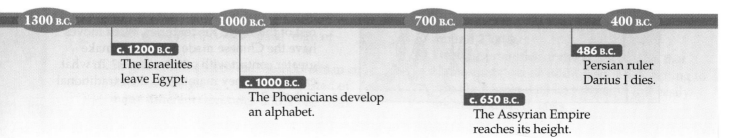

1300 B.C.	1000 B.C.	700 B.C.	400 B.C.

c. 1200 B.C.
The Israelites leave Egypt.

c. 1000 B.C.
The Phoenicians develop an alphabet.

c. 650 B.C.
The Assyrian Empire reaches its height.

486 B.C.
Persian ruler Darius I dies.

Ashurbanipal hunting on horseback. Relief from the NW Palace at Nineveh, c. 640 B.C.

Your History Journal

The kingdoms of the Middle East provide rich accounts of the struggle for peace and justice. Read the quotations on pages 86 and 93 and write similar verses about several events in this chapter.

c. 1200 B.C.
Aramaeans settle
in central Syria.

c. 1100 B.C.
Phoenicians reach Spain and
western Africa.

c. 600s B.C.
Lydians develop a
wealthy kingdom
in Asia Minor.

Section 1

Trading Peoples

Setting the Scene

▶ **Terms to Define**
confederation, alphabet, colony, barter

▶ **People to Meet**
the Aramaeans, the Phoenicians, the Lydians

▶ **Places to Locate**
Syria, Damascus, Tyre

Find Out How did trading peoples influence
the development of the Middle East?

The Storyteller

*King Hiram was pleased. Tyre, his capital city,
was a bustling seaport: sophisticated, cosmopoli-
tan, and rich. Not only did the kings of Egypt and
Babylon send ambassadors to Hiram's court, they
also brought business to his land. Gold, copper,
ivory, and linen from Egypt; precious stones from
Babylon; silver from Asia Minor; and pottery from
Crete enriched Tyre. In return, Tyre exchanged
cedar, cut from the nearby mountains, and a vivid
purple dye, harvested from murex shells found in
the seas near the rocky coast. Hiram's people were
Phoenicians, the people of the purple, the color—
beautiful, costly, and rare—which throughout the
ancient world marked an individual as one of
immense wealth and high rank.*

—adapted from
*The Bible as
History,* Werner
Keller, translated
by William Neil,
1969

Phoenician ship

The magnificent civilizations of
Mesopotamia and Egypt greatly influenced neighboring peoples in the
Fertile Crescent—among them **the Aramaeans**
(AR•uh•MEE•uhnz) and **the Phoenicians** (fih
•NEE•shuhnz). In turn, these trading peoples
helped to spread their own cultures throughout the
region and into much of the ancient world.
Traveling on sailing ships and by caravan, traders
from the Fertile Crescent brought languages, customs, and ideas along with their trade goods.

The Aramaeans

One of the most active peoples in early Middle
Eastern trade, the Aramaeans settled in central
Syria around 1200 B.C. Although Aramaean kings
established a capital at **Damascus**, provincial leaders frequently challenged their authority. Despite
political weaknesses, the Aramaeans gained control
of the rich overland trade between Egypt and
Mesopotamia.

Because Aramaean caravans crossed and
recrossed the Fertile Crescent on business, people
throughout the region learned Aramaic, the language of the Aramaeans. Until the A.D. 800s, the
majority of the people living in the Fertile Crescent
spoke Aramaic, a language closely related to
Hebrew and Arabic. In addition, some parts of the
Bible were written in Aramaic.

The Phoenicians

Between ancient Egypt and Syria lay the land
of Canaan, today made up of Lebanon, Israel, and
Jordan. The Phoenicians, one of the Semitic groups
that migrated from the Arabian Peninsula about
3000 B.C., settled in the northern part of Canaan.
Their neighbors in Canaan, the Philistines, came
from the eastern Mediterranean. The Greeks would

Lloyd K. Townsend

Merchants of the Mediterranean

In this illustration sturdy cargo boats dock in their North African home port of Carthage, and war galleys in the harbor lie in wait for any rivals caught in Phoenician waters. A captain bargains over the price of a bale of purple cloth for the next voyage as his crew unloads grain from Sardinia and cedar logs from North Africa. Above deck sit clay jars of olive oil and wine; below, silver, tin, gold, and ivory are stored. Departing vessels take on terra-cotta figurines, decorated ostrich eggshells, metal utensils, and perfume vials.

From their cities nestled along the coast of the eastern Mediterranean Sea, Phoenicians launched a trading empire. They soon became middlemen for their neighbors in Mesopotamia, Arabia, and Egypt. By 800 B.C., Phoenician trade had spread into the western Mediterranean. From Carthage and other Mediterranean cities, the Phoenicians manned supply depots, guarded sea lanes, and expanded their trading empire. ⏾

later call Canaan *Palestine*, the Greek name for the Philistines.

In contrast to the Aramaeans, who trekked overland to reach their markets, the Phoenicians sailed the seas. On a narrow strip of land between the mountains of western Syria and the Mediterranean Sea, Phoenicia lacked enough arable land for farming, and many Phoenicians turned to the sea to earn a living. They harvested timber from the cedar forests on nearby slopes to build strong, fast ships.

By 1200 B.C. the Phoenicians had built a string of cities and towns along their coast. Many of these scattered ports grew to become city-states, the largest of which were **Tyre**, Byblos, Sidon, and Berytus (modern Beirut). The city-state of Tyre often provided the leadership for what remained a confederation, or loose union, of independent Phoenician city-states. According to the Bible:

> ❝ Who was like Tyre.… In the midst of the
> sea? When your wares were unloaded
> from the seas, You satisfied many peoples;
> With your great wealth and merchandise
> You enriched the kings of the earth. ❞
> —Ezekiel 27:32-33

The Phoenicians sailed from their coastal city-states throughout the Mediterranean. Expert navigators, they learned to plot their voyages with great accuracy by means of the sun and the stars. By 1100 B.C. Phoenicians reached the southern coast of Spain and the western coast of Africa. Some historians believe they even ventured as far as the British Isles in northwestern Europe.

Astute traders and businesspeople, the Phoenicians soon took charge of Mediterranean shipping and trade. At ports of call, they exchanged cedar logs, textiles dyed a beautiful purple, glass objects, and elegant jewelry for precious metals. They also brought new business practices, such as bills of sale and contracts.

An advantage that Phoenician merchants held over their competitors when keeping track of complex business deals was an improved alphabet—a series of written symbols that represent sounds. Phoenicians developed their efficient alphabet about 1000 B.C. from earlier, more complicated systems from southern Canaan and northwest Syria. The concise Phoenician alphabet used just 22 characters, each character representing a consonant sound. Readers mentally supplied vowels in the proper places.

The Phoenician system later became the foundation of several alphabets, including Greek, which in turn became the basis of all Western alphabets. Because the Phoenician alphabet did not require years of study to master, merchants no longer needed the services of specially trained scribes to keep records.

To protect and resupply their ships, Phoenician sailors and traders set up along the coasts of the Mediterranean a network of temporary trading posts and colonies, or settlements of Phoenician emigrants. For example, about 814 B.C., people from Tyre founded a colony named Carthage on the coast of present-day Tunisia. Carthage eventually became the most powerful city in the western Mediterranean.

The Lydians

The **Lydians** (LIH•dee•uhnz) lived in Asia Minor—the peninsula jutting westward between the Mediterranean, Aegean, and Black Seas. Lydian merchants and artisans were well situated to prosper in the growing regional trade. By the late 600s B.C., the Lydians had developed a wealthy and independent kingdom famous for its rich gold deposits.

Most traders from neighboring cultures still relied on a system of barter for their transactions, exchanging their wares for other goods. The Lydians, however, began to set prices and developed a money system using coins as a medium of exchange. Soon Greek and Persian rulers began to stamp their own coins, and the concept of money spread beyond Lydia.

SECTION 1 REVIEW

Recall
1. **Define** confederation, alphabet, colony, barter.
2. **Identify** the Aramaeans, the Phoenicians, the Lydians.
3. **Describe** the bodies of water bordering the regions of Canaan and Asia Minor.

Critical Thinking
4. **Evaluating Information** What factors enabled the Phoenician city-states to remain independent of each other and to prosper?

Understanding Themes
5. **Cultural Diffusion** Why was the Phoenician alphabet a significant development?

c. 1900 B.C.
Abraham settles in Canaan.

c. 1200 B.C.
The Israelites first celebrate Passover.

c. 1000 B.C.
David sets up capital at Jerusalem.

c. 530s B.C.
Jews rebuild the Temple in Jerusalem.

Section 2

Early Israelites

Setting the Scene

▶ **Terms to Define**
monotheism, covenant, exodus, prophet, Diaspora

▶ **People to Meet** the Israelites, Abraham, Moses, Deborah, David, Solomon

▶ **Places to Locate** Canaan, Jerusalem

 **Find Out** What part do slavery, exile, and return play in the history of the Israelites?

The Storyteller

This battle would be decisive, Jael was certain. Before the sun set, the Israelites would be recognized as Yahweh's chosen people. Unlike the nomads who had passed through Canaan for generations, the 12 tribes of Israel now sought permanent settlement. However, to remain and prosper, the Israelites had to join together and defeat the threatening Canaanites. Several tribes of Israel, held together only by their common covenant with Yahweh, were sending armed men to battle. Jael, resolving to take action herself, if necessary, was sure that Yahweh would muster the heavens themselves to confound the enemies of the covenant, give victory to the Israelites, and bring peace to the land.

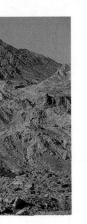

Mount Sinai

—adapted from the *Holy Bible*, Judges

People in the ancient world usually worshiped many deities. The Phoenicians, for example, worshiped a chief god known as El, Baal, or Melqart; an earth-mother goddess called Astarte; and a young god of rebirth named Adonis.

The **Israelites**—another people living in **Canaan**—were an exception among the polytheistic cultures of the ancient world. They brought a new idea to the world, monotheism, or the belief in one all-powerful God. The Israelites believed that God, whom they called Yahweh, determined right and wrong and expected people to deal justly with each other and to accept moral responsibility for their actions. The teachings of the Israelites exist today as the religion of Judaism, which in turn has influenced two other monotheistic religions—Christianity and Islam.

The Land of Canaan

The Bible remains one of the main sources of ancient history in the Fertile Crescent. As a record of the early Israelites, the Bible traces their origins to Abraham, a herder and trader who lived in the Mesopotamian city of Ur. Around 1900 B.C. **Abraham** and his household left Ur and settled in Canaan at the command of Yahweh, or God. The Israelites believed that God made a covenant, or agreement, with Abraham at this time. "I will make of you a great nation" was God's promise to bless Abraham and his descendants if they would remain faithful to God.

According to the Bible, once in the land of Canaan, the descendants of Abraham shared the land with other related peoples, such as the Phoenicians and Philistines. Canaan contained rocky hills and desert, fertile plains and grassy slopes, with the best farming in the valley of the Jordan River. Many people lived as nomads herding sheep and goats.

The Exodus From Egypt

Abraham's grandson Jacob, also known as Israel, raised 12 sons in Canaan, and each son led a separate family group, or tribe. These groups became the 12 tribes of Israel. After a severe drought brought a terrible famine to Canaan, the Israelites migrated to Egypt, perhaps during the time that the Hyksos ruled. The Israelites lived peacefully there for several generations, until the pharaohs decided to enslave them.

In the 1200s B.C., the Israelite leader **Moses** led his people out of Egypt in an exodus, or departure, into the Sinai Desert. Every year during the festival of Passover, Jews today retell the story of the Exodus from Egypt.

According to the Bible, during the long trek across the desert of the Sinai Peninsula, God renewed the covenant made with Abraham. Moses and the Israelites pledged to reject all gods other than the one true God and to obey God's laws, the most important of which would be called the Ten Commandments.

> **❝** I the Lord am your God who brought you out of the land of Egypt, the house of bondage: You shall have no other gods beside Me.
> You shall not make for yourself a sculptured image.... ❡
> You shall not swear falsely by the name of the Lord your God....
> Remember the sabbath day and keep it holy....
> Honor your father and your mother, that you may long endure on the land that the Lord your God is giving you.
> You shall not murder.
> You shall not commit adultery.
> You shall not steal.
> You shall not bear false witness against your neighbor.
> You shall not covet ... anything that is your neighbor's. **❞**
>
> —Exodus 20:2–14

In return for their loyalty, God promised the Israelites a safe return to the land of Canaan.

Settling the Land

Moses died before reaching Canaan, but his successor, Joshua, led the Israelites across the Jordan River into Canaan. For about 200 years, the

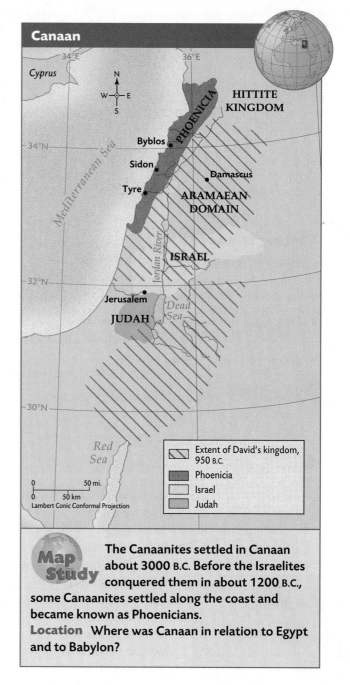

Canaan

Extent of David's kingdom, 950 B.C.
Phoenicia
Israel
Judah

Map Study The Canaanites settled in Canaan about 3000 B.C. Before the Israelites conquered them in about 1200 B.C., some Canaanites settled along the coast and became known as Phoenicians.
Location Where was Canaan in relation to Egypt and to Babylon?

Israelites fought the Philistines and the Canaanites who now occupied the land.

The Fighting Judges

Lack of unity among the 12 tribes of Israel prolonged the campaign to acquire Canaan. Leaders known as "judges" ruled each tribe. Serving as both judicial and military leaders, some of the judges attempted to rally the Israelites. The Bible relates how **Deborah**, a judge widely admired for her wisdom, planned an attack on a Canaanite army camped near Mount Tabor. The Israelites believed that through God's help, they won the battle.

The Davidic Monarchy

Around 1020 B.C. continual warfare led most of the Israelite tribes to unite under one king, Saul. Although he was popular at first, Saul's power waned when he proved unable to defeat the Philistines. **David**, who had once fought the Philistine Goliath on Saul's behalf, took the throne in 1012 B.C. and ruled for the next 40 years. King David set up a capital at **Jerusalem**, organized a central government, and enlarged his kingdom's borders. During his reign, the Israelites enjoyed economic prosperity.

David's son **Solomon** succeeded his father in 961 B.C. Solomon founded new cities and lavished money on the construction of a magnificent temple to God in Jerusalem. The Israelites resented Solomon's high taxes and harsh labor requirements. After Solomon's death in 922 B.C., the 10 northern tribes broke away from the 2 tribes in the south. The northern tribes continued to call their kingdom Israel. The 2 southern tribes called their kingdom Judah, and kept Jerusalem as their capital. The word *Jew* comes from the name *Judah*.

Exile and Return

Although split politically, the people of Israel and Judah continued to share one religion. The 2 kingdoms, however, were too weak to resist invasions by powerful neighbors. In 722 B.C. the Assyrians of Mesopotamia swept in and conquered Israel, scattering the people of the 10 northern tribes throughout the Assyrian Empire. Then, in 586 B.C., another Mesopotamian people, the Chaldeans (kal•DEE•uhnz), gained control of Judah and destroyed the Temple in Jerusalem. They enslaved some of the city's residents and carried them off to exile in the Chaldean capital city of Babylon.

Exile in Babylon

During this difficult period, prophets—preachers who interpreted God's will—arose among the Israelites, who were called Jews after the Babylonian exile. Some prophets, such as Jeremiah, condemned abuses in society and blamed the exile on the Jews' forgetting their duties to God and to one another. The prophets also helped the people of

CONNECTIONS

Science and Technology

Counting the Days

How many days are there in a week? Different ancient peoples had more than one answer to this question. The Assyrians used a five-day week, while the Egyptians favored groupings of seven.

The modern week may trace its origins to the Jewish custom of observing a Sabbath day every seven days. Alternatively, our week may have originated in the Babylonian belief in the sacredness of the number seven—a belief probably linked either to the four seven-day phases of the moon or to the seven planets then visible in the heavens.

Ancient peoples often developed lunar calendars, based on the length of time it takes the moon to circle Earth, about 29 days. Of course, the lunar year of about 354 days did not

A modern sundial

correspond to the solar, or agricultural, year of 365 days. To solve this problem, Babylonian rulers added an extra month to certain years by royal decree.

Astronomers continued to try to adjust calendars to match the annual cycle of seasons. In 46 B.C. the Roman ruler Julius Caesar decreed that months should be longer than a lunar month. He also introduced January 1 as the first day of a new year. But not until A.D. 1582 were errors in the Julian calendar corrected by Pope Gregory XIII, who formalized a self-correcting system of leap years. The Gregorian calendar used today by most people in the Western world closely matches the solar year.

MAKING THE CONNECTION

1. How did the Babylonians resolve differences between the lunar year and the solar year?
2. How does our modern calendar differ from the ancient Babylonian calendar?

Judah retain their culture during the exile.

While in Babylon, the Jews no longer had a temple in which to worship God. Instead, small groups of Jews began to meet on the Sabbath, the holy day of rest, for prayer and discussion. The rise of local synagogues developed from these gatherings.

Rebuilding Jerusalem

Many Jews continued to hope for a return to Jerusalem. Finally, in 539 B.C., the Persians conquered the Chaldeans. The Persian king, Cyrus II, allowed the Jewish exiles to return to Judah and to rebuild the Temple in Jerusalem. In the 400s B.C., Jewish holy writings were collected and organized into the Torah, made up of the first five books of the Bible: Genesis, Exodus, Leviticus, Numbers, and Deuteronomy.

Although a new Jewish community arose in Jerusalem, many Jews chose to remain in Babylon, and some migrated to other areas in the Middle East. Ever since this time, communities of Jews have existed outside their homeland in what has become known as the Diaspora, a Greek word meaning "scattered."

Visualizing History Scribes recopied the Torah carefully, comparing each letter and word to the original copy. *What was the prophet Micah's vision for the world?*

A Lasting Legacy

Their troubled history—with cycles of slavery, exile, and return—made the Jews keenly aware of their past. Seeing events as having a God-directed purpose, the Jews recorded their history and examined it for meaning. The Jewish Scriptures begin with the Torah and include the writings of the prophets. As the Jews scattered beyond Canaan, they took the Torah with them, and its teachings spread around the world.

From the Torah has come the concept that every human being, made in the image of God, has infinite worth. Further, humans work in partnership with God, striving to achieve a perfect world, and this link makes people accountable for what happens in the world. The Jewish prophet Micah expressed his vision for the world as follows:

> ❝ And they shall beat their swords
>   into plowshares,
> And their spears into pruning hooks.
> Nation shall not take up
> Sword against nation;
> They shall never again know war;
> But every man shall sit
> Under his grapevine or fig tree
> With no one to disturb him. ❞
>
> —Micah 4:3–4

SECTION 2 REVIEW

Recall
1. **Define** monotheism, covenant, exodus, prophet, Diaspora.
2. **Identify** the Israelites, Abraham, Moses, Deborah, David, Solomon.
3. **Locate** Jerusalem on the map on page 84. What was the significance of Jerusalem to Jews in exile in Babylon?

Critical Thinking
4. **Analyzing Information** Create a chronology of the migrations of the Israelites.

Understanding Themes
5. **Innovation** What religious beliefs set the Israelites apart from other ancient peoples? How have these beliefs helped the Jews to survive in spite of exile and persecution?

Taking Notes

Your history teacher has assigned 20 pages of text to read for homework tonight. You will be tested on the material tomorrow. How will you remember all those facts?

Learning the Skill

Taking notes will help you remember what you have read. Effective note taking, however, is more than just writing facts in short phrases. When taking notes, you must group facts in a logical order. This order can be chronological—what happened first, next, last. It can be based on relationships between events—for example, causes and effects or problems and solutions. By arranging notes logically, you will have better recall and understanding of the information.

Before taking notes, read the material to identify the main ideas. Look for patterns and connections between ideas. Then decide on a note-taking method. Whenever possible, use a graphic organizer to take notes. For example, use a time line to take notes on the sequence of events. A cause-and-effect chart with arrows identifies connections between events. A semantic web shows different aspects of a general topic or theme. A category chart arranges data about groups of people and places into specific categories. Once you have selected an appropriate method, paraphrase your notes in brief headings and short phrases.

Practicing the Skill

Reread Section 2 on pages 83-86 about the early Israelites. Use that information and the semantic web below to answer the following questions.
1. What subtopics belong in the two upper boxes of this web?
2. What religions belong in the lower boxes?
3. What subtopics can you add to the upper left box?
4. What subtopics can you add to the upper right box?

Applying the Skill

Use a semantic web to take notes on Section 1, Trading Peoples.

For More Practice

Turn to the Skill Practice in the Chapter Review on page 95 for more practice in taking notes.

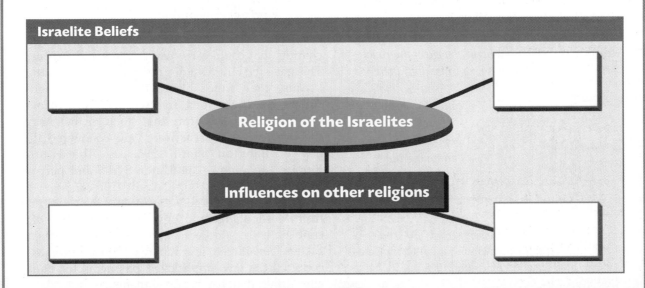

Israelite Beliefs

Religion of the Israelites

Influences on other religions

2000 B.C.   1500 B.C.   1000 B.C.   500 B.C.

c. 1600 B.C.
Hittite Empire reaches
its height.

c. 605 B.C.
Nebuchadnezzar
begins reign in
Babylon.

525 B.C.
Persian armies
conquer Egypt.

Section 3

Empire Builders

Setting the Scene

▶ **Terms to Define**
    satrap

▶ **People to Meet**
    the Hittites, the Assyrians, the Chaldeans,
    Nebuchadnezzar, the Persians, Cyrus II,
    Darius I, Zoroaster

▶ **Places to Locate** Anatolia, Babylon, Nineveh,
    Persepolis

 **Find Out** How did a series of powerful
empires extend their rule throughout the
Middle East?

The Storyteller

*The scribe carefully recorded King
Ashurbanipal II's proclamation. The royal
archives would preserve an accurate account of
the actions taken against the cities that had dared
to revolt. The king dictated: "With the fury of my
weapons I stormed the city. I flayed all the chief
men who had revolted, and I covered a pillar with
their skins. Some I impaled on the pillar on
stakes.... I fashioned a heroic image of my royal
self, my power and my glory I inscribed there-
on...." Ashurbanipal
called the gods to
destroy all who
opposed him, over-
throwing their
kingdoms and blot-
ting out their
names from the land.*

*Hittite hunting
scene*

—from *Ancient Records of Assyria and
Babylonia*, Volume 1, edited by Daniel
David Luckenbill, 1968

The Phoenicians, Aramaeans, Lydians,
and Israelites gave the world their
alphabets, languages, commercial prac-
tices, and religious beliefs. These peoples, however,
lacked the military power of their neighbors, and
the conquering armies of a series of warlike
empires came to rule the Fertile Crescent.

The Hittites

Around 2000 B.C., **the Hittites**—perhaps coming from areas beyond the Black Sea—conquered
the local people of Asia Minor. The Hittites set up
several city-states on a central plateau called
Anatolia, and by about 1650 B.C., they had built a
well-organized kingdom. Archaeologists have deci-
phered the writing on some of the clay tablets
found in the ruins of Hattusas, the Hittite capital.
Other information about the Hittites comes from
records of peoples they confronted as they expanded their empire. An Egyptian source, for example,
described the Hittites' custom of wearing their hair
in a long, thick pigtail that hung down in the back.

Hittite kings assembled a fearsome army—the
first in the Middle East to wield iron weapons
extensively. The army used light, spoked-wheel
chariots that could carry two soldiers and a driver.
This gave the Hittites a decided advantage in battle,
because they were able to field twice as many
troops as their foes in two-person chariots.
Overwhelming any army that stood in their way,
the Hittites pushed eastward and conquered the
city of **Babylon** about 1595 B.C. The Hittite
Empire—spanning Asia Minor, Syria, and part of
Mesopotamia—lasted until about 1200 B.C.

The Hittites largely borrowed their culture
from Mesopotamia and Egypt. However, they did
contribute to Middle Eastern civilization a legal
system considered less harsh than Hammurabi's
code. Hittite law emphasized payments for damages rather than harsh punishments.

The Assyrians

The Assyrians, a people living in northern Mesopotamia, had faced constant invasions from adjoining Asia Minor—including those by the Hittites. About 900 B.C. the Assyrians finally became strong enough to repel attacks from the west. They also began to launch their own military campaigns to subdue their Mesopotamian neighbors.

A Powerful Army

The Assyrian army earned a reputation as the most lethal fighting force in the Middle East. The Assyrians organized their warriors into units of foot soldiers, charioteers, and fast-moving cavalry fighting on horseback. They were described as fighters "whose arrows were sharp and all their bows bent, the horses' hooves were like flint, and their [chariot] wheels like a whirlwind." The Assyrians fought with iron weapons and used battering rams against the walls of the cities they attacked.

The Assyrians treated conquered peoples cruelly. They burned cities and tortured and killed thousands of captives. The Assyrians routinely deported entire populations from their homelands. Resettling the land with people from other parts of the empire, the Assyrians forced these settlers to pay heavy taxes.

The Assyrian Empire

By about 650 B.C., the Assyrian kings governed an empire stretching from the Persian Gulf to Egypt and into Asia Minor. They divided their empire into provinces, each headed by a governor directly responsible to the king. Officials sent from the central government collected taxes to support the army and to fund building projects in **Nineveh**, the Assyrian capital. To improve communication, the Assyrians built a network of roads linking the provinces. Government messengers and Aramaean merchants traveled these roads, protected by soldiers from bandits.

In spite of these links, the Assyrian Empire eventually began to fracture as conquered peoples continually rebelled. In 612 B.C. **the Chaldeans**, who lived in the ancient city of Babylon, formed an alliance with the Medes from the east. The alliance captured Nineveh and brought down the Assyrian Empire.

The Chaldeans

Soon after the Assyrians fell, the Chaldean Empire succeeded in dominating the entire Fertile Crescent. Most of the Chaldeans—sometimes called the New Babylonians—were descended from people of Hammurabi's Babylonian Empire of the 1700s B.C.

The Chaldeans reached the height of their power during the reign of one of their greatest

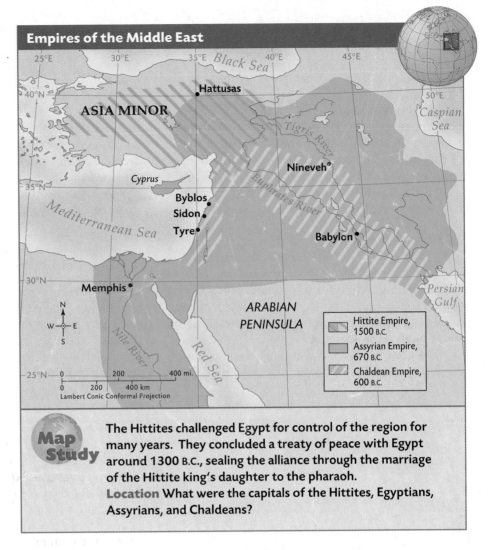

Empires of the Middle East

Hittite Empire, 1500 B.C.
Assyrian Empire, 670 B.C.
Chaldean Empire, 600 B.C.

Map Study

The Hittites challenged Egypt for control of the region for many years. They concluded a treaty of peace with Egypt around 1300 B.C., sealing the alliance through the marriage of the Hittite king's daughter to the pharaoh.
Location What were the capitals of the Hittites, Egyptians, Assyrians, and Chaldeans?

rulers, King **Nebuchadnezzar** (NEH•byuh•kuhd•NEH•zuhr), from 605 B.C. to 562 B.C. He extended the boundaries of the Chaldean Empire as far west as Syria and Canaan, conquering the city of Jerusalem and the Phoenician city-state of Tyre and forcing the people of the kingdom of Judah into a Babylonian exile in 586 B.C. Nebuchadnezzar also amassed great wealth and rebuilt Babylon into one of the largest, most beautiful cities of the ancient world.

Historians of the time counted two features of Babylon among the so-called Seven Wonders of the World—its wall and its Hanging Gardens. An immense wall snaked around the city, standing 50 feet (15 m) high and bristling with watchtowers every 100 yards (90 m). Nebuchadnezzar created the Hanging Gardens for his wife. Constructed on several levels and designed to be visible from any point in Babylon, the elaborate park was fed by water pumped from a nearby river.

The Chaldeans were also noted for their interest in astrology. They recorded their observations of the stars and made maps that showed the position of the planets and the phases of the moon. Their studies laid the foundations for the science of astronomy.

After Nebuchadnezzar's death, a series of weak kings held the throne. Poor harvests and slow trade further sapped the strength of an empire whose people had been severely taxed and plundered. Then, in 539 B.C., **the Persians** under **Cyrus II** came from the mountains to the northeast, seized Babylon, and then conquered the rest of the Chaldean Empire.

The Persians

The Persians originated from a larger group of people now called Indo-Europeans. As warriors and cattle herders in search of new grasslands, the Persians and the Medes, another Indo-European group, left central Asia about 2000 B.C. They settled on a plateau between the Persian Gulf and the

Images of the Times

Ancient Persepolis

The most luxurious palace of Darius was built at Persepolis. Completed by Xerxes, the palace was a monument to the king's power.

Alexander the Great destroyed most of the palace in 331 B.C., but the stone monumental gateways and terraces survived.

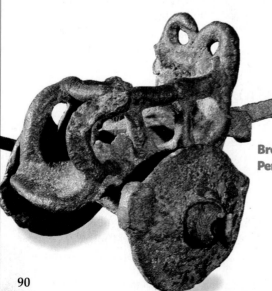

Bronze image of a Persian chariot

Caspian Sea, in the area of present-day Iran.

Cyrus's Conquests

During the 540s B.C., Cyrus had developed a strong army, conquered the Medes, and advanced into neighboring lands. He added northern Mesopotamia, Syria, Canaan, and the Phoenician cities to his empire. Cyrus also took over the kingdom of Lydia and the Greek city-states in Asia Minor. In 525 B.C. Cyrus's son Cambyses (kam•BY•seez) conquered Egypt, bringing all of the Middle East under Persian control.

The Persian Empire, then second to none, stretched from the Nile River to the Indus River, a distance of 3,000 miles (4,800 km). Within this immense empire, the Persians ruled more than 50 million people.

Darius's Empire

The best organizer among the Persian kings was **Darius I**, who reigned from 522 B.C. to 486 B.C. To administer his empire, Darius effectively divided the realm into provinces and assigned satraps, or provincial governors, to rule. Military officials and tax inspectors, chosen by the king from among the conquered people themselves, assisted the satraps in carrying out the king's decrees in the provinces. In addition, inspectors called "Eyes and Ears of the King" made unannounced tours of the provinces and reported directly to the king on the activities of officials. In this way, the king's court was able to keep watch on local government.

In contrast to the Assyrians, the Persians were tolerant rulers who allowed conquered peoples to retain their own languages, religions, and laws. The Persians won the loyalty of conquered peoples by respecting local customs. They believed that this loyalty could be won more easily with fairness than by fear or force. When faced with rebellion, however, the Persians did not hesitate to take extreme military measures.

Commerce and Roads

Darius brought artisans from many of his

Persian god and goddess protecting a palm tree

More than 1,000 years after Alexander destroyed Persepolis, the first curious travelers rediscovered the impressive remains of the city. The Apadana hall at the northern end of the palace contains stairways with beautiful reliefs of Persian nobles, guards, and tribute bearers.

REFLECTING ON THE TIMES

1. About what year did travelers rediscover Persepolis?
2. What ruins reveal the wealth of Persian kings?

91

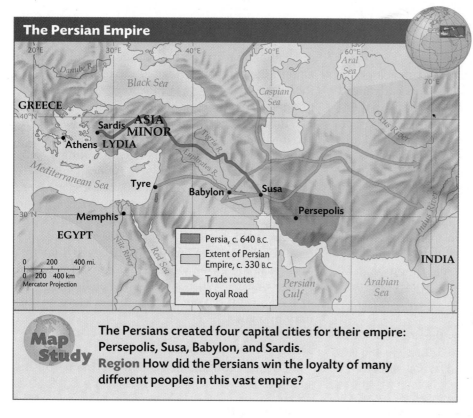

The Persian Empire

Persia, c. 640 B.C.
Extent of Persian Empire, c. 330 B.C.
→ Trade routes
— Royal Road

0   200   400 mi.
0   200   400 km
Mercator Projection

Map Study

The Persians created four capital cities for their empire: Persepolis, Susa, Babylon, and Sardis.
Region How did the Persians win the loyalty of many different peoples in this vast empire?

conquered lands to build **Persepolis**, the most magnificent city in the empire. The Persians themselves did not engage in trade, which they considered an indecent occupation. However, they did encourage trade among the peoples of their empire. To advance trade throughout the empire and aid the movement of soldiers, Darius had Persian engineers improve and expand the network of roads first laid down by the Assyrians. Royal messengers also journeyed on the roads allowing "neither snow, nor rain, nor heat, nor the darkness of night to hinder them in the prompt completion of their … tasks."

The Royal Road, the most important thoroughfare in the Persian Empire, stretched more than 1,500 miles (2,400 km) from Persia to Asia Minor. Every 14 miles (22.4 km), stations along the Royal Road provided travelers with food, water, and fresh horses. Royal messengers could travel the length of the road in just seven days, a journey that had taken three months before the road was built.

A Persian Disaster

During his reign, Darius waged war against the Greeks over the control of city-states in Asia Minor. After Darius died, his son Xerxes (ZUHRK •SEEZ) led the forces of Persia in a disastrous campaign to conquer Greece in 480 B.C. Xerxes' defeat stopped Persian expansion into Europe.

Persian Religion and Culture

The Persians followed a strict moral code that stressed bravery and honesty. They taught their sons to "ride horses, to draw a bow, and to speak the truth." Before the 500s B.C., the Persian people worshiped many deities associated with the sky, sun, and fire. Then, about 570 B.C., a prophet named **Zoroaster** (ZOHR•uh•WAS •tuhr) began to call for reform of the Persian religion. Zoroaster preached that the world was divided by a struggle between good and evil. The god Ahura Mazda led the forces of good, and a lesser deity, Ahriman, represented the spirit of darkness. At the end of time, Ahura Mazda would triumph over Ahriman.

Zoroaster also taught that humans were caught up in this struggle and had to choose between good and evil. All humans who fought on the side of Ahura Mazda against evil would be rewarded with eternal life. Those who chose Ahriman would be condemned after death to eternal darkness and

WORLD Spread of Celtic Culture

Central Europe, c. 600 B.C.
The Hallstatt Celts spread their influence from Austria to the British Isles. They were among the first people in northern Europe to make iron. Their warlike chieftains relied on horses and slept on animal skins in crude houses. Their weapons and artifacts, however, were decorated with elaborate patterns. Celtic art featured highly stylized plants and animals.

Central Europe

This relief of King Darius and Xerxes is one of many at the palace of King Darius. The rigidity of posture and arrogance of the figures conveys the grandeur and ceremony of the royal court. *How did the Royal Road affect travel time?*

misery. These teachings were contained in a book called the Avesta.

Persian rulers believed that they ruled by the power of Ahura Mazda and were responsible to him alone. Darius I had the following statement carved on a cliff:

66 On this account Ahura Mazda brought me health…. Because I was not wicked, nor was I a liar, nor was I a tyrant, neither I nor any of my line. We had ruled according to righteousness. 99

Zoroaster's teachings were eventually linked to the glorification of the Persian monarchy. Because the monarchy was viewed as a sacred institution, Persian kings commanded great respect and were surrounded by pomp and pageantry. This style of kingship later shaped the development of monarchies in the Western world.

Zoroaster's beliefs also may have shaped beliefs in the Mediterranean world. Some scholars believe that Zoroaster's teachings about paradise, hell, and the Last Judgment—or the separation of good and evil at the end of time—may have influenced Judaism, Christianity, and Islam. Other aspects of Persian culture lived on as well, and mixed with Greek culture when Alexander the Great absorbed the Persians into his own empire in the 300s B.C.

SECTION 3 REVIEW

Recall
1. **Define** satrap.
2. **Identify** the Hittites, the Assyrians, the Chaldeans, Nebuchadnezzar, the Persians, Cyrus II, Darius I, Zoroaster.
3. **Locate** the Hittite, Assyrian, Chaldean, and Persian Empires on the maps on pages 89 and 92. Rank them in order of approximate size.

Critical Thinking
4. **Evaluating Information** Why might other religions have adopted features of the Zoroastrian religion?

Understanding Themes
5. **Conflict** How did the military exploits of the Hittites and the Assyrians both change the way peoples of the time fought military battles and the way in which they dealt with conquered peoples?

Historical Significance

Trading peoples and empire builders both enriched the culture of the ancient Middle East and strongly influenced later civilizations. One of the most significant innovations, for example, was the concise and easy-to-learn Phoenician alphabet, which spread communication, enhanced trade, and eventually evolved into the alphabet used to spell the words on this page.

Spiritual life also evolved dramatically, through the adherence of the Israelites to a belief in one God, who required people to live justly. The concepts of monotheism and ethical laws have endured in the modern religions of Judaism, Christianity, and Islam.

Using Key Terms

Write the key term that completes each sentence.

a. alphabet
b. monotheism
c. colony
d. covenant
e. barter
f. satraps
g. exodus
h. prophets
i. Diaspora
j. confederation

1. The belief in one all-powerful god is known as _____ .
2. In the 1200s B.C., the Israelite leader Moses rallied his people and led them out of Egypt in a _____ into the Sinai Desert.
3. The Phoenicians were organized into a _____ of independent city-states along the coast of northern Canaan.
4. Israelite _____ condemned abuses in society and urged people not to forget their duties to God and to one another.
5. Persian kings appointed a number of _____ to govern the provinces of the Persian Empire.
6. Jewish communities existing outside of their homeland have become known as the _____, after a Greek word meaning "scattered."
7. The Phoenicians developed an improved, efficient_____—a series of written symbols that represent sounds.
8. About 814 B.C. Phoenician emigrants founded the _____ of Carthage on the coast of present-day Tunisia in North Africa.
9. In early Asia Minor, most traders relied on a system of _____ for their transactions—exchanging their wares for other goods.
10. According to the Bible, God made a _____ with Abraham, stating that Abraham's descendants would be blessed as a great nation if they remained faithful to God.

Using Your History Journal

Choose one of the verses that you have written for your journal dealing with an event mentioned in the chapter. After research expand the verse into an epic poem about the event.

Reviewing Facts

1. **Explain** how Aramaic came to be spoken throughout the Fertile Crescent.
2. **Identify** the practices that the Phoenicians introduced to Mediterranean business and trade. What advantage did the Phoenicians have over their competitors?
3. **Describe** how the Israelites interpreted and applied the new idea of monotheism.
4. **List** the peoples with whom the Israelites came into conflict after the Exodus from Egypt and the return to Canaan.
5. **Identify** the contribution that the Hittites made to Middle Eastern civilization.

Critical Thinking

1. **Apply** What natural resource supported the Lydians' development of a money system to replace the barter system?
2. **Analyze** How were the deities and beliefs of the Phoenicians, the Israelites, and the Persians different from one another?
3. **Analyze** What actions taken by Darius I made his rule so effective?

4. Evaluate Which development of this period do you believe was most important for the future of world history? Why?

Geography in History

1. **Movement** What event led to the establishment of a large Jewish community in Babylon after 586 B.C.?
2. **Human/Environment Interaction** How did the people of Babylon provide water to various locations inside the city walls?
3. **Human/Environment Interaction** How did the people of Babylon fortify the city against attack from outsiders?

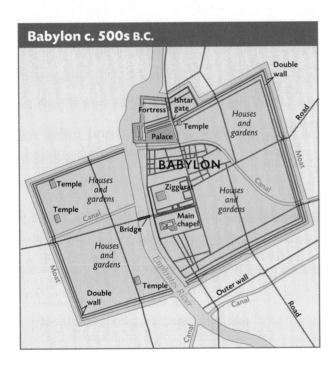

Babylon c. 500s B.C.

Understanding Themes

1. **Cultural Diffusion** Based on your knowledge of the ancient trading peoples of the Middle East, what kinds of ideas might people be likely to adopt from other cultures?
2. **Innovation** From a modern perspective, do you see any advantages or disadvantages to the development of a religious belief system based on monotheism?

3. Conflict Make a list of what aims might have motivated conquerors such as the Hittites, Assyrians, Chaldeans, and Persians to incorporate their neighbors into empires.

Linking Past and Present

1. Does the legal system of our country parallel Hittite law or Hammurabi's code? Provide a brief explanation of your view.
2. The Israelites, ancestors of the Jews, shared Canaan with several other peoples, such as the Phoenicians and the Philistines. What peoples live today in what was formerly the land of Canaan? Give a brief summary of their history in recent decades.
3. Solomon built a magnificent temple at Jerusalem. The last Jewish temple on the Temple Mount was destroyed in A.D. 70. What building stands on that site now?

Skill Practice

The various peoples in this chapter all lived in the Middle East. The beginning dates of their civilizations, the achievements of their cultures, and their contributions to history all differ. Use the category chart below to arrange data about each group.

Peoples	Beginning Dates	Cultural Achievements and Contributions
Aramaeans		
Phoenicians		
Lydians		
Israelites		
Hittites		
Assyrians		
Chaldeans		
Persians		

The bones of early human beings as well as other fossil remains, archaeological artifacts, and written records hold many clues for researchers studying the past. Although historians consider history to have begun about 5,500 years ago, when early civilizations created writing systems, the human story extends much further into the past—into more than 2 million years of prehistory.

In prehistoric times, early human beings set many cultural patterns that continued into historic times. They adapted to their changing environment. They migrated in search of more hospitable living conditions. They cooperated with one another to obtain food and came into conflict over land and water. They invented new ways of doing things and adopted from one another new methods and ideas.

Some early peoples quit their wandering life and settled down as farmers. They began to live together in villages and later built cities. Many historians set the beginning of history at the formation of cities, for it was there that writing and other activities of early civilization evolved. The ancient cities founded in the river valleys of the Nile, the Tigris-Euphrates, the Indus, and the Huang spawned several great civilizations. Some of these civilizations shared their ideas and way of life with other peoples through trade, conquest, and empire. Some disappeared; some were overcome but rose again; some have continued in one form or another to the present day.

Chapter 1
Human Beginnings

Using research techniques such as radiocarbon dating to date plant and animal matter, anthropologists and archaeologists have been able to establish a time frame for prehistoric human life. Scientists do not agree about all aspects of how or when the first human beings became truly human, but fossil evidence suggests that the first prehuman hominids lived about 4.4 million years ago. Over the next few million years, the hominids gradually adapted to changes in their environment, such as a colder climate, in various ways. Some hominids evolved larger brains.

Visualizing History **Archaeologist working at a grave site in Jerusalem.** *What allowed people to give up their nomadic life and settle in cities?*

Early Humans

Two large-brained hominids, *Homo habilis* and *Homo erectus*, as well as all modern human beings, are scientifically classified in the genus *Homo*—human. During the Ice Ages—periods of cold climate and glaciation—some early people migrated to warmer areas, and others perished from the cold or lack of food. Others learned techniques for staying warm. Clothing and fire became part of the culture of prehistoric people, as did the use of stone tools. The early human beings of the Stone Age invented many new technological and social skills, including spoken language. Changes were relatively slow, however, until the modern human species, *Homo sapiens*, appeared around 200,000 years ago. Two groups of *Homo sapiens*, the Neanderthals and Cro-Magnons, made significant advances in housing and in tool and weapon making, but the greatest achievement came late in the Stone Age, during the Neolithic period, with the shift from hunting and food gathering to agriculture. This change in the way of life was so radical that it is often referred to as the Neolithic Revolution.

Civilizations

The development of agriculture was an essential stepping-stone to civilization. Initially farming allowed people to give up their nomadic life and settle in communities. Eventually, with a relatively steady food supply, many men and women could devote their time to economic activities other than farming. As time passed, some of the early agricultural villages grew into the first cities, which were home to highly organized societies, or civilizations. All early civilizations shared some basic features. They had specialized labor; cooperative methods for producing surplus food, such as irrigation; and metalworking technology. Under an organized government they formed social classes and maintained an army. They undertook long-distance trade. With a system of values and religious beliefs, they were sophisticated enough to have written records.

SURVEYING CHAPTER I

1. **Analyzing Information** How did climate affect where early hominids lived?
2. **Making Connections** How did the Neolithic Revolution become a stepping-stone to the rise of the first civilizations?

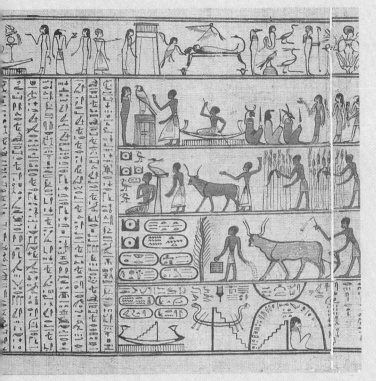

Chapter 2
Early Civilizations

Cities and civilizations arose at different times in different parts of the world. Many of the earliest civilizations had one thing in common, however: they grew out of agricultural settlements in river valleys. Civilization appeared around 3500 B.C. in the Tigris-Euphrates River valley in the Fertile Crescent, but it also arose soon thereafter in the Nile River valley of Egypt, and again later in the Indus River valley of the South Asian subcontinent and in the Huang He valley in China.

Ancient Egypt and Mesopotamia

In northeastern Africa, nomads left the desert to settle along the fertile banks of the Nile and founded villages. These villages then banded together in small kingdoms, which were later united under a king, who was a religious and political leader and head of a government bureaucracy.

The ancient Egyptians built a magnificent civilization. With innovative irrigation and flood control techniques, they used the seasonally fluctuating Nile waters to their advantage. They undertook ambitious building projects, such as the Pyramids, which required new engineering skills. The writing system early Egyptians invented and the script that formed from it were put to use both for everyday purposes and for decorating their massive monuments. The prosperity achieved by Egyptian civilization encouraged later pharaohs to expand the frontiers of their country and to build an empire. The cultural diffusion made possible by the empire further enriched Egyptian civilization.

In Mesopotamia, the land between the Tigris and Euphrates Rivers, the pattern of development was much the same. Peoples fleeing war and overpopulation, as well as poor climate, settled in villages on the fertile river plain. Although the early peoples of Mesopotamia, unlike the Egyptians, could not depend on a regular supply of water, they managed to meet the challenges of the twin rivers by cooperating with one another and devising methods of irrigation and flood control. The Sumerians, a group who migrated to the region from central Asia, built the world's first cities and a civilization that reached its height sometime before that of the Egyptians. The complex organization of

Visualizing History A funeral papyrus from the *Book of the Dead*, Egypt. *Along what river are most ancient Egyptian monuments found?*

their civilization was evident in the governments of the Sumerian city-states and their laws and religion. The innovative Sumerians created cuneiform, perhaps the world's oldest writing system, and they also invented the wheel. The prosperous Sumerian city-states eventually fell to empire builders, first the Akkadians and later the Babylonians.

South and East Asian Civilizations

At about the same time as the rise of empires in Mesopotamia, a third river valley civilization to the east, the Harappans, reached its peak. Adapting to the unique seasonal winds and flood patterns of their environment, the people of the South Asian subcontinent prospered in the Indus River valley. They produced a surplus of food and various goods, which they traded with the people of Mesopotamia, among others. The pictograms on the seals used to identify merchandise from the Indus Valley suggest that the Harappan people also exchanged ideas with their trading partners. Although the remains of Harappan cities such as Mohenjo-Daro indicate that the people of the Indus Valley were expert urban planners, why the cities were destroyed and what caused their civilization to collapse remains a mystery.

The fourth river valley civilization, which began in ancient China, has continued to the present day. Isolated from other cultures for many centuries by formidable landforms, the Chinese formed one culture and a strong sense of national identity. From Neolithic times, people settled and flourished in the Huang He valley. Written records and other finds indicate that under the Shang dynasty, which controlled the river valley from about 1700 B.C. to 1000 B.C., the Chinese built their first cities, created a complex writing system, and perfected their skill in casting bronze. The replacement of the Shang dynasty by the Zhou dynasty was just one of many transitions between the dynasties that successively ruled China.

SURVEYING CHAPTER 2

1. **Relating to the Environment** How did the ancient Egyptians and Sumerians meet the challenges of their river environments?
2. **Defending a Point of View** Do you think cultural diffusion benefits or hinders the growth of a civilization? Explain your reasoning, supporting your point of view by citing examples from ancient Egypt and Mesopotamia.

Chapter 3
Kingdoms and Empires in the Middle East

The Fertile Crescent, where civilization began, continued to be home for diverse peoples after the earliest river valley civilizations fell. Many people in the region were active in trade and thus promoted cultural diffusion and also made lasting cultural and economic contributions to later civilizations.

Traders and Herders

Prominent among the trading peoples of the Middle East were the Phoenicians. They not only navigated the Mediterranean Sea and beyond with ease, controlling shipping and trade and founding colonies, but created an alphabet that was a major breakthrough in writing and the model for later alphabets. Among the other trading peoples in the region, the Aramaeans introduced the Aramaic language into the everyday life of many other peoples, and the Lydians left a lasting mark on the economies of other civilizations by using coins as a medium of exchange.

The Israelites, a nomadic people in this region, made lasting cultural contributions. Foremost among these was monotheism—the belief in one

Ruins of ancient Babylon, capital of the Chaldeans. *How long did the Chaldean Empire last before being overthrown by the Persians?*

all-powerful God—an idea that formed the basis of Judaism, Christianity, and Islam. During their long history, the Israelites several times came into conflict with neighboring peoples. Although they were enslaved and exiled, they kept close ties to their homeland.

Empire Builders

Many peoples in the Fertile Crescent suffered as warlike empires successively dominated the region and neighboring regions as well.

In spite of their emphasis on war, these empires also advanced trade, created new methods of government, and carried out building projects. The Hittites were the first of these aggressors, coming to Asia Minor from Europe or central Asia. With many advantages in military tactics, the Hittites established an empire spanning Asia Minor, Syria, and part of Mesopotamia.

The Assyrians, a Mesopotamian people, were the next conquerors in the Middle East. They too had great expertise on the battlefield, and cruelly treated the peoples they conquered. They controlled an empire stretching from the Persian Gulf to Egypt and into Asia Minor.

The well-organized and extensive Assyrian Empire fell to the Chaldeans (descendants of the Babylonians). The Chaldeans built their capital,

Babylon, into one of the largest, most stunning cities of the ancient world. In less than 100 years, however, the Chaldean Empire was in turn overthrown by the Persians.

The Persians, who originated in central Asia and settled in the area of present-day Iran, built an empire that was second to none, stretching from the Nile River to the Indus River. The Persians surpassed their predecessors in administering a vast area and in tolerating the languages, religions, and customs of subject peoples. Communication and cooperation characterized the Persian approach to ruling an empire. The teachings of the Persian prophet Zoroaster may have later influenced certain beliefs of the religions of Judaism, Christianity, and Islam.

SURVEYING CHAPTER 3

1. **Analyzing Information** How did the Hittites, Assyrians, Chaldeans, and Persians acquire their empires?
2. **Making Comparisons** Compare and contrast the empires that came to dominate the Fertile Crescent and neighboring regions, from the Akkadians to the Persians.

Flowering of Civilizations

Then & Now

As people developed agricultural technology, nomadic life gave way to living in communities. Emerging cities became centers of trade and commerce, characterized by highly organized social structures and governments. Commerce brought wealth that allowed more people time for leisure and study. Ancient civilizations contributed much that remains in the modern world. China developed a civil service system based on merit. The city of Alexandria in Egypt had a great library. The Greeks refined geometry to calculate the size of the earth. Architecture, theater, and education all have their roots in ancient civilizations.

A Global Chronology

2000 B.C.	1500 B.C.	1000 B.C.
Political	**c. 1500 B.C.** Aryans cross the Hindu Kush into South Asia.	
Scientific	**c. 1700 B.C.** Babylonian Empire adopts Sumerian calendar.	
Social/Cultural		**c. 1200 B.C.** Vedic Age begins in India.

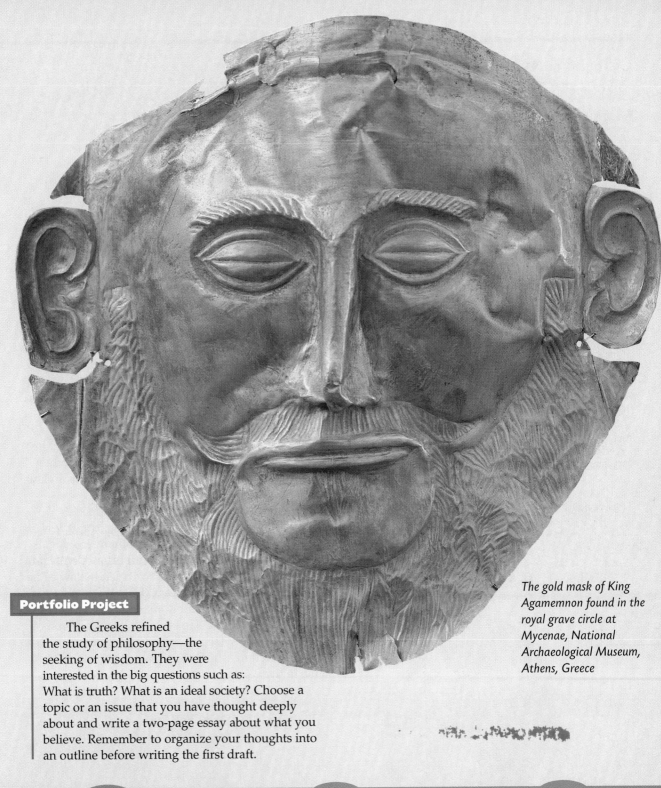

The gold mask of King Agamemnon found in the royal grave circle at Mycenae, National Archaeological Museum, Athens, Greece

Portfolio Project

The Greeks refined the study of philosophy—the seeking of wisdom. They were interested in the big questions such as: What is truth? What is an ideal society? Choose a topic or an issue that you have thought deeply about and write a two-page essay about what you believe. Remember to organize your thoughts into an outline before writing the first draft.

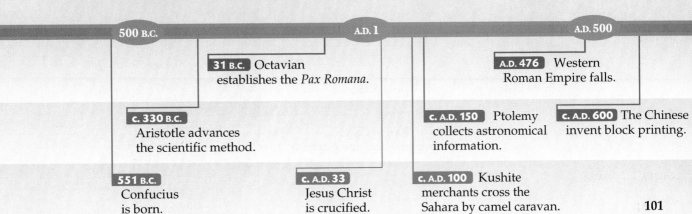

500 B.C.   A.D. 1   A.D. 500

31 B.C. Octavian establishes the *Pax Romana*.

A.D. 476 Western Roman Empire falls.

c. 330 B.C. Aristotle advances the scientific method.

c. A.D. 150 Ptolemy collects astronomical information.

c. A.D. 600 The Chinese invent block printing.

551 B.C. Confucius is born.

c. A.D. 33 Jesus Christ is crucified.

c. A.D. 100 Kushite merchants cross the Sahara by camel caravan.

101

The Spread of Ideas

Systems of Law

Law is a code of conduct and rights accepted or formally recognized by a society. Law provides social control, order, and justice. It enables people to know their rights and responsibilities. Law also forms the cornerstone of constitutional government. A constitutional government based upon law helps ensure justice, or the fair treatment of all citizens. "Where law ends, tyranny begins," said William Pitt, an English leader, in A.D. 1770.

United States *France* *Roman Empire*

Roman Empire
Laying the Foundation

Sometime around 451-450 B.C., a group of judges posted 12 tablets in Rome's main forum, or marketplace. According to legend, the common people of Rome had demanded that the laws be written down for all to see. People would then know their rights. The tablets listed the unwritten laws that guided judges. They also included penalties imposed on people who broke the law.

Although a group of invaders smashed the so-called Twelve Tables in 390 B.C., the basic code of law remained in effect for almost 1,000 years. When Roman armies marched out to conquer a huge empire, they carried their belief in law with them. By A.D. 120 Roman law governed the entire Mediterranean world and much of western Europe.

In theory, Roman law applied to all people, regardless of wealth or power. Not everyone honored Roman legal ideals. Nonetheless, the Romans developed an important democratic principle. They believed people should be ruled by law rather than by the whims of leaders. In A.D. 533-534 the Byzantine emperor Justinian consolidated all Roman law into a single written code. The Justinian Code became the foundation of the present civil law system. Civil law and common law, which originated in England, are two of the major legal systems in the world today.

Cicero

Independence Hall,
Philadelphia

The United States
A Model for Constitutional Government

The Founders of the United States knew about and admired the Romans. They understood what the Roman orator Cicero meant when he spoke of the need to limit the power of government. When it came time to draw up a plan of government, they wrote a constitution that balanced the powers of government among three branches.

To ensure that rulers did not place themselves above the law, the Framers included a provision that made the Constitution "the supreme law of the land." The Framers used the example of Rome to defend the Constitution. "The Roman republic attained ... the utmost height of human greatness," declared Alexander Hamilton. He then explained how government under the Constitution would do the same.

A second system of legal justice, common law, evolved in England. Trial by jury, the right to petition the government, and many other rules governing trials originated in this system. Common law is not a written code but rather is based on written judicial decisions. Common law was established in the American colonies and continued to develop when the colonies became states of the United States.

France
Unifying the Law

In A.D. 1799 a French general named Napoleon Bonaparte set out to build an empire even larger than Rome's. By A.D. 1802 he had conquered much of Europe. Napoleon then tried to extend his reach into the Americas.

In seeking to rule this empire, Napoleon followed the Roman example. He took part in a commission to draw up a uniform code of laws. This code, known as the Napoleonic Code, was completed in A.D. 1807.

Although Napoleon ruled as emperor, the code named in his honor reaffirmed the principle that the same laws should be used to govern all people. In drafting these laws, Napoleon drew upon many of the legal precedents first introduced by the Romans. Under Napoleon, this code became applied in lands as far-flung as present-day Belgium, Quebec, Spain, and some Latin American nations.

Assemblée Nationale, Paris

LINKING THE IDEAS

1. What important democratic principle did the Romans develop?

Critical Thinking

2. How did the United States hope to ensure that rulers would not place themselves above the law?

2000–350 B.C.

The Rise of Ancient Greece

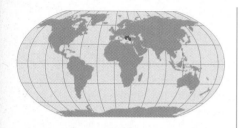

Chapter Themes

▶ **Relation to Environment** Closeness to the sea helps make the early Greeks seafarers. *Section 1*

▶ **Movement** The Greeks found colonies throughout the area of the Mediterranean and Black Seas. *Section 2*

▶ **Regionalism** Two leading Greek city-states—Athens and Sparta—differ greatly from each other in their values, cultures, and achievements. *Section 3*

▶ **Conflict** Greek city-states together fight the Persians; then the city-states, led by rivals Athens and Sparta, fight each other. *Section 4*

The Storyteller

An eager crowd gathered in the sun-drenched sports arena just outside King Minos's palace at Knossos on the Aegean island of Crete. According to legend, Minos ruled over the Minoan civilization in the 2000s B.C. The Minoans' favorite event—bull leaping—was about to begin. The crowd gasped as a raging bull, representing the earthquakes that shook Crete, charged a young male gymnast who stood motionless. Just before the collision, the gymnast grabbed the bull's horns and somersaulted onto the bull's back. Then his body arched into the air, and he completed a back flip, landing in the arms of his female partner waiting nearby. The crowd cheered at the end of this spectacle, part sport and part religious ritual. By leaping over the bull, the gymnast had shown that no matter how much the earth trembled, the Minoans would stay on Crete.

Historical Significance

What kinds of governments and societies developed in ancient Greece? How have Greek political ideas shaped the development of Western civilization?

1600 B.C.	1200 B.C.	800 B.C.	400 B.C.

c. 1600 B.C. Minoan civilization reaches its peak.

c. 1100 B.C. Dorians invade Greece.

c. 700 B.C. Greeks found colonies in the Mediterranean area.

c. 460 B.C. Golden Age of Athens begins.

Minoan wall painting of a fleet of ships entering port.
National Archaeological Museum, Athens, Greece

Your History Journal

Athens laid the foundation for the Western concept of democratic government. After reading about Athenian democracy, write an essay entitled "What Democracy Means to Me."

c. 2000 B.C. Mycenaean civilization begins.

c. 1450 B.C. Mycenaeans control the Aegean area.

c. 750 B.C. Homer composes epics.

Section 1

Beginnings

Setting the Scene

▶ **Terms to Define**
  labyrinth, bard

▶ **People to Meet**
  Sir Arthur Evans, the Minoans, the Mycenaeans, Homer, Heinrich Schliemann

▶ **Places to Locate**
  Crete, Mycenae

Find Out Where and how did the early civilizations of Greece develop?

The Storyteller

The hero Sarpedon was a son of Zeus, but destined to die in the Trojan War. He held before him the perfect circle of his shield, a lovely thing of beaten bronze, which the bronze-smith had hammered out for him. On its inward side were stitched ox-hides in close folds with golden staples all around the circle…. And now Sarpedon spoke to Glaukos, son of Hippolochos: "Glaukos, why are we honored before others with the best seats, choice cuts of meat, brimming wine cups, and the best plots of land? Because we stand in the front line of blazing battle. Friend, if we could escape, and live forever ageless and immortal, I would not go on fighting, or encourage you to fight. But now, since the spirits of death stand close by us, let us go win glory for ourselves, or yield it to others."

Entrance to the ancient silver mines at Siphnos, Greece

—adapted from *The Iliad of Homer,* translated by Richmond Lattimore, 1951

The ancient Greeks became the people who set their stamp on the Mediterranean region and who also contributed greatly to the way we live today. Every time you go to the theater or watch the Olympic Games on television, you enjoy an activity that has its roots in ancient Greece. Modern public buildings often reflect Greek architectural styles. Above all, the ancient Greeks developed the Western concept of democracy.

The Aegean Area

Ancient Greece included the southern part of Europe's Balkan Peninsula and a group of small, rocky islands, most of which dot the Aegean (ih•JEE•uhn) Sea near Asia Minor. Low-lying, rugged mountains make up about three-fourths of the Greek mainland. Between the mountain ranges and along the coast lie fertile plains suitable for farming. Short, swift rivers flow from the interior to the sea, and the long, indented coastline provides many fine harbors. The climate is mild, with rainy winters. Afternoon breezes carrying cooler air from the sea offset the hot, dry summers.

The mountains both protected and isolated Greeks on the mainland. Besides making attacks by foreigners difficult, the mountains limited travel and communication between communities. The Greek people, therefore, never united under one government, although they spoke one language and practiced the same religion.

Because of the numerous harbors and since no place in Greece is more than 50 miles (80 km) from the coast, many Greeks turned to the sea to earn their living. They became fishers, traders, and even pirates.

In addition, the mild climate allowed the ancient Greeks to spend much of their time outdoors. People assembled for meetings in the public square, teachers met their students in public gardens, and actors performed plays in open-air theaters.

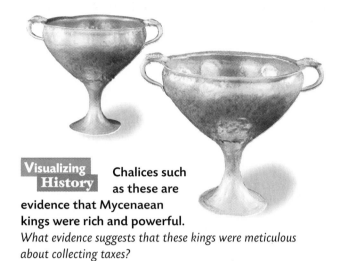

Chalices such as these are evidence that Mycenaean kings were rich and powerful.

What evidence suggests that these kings were meticulous about collecting taxes?

Aegean Civilizations

Greek myths referred to an early civilization on the island of **Crete**, southeast of the Greek mainland, but for a long time historians disputed this claim. Then, about A.D. 1900, British archaeologist **Sir Arthur Evans** unearthed remains of the Minoan civilization, which flourished from about 2500 B.C. to 1450 B.C.

The Minoans

At Knossos (NAH•suhs) on Crete, Evans uncovered the palace of legendary King Minos. Throughout the palace, passageways twist and turn in all directions to form a labyrinth, or maze. Brightly colored murals that decorate palace walls show that **the Minoans**—both men and women—curled their hair, bedecked themselves with gold jewelry, and set off their narrow waists with wide metal belts. The murals also show that they were fond of dancing and sporting events, such as boxing matches.

Minoan women apparently enjoyed a higher status than women in other early civilizations. For example, Minoan religion had more goddesses than gods. The chief deity of Crete was the Great Goddess, or Earth Mother, whom the Minoans believed caused the birth and growth of all living things.

The Minoans earned their living from sea trade. Crete's oak and cedar forests provided wood for ships. In addition, the island's location enabled Minoan traders to reach Egypt and Mesopotamia. By 2000 B.C., Minoan fleets dominated the eastern Mediterranean, carrying goods and keeping the seas free from pirates. The ships also guarded Crete

against outside attack, which explains why the Minoans did not build walls around their cities.

Minoan civilization reached its peak around 1600 B.C. About 250 years later it collapsed. Some historians think its cities were destroyed by huge tidal waves resulting from an undersea earthquake. Others think that a people from the Greek mainland, **the Mycenaeans** (MY•suh•NEE•uhnz), succeeded in invading Crete.

The Mycenaeans

The Mycenaeans originated among the Indo-European peoples of central Asia. About 2000 B.C., as a result of the rapid growth of their population, the Mycenaeans began moving out from their homeland. Upon entering the Balkan Peninsula, they gradually intermarried with the local people——known as Hellenes (HEH•leenz)––and set up a group of kingdoms.

Each Mycenaean kingdom centered around a hilltop on which was built a royal fortress. Stone walls circled the fortress, providing a shelter for the people in time of danger. Nobles lived on their estates outside the walls. They would turn out in armor when the king needed them to supply horse-drawn chariots. The slaves and tenants who farmed the land lived in villages on these estates.

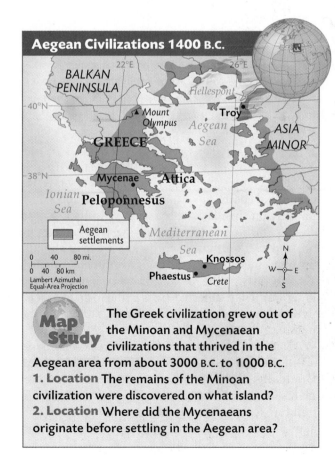

Aegean Civilizations 1400 B.C.

Map Study

The Greek civilization grew out of the Minoan and Mycenaean civilizations that thrived in the Aegean area from about 3000 B.C. to 1000 B.C.
1. Location The remains of the Minoan civilization were discovered on what island?
2. Location Where did the Mycenaeans originate before settling in the Aegean area?

Heinrich Schliemann discovered six tombs at the royal grave circle near the lion gate at Mycenae. They contained 16 skeletons and a large hoard of gold. *What events ended Mycenaean civilization?*

By the mid-1400s B.C., the Mycenaeans had conquered the Minoans and controlled the Aegean area. By 1100 B.C., however, fighting among the Mycenaeans had destroyed the great hilltop fortresses. Soon after, a new wave of invaders, the Greek-speaking Dorians, entered Greece from the north. Armed with iron weapons, the Dorians easily overran the mainland.

Historians call the next 300 years of Greek history a "dark age." During this period, overseas trade stopped, poverty increased, and people lost skills such as writing and craft making. Thousands of refugees fled the mainland and settled in Ionia—the west coast of Asia Minor and its adjoining islands.

By 750 B.C. the Ionians had reintroduced culture, crafts, and skills to their homeland, including the alphabet used by Phoenician traders. The "dark age" of the Dorians ended, and a new Greek civilization with Mycenaean elements emerged. The new civilization—called Hellenic, after the original people of Greece—flourished from about the 700s B.C. until 336 B.C.

Poets and Heroes

During the "dark age," bards, or singing storytellers, had kept alive Mycenaean traditions. With their new ability to write, the Greeks began to record the epic poems that the bards had passed from generation to generation.

The *Iliad* and the *Odyssey*

According to tradition, a blind poet named **Homer** who lived during the 700s B.C. composed the two most famous Greek epics—the *Iliad* and the *Odyssey*. Homer set the *Iliad* and the *Odyssey* during and after the legendary Trojan War. The Mycenaeans had supposedly fought the people of Troy in the mid-1200s B.C. In A.D. 1870 **Heinrich Schliemann**, a German archaeologist, proved that Troy actually existed and was a major trading city in Asia Minor.

The *Iliad* begins when a Trojan prince named Paris falls in love with Helen, the wife of a Mycenaean king, and takes her with him to Troy. To avenge Helen's kidnapping, the Mycenaeans lay siege to Troy for 10 years, but they cannot capture the city. Finally, they trick the Trojans by building a huge, hollow wooden horse. The best Mycenaean soldiers hide inside the horse, while the rest board their ships and pretend to sail away. The joyful Trojans, thinking themselves victorious, bring the gift horse into the city. That night, the Greeks creep out of the horse, slaughter the Trojan men, enslave

The palaces in the city of **Mycenae** served as centers of both government administration and production. Inside, artisans tanned leather, sewed clothes, fashioned jars for storing wine and olive oil, and made bronze swords and ox-hide shields. To help in collecting taxes, government officials kept records of the wealth of every person in the kingdom. They collected taxes in the form of wheat, livestock, and honey, which were stored in the palace.

Minoan traders visited the Greek mainland soon after the Mycenaeans set up their kingdom. Gradually, the Mycenaeans adopted many elements of Minoan culture—metalworking and shipbuilding techniques and navigation by the sun and stars. The Mycenaeans worshiped the Minoan Earth Mother as well.

Erich Lessing, Magnum

Trojan Horse

On this Greek vase from the 600s B.C. the Trojan horse of myth and epic stands tall. According to the Greek poet Homer—who described the Trojan War in his epic poem the *Iliad*—for ten long years the Mycenaeans of Greece battled their enemies who lived within the walls of the Turkish city of Troy. The two sides were so well matched that only a clever strategy of war could produce victory. So the Greeks came up with one: They built a great wooden horse, so large that a cargo of soldiers could hide in its belly. Then they set the horse on wheels and gave it to Troy as a "gift." Having tricked their way into Troy, the Greek soldiers leapt out of the horse and conquered their foe.

While time has blurred the line between historic fact and Homeric epic (written centuries after the struggle), an important war did take place in which a loose federation of Greek kings set out to conquer the city-state of Troy. Homer's epic reveals that piracy and plunder were part of that era's commerce. Archaeologists have uncovered the ruins of a mighty Turkish fortress that once commanded the narrows of the Hellespont. Modern opinions, however, differ as to whether or not this was the site of Homer's Troy. ⊕

the women and children, and burn the city to the ground.

The *Odyssey* describes the homeward wanderings of the Mycenaean king Odysseus after the fall of Troy. Because it took him 10 years to return to Greece, people refer to any long, adventure-filled journey as an *odyssey*.

Teaching Greek Values

Eventually, schools in ancient Greece used the *Iliad* and the *Odyssey* to present to students many of the values of Hellenic civilization. For example, in an exciting description of men marching to war, the *Iliad* taught students to be proud of their Greek heritage and their heroic ancestors:

> ❝ As a ravening fire blazes over a vast forest and the mountains, and its light is seen afar, so while they marched the sheen from their forest of bronze [spears] went up dazzling into high heaven.
>
> As flocks of wildfowl on the wing, geese or cranes or long-necked swans fly this way and that way over the Asian meadows, proud of the power of their wings, and they settle on and on honking as they go until they fill the meadow with sound: so flocks of men poured out of their camp onwards over the Scamandrian plain, and the ground thundered terribly under the tramp of horses and of men. ❞
>
> —Homer, from the *Iliad*, mid-700s B.C.

The *Iliad* and the *Odyssey* also represented other values of Hellenic civilization, such as a love for nature, the importance of husband-wife relationships and tender feelings, and loyalty between friends. Hellenic schools also used the two epics to teach students to always strive for excellence and to meet with dignity whatever fate had in store.

A Family of Deities

In Greek religion, the activities of gods and goddesses explained why people behaved the way they did and why their lives took one direction rather than another. The Greeks also believed that their powerful deities caused the events of the physical world to occur—such as the coming of spring or violent storms with thunder and lightning.

Most ancient peoples feared their deities. They believed that people were put on the earth only to obey and serve the gods and goddesses. The Greeks were the first people to feel differently. They placed importance on the worth of the individual. Because they believed in their own value, the Greeks had a great deal of self-respect. This allowed them to approach their gods with dignity.

Much more than other civilizations did, the Greeks humanized their deities. Unlike the half-animal gods and goddesses of Egypt, Greek deities had totally human forms. They behaved like humans, too—marrying, having children, lying, and murdering. Frequently jealous of one another, the Greek deities quarreled and sometimes played tricks on one another. They also possessed super-human powers. Since the Greeks saw their deities as sources of power, both physical and mental, they tried to be like them by doing everything to the best of their ability.

Gods and Goddesses

The gods and goddesses of ancient Greece combined features of both Minoan and Mycenaean deities. For example, different Greek goddesses took over different aspects of the Earth Mother. Athena became the goddess of wisdom and art, Demeter became the goddess of agriculture, and Aphrodite became the goddess of love and beauty. Each community chose a particular god or goddess as its patron and protector, but all Greeks worshiped as their chief deity the Mycenaean god Zeus.

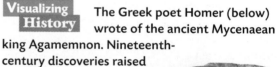 The Greek poet Homer (below) wrote of the ancient Mycenaean king Agamemnon. Nineteenth-century discoveries raised Homer's work from the rank of myth to that of history. *Who was Helen of Troy?*

Greeks believed that the 12 most important Greek deities lived on high Mount Olympus, an actual mountain in Greece. Each of the deities controlled a specific part of the natural world. For example, Zeus, the chief god, was thought to rule the sky, weather, and thunderstorms. His brother Pluto was thought to rule the underworld, where the dead spent eternity.

Zeus's son Apollo, the god of light, drove the sun across the sky every day in his chariot. Because the Greeks also considered Apollo to be the god of prophecy, they would bring gifts to the oracle at Delphi—a holy place to honor Apollo—and ask to have hidden knowledge revealed. Like the Shang in ancient China, the Greeks believed that oracles could predict the future. At the Delphic oracle, they would ask questions, and the priests and priestesses would interpret Apollo's replies.

Festivals

As Hellenic civilization developed, certain religious festivals became an important part of Greek life. Every four years the Greeks held a series of athletic contests "for the greater glory of Zeus." Because these contests were held at the city of Olympia, they were called the Olympic Games. The Greeks also originated the play—a celebration in honor of Dionysus, the god of wine and fertility. At these events, the audience sat on a hillside around an open space, where a chorus chanted a story about Dionysus and danced to the sound of a flute. As the years passed, cities began building permanent amphitheaters, carving a hillside into a semicircle, adding rows of stone seats, and paving the stage area. Actors began to recite poems explaining the songs and dances of the chorus. The words they recited eventually evolved into dialogue.

SECTION 1 REVIEW

Recall
1. **Define** labyrinth, bard.
2. **Identify** Sir Arthur Evans, the Minoans, the Mycenaeans, Homer, Heinrich Schliemann.
3. **Describe** the routes the Mycenaeans would have taken to reach Troy and Knossos from their home city of Mycenae.

Critical Thinking
4. **Applying Information** Using Zeus, Athena, and Apollo, illustrate how the Greeks viewed their gods and goddesses.

Understanding Themes
5. **Relation to Environment** How did the geography and climate of Greece and the Aegean islands affect the development of the Minoan and Mycenaean civilizations?

700 B.C.

c. 700s B.C. Greek kings
lose power to aristocrats.

600 B.C.

c. 600s B.C. Greeks learn
coinage from the Lydians.

500 B.C.

c. 500 B.C.
The rule of
tyrants in Greek
city-states ends.

Section 2

The Polis

Setting the Scene

▶ **Terms to Define**
polis, citizen, aristocrat, phalanx, tyrant,
oligarchy, democracy

▶ **Places to Locate**
Athens, Sparta

 **Find Out** How did economic prosperity bring
significant political and social changes to the
Greek city-states?

The Storyteller

*An Athenian ruler had to be careful of plots
hatched by jealous nobles. The tyrant Hippias, the
once-mild ruler of Athens, learned this lesson. He
was with his bodyguard, arranging a citywide
parade, when two
assassins approached.
Pretending to take
part in the proces-
sion, they had dag-
gers ready, hidden
behind their shields.
Suddenly, seeing one
of their accomplices
casually talking with
Hippias, they halted,
thinking that he had
betrayed the plot to the tyrant. Turning, they
rushed within the gates, met Hippias's brother,
and killed him. Afterward, Athenians found
Hippias harsher, ever fearful of revolt.*

The Parthenon on the Acropolis

—adapted from *The Peloponnesian
War,* Thucydides, Crawley translation revised by T.E. Wick, 1892

The English language offers evidence of
how ancient Greeks have influenced
modern life. Words such as *police* and
politics, for example, derive from the Greek word
polis. The polis, or city-state, was the basic political
unit of Hellenic civilization. Each polis developed
its own pattern of life independently but shared
certain features with other city-states.

The Typical Polis

A typical polis included a city and the surrounding villages, fields, and orchards. At the center
of the city on the top of an acropolis (uh•KRAH•puh
•luhs), or fortified hill, stood the temple of the local
deity. At the foot of the acropolis the agora, or public square, served as the political center of the polis.
Citizens—those who took part in government—
gathered in the agora to carry out public affairs,
choose their officials, and pass their laws. Artisans
and merchants also conducted business in the agora.

The citizens of a polis had both rights and responsibilities. They could vote, hold public office, own
property, and speak for themselves in court. In return,
the polis expected them to serve in government and
to defend the polis in time of war.

Citizens, however, made up only a minority of the
residents of a polis. In Athens, slaves and those who
were foreign-born were excluded from citizenship,
and before 500 B.C. so were men who did not own
land. Greek women had no political or legal rights.

Greek Colonies and Trade

The return of prosperity after the "dark age"
led to an increase in Greece's population. By 700
B.C. Greek farmers no longer grew enough grain to
feed everyone. As a result, each polis sent out
groups of people to establish colonies in coastal
areas around the Mediterranean and Black Seas.

Colonies

Each colony kept close ties with its metropolis, or "parent city." A colony supplied its metropolis with grain—wheat and barley. Farmers on the Greek mainland produced wine, olive oil, and other cash crops for export. Because vineyards and olive groves needed fewer workers than did grain fields, many farmers moved to the cities, where they learned crafts. With more goods to sell, Greek merchants began trading throughout the Mediterranean region.

Economic Growth

During the 600s B.C. the Greeks replaced their barter system with a money economy, and their overseas trade expanded further. Merchants issued their own coins, but eventually individual city-states took over this responsibility.

The cities of Ionia in Asia Minor assumed leadership in a growing textile industry. Sheep in the interior of Asia Minor furnished the raw material. Purple dye obtained from mollusks, a type of shellfish, gave the woven materials color.

Pottery developed as a local industry wherever sufficient clay was found. Pottery made in Ionia was the earliest Greek pottery to be exported. Ionian pottery styles were based on Mycenaean and Middle Eastern influences. The artists who made and decorated the vases painted figures of birds and humans interspersed with line or geometric decorations.

Political and Social Change

Economic growth changed Greek political life. Greek communities at first were ruled by kings. By the 700s B.C., however, the kings had lost power to landholding aristocrats, or nobles, who as members of the upper class provided cavalry for the king's military ventures.

By 650 B.C. disputes arose between the aristocrats and the common people. Farmers often needed credit until harvest time. To obtain loans from the wealthy aristocrats, they had to pledge their fields as security. When they could not repay the loans, many farmers lost their land to the aristocrats and became either sharecroppers or day laborers in the cities. Some even had to sell themselves into slavery. In protest, farmers demanded political reforms.

Geography

Sailing the Aegean

Because of their many natural harbors, the Greeks transported most goods by sea. Sea travel made good sense, given the rugged mountains of the Greek mainland. Besides, pack animals could carry only small loads short distances. Merchants found sea transport of bulky cargo—grain, timber, and even jugs of olive oil—to be practical and inexpensive. Greek sailors could sail easily only when the wind was behind them. The prevailing northerly winds made the voyage from Athens to the Black Sea slow and difficult, but the return trip was quick and easy. Likewise, Greek ships could coast to Egypt, but they had to struggle to get home. Most ships managed only one round-trip per year.

Pottery jar showing a merchant ship

The typical Greek freighter was broad—about 25 feet (7.5 m) wide compared to a length of 80 feet (24 m). Rigged with a large square sail, this sturdy ship averaged only about 5 knots with the wind. Merchant ships usually sailed in fleets escorted by warships—galleys propelled by oarsmen.

Compare the ancient ships with today's diesel-driven giants. A container ship makes the round-trip between the United States and Europe in 21 days. It holds cargo in 1,000 containers—four of which are the size of one Greek freighter. Some things have not changed, however. The Greek merchant fleet of today ranks among the largest in the world.

MAKING THE CONNECTION

1. Why were the prevailing winds a problem for Greek sailors?
2. Besides larger, faster ships, how has cargo transport changed since ancient times?

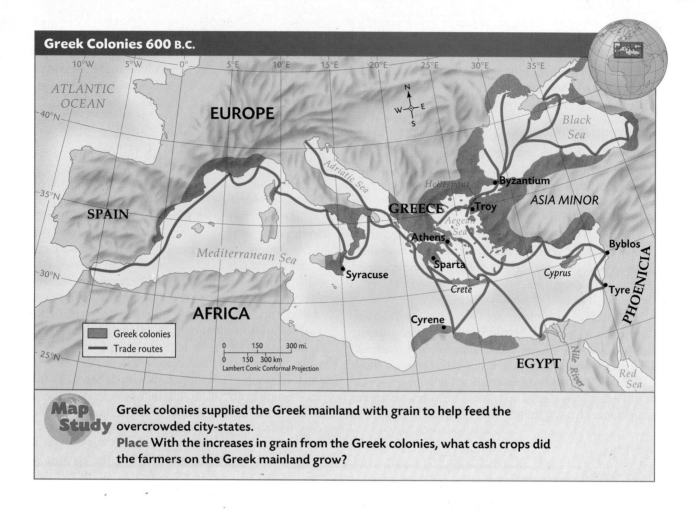

Greek Colonies 600 B.C.

Greek colonies
Trade routes

0   150   300 mi.
0   150 300 km
Lambert Conic Conformal Projection

Map Study Greek colonies supplied the Greek mainland with grain to help feed the overcrowded city-states.

Place With the increases in grain from the Greek colonies, what cash crops did the farmers on the Greek mainland grow?

The farmers, who were foot soldiers, were becoming more valuable to Greek armies than the aristocrats, who were cavalry. As Greek armies came to rely on the phalanx—rows of foot soldiers closely arrayed with their shields forming a solid wall—aristocrats began to lose influence. Middle-class, non-landowning merchants and artisans, thus far excluded from citizenship, wanted a voice in the government and joined the farmers in their demands. Merchants and artisans also wanted the polis to advance their interests by encouraging industry and by protecting profitable overseas trade routes.

As a result of the unrest, tyrannies arose. A tyranny was created when one man, called a tyrant, seized power and ruled the polis single-handedly. Although most tyrants ruled fairly, the harshness of a few gave *tyranny* its present meaning—rule by a cruel and unjust person.

Tyrants ruled various Greek city-states until about 500 B.C. From then until 336 B.C., most city-states became either oligarchies or democracies. In an oligarchy, a few wealthy people hold power over the larger group of citizens. In a democracy, or government by the people, power lies in the hands of all the citizens. Two democracies of ancient Greece—**Athens** and **Sparta**—became the most famous of the city-states.

SECTION 2 REVIEW

Recall
1. **Define** polis, citizen, aristocrat, phalanx, tyrant, oligarchy, democracy.
2. **Identify** Athens, Sparta.
3. **Describe** the social and politi-cal functions of an acropolis and an agora in a Greek polis.

Critical Thinking
4. **Synthesizing Information** What arguments might a citi-zen of a polis present for or against changing citizenship?

Understanding Themes
5. **Movement** What kind of rela-tionship existed between a Greek colony and its metropo-lis on the Greek mainland?

Results of Militarism

The Spartans succeeded in maintaining their power over the helots and *perioeci* for nearly 250 years. They paid a price, however. Suspicious of any new ideas that might change their society, the Spartans lagged far behind other city-states in developing trade and manufacturing. As a result, they were much poorer than the other Greeks. The Spartans also lagged in intellectual accomplishments. The Athenians created a vast body of literature and made important discoveries in science. The Spartans did not. The Spartans were, however, exceptional athletes who almost always won the Olympic Games, and Spartan soldiers played key roles in defending Greece against invaders.

Athens

Northeast of the Peloponnesus—on a peninsula of central Greece named **Attica**—people descended from the Mycenaeans established the city-state of Athens. They named their polis after the goddess Athena. Like the early rulers of the other city-states, Athenian kings and aristocrats in the 600s B.C. faced demands by small farmers, merchants, and artisans for economic and political reforms.

Around this time, the governing methods of Athens and Sparta diverged. Athens gradually expanded its definition of citizenship to encompass more people. Initially, only a man whose father and maternal grandfather had been citizens could be a citizen; however, non-landowning citizens could not participate in Athens's Assembly. Athenians called the many free (non-enslaved) foreigners who lived in Athens *metics*. These people could not own land or participate in government. By 507 B.C., however, the constitution of Athens stated that all free men were citizens regardless of what class they belonged to, and that they could participate in the Assembly regardless of whether they owned land. This political change reduced much of the friction between social classes and enabled Athens to forge ahead.

The goddess Athena, according to Greek tradition, won the contest for control of Athens over the sea god Poseidon.

REFLECTING ON THE TIMES

1. What innovation did Greek sculptors introduce in the classical period?
2. Why was Athena's name rather than Poseidon's given to the city of Athens?

Draco's Law Code

Four successive tyrants brought most of the changes in Athenian government. **Draco**, the first of these tyrants, issued an improved code of laws in 621 B.C. The penalties given to offenders were extremely harsh. Even minor offenses, like stealing a cabbage, were punishable by death.

Over time, the word *draconian* has come to describe something that is very cruel and severe. On the other hand, because Draco's laws were written down, everyone knew exactly what the laws were. Aristocrats could no longer dictate what was legal and what was not.

Solon's Reforms

The next series of reforms took place under the tyrant **Solon**, who became the leader of Athens in 594 B.C. To improve economic conditions, Solon canceled all land debts and freed debtors from slavery. He also placed limits on the amount of land any one individual could own. By urging farmers to grow cash crops rather than grain, Solon promoted trade. He also promoted industry by ordering fathers to teach their sons a trade and by extending citizenship to artisans and merchants who were not born Athenians.

Next, Solon turned his attention to the political conflict between aristocrats and commoners. He did this by setting up a two-house legislature. Aristocrats belonged to the Council of 400, while landowning commoners made up the Assembly. The Council drafted measures that then went to the Assembly for approval.

Radical Reformers

In 546 B.C. the tyrant **Peisistratus** (pih•SIHS•truh•tuhs) took over the government of Athens. Peisistratus pushed reforms in an even more radical

direction than had Solon. He divided large estates among landless farmers and extended citizenship to men who did not own land. Peisistratus provided the poor with loans and put many of them to work building temples and other public works projects.

Cleisthenes (KLYS•thuh•NEEZ), the fourth tyrant to help reform Athens, came to power in 508 B.C. The following year he introduced a series of laws that established democracy for Athens. Through his reforms, Cleisthenes sought to end local rivalries, break the power of the aristocracy, and extend citizenship guarantees to more people living in Athens. He also set out to reorganize the structure of Athenian government.

Athenian Democracy

The Assembly remained the major political institution in Cleisthenes' democracy. All citizens could belong to the Assembly, in which they were considered equal before the law and guaranteed freedom of speech. The Assembly passed laws and also served as a supreme court. In addition, each year the Assembly chose 10 generals to run the army and navy. A Council of 500 administered everyday government business such as taxes, treaties, and public works.

Each year in a lottery, Athenians chose members of the Council. They favored a lottery over the ballot, believing that, except for running a military campaign, all citizens were competent to hold public office. In addition, they considered elections unfair because rich men, men who boasted a well-known family name, or men who spoke effectively in public would have an advantage. Besides, all citizens were supposed to take part in government.

Athenian democracy included a jury system to decide court cases. Juries contained from 201 to

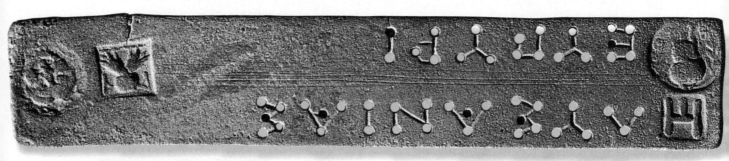

Visualizing History A juror's token is shown above. Athenian courts demonstrated faith in the ordinary man's ability. Groups of hundreds of citizens sat on panels called *dicasteries* and decided cases by majority vote. *Why were juries so large?*

1,001 members, with a majority vote needed to reach a verdict. The Athenians reasoned that the large size of their juries would keep jurors from being influenced by threats, bribes, or prejudice.

Athenian democracy also included a system called ostracism. Each year, citizens could write the name of an undesirable politician on a piece of baked clay called an ostracon. If a person's name appeared on 6,000 ostraca, the polis exiled him for 10 years.

Cleisthenes' reforms lasted for almost 200 years, until the Macedonians living to the north conquered the Greeks. Even though the Athenians excluded several groups from citizenship, ancient Athens nevertheless laid the foundation for the Western concept of democratic government.

Athenian Education

The training an Athenian received depended on social and economic status. About a week after being born, a male child received a name and was enrolled as a citizen. Because Athens expected every citizen to hold public office at some time in his life, it required Athenian citizens to educate their sons. With few exceptions, Athenian girls—who would not participate in governing the democracy of Athens—did not receive a formal education. Instead, a girl learned household duties, such as weaving and baking, from her mother.

Private tutors educated the boys from wealthy upper-class families, while other students paid a small fee to attend a private school. Much of their education was picked up in the agora, through daily conversations and discussions in the Assembly.

Athenian boys entered school at age 7 and graduated at age 18. Their main textbooks were the *Iliad* and the *Odyssey*, and students learned each epic by heart. They studied arithmetic, geometry, drawing, and music in the morning and gymnastics in the afternoon. When boys reached their teens, they added **rhetoric**, or the art of public speaking, to

Zapotec Temple Complex at Monte Albán

Mexico, c. 500 B.C.
Monte Albán in the valley of Oaxaca in southern Mexico became an important center of Zapotec culture. The Zapotecs flattened the mountaintop to create a large plaza, around which they designed a temple complex. They carved the slopes of the mountain into terraces for agriculture and housing. An estimated 5,000 people, or about 50 percent of the valley's population, lived at Monte Albán.

their studies. Because lawyers did not represent participants in a court case, an Athenian needed to be accomplished in rhetoric to argue his own position.

When young Athenian men reached 18, they left for two years of military service. Before entering the army, however, they went with their fathers to the temple of Zeus, where they swore the following oath:

> ❝ I will not bring dishonor upon my weapons nor desert the comrade by my side. I will strive to hand on my fatherland greater and better than I found it. I will not consent to anyone's disobeying or destroying the constitution but will prevent him, whether I am with others or alone. I will honor the temples and the religion my forefathers established. ❞
>
> —oath of enrollment in Epheboi corps, early 400s B.C.

SECTION 3 REVIEW

Recall
1. **Define** rhetoric.
2. **Identify** Draco, Solon, Peisistratus, Cleisthenes.
3. **Locate** Athens and Sparta on the map on page 121. In which peninsula was each located?

Critical Thinking
4. **Evaluating Information**
   Do you think the reasons the Athenians gave for choosing government officials by lottery were good reasons? What other method would you propose if you were an Athenian reformer?

Understanding Themes
5. **Regionalism** Contrast Athens and Sparta in their idea of citizenship, type of education, and position of women.

550 B.C.　　　　　500 B.C.　　　　　450 B.C.　　　　　400 B.C.

546 B.C.
Persian armies
conquer Ionia.

499 B.C. Athenians
and Persians fight
the Battle of Marathon.

447 B.C. Pericles
begins rebuilding
of Athens.

431 B.C.
Peloponnesian
War begins.

Section 4

War, Glory, and Decline

Setting the Scene

▶ **Terms to Define**
  symposium, mercenary

▶ **People to Meet**
  Darius I, Xerxes, Themistocles, Leonidas,
  Pericles, Aspasia

▶ **Places to Locate**
  Marathon, Thermopylae, Salamis, Delos

Find Out How did the Persian Wars and the
Peloponnesian War affect democracy in the
Greek city-states?

The Storyteller

*The Greek historian Herodotus reported that
during the Persian Wars, some Greek deserters
approached the Persian king Xerxes. Questioned
about what the Greeks were about to do, they told
him the truth: The Olympic Games were being held.
They were going to watch the athletic competitions
and chariot races. When asked what the prize
was for such contests, they responded that the
Olympic prize was an olive wreath. Upon
hearing this, a Persian noble cried out
in fear: "What kind of men are
these? How can we be expected to
fight against men who compete
with each other for no material
reward, but only for honor!"*

—adapted from *The Histories*,
Herodotus, translated by
Aubrey de Selincourt

Themistocles

As the 400s B.C. opened, the Persian
Empire—then the strongest military
power in the ancient world—stood
poised to extend its influence into Europe.
Surprisingly, the Greek city-states not only cooperated with each other in resisting the Persian attack,
but they also succeeded in throwing Persia's armed
forces back into Asia.

After their victory against Persia, the Greeks—
especially the Athenians—enjoyed a "golden age"
of remarkable cultural achievements. Then, the
Greek city-states began to fight among themselves.
This bitter and devastating war lasted for more
than 27 years.

The Persian Wars

In 546 B.C. the Persian armies, led by Cyrus II,
conquered the Greek city-states of Ionia, in Asia
Minor. Despite the mildness of Persian rule, the
Ionians disliked the conquerors. The Ionians considered the non-Greek-speaking Persians to be barbarians. In addition, an all-powerful king ruled the
Persian Empire, whereas the Greek population of
Ionia believed that citizens should choose their own
government.

Finally, in 499 B.C., the Ionians revolted against
the Persians. Even though Athens and another
mainland polis sent some warships to help the
Ionians, **Darius I** of Persia soon defeated the
Ionians. Darius then decided to punish the mainland Greeks for helping the rebels.

Marathon

Darius first tried to send an army around the
northern coast of the Aegean Sea. However, a storm
destroyed his supply ships, forcing him to turn
back. Two years later, in 490 B.C., Darius tried again.

This time he sent his fleet directly across the Aegean to the coastal plain of **Marathon**, about 25 miles (40 km) north of Athens. For several days the Persians awaited the Athenians. However, the Athenians, outnumbered 20,000 to 10,000, did nothing. Finally, the Persians decided to attack Athens directly. They loaded their ships with the cavalry—the strongest part of their army—and then began loading the infantry.

Not waiting for the Persians to take the offensive, the Athenians struck. The Athenian general ordered his well-disciplined foot soldiers to charge down the hills above Marathon at the Persian infantry, which stood in shallow water waiting to board the ships. This tactic astounded the Persians, who believed that infantrymen would fight

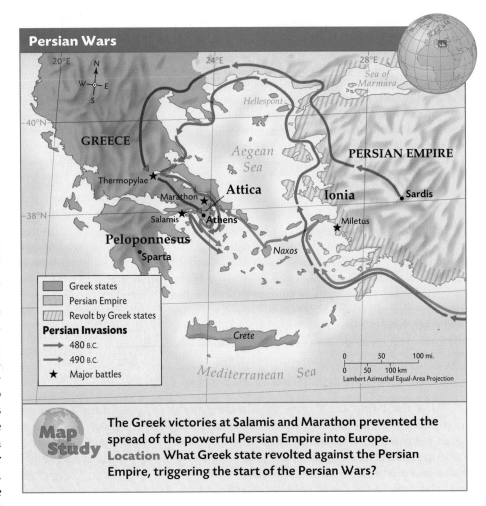

Persian Wars

Greek states
Persian Empire
Revolt by Greek states

Persian Invasions
→ 480 B.C.
→ 490 B.C.
★ Major battles

The Greek victories at Salamis and Marathon prevented the spread of the powerful Persian Empire into Europe.
Location What Greek state revolted against the Persian Empire, triggering the start of the Persian Wars?

only with the support of horsemen and archers. Marathon was a terrible defeat for the Persians, who reportedly lost 6,400 men compared to only 192 Greek casualties.

Salamis

After Marathon, the Persians withdrew to Asia Minor, but they returned 10 years later. In 480 B.C. Darius's son and successor, **Xerxes**, invaded Greece from the north, this time with 200,000 soldiers. Because so huge an army could not live off the land, offshore supply ships accompanied them.

Once again the Greeks, this time under the leadership of Sparta, faced the Persians. A few years before, the oracle at Delphi had said that Greece would be safe behind a "wooden wall." The Athenian general **Themistocles** (thuh•MIHS•tuh •KLEEZ) tried to convince his Greek allies that a "wooden wall" meant a fleet of ships and that the way to defeat the Persians was to challenge them at sea.

To do this, the Greek army had to set up a delaying action on land. They chose **Thermopylae** (thuhr•MAH•puh•lee) as the place—a mountain

pass north of Athens. There, 7,000 Greeks led by King **Leonidas** of Sparta stood firm against the Persians for three days. Then a Greek traitor showed the enemy a trail over which they could attack the Greeks from the rear. Realizing that he would soon be surrounded, Leonidas sent off most of his troops. But he and 300 fellow Spartans remained obedient to the law of their polis—never

Footnotes to History

Marathon
According to legend, a messenger named Pheidippides (fy•DIH•puh•DEEZ) carried the news of the victory at Marathon back to Athens. Because Pheidippides had previously run 280 miles (448 km) in four days, he barely managed to reach the city and deliver his message before he fell to the ground, dead from exhaustion. Ever since, people have used the word *marathon* to describe a long-distance race.

surrender on the battlefield, but fight until victory or death.

> 66 They [the Spartans] defended themselves to the last, such as still had swords using them, and the others resisting with their hand and teeth; till the barbarians [Persians] … overwhelmed and buried the remnant left beneath showers of missile weapons. 99
>
> —Herodotus, from *History*, 400s B.C.

The heroic stand of Leonidas and the Spartans gave Themistocles enough time to carry out his plan. He drew the Persian fleet into the strait of Salamis, a narrow body of water between Athens and the island of **Salamis**. Themistocles reasoned that the heavy Persian ships would crowd together in the strait and make easy targets for the lighter but faster and more maneuverable Greek ships. The plan worked, and the outnumbered ships of the Greek navy destroyed almost the entire Persian fleet.

After the battle at Salamis, the Greeks gained the upper hand. By 479 B.C., the Persians had once again retreated to Asia Minor, this time for good. With the end of the Persian Wars, the Greek city-states resumed their traditional quarrels.

The Golden Age of Athens

Greek culture reached its peak after the Persian Wars. Most historians refer to the period from 461 B.C. to 429 B.C. as the Golden Age of Athens because most Greek achievements in the arts and sciences took place in Athens during this time.

Pericles in Charge

The Athenian general **Pericles**, beginning in the 450s B.C., led Athens through its Golden Age. The Persians had burned Athens during the Persian Wars, but beginning in 447 B.C., Pericles was determined to rebuild the city. When the rebuilt temples and palaces crowned its acropolis, Athens became the most beautiful city in Greece. The most famous structure built under Pericles, the Parthenon (the temple of Athena), still stands.

Pericles wanted the polis of Athens to stand for all that was best in Greek civilization. A persuasive speaker, he expressed his ideas in a famous funeral oration quoted by the Greek historian Thucydides (thoo•SIH•duh•DEEZ):

> 66 We are called a democracy [because power] is in the hands of the many and not the few.… When it is a question of putting one person before another in positions of public responsibility, what counts is not membership of a particular class, but the actual ability which the man possesses.… We are prevented from doing wrong by respect … for the laws.… We are lovers of the beautiful, yet simple in our tastes, and we cultivate the mind without loss of manliness.… To avow poverty with us is no disgrace; the true disgrace is in doing nothing to avoid it.… Athens is the school of Hellas [Greece]. 99

Athenian Daily Life

Athenians lavished money on public buildings, but they kept their individual homes simple. The typical Athenian house contained two main rooms and several smaller ones built around a central courtyard. In one main room, the dining room, the men entertained guests and ate while reclining on couches. An Athenian woman joined her husband for dinner only if company was not invited. In the other main room, the wool room, the women spun and wove cloth. In the courtyard stood an altar, a wash basin, and sometimes a well. The courtyard also contained the family's chickens and goats.

Athenian men usually worked in the morning as farmers, artisans, and merchants. Then they spent the afternoon attending the Assembly or exercising in the gymnasium. Slaves—who were mostly foreigners and prisoners of war and who made up one-third of the population—did most of

Visualizing History Pericles held virtual control over Athenian affairs for the last 15 years of his life, being elected each year as one of the 10 city generals. *How did Pericles identify his faith in democracy?*

the heavy work in craft production and mining. Many slaves also worked as teachers and household servants. Most Athenian women spent their time at home, cooking and making wool cloth, but poor women worked in the open-air markets as food sellers and cloth weavers.

Upper-class Athenian men—as well as citizens from other city-states—enjoyed the symposium as a form of recreation. Wives were excluded from a symposium, which was a drinking session following a banquet. The men at a symposium were entertained by female dancers and singers as well as by acrobats and magicians. The guests also spent much of the evening entertaining each other, telling riddles and discussing literature, philosophy, and public issues.

Athenian Women

In spite of restrictions, many Athenian women were able to participate in public life—especially in city festivals—and learned to read and write. Public opinion allowed greater freedom to women of the *metic* class than to those of other groups. The most famous of *metic* women was **Aspasia**, who was known for her intelligence and personal charm. To her house came many of the women of Athens, and she apparently gave advice on home life while attempting to gain more education and greater freedom for Athenian women. Her views aroused great opposition among some Athenians of both sexes, and she was prosecuted on a charge of "impiety," or disloyalty to the gods. Aspasia was finally acquitted after an impassioned plea to the jury by Pericles himself.

The Peloponnesian War

Even after the Persian Wars ended, the Persian threat remained. Athens persuaded most of the city-states—but not Sparta—to ally against the enemy. This alliance became known as the Delian League because the treasury was kept on the sacred island of **Delos**. Athens provided the principal naval and land forces, while the other city-states furnished money and ships. Over the next several decades, the Delian League succeeded in freeing Ionia from Persian rule and sweeping the Aegean free of pirates. Overseas trade expanded, and Greece grew richer.

The Athenian Empire

Athens gradually began to dominate the other city-states. Pericles, for example, used part of the Delian League's treasury to build the Parthenon.

Visualizing History A Spartan soldier poises for battle. The Spartans developed a chain of orders to be shouted above the din of battle. *How did Sparta attain a navy?*

He insisted that criminal cases be tried only in Athens and that other city-states adopt the Athenian coinage system. He also sent Athenian troops to support revolts by commoners against aristocrats in other city-states. In short, the policies of Pericles more or less transformed the Delian League from what had been an anti-Persian defense league into an Athenian empire.

As Athen's trade and political influence grew, several city-states reacted by forming an alliance opposed to Athens. Sparta, a long-standing Athenian rival, became the leader of the anti-Athens alliance. Since Sparta was located in the Peloponnesus, historians have called the war against Athens and its allies the Peloponnesian War.

The Conflict

The Peloponnesian War lasted from 431 B.C. to 404 B.C., excluding one brief period of peace. At first it seemed as if Athens could hold out indefinitely, since Sparta had no navy. Sparta's fear and jealousy of Athens, however, were so strong that the Spartans made a deal with the Persians to return Ionia to Persian control. In exchange, Sparta received gold to build its own fleet. Then, in 430 B.C., a disastrous plague—probably typhus—weakened Athens. More

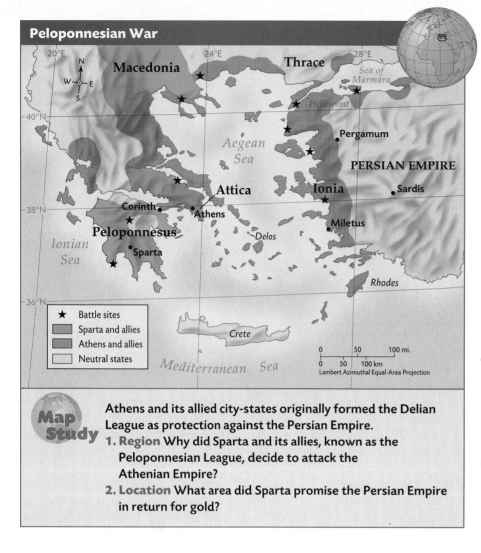

Peloponnesian War

Map Study

Athens and its allied city-states originally formed the Delian League as protection against the Persian Empire.

1. **Region** Why did Sparta and its allies, known as the Peloponnesian League, decide to attack the Athenian Empire?
2. **Location** What area did Sparta promise the Persian Empire in return for gold?

fleet. After the Spartans laid siege to Athens itself, the Athenians finally surrendered in 404 B.C.

Effects of the War

The Peloponnesian War brought disaster to the Greek city-states, both victors and vanquished. Many city-states declined in population. Fighting had destroyed many fields and orchards. Unemployment became so widespread that thousands of young men emigrated and became mercenaries, or hired soldiers, in the Persian army.

Worst of all, the Greeks lost their ability to govern themselves. The length and cost of the war made people forget about the common good of their polis and think only about making money. Feelings between aristocrats and commoners grew increasingly bitter. Many Greeks, losing faith in democracy, even came to look down on free political discussion and began to believe that might makes right.

than a third of its population died, including Pericles.

After Pericles died in 429 B.C., some Athenians wanted to make peace with Sparta and its allies, while other Athenians wanted to keep on fighting. No decision was made, and the war continued deadlocked for many more years. Eventually, several allies of Athens switched sides and joined the Spartan-led alliance. Then, with their Persian-financed navy, the Spartans destroyed the Athenian

For a time, Sparta tried to rule the other city-states. Then, in 371 B.C., a new alliance of city-states led by Thebes overthrew the harsh, incompetent Spartan rulers. The Thebans, however, also made poor rulers and were also overthrown. As a result of almost continual fighting, the city-states became weaker than ever. When a new invader, the Macedonians, threatened Greece in the 350s B.C., the city-states were unable to resist.

SECTION 4 REVIEW

Recall
1. **Define** symposium, mercenary.
2. **Identify** Ionia, Darius I, Marathon, Xerxes, Themistocles, Thermopylae, Leonidas, Salamis, Pericles, Aspasia.
3. **Describe** the daily activities of an Athenian husband. What were those of an Athenian wife?

Critical Thinking
4. **Evaluating Information** Judge whether Pericles' rule was beneficial for Athens. Give reasons to support your answer.

Understanding Themes
5. **Conflict** Why didn't loyalty to the polis prevent Greeks from uniting against Persia?

Critical Thinking SKILLS

Making Comparisons

In shopping for athletic shoes, you have narrowed your selection to two pairs. Which pair should you buy? To decide this question, you must make a comparison.

Learning the Skill

Making comparisons means finding similarities and differences. In the above example, you might first notice the similarities between the shoes. Both pairs are the same price and the same color. Then, you would look for differences. One pair extends above the ankle, the other pair does not. One pair is designed for jogging, the other for aerobics. Once you have compared the shoes, you can draw a conclusion about which pair will best suit your needs.

Apply the same method in comparing any two objects, groups, or concepts. First, determine the purpose of your comparison. What question do you want to answer? Then determine the bases for comparison. In the shoe example, we compared on the bases of price, color, style, and athletic function. Then identify similarities and differences in each of these categories. Finally, use the comparison to draw conclusions or to answer your question.

Practicing the Skill

The excerpts on this page discuss the military strength of Sparta and Athens. Read the excerpts and answer the questions below.

1. Identify three bases for comparing the military strength of Athens and Sparta.
2. Do both city-states have armies and navies?
3. What are two differences in the military strength of Athens and Sparta?
4. Based on this comparison, which city-state has greater military strength? Why?

❝ We [Spartans] have many reasons to expect success,—first, superiority in numbers and in military experience, and second, our general and unvarying obedience in the execution of orders. The naval strength which they [Athens] possess shall be raised by us from ... the monies at Olympia and Delphi. A loan from these enables us to seduce their foreign sailors by the offer of higher pay.... A single defeat at sea is in all likelihood their ruin. ❞

—Thucydides, account of a Corinthian envoy to the Congress at Sparta, 432 B.C.

❝ Personally engaged in the cultivation of their land, without funds either private or public, the Peloponnesians [Spartans] are also without experience in long wars across the sea.... Our naval skill is of more use to us for service on land, than their military skill for service at sea. Even if they were to ... try to seduce our foreign sailors by the temptation of higher pay ... none of our foreign sailors would consent to become an outlaw from his own country, and to take service with them. ❞

—Pericles, account to Athenian Ecclesia, 432 B.C.

Applying the Skill

Choose a topic or activity that interests you, such as baseball, rock music, politics, etc. Research and compare two individuals, groups, or organizations involved in this activity. Write a short essay or make a chart outlining at least five similarities and five differences.

For More Practice

Turn to the Skill Practice in the Chapter Review on page 127 for more practice in making comparisons.

Historical Significance

Ancient Greece provided the world with its first example of democratic government. Because the limited number of citizens in a Greek polis permitted direct participation by all citizens, Athens can be described as a *direct* democracy. In the United States today, where we elect senators and representatives who are responsible to us, the form of government is called a *representative* democracy. In contrast to citizenship in ancient Greece, United States citizenship has broadened to include women and people of all races, as well as naturalized foreign-born citizens.

Using Key Terms

Write the key term that completes each sentence.

a. aristocrats
b. citizen
c. democracy
d. oligarchy
e. mercenary
f. polis
g. rhetoric
h. tyrant
i. symposiums
j. labyrinth
k. phalanx
l. bards

1. The _____, the basic political unit of ancient Greece, included a city and the surrounding villages, fields, and orchards.
2. A woman in ancient Greece was not considered to be a full _____ with the right to take part in political affairs.
3. A leader known as a _____ came to power in many Greek city-states and usually promised to introduce reforms to help farmers, merchants, and artisans.
4. Upon reaching their teens, Athenian boys studied _____, or the art of public speaking, as part of their education.
5. Sir Arthur Evans discovered that intricate passageways in Minos's palace at Knossos on Crete form a _____, or maze.
6. By the 700s B.C., kings in Greece had lost power to landholding members of the upper class known as _____.
7. Athenian men entertained each other at _____, telling riddles and discussing literature, philosophy, and public issues.
8. In an _____, a few wealthy people hold power over a larger group of citizens.
9. _____, or singing storytellers, kept alive Mycenaean literary traditions during Greece's "dark age."
10. In a _____, or government by the people, political power lies in the hands of all citizens.

Using Your History Journal

Democracy is not easy to achieve or to maintain. Make a list of the issues that challenge democracy in America. Write a paragraph entitled "Maintaining Democracy" or "Achieving Democracy" that responds to this issue.

Reviewing Facts

1. **List** the elements of Minoan culture that were adopted by the Mycenaeans.
2. **State** the values of Hellenic civilization that were found in the *Iliad* and the *Odyssey*.
3. **Explain** how the attitude of the Greeks toward their deities differed from the attitude of the Egyptians.
4. **Explain** how Sparta's response in the 700s B.C. to the problems of increased population and a shortage of arable land differed from the response of most other Greek city-states.
5. **Describe** the major difference between the Greeks and the Persians, according to the Ionians.

Critical Thinking

1. **Apply** How did Sparta's values affect its educational system?
2. **Analyze** How did increased trade affect Greek political life?
3. **Synthesize** What might have been the outcome of the Persian Wars if Themistocles had not convinced the Greeks to build a fleet of ships?

4. **Analyze** Shown below, the south porch of the Erechtheum near the Parthenon uses figures of maidens to replace conventional columns. The buildings on the Acropolis are examples of early classical architecture and sculpture. What might these figures suggest about the role of women in Athenian life?

Understanding Themes

1. **Relation to Environment** What aspects of Crete's environment enabled the Minoans to become skilled seafarers?
2. **Movement** What role did trade play in the development of Greek civilization?
3. **Regionalism** What effect did Sparta's emphasis on military values have on its development as a city-state?
4. **Conflict** Why did several Greek city-states, led by Sparta, form an alliance in the mid-400s B.C. to fight against Athens and the Delian League?

Linking Past and Present

1. During times of unrest in ancient Athens, tyrants seized power to introduce political and economic reforms. Do you think a tyrant could establish a dictatorship in the United States at a time of crisis? Explain your answer.
2. Why might students at the United States Naval Academy study the Persian Wars?

Skill Practice

Reread Section 3 and compare the two leading city-states in ancient Greece.

1. What are two similarities in the education of young people in Athens and Sparta?
2. What are two differences in their education?
3. What are two similarities in the political structure of Athens and Sparta?
4. What are two differences in their political structure?
5. What are two differences in the role of women in Athens and Sparta?
6. What are two similarities in women's roles?

Geography in History

1. **Place** Although it is a small island, Crete has what two landforms?
2. **Location** Refer to the map on page 124. What is the relative location of Crete? What is Crete's absolute location?
3. **Location** Where was the palace of the legendary king Minos?
4. **Human/Environment Interaction** How did the early people of Crete earn their living?

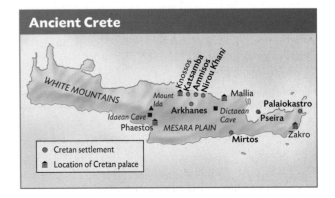

Ancient Crete

WHITE MOUNTAINS
Mount Ida
Idaean Cave
Phaestos
Knossos
Katsamba
Amnisos
Nirou Khani
Arkhanes
MESARA PLAIN
Mallia
Dictaean Cave
Mirtos
Palaiokastro
Pseira
Zakro

● Cretan settlement
🏛 Location of Cretan palace

Chapter

5

750–150 B.C.

The Height of Greek Civilization

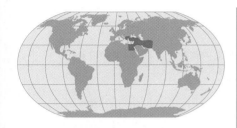

Chapter Themes

▶ **Innovation** The ancient Greeks develop a culture that becomes one of the foundations of Western civilization. *Section 1*

▶ **Innovation** Ancient Greek thinkers believe in reason and the importance of the individual. *Section 2*

▶ **Cultural Diffusion** Alexander's empire brings about a mix of Greek and Middle Eastern cultures. *Section 3*

The Storyteller

An outwardly unimpressive man, Socrates was nonetheless an intellectual giant in the Athens of the late 400s B.C. One of his devoted followers described Socrates' day: "At early morning he was to be seen betaking himself to one of the promenades or wrestling grounds; at noon he would appear with the gathering crowds in the marketplace; and as day declined, wherever the largest throng might be encountered, there was he to be found, talking for the most part, while anyone who chose might stop and listen." Socrates was a supreme questioner who succeeded in getting people to analyze their own behavior. Today, Socrates' reputation lives on as one of the greatest teachers of all time.

Historical Significance

What were the principal beliefs and values of the ancient Greeks? How did their achievements in art, philosophy, history, and science shape the growth of Western civilization?

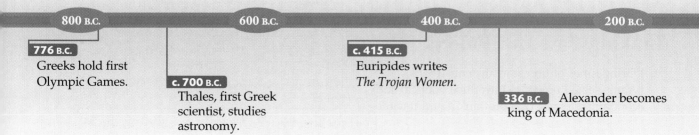

800 B.C.	600 B.C.	400 B.C.	200 B.C.

776 B.C.
Greeks hold first Olympic Games.

c. 700 B.C.
Thales, first Greek scientist, studies astronomy.

c. 415 B.C.
Euripides writes *The Trojan Women*.

336 B.C. Alexander becomes king of Macedonia.

History & Art Actors preparing for a performance, a mosaic from the House of the Tragic Poet, Pompeii. National Museum, Naples, Italy

Your History Journal

The word thespian, *meaning "actor," derives from the Greek dramatist Thespis. Many Greek innovations in staging productions are still used today. Research the history of early Greek drama. Write a comparison with modern theater.*

600 B.C.   500 B.C.   400 B.C.

c. 600 B.C.
Greeks perform
the earliest plays.

459 B.C. Aeschylus
writes the *Oresteia*.

432 B.C. Athenians
finish building the
Parthenon.

Section 1

Quest for Beauty and Meaning

Setting the Scene

▶ **Terms to Define**
classical, sanctuary, perspective, amphora, tragedy, comedy

▶ **People to Meet**
Myron, Phidias, Praxiteles, Aeschylus, Sophocles, Euripides, Aristophanes

▶ **Places to Locate**
Olympia

Find Out How did the Greeks express their love of beauty and meaning?

The Storyteller

An early Greek actor remembers performing in his first tragedy: "I put on the robe of Zeus for the prologue, a lovely thing, purple worked with golden oak leaves.... The next thing I remember is sitting enthroned down center on the god-walk, eagle on left fist, scepter in right hand ... and all the eyes of Athens skinning me to the bone." The actor felt as though he had sleepwalked into the scene. Gripped by fear, he tried to remember his lines: "My father would die of shame.... He was twice the artist I am. At once my lines came back to me. I started my speech...."

Vase depicting actors preparing for a play

—adapted from *The Mask of Apollo*, Mary Renault, 1974

During the mid-400s B.C., Greek civilization reached its cultural peak, particularly in the city-state of Athens. This period of brilliant cultural achievement has been called ancient Greece's Golden Age. Artists of the Golden Age excelled in architecture, sculpture, and painting. They created works characterized by beautiful simplicity and graceful balance, an artistic style now called classical.

Classical Greek art, copied soon after in Roman artistic styles, set lasting standards of beauty still admired today. The writers and thinkers of ancient Greece also made enduring achievements in literature and drama, creating works read through the centuries and still considered classics today. Many cultural traditions of Western civilization—the civilization of Europe and those parts of the world influenced by Europeans—began with Greece's Golden Age.

Building for the Gods

The Greeks, wrote the Athenian leader Pericles, were "lovers of the beautiful." Each Greek city-state tried to turn its acropolis into an architectural treasure.

The Parthenon—the temple to Athena built on the summit of the Acropolis in Athens—best exemplified classical Greek architecture. It was begun in 447 B.C. and finished in 432 B.C., under the rule of Pericles. Because the Greeks worshiped either in their homes or at outdoor altars, they did not need large sanctuaries, or places of worship. Instead, they built temples as places where their deities would live.

The Parthenon has an ingeniously simple design. It is a rectangle surrounded by 46 fluted columns. At the same time, the Parthenon is extremely beautiful. In the right light, because of

Visualizing History An ancient Greek krater (vase) illustrates a scene from Odysseus and the Sirens. *What kinds of vases did the Greeks decorate with scenes from mythology?*

iron in its white marble, the Parthenon gleams a soft gold against the blue sky.

The Parthenon's graceful proportions perfectly balance width, length, and height. To the Greeks the Parthenon represented the ideal of "nothing to excess," an ideal sometimes called the Golden Mean, or the midpoint between two extremes.

The architects of the Parthenon also understood optical illusions and perspective, or the artistic showing of distances between objects as they appear to the eye. Thus, they made the temple's columns thicker in the middle and thinner at the top so that the columns appeared straight when viewed from a distance. The steps leading up to the Parthenon, actually lower in the center than at either end, likewise appear straight. The Athenians wanted to create the impression of perfection—and they succeeded.

Greek Arts

The Greek love of beauty was expressed in the fine arts as well as in architecture. In both painting and sculpture, the Greeks—because they emphasized the individual—excelled at portraying the human form.

Painting on Vases

Although the Greeks painted murals, as had the Minoans, no originals have survived. We know of Greek murals only from written descriptions or Roman copies. But today we can still see examples of their work in the paintings on Greek vases.

The Greeks designed their pottery with different shapes that were suited for different functions. For example, Greek potters gave the *krater*—a small two-handled vase—a wide mouth in which it was easy to mix wine with water. On the other hand, they gave the *leythos* a narrow neck so that oil could be poured out slowly and in small quantities.

Most Greek pottery remaining from the classical period is either red on a black background or black on a red background. The varied subjects of the paintings depended on the size and use of the vase. Potters usually decorated an amphora—a large vase for storing oil and other bulk supplies—with scenes from mythology. In contrast, a *kylix*—a wide, shallow two-handled drinking cup—showed scenes of everyday life: children attending school, shoemakers and carpenters plying their trades, a farmer guiding the plow behind a team of oxen, a merchant ship braving the winds. Greek potters skillfully adapted their designs and decorations to the curves and shape of the vase.

Sculpting the Human Body

Greek sculpture, like Greek architecture, reached its height in Athens during the time of Pericles. **Myron**, one of the greatest sculptors of Greece's Golden Age, portrayed in his statues idealized views of what people *should* look like rather than actual persons. When Myron sculpted his *Discus Thrower* poised to hurl the discus, he carved the lines of the body to indicate an athlete's excellent physical condition as well as his mental control over what he was doing.

The great sculptor **Phidias** (FIH•dee•uhs) was in charge of the Parthenon's sculptures. Phidias himself carved the towering statue of Athena that was placed inside the Parthenon. The statue, made of gold and ivory plates attached to a wooden framework, showed the goddess in her warlike aspect, carrying a shield, spear, and helmet.

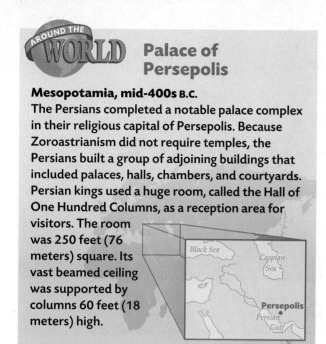

AROUND THE WORLD

Palace of Persepolis

Mesopotamia, mid-400s B.C.
The Persians completed a notable palace complex in their religious capital of Persepolis. Because Zoroastrianism did not require temples, the Persians built a group of adjoining buildings that included palaces, halls, chambers, and courtyards. Persian kings used a huge room, called the Hall of One Hundred Columns, as a reception area for visitors. The room was 250 feet (76 meters) square. Its vast beamed ceiling was supported by columns 60 feet (18 meters) high.

A hundred years after the Golden Age of Athens, the work of another famous Greek sculptor—**Praxiteles** (prak•SIH•tuhl•EEZ)—reflected the changes that had occurred in Greek life. The sculptures of Myron and Phidias had been full of power and striving for perfection, as befitted a people who had defeated the mighty Persian Empire. By the time of Praxiteles, the Greeks had suffered through the Peloponnesian War and had lost their self-confidence. Accordingly, Praxiteles and his colleagues favored life-sized statues rather than massive works. They emphasized grace rather than power. The sculptors of the Golden Age had carved only deities and heroes, but the sculptors of the 300s B.C. carved ordinary people too.

Drama and Theater

The Greeks also explored the human condition through theatrical dramas. They were the first people to write and perform plays, which they presented twice a year at festivals to honor Dionysus, the god of wine and fertility.

Aeschylus

The earliest Greek plays were tragedies. In a tragedy, the lead character struggles against fate only to be doomed—after much suffering—to an unhappy, or tragic, ending. **Aeschylus** (EHS•kuh•luhs), the first of the great writers of tragedies in the 400s B.C., wrote 90 plays. Seven have survived. His *Oresteia* is a trilogy—a set of three plays with a related theme—and is famous for the grandeur of its language.

The *Oresteia* shows how the consequences of one's deeds are carried down from generation to generation. The first play in the trilogy tells about the return of King Agamemnon from the Trojan War and his murder by his wife Clytemnestra in revenge for Agamemnon's sacrifice of their daughter Iphigenia before the Greeks sailed for Troy. The second play describes how Agamemnon's son Orestes in turn avenges his father's death by killing his mother. The third play has Orestes standing trial in Athens for his bloody deed. When the jury splits six to six, the goddess Athena intervenes and casts the deciding vote in favor of mercy. The moral of the trilogy is that the law of the community, not personal revenge, should decide punishment.

Sophocles

The next great tragedian, **Sophocles** (SAH•fuh•KLEEZ), had served as a general in the Athenian army and had lived through most of the Peloponnesian War. Sophocles accepted human suffering as an unavoidable part of life. At the same time, he stressed human courage and compassion.

In one of his most famous plays, *Oedipus Rex*, Sophocles deals with the plight of Oedipus, a king who is doomed by the deities to kill his father and marry his mother. Despite Oedipus's efforts to avoid his fate, the deities' decree comes true. When Oedipus discovers what he has done, he blinds himself in despair and goes into exile.

Euripides

The last of the three great Greek tragedians—**Euripides** (yu•RIH•puh•DEEZ)—rarely dealt with the influence of the gods and goddesses on human lives. Instead, he focused on the qualities human beings possess that bring disaster on themselves.

Euripides also hated war, and many of his 19 surviving plays show the misery war brings. In *The Trojan Women*, the Trojan princess Cassandra explains why the Greeks, despite their victory, are not better off than the Trojans:

❝ And when [the Greeks] came to the banks
   of the Scamander those thousands died.
   And why?
   No man has moved their landmarks or
   laid siege to their high-walled towns.
   But those whom war took never saw their
   children.
   No wife with gentle hands shrouded them
   for their grave.
   They lie in a strange land. And in their

Fulvio Rizzo

Liberto Perugi

Greek Soldier

A Greek warrior, sculpted in bronze, gazes at the world with a determined stare. For more than 1,500 years, the soldier rested under the waters of the Mediterranean Sea. Then in 1972 an Italian chemist from Rome, diving off the coast of southern Italy, found this statue and a companion bronze of an older Greek soldier. The statues were probably lost at sea en route to Rome—perhaps thrown overboard to lighten a storm-tossed ship. Rescued by divers (upper left) and carefully restored, the statues now stand guard in an Italian museum.

The Greeks began casting statues in bronze in the mid-500s B.C. Within a century ancient Greek civilization entered its Golden Age, the era in which Plato (427–347 B.C.) and Aristotle (384–322 B.C.) laid the foundations of Western philosophy; Sophocles (495–405 B.C.) wrote tragedies; Thucydides (471–c. 400 B.C.) recorded Greek history; and Phidias of Athens (500–431 B.C.) created statues—perhaps even these rare examples. It was an age in which sculptors created new modes of artistic expression and began to depict the human body with precision. ⊕

Chapter 5 *The Height of Greek Civilization* **133**

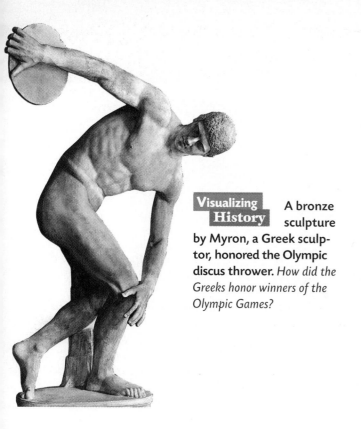

A bronze sculpture by Myron, a Greek sculptor, honored the Olympic discus thrower. *How did the Greeks honor winners of the Olympic Games?*

about issues of his day. In his play *The Clouds*, Aristophanes had a character named Strepsiades ask where Athens was on a map. When the polis's location was pointed out to him, Strepsiades replied: "Don't be ridiculous, that can't be Athens, for I can't see even a single law court in session."

The Olympic Games

Believing that healthy bodies made the best use of nature's gifts, the ancient Greeks stressed athletics in their school curriculum. Greek men who could afford the leisure time usually spent all or part of their afternoons practicing sports in their polis's gymnasiums.

The ancient Greeks held the Olympic Games—their best-known sporting event—in **Olympia** every four years. Because the Olympic Games were a religious festival in honor of Zeus, trading and fighting stopped while they were going on. The Greek calendar began with the supposed date of the first Olympic Games: 776 B.C.

Athletes came from all over the Greek-speaking world to compete in the Olympics. Only male athletes, however, were allowed to take part, and women were not permitted even as spectators. Games that honored the goddess Hera were held at a different location than Olympia and gave Greek women an opportunity to participate in races.

In line with the Greek emphasis on the individual, Olympic competition took the form of individual rather than team events. These consisted at first of only a footrace. Later other events—the broad jump, the discus throw, boxing, and wrestling—were added. An activity called the pentathlon (pehn•TATH•luhn) combined running, jumping, throwing the discus, wrestling, and hurling the javelin.

The Greeks crowned Olympic winners with wreaths of olive leaves and held parades in their honor. Some city-states even excused outstanding athletes from paying taxes.

homes are sorrows, too, the very same.
Lonely women who died, old men who
waited for sons that never came—no
son left to them to make the offering at
their graves.
That was the glorious victory they won. 〞

——Euripides, from his tragedy
The Trojan Women, c. 415 B.C.

A Comedy Tonight

Eventually the Greeks also wrote comedies, plays with humorous themes and happy endings. **Aristophanes** (ar•uh•STAH•fuh•NEEZ), the most famous writer of comedies, created imaginative social satire. In his works he made witty comments about leading figures—such as Euripides—and

---

SECTION 1 REVIEW

Recall
1. **Define** classical, sanctuary, perspective, amphora, tragedy, comedy.
2. **Identify** Myron, Phidias, Praxiteles, Aeschylus, Sophocles, Euripides, Aristophanes.
3. **Describe** how worship of Greek deities influenced architecture, art, and athletics.

Critical Thinking
4. **Applying Information** Show how the Greek emphasis on the individual was demonstrated both in the Olympic Games and in the fine arts.

Understanding Themes
5. **Innovation** How was the ancient Greeks' emphasis on reason and individuality revealed in their arts? Cite examples from architecture, sculpture, and drama.

c. 500s B.C.
Pythagoras develops mathematical theories.

435 B.C.
Herodotus writes history of the Persian Wars.

399 B.C.
Athenians try Socrates for treason.

335 B.C.
Aristotle opens the Lyceum in Athens.

Section 2

The Greek Mind

Setting the Scene

▶ **Terms to Define**
philosopher, logic, hygiene

▶ **People to Meet**
Sophists, Socrates, Plato, Aristotle, Herodotus, Thucydides, Thales, Pythagoras, Hippocrates

Find Out What did the ancient Greeks achieve in philosophy, history, and science?

The Storyteller

Socrates was on trial for his life, for crimes against religion and for corrupting the youth of Athens. He spoke in his own defense: "I have done nothing but try to persuade you all, young and old, not to be concerned with body or property first, but to care chiefly about improvement of the soul. I tell you that virtue does not come from money, but that money comes from virtue, as does every other good of man, public and private. This is my teaching, and if this corrupts the youth, then I am a mischievous person. O men of Athens, either acquit me or convict me; but whichever you do, understand that I shall never alter my ways, not even if I have to die many times."

—adapted from
The Apology of Socrates, Plato

Socrates

The Greeks believed the human mind capable of understanding everything. As a result, the **philosophers**, or thinkers, of ancient Greece produced some of the most remarkable ideas the world has ever known. Through philosophy—which means "the seeking of wisdom"—they laid the foundations for such disciplines as history, political science, biology, and **logic**, or the science of reasoning.

The Sophists

In the 400s B.C. higher education was provided by professional teachers known as **Sophists**. Although Sophists traveled from polis to polis, many gathered in Athens, possibly for the freedom of speech allowed there. Sophists, meaning "knowers," claimed that they could find the answers to all questions.

Many Sophists rejected the belief that the gods and goddesses influenced human behavior. They also did not believe in absolute moral and legal standards. Instead, they asserted that "man is the measure of all things" and that truth is different for each individual.

Not only did Sophists challenge certain traditional Greek beliefs, they also took money for their teaching. Many of them seemed most intent on teaching young men how to win a political argument and get ahead in the world. Many Greeks, including two of Greece's greatest philosophers—**Socrates** (SAH•kruh•TEEZ) and his pupil **Plato**—criticized the Sophists severely.

Socrates

Socrates was born to a poor Athenian family in 470 B.C. Athough a sculptor by trade, he spent most of his time teaching. Unlike the Sophists, Socrates believed in absolute rather than relative truth. His main interest did not lie in teaching rhetoric or in imparting information. Rather, Socrates was attracted to the process by which people learned how to think for themselves.

To encourage his students to clear away mistaken ideas and discover the truth, Socrates developed a teaching technique known as the Socratic method. He would ask students pointed questions without giving them answers and then oppose the students' answers with clear logical arguments. Through this method, he forced his students to defend their statements and to clarify their thinking. For example, in discussing the topic of justice, Socrates proceeded as follows:

> 66 Socrates: Does falsehood then exist among mankind?
> Euthydemus: It does assuredly.
> Socrates: Under which head [justice or injustice] shall we place it?
> Euthydemus: Under injustice, certainly.
> Socrates: Well then … if a father, when his son requires medicine, and refuses to take it, should deceive him, and give him the medicine as ordinary food, and, by adopting such deception, should restore him to health, under which head must we place such an act of deceit?
> Euthydemus: It appears to me that we must place it under [justice].… I retract what I said before. 99
>
> —Xenophon, from *Memorabilia*, early 300s B.C.

Some prominent Athenians viewed Socrates' teachings as a threat to the polis. In 399 B.C. they accused him of "corrupting the young" and of "not worshiping the gods worshiped by the state" and had him brought to trial.

Socrates argued in his own defense that a person who *knew* what was right would always *do* what was right and that the intellectual search for truth was the most important thing in the world. "A man who is good for anything ought not to calculate the chance of living or dying; he ought only to consider whether … he is doing right or wrong."

Despite Socrates' eloquence, a jury of citizens found him guilty and sentenced him to death. Although Socrates had the right to ask for a lesser penalty, such as exile, he refused to do so. He had lived his life under the laws of his polis, and he would not avoid obeying them now.

Socrates carried out the sentence of his fellow citizens himself. He drank poisonous hemlock juice and died quietly among his grieving followers.

Plato

Born an Athenian aristocrat, Plato thought at first of entering politics. However, after Socrates' death, Plato—at age 30—became a teacher and opened his Academy, a school that remained in existence until A.D. 529.

From memory Plato recorded dialogues, or conversations, between Socrates and fellow Athenians, and he also wrote the earliest book on political science, *The Republic*. In this book, he presented a plan for what he considered would be the ideal society and government.

Plato disliked Athenian democracy and preferred the government of Sparta. He gave more importance to the state than to the individual. Like the Spartans, he believed that each person should place service to the community above strictly personal goals. Plato also believed that the result of people having too much freedom is social disorder. He distrusted the lower classes and wanted only the most intelligent and best-educated citizens to participate in government. As he explained in *The Republic*:

> 66 Until philosophers are kings, or the kings and princes of this world have the spirit and power of philosophy, and political greatness and wisdom meet in one, and those commoner natures who pursue either to the exclusion of the other are compelled to stand aside, cities will never have rest from their evils, no, nor the human race. 99

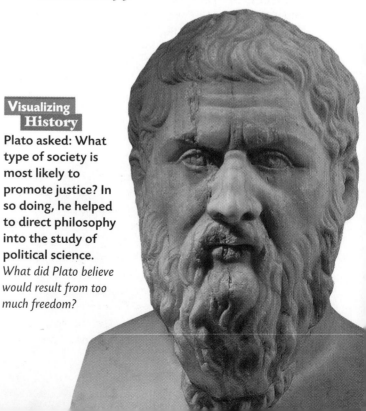

Visualizing History

Plato asked: What type of society is most likely to promote justice? In so doing, he helped to direct philosophy into the study of political science. *What did Plato believe would result from too much freedom?*

Plato's political views were part of an all-embracing philosophy by which he tried to search for "truth." Plato rejected the senses—seeing, hearing, touch, smell, and taste—as a source of truth, believing that the many things that could be perceived by these senses were only "appearance." Reality, the "real" world, was constructed from ideas, or ideal "forms," which could be understood through logical thought and reasoning.

Aristotle

The third great philosopher of ancient Greece was **Aristotle** (AR•uh•STAH•tuhl), who had studied with Plato at the Academy for 20 years. Aristotle then tutored the young Alexander of Macedonia, who later would be known as Alexander the Great. In 335 B.C. Aristotle opened a school in Athens called the Lyceum. Besides teaching, he wrote or edited more than 200 books on topics ranging from astronomy to poetry and from political science to the weather. Because of Aristotle's wide range of knowledge, the Italian poet Dante later called him "the master of those who know."

Aristotle influenced later philosophers with his work on logic. He developed the syllogism, a means for presenting an argument in such a way that one can determine whether or not the conclusion follows logically from the premises, or basic statements.

Aristotle and Science

Aristotle also influenced scientific work. He was the first person to observe facts, then classify them according to their similarities and their differences, and finally develop generalizations from his data. Some of his specific beliefs—notably, that Earth is the center of our solar system—were incorrect. Aristotle's views and his method of inquiry, however, would continue to dominate European scientific thinking for centuries.

Aristotle and Government

Many of Aristotle's writings were focused on political science. Unlike Plato, he did not theorize about idealized principles of government. Instead, he examined the political structure of various city-states, analyzing their advantages and disadvantages. Only then did he spell out his conclusions in a book called *Politics*. Aristotle believed that democracies, oligarchies, and tyrannies are all workable, depending on circumstances. He preferred, however, to have power rest with the middle class, because they knew both how to command *and* obey.

Writers of History

The Greeks also used their intellectual skills in writing history. Until the 400s B.C. the Greeks had considered literary legends as history. **Herodotus** (hih•RAH•duh•tus), the first Greek historian, decided to separate fact from legend. Historians still consider him "the father of history."

Herodotus

Herodotus chose as his subject the Persian Wars and called his work the *Historia*, or "investigation." Herodotus traveled throughout the Persian Empire and also visited many Greek colonies. Everywhere he went, he asked questions, recorded answers, and checked the reliability of his sources. However, he accepted some statements that were not true, especially exaggerated numbers—such as how many Persians died at Marathon. He also sometimes offered supernatural explanations of events.

Herodotus did not limit himself to describing military and political events. He also wrote about outstanding individuals, social customs, and religious beliefs and practices. Later historians have learned a great deal from the *Historia* about the culture of the period and about the civilizations that Herodotus visited.

Thucydides

The second noted historian of ancient Greece, **Thucydides** (thoo•SIH•duh•DEEZ), wrote about the Peloponnesian War. Thucydides is regarded as the first scientific historian because he completely rejected the idea that the deities played a part in human history. Only human beings make history, Thucydides said. He also was as accurate and impartial as possible. He visited battle sites, carefully examined documents, and accepted only the evidence of actual eyewitnesses to events.

Footnotes to History

The Atom
The Greek thinker Democritus came up with the idea of a solid particle of matter so small that it was both invisible and not divisible. He named this particle *atom*, meaning "invisible." Today scientists know that atoms are in fact divisible and include many separate and smaller types of matter. But the basic idea of atomic physics can be traced back to Democritus.

Greek physicians observed the many symptoms of disease and concluded that illnesses are not caused by evil spirits, but have natural causes. *What three prescriptions for health did Hippocrates suggest?*

guish mathematics as a pure science apart from everyday practical uses. They constructed systematic methods of reasoning to prove the truth of mathematical statements. Through the study of mathematics, Greek thinkers believed that they could find absolutely certain and eternal knowledge.

The first prominent Greek scientist was **Thales** (THAY•leez) of Miletus, a Greek city-state in Ionia. Born in the mid-600s B.C., Thales studied astronomy at Babylon and mathematics in Egypt and could foretell a solar eclipse. He also formulated a theory that water was the basic substance of which everything in the world is made.

During the 500s B.C., **Pythagoras** (puh •THA•guh•ruhs) tried to explain everything in mathematical terms. He explored the nature of numbers, especially whole numbers and their ratios. Students of geometry still learn the Pythagorean theorem about the relationship of sides of a right-angled triangle. Pythagoras also taught that the world was round and revolved around a fixed point.

Thucydides did not simply recite facts, however. He also offered explanations for why events took place and what motivated political leaders. He believed that future generations could learn from the past.

The First Scientists

The ancient Greeks passed on a great scientific heritage. They believed that the world is ruled by natural laws and that human beings can discover these laws by using reason. Lacking scientific equipment, the Greek scientists made most of their discoveries by observation and thought. They then went on to develop general theories or statements about the workings of nature.

Greek Mathematicians

The Greeks became the first people to distin-

Greek Medicine

Greek scientists also contributed to the field of medicine. Called "the father of medicine," the physician **Hippocrates** (hih•PAH•kruh•TEEZ) believed that diseases had natural, not supernatural, causes and that the body could heal itself. He was the first doctor to view medicine as a science separate from religious beliefs or mythological explanations.

Basing his work in the late 400s B.C. on observation, he traveled all over Greece diagnosing illnesses and treating sick people. He urged fellow doctors to keep records of their cases and to exchange information with one another. He strongly advocated proper *hygiene*, or health care, a sound diet, and plenty of rest.

According to tradition, Hippocrates drafted a code for ethical medical conduct that has guided the practice of medicine for more than 2,000 years. Many doctors today recite the Hippocratic oath when they receive their medical degree.

Recall
1. **Define** philosopher, logic, hygiene.
2. **Identify** Sophists, Socrates, Plato, Aristotle, Herodotus, Thucydides, Thales, Pythagoras, Hippocrates.

3. **Explain** how Plato, Socrates, and Aristotle were related as philosophers. •
Critical Thinking
4. **Making Comparisons** Compare the political views of Plato and Aristotle and their

attitudes regarding observations made through the senses.
Understanding Themes
5. **Innovation** How did Socrates and Hippocrates each contribute to the intellectual life of ancient Greece?

Finding Exact Location on a Map

Your new friend invites you to her house. In giving directions, she says, "I live at the northwest corner of Vine Street and Oak Avenue." She has pinpointed her exact location. We use a similar system to identify the exact location of any place on Earth.

Learning the Skill

Over many centuries, cartographers developed a grid system of imaginary lines—the lines of latitude and lines of longitude. Lines of latitude run east and west around the earth. Because they always remain the same distance from each other, they are also called parallels. The parallel lines of latitude measure distance north and south of the Equator, located at 0° latitude. Each line of latitude is one degree, or 69 miles (110 km), from the next. There are 90 latitude lines between the Equator and each Pole. For example, New York City lies 41° north of the Equator, or 41° N.

Lines of longitude, or meridians, run north and south from Pole to Pole. Unlike lines of latitude, lines of longitude are not always the same distance from each other. Lines of longitude are farthest apart at the Equator and intersect at each Pole. Longitude measures distance east and west of the Prime Meridian, located at 0° longitude. That line runs through Greenwich, England, in western Europe and through western Africa. Longitude lines increase east and west of the Prime Meridian to 180°. This meridian runs through the Pacific Ocean. New York City, for example, lies 74° west of the Prime Meridian, or 74° W.

With this system, we can pinpoint the "grid address" of any place on Earth. On a map, find the nearest line of latitude to the designated place. Then follow along this line until it crosses the nearest line of longitude. The point where the lines intersect is the grid address. For example, New York City has this grid address: 41° N, 74° W.

Practicing the Skill

Use the map below to answer the following questions:
1. What is the approximate grid address of Babylon?
2. What city is located at approximately 31° N, 30° E?
3. What is the approximate grid address of Nineveh?
4. What is the approximate grid address of Tyre?

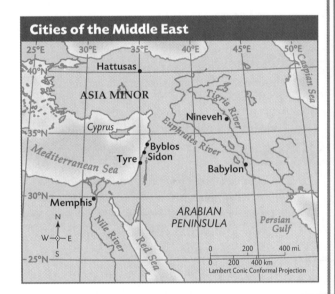

Applying the Skill

Create a travel itinerary for a tour of the ruins of ancient Egypt, Greece, or the Middle East. Choose at least 10 locations you would like to visit. Draw a map of the region, including grid lines. On the map, identify the approximate grid location of each place.

For More Practice

Turn to the Skill Practice in the Chapter Review on page 151 for more practice in finding exact location on a map.

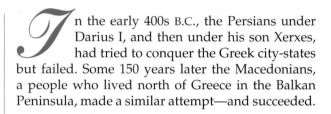

400 B.C.	300 B.C.	200 B.C.	100 B.C.

359 B.C. Philip II becomes king of Macedonia.

331 B.C. Alexander the Great defeats the Persians in the battle of Gaugamela.

250 B.C. Jewish scholars translate the Hebrew Bible into Greek.

c. 100 B.C. Roman Empire begins to conquer the Hellenistic world.

Section 3

Alexander's Empire

Setting the Scene

▶ **Terms to Define**
domain

▶ **People to Meet**
Philip II, Demosthenes, Alexander the Great, Zeno, Menander, Eratosthenes, Euclid, Archimedes

▶ **Places to Locate**
Macedonia, Alexandria

Find Out ▶ What were Alexander's goals for his empire, and how successful was he in achieving them?

The Storyteller

Hellenistic poets who lived in bustling cities loved to tell simple fables about love in a country-side setting:

*A bee once stung the god of love [Cupid]
as he was stealing honey.
His fingertips began to smart,
and he blew upon his hand,
stamped and danced.
When he showed his wound to his mother,
she laughed. "Aren't you just like the bee,
so small, yet inflict-
ing great pain?"*

—adapted from *The Idylls of Theocritus,* (no. 19, "The Honey-Thief"), in *Greek Pastoral Poetry,* Anthony Holden, 1974

Cupid, wall painting, Pompeii, Italy

In the early 400s B.C., the Persians under Darius I, and then under his son Xerxes, had tried to conquer the Greek city-states but failed. Some 150 years later the Macedonians, a people who lived north of Greece in the Balkan Peninsula, made a similar attempt—and succeeded.

Rise of Macedonia

The Macedonians, like the Spartans, were descended from the Dorians, and the Macedonian language incorporated many Greek words. The Greeks, however, looked down on the Macedonians as backward mountaineers.

In 359 B.C. **Philip II** became king of **Macedonia**. During his youth he had been a hostage for three years in the Greek city-state of Thebes. There he had learned to admire both Greek culture and military organization. As king, Philip determined to do three things: create a strong standing army, unify the quarreling Greek city-states under Macedonian rule, and destroy the Persian Empire.

Philip increased his army's fighting power by organizing his infantry into Greek-style phalanxes. Arrayed in close formation 16 rows deep, Philip's lance-bearing foot soldiers fought as a single unit.

For the next 23 years, Philip pursued his ambition. Sometimes he conquered a polis or bribed a polis's leaders to surrender. Sometimes he allied a polis through marriage; Philip had a total of six or seven wives.

The Greek city-states, weakened by the Peloponnesian War, would not cooperate in resisting Philip. The great Athenian orator **Demosthenes** (dih•MAHS•thuh•NEEZ) appealed to his fellow citizens to fight for their liberty. But Demosthenes' words were to no avail. By 338 B.C. Philip had conquered all of Greece except Sparta.

Philip then announced that he would lead the Greeks and Macedonians in a war against Persia. But in 336 B.C., just as he was ready to carry out his

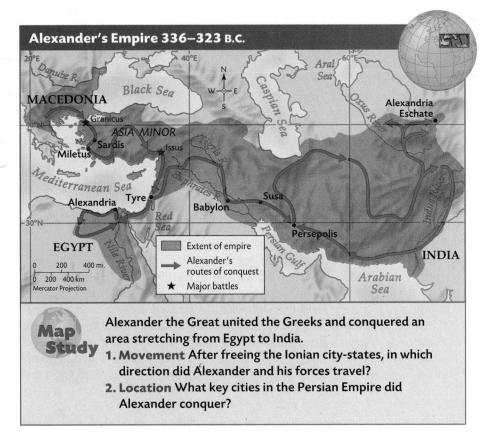

Alexander's Empire 336–323 B.C.

Extent of empire

Alexander's routes of conquest

★ Major battles

Map Study

Alexander the Great united the Greeks and conquered an area stretching from Egypt to India.

1. **Movement** After freeing the Ionian city-states, in which direction did Alexander and his forces travel?
2. **Location** What key cities in the Persian Empire did Alexander conquer?

plans, Philip was murdered—either by a Persian agent or by an assassin hired by his first wife, Olympias. Olympias's son Alexander, later known as **Alexander the Great**, became king.

Alexander the Great

Alexander was only 20 when he became the ruler of Macedonia and Greece. A commander in the Macedonian army since he was 16, Alexander was highly respected by his soldiers for his courage and military skill. He was also extremely well educated, for his father had him tutored by Aristotle for four years.

Early Conquests

In 334 B.C. Alexander led 30,000 soldiers and 5,000 cavalry into Asia to open his campaign of "West against East." The first major encounter with the Persians took place at the Granicus River in western Asia Minor. Alexander's forces won, and he sent 300 suits of Persian armor to Athens as an offering to the goddess Athena. He then marched along the coast of Asia Minor, freeing the Ionian city-states from Persian rule.

The second major battle between the Greeks and Persians took place in 333 B.C. at Issus, Syria. Once again, Alexander's superb tactics resulted in victory, forcing the Persian king Darius III to flee.

Instead of pursuing Darius, Alexander and his troops moved south along the Mediterranean coast. First they captured the seaports of Phoenicia and cut off the Persian fleet from its main supply bases. The fleet soon surrendered. Next, turning west, they invaded Egypt where the people, discontented under Persian rule, welcomed them and declared Alexander a pharaoh. In Egypt, Alexander established a new city and named it **Alexandria** after himself.

Final Campaigns

In 331 B.C. Alexander again turned his attention eastward. He invaded Mesopotamia and smashed Darius's main army in the battle of Gaugamela near the Tigris River. He went on to capture the key cities of the Persian Empire: Babylon, Persepolis, and Susa. When Darius was killed by one of his own

Alexander the Great

generals, Alexander declared himself ruler of the Persian Empire.

Even this success was not enough for the young conqueror. In 327 B.C. he led his soldiers into India, and after three years they reached the Indus River valley. Alexander hoped to go farther yet, but his Macedonian veterans refused. Alexander therefore reluctantly turned around and went to Babylon, which he had made the capital of his empire. But the hardships of the journey had undermined his health, and he fell ill with a fever, probably malaria. In 323 B.C. Alexander the Great died at the age of 33.

Imperial Goals

When Alexander first set out with his army, his goal was to punish Persia for its invasion of Greece 150 years earlier. But as more and more territory came under his control, Alexander's views changed. His new vision was to create an empire that would unite Europe and Asia and combine the best of Greek and Persian cultures.

Alexander tried to promote this goal by example. He wore Persian dress and imitated the court life of Persian kings. He married a daughter of Darius III and encouraged 10,000 of his soldiers to marry Persian women. He enrolled 30,000 Persians in his army. He also founded about 70 cities that served both as military outposts and as centers for spreading the Greek language and culture throughout his empire.

Divided Domain

Following Alexander's death, three of his generals—Ptolemy (TAH•luh•mee), Seleucus (suh•LOO•kuhs), and Antigonus (an•TIH•guh•nuhs)—eventually divided his vast empire into separate domains, or territories. Ptolemy and his descendants ruled Egypt, Libya, and part of Syria. The most famous Ptolemaic ruler was Cleopatra VII, who lost her kingdom to the Romans in 31 B.C.

Images *of the* Times

The Hellenistic Age

Hellenistic culture blended mythology with real live heroes.

The Greeks retold tales of mythological figures on pottery. This scene shows the god of wine, Dionysus, in a boat.

Bronze statuette of Hellenistic dancer, said to be from Alexandria.

This Pompeiian mosaic honors Alexander the Great, who extended his empire to the Indus River valley.

Seleucus and his descendants—the Seleucids (suh•LOO•suhds)—at first controlled the rest of Syria, as well as Mesopotamia, Iran, and Afghanistan. After a while, however, they were forced to give up their eastern territory and withdraw to Syria. In 167 B.C. Jewish guerrillas led by Judah Maccabees challenged the Seleucid control of Palestine. The Seleucid Antiochus IV had ordered the Jews to worship the Greek deities, but many Jews refused to abandon their religion. In 165 B.C. Judah Maccabees succeeded in reoccupying Jerusalem and rededicating the Temple, an event commemorated by the Jewish festival of Hanukkah. The kingdom of Judah would remain independent until its defeat by Rome in 63 B.C. The Seleucids likewise ruled in Syria until the Romans came.

The domain of Antigonus and his heirs consisted at first of Macedonia and Greece. But the Greek city-states soon declared their independence and once again began fighting with each other. In the 100s B.C., the growing Roman Empire would conquer Macedonia and Greece.

Hellenistic Culture

The political unity of Alexander's empire disappeared with his death, but the Greek language and culture continued to spread and flourish in the lands he had conquered. There, Hellenic ways of life mixed with elements of Middle Eastern culture to form a new culture, called Hellenistic.

City Life

Hellenistic culture was concentrated in cities. The largest and wealthiest of these was Alexandria in Egypt. Alexandria's straight streets intersected each other at right angles, in contrast to the crooked streets of older cities. Its white stucco stone palaces and temples gleamed brilliantly in the sun.

The city's economic position benefited from a double harbor that could hold 1,200 ships at a time. Another asset to trade was the city's lighthouse, which was visible from 35 miles (56 km) out at sea.

Alexandria also was a major intellectual center. Its museum was the first ever and included a

Woman and servant, a Hellenistic funerary stela from Kerameikos cemetery.

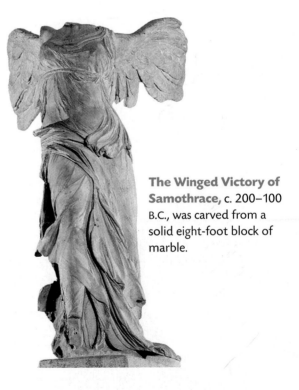

The Winged Victory of Samothrace, c. 200–100 B.C., was carved from a solid eight-foot block of marble.

REFLECTING ON THE TIMES

1. How did Greek pottery promote popular myths?
2. What was the easternmost border of Alexander's empire?

library of nearly a million volumes, an institute for scientific research, a zoo, and a botanical garden. Scientists came from all over the Hellenistic world. Around 250 B.C. Jewish scholars in Alexandria translated the Hebrew Bible into Greek. This translation, known as the Septuagint (sehp•TOO •uh•juhnt), was later used by the apostle Paul and is still used in the Eastern Orthodox Church.

During Hellenic times, the Greeks had been intensely involved with their particular polis. In Hellenistic society, however, the Greeks formed the upper class of Alexandria and other cities in the Middle East and Asia Minor that were ruled by kings. Rather than being loyal to their king or kingdom, professional Greek soldiers and bureaucrats moved from place to place, wherever job opportunities were best.

In Alexandria and other Hellenistic cities, the social status of upper-class Greek women improved over their traditional status in Athens. No longer secluded, women could move about freely. They learned how to read and write and entered such occupations as real estate, banking, and government. Such opportunities were not, however, available to commoners.

Hellenistic Philosophers

Hellenistic philosophers focused on personal behavior, especially the question of how to achieve peace of mind. Three systems of thought attracted most Hellenistic intellectuals: Cynicism, Epicureanism (EH•pih•kyu•REE•uh•NIH•zuhm), and Stoicism.

The best known Cynic was Diogenes (dy•AH •juh•NEEZ). He criticized materialism and asserted that people would be happy if they gave up luxuries and lived simply, in accord with nature. The scholar Epicurus started the philosophy of Epicureanism. He argued that people should avoid both joy and pain by accepting the world as it was, ignoring politics, and living simply and quietly with a few close friends.

Zeno founded Stoicism. The name *Stoicism* comes from the *Stoa Poikile*, or "painted porch," in which Zeno lectured. The Stoics believed that what happened to people was governed by natural laws. Accordingly, people could gain happiness by ignoring their emotions, and instead following their reason. In this way, they were able to accept even the most difficult circumstances of life and do their duty. Stoicism later affected both Roman intellectuals and early Christian thinkers.

CONNECTIONS

Economics

An Economic Region

Coin bearing the face of Alexander the Great

Geographers, historians, and economists often divide the world into regions based on physical features, political characteristics, or economic factors, such as trade routes and uniform currency. The empire of Alexander the Great came to be one economic region.

International sea trade expanded greatly under Alexander's empire and its successor domains. The Ptolemies, in particular, began using the monsoons to sail directly across the Indian Ocean between Africa and Asia instead of hugging the coast. As a result, luxury items from India and Arabia became common in Mediterranean cities.

An increase in public works projects also spread throughout the empire. Alexander and his successors used the vast sums of gold and silver captured in Persia to finance road construction and harbor development.

A uniform currency held Alexander's empire together economically. Before Alexander, the Greek city-states, Egypt, and Persia all had coined their own money. Alexander circulated a coin bearing his profile, which merchants could use everywhere.

After Alexander's death, his empire divided into rival kingdoms. The people in the overall geographic area, however, still enjoyed a common culture. Extensive trade routes also helped to maintain close economic links among the cities built by Alexander.

MAKING THE CONNECTION

1. List three regional economic characteristics of Alexander's empire.
2. What are the boundaries of the region in which you live?

Hellenistic Art and Literature

During the Hellenistic era, artists departed from Hellenic styles. Instead of carving idealized individuals, Hellenistic sculptors showed people in the grip of powerful emotions. They also carved portrait heads, because art had become a business.

Hellenistic playwrights usually wrote comedies rather than tragedies. Like Hellenistic philosophers, they ignored the problems of the outside world as much as possible. **Menander**, the most renowned Hellenistic playwright, specialized in comedies about everyday life. Well-known lines from his works include "Whom the gods love die young" and "We live not as we will, but as we can."

Science, Medicine, and Mathematics

Although limited by their simple instruments, Hellenistic scientists performed many experiments and formed new theories. Aristarchus (AR•uh•STAHR•kuhs) of Samos concluded that the sun is larger than the earth, that the earth revolves around the sun, and that the stars lie at immense distances from both. **Eratosthenes** (EHR•uh•TAHS•thuh•NEEZ) estimated the earth's circumference to within 1 percent of the correct figure. Hellenistic doctors dissected corpses in order to learn more about human anatomy. They discovered the nervous system, studied the brain and the liver, and learned how to use drugs to relieve pain.

The Hellenistic period also saw great developments in mathematics and physics. **Euclid** of Alexandria wrote *The Elements of Geometry*, a book that organized all information about geometry. **Archimedes** (AHR•kuh•MEE•deez) invented the compound pulley, which moves heavy objects easily, and the cylinder-screw, which is still used to lift water for irrigation. He also discovered the principle of buoyancy and demonstrated the principle of the lever.

SECTION 3 REVIEW

Recall
1. **Define** domain.
2. **Identify** Philip II, Demosthenes, Alexander the Great, Zeno, Menander, Eratosthenes, Euclid, Archimedes.
3. **Locate** Macedonia and Alexandria on the map on page 141. What does Alexandria owe to the Macedonians?

Critical Thinking
4. **Making Comparisons** Compare and contrast Alexander the Great's original goal and the goal he finally chose for his empire. Why did his goals change?

Understanding Themes
5. **Cultural Diffusion** Explain how and why Hellenistic arts differed from Hellenic arts.

6

750 B.C.–A.D. 500
Ancient Rome and Early Christianity

Chapter Themes

▶ **Change** The Roman political system evolves as Rome allows more of its people to participate in government. *Section 1*
▶ **Conflict** Roman armies conquer most of the Mediterranean world. *Section 2*
▶ **Cultural Diffusion** The Romans build an empire and spread Latin culture. *Section 3*
▶ **Innovation** Christianity becomes the dominant religion in the West. *Section 4*
▶ **Change** Germanic invasions and cultural weaknesses destroy the Roman Empire. *Section 5*

𝒮toryteller

War trumpets rang over the cheers of the people of Rome who gathered to view the triumphal grand parade. Then sweating horses jerking at their harnesses rattled the victor's chariot over the paving stones, and the people's cries became louder. On this day in 146 B.C., the Romans were celebrating their conquest of the last of the free Greek city-states.

Ironically, however, over the next several centuries Greek culture would come to form the base of Roman culture and society. Texts written by Greeks would shape Roman knowledge in many areas of study. Even after years of Roman rule, the eastern Mediterranean world would retain Greek as its primary language.

Historical Significance

How did the small city-state of Rome become the center of a vast, diverse empire that spanned the Mediterranean world? What were Rome's last legacies to Europe, Africa, the Middle East, and other parts of the world?

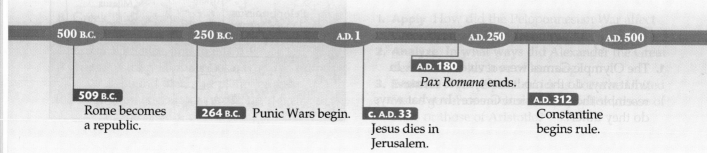

500 B.C.	250 B.C.	A.D. 1	A.D. 250	A.D. 500

509 B.C.
Rome becomes a republic.

264 B.C. Punic Wars begin.

c. A.D. 33
Jesus dies in Jerusalem.

A.D. 180
Pax Romana ends.

A.D. 312
Constantine begins rule.

Woman playing the cithera, painted on the east wall of a room in
the villa of Publius Fannius Synistor, Pompeii, Italy

Your History Journal

The European cities of Bonn, Vienna,
London, and Paris were each founded by
the Romans. Research the early history of
one of these cities and describe the Roman
influence on its early architecture and
lifestyle.

c. 753 B.C.
Romulus
founds Rome.

c. 620 B.C.
Etruscans
gain control
of Rome.

451 B.C.
The patricians of
Rome enact the
Twelve Tables.

287 B.C.
The plebeians
begin to make
laws for Rome.

Section 1

The Roman Republic

Setting the Scene

▶ **Terms to Define**
patrician, republic, plebeian, consul, dictator, tribune

▶ **People to Meet**
the Etruscans, the Latins, Romulus, the Tarquins

▶ **Places to Locate**
Italy, Sicily, Rome

 How was Rome governed as a republic? How did the Roman Republic change over the years?

The Storyteller

The city of Rome was besieged by Lars Porsena, king of Clusium, and the time had come for decisive action. One young Roman hoped to break the siege by killing Porsena. After laying his plan before the Senate, he set out alone toward enemy lines. However, he was seized as a spy and dragged by guards before the very man he had hoped to kill—Porsena. He spoke boldly: "I am a Roman, my name is Gaius Mucius. I came here to kill you—my enemy. I have as much courage to die as to kill. It is our Roman way to do and to suffer bravely."

The Forum

—adapted from *Early History of Rome,* Titus Livy, in *The Global Experience, Readings in World History to 1500,* 1987

The peoples of **Italy** first came into contact with the Greeks around 900 B.C., when Greek traders sailed up both the east and west coasts of the Italian Peninsula. From about 750 B.C. to 500 B.C., the Greeks set up farming communities in southern Italy and in **Sicily,** an island southwest of the Italian Peninsula. These Greek colonists planted olive trees for the oil yielded and grapevines from which they could produce wine, thus introducing these two major products to Italy. The Greeks also introduced the Greek alphabet to the Italians.

The Italian Peninsula

The Greeks were interested in colonizing Italy for several reasons, one of which was Italy's central location in the Mediterranean. A narrow, boot-shaped peninsula, Italy extends from Europe toward the shores of Africa, dividing the Mediterranean almost in half. Thus, Italy was ideally situated to be the center of trade among three continents: Asia, Europe, and Africa. Italy's rich soil and mild, moist climate also attracted the Greek colonists. Beyond the mountains and foothills that covered three-quarters of the peninsula lay plains with soil enriched by the silt deposits of mountain streams.

However, the silt washing down Italy's short and shallow rivers blocked the mouths of many rivers, creating mosquito-infested swamps. The people of Italy suffered recurrent epidemics of malaria and other diseases carried by mosquitoes.

Because of Italy's mountains, the early inhabitants of the peninsula generally traded among themselves. Italy's only land connection—to the north—was cut off by the Alps. Furthermore, Italy's rocky and marshy coastline lacked good harbors. To increase trade, the Italians eventually turned to the sea, but until that time came, they remained attached to the land.

Early Peoples

Archaeological evidence suggests that people lived in Italy long before the Greeks arrived or Roman civilization began. The remains of human settlements reveal that Neolithic cultures may have begun to form in Italy as early as about 5000 B.C. Early peoples in the Italian Peninsula built villages and farms, moving on whenever they had exhausted the land around their settlements.

Indo-Europeans

Between 2000 B.C. and 1000 B.C., waves of Indo-European immigrants arrived and overwhelmed these Neolithic peoples. By the time Greek colonists came to Italy, many peoples inhabited the peninsula—including Umbrians in the north, Latins in the central plain called Latium (LAY•shee•uhm), and Oscans in the south. Like the Greeks, most of these people spoke Indo-European languages.

The Etruscans

The most mysterious of the early peoples were **the Etruscans** who, from about 900 B.C. to 500 B.C., ruled northern Italy from the plains of Etruria. No one knows definitely where the Etruscans came from. They did not, at any rate, speak an Indo-European language as did many of the inhabitants of the peninsula. Although Etruscans wrote in an alphabet borrowed from the Greeks, modern scholars have been able to decipher only a few Etruscan words.

Although Etruscan writings still baffle our understanding, Etruscan art is expressive, needing no translation. In wall paintings, Etruscan figures dance and play music, enjoying a rich and pleasant life. In Etruscan sculpture, men and women feast and converse, triumphant soldiers revel in their victories, and hauntingly beautiful deities smile and gesture.

Such sculptures ornamented the homes of the Etruscan upper classes. Historians believe that Etruscan society probably consisted of wealthy overlords, aristocratic priests, and a slave labor force made up of conquered peoples. Wealthy overlords enslaved these peoples to provide themselves with comforts, and aristocratic priests sacrificed prisoners of war or forced them to duel to the death to appease angry gods.

After repeated revolts, the Etruscan lower classes and the other Italian peoples under Etruscan rule finally freed themselves from

CONNECTIONS The Arts

Etruscan Culture

Etruscan tomb art

Although archaeologists have unearthed the remains of some Etruscan cities, these tell little about Etruscan culture. Only the many burial chambers that have been uncovered provide clues about the Etruscans.

The murals and sculptures in these tombs depict the daily life of the Etruscans. Many tomb paintings show sports, religious ceremonies, and people enjoying music and feasts. Some tombs have murals that show funeral banquets. In these, the scene on one wall shows banqueters, and on the other walls dancers or musicians.

The many objects in Etruscan tombs—furniture, clothing, jewelry, pottery, and tools—also reveal much about Etruscan culture. Because many of the objects seem Greek or Middle Eastern, the Etruscans probably traded with these peoples. The luxury items also suggest that Etruscan society had a wealthy upper class.

MAKING THE CONNECTION

1. Why are Etruscan tombs so vital in studying ancient Etruria?
2. What conclusions have historians drawn from objects in Etruscan tombs?

domination by these wealthy overlords and priests. Chief among those who overthrew the Etruscans were **the Latins**, whose center was the city of **Rome** in the central plain of Latium.

The Rise of Rome

According to legend, in 753 B.C., a stocky man named **Romulus** was building the wall of a city on a hill overlooking the Tiber River. His twin brother, Remus, came over from the hillside opposite, where he too had been laying the foundations for a city. The Roman historian Livy tells what happened next:

> 66 Remus, by way of jeering at his brother, jumped over the half-built walls of the new settlement, whereupon Romulus killed him in a fit of rage, adding the threat, 'So perish whoever else shall over-leap my battlements.' 99
>
> —Livy, *Ab Urbe Condita*, 29 B.C.

Setting more stone on the stains of his brother's blood, Romulus is said to have continued his building. In time, his namesake city—Rome—grew to include his brother's hill and the other nearby hills. Romulus was so effective a military ruler, the myth tells us, that Rome became the greatest city in that part of the peninsula.

In fact, the origins of Rome were probably much less violent. At some time between 800 B.C. and 700 B.C., the Latins huddled in straw-roofed huts in the villages on the seven hills apparently agreed to join and form one community. It was this community that came to be called Rome.

Etruscan Rule

About 620 B.C. the Etruscans gained control of Rome. A wealthy Etruscan family, **the Tarquins**, provided kings to rule over the Romans. The Tarquins taught the Latins to build with brick and to roof their houses with tile. They drained the marshy lowlands around Rome and laid out city streets. At the center of the city they created a square called the Forum, which became the seat of Roman government. The Tarquins also built temples, taught the Romans many of the Etruscans' religious rituals, and elevated Rome to a position among the wealthiest cities in Italy.

Then in 534 B.C. Tarquin the Proud came to the throne. This king's cruelties so angered the Romans that in 509 B.C. they drove the Tarquins out. Skilled Etruscan artisans stayed on in Rome, however, helping the city continue to prosper.

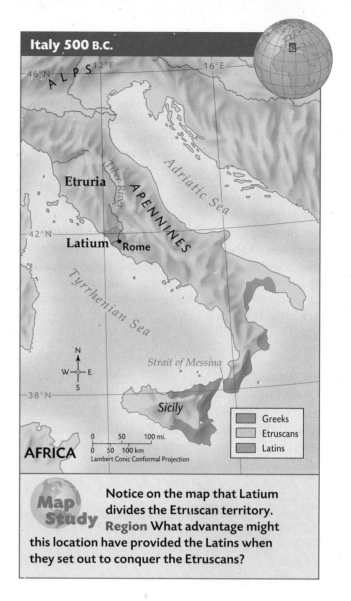

Italy 500 B.C.

Greeks
Etruscans
Latins

Map Study Notice on the map that Latium divides the Etruscan territory. **Region** What advantage might this location have provided the Latins when they set out to conquer the Etruscans?

Social Groups

Under Etruscan rule, a new wealthy aristocratic class had come into being in Rome—Latin nobles called patricians. Once the Etruscan rulers were driven out, the patricians declared Rome a republic, a community in which the people elect their leaders.

Most of Rome's inhabitants, however, were plebeians (plih•BEE•uhns), who included wealthy, nonaristocratic townspeople and landowners as well as merchants, shopkeepers, small farmers, and laborers. As citizens, both the plebeians and the patricians had rights, such as the right to vote, and responsibilities, such as paying taxes and serving in the military. Plebeians, however, could not hold public office as patricians could.

The Roman Republic

The patricians organized Rome's government into executive and legislative branches. Two patrician officials elected for one-year terms headed the executive branch, running the city's day-to-day affairs. These officials were called consuls because they had to consult each other before acting. They understood that either consul could veto the other's decisions. The word *veto* is Latin for "I forbid." The consuls oversaw other executive officials, such as praetors, or judges, and censors, or keepers of tax and population records. Only a dictator, a leader whose word was law, could overrule the consuls. But dictators were temporarily appointed to lead the Romans only in time of crisis.

The Roman legislative branch at first consisted of the Assembly of Centuries and the Senate, both under patrician control. Members of the Assembly of Centuries (named for a military formation of 100 soldiers) elected officials of the executive branch. However, the power of the Senate—a group of 300 patrician men who served for life—outweighed the Assembly of Centuries. The senators advised the consuls, debated foreign policy, proposed laws, and approved contracts for constructing roads, temples, and defenses.

Plebeians Against Patricians

The plebeians resented their lack of power in the new republic—especially because they knew that the patricians could not maintain the republic without them. In 494 B.C., to obtain a greater voice in the government, the plebeians went on strike—at first refusing to serve in the army and then leaving the city altogether to set up a republic of their own.

Tribunes

The patricians, frightened at the loss of their military and work forces, soon agreed to meet some of the plebeians' demands. The patricians agreed to recognize the plebeians' chosen representatives, the tribunes. They also granted tribunes the power to veto any government decision and ensured that they would be protected by law. Tribunes could not be arrested, and any person who dared to injure a tribune could be put to death. The patricians also formally recognized the Assembly of Tribes, the plebeians who elected the tribunes.

Old and New Laws

The plebeians did not stop fighting for their rights after winning these concessions. Until that time, no one had ever put Roman laws into writing—and only the patricians knew what the laws said. As a result, plebeians usually found out about a law only upon being charged with breaking that law. To make sure that judges applied the laws fairly, the plebeians insisted that the government write down the laws.

After decades of struggle, the plebeians in 451 B.C. finally got the patricians to engrave the laws on 12 bronze tablets and to set them in the Forum for all to see. The Twelve Tables, as these tablets were called, became the basis for all future Roman law.

Soon after, plebeians also won the right to serve in some public offices, although few of them could bear the cost of an unsalaried public position. Then, in 287 B.C., plebeians won their greatest success, establishing their right to make laws for the republic in the Assembly of Tribes.

Changes for Plebeians

Other changes followed that improved the status of plebeians. Among these, plebeians were allowed to marry patricians, and failure to pay debts was no longer penalized by slavery. In spite of these benefits for the common people, the republic continued to be dominated by a small group of powerful and wealthy citizens. However, through their struggles the plebeians had moved Rome closer to democracy.

Religion

Early Romans worshiped nature spirits. Under Etruscan influence, they came to think of these spirits as gods and goddesses. They also adopted the practice of foretelling the future. Priests known as soothsayers believed that they could gain knowledge of future events by observing the flight of birds or the intestines of animals.

For almost 500 years, Rome thrived as a republic. During this time, the Romans were influenced by Greek culture. They borrowed Greek deities, giving them Roman names. Aphrodite, the Greek

 **Footnotes to History**

A Roman Dinner Party In ancient Rome, dinner guests of wealthy Romans would recline on couches while slaves served them delicacies. Main course dishes might include boiled stingray garnished with hot raisins; boiled crane with turnips; roast hare in white sauce; leg of boar; wood pigeon baked in a pie; or roast flamingo cooked with dates, onions, honey, and wine.

Visualizing History An Etruscan farmer and his animals, c. 300 B.C. Etruscan literature, music, painting, metalwork, and jewelry were admired by the Romans. *Why did the Romans drive the wealthy Etruscan family, the Tarquins, from the city?*

goddess of love, became the Roman goddess Venus. Ares, the Greek god of war, became Mars. They also made their old gods look Greek, giving the Etruscan god Jupiter the characteristics of the Greek Zeus.

Roman life remained distinctly Roman, however. Families privately worshiped their ancestral spirits and their storeroom guardians, as well as Vesta, goddess of the hearth.

Family

The family was the basic unit of Roman society. Roman households were large and close-knit. They included all unmarried children, married sons and their families, all dependent relatives, and household slaves.

In Roman families the father was absolute head of the household. He conducted the religious ceremonies, controlled property, and supervised the education of his sons. He also had the power to sell family members into slavery, or even kill them. However, fathers also felt a deep sense of responsibility for the welfare of all family members.

Roman wives had few legal rights, but they had more freedom than Greek women. They acted as hostesses for parties, did their marketing, and ran their households with little or no interference. Occasionally, however, they did acquire their own property and businesses. Wealthy women, with slaves to do their work, could study Greek literature, arts, and fashions. Lower-class women spent their time at household tasks and in family-run shops.

Roman children grew up with firm discipline and had to give complete loyalty to their family. In early Rome, parents taught their children reading, writing, and moral standards. Boys were trained by their fathers to be good farmers and soldiers. Mothers taught their daughters how to run households.

Rich or poor, most Romans held the same values: thrift, discipline, self-sacrifice, and devotion to the family and the republic. Long after the Roman Republic ended, nostalgic reformers saw these as traditional Roman values.

SECTION 1 REVIEW

Recall

1. **Define** patrician, republic, plebeian, consul, dictator, tribune.
2. **Identify** the Etruscans, the Latins, Romulus, the Tarquins.

3. **Locate** Etruria, Latium, and Rome on the map on page 156. How were the people of these three places connected?

Critical Thinking

4. **Evaluating Information** How might the struggle between patricians and plebeians have weakened Rome? Give examples to support your case.

Understanding Themes

5. **Change** Why did political change occur in the Roman Republic?

C. 264 B.C. Rome rules the entire Italian Peninsula.

202 B.C. Roman forces defeat Carthage at the battle of Zama.

133 B.C. The reformer Tiberius Gracchus becomes tribune.

44 B.C. Group of senators assassinate Julius Caesar.

Section 2

Expansion and Crisis

Setting the Scene

▶ **Terms to Define**
indemnity, triumvirate

▶ **People to Meet**
Hannibal, Scipio, Tiberius Gracchus, Gaius Gracchus, Marius, Sulla, Julius Caesar, Octavian, Marc Antony

▶ **Places to Locate**
Carthage

 **ind Out** How did economic and social problems bring down the Roman Republic?

The Storyteller

The government of Rome had become cumbersome and corrupt. Maecenas, the richest man in Rome, was about to propose a radical change.

Marc Antony

Called before Mark Anthony, Marcus Lepidus, and Octavian, the most powerful men in Rome, he spoke persuasively. "Ever since we were led outside the peninsula, filling the whole earth with our power, nothing good has been our lot. Our city, like a great ship manned with a crew of every race and lacking a pilot, has been rolling and plunging as it has drifted in a heavy sea." Maecenas looked at his hearers. One of them must assume all authority. Rome had to cease being a republic.

—from Roman History, Dio Cassius, in Readings in Ancient History from Gilgamesh to Diocletian, 1969

From about 500 B.C. to 300 B.C., Rome faced threats from its many neighbors in Italy. To protect their republic, the Romans either conquered these opponents or forced them to ally with Rome. In this way the Romans subdued one rival after another, until by 264 B.C., Rome ruled the entire peninsula.

Roman Legions

Rome's success in war was due to its strong army. In the early days of the republic, every male citizen had to serve in the military when needed. Early Roman armies also used the tactics of Greek phalanx warfare. Roman generals, however, learned that phalanxes were too large and slow to be effective. They reorganized their troops into legions of 6,000 men and divided these further into small, mobile units of 60 to 120 soldiers. With this new organization, the Romans could shatter the phalanxes of their enemies.

Roman soldiers—called legionaries—were well trained, and deserters were punished by death. With such iron discipline, the legionaries would conquer an empire. In a time when victors routinely slaughtered or enslaved whole cities, Rome treated conquered foes remarkably well. Some conquered peoples were allowed to keep their own governments if they helped fight Rome's wars. Rome gave other peoples partial rights, and to some peoples even granted citizenship.

The Romans set up permanent military settlements—called *coloniae*—throughout Italy to defend strategic heights and river crossings. To link these *coloniae*, the legions forged a chain of roads up and down the Italian Peninsula. As war yielded gradually to peace, some of these roads became major trade routes.

Chapter 6 *Ancient Rome and Early Christianity* **159**

Visualizing History Roman legionaries, shown in a colorful mosaic, were well trained. *How did Rome defeat the Carthaginian navy?*

Rome Against Carthage

In Chapter 3 you read how **Carthage** became the Mediterranean area's wealthiest city. To expand their commerce, the Carthaginians had then gone on to conquer the Spanish coast and most of Sicily by about 300 B.C. The Romans decided to check the expansion of the Carthaginians—the *Punici*, as the Romans called them.

The First Punic War

In 264 B.C. Carthage threatened to seize the Strait of Messina, a narrow passage between Sicily and Italy. When the Romans sent a force to secure the strategic waterway, a full-scale war erupted.

The Romans' strong army conquered most of Carthage's colonies in Sicily. However, the Carthaginians lashed out at the Romans with their huge and powerful fleet. For a time this naval superiority gave Carthage the advantage.

Undaunted, the Romans built a larger fleet. In a battle off the African coast, they stunned the Carthaginians with a new tactic. They snared the enemy's ships with grappling hooks, boarded them, and defeated the enemy in hand-to-hand combat. This enabled the Romans to fight on sea as well as they did on land. Thus, they were able to force the Carthaginians to retreat.

The war raged on until 241 B.C., but the Carthaginians never regained control of Sicily or the sea. Threatened with invasion of their homeland, they agreed to hand the Romans a huge indemnity, or payment for damages.

The Second Punic War

In 221 B.C. a young soldier named **Hannibal** became general of the Carthaginian army in Spain. In 218 B.C. Hannibal grabbed one of Rome's allied cities in Spain. His next move was even more audacious—to take the war into Italy itself. Leading 40,000 soldiers and about 40 elephants, he marched out of Spain, crossed southern Gaul, and started up the Alps. His soldiers, however, were terrified by the sight of those chilly heights, and their fears were well-founded. Before they reached Italy, cold, snow, hunger, sickness, and attacks by mountain peoples killed half of Hannibal's army and most of the elephants.

Although outnumbered, Hannibal's troops defeated the Roman armies sent against them. By 216 B.C., in a battle at Cannae in southeastern Italy, Hannibal's soldiers had nearly destroyed the Roman army. But the Romans rallied, refusing to admit defeat, and raised dozens of new volunteer legions. Their general, Publius **Scipio** (POO•blee •uhs SIH•pee•OH), attacked Carthage and forced Hannibal's recall to Africa.

In 202 B.C. Scipio's forces defeated Hannibal's army at Zama, near Carthage. At Scipio's demand, the Carthaginians gave up their lands in Spain, handed over most of their warships, and agreed to another indemnity.

The Third Punic War

After 50 years of peace, Carthage regained its prosperity. Although Carthage was still no threat, Rome decided to end Carthaginian independence. In 146 B.C. the Romans burned Carthage, sold its surviving population into slavery, and sowed salt in its soil so that no crops would grow. This victory gave Rome complete control of the western Mediterranean.

The Republic in Crisis

While Roman armies were fighting the Punic Wars in the west, their forces were also engaged in conflicts in the east. Between 230 B.C. and 130 B.C., Rome brought the eastern Mediterranean area under its rule. Although the Romans left Syria and Egypt independent, they forced the rulers into obedient alliances. With these eastern conquests, the Romans emerged as the undisputed masters of the Mediterranean from Spain to Asia Minor. As a result, they had begun to call the Mediterranean *mare nostrum*—"our sea."

Ruling such a vast territory, however, created considerable difficulties. Political leaders could not readily adapt Rome's form of government—which had been created to meet the needs of a small city-state—to govern these numerous peoples. Political problems led to social and economic upheaval as well.

Exploiting the Provinces

Rome organized its non-Italian territories into provinces that had to pay tribute to Rome and recognize its authority. At first the provinces seemed a source of endless wealth. The Senate-appointed governors, called proconsuls, often accepted bribes and robbed the provincial treasuries. The publicans—officials who collected the taxes—also took money from the provinces. Soon, taking money from the provinces became an accepted way for the rich to become richer.

In response to this treatment, the provinces rebelled. It became necessary to permanently station Roman legions in most provinces. Because putting down revolts cost Rome troops and money, the provinces began to strain Rome's resources. While the people in most provinces adjusted to Rome's rule, the Jews in Palestine stubbornly resisted. The Romans sacked Jerusalem in A.D. 70.

Changing the Countryside

By expanding, the Roman government acquired properties in the provinces. These holdings were rented to wealthy Romans, who joined individual units into large estates called latifundia (LA•tuh•FUHN•dee•uh). Latifundia owners used enslaved people to work the land. Because slave labor was less expensive than paid labor, latifundia owners could produce crops that cost less than those grown by small farmers in Italy. By offering low prices for grain, latifundia owners in the provinces captured the grain market and thus brought great wealth to the provinces.

The latifundia owners also forced small farmers out of business. Then, just as they had done in the provinces, proconsuls and publicans began buying up small farms in Rome to create latifundia. Wisely, rather than try to compete in the grain market against provincial latifundia, these owners devoted their estates to sheep ranching and to raising olives and fruits. Thus, latifundia owners captured these markets too, putting even more farmers out of work.

Visualizing History Rome's legions put down revolts in the provinces, but not without cost. Here, women funeral dancers mourn losses. *Why were the provinces not an endless source of wealth to Rome?*

Crowding the Cities

Landless farmers streamed into Rome, where bread was cheap and public shows were free. In the cities the poor discovered that many jobs were already being done by enslaved people. Angry and without hope, the free poor eked out a living and voted for any leader who promised cheaper food and more amusements. Although often jobless, these people clung proudly to their status as free citizens.

While the urban poor increased in numbers, so too did a new class between the plebeians and the patricians. Made up of people who had obtained wealth in working their latifundia or in business, this new social class took the old title of *equites* (EH •kwuh•TEEZ). The title *equites*, or knights, had once applied to those wealthy enough to ride horses in battle but not noble enough to be patricians. The new *equites* saw more value in wealth than in nobility or character, influencing most Romans to adopt similar values.

Reformers and Generals

Many Romans viewed with dismay the changes brought on by Roman expansion. They feared that the growth of latifundia and the spread of corruption threatened the republic's institutions. They also thought that someone had to help the urban poor before these plebeians toppled the state.

The Gracchi

As grandson of General Scipio, a patrician career lay open to **Tiberius Gracchus**. Instead, he threw in his lot with the plebeians, winning the office of tribune in 133 B.C. As tribune, Tiberius at once proposed a law to limit the size of the latifundia and to redistribute land to the poor. Despite stiff opposition from the patrician Senate, Tiberius passed the law through the plebeian Assembly of Tribes. Opponents organized a riot in which Tiberius and 300 of his followers were killed. His murder, the first political violence in Rome in 400 years, would begin a trend.

Elected tribune a decade later, Tiberius's brother **Gaius** pushed through more reforms. A fiery orator, he persuaded the plebeian Assembly to give more land to farmers. To help the urban poor, he set up a government program to sell grain at low prices. Because the Senate refused to convict corrupt provincial governors, Gaius started a new court with members drawn from the *equites*.

Gaius too met with a violent end. In 121 B.C. he was killed in a riot planned by his enemies. By 111 B.C., the Senate had put a stop to the land reforms.

Marius and Sulla

In 107 B.C. General Gaius **Marius** was elected consul. A reformer, he gave poor people jobs by enlisting them in the army. He paid them money for their service and promised them land when they were discharged. For the first time, Rome had a professional army in which soldiers owed allegiance to their commander, not to the republic.

In 88 B.C. this new army was used against Gaius Marius. General Lucius Cornelius **Sulla** sought to end his dispute with Marius over who should command the army in the east. Sulla persuaded his legions to capture Rome and drive Marius into exile. After seven years of civil war, Sulla appointed himself dictator. He tried to strengthen the Senate and take power away from the Assembly of Tribes. But by then the army had become the most powerful element in Roman politics, and violence overtook law.

Visualizing History Political strife in the period following the murders of the Gracchi gave the young Julius Caesar the opportunity to rise to power. *Why did Caesar's crossing the Rubicon River lead to civil war?*

The First Triumvirate

In 70 B.C. General Gnaeus Pompey (NEE•uhs PAHM•pee) and the politician Marcus Licinius Crassus were elected consuls. They gained the support of **Julius Caesar**, a rising young aristocrat. Then, in 60 B.C., the three formed a triumvirate, a group of three persons with equal power, to control the government. The triumvirate proved to be unstable, however.

Politically ambitious, Caesar took a military command in Gaul, which was inhabited by Indo-Europeans known as Celts (KEHLTS). Caesar conquered the Celts, forcing them to accept Roman rule. He then pushed northward, greatly increasing Rome's landholdings in northwestern Europe and elevating his own status as well.

Meanwhile Crassus, attempting to prove that he too was a great military leader, was killed in battle in 53 B.C. Fearing that Caesar might use his own legions to seize power, Pompey and the Senate then ordered Caesar to leave his legions north of the Rubicon River, the legal border of Roman Italy, and return to Rome. According to legend, however, upon arriving at the Rubicon, Caesar saw a vision that encouraged him to cross, and exclaimed to his troops, "Let us accept this as a sign from the gods, and follow where they beckon, in vengeance on our double-dealing enemies. The die is cast."

By crossing the Rubicon, Caesar officially committed treason and started civil war. Within two months he had captured all of Italy and driven Pompey and his allies out of the country. The fighting eventually spread to the entire Mediterranean region, with Caesar finally overwhelming Pompey's armies.

Julius Caesar

In 45 B.C. Caesar took over the government as dictator for life, to rule very much like a monarch. Under his leadership, the government gave jobs to the unemployed, public land to the poor, and citizenship to many people in the provinces. Caesar also added representatives from the provinces to the Senate. Finally, Caesar adopted a new calendar based on the Egyptian year of $365\frac{1}{4}$ days. This calendar was called Julian in honor of Caesar. It was used in western Europe until early modern times.

Many Romans believed that Caesar was a wise ruler who had brought order and peace back to Rome. Others, however, considered him to be a tyrant who meant to end the republic and make himself king. To prevent this, on March 15, 44 B.C., a group of senators led by Marcus Brutus and Gaius Cassius assassinated Caesar as he entered the Senate.

End of the Republic

After the death of Julius Caesar, his 18-year-old grandnephew **Octavian** joined forces with **Marc Antony** and Marcus Lepidus, two of Caesar's top government officers. Together this second triumvirate defeated Caesar's assassins in 42 B.C. Then, while keeping up the appearance of republican government, these three generals divided the Roman world among themselves. Octavian took command in Italy and the west, Antony ruled in Greece and the east, and Lepidus took charge of North Africa.

The second triumvirate did not last long, however. Octavian forced Lepidus to retire from political life. When Antony married Cleopatra, the queen of Egypt, Octavian persuaded the Romans that Antony intended to rule them with his foreign queen by his side, and so Octavian declared war on Antony in Rome's name. In 31 B.C. Octavian scattered the forces of his enemies in a critical naval battle at Actium in Greece. A year later, to evade capture by Octavian, Antony and Cleopatra committed suicide in Egypt. With Antony dead, Octavian became the undisputed ruler of Rome.

SECTION 2 REVIEW

Recall
1. **Define** indemnity, triumvirate.
2. **Identify** Hannibal, Scipio, Tiberius Gracchus, Gaius Gracchus, Marius, Sulla, Julius Caesar, Octavian, Marc Antony.
3. **Locate** Carthage and Gaul on the map on page 165. What was the importance of each place in the military history of the Roman Republic?

Critical Thinking
4. **Making Comparisons** Compare the events that started the First and Third Punic Wars. Why might one war be called justified and the other unjustified?

Understanding Themes
5. **Conflict** Explain how Roman conquests overseas affected Rome's development.

| A.D. 1 | A.D. 50 | A.D. 100 | A.D. 150 | A.D. 200 |

A.D. 14
Augustus Caesar dies.

A.D. 79
Volcanic eruption
destroys Pompeii.

A.D. 96 Rule of the
Good Emperors begins.

A.D. 180
Pax Romana ends.

Section 3

The Roman Empire

Setting the Scene

▶ **Terms to Define**
aqueduct

▶ **People to Meet**
Augustus, Tiberius, Claudius, Nero, Marcus
Aurelius, Galen, Ptolemy, Virgil, Livy

▶ **Places to Locate**
Appian Way

 **ind Out** What was life like in the Roman
Empire during the *Pax Romana*?

The Storyteller

*The visitor, Aelius Aristides, an educated and
well-travelled man, had never seen anything to
rival Rome. And it was not just the city—it was
everything that Rome represented: military might,
sensible government, and an elegant lifestyle.
Who could help but admire an empire that commanded vast territories and diverse peoples, a military that conquered both armed forces and selfish
ambition, a government where officials ruled not
through arbitrary power but by law. Romans
"measured out the world, bridged rivers, cut
roads through mountains, filled the wastes with
posting stations, introduced orderly and refined
modes of life." They
were, he declared,
natural rulers.*

Augustus
Caesar

—adapted from
*Oration on the Pax
Romana,* Aelius
Aristides, reprinted
in *Sources of the
Western Tradition,*
Marvin Perry, 1991

Under the Roman Republic, laws had
proven too weak to control social
changes, while generals had taken
power away from elected officials. Thus, Octavian
believed that Rome needed one strong leader. The
Senate agreed and appointed Octavian consul, tribune, and commander in chief for life in 27 B.C.
Octavian gave himself the title *Augustus*, or
"Majestic One."

The First Emperors

Augustus claimed to support the republic, but
he actually laid the foundation for a new state
called the Roman Empire. In practice, he became
Rome's first emperor, or absolute ruler.

Augustus Caesar

In the 40 years of his reign—from 27 B.C. to A.D.
14—Augustus rebuilt the city of Rome and became
a great patron of the arts. He also introduced many
reforms to the empire. Proconsuls could no longer
exploit the provinces. Publican tax collectors were
replaced with permanent government employees.
Grain was imported from North Africa so that all in
Rome would be fed. New roads were built and old
ones repaired. Magnificent public buildings were
constructed throughout the empire. Augustus
boasted that he had "found Rome a city of brick
and left it a city of marble."

In 31 B.C. there began the *Pax Romana*, or
Roman Peace, which lasted about 200 years. The
only major disturbances during those years
occurred when new emperors came to power. For,
although Augustus chose his own successor carefully, he failed to devise any law for the selection of
later emperors.

The Julian Emperors

Historians call the four emperors who ruled
from A.D. 14 to A.D. 68 the Julians because each was

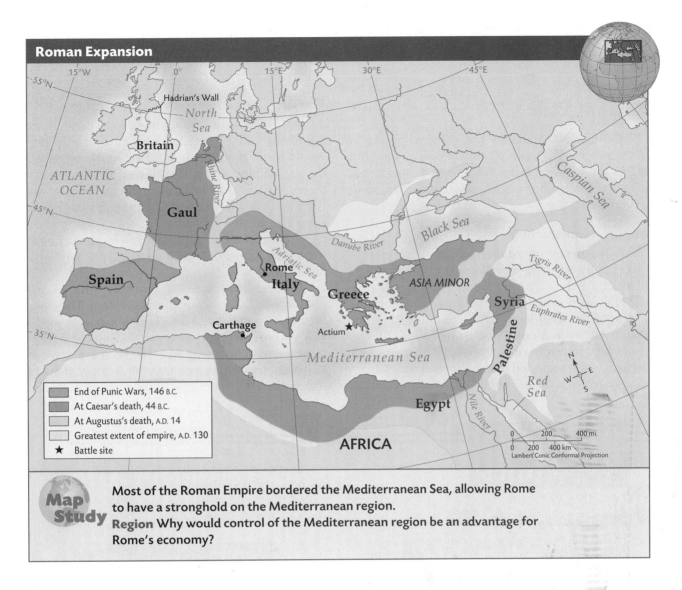

North Sea

Hadrian's Wall

Britain

ATLANTIC OCEAN

Gaul

Rhine River

Spain

Rome
Italy

Adriatic Sea

Danube River

Black Sea

Caspian Sea

Tigris River

ASIA MINOR

Greece

Syria

Euphrates River

Palestine

Carthage

Actium

Mediterranean Sea

Red Sea

Egypt

Nile River

AFRICA

Legend:
- End of Punic Wars, 146 B.C.
- At Caesar's death, 44 B.C.
- At Augustus's death, A.D. 14
- Greatest extent of empire, A.D. 130
- ★ Battle site

0   200   400 mi.
0 200 400 km
Lambert Conic Conformal Projection

Map Study
Most of the Roman Empire bordered the Mediterranean Sea, allowing Rome to have a stronghold on the Mediterranean region.
Region Why would control of the Mediterranean region be an advantage for Rome's economy?

related in some way to Julius Caesar. Each showed promise when he became emperor, but later revealed great faults.

Augustus's adopted son **Tiberius**, who succeeded Augustus Caesar as emperor, spoiled his able leadership by accusing many innocent people of treason against him. Caligula, Tiberius's grandnephew and successor in A.D. 37, became mentally disturbed and was killed by a palace guard in A.D. 41. Caligula's uncle, **Claudius**, was a renowned scholar, but as he grew older he had difficulty focusing on affairs of state.

Nero, Claudius's stepson, who became emperor in A.D. 54, was cruel and probably insane. Nero was willing to bankrupt Rome to pay for his twin pleasures—horse racing and music. Suspecting others of plotting against him, he killed his wife and his mother and executed many senators. In A.D. 68 the Senate sentenced Nero to death for treason. Before he committed suicide, reportedly he cried, "What a loss I shall be to the arts!"

The Good Emperors

For 28 years following Nero's death, Rome was governed by a number of emperors who were backed by the army. Then, in A.D. 96 the Senate chose its own candidate for emperor: Nerva. Historians consider Nerva the first of the so-called Good Emperors; the others were Trajan, Hadrian, Antoninus Pius, and **Marcus Aurelius** (aw•REE •lee•uhs). The Good Emperors were known for their skills as effective administrators and their support of large building projects.

The Emperor Trajan, who succeeded Nerva, increased the empire to its greatest size. Hadrian then strengthened Rome's fortifications along the frontiers. Antoninus Pius succeeded him, maintaining the empire's prosperity. The philosopher-ruler Marcus Aurelius brought the empire to the height of its economic prosperity. All of these Good Emperors lived by the principle of Stoic philosophy best expressed by Marcus Aurelius in *Meditations*: "Every moment think steadily as a Roman and a human being how to do what you have in hand with perfect and simple dignity."

Roman Rule

By the time Augustus had come to power in 27 B.C., between 70 and 100 million people were living in the Roman Empire. To rule so many people effectively, Augustus had to make many changes in government.

Imperial Government

Augustus improved the working of the empire by carefully choosing professional governors rather than letting the Senate appoint inexperienced proconsuls every year. In some provinces, such as Judea, he left local kings in charge under his command. Augustus ordered new roads built so that he could keep in touch with all parts of the empire, and he personally inspected the provinces frequently.

Augustus also dignified his own position by serving as *pontifex maximus*, or chief priest of Rome. Thus he and each later emperor became the head of a national, unifying religion.

The Law

As the Romans won more provinces, they found that they needed a new kind of law that would apply to noncitizens. They therefore created the *jus gentium*, or law that dealt with noncitizens, as opposed to the *jus civile*, or citizen law. By the early A.D. 200s, however, emperors had granted citizenship to the peoples of so many nearby provinces that all free males in the empire had been made full citizens of Rome, and the two laws became one.

In their laws Romans generally stressed the authority of the state over the individual. They also accorded people definite legal rights, one of which was that an accused person should be considered innocent until proven guilty. The Roman system of law has formed the basis for the legal systems of many Western nations and of the Christian Church.

Images *of the* Times

Pompeii, A.D. 79

On August 23-25, A.D. 79, the volcano Vesuvius erupted in southern Italy. The city of Pompeii was buried in a single day.

A detail from the Villa of the Mysteries shows that life for many in Pompeii offered many comforts and pleasures.

An Imperial Army

Augustus and later emperors maintained the professional army. As conditions became more peaceful, however, Augustus reduced the number of legions and supplemented this fighting force with troops recruited from the provincial peoples. Even with forces combined, the emperor could count on having only about 300,000 troops, which was not enough to defend a border with a length of about 4,000 miles (6,440 km). Therefore, by A.D. 160, invasions by peoples outside the empire had become a continuing problem.

Roman Civilization

From about 31 B.C. to A.D. 180, the Roman world enjoyed a period of prosperity known as the *Pax Romana*, or Roman Peace. The stability of the *Pax Romana* boosted trade, raised standards of living, and generated many achievements in the arts. The Latin author Tertullian described this time:

> " Everywhere roads are built, every district is known, every country is open to commerce … the [fields] are planted; the marshes drained. There are now as many cities as there were once solitary cottages…. Wherever there is a trace of life, there are houses and human habitations, well-ordered governments, and civilized life. "
>
> —Tertullian, *Concerning the Soul*, c. A.D. 180

The Empire's Economy

Tertullian's description of economic growth under the empire was not exaggerated. In the first century A.D., artisans in Italy made pottery, woven cloth, blown glass, and jewelry for sale throughout the empire. The provinces in turn sent to Italy luxury items, such as silk cloth and spices, gathered in trade with China, India, and Southeast Asian countries. Dockworkers at Rome's harbor, Ostia, unloaded raw materials such as tin from Britain,

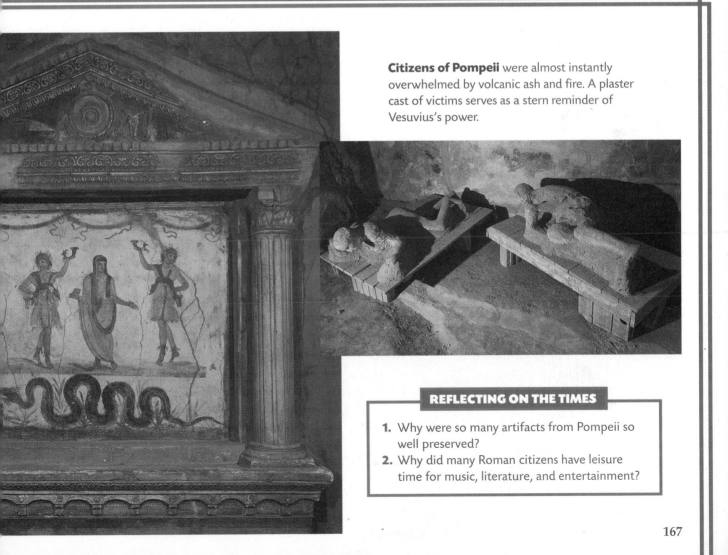

Citizens of Pompeii were almost instantly overwhelmed by volcanic ash and fire. A plaster cast of victims serves as a stern reminder of Vesuvius's power.

REFLECTING ON THE TIMES

1. Why were so many artifacts from Pompeii so well preserved?
2. Why did many Roman citizens have leisure time for music, literature, and entertainment?

iron from Gaul, and lead from Spain. Soon skillful Greek traders within the empire were doing business in distant areas, such as eastern Africa, Southeast Asia, and China.

Life During the *Pax Romana*

These economic changes brought changes in lifestyles. The family gradually became less significant than it had been during the republic. Romans had fewer children and were likely to divorce and remarry several times. Fathers lost some of the absolute power they had during the republic, and wives gained some legal rights. Society became less stable. Patricians might go bankrupt, *equites* might take a place in the Senate, and a poor man might even make a fortune in manufacturing.

Within each class, a consistent pattern of life formed. The wealthy often held public office, owned large farms outside the cities, ran factories, or directed trading firms. They lived comfortably in luxurious homes with marble walls, mosaic floors, running water, and baths.

The prosperity of the *Pax Romana* sometimes reached people of average means—shopkeepers and artisans. Although fewer people became very rich, more became moderately well off. The majority in Rome, however, were still poor. There were no private baths for them; instead they bathed at crowded public areas built under Augustus and later emperors. Most Romans lived in flimsy wooden apartment buildings of six or seven stories that readily collapsed or caught fire.

Public Amusements

Despite these trying conditions, the poor did not rebel against the government, because it offered them both free bread and free entertainment. By A.D. 160, Romans were celebrating 130 holidays a year. On some days, teams of charioteers competed in races in the Circus Maximus, an arena seating more than 150,000. On other holidays, crowds could watch gladiators fight each other to the death or battle wild animals in stadiums like the Colosseum.

Architecture, Engineering, and Science

The Romans erected many impressive buildings during the *Pax Romana* besides the Circus Maximus and the Colosseum. Between A.D. 118 and A.D. 128, Hadrian rebuilt the Pantheon, a temple for all the deities, with a soaring dome and a huge skylight. To build the Pantheon, the Romans mixed concrete—a new building material—with various kinds of stone.

The Romans also excelled in road building. The first major Roman road was the **Appian Way**. Constructed in the 300s B.C., it connected Rome and southeastern Italy. During the *Pax Romana*, a network of roads was built to link Rome with the provinces. Reaching a total length of 50,000 miles (80,000 km), the road network contributed to the empire's unity.

As they constructed public buildings and a vast network of roads, the Romans engineered aqueducts, or artificial channels for carrying water.

Visualizing History Entertainment at the giant arena Circus Maximus, depicted in this bas-relief, was free to Roman citizens. *What new building material did the Romans use to construct the Pantheon?*

© Sonia Halliday Photographs

Roman Forum

The ruins of the Roman Forum are a major tourist attraction of modern Rome. In ancient times, the Forum was the center of both politics and commerce. The Forum contained a number of separate buildings: In the foreground the Temple of Castor and Pollux, built in the 400s B.C., honored Roman gods. Behind is the Arch of Titus, the ruler whose military victory is enshrined in the arch built about A.D 70. Beyond the Arch stand the walls of the Colosseum. The largest amphitheater built in ancient Rome, the Colosseum took a decade to construct and could seat 50,000. Here the Romans watched gladiators battle lions and later vanquish Christians.

The rise of the Roman state began with the city of Rome itself hundreds of years before the birth of Christ. Slowly the Romans consolidated control over Italy and built a great army. By 200 B.C. Rome had become a vast empire. Power brought wealth and great monuments such as these in the Forum. ⊕

These lofty arches built out of stone enabled water to flow into Rome from as far away as 57 miles (about 92 km). One Roman-built aqueduct in Segovia, Spain, was so well constructed that it is still used today—nearly 1,900 years after it was completed.

The Romans excelled at adapting the discoveries of others and using them in new and more practical ways. They made use of the Etruscan arch and dome to build aqueducts and the Pantheon, and borrowed the Greek design for columns to support porches built around city squares.

Roman scientists also relied upon information that had been gathered from other cultures. The medical ideas of the ancient world compiled by the Greek physician **Galen** formed the basis of Roman medical science. Likewise, the observations of the Egyptian astronomer **Ptolemy** formed the foundation of Roman astronomy. Galen's works influenced medical science for many centuries, and Ptolemy's work made it possible for later astronomers to predict with accuracy the motion of the planets.

Roman Education

The Romans studied their borrowed knowledge avidly. Wealthy boys and girls received private lessons at home. Young men from wealthy families went on to academies—where former Greek slaves often taught—to learn geometry, astronomy, philosophy, and oratory. The daughters of the wealthy did not attend academies. Many upper-class women continued to study at home, however, and often became as well educated as Roman men. People in the lower classes usually had at least the basic knowledge of reading, writing, and arithmetic they needed to conduct business.

Language and Literature

Latin, Rome's official language, had a vocabulary far smaller than that of Greek or modern English; thus, many words expressed several meanings. Nevertheless, Latin remained the *lingua franca*, or common language, of Europe as late as the A.D. 1500s. Latin also forms the basis of the so-called Romance languages, such as Italian, French, Spanish, Portuguese, and Romanian, and supplies the roots for more than half of English words.

Although Romans learned from Greek literature, during the reign of Augustus Latin literature achieved an elegance and power of its own. Cicero, a Roman senator, published beautifully written speeches. Ovid wrote the *Metamorphoses*, a collection of verses based on Greek mythology. Horace, a poet, wrote about the shortness of life and the rewards of companionship. Horace's friend **Virgil** wrote the *Aeneid*, an epic poem comparable to those of Homer. In one passage of this poem, Virgil expresses both the humility and pride of Romans:

    " Others, no doubt, will better mould the bronze
      To the semblance of soft breathing, draw, from marble,
      The living countenance; and others plead
      With greater eloquence, or learn to measure,
      Better than we, the pathways of the heaven,
      The risings of the stars: remember, Roman,
      To rule the people under law, to establish
      The way of peace, to battle down the haughty,
      To spare the meek. Our fine arts, these, forever. **"**

           —Virgil, the *Aeneid*, c. 20 B.C.

Livy, a later writer, wrote a monumental history of Rome that glorified the early Romans. The historian Tacitus, on the other hand, condemned the tyranny of the Julian emperors with subtle but scathing irony. In *Germania*, Tacitus contrasted the robust life of the Germans with what he felt was the weak and pleasure-loving life of the Romans.

SECTION 3 REVIEW

Recall
1. **Define** aqueduct.
2. **Identify** Augustus, *Pax Romana*, Tiberius, Claudius, Nero, Marcus Aurelius, Galen, Ptolemy, Virgil, Livy.
3. **Use** the map on page 165 to identify Roman expansion. When did the empire reach its greatest extent?

Critical Thinking
4. **Synthesizing Information** The expression "bread and circuses" has been used to describe hasty measures taken by a government to prevent discontent among the poor. Explain whether you believe this expression applies to any aspects of life in the modern United States. If so, to what aspects does it apply?

Understanding Themes
5. **Cultural Diffusion** List some of the advantages and disadvantages to a province of adopting Roman culture.

A.D. 1	A.D. 150	A.D. 300	A.D. 450

c. A.D. 30
Jesus preaches in Palestine.

A.D. 70 Jews in Palestine unsuccessfully revolt against Roman rule.

A.D. 312
Constantine becomes Roman emperor.

A.D. 392
Christianity becomes Rome's official religion.

Section 4

The Rise of Christianity

Setting the Scene

▶ **Terms to Define**

sect, messiah, disciple, martyr, bishop, patriarch, pope

▶ **People to Meet**

Jesus, Paul, Peter, Constantine, Theodosius, Augustine

 **Find Out** What did Jesus of Nazareth teach, and how did the early Christians influence the later Roman Empire?

The Storyteller

How could Justin, a man well versed in philosophy and intellectual pursuits, explain to the emperor why he had embraced Christianity? He had opened a school to teach others about this religion, although most educated people dismissed it as a dangerous superstition. He had to convince the emperor that, just as the ancient philosophers had sought truth, Christians sought it too. Since both scholars and Christians shared this quest, following Christian teachings could only help in the search for understanding. He set his pen to paper and began to write a defense of the Christian faith.

—from *Apology*, Justin, reprinted in *Readings in Ancient History from Gilgamesh to Diocletian*, Nels M. Bailkey, 1969

Mosaic of Jesus as shepherd

The early Romans worshiped nature spirits. Under Etruscan influence they came to think of these spirits as deities. Later, the Romans adopted much of Greek religion, identifying Greek deities with their own. Beginning with Augustus, the government also expected people to honor the emperor as Rome's chief priest. Nevertheless, the empire's people were still allowed to worship freely, and a variety of religions flourished.

Meanwhile, a new monotheistic religion called Christianity began to be practiced by some of the Jews in the eastern Mediterranean. At first, both the Romans and the earliest Christians thought of the new religion as a sect, or group, within Judaism. As Christians won over non-Jewish followers, however, the faith diverged from its Jewish roots and became a separate religion.

Judaism and the Empire

In A.D. 6 the Emperor Augustus turned the kingdom of Judah into the Roman province of Judea. The Romans in Judea still allowed the Jews to practice their religion, but they treated them cruelly. Many Jews therefore strengthened their hope that a messiah, or savior, would help them regain their freedom. The coming of a messiah had long been foretold by Jewish prophets.

Believing that God would intervene on their behalf, some Jews took matters into their own hands. In A.D. 66 they rebelled against the Romans and overpowered the small Roman army in Jerusalem. But only four years later, in A.D. 70, the Romans retook Jerusalem, destroying the Temple and killing thousands of Jews.

Then, after another unsuccessful rebellion in A.D. 132, the Romans banned the Jews from living

Chapter 6 *Ancient Rome and Early Christianity* **171**

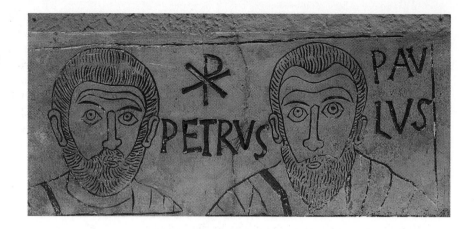

An engraving of the apostles Peter and Paul decorates the sepulchre of the child Asellus. *Why did the apostles form churches?*

in Jerusalem. The Jews were forced to live in other parts of the Mediterranean and the Middle East. In their scattered communities, the Jews continued to study the Torah, the entire body of Jewish religious law and learning. They set up special academies called yeshivas to promote its study. Furthermore, between A.D. 200 and A.D. 500, rabbis—scholars trained in the yeshivas—assembled their various interpretations of the Torah into a book known as the Talmud. To this day the Talmud remains an important book of Jewish law.

Jesus of Nazareth

A few decades before the Jewish revolts, a Jew named **Jesus** grew up in the town of Nazareth. With deep spiritual fervor, Jesus traveled through Galilee and Judea from about A.D. 30 to A.D. 33, preaching a new message to his fellow Jews and winning **disciples**, or followers.

Proclaiming that God's rule was close at hand, Jesus urged people to turn away from their sins and practice deeds of kindness. He said that God was loving and forgiving toward all who repented, no matter what evil they had done or how lowly they were. In his teaching, Jesus often used parables, or symbolic stories. With the parable below, Jesus urged his followers to give up everything so that they would be ready for God's coming:

> ❝ The kingdom of heaven is like treasure lying buried in a field. The man who found it, buried it again; and for sheer joy went and sold everything he had, and bought that field. ❞
>
> —Matthew 13:44-46

Jesus' disciples believed that he was the messiah; other Jews, believing that the messiah had yet to come, disputed this claim. The growing controversy over Jesus troubled Roman officials in Palestine. They believed that anyone who aroused such strong public feelings could endanger Roman rule in the region. In about A.D. 33, the Roman governor Pontius Pilate arrested Jesus as a political rebel and ordered that he be crucified—hung from a cross until dead. This was a typical Roman way of punishing criminals.

The Spread of Christianity

After Jesus' death, his disciples proclaimed that he had risen from the dead and had appeared to them. They pointed to this as evidence that Jesus was the messiah. His followers began preaching that Jesus was the Son of God and the way of salvation. Small groups in the Hellenistic cities of the eastern Mediterranean world accepted this message. Jews and non-Jews who accepted Jesus and his teachings became known as Christians—*Christos* was Greek for "messiah." They formed churches—communities for worship, fellowship, and instruction.

A convert named **Paul** aided Christianity's spread, especially among non-Jews. He traveled widely and wrote on behalf of the new religion. Paul's letters to various churches were later combined with the Gospels, or stories about Jesus, and the writings of other early Christian leaders. Together, these works form the New Testament of the Bible.

Meanwhile, other apostles, or Christian missionaries, spread Christianity throughout the Roman world. It is believed that **Peter**, the leader of the group, came to Rome and helped found a church in that city. Other churches were set up in Greece, Asia Minor, Egypt, and later in Gaul and Spain.

Persecution and Competition

Christians taught that their religion was the only true faith. They refused to honor the emperor as a god and rejected military service. As a result, many Romans disliked the Christians and accused them of treason.

The Romans feared that Christian rejection of their deities would bring divine punishment. Therefore, although they did not hunt out the Christians, if local officials thought Christians were causing trouble, they might have the Christians killed. The Romans frequently threw these Christian martyrs—people who chose to die rather than give up their beliefs—into the stadiums to be killed by wild beasts in front of cheering crowds.

Such persecution, which lasted until the early A.D. 300s, kept many people from becoming Christians. To win converts, Christians had to overcome this obstacle. Christianity also had to compete for followers with polytheistic religions and mystery religions—so named for their mythical heroes and secret rituals—and with Judaism.

During the A.D. 200s and 300s, different varieties of Christianity flourished in the Mediterranean world along with these other religions. Like Judaism, Christianity was mainly a religion of the cities, while traditional Roman religions retained their hold in the countryside. Even though the number of Christians was relatively small during this period, their strength in the cities of the Roman Empire gave Christianity an influence that was far beyond its size.

Romans Adopt Christianity

According to legend, in A.D. 312, as the Roman general **Constantine** led his army into battle, a flaming cross appeared in the sky and beneath it in fiery letters appeared the Latin words *In hoc signo vinces*: "With this as your standard you will have victory." Apparently because of this vision, Constantine ordered his soldiers to paint the Christian symbol of the cross on their shields. When his army won the battle, Constantine credited the victory to the Christian God.

Named emperor of Rome in A.D. 312, Constantine thus became a protector of Christianity. Through his influence all religious groups throughout the empire, including Christians, gained complete freedom to worship as they pleased. Constantine attended meetings of Christian leaders and ordered churches to be built in Rome and Jerusalem.

Because of effective missionary work and growing government support, Christianity further increased in size and influence throughout the entire Roman world. It became as important in the western part of the empire as it was in the eastern part. In A.D. 392 the Emperor **Theodosius** (THEE•uh•DOH•shuhs) made Christianity the official religion of the Roman Empire. At the same time, he banned the old Hellenistic and Roman religions.

The Early Church

From early times Christians recognized that their organization, the Church, would prosper only if it was united. They also felt that Christian teachings had to be stated clearly to avoid differences of opinion that might divide the Church. Consequently, Christians turned to important religious thinkers who attempted to explain many Christian beliefs. Between A.D. 100 and A.D. 500, various scholars known as Church Fathers wrote books explaining Christian teachings. They greatly influenced later Christian thinkers.

Teachings of Augustine

Christians in the western part of the empire especially valued the work of **Augustine**, a scholar born in North Africa in A.D. 354. Augustine is considered to have written one of the world's first great autobiographies. In this work called *Confessions*, Augustine describes how he was converted to Christianity:

> ❝ I heard from a neighboring house a voice, as of a boy or girl, I know not, chanting, and oft repeating, 'Take up and read; Take up and read.'… So … I arose, interpreting it to be no other than a command from God, to open the book [the Bible], and read the first chapter I should find. ❞
>
> —Augustine, *Confessions*, c. A.D. 398

Visualizing History **Constantine became a defender of Christianity.** *How did the status of Christians living in the Roman Empire change under the rule of Constantine?*

The walls of Roman catacombs host many depictions of Christian art such as the Eucharistic Banquet version of the Last Supper. *What kind of literature was the* City of God?

So powerful was Augustine's influence that he became a leading church official in North Africa. In this post he wrote books, letters, and sermons that shaped Christian thought during his own time and afterward. For instance, he wrote *City of God*—the first history of humanity from the Christian viewpoint.

Church Structure

By Augustine's time, Christian leaders had organized the Church as a hierarchy—into levels of authority, each level more powerful than the level below it. Local gatherings of Christians, called parishes, were led by priests. Priests conducted worship services and supervised parish activities. Several parishes together formed a diocese, each overseen by a bishop. Bishops interpreted Christian beliefs and administered regional church affairs. The most powerful bishops governed Christians in the empire's larger cities. The bishops of the five leading cities—Rome, Constantinople, Alexandria, Antioch, and Jerusalem—were called patriarchs.

The bishops of the Christian Church met in councils to discuss questions and disputes about Christian beliefs. The decisions they reached at these councils came to be accepted as doctrine, or official teachings. The points of view the council did not accept were considered heresy, or false doctrine.

During the A.D. 400s, the bishop of Rome began to claim authority over the other patriarchs. Addressed by the Greek or Latin word *papa*, his name today is rendered *pope* in the English language. Latin-speaking Christians in the West regarded the pope as head of all of the churches. Greek-speaking Christians in the East, however, would not accept the authority of the pope over their churches. The bishops of Alexandria and Antioch claimed to exercise a paternal rule equal to that of the pope. Eventually these churches and those of the Latin West separated from each other. In time, the Latin churches as a group became known as the Roman Catholic Church. The Greek churches as a group became known as the Eastern Orthodox Church.

Recall
1. **Define** sect, messiah, disciple, martyr, bishop, patriarch, pope.
2. **Identify** the Talmud, Jesus, Paul, Peter, Constantine, Theodosius, Augustine.
3. **Use** a chart to describe the hierarchy of the Christian Church by the time of Augustine. What were the functions of bishops? Of priests?

Critical Thinking
4. **Evaluating Information** Why might the Romans in Judea especially have responded harshly toward anyone arousing strong feelings among the Jewish people?

Understanding Themes
5. **Innovation** List some of the ways in which Christianity diverged from Judaism to become a distinct religion rather than a sect.

A.D. 284 Diocletian becomes Roman emperor.

A.D. 330 Constantine moves capital to Byzantium, renamed Constantinople.

A.D. 395 Theodosius divides Roman Empire.

A.D. 476 German soldier Odoacer seizes Rome.

Section 5

Roman Decline

Setting the Scene

▶ **Terms to Define**
  inflation

▶ **People to Meet**
  Diocletian, Constantine, Theodosius I, Alaric, Attila

▶ **Places to Locate**
  Constantinople

Find Out What caused the decline of the western Roman Empire?

The Storyteller

The old world had ended. There was no longer any doubt of that. Gregory, whose family had for countless generations served Rome as Senators and consuls, looked out the window at the city which had once ruled the world. Now it was in the hands of warlike tribes who had no appreciation for Roman virtue, achievements, or culture.

"Cities are destroyed," he mused, "fortifications razed, fields devastated. Some men are led away captive, others are mutilated, others slain before our eyes." The pride of Rome was reduced to memories of a vanished glory.

—from Homiliarum in Ezechielem, Pope Gregory I, reprinted in Sources of the Western Tradition, Marvin Perry, Joseph Peden, and Theodore Von Laue, 1991

Marcus Aurelius

During the A.D. 200s, while Christianity was spreading through the Roman Empire, Germanic tribes began to overrun the western half of the empire. Many inhabitants in this area reported widespread devastation and chaos. The Germanic tribes had always been a threat to the empire. Why were they so much more successful now than they were during the times of Marcus Aurelius?

The Empire's Problems

The Romans had a brief rest from political violence during the reign of the five Good Emperors. When Marcus Aurelius died in A.D. 180, however, a new period of violence and corruption brought the *Pax Romana* to an end.

Political Instability

The time of confusion began with the installation of Emperor Commodus, Marcus Aurelius's son. Like Nero, he spent so much state money on his own pleasures that he bankrupted the treasury. In A.D. 192 Commodus's own troops plotted to kill him.

From A.D. 192 to A.D. 284, army legions installed 28 emperors, only to kill most of them off in rapid succession. During this time of political disorder, Rome's armies were busier fighting each other than they were defending the empire's borders. Germanic tribes such as the Goths, the Alemanni, the Franks, and the Saxons repeatedly and successfully attacked the empire.

Economic Decline

Political instability led to economic decline. Warfare disrupted production and trade. For artisans and merchants, profits declined sharply, forcing many out of business. Warfare also destroyed farmland, causing food shortages that sent food prices soaring.

Chapter 6 *Ancient Rome and Early Christianity* **175**

To cope with falling incomes and rising prices, the government minted more coins. It hoped the increase would make it easier to pay its soldiers. However, because the government had already drained its stores of gold and silver, the new coins contained less of the precious metals—cutting their value. To continue getting the same return for their goods, merchants raised prices. Thus, the government's policy sparked severe inflation—a rise in prices corresponding to a decrease in the value of money.

The spiraling decline in wealth affected almost all parts of the empire. To sustain a fighting force, the Roman government had to continually raise soldiers' wages. Taxing landowners heavily seemed the only way to meet this expense, but as increased taxes made farming less profitable, more and more farmers abandoned their lands. As a result, the output of crops shrank even more, worsening the food shortage.

Unsuccessful Reforms

During the late A.D. 200s and early A.D. 300s, two emperors—**Diocletian** (DY•uh•KLEE•shuhn) and later, **Constantine**—struggled to halt the empire's decline. Their reforms preserved the government in the eastern part of the empire for more than 1,000 years. In the west, they succeeded only in briefly delaying the Germanic tribes' invasion of Rome.

Diocletian

General Diocletian came to power in A.D. 284 by slaying the murderer of the preceding emperor. To hold back invasions, he raised the number of legions in the army and spent his time traveling throughout the empire to oversee defenses. Recognizing, however, that the empire was too large for one person to govern, Diocletian divided the empire into two administrative units. Diocletian set himself up as coemperor of the eastern provinces and set up General Maximian as coemperor of the western provinces.

Diocletian also tried to stop the empire's economic decline. To slow inflation, he issued an order called the Edict of Prices. In this edict, Diocletian froze wages and set maximum prices for goods. Yet, even though the penalty for breaking the law was death, his effort failed completely. Citizens merely sold their goods through illegal trade. To stop farmers from leaving their lands and heavily taxed people from changing their

 As this relief sculpture shows, tax collectors in Roman times were very visible. *Why did the Roman government have to increase taxes?*

professions to avoid taxation, Diocletian required farmers who rented land never to leave their property and all workers to remain at the same job throughout their lives.

Constantine

When Diocletian retired in A.D. 305, civil wars broke out again. They continued until Constantine came to power in A.D. 312.

Constantine worked to stabilize the empire once more. He made it legal for landowners to chain their workers to keep them on the farm. He declared most jobs hereditary; sons had to follow their fathers' occupations. In A.D. 330 he moved the capital of the eastern empire to the Greek town of Byzantium—an ideal site for trade and well protected by natural barriers—and renamed it **Constantinople**.

Theodosius

After Constantine's death in A.D. 337, civil war flared anew until **Theo-**

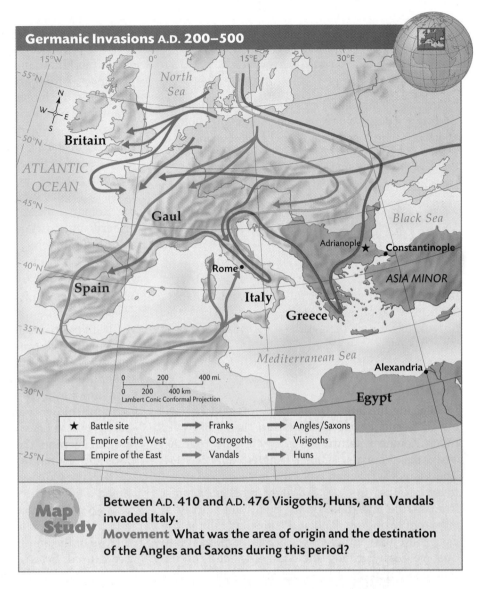

Germanic Invasions A.D. 200–500

★ Battle site | → Franks | → Angles/Saxons
☐ Empire of the West | → Ostrogoths | → Visigoths
☐ Empire of the East | → Vandals | → Huns

Map Study
Between A.D. 410 and A.D. 476 Visigoths, Huns, and Vandals invaded Italy.
Movement What was the area of origin and the destination of the Angles and Saxons during this period?

dosius I succeeded Constantine. During Theodosius's rule, the empire still suffered internal problems, and again the western half suffered more. To lessen the problems, Theodosius willed upon his death that the eastern and western parts should be declared separate empires. In A.D. 395 this division came to pass. To distinguish the two, historians refer to the eastern empire as the Byzantine Empire—after Byzantium, the town that became the capital—and the western empire as the Roman Empire.

Barbarian Invasions

Germanic tribes entered the Roman Empire for many reasons. Beginning in the late A.D. 300s, large numbers of Germanic peoples migrated into the empire because they sought a warmer climate and better grazing land. Others crossed the empire's borders wanting a share of Rome's wealth. Most, however, came because they were fleeing the Huns, fierce nomadic invaders from central Asia.

Warrior Groups

Germanic warriors lived mostly by raising cattle and farming small plots. Despite their interest in the empire's goods, they themselves had little surplus to trade and were poor compared to the Romans. Each warrior group consisted of warriors, their families, and a chief. This chief governed the group and also led the warriors into battle. As the bands of warriors were numerous, so too were the chiefs. Often the only unifying factor among these Germanic groups was their language, which to the Romans sounded like unintelligible babbling. The Romans labeled the Germanic peoples barbarians, a reference to the sounds they made.

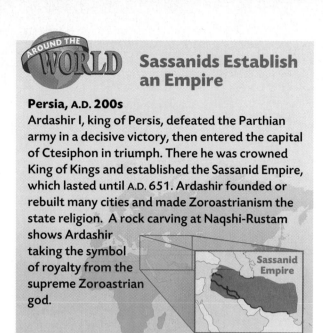
The Visigoths

During the late A.D. 300s and A.D. 400s, a variety of Germanic groups extended their hold over much Roman territory. They were the Ostrogoths, Visigoths, Vandals, Franks, Angles, and Saxons. The Visigoths, at first, were the most important of these groups. In A.D. 378 they rebelled against Roman rule and defeated a large Roman army at Adrianople in the Balkan Peninsula, killing the eastern Roman emperor. His successor managed to buy peace by giving the Visigoths land in the Balkans. Then in A.D. 410 the Visigothic chief, **Alaric**, led his people into Italy, capturing and sacking Rome. After Alaric's death the Visigoths retreated into Gaul.

The Huns

The next threat to the empire was invasion by the Huns. This nomadic group streamed westward from the grasslands of central Asia. Led by their chief, **Attila**, the Huns raided the eastern empire; then they moved north into Gaul. In A.D. 451 the Romans and the Visigoths combined to fight and stop the Huns in central Gaul. Foiled in the provinces, Attila turned upon Italy. There his horde plundered the larger cities and terrified the people. Eventually plague and famine took their toll on the Huns. After Attila died in A.D. 453, they retreated to eastern Europe.

The end of the empire of the Huns brought new troubles to the Romans. Wandering Germans, Persians, Slavs, and Avars battered continually at the Roman Empire's eastern frontier. Diplomacy, bribery, and warfare kept them at bay for only a short time.

End of the Western Empire

With the Huns gone and Italy devastated, nothing remained to prevent Germanic tribes from taking over. The Vandals raided and thoroughly sacked Rome in A.D. 455. Franks and Goths divided Gaul among themselves. Finally, in A.D. 476, a German soldier named Odoacer (OH•duh•WAY•suhr) seized control of Rome by killing the emperor and keeping the emperor's son from power. Odoacer then named himself king of Italy.

Because Odoacer called himself king and never named a substitute emperor, people today refer to A.D. 476 as the year in which the Roman Empire "fell." However, this event no more signifies the collapse of the empire than any other event. Its end was caused by a complex interaction of events between A.D. 200 and A.D. 500.

More accurately, the Roman Empire ended in the late A.D. 400s. Yet it did not mean the end of Roman culture, for the new Germanic rulers accepted the Latin language, Roman laws, and the Christian Church. In the Byzantine Empire, however, aspects of Roman culture were gradually supplanted by Hellenistic culture. By the A.D. 700s, Greek had even replaced Latin as the language of the Byzantine Empire.

SECTION 5 REVIEW

Recall
1. **Define** inflation.
2. **Identify** Diocletian, Constantine, Theodosius I, Alaric, Attila, Odoacer.
3. **Locate** Adrianople on the map on page 177. What significant event occurred there during the time of the "fall" of the Roman Empire?

Critical Thinking
4. **Synthesizing Information** Which do you think had a greater impact on the fall of the Roman Empire, internal difficulties or outside invaders? Why?

Understanding Themes
5. **Change** How did warfare both create and destroy the Roman Empire?

Relevant and Irrelevant Information

Suppose you go to a department store sale and see a CD player that you like. You ask the salesperson, "How much does it cost?"

"It's a great price—lower than it has been all year!"

"But how much is it?" you repeat.

"It comes with a two-year warranty."

"You've told me that it's discounted and has a warranty, but how much is it?" you insist.

"It's on sale for $129.95 plus tax."

Finally, you have the information you need.

Learning the Skill

For any subject or area of interest, information that is available may be either relevant or irrelevant. Relevant information is connected, or related, to the subject. Any facts that define, explain, or illustrate the subject are relevant. Irrelevant information is just the opposite—facts unrelated to the subject. Irrelevant information is not necessarily wrong; it is just not useful to the subject. In the example above, you wanted to know the price of the CD player. All other information was irrelevant.

History contains masses of factual information. To avoid being overwhelmed by the quantity, you must learn to distinguish between relevant and irrelevant material. This is very important when studying for an exam or writing a report. First, clearly define your topic, question, or main idea. Write this topic in your own words. When studying written material, examine each sentence and look for facts that define, explain, or illustrate your topic. Take notes on these items. When listening to a lecture or other oral presentation, look for the same kinds of material and take notes on relevant statements. As soon as possible, rewrite your notes in full sentences.

Practicing the Skill

Decide whether each statement below is relevant or irrelevant to the following topic: the decline of the Roman Empire. Explain each answer.

1. During the A.D. 200s, Germanic peoples began to overrun the western half of the empire.
2. From A.D. 192 to A.D. 284, army legions installed 26 emperors, only to kill most of them off in rapid succession.
3. The Romans built aqueducts throughout Europe.
4. The Roman baths served as popular meeting places for social and business purposes.
5. Political instability led to economic decline.
6. Long after the collapse of the empire, Latin remained the written language of the Roman Catholic Church.
7. Corruption and disunity within the Roman Empire made it easier for external forces to overrun it.
8. Roman citizens had the duty to be ready for army service at any time.
9. As the empire grew, the rule limiting citizenship to members of the original peoples of Rome was changed.
10. The emperors of Rome became so weak that they were puppets of the army—a military that allowed men of German birth to become commanders.

Applying the Skill

Choose one of the following aspects of the Roman Empire: economy, daily life, public amusement, science and engineering, arts and literature. Using books and/or encyclopedias, find at least five pieces of relevant information on your chosen topic. List your sources for each piece of information.

For More Practice

Turn to the Skill Practice in the Chapter Review on page 181 for more practice in distinguishing between relevant and irrelevant information.

Historical Significance

The Romans established a common culture among the diverse peoples of the Mediterranean world. Their legal system, forms of government, engineering feats, and arts formed the foundation of many provincial cities. Frequent civil wars triggered a chain of events that ultimately led to the Roman Empire's economic and political ruin.

The lasting legacies of the Roman Empire, however, are its Latin language, which provided the root of the Romance languages; its engineering skills; its transmission of Greek culture; and Christianity.

Using Key Terms

Write the key term that completes each sentence.

a. indemnity
b. bishop
c. plebeians
d. sect
e. inflation
f. aqueducts
g. republic
h. patricians
i. triumvirate
j. messiah
k. pope
l. consul
m. dictator

1. After years of rule by kings, the Romans declared their city-state a _____, a form of government in which people elect their leaders.
2. In 60 B.C. Pompey, Crassus, and Julius Caesar formed a _____, a group of three persons with equal power, to control the government.
3. Throughout the Roman Empire, Roman engineers built _____, or artificial channels for carrying water from one area to another.
4. After their defeat, the people of Carthage agreed to pay the Romans a huge _____, or payment for damages.
5. Early Christianity was thought of as a _____, or group, within Judaism.
6. Many Jews hoped for a _____, or savior, to deliver them from Roman rule.
7. A church official known as a _____ oversaw a diocese, interpreted Christian beliefs, and administered church affairs.
8. The majority of people in the Roman Republic were _____ —nonaristocratic landowners, merchants, shopkeepers, small farmers, and laborers.
9. During the period of economic decline, the Roman government's debasing of coinage sparked severe _____ —a rise in prices that reflected a decrease in the value of money.
10. Latin nobles called _____ drove out the Etruscans and changed Rome's form of government.

Using Your History Journal

Imagine that you are either a young Roman legionary stationed in a remote outpost of the empire in A.D. 130 or you are a friend of the legionary, awaiting his return to Rome. Write a letter describing what you have been doing in the past week.

Reviewing Facts

1. **Explain** what was the main source of conflict between Rome and Carthage.
2. **Describe** how Rome's political system changed when Augustus Caesar came to power.
3. **Explain** the difference between the *jus gentium* and the *jus civile*.
4. **Discuss** how Roman governors made provincial cities throughout the empire more like Rome.
5. **Tell** how Augustus strengthened the bonds between the city of Rome and provincial cities.

Critical Thinking

1. **Apply** How did the reforms introduced during Marius's rule hasten the end of the Roman Republic?
2. **Analyze** What evidence suggests that Roman society was more stable during the republic than during the time of the empire?
3. **Evaluate** In what ways did the Romans' treatment of the peoples they conquered differ from the ways in which other victors usually treated the peoples they conquered? How might Roman attitudes have strengthened the empire?

4. Analyze The vase shown here incorporates the Etruscan alphabet. Why have scholars been unable to decipher Etruscan words?

Geography in History

1. **Location** Refer to the map below. Which area (east or west) was more heavily influenced by Christianity by A.D. 200?
2. **Movement** How did Constantine encourage the spread of the Christian religion in the Roman Empire?
3. **Place** According to the map below, which city in western Europe had the largest concentration of Christians by A.D. 200?

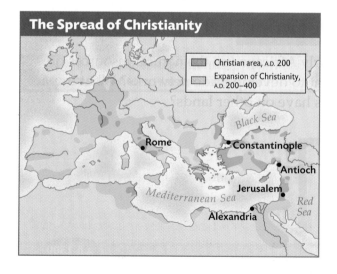

The Spread of Christianity

Christian area, A.D. 200
Expansion of Christianity, A.D. 200–400

Rome
Black Sea
Constantinople
Antioch
Jerusalem
Mediterranean Sea
Alexandria
Red Sea

Understanding Themes

1. **Change** How did the Roman government change from the time of the Etruscans to Augustus Caesar?
2. **Conflict** Describe a conflict between nations that has occurred in the recent past and explain the ways in which it is similar to conflicts between the Romans and other peoples of the Mediterranean region.
3. **Cultural Diffusion** How might Roman roads have helped to foster cultural diffusion?
4. **Innovation** What was the basis of the religious controversy between Jesus' followers and some of the Jews in Palestine? How might this division have furthered Christianity's evolution as a separate religion?
5. **Change** Which half of the Roman Empire would have benefited most by becoming politically separate from the other? Why?

Linking Past and Present

United States government officials recently have proposed legislation to allow the President to veto parts of budget laws passed by Congress. Do you think the President should be granted this power? Why or why not? Use examples from Roman history to support your answer.

Skill Practice

Read the following paragraph of numbered sentences. For each sentence, determine whether or not it is relevant to this topic: the importance of the Italian Peninsula in ancient times. Explain each answer.

1. The Greeks were interested in colonizing Italy for several reasons, the most important of which was Italy's central location in the Mediterranean. 2. A narrow boot-shaped peninsula, Italy extends from Europe toward Africa, dividing the Mediterranean almost in half. 3. Thus Italy was ideally suited to be the center of trade among three continents. 4. Italy's rich soil and moist climate also attracted Greek colonists. 5. The silt washing down Italy's rivers, however, created mosquito-infested swamps at the mouths of rivers. 6. By the time Greek colonists arrived, many peoples inhabited Italy, including Umbrians, Latins, and Oscans.

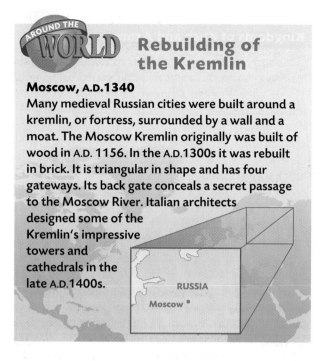

AROUND THE WORLD Rebuilding of the Kremlin

Moscow, A.D.1340
Many medieval Russian cities were built around a kremlin, or fortress, surrounded by a wall and a moat. The Moscow Kremlin originally was built of wood in A.D. 1156. In the A.D.1300s it was rebuilt in brick. It is triangular in shape and has four gateways. Its back gate conceals a secret passage to the Moscow River. Italian architects designed some of the Kremlin's impressive towers and cathedrals in the late A.D.1400s.

RUSSIA

Moscow •

age, called age sets. Boys younger than 10 or 12 herded cattle; girls of the same age helped their mothers plant as well as tend and harvest crops. At about 12 years old, boys and girls took part in ceremonies initiating them into adulthood. A boy remained with his age set throughout his life. After marriage, a girl joined an age set in her husband's village.

Religious Beliefs

To most Africans, marriage customs and all other social laws and traditions were made by a single supreme god who created and ruled an orderly universe. The god rewarded those who followed social rules with abundant harvests and the birth of healthy children, and punished those who violated tradition with accidents, crop failures, or illness.

Beneath the supreme god were many lesser deities who influenced the daily affairs of men and women. These deities were present in natural phenomena such as storms, mountains, and trees.

Many Africans also believed that spirits of dead ancestors lived among the people of the village and guided their destiny.

The religious beliefs and family loyalties of most Africans maintained stability and support within villages. Most communities expected their members to obey the social rules they believed to have come from the supreme god.

Although African communities relied heavily on religious and family traditions to maintain a stable social structure, outside influences through trade and learning still affected them. North Africans absorbed influences from the Arab world, whereas sub-Saharan people adapted to Persian, Indian, and later, European influences. From these outsiders, African communities adopted many new customs, ideas, and languages.

The Arts

Various arts developed in early sub-Saharan Africa. Sculpture was an important art form. African sculpture included figures, masks, decorated boxes, and objects for ceremonial and everyday use. Most of these items were made of wood, bronze, ivory, or baked clay. The wearing of masks at ceremonial dances symbolized the link between the living and the dead. Those wearing the masks and performing the dances called upon ancestral spirits to guide the community.

Music rich in rhythm was interwoven with the fabric of everyday African life. It included choral singing, music performed at royal courts, and songs and dances for ceremonies. In villages, where many activities were performed by groups, music often provided the motivation and rhythm for various tasks, such as digging ditches or pounding grain. African musicians used a variety of drums as well as harps, flutes, pipes, horns, and xylophones.

Early sub-Saharan Africa excelled in oral literature passed down from one generation to another. The stories included histories, fables, and proverbs. Oral literature not only recorded the past but also taught traditions and values.

SECTION I REVIEW

Recall
1. **Define** oral tradition, plateau, savanna, matrilineal, age set.
2. **Identify** Sahel, Nubia, Kush, Piankhi, Axum, Ezana, the Nok, Bantu.
3. **Locate** the Nile River valley on the map on page 187. Why did the Nubians settle in the Upper Nile Valley?

Critical Thinking
4. **Applying Information** Explain how Mediterranean trade influenced the economy of the kingdom of Axum.

Understanding Themes
5. **Movement** How does the Bantu migration in early sub-Saharan Africa contrast with the Aryan migration in early South Asia?

Section 2

Kingdoms in West Africa

Setting the Scene

▶ **Terms to Define**
  monotheism, ghana, mosque

▶ **People to Meet**
  Sundiata Keita, Mansa Musa, Askia Muhammad

▶ **Places to Locate**
  Ghana, Mali, Timbuktu, Songhai

Find Out How was trade carried out in West Africa?

The Storyteller

The poets of Mali preserved the history of their people. Hear one speak: "I teach kings the history of their ancestors so that the lives of the ancients might serve them as an example, for the world is old, but the future springs from the past. My word is pure and free of all untruth.... Listen to my word, you who want to know, by my mouth you will learn the history of Mali. By my mouth you will get to know the story of the ancestor of great Mali, the story of him who ... surpassed even Alexander the Great.... Whoever knows the history of a country can read its future."

Horn player, Benin

—from *Sundiata: An Epic of Old Mali* in *The Humanistic Tradition*, Gloria K. Fiero, 1992

Sub-Saharan Africa provided rich natural resources for the early kingdoms of West Africa. Africans living in this area between A.D. 300 and A.D. 1500 mined gold and other mineral resources found in the region. An active trade developed between them and peoples outside the region who practiced a religion called Islam. Islam preached monotheism, or the belief in one God, and spread throughout the Middle East, North Africa, and Spain during the A.D. 600s and A.D. 700s. Through their trade contacts with Muslims, the followers of Islam, African cultures gradually adopted Islamic cultural elements such as language and religion.

Kingdom of Ghana

The kingdom of **Ghana** became one of the richest trading civilizations in sub-Saharan Africa due to its location midway between Saharan salt mines and tropical gold mines. Between A.D. 300 and A.D. 1200 the kings of Ghana controlled a trading empire that stretched more than 100,000 square miles (260,000 sq. km). They prospered from the taxes they imposed on goods that entered or left their kingdom. Because the ghana, or king, ruled such a vast region, the land became known by the name of its ruler—Ghana.

There was two-way traffic by caravan between cities in North Africa and Ghana. Muslim traders from North Africa sent caravans loaded with cloth, metalware, swords, and salt across the western Sahara to northern settlements in Ghana. Large caravans from Ghana traveled north to Morocco, bringing kola nuts and farming produce. Ghanaian gold was traded for Saharan salt brought by Muslim traders.

Salt was an important trade item for the people of Ghana. They needed salt to preserve and flavor their foods. Using plentiful supplies of gold as a

Chapter 7 *Flowering of African Civilizations* **189**

medium of exchange, Ghanaian merchants traded the precious metal for salt and other goods from Morocco and Spain.

Masudi, a Muslim traveler, writing about A.D. 950, described how trade was conducted:

> 66 The merchants … place their wares and cloth on the ground and then depart, and so the people of [Ghana] come bearing gold which they leave beside the merchandise and then depart. The owners of the merchandise then return, and if they are satisfied with what they have found, they take it. If not, they go away again, and the people of [Ghana] return and add to the price until the bargain is concluded. 99

Ghana reached the height of its economic and political power as a trading kingdom in the A.D. 800s and A.D. 900s. The salt and gold trade moving through Ghana brought Islamic ideas and customs to the kingdom. Muslim influence increased as Muslims held court positions, and many Ghanaians converted to Islam.

At the end of the A.D. 1000s, an attack on the Ghanaian trade centers by the Almoravids, a Muslim group from North Africa, led to the eventual decline of Ghana as a prosperous kingdom. Groups of Ghanaians broke away to form Islamic communities that developed into many small independent states.

Footnotes to History

Golden Monarchs
Ghana's rulers became very wealthy from the taxes they imposed on the gold and salt trade. They wore elaborate gold headdresses and adorned themselves with jewelry. One ruler's dogs even wore collars and bells made of silver and gold.

Images of the Times

Africa's Religious Heritage

Religion played a central role in the development of African cultures. Islam became the dominant religion in the north.

The Great Mosque at Timbuktu
Founded around A.D. 1100, the city of Timbuktu became a major center of trade and site of an important Islamic school.

Altar of the Hand, Benin
Beginning in the A.D. 1200s the kingdom of Benin emerged as a wealthy trading state. The *oba*, or king, became the political, economic, and spiritual leader of the people.

Kingdom of Mali

Mali, one of the small states to break away from Ghana, became a powerful kingdom that eventually ruled much of West Africa. The word *Mali* means "where the king resides" and is an appropriate name for a kingdom that gained much of its power and influence from its kings. **Sundiata Keita**, one of Mali's early kings, defeated his leading rival in A.D. 1235 and began to conquer surrounding territories. By the late A.D. 1200s, Mali's territory included the old kingdom of Ghana.

Sundiata worked to bring prosperity to his new empire. He sought to improve agricultural production, and he restored the trans-Saharan trade routes that had been interrupted by the Almoravid attacks. Sundiata ordered soldiers to clear large expanses of savanna and burn the grass that had been cleared to provide fertilizer for crops of peanuts, rice, sorghum, yams, beans, onions, and grains. With the benefit of adequate rainfall, agriculture flourished in Mali. With larger tracts of land under cultivation, farmers produced surplus crops that Mali's kings then collected as taxes.

Mali's greatest king was **Mansa Musa**, who ruled from A.D. 1312 to A.D. 1332. By opening trade routes and protecting trade caravans with a powerful standing army, Musa maintained the economic prosperity begun by Sundiata. He also introduced Islamic culture to Mali.

A Muslim himself, Musa enhanced the prestige and power of Mali through a famous pilgrimage to Makkah in A.D. 1324. Arab writers report that Musa traveled in grand style. He took with him 12,000 slaves, each dressed in silk or brocade and carrying bars of gold. Musa gave away so much gold on his journey that the world price of gold fell. At Makkah, Musa persuaded a Spanish architect to return with him to Mali. There the skilled architect built great mosques—Muslim houses of worship—and other fine buildings, including a palace for Musa in the capital of **Timbuktu** (TIHM•BUHK•TOO). Timbuktu became an important center of Muslim art and learning mainly through the efforts of Mansa Musa, who

Terra-cotta heads, c. early 1600s, commemorate the deceased members of the royal family among the Akan peoples of southern Ghana.

REFLECTING ON THE TIMES

1. What is the dominant religion of northern Africa?
2. Why did the Akan people of Ghana place terra-cotta heads on graves?

James L. Stanfield

West African Empire

This turreted mosque in Djenné, Mali, harks back to the A.D. 1300s, when the town thrived as a center of trade and Islamic learning. A masterpiece of African-Muslim architecture, the great mosque boasts massive mud ramparts broken by patterns of protruding beams. Its tall spires are crowned not with the traditional Islamic crescent but with ostrich eggs, symbol of fertility and fortune. Every year, after the rainy season, the town turns out 4,000 people to replaster the walls of the mosque with their bare hands. The job is done in a day.

Almost two centuries before Columbus set off for the Americas, an Arab traveler and author named Ibn Battuta began his travels in A.D. 1325 to the far corners of the Islamic world—from North Africa to China and back. He returned home three decades later as one of history's great travelers and travel writers. His journeys totaled 75,000 miles (121,000 km)—three times the distance logged by his European predecessor, Marco Polo. Ibn Battuta's final journey brought him here to the West African empire of Mali where he praised the piety of the Muslims. Battuta sought out the ruler, Mansa Sulayman, at his capital but was not impressed with the king's generosity. Mansa Sulayman, he wrote, "is a miserly king." Battuta also traveled to Timbuktu—about a hundred years before the city really started to prosper. At its height, in the A.D. 1500s, the city could boast three universities and perhaps 50,000 residents. ⊕

encouraged Muslim scholars to teach at his court.

After Mansa Musa died in A.D. 1332, the empire came under attack by Berbers, a people living in the Sahara region to the north. They raided Mali and captured Timbuktu. From the south, warriors from the rain forest also attacked Mali. Inside the kingdom, people living in the **Songhai** region of the Niger River valley had long resented losing control over their region and rebelled against the empire. By the middle of the A.D. 1500s, Mali had split into several independent states.

Kingdom of Songhai

The rebellious Songhai, who were skilled traders, farmers, and fishers, were led by strong leaders. During the late A.D. 1400s their ruler, Sunni Ali, fought many territorial wars and managed to conquer the cities of Timbuktu and Djenné, expanding his empire to include most of the West African savanna. Sunni Ali was a Muslim ruler, but when he died, rule fell to his son, a non-Muslim. The Muslim population of Songhai overthrew Ali's son and brought a Muslim ruler to the throne.

Under the new ruler, **Askia Muhammad**, the Songhai Empire reached the height of its glory. Ruling from A.D. 1493 to A.D. 1528, Askia Muhammad divided Songhai into five huge provinces, each with a governor, a tax collector, a court of judges, and a trade inspector—very much like the government structure of China in the A.D. 1400s. The king maintained the peace and security of his realm with a cavalry and a navy. Timbuktu became a center of learning.

Devoted to Islam, Muhammad introduced laws based on the teachings of the holy book of Islam, the Quran (kuh•RAHN). Lesser crimes were sometimes overlooked, but those who committed major crimes such as robbery or idolatry received harsh punish-

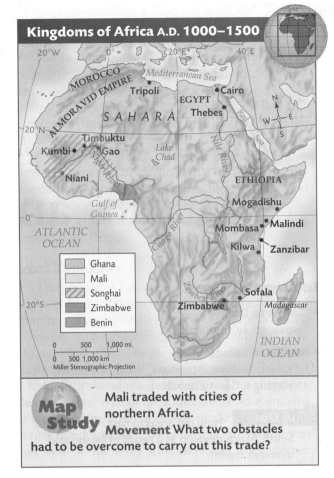

Kingdoms of Africa A.D. 1000–1500

Legend:
- Ghana
- Mali
- Songhai
- Zimbabwe
- Benin

0   500   1,000 mi.
0   500 1,000 km
Miller Stereographic Projection

Map Study Mali traded with cities of northern Africa. **Movement** What two obstacles had to be overcome to carry out this trade?

ments. Askia Muhammad appointed Muslim judges, assuring that Islamic laws would be upheld.

In A.D. 1528 Askia Muhammad was overthrown by his son. A series of struggles for the throne followed, leading to a weakened central government. Around A.D. 1589 the rulers of Morocco sent an army across the Sahara to attack Songhai gold-trading centers. Moroccan soldiers, armed with guns and cannons, easily defeated the Songhai forces fighting with only swords, spears, and bows and arrows. By A.D. 1600 the Songhai Empire had come to an end.

190
191
191
193

SECTION 2 REVIEW

Recall
1. **Define** monotheism, ghana, mosque.
2. **Identify** the Almoravids, Sundiata Keita, Mansa Musa, Askia Muhammad.
3. **Locate** Timbuktu on the map on this page. How did Timbuktu become an important center of Islamic art and learning during the A.D. 1300s?

Critical Thinking
4. **Analyzing Information** Why was trade vital to the economies of the West African kingdoms?

Understanding Themes
5. **Cultural Diffusion** What goods were traded, and how did trade between West Africa and the Islamic world influence the development of West African cultures between A.D. 900 and A.D. 1500?

This view shows the circular stone ruins of the Great Zimbabwe with an exterior wall more than 800 feet in circumference.

What functions did this "stone house" serve?

passages that protected the circular house of the Zimbabwe chief. Near the house, archaeologists have uncovered a platform with several upright stones that may have been the place where the chief held court.

Territorial Divisions

For nearly five centuries, Karanga and the other Bantu states grew wealthy from their control of the chief routes between the gold mines and the sea. However, during the A.D. 1400s, Bantu states in South Africa struggled in civil wars that brought disorder to the kingdoms and disrupted trade.

The Karanga territories were split between two rival forces. The northern territory was called Monomotapa. The southern territory was taken over by the Changamire dynasty.

The Changamire Empire became stronger than the Monomotapa Empire. Changamire rulers took over Great Zimbabwe and built the fortress's largest structures. At the same time, European explorers arrived along the East African coast. Eager to control the sources of gold, ivory, and copper, the Europeans attacked the Monomotapa Empire, threatening the survival of the African civilizations in the continent's interior.

SECTION 3 REVIEW

Recall
1. **Define** monopoly, multicultural.
2. **Identify** Kilwa, Malindi, Mombasa, Sofala, Zanzibar, Karanga, Great Zimbabwe.
3. **Explain** why the Bantu kingdoms of Central and South

Africa prospered.

Critical Thinking
4. **Synthesizing Information** Imagine that you are an Arab merchant visiting an East African coastal city-state in the A.D. 1300s. What aspects of the people's culture would be

familiar to you? What parts might seem different?

Understanding Themes
5. **Innovation** What new aspect of cultural life developed in the city-states of East Africa as a result of African and Middle Eastern contacts?

Answering Test Questions

How do you react when your teacher announces a test? For many students, taking a test is a dreaded ordeal. Learning test-taking strategies, however, can make this unavoidable experience easier and more successful.

Learning the Skill

Preparation: Good test preparation requires time. Don't try to cram all the facts into your mind at the last minute. Before beginning to study, identify what material the test will cover.

Review: To review the material, list main topics and concepts from your class notes and other material. From your textbook, list headings, map and graph titles, preview items, and review questions. These textbook items usually contain the main concepts of the chapter. Under each main topic or concept, add important details such as terms, people, places, events, movements, and dates. Finally, review previous tests and quizzes to find out what kinds of questions to expect.

Practice: Now turn your list of topics into questions and test yourself. Write your answers and evaluate them. Find areas that require further study. If you need help, ask a parent, teacher, or friend to resolve confusing issues or to quiz you again. Repeat the process of self-testing and checking your answers until you can answer most questions quickly and easily.

Taking the Test: When taking a test, preview all of its parts. Estimate how much time you will need to complete each section. Allow more time for essay questions than for short answer questions. Answer easy questions first. Then complete those that need more work. Read all test directions carefully and follow them correctly. Allow time at the end to review your answers and make additions or corrections.

A. Multiple-Choice Questions: Read all choices before marking one. If you are not sure of an answer, make your best guess.

B. Analogy Questions: First identify the relationship between the first set of items. Then look for a term that will show the same relationship in the second pair of items. Here's an example: Mansa Musa is to Mali as Askia Muhammad is to _____. Mansa Musa was Mali's greatest king. This is the relationship between the first pair. To complete this analogy, you must know that Askia Muhammad was the greatest king of another African kingdom—Songhai.

C. Essay Questions: Make sure you understand the question. In the margin or on a notepad, briefly jot down the main points to include in your answer. Decide how to arrange these ideas and then write a complete answer.

Practicing the Skill

Imagine that you are taking a test on Chapter 7. Answer the following questions about preparing for and taking the test.

1. What topics, terms, and concepts would you list as study topics for Section 1, "Early Africa"?
2. Write a self-test question for each subheading in Section 2, "Kingdoms in West Africa."
3. How would you study the information in the map entitled "Kingdoms of Kush and Axum"?
4. Suppose you expect a test question comparing the Bantu and Ghana kingdoms. How would you study for this question?

Applying the Skill

Write five self-test questions on the material in Chapter 7. Without consulting the textbook, write answers to all questions. Then refer to the textbook to decide which topics need further study and rewrite your answers to those questions.

For More Practice

Turn to the Skill Practice in the Chapter Review on page 199 for more practice in answering test questions.

India's Great Civilization

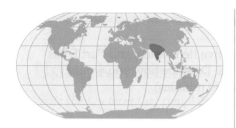

Chapter Themes

▶ **Movement** Aryans invade the Indian subcontinent and bring new ideas and practices. *Section 1*

▶ **Innovation** Hinduism and Buddhism emerge and become the dominant religions in much of Asia. *Section 2*

▶ **Cultural Diffusion** Mauryan and Gupta rulers bring unity to northern India and encourage cultural achievements. *Section 3*

The Storyteller

The Mahabharata, *an epic poem of ancient India, relates an amazing event. A battle raged, but the prince Arjuna did not want to fight. After all, among his foes were relatives. Arjuna took his case to the god Krishna: "O Krishna, when I see my own people … eager for battle, my limbs shudder, my mouth is dry, my body shivers, and my hair stands on end…. I can see no good in killing my own kinsmen."*

Krishna answered, "As a [warrior], your duty is to fight a righteous battle…. Arise, O Arjuna, and be determined to fight. Get ready for battle without thought of pleasure and pain, gain and loss, victory and defeat."

As a warrior, Arjuna understood Krishna's words. A warrior must fight. It was his duty.

Historical Significance

What were the achievements of India's early civilization? What religions emerged from early India that have shaped the cultures of Asia and, in many ways, the rest of the world?

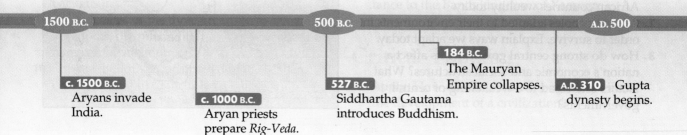

1500 B.C.	500 B.C.	A.D. 500
c. 1500 B.C. Aryans invade India.	**c. 1000 B.C.** Aryan priests prepare *Rig-Veda*.	**527 B.C.** Siddhartha Gautama introduces Buddhism.	**184 B.C.** The Mauryan Empire collapses.	**A.D. 310** Gupta dynasty begins.

Visualizing History Hindus communicated their beliefs through poems, tales, songs, and art. This painting of Vishnu on a bird honors one of the three main gods of Hinduism.

Your History Journal

Using a recent edition of an almanac, make a chart of the world's major religions, including the number of people who today are adherents of each religion.

c. 1200 B.C.
Vedic Age begins.

c. 1000 B.C.
Rig-Veda records
Aryan legends.

c. 700 B.C.
Religious thinkers
compile the *Upanishads*.

Section 1

Origins of Hindu India

Setting the Scene

▶ **Terms to Define**
  rajah, epic, *varna*, *jati*, dharma, reincarnation,
  karma, ahimsa

▶ **People to Meet**
  the Aryans

▶ **Places to Locate**
  Hindu Kush, Ganges Plain

nd Out How did the cultures of the Aryans
and the peoples they conquered develop into the
culture of Hindu India?

The Storyteller

*The bleeding warrior lay helpless with a bro-
ken arm. Only proper words and medicines could
save him now. The priest, sprinkling him with
water and herbs chanted: "He who drinks you,
medicine, lives. Save the man. You are mender of
wounds inflicted by club, arrow, or flame. Mend
this man. O most beautiful one, go to the fracture."
Next would come the grass and termite mud mixture to drink, then water in a cow's horn, and
pepper-corns to eat. The
warrior breathed quietly,
thankful that he had
found a healer who knew
the ritual.*

—adapted from *Religious
Healing in the Veda*,
Kenneth Zysk, 1985

Hindu Kush

*T*nto the Indus River valley raced horse-
drawn chariots carrying tall, light-
skinned warriors—**the Aryans** from
areas north of the Black and Caspian Seas. The invasion began around 1500 B.C. For several generations,
waves of Aryans swept through passes in the mountains known as the **Hindu Kush** into the Indus
River valley and from there into northern India.

Aryans

After conquering the people of the Indus River
valley, the Aryans moved southeast into the
Ganges Plain. There they subdued the local inhabitants and developed a new civilization that eventually spread over much of South Asia. Aspects of
this civilization—especially its religious contributions—endure today.

Ways of Life

The Aryans were loosely organized into tribes
of nomadic herders. Each tribe was led by a rajah,
or chief. Ancient Aryan legends and hymns
describe people who delighted in waging war,
gambling on chariot races, and singing and dancing
at festivals. Cattle were the basis of their diet and
economy, even serving as money. Wealth was measured in cattle, and so the Aryans raided each
other's herds. They were often at war.

The fertile Indus Valley was ideal for farming,
and the Aryans soon settled down into an agricultural way of life. Dozens of Aryan words describe
cattle, indicating their continued prominence in
Aryan life. Cattle provided meat, fresh milk, and
ghee, or liquid butter. The Aryans also hunted
game and butchered sheep and goats from their
herds. Later, their herds would be considered so
sacred that a ban was placed on eating meat. The

Aryans also ate cucumbers, bananas, and barley cakes.

Men dominated the Aryan world. Although a woman had some say in choosing a husband, the man she married expected no challenge to his authority. Even so, women took part in religious ceremonies and social affairs, and they were allowed to remarry if they were widowed—freedoms they would lose in the centuries to come. Both girls and boys from families of high rank attended school, where they learned Aryan traditions.

Language and Traditions

As a nomadic people, the Aryans had no written language. Sanskrit, their spoken language, evolved slowly and became one of the major languages of India. As part of the great Indo-European language family, Sanskrit has many of the same root words as English, Spanish, French, and German. It also includes many words from the languages of the peoples living in India before the Aryan invasions.

The Aryan warrior-herders sang rousing hymns and recited epics, long poems celebrating their heroes. For centuries these hymns and poems were passed by word of mouth from generation to generation. Families of warriors and priests were responsible for preserving this oral heritage. Over and over they repeated the legends, striving for complete accuracy.

Eventually, the Aryans developed a written form of Sanskrit. Priests collected the hymns, poems, legends, and religious rituals into holy books known as Vedas (VAY•duhz), or "Books of Knowledge," which formed the basis of Aryan religious practices.

Indeed, the Vedas are extremely valuable sources of knowledge, for without them historians would know little about the Aryans. Unlike the Indus River valley people, the Aryans left no artifacts or structures. Whatever we know of their life and culture we know from the Vedas. Indeed, Indian history from 1200 B.C. to 500 B.C. is known as the Vedic Age. The oldest of the four Vedas, the *Rig-Veda*, dates from around 1000 B.C. It records legends that tell us about Aryan life. The *Rig-Veda* is one of the world's oldest religious texts still in use.

Social Structure

The Vedas reveal the complex social system of ancient India. The invading Aryans brought a system of four main social classes, or *varnas*. At first the warriors, called Kshatriyas (KSHA•tree•uhz), were the most honored *varna*. They were followed by the priests, or Brahmans; merchants, artisans, and farmers, called Vaisyas (VYSH•yuhz); and

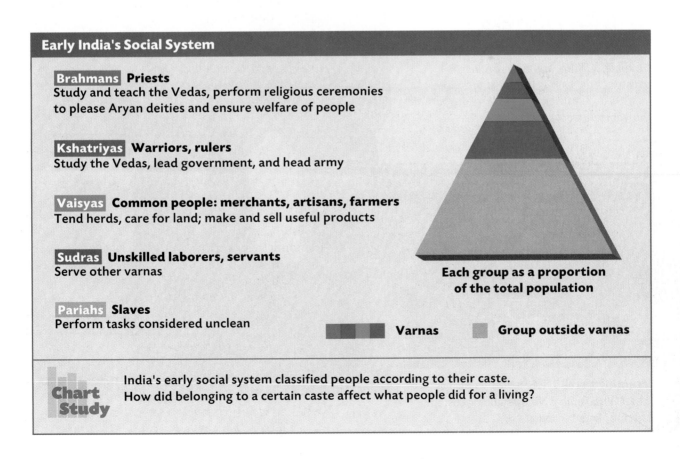

Early India's Social System

Brahmans Priests
Study and teach the Vedas, perform religious ceremonies to please Aryan deities and ensure welfare of people

Kshatriyas Warriors, rulers
Study the Vedas, lead government, and head army

Vaisyas Common people: merchants, artisans, farmers
Tend herds, care for land; make and sell useful products

Sudras Unskilled laborers, servants
Serve other varnas

Pariahs Slaves
Perform tasks considered unclean

Each group as a proportion of the total population

■ Varnas   ■ Group outside varnas

Chart Study
India's early social system classified people according to their caste.
How did belonging to a certain caste affect what people did for a living?

unskilled laborers and servants, known as Sudras (SHOO•druhz).

Only priests and warrior families were allowed to hear and recite the Vedas. Over the years, rituals grew more secret and complex, and priests replaced warriors as the most honored members of society. The priests alone knew how to make sacrifices properly and to repeat the appropriate hymns. The social system changed to reflect the importance of priests.

Each *varna* had its own duties and took pride in doing them well. The Brahmans performed the elaborate rituals and studied the Vedas; only they could teach the Vedas. As warriors, Kshatriyas took charge of the army and the government. They led the councils of elders who ran small villages. Kshatriyas could study the Vedas but were not allowed to teach them. Vaisyas had the important tasks of tending the cattle, lending money, trading goods, and caring for the land. The Sudras' job was to serve the other varnas. They worked in the fields and acted as servants.

By 500 B.C. the division among the four *varnas* had become more rigid. Varnas were divided into smaller groups knows as *jati*. *Jati* were formed according to occupations: shoemakers, potters, farmers, and so on. Priests were higher than cultivators, and cultivators were higher than carpenters, for example. *Jati* had their own rules for diet, marriage, and social customs. Groups lived in separate neighborhoods and did not mix socially with others.

Centuries later, Europeans named the Indian system of *varnas* and *jati* the caste system. The word *caste* has no one definition, but how it worked is clear. Within the system people were always ranked. They were born into a group, and that group could not be changed. People married within their own group. Moreover, that group determined a great deal about people's everyday lives. Members of the group lived in the same neighborhoods and did not mix socially with those outside.

Outside the system of *varnas* and *jati* were a group later called the pariahs. They did work that

Images
of the Times

Hindu Beliefs

The three main gods of Hinduism are Brahma, Vishnu, and Siva. Brahma is creator of the world, Vishnu is preserver, and Siva is destroyer. These three are part of the same universal spirit.

Meeting to read holy writings such as the *Mahabharata* is a long-standing custom among Hindus in India.

was considered unclean, such as skinning animals and tanning their hides for leather. Sometimes called "outcastes" or "untouchables," the pariahs lived outside the villages and were shunned by most other people.

Concept of Duty

The Vedas outlined the dharma, or duties, of the males who belonged to each *varna*. Members of each *varna* were urged to do their duty. The epic poem called the *Mahabharata* (muh•HAH•BAH •ruh•tuh) makes the concept clear. One eloquent section, called the *Bhagavad Gita* (BAH•guh•VAHD GEE•tuh), or "Song of the Lord," includes the story you read at the beginning of this chapter. Arjuna's decision—to fight no matter what the personal cost—illustrates the importance of dharma in Indian life. As a warrior, Arjuna had to do his duty, even if it meant fighting against family.

The concept of dharma included doing what was proper for one's age. For instance, a male student would follow an occupation that was appropriate for his class. He then took a wife, and assumed responsibility for a family. In old age, he retired. As he neared death, he withdrew from his friends and family to pray. A woman was educated in household tasks. She married and served her husband and family until he died or retired, at which time she was expected to retire from active life and be taken care of by her sons and daughters-in-law. This concept of duty affected every member of society.

India's Two Epics

Two epics addressed the concepts of good and evil and became the spiritual forebears of India's main religions. The tale of Arjuna is a small part of the *Mahabharata*, which is 100,000 verses in length—as long as the first five books of the Bible. The epic—like the Bible—is a collection of writings by several authors. Some characters are historical, while others represent human ideals and various deities. Woven into the story of two families' struggle for power are discussions of religion and philosophy.

Much of India's fine art is related to its religions. Hindus built elaborate temples, such as this Mehsana Sun Temple (interior shown).

This sculpture of Ganesha, god of good fortune and auspicious beginnings, was done in the A.D. 1700s.

REFLECTING ON THE TIMES

1. How did Hinduism contribute to the development of fine art in India?
2. What epic describes the concept of duty that affects every member of Hindu society?

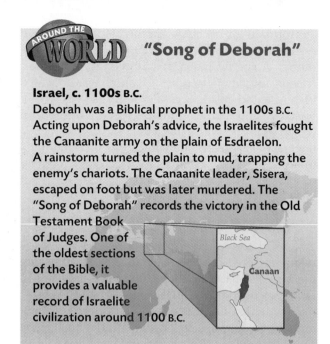

AROUND THE **WORLD** "Song of Deborah"

Israel, c. 1100s B.C.
Deborah was a Biblical prophet in the 1100s B.C. Acting upon Deborah's advice, the Israelites fought the Canaanite army on the plain of Esdraelon. A rainstorm turned the plain to mud, trapping the enemy's chariots. The Canaanite leader, Sisera, escaped on foot but was later murdered. The "Song of Deborah" records the victory in the Old Testament Book of Judges. One of the oldest sections of the Bible, it provides a valuable record of Israelite civilization around 1100 B.C.

Black Sea

Canaan

One passage tells of how the need for a king arose when dharma no longer guided people in everyday life:

> Bhishma said: … Neither kingship nor king was there in the beginning, neither scepter nor the bearer of the scepter. All people protected one another by means of righteous conduct (dharma). Thus, while protecting one another by means of righteous conduct, O Bharata, men eventually fell into a state of spiritual lassitude [weariness]. Then delusion overcame them … their sense of righteous conduct was lost. When understanding was lost, all men … became victims of greed.

Later, the God Vishnu chooses "… that one person among mortals who alone is worthy of high eminence." A man named Virajas is brought forth, and he becomes the first king.

A second epic, the well-loved *Ramayana*, grew to 24,000 verses before it was written down. It presents the moving tale of Rama and Sita (SEE•tuh). Rama was the ideal king; Sita, his faithful wife. Vividly describing the struggle between good and evil, the *Ramayana* tells how the demon Ravana captures Sita. When Rama finds that she is missing, he cries:

> Sita! Gentle Sita! If you have wanted to prove my love, if you are hiding from us, let the agony of my fear suf-

fice. Come to me, my love, come to me!"
He stood there, both his arms held wide, as though half hoping she might run forward to his embrace. The country lay very still around him. Only the old tree shivered in every leafy spray and seemed to wring its hands for pity.
Slowly that gleam of hope quite faded, and his arms fell to his sides.

Rama at first doubts Sita; but later she is saved, and they reunite. Like other Indian epics, the *Ramayana* ends with good winning over evil.

Indian Beliefs

The Aryan conquerors believed in many deities and thought their gods and goddesses had power over the forces of nature. They worshiped Agni, the god of fire; Indra, the god of thunder and war; and Usha, the goddess of dawn. Aryan priests created elaborate rituals and offered sacrifices to appease the gods and win their favor.

Over the centuries, as political and social organizations evolved, the Aryan religion slowly changed into Hinduism and became the national religion of India.

Universal Spirit

Hinduism was not founded on the teachings of one person, nor did it have one holy book. Instead it was based on different beliefs and practices, many of which had their roots in the Vedas and the Indian epics.

Other ideas that became part of Hinduism came from religious thinkers who had grown discontented with complex Vedic rituals. Between 800 B.C. and 400 B.C., their search for wisdom and truth was reflected in the religious writings known as the *Upanishads* (oo•PAH•nih•SHAHDZ).

The *Upanishads* tell of a universal spirit present within all life, "a light that shines beyond all things on earth." All living things, according to these writings, have souls. Thus, Hindus came to regard animals as sacred and forbade killing them. All souls, say the *Upanishads*, are part of the one eternal spirit, sometimes called Brahman Nerguna. Their bodies tie them to the material world, but only for a short time. To know true freedom, a soul must be separated from the material world and united with Brahman Nerguna: "As a lump of salt thrown in water dissolves, and cannot be taken out again as salt, though wherever we taste the water it is salt."

The authors of the *Upanishads* taught that forms of self-denial such as fasting helped people achieve union with the universal spirit. They encouraged the practice of yoga, a discipline that combines physical and mental exercises designed to help one achieve a state of tranquility.

Cycle of Rebirth

Another idea that came from the *Upanishads* was that of reincarnation, or the rebirth of the soul. Hindus believe the soul passes through many lifetimes before it finally achieves union with the universal spirit. The *Upanishads* offer this picture of rebirth:

> 66 As a caterpillar, having reached the end of a blade of grass, takes hold of another blade, then draws its body from the first, so the Self, having reached the end of his body, takes hold of another body, then draws itself from the first. 99

The cycle of rebirth is determined by a principle called karma. According to this principle, how a person lives his or her life determines what form the person will take in the next life. To move toward the universal spirit, one must live a good life and fulfill one's dharma. For example, a conscientious diplomat, a Kshatriya, might be reborn as a Brahman. The souls of those who fail to fulfill their dharma, however, might be reborn in a lower *varna*, or perhaps even as snakes or insects.

The concept of karma creates the desire to live a good life, for "By good deeds a man becomes what is good, by evil deeds what is bad." Out of that desire arose the practice of nonviolence toward all living things—still important to Hindus today. Called ahimsa (uh•HIHM•SAH), this practice requires the believer to protect humans, animals, and even insects and plants.

The cycle of reincarnation continues until a person reaches spiritual perfection. The ultimate aim of life is *moksha*, or release from the pain and

History & Art Siva, ringed by a circle of flames, dances on the back of the dwarf Apasmara. *Why do Hindus regard animals as sacred?*

suffering of rebirth after rebirth. In *moksha* a person finds freedom from reincarnation in a state of complete oneness with Brahman Nerguna. Hindus teach that a life committed to prayer, religious rituals, strict self-denial, and rejection of all worldly possessions will help a person to achieve the final goal of *moksha*.

SECTION 1 REVIEW

Recall
1. **Define** rajah, epic, *varna*, *jati*, dharma, reincarnation, karma, ahimsa.
2. **Identify** the Aryans, Sanskrit, *Vedas*, *Mahabharata*, *Bhagavad Gita*, *Ramayana*, Hinduism,

Upanishads.
3. **Explain** how geography affected the life of the Aryan groups that invaded India.

Critical Thinking
4. **Applying Information** Illustrate the Hindu concept of

dharma by telling the story of the warrior-prince Arjuna.

Understanding Themes
5. **Movement** How did the Aryan invasion beginning about 1500 B.C. affect the development of Indian culture?

600 B.C.	550 B.C.	500 B.C.

c. 566 B.C.
Siddhartha
Gautama is born.

c. 540 B.C.
Gautama begins
spiritual search.

c. 500 B.C. Gautama
(the Buddha) dies.

Section 2

Rise of Buddhism

Setting the Scene

▶ **Terms to Define**
   nirvana, stupa

▶ **People to Meet**
   Siddhartha Gautama

Find Out Why did Buddhism appeal to many people in India, Southeast Asia, and East Asia?

The Storyteller

Siddhartha stood still, as if a snake lay in his path. Suddenly the icy thought stole over him: he must begin his life completely afresh. "I am no longer what I was, ... I am no longer a hermit, no longer a priest, no longer a Brahmin. How can I return home? What would I do at home with my father? Study? Offer sacrifices? Practice meditation? All this is over for me now." He realized how alone he was. Now he was Siddhartha, the awakened. He must begin his life afresh. He began to walk quickly, no longer homewards, no longer looking back.

—from *Siddhartha*, Herman Hesse, translated by Hilda Rosner, 1957

Gautama, the Buddha

During the 500s B.C., changes occurred in Indian religious life. Many devout Hindus became dissatisfied with external rituals and wanted a more spiritual faith. They left the towns and villages and looked for solitude in the hills and forests. Through meditation, many of these religious seekers developed new insights and became religious teachers. Their ideas and practices often led to the rise of new religions. The most influential of the new religions was Buddhism.

The Buddha

Siddhartha Gautama (sih•DAHR•tuh GOW•tuh•muh), the founder of Buddhism, began his life as a Kshatriya prince. Born around 566 B.C., Gautama was raised in luxury. As a young man he continued to live a sheltered life, shielded from sickness and poverty. Tradition states that one day Gautama's charioteer drove him around his estates, and for the first time Gautama saw sickness, old age, and death. Shocked at these scenes of misery, Gautama decided to find out why people suffered and how suffering could be ended. At the age of 29, he left his wife and newborn son and wandered throughout India.

For seven years Gautama lived as a hermit, seeking the truth through fasting and self-denial. This did not lead him to the truth, however. One day, while meditating under a tree, Gautama gained a flash of insight that he felt gave him an answer to the problem of suffering. He began to share with others the meaning of his "enlightenment." Dressed in a yellow robe, he preached his message to people and began to gather followers. His closest friends began calling him the Buddha, or "Enlightened One."

Rajesh Bedi

The Buddha's First Sermon

From this stupa, or domed shrine, in Isipatana, a village in northern India, the Buddha is said to have delivered his first sermon. Once a small village, Isipatana is now Sarnath, a suburb of the city of Varanasi. Here, Buddhists believe, in the 500s B.C. the Buddha delivered his first sermon to five followers. A large monastery, which once housed 1,500 monks, was founded on this sacred spot. Today the shrine stands empty.

The Buddha began India's second religion, after the far older Hindu religion had become entrenched. He lived in a unique moment of history. The 500s B.C. gave birth not only to Buddhism in India but also to Confucianism in China and to new rationalist philosophies in Greece. Buddhism became one of the world's major religions and the Buddha one of the most notable spiritual leaders in the history of the world. ⊕

Four Noble Truths

The Buddha developed a new religious philosophy. He outlined his main ideas in the Four Noble Truths. First, as he had discovered, all people suffer and know sorrow. Next, said the Buddha, people suffer because their desires bind them to the cycle of rebirth. He told his followers:

> **❝** The thirst for existence leads from rebirth to rebirth; lust and pleasure follow. Power alone can satisfy lust. The thirst for power, the thirst for pleasure, the thirst for existence; there, O monks, is the origin of suffering. **❞**

The third truth, said the Buddha, was that people could end their suffering by eliminating their desires. And according to the fourth truth, one could eliminate desire by following the Eightfold Path.

The Eightfold Path

The Buddha urged his disciples to do eight things: know the truth, resist evil, say nothing to hurt others, respect life, work for the good of others, free their minds of evil, control their thoughts, and practice meditation. By avoiding extremes and following the Eightfold Path, a person could attain nirvana, a state of freedom from the cycle of rebirth. Nirvana is not a place, like heaven, but a state of extinction. In fact, the root meaning of the word *nirvana* is a "blowing out," as of a candle. In nirvana, a person would be in a state of oneness with the universe.

The Buddha rejected the *varna* system. He taught that a person's place in life depended on the person, not on the person's birth. He taught that anyone, regardless of caste, could attain enlightenment. He did not believe in the Hindu deities. He believed in reincarnation but taught that one could escape the cycle of suffering and reach nirvana by following the Eightfold Path.

Spread of Buddhism

The Buddha spent 45 years teaching the Four Noble Truths and the Eightfold Path. He gathered thousands of disciples around him. After their master's death, traveling monks carried the new religion beyond India to other parts of Asia, especially to China, Japan, Korea, and the Middle East.

Architecture and the Arts

The rise of Buddhism led to a flowering of architecture and the arts. Buddhist architects built stupas, or large stone mounds, over the bones of Buddhist holy people. Stupas were known for their elaborately carved stone railings and gateways. Paintings and statues of the Buddha, carved of polished stone or wood covered with gilt, adorned stupas and cave temples. Exquisite smaller statues were made from fine porcelain. Books about the Buddha's life and teachings were often beautifully illustrated.

Divisions

As Buddhism spread, disagreements developed among the Buddha's followers. Two distinct branches of Buddhism soon arose. One branch, known as Theravada, was established in South Asia and Southeast Asia. It remained fairly close in practice to the original teachings of the Buddha, regarding him as simply a teacher.

The other branch of Buddhism was known as Mahayana. It became dominant in China, Korea, and Japan. Mahayana encouraged the worship of the Buddha as a divine being and savior.

Today, only a few Indians are Buddhists. Most are Hindus. Muslims, Jains, Christians, and others make up the rest of the population. Recently, however, Buddhism has gained new followers in India, especially among the pariahs. Outside India, Buddhism has followers in the West as well as in the East.

SECTION 2 REVIEW

Recall
1. **Define** nirvana, stupa.
2. **Identify** Siddhartha Gautama, Four Noble Truths.
3. **Locate** on a map in the Atlas the Asian countries to which monks and merchants carried the teachings of the Buddha: China, Japan, Korea, Burma, Malaysia, Indonesia. How did the monks and merchants help to assure the survival of Buddhism as a worldwide religion?

Critical Thinking
4. **Synthesizing Information** Compare the religions of Hinduism and Buddhism, explaining which Hindu beliefs and practices the Buddha accepted and which he rejected in his teaching.

Understanding Themes
5. **Innovation** Decide how your own life and goals would be different if you tried to live by the Four Noble Truths and the Eightfold Path.

Section 3

Indian Empires

Setting the Scene

▶ **Terms to Define**
  "Arabic numerals"

▶ **People to Meet**
  Chandragupta Maurya, Asoka, Chandragupta I, Chandragupta II

▶ **Places to Locate**
  Magadha

Find Out What were the cultural achievements of the Mauryan and Gupta Empires?

The Storyteller

It troubled King Asoka that criminals continued their wrongdoing within his empire. Therefore he was proud of his latest merciful decree, carved on stone monuments: "Thus speaks the Beloved of the Gods.... This is my instruction from now on: Men who are imprisoned or sentenced to death are to be given three days respite. Thus their relations [relatives] may plead for their lives, or, if there is no one to plead for them, they may make their donations or undertake a fast for a better rebirth in the next life. For it is my wish that they should gain the next world."

—from Asoka and the Decline of the Mauryas, Romila Thapar, 1961

Lion-headed capital atop a Rock Edict pillar of Asoka

Despite the high mountain barriers in the north, India has never been completely cut off from other lands. The Aryans marched through the mountain passes to invade the Indus River valley; later, others followed. In the 500s B.C., Persian ruler Darius I conquered lands in the Indus River valley. Alexander the Great invaded the same area in 327 B.C., and Indian merchants carried on a busy trade with the Roman Empire. In all that time, however, no Indian king or foreign conqueror had ever succeeded in uniting the separate kingdoms into one Indian nation.

At the time of Darius's invasion, one Indian kingdom, **Magadha**, was expanding in the north. King Bimbisara, who ruled Magadha from 542 B.C. to 495 B.C., added to its territory by conquest and marriage. Although Magadha declined after Bimbisara's death, it was to become the center of India's first empire.

The Mauryan Empire

At the time of Alexander's invasion, Magadha was only one of many small warring states in northern India. Then, in 321 B.C., a military officer named **Chandragupta Maurya** (CHUHN •druh•GUP•tuh MAH•oor•yuh) overthrew the Magadhan king and proclaimed himself ruler.

Chandragupta Maurya was a skilled administrator whose achievements included the development of an efficient postal system. He kept control of his empire by maintaining a strong army and by using an extensive spy network. He founded a Mauryan kingdom that included most of northern and central India and lasted until 184 B.C.

Asoka's Enlightened Rule

Indian civilization blossomed during the reign of Chandragupta's grandson, **Asoka** (uh•SHOH •kuh). Asoka's rule began in 274 B.C. with fierce wars of conquest. His merciless armies swept

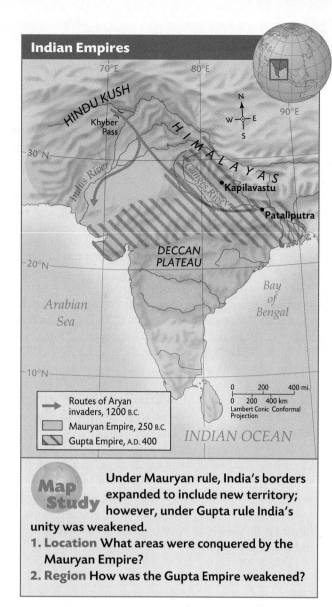

Indian Empires

HINDU KUSH
Khyber Pass
Indus River
HIMALAYAS
Ganges River
• Kapilavastu
• Pataliputra
DECCAN PLATEAU
Arabian Sea
Bay of Bengal
INDIAN OCEAN

70°E 80°E 90°E
30°N 20°N 10°N

0   200   400 mi.
0   200 400 km
Lambert Conic Conformal Projection

→ Routes of Aryan invaders, 1200 B.C.
▨ Mauryan Empire, 250 B.C.
▧ Gupta Empire, A.D. 400

Map Study Under Mauryan rule, India's borders expanded to include new territory; however, under Gupta rule India's unity was weakened.
1. **Location** What areas were conquered by the Mauryan Empire?
2. **Region** How was the Gupta Empire weakened?

across the plains and into the forests and cities, hunting down and killing their enemies. He built an empire that covered two-thirds of the Indian subcontinent.

After one particularly brutal battle, Asoka rode out to view the battlefield. The experience changed his life. As he looked on the bloodied bodies of the dead and maimed, the Indian ruler was horrified. Determined never again to rule by force and terror, Asoka renounced war. Henceforth, he announced, he would follow the teachings of the Buddha and become a man of peace. Asoka kept his word. During his reign, missionaries spread Buddhism throughout India and other parts of Asia.

Asoka issued laws stressing concern for other human beings. To make sure these laws became widely known, Asoka wrote them in the local languages rather than in Sanskrit. The laws, known

today as the Rock Edicts, were carved on rocks and on tall stone pillars throughout the vast empire.

Asoka's public projects reflected the same care for people. He provided free hospitals and veterinary clinics. He built fine roads, with rest houses and shade trees for the travelers' comfort.

Although he promoted Buddhism, Asoka permitted his non-Buddhist subjects to continue to practice Hinduism if they wished. The Hindu caste system continued.

Collapse of Mauryan Empire

The Mauryan Empire declined after Asoka's death in 232 B.C. because his successors were not as enlightened as he was. They levied heavy taxes on the goods sold by merchants and seized large portions of the crops grown by peasants. Such harsh policies caused the people to turn against the Mauryas. When the last Mauryan ruler was murdered in 184 B.C., northern India again split into many small warring kingdoms.

The Gupta Empire

After the Mauryan Empire, 500 years passed before much of India was again united. About A.D. 310, **Chandragupta I** began to build an empire. He was not related to Chandragupta Maurya, but like that earlier ruler he made Magadha the base of his kingdom.

Chandragupta I introduced the Gupta dynasty, which ruled northern India for more than 200 years. The arts and sciences flourished, and the Gupta period would later be called India's Golden Age.

The Guptas governed a much smaller empire than the Mauryas. They never gained control of the Indus Valley or of the Deccan, the broad plateau that forms most of India's southern peninsula. The Guptas did manage to build a strong state, however, and worked to maintain unquestioned authority. They trained soldiers and used spies and political assassins. In short, they did whatever they felt had to be done to maintain power.

Gupta Religion

The Gupta rulers encouraged learning based on the ideas found in the *Upanishads*. They made Hinduism the religion of their empire. Hindu temples were built—elaborate structures with brightly painted sculptures depicting tales in the *Mahabharata* and the *Ramayana*. Although each temple had its presiding god or goddess, the Hindus viewed the many deities as different ways of worshiping Brahman Nerguna, the eternal spirit.

The Ajanta Caves

On the inner side of a 70-foot (22-m) granite cliff in central India are a number of spectacular caves carved into the rock. Known today as the Ajanta caves, these wonders were built by Buddhist monks between A.D. 300 and A.D. 600.

The monks carved out the caves to serve as monasteries and temples. They first fashioned the ceilings of the chambers. Then they worked their way

Royal Procession, cave 17

downward, cutting out the walls and floors. Finally, sculptors and painters decorated cave entrances and interiors with murals, statues, and carved pillars.

Most of the Ajanta cave paintings illustrate tales and stories from the Buddha's previous lives. Some paintings show everyday life in early India. Others show Gupta kings and queens and their royal courts. Still others are images of ships, elaborate buildings, and animals such as elephants, bulls, and tigers. Art historians believe that the styles and subjects of the Ajanta cave paintings spread to other parts of India and eventually influenced Buddhist art throughout Asia.

MAKING THE CONNECTION

1. Who built the Ajanta caves? How and why did they build them?
2. What subjects do the sculptures and paintings show?

Gupta Life

The Gupta Empire reached its height under **Chandragupta II**, who ruled from A.D. 375 to A.D. 415. Faxian (FAH•SYEN), a Buddhist monk from China, traveled to India and recorded in his diary:

❝ In the Gupta Empire, people are numerous and happy; only those who cultivate the royal land have to pay [in] grain.... If they want to go, they go; if they want to stay, they stay. The king governs without decapitation [cutting off heads] or corporal [bodily] punishment.... The leaders of Vaisya families have houses in the cities for dispensing charity and medicine. ❞

Faxian may have exaggerated the benefits of Gupta rule, but he provided a useful glimpse into Indian life. By easing tax burdens, Chandragupta II gave people more freedom. Of all the Gupta monarchs, he was the most chivalrous and heroic. Though he expanded the empire, he is remembered for more than conquest. Gupta rulers believed they had reached a high level of civilization. They began to write down rules for everything, from grammar to drama to politics. The Sanskrit of the Gupta court

became the major language in the north.

In one respect, though, daily life did not improve during the Gupta period. The status of Indian women had declined since Aryan times. Aryan women at first often had a say about whom they would marry. By Gupta times, parents were choosing mates for their children, and child marriages were common. Women and mothers were

Highway Rest Stops

Asoka's highway rest stops were marked by stone pillars engraved with Buddhist teachings. On one of these pillars, Asoka explained:

I have ordered banyan trees to be planted along the roads to give shade to men and animals. I have ordered mango groves to be planted. I have ordered wells to be dug every [half-mile], and I have ordered rest houses built.

—The Edicts of Asoka

Gupta rulers decorated Hindu temples with elaborate scenes from the *Ramayana*, such as this painting of Rama and Lakshamana accompanied by Visvamitra. *What was the purpose of the* Panchatantra?

highly respected, but they had little power or independence.

Art and Learning

Learning flourished under the Guptas. The court welcomed poets, playwrights, philosophers, and scientists. Much of the writing was concentrated on religion, but folk tales were also popular. A collection of tales called the *Panchatantra* presented moral lessons through animals who acted like humans. Many of these stories eventually spread to the Middle East and the West, where they were retold by other authors. Drama was also important during Gupta times. Kalidasa, the most famous playwright, wrote *Shakuntala*, a play about romantic love between a king and a forest maiden.

Gupta mathematicians contributed significantly to mathematics as it is today, making major advances in developing the principles of algebra. They also explained the concept of infinity and invented the concept of zero. The symbols they devised for the numbers 1 to 9 were adopted by traders from the Middle East and so came to be called "Arabic numerals" in the West.

Gupta astronomers used these mathematical discoveries to advance their understanding of the universe. They realized that the earth is round, and they had some knowledge of gravity. In medicine, Gupta doctors set bones, performed operations, and invented hundreds of medical instruments.

Many countries benefited from Gupta achievements, as both ideas and products traveled the land and sea trade routes that connected India to the rest of the world. Indian exporters traded such items as gems, spices, cotton, teak, and ebony for horses from Arabia and central Asia, silk from China, and gold from Rome.

The Golden Age Ends

After Chandragupta II's death in A.D. 415, the Gupta Empire began to fail. As the government weakened, the Guptas faced invasions along India's northwestern border. By A.D. 600, the Gupta Empire had dissolved into a collection of small states.

However, much of the culture that was uniquely Indian survived. Many aspects of India's life today grew out of the social structures and religions, the arts and sciences, that were born during the 2,000 years that followed the Aryan invasions.

SECTION 3 REVIEW

Recall
1. **Define** "Arabic numerals."
2. **Identify** Chandragupta Maurya, Asoka, Chandragupta I, Chandragupta II, *Panchatantra*, *Shakuntala*.
3. **Locate** the map on page 212, and find the Mauryan Empire and the Gupta Empire. Compare and contrast their sizes and features.

Critical Thinking
4. **Analyzing Information** How did the rulers of India's empires have an effect on the religious life of the Indian people?

Understanding Themes
5. **Cultural Diffusion** What aspects of early Indian empires have had a lasting impact on India and the rest of the world?

Determining Cause and Effect

As you read a mystery novel, you may try to figure out which events or actions caused the main character to act in specific ways. Understanding history is a similar process. We try to find reasons behind people's actions. Looking for cause-effect relationships unlocks the mystery of history.

Learning the Skill

To identify cause-effect relationships in history, first select an event. Then examine the situation before this event. How was it different? Look for related problems and actions. These are likely causes of the event. Suppose you select the following event: Asoka's renunciation of war. What events preceded Asoka's decision? In earlier years, Asoka had led many brutal wars of conquest. Eventually, he was horrified by the bloody results of war. This combination of underlying and specific events caused him to renounce war altogether.

Now examine what happened after Asoka renounced war. He became a Buddhist, promoted Buddhist ideas of compassion, and passed laws

based on this philosophy. He also built hospitals and roads and worked to improve conditions for his people. These were direct and indirect effects of Asoka's change of direction.

Certain words and phrases often indicate cause-effect relationships; these include *because, due to, therefore, as a result of, led to, and brought about*. It can be hard to determine causes and effects of historical events. Facts may be missing. Moreover, we can't test our ideas as we can in science experiments. Instead, we must rely on logic and common sense.

Practicing the Skill

Read the paragraph below. Then answer the questions that follow.

> **"**Cattle were the basis of the Aryan diet and economy, even serving as money. Wealth was measured in cattle, and so the Aryans raided each other's herds. They were often at war.... Dozens of Aryan words describe cattle, indicating their continued prominence in Aryan life. Later, their herds would be considered so sacred that a ban was placed on eating meat. **"**

1. What were causes of conflict among Aryans?
2. How did the importance of cattle affect the culture and language of Aryans?

Applying the Skill

Reread Section 2, "Rise of Buddhism." Then describe causes of Buddhism's rise in India and its effects on India and other parts of the world.

For More Practice

Turn to the Skill Practice in the Chapter Review on page 217 for more practice in determining cause and effect.

Lion-headed capital atop a Rock Edict pillar of Asoka

Historical Significance

The civilization that developed in India between 1500 B.C. and A.D. 500 produced two of the world's great religions: Hinduism and Buddhism. Hinduism became not only India's major faith but also its way of life. Buddhism rejected many Hindu social practices and affirmed a disciplined life to achieve peace and deliverance from suffering. The belief in nonviolence has influenced modern leaders in their struggle for peace and human rights. Over the centuries, the two religions have inspired magnificent achievements in architecture and the arts.

Using Key Terms

Write the key term that completes each sentence.

a. ahimsa
b. dharma
c. epics
d. *jati*
e. karma
f. nirvana
g. rajah
h. reincarnation
i. stupas
j. *varna*

1. In following the Buddha's teachings, Buddhists strive to attain freedom from the cycle of rebirth, a state called _____.
2. The Aryans were loosely organized into a number of tribes, each of which was led by a _____, or chief.
3. The invading Aryans brought to the Indian subcontinent a system of four main social classes, or _____.
4. To ensure rebirth in a higher state, people in each Hindu group must properly perform their duty, or _____.
5. Early literary works, such as the *Mahabharata* and the *Ramayana*, are _____ that reflect basic Hindu beliefs and values.
6. Hindus believe in _____, a process of rebirth in which the soul resides in many bodies before it finally unites with Brahman Nerguna, or the universal spirit.
7. A person's _____ determines whether he or she will be closer to the universal spirit in the next life.
8. For purposes of prayer, Buddhist architects built large elaborate _____ over the remains of holy people.
9. Each *varna* was made up of social groups called _____ that were defined and ranked by occupation.
10. The practice of _____, or nonviolence, requires the believer to protect all living things—humans, animals, and even insects and plants—from harm.

Using Your History Journal

Refer to a world almanac to determine how many Buddhists and how many Hindus live in each region of the world today. Build a graph or create a world map that illustrates this information.

Reviewing Facts

1. **Identify** Chandragupta Maurya and his role in developing early Indian civilization.
2. **Explain** in your own words the Four Noble Truths of Buddhism.
3. **Define** *ahimsa* and describe how it is practiced in Indian society.
4. **Identify** the *Bhagavad Gita* and its major theme.
5. **Locate** where the Aryan invaders came from, and how they entered what later became Pakistan and northern India.
6. **List** some of the achievements of Indian mathematicians during the Gupta Empire.
7. **Identify** Siddhartha Gautama and his social background.

Critical Thinking

1. **Apply** How could a person use the principle of nonviolence, or ahimsa, as a force for social change?
2. **Analyze** How did ideas in the Hindu religion help to maintain the separation of classes in Indian society?
3. **Synthesize** What might have happened if Asoka had not been horrified while viewing the carnage after a fierce battle?

4. Analyze Here, two Brahman cattle stand in a street of Bombay, India. Why do Hindus abstain from eating meat?

Understanding Themes

1. **Movement** How was India affected by the Aryan invasions?
2. **Innovation** What might make Buddhism attractive to people from different cultures?
3. **Cultural Diffusion** Why did Gupta achievements in science and the arts spread quickly to other parts of the world, both Eastern and Western?

Linking Past and Present

1. The *varna* system created a huge underclass that Europeans called "the untouchables." How do you think this system created problems for modern India?
2. Religion has always had a major part in Indian society. How have religious differences hindered Indian unity in modern times?
3. Early in the 1900s, India applied the Hindu principle of nonviolence to help win its independence from Great Britain. Do you think people can still use nonviolence effectively to win freedom and human rights?

Geography in History

1. **Location** What mountain range forms India's northern border?
2. **Movement** What routes did the Aryan invaders take to the interior of India?
3. **Region** What effect did the invasion of the Aryans have on the developing culture of India?
4. **Human/Environment Interaction** What physical features made it difficult for one empire to unify all of northern and southern India?

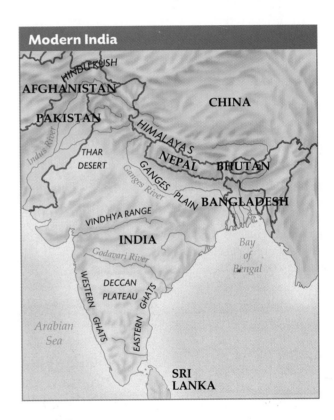

Modern India

Skill Practice

Reread the discussion of "The Gupta Empire" in Section 3. Then answer the following questions.

1. What caused the Gupta rulers to use spies and assassins?
2. The Guptas adopted Hinduism as India's religion. What effects did this have on art and architecture?
3. What were the effects of Gupta culture on science and mathematics?
4. What caused the breakup of the Gupta Empire?

Chapter 9

1100 B.C.–A.D. 200
China's Flourishing Civilization

Chapter Themes

▸ **Uniformity** The Qin and Han dynasties establish and maintain a strong central government. *Section 1*
▸ **Innovation** The Chinese formulate ethical philosophies and make scientific and technological advances. *Section 2*
▸ **Cultural Diffusion** Traders carry ideas and products along the Silk Road. *Section 3*

The Storyteller

Whom do you agree with in the following conversation, dating from the 500s B.C.? What is right, or "straightness," in this case?

The Governor of She said to Confucius: "In our village there is a man nicknamed Straight Body. When his father stole a sheep, he gave evidence against him." Confucius answered, "In our village those who are straight are quite different. Fathers cover up for their sons, and sons cover up for their fathers...."

This conversation involves a conflict between law and family. Confucius's view—that family should always take precedence—reflects an attitude toward families that was dominant in Chinese culture for a long time.

Historical Significance

How did the ideas of Confucius and other Chinese thinkers affect behavior in Chinese society for centuries? How have their ideas influenced China's development and its relationship with other parts of the world?

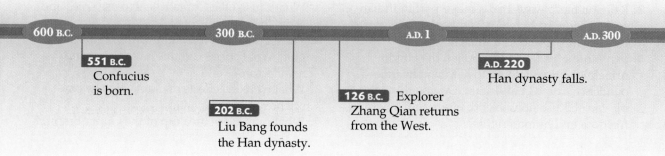

600 B.C. | 300 B.C. | A.D. 1 | A.D. 300

551 B.C. Confucius is born.

202 B.C. Liu Bang founds the Han dynasty.

126 B.C. Explorer Zhang Qian returns from the West.

A.D. 220 Han dynasty falls.

218

The Great Wall of China at Huang Ya Guan, a view of a section of the 4000-mile-long wall

Your History Journal

Chinese inventions and discoveries include many "firsts" such as printed books, the compass, and gunpowder. Choose one Chinese invention or discovery reported in this chapter and write a short research report on its early history.

771 B.C. Zhou political power begins to decline.

221 B.C. Qin Shihuangdi founds the Qin dynasty.

141 B.C. Wudi becomes the sixth Han emperor.

Section 1

Three Great Dynasties

Setting the Scene

▶ **Terms to Define**
   cavalry, civil service, mandarin

▶ **People to Meet**
   Qin Shihuangdi, Liu Bang, Wudi, Zhang Qian

▶ **Places to Locate**
   Great Wall of China, Silk Road

Find Out What major advances did China make under the Zhou, Qin, and Han dynasties?

The Storyteller

Seeing the Marquis Chao of Han asleep on the cold floor, the keeper of the royal hat covered him with a robe. Upon awakening, the marquis demanded to know who had covered him. Learning the keeper of the hat was responsible, the marquis punished the keeper of the robe for failing to perform his duty. Then he punished the keeper of the hat for undertaking tasks not his to perform. The trespass of one official upon the duties of another was considered a great danger.

—adapted from *Basic Writing of Mo Tzu, Hsün Tzu, and Han Fei Tzu,* reprinted in *The Global Experience: Readings in World History to 1500,* 1987

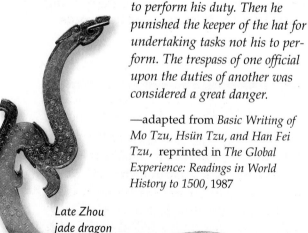

Late Zhou jade dragon

Around 1100 B.C., the Chinese people were fashioning ideas that would result in a unique civilization. From then until the A.D. 200s, the Chinese lived under three dynasties, or ruling families—the Zhou (JOH), the Qin (CHIN), and the Han (HAHN). The first of these, the Zhou, ruled the nation for more than 800 years, longer than any other Chinese dynasty.

The Enduring Zhou

The Zhou conquered the last Shang dynasty king around 1028 B.C., claiming the Mandate of Heaven, or heaven's approval. They called their king the Son of Heaven, saying that the Shang had lost the mandate by ruling poorly.

Eventually, the Zhou held a vast realm. To control their holdings, Zhou kings set up an agricultural system in which nobles owned the land and peasants worked it. They appointed their relatives to govern, giving each one a city-state.

Each local lord had total authority on his own lands and built his own army. At first all the lords pledged allegiance to the Son of Heaven. In time, though, some grew strong enough to challenge the king's authority.

In 771 B.C. the Zhou suffered a severe defeat in a conflict with their enemies. After that, political power fell increasingly to local nobles. In the next centuries, the nobles fought small wars until by the 200s B.C., several city-states were locked in a struggle that ended the Zhou era.

Even though Zhou rulers lost their power, the Zhou are remembered for many technological advances. During the Zhou period the Chinese built roads and expanded foreign trade. They obtained horses from western nomads, forming a

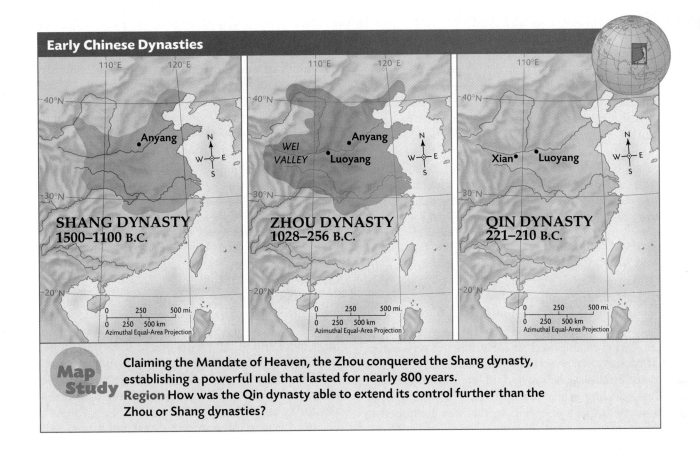

Early Chinese Dynasties

SHANG DYNASTY
1500–1100 B.C.

ZHOU DYNASTY
1028–256 B.C.

QIN DYNASTY
221–210 B.C.

Map Study Claiming the Mandate of Heaven, the Zhou conquered the Shang dynasty, establishing a powerful rule that lasted for nearly 800 years. **Region** How was the Qin dynasty able to extend its control further than the Zhou or Shang dynasties?

cavalry, or group of mounted warriors, along with horse-drawn chariots. The Zhou also added a deadly weapon: the crossbow. They further elaborated the system of picture writing begun by the Shang, a system that is the ancestor of modern Chinese writing. Under the Zhou, iron plows were invented, irrigation systems were developed, and flood-control systems were initiated. These and other advances led to population growth, and Zhou China became the world's most densely populated country.

The Mighty Qin

Meanwhile, several small states were struggling for control in China. Among them was a state on the western border ruled by the Qin. By 221 B.C., the Qin had wiped out the Zhou and conquered the rest of northern China, uniting much of the nation under a strong central authority for the first time. Westerners would later call the nation *China* after the Qin, whose first ruler added the title Shihuangdi (SHUR•HWONG•DEE), or First Emperor, to his name.

A tireless ruler, **Qin Shihuangdi** set out to create a government directly under his control. He reorganized the empire into military districts, appointing officials to govern them. This system

prevented local lords from becoming strong enough to challenge the power of the central government—the problem that had led to the downfall of the Zhou.

The First Emperor made other changes to further centralize his control. He devised a system of weights and measures to replace the various systems used in different regions. He standardized coins, instituted a uniform writing system, and set up a law code throughout China.

Qin had grandiose plans for his empire, and he used forced labor to accomplish them. Gangs of Chinese peasants dug canals and built roads.

Footnotes to History

Court Magic
A court magician made a potion for Wudi, claiming that it would give immortality. Before the emperor got the potion, a scholar drank it. The scholar was immediately sentenced to death but told Wudi that, if the potion was genuine, Wudi would not be able to kill him. If the potion was a fake, he had done no harm. Wudi had to agree. Needless to say, the scholar had exposed a fraud.

The Great Wall

To Qin, one building project seemed especially urgent—shoring up China's defenses to the north. Earlier rulers had built walls to prevent attacks by nomadic invaders. Qin ordered those walls connected. Over several years some 300,000 peasants toiled—and thousands died—before the work was done. Eventually the wall stretched more than 4,000 miles (6,437 km). Rebuilt by later rulers, the **Great Wall of China** stands today as a monument to Qin's ambition and to the peasants who carried out their emperor's will.

Qin's Strict Rule

Qin Shihuangdi imposed a new order on China. He ended the power of the local lords by taking land from many of them and imposing a tax on landowners. He appointed educated men instead of nobles as officials to run his government.

Qin even imposed an early form of censorship, clamping down on scholars who discussed books and ideas. In 213 B.C. he ordered all books burned except those dealing with "practical" subjects like agriculture, medicine, and magic. In this way he hoped to break people's ties to the past. He agreed with his adviser, who said, "anyone referring to the past to criticize the present … should be put to death." About 460 scholars resisted and were executed.

Qin's subjects saw him as a cruel tyrant who had lost the Mandate of Heaven. Nobles were angry because he had destroyed the aristocracy; scholars detested him for the burning of books; and peasants hated his forced-labor gangs. In 210 B.C. Qin died, and soon the dynasty itself came to an end. Even so, the rule of the Qin brought lasting changes. The most influential changes were new ways of organizing the nation, establishing foundations for the Chinese state that would last 2,000 years.

The Glorious Han

In 207 B.C. **Liu Bang** (LYOH BONG) overthrew the Qin government. A military official from a peasant background, Liu defeated his most powerful rival in 202 B.C. and declared himself the emperor of a new dynasty, the Han.

The Han governed China until A.D. 220, more than 400 years. The Han emperors used the same forms of centralized power that the Qin had set up, but without the harshness of Qin rule. Han China rivaled the Roman Empire in its power and achievement.

Advances Under Wudi

The Han dynasty reached its peak during the reign of **Wudi** (WOO•DEE), who ruled from 141 B.C. to 87 B.C. Wudi, one of the most talented and dynamic rulers in Chinese history, personally supervised all aspects of his government.

An ambitious ruler, Wudi extended his empire. He sent huge armies against the nomadic invaders and other non-Chinese peoples. He conquered lands to the north, including Korea and Manchuria, south into Southeast Asia, and west as far as northern India.

In 139 B.C. Wudi sent out an expedition led by **Zhang Qian** (JAHNG CHYEN), a general and explorer. Thirteen years later, Zhang staggered back. His troops had been nearly wiped out by barbarian attacks, and the general had endured more than 10 years of captivity.

Although he had made no conquests, Zhang brought back amazing tales he had heard on his travels. He told of a great empire to the west, with huge cities full of people "who cut their hair short, wear embroidered garments, and ride in very small chariots." Zhang, who was describing Rome, gave Han rulers their first hint of another civilization as advanced as their own.

Wudi's new interest in the West, fed by news of Zhang Qian's explorations, led to the expansion of trade routes later known as the **Silk Road**. Winding past deserts and through mountain passes, the Silk Road linked East and West. It allowed traders to exchange China's fine silk for Middle Eastern and European products, such as gold, glassware, and wool and linen fabrics.

Pax Sinica

Under the Han, China enjoyed a 400-year period of prosperity and stability, later referred to as the *Pax Sinica* (PAHKS SIH•nuh•kuh), the Chinese Peace. The *Pax Sinica* coincided with the *Pax Romana* in the West.

During the *Pax Sinica*, Wudi adopted an economic policy designed to prevent food shortages and high prices. Government agents stored surplus food during years of plenty and sold it when harvests were poor. Under this system, China was able to feed its growing population.

Before Wudi, emperors had chosen as their officials members of their families or of the aristocracy, a practice that led easily to corruption in government. Wudi wanted talented people to govern, and so he initiated changes. First, he asked people to recommend candidates for public posts. These candidates took long, difficult written examinations. After an official "graded" the tests, the emperor evaluated the results and appointed those with the highest scores.

Thomas J. Abercrombie

Silk Road

The Silk Route

National Geographic Publications
Art Division

A caravan of men and mules walk a trail that once formed part of the old Silk Road, a network of paths cutting across Asia from the Pacific coast of China to the Mediterranean Sea. The route, first traveled many years before the Christian era, was the passageway not only for Chinese silk but for a great range of products including jade and fruit, ideas and paintings. Today it is still possible to see how poles and rocks created the actual highway over which goods moved throughout many centuries—before ships, trains, buses, and airplanes replaced mules and packs.

You can trace the length of the trip on the accompanying map. A trader setting forth from the Chinese city of Nanjing would soon leave Chinese territory and enter a world of Muslim ethnic groups and treacherous terrain. The trail loops south and north of the scorching Takla Makan Desert and rises high through mountain passes across the Pamir Mountains. The whole trip was far too long for a single caravan to undertake. Instead, Chinese or Persian merchants dealt with central Asian middlemen from lands such as Afghanistan and Turkestan. ⊕

Chapter 9 *China's Flourishing Civilization* **223**

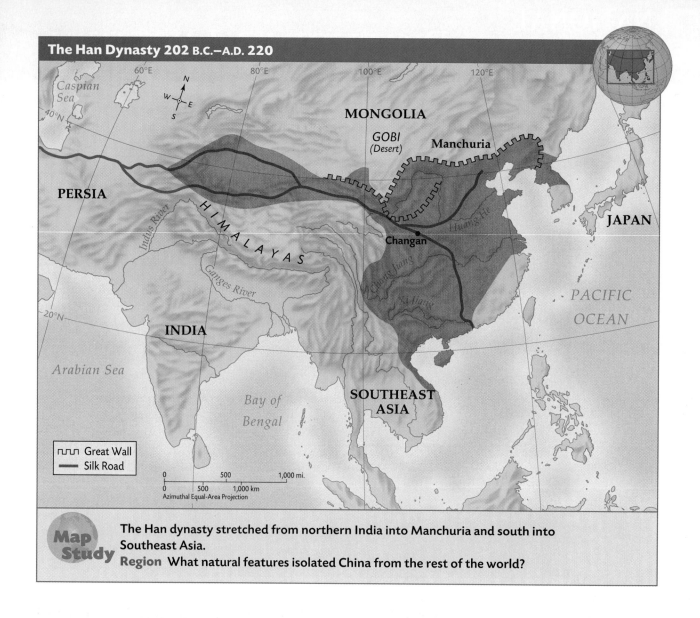

MONGOLIA

GOBI (Desert)

Manchuria

PERSIA

HIMALAYAS

Indus River

Huang He

Changan

Chang Jiang

Xi Jiang

JAPAN

PACIFIC OCEAN

Ganges River

INDIA

Arabian Sea

Bay of Bengal

SOUTHEAST ASIA

⌐⌐⌐ Great Wall
— Silk Road

0   500   1,000 mi.
0   500   1,000 km
Azimuthal Equal-Area Projection

Map Study The Han dynasty stretched from northern India into Manchuria and south into Southeast Asia.
Region What natural features isolated China from the rest of the world?

Wudi's examinations evolved into the civil service, a system that allowed anyone with ability to attain public office. At least, that was the theory. In practice, the system favored the wealthy, for education was expensive, and usually only the wealthy could afford to obtain enough education to pass the exams.

The civil service system made scholars the most respected members of Chinese society. A new class of well-educated civil servants, called mandarins, controlled the government, and they would continue to do so until the early 1900s.

After Wudi's reign, Han power declined until the dynasty eventually fell in A.D. 220. However, Han achievements in government, technology, science, and the arts were lasting.

SECTION 1 REVIEW

Recall
1. **Define** cavalry, civil service, mandarin.
2. **Identify** Qin Shihuangdi, Liu Bang, Wudi, Zhang Qian.
3. **List** two of the major achievements the Chinese people made under each dynasty—the Zhou, the Qin, and the Han.

Critical Thinking
4. **Analyzing Information** Did Wudi's civil service system offer equal opportunity to all Chinese? Explain.

Understanding Themes
5. **Uniformity** How did Qin Shihuangdi unify China?

c. 522 B.C. Confucius begins to teach.

c. 500 B.C. Daoism emerges as a major Chinese philosophy.

c. A.D. 400 Buddhism becomes a popular religion in China.

Section 2

Three Ways of Life

Setting the Scene

▶ **Terms to Define**
ethics, filial piety, yin and yang

▶ **People to Meet**
Confucius (Kongzi), Laozi

Find Out What philosophic ideals shaped China's government, and how did they shape it?

The Storyteller

One of the duties of Prince Wei-hui's cook was to slaughter cattle for the royal table. When he performed this task, all his movements were harmonious, like a dance. The prince was amazed and asked his servant how he was able to do such heavy work so effortlessly. The cook explained, "What your servant loves is the Tao, which I have applied to the skill of carving. I work with my mind, and not with my eyes." In this way, the toughest cuts yielded easily before his skill. He had learned how to nurture his spirit while maintaining his livelihood.

—adapted from *A Source Book in Chinese Philosophy*, reprinted in *Lives and Times: A World History Reader*, James P. Holoka and Jiu-Hwa L. Upshur, 1994

Confucius

In the latter half of the Zhou era, two major philosophies appeared in China—Confucianism and Daoism. Neither dealt with the supernatural or with eternal life; both were focused instead on life in this world.

Confucianism

Confucianism grew out of the teachings of **Kongzi** (KOONG•DZUH), a government official from Shandong Province. Known in the West as **Confucius**, he was born about 551 B.C. to a poor family. For over 12 years, Confucius traveled throughout northern China, seeking a position as an adviser to a ruler. He hoped that in such a position he could help end China's political and social disorder. Never able to get the post he wanted, Confucius finally found a way to spread his ideas by becoming a teacher.

Family and Government

Promoting order was Confucius's principal concern. He believed that everyone had a proper role in society. If each person would accept that role and perform the related duties, social and political disorder would end. Confucius did not write books, but his followers collected his sayings and later published them in a collection called the *Analects*.

Individuals, Confucius taught, should live according to principles of ethics—good conduct and moral judgment. Ethics began with respect for family, especially elders, and reverence for the past and its traditions. Ethics should govern each person's behavior in these five primary relationships: ruler and subject, parent and child, husband and wife, old and young, friend and friend. Each person, Confucius believed, owed respect and obedience to those above him or her. Those above were expected to set a good example for those below.

Confucius cared especially about filial piety, or children's respect for their parents. For Confucius,

Chapter 9 *China's Flourishing Civilization* **225**

the family represented society in miniature. He said:

> **❝** The superior man spreads his culture to the entire nation by remaining at home.... The teaching of filial piety is a preparation for serving the ruler of the state; the teaching of respect for one's elder brothers is a preparation for serving all the elders of the community; and the teaching of kindness in parents is a training for ruling over people.... When individual families have learned kindness, then the whole nation has learned kindness. **❞**

Governments too had a duty: to set an example of right conduct. The ethical ruler had integrity, was righteous, inspired loyalty, understood proper behavior, and appreciated culture.

When a student asked Confucius for one single word that could serve as a principle for conduct, he responded: "Perhaps the word *reciprocity* will do. Do not do unto others what you would not want others to do unto you." This rule is similar to a familiar teaching of Judaism and Christianity, sometimes called the Golden Rule: "Do unto others as you would have others do unto you."

Confucianism After Confucius

The Zhou government did not accept Confucius's teachings during his lifetime. Within a century after his death in 479 B.C., however, Confucian ethics were widely followed in China. Later scholars added their ideas, and Confucianism eventually became a religion.

During the Han dynasty, Confucius's teachings provided the basis for Wudi's civil service system. Though Han scholars reinterpreted Confucianism, they retained its devotion to ethical behavior and just government. Indeed, Confucius's teachings would serve as a basis for Chinese society and government until the 1900s.

Daoism

During the time of Confucius, a man called **Laozi** (LOW•DZUH), or "Old Master," taught ideas that in some ways seem the opposite of Confucianism. He rejected formal social structures and the idea that people must fill specific roles in society. Unlike Confucius, Laozi shunned public

The First Seismograph

Zhang Heng's seismograph

In 1994 a powerful earthquake struck Los Angeles, California. A year later, the city of Kobe in Japan was rocked by a major quake that brought death and destruction throughout the city's metropolitan area.

Today we know that shifting in the earth's crust causes earthquakes. This movement sends seismic waves across the earth's surface, much as dropping a pebble in a pond sends ripples across water.

People in Han China believed that angry spirits caused earthquakes to express their displeasure with society. Scholars studied quakes closely in hope of finding a divine message.

In A.D. 132 Zhang Heng invented the world's first seismograph, an instrument for detecting and measuring earthquakes. Zhang's device resembled a domed, cylindrical urn. Each of eight dragons around the top held a ball in its jaws. At the base of the urn sat eight toads with upturned heads and open mouths, each directly under a dragon.

When a tremor occurred, a mechanism caused one of the balls to fall into a toad's mouth. This action showed that somewhere an earthquake was taking place. The side of the seismograph where that toad was sitting indicated the quake's direction. As the ball popped into the toad's mouth, the loudness indicated the tremor's strength.

MAKING THE CONNECTION

1. How did Zhang Heng's seismograph work?
2. Why might Han emperors want to know about earthquakes?

life, leaving anything we know of him heavily mixed with legend.

Daoist Ideas

Laozi's ideas were recorded in the *Dao De Jing*, one of the Chinese classics. Daoists believed that people should renounce worldly ambitions and turn to nature and the Dao—the eternal force that permeates everything in nature. They followed examples from nature, as these lines suggest:

> **"** The highest good is like water.
> Water gives life to the ten thousand things
>   and does not strive.
> It flows in places men reject and so is like
>   the Dao.
> In dwelling, be close to the land.
> In meditation, go deep in the heart.
> In dealing with others, be gentle and kind.
> In speech, be true.
> In ruling, be just. **"**

By emphasizing harmony with nature, Daoists deeply influenced Chinese arts, particularly painting and poetry.

Daoist simplicity seems to oppose Confucian formalism, but a person could be both a Confucianist and a Daoist. Confucianism provided the pattern for government and one's place in the social order, and Daoism emphasized harmony within the individual attuned to nature. Because the emphasis of each was different, a person could easily be both.

Yin and Yang

A Chinese theory related to Daoist ideas was the concept of yin and yang, the two opposing forces believed to be present in all nature. Yin was cool, dark, female, and submissive, while yang was warm, light, male, and aggressive. Everything had both elements. For harmony the two elements had to be in balance. Human life and natural events, including the changing seasons, resulted from the interplay between yin and yang.

History & Art Laozi on his buffalo. Guimet Museum, Paris, France. *How did the teaching of Laozi as recorded in the Dao De Jing influence Chinese arts and poetry?*

The concept of yin and yang helped the Chinese reconcile seeming opposites—like Dao simplicity and Confucian formalism. It also helped them accept Buddhist ideas brought to China by monks and traders from India.

Buddhism

Buddhism reached China just as the Han Empire was collapsing, and its emphasis on personal salvation in nirvana appealed to many people seeking an escape from suffering. Confucianists could follow its Eightfold Path, and Daoists admired its use of meditation. By the A.D. 400s, Buddhism was widely embraced in China.

SECTION 2 REVIEW

Recall
1. **Define** ethics, filial piety, yin and yang.
2. **Identify** Confucius, Laozi.
3. **Explain** why Confucius wanted to become an adviser to a ruler. What was his goal in life, and was he successful?

Critical Thinking
4. **Making Comparisons** How would you compare the philosophers Confucius and Laozi in their ideas and also in their ways of life?

Understanding Themes
5. **Innovation** How did the concept of yin and yang help the Chinese people reconcile ideas in the thought of Daoism that seemed opposed to Confucianism?

1000 B.C. 500 B.C. A.D. 1

1000 B.C. Chinese begin poems in the *Book of Songs*.

240 B.C. Chinese astronomers record appearance of Halley's comet.

c. 100 B.C. Chinese invent paper.

Section 3

Society and Culture

Setting the Scene

▶ **Terms to Define**
hierarchy, extended family, nuclear family, acupuncture

▶ **People to Meet**
Sima Qian

Find Out How was early Chinese society organized, and what scientific and technological breakthroughs took place in early China?

The Storyteller

Wu Phu was a physician, trained by Hua Tho, an outstanding medical theorist. Hua Tho impressed upon his pupils the importance of physical exercise as a means of obtaining good health. He compared an exercised body to running water, which never became stale. "When the body feels ill," he counseled, "one should do one of these exercises. After perspiring, one will sense the body grow light and the stomach will manifest hunger." There was merit in those recommendations. Wu Phu had carefully followed his master's regimen, and although he was past ninety years of age, his hearing, vision, and even his teeth were all still excellent.

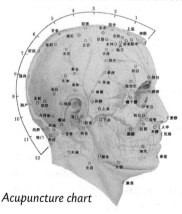

—adapted from "Hygiene and Preventive Medicine in Ancient China," reprinted in *Reflections on World Civilization*, edited by Ronald H. Fritze, James S. Olson, and Randy W. Roberts, 1994

Acupuncture chart

Confucian values governed all aspects of personal and social life in Han China. "With harmony at home, there will be order in the nation," Confucius had said. "With order in the nation, there will be peace in the world." And indeed, the family was supreme in Chinese society. It was the focus of life, bound together strongly by mutual love, loyalty, and dependence.

Family Life

The members of a Chinese family of the Han era lived and worked together. In an ideal family every member knew his or her role and the duties that went with it.

Relationships

Family members did not relate to each other as equals; instead, the family was a strict hierarchy, organized into different levels of importance. The oldest male in the home, usually the father, was dominant. Next in rank was the oldest son, followed by all the younger sons and all the females. The mother came before the daughters, and finally—at the bottom—the youngest daughter or childless daughter-in-law. Each family member expected obedience from those who were further down in the hierarchy, and each obeyed and respected those who were above.

Family Rules

Strict rules governed the relationships between husbands and wives, parents and grandparents, uncles and aunts, brothers and sisters, and other relatives. Each family member knew his or her place and understood its duties, and each was careful not to bring dishonor on the family by failing in those duties. Moreover, the duty to family members did not stop at death; all were expected to pay respect to departed ancestors.

Typical homes in Han China did not have the extended families, or families of many generations living together, that would later be typical. Rather, they had what we call today nuclear families, each consisting of parents and their children. The father assigned his children's careers, determined their education, arranged their marriages, meted out rewards or punishments, and controlled the family finances. The family also provided support for members who themselves could not contribute—the aged, the young, the sick, and even the lazy.

No doubt the system offered many opportunities for exploiting those further down in the hierarchy. Nevertheless, few fathers were tyrants. Like other family members, they practiced ethical principles of kindness and compassion, either from genuine love or from fear of the disapproval of others and the scorn of their ancestors.

Status of Women

Under the Confucian social system, women were subordinate to men. Confucius himself had little regard for women, saying, "Women and uneducated people are the most difficult to deal with."

Girls began life subservient to their fathers and brothers. Later their husbands and in-laws were their superiors, and eventually even a mother came under the authority of her own sons. Parents valued baby girls far less than baby boys. A poor family had to work hard to raise and support a child, and if that child was a daughter, she left home to become part of her husband's family as soon as she married.

Some women were able to gain respect in Chinese homes. With marriage and motherhood, they became revered. Other opportunities for women, such as education, were limited. In spite of Confucianism's predominance, women fared far better under the Han than they would in later centuries. They could inherit property, even own it after they married, and they could remarry after a husband's death.

Society and Economy

Chinese society consisted of three main classes: landowners, peasants, and merchants. Landowning families were wealthy. They lived in tile-roofed mansions with courtyards and gardens. They surrounded their homes with walls to protect them from bandits. They filled their rooms with fine furniture and adorned them with silk wall hangings and carpets. Wealthy families feasted on a rich variety of foods.

The landholders' wealth was generally limited, however, and families rarely kept their holdings for

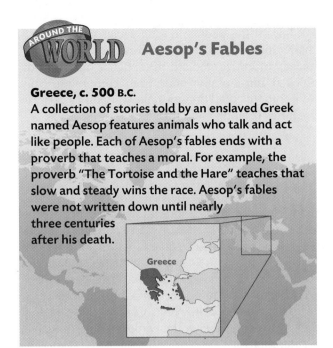

AROUND THE WORLD **Aesop's Fables**

Greece, c. 500 B.C.
A collection of stories told by an enslaved Greek named Aesop features animals who talk and act like people. Each of Aesop's fables ends with a proverb that teaches a moral. For example, the proverb "The Tortoise and the Hare" teaches that slow and steady wins the race. Aesop's fables were not written down until nearly three centuries after his death.

Greece

more than a few generations. When a family's land was divided, it went to all the sons, not just the oldest, with the result that in time individual landowners had less and less property.

Probably 90 percent of the Chinese people were peasants. The wealth that supported the lifestyles of the rich was gained from the hard labor of the peasants who cultivated the land. Unlike Western farmers, who usually lived on the land they farmed, most Chinese peasants lived in rural villages and worked fields outside their mud walls. Their homes were simple, and they ate a plain diet that featured millet, rice, beans, turnips, and fish.

The peasants raised livestock and toiled long hours in the grain fields. They faced constant threats from floods and from famines. As rent for the land, peasants turned over part of their produce to the landowner. The government required them to pay taxes and to work one month each year on public works projects such as road building. In times of conflict, peasants were drafted into the army as soldiers.

At the bottom of the social hierarchy were merchants—a group that included shopkeepers, traders, service workers, and even bankers. The merchants lived in towns and provided goods and services for the wealthy. In spite of the great wealth that many merchants accumulated, Chinese society generally held them in contempt. Confucianism taught that the pursuit of profit was an unworthy pastime for the "superior" individual. Merchants were not allowed to take the civil service examinations and enter government service.

For all the people in Han society except merchants, the civil service system provided opportunities for advancement, though the expense of education blocked most of the poor from competing. Still, poor but talented individuals sometimes rose to positions of power and influence.

Literature

Although the Qin burned thousands of books, many survived in royal libraries and secret private collections. Particularly prized was a collection of books called the Five Classics, some of which were written before Confucius. All candidates for the civil service were required to master them. No better example is recorded of the Chinese reverence for history.

The oldest of the Five Classics, the *Book of Songs*, preserves 305 of the earliest Chinese poems, written between 1000 B.C. and 600 B.C. The poems deal with political themes, ritual, and romance. Many seem modern, with their everyday topics and simple, concrete imagery—this one, for example:

> " Near the East Gate
> Young women go
> Like so many clouds all day.
> Like drifting clouds
> A thought of them
> Soon blows away.
>
> There. White robe
> and a blue scarf—
> she makes my day.
>
> Near the Great Tower and Wall
> Go slender girls
> Like reeds by river's edge:
> Like bending reeds
> A thought of them
> Soon passes by. "

The *Book of Documents* records political speeches

Han China

The Han dynasty was a golden age of Chinese history. Important political, economic, and cultural changes took place.

Wudi's examinations developed into a civil service system, leading to a wealthy class of mandarins who controlled the government.

and documents from early in the Zhou dynasty, including the earliest statement of the Mandate of Heaven. The *Book of Changes* presents a complex system for foretelling the future and choosing a course of action. In *Spring and Autumn Annals* Confucius reported major events that occurred in the state of Lu between 722 B.C. and 481 B.C.

The Five Classics were thought to carry solutions to most problems. Officials studied them closely to find support for their positions, such as the conduct of political leaders. Accounts of solar eclipses, meteor showers, and droughts were used to show what terrifying events and disasters could befall poor political leaders.

Another great collection of books, the Thirteen Classics, included the *Analects*—Confucius's sayings compiled by his students after his death. Many appeared as answers to questions. For example, Confucius was asked about the gentleman, or the "superior man." Among other replies he gave this one: "What the gentleman seeks, he seeks within himself; what the small man seeks, he seeks in others."

The Han Chinese encouraged literary pursuits and made literature available to everyone. An especially valuable work produced during the Han dynasty period was the *Historical Record*. Written by **Sima Qian** during the reign of Wudi, it is the first true history of ancient China.

Science and Technology

Besides literature and philosophy, China made major contributions in science and technology. By the 300s B.C., Chinese astronomers had calculated the length of the solar year as $365\frac{1}{4}$ days. They gazed through bronze tubes equipped with a device that divided the sky into measured segments, allowing them to make accurate measurements. They kept valuable records of solar and lunar eclipses and comet sightings. In 240 B.C. Chinese astronomers recorded the appearance of the object that would later be called Halley's comet—many centuries before Halley's birth.

Fine Han pottery, produced during 400 years of prosperity and stability, served wealthy landowners and merchants.

A terra-cotta horseman from Yang-kia-Wan was created as a funerary statuette.

REFLECTING ON THE TIMES

1. How did mandarins come to control the government of China?
2. Why do the arts develop during periods of prosperity?

Visualizing History Women prepare newly woven silk. Han weavers created beautiful damasks of many colors. *What was the name of one of history's greatest trade routes out of China?*

Medicine

Chinese physicians recognized nutrition as vital and realized that some diseases resulted from vitamin deficiencies. Although they did not identify vitamins as such, they discovered and prescribed foods that would correct some problems. They also understood that many herbs had medicinal value.

Chinese doctors treated ailments and relieved pain with acupuncture, a technique in which the skin is pierced with thin needles at vital points. They believed acupuncture restored the balance between yin and yang in a person's body.

Farming and Transport

Under the Han, many improvements occurred in agriculture and transportation. Complex irrigation systems drained swamps and diverted rivers to quench parched fields. Advances in fertilizing crops helped farmers produce enough to feed China's growing population. Veterinary medicine helped save many farm animals. New canals and improved roadways reduced the cost of distributing food and permitted ideas to spread more rapidly.

Inventions

Many inventions in ancient China were especially vital to Chinese life and the economy. Made by the Chinese since prehistoric times, silk was in great demand as a trade item; its worth was attested to by the name of one of history's greatest trade routes—the Silk Road. Caravans carried the precious cargo as far as Rome.

Paper was probably invented by 100 B.C., although it was officially credited to an inventor of about 200 years later. Artisans pounded tree bark, hemp, or rags into a pulp. By treating it with gelatin, they discovered that they could then make paper. Used first for wrapping and clothing, paper was soon recognized as an ideal writing material.

The invention of paper benefited the bureaucratic Han government. Its centralized structure resulted in an explosion in the number of documents. Most were written on strips of wood, which were fragile and cumbersome to work with. The use of paper had many obvious advantages.

Other inventions improved mining and construction. Miners, using iron drill bits driven by workers on seesawlike levers, drilled boreholes to obtain salt from the earth. Another invention was the wheelbarrow, which was first used on building sites around 100 B.C.

These are only a few examples from a list of Chinese "firsts," which also includes the first printed books, the earliest technologies for casting bronze and iron, the suspension bridge, the compass, and gunpowder. Such achievements caused China to remain far ahead of Europe in science and technology until the A.D. 1300s.

SECTION 3 REVIEW

Recall
1. **Define** hierarchy, extended family, nuclear family, acupuncture.
2. **Identify** the Five Classics, *Spring and Autumn Annals*, the *Analects*, Sima Qian.
3. **Explain** how families and government during the Han era reflected the Confucian idea of order.

Critical Thinking
4. **Making Comparisons** Compare a typical Han Chinese family with families you consider typical of America today.

Understanding Themes
5. **Cultural Diffusion** What ideas and products from ancient China have become popular in the West in recent years? What factors account for their popularity among Western thinkers and consumers?

Critical Thinking SKILLS

Identifying Central Issues

The saying "He can't see the forest for the trees" refers to someone so focused on separate details that he cannot see the entire situation. Sometimes we face this problem when studying history. It is easy to focus on details such as names, dates, and places, thus losing sight of the bigger picture. To avoid this, it is important to identify the central issues. Central issues are the main ideas of historical material.

Learning the Skill

First, skim the material to identify its general subject. Look for headings and subheadings; often they highlight central issues. A central issue may also appear in the topic sentence of a paragraph. The other sentences in the paragraph usually explain and support the central issue.

When looking for central issues, ask yourself these questions: What is the general topic of this material? What ideas have the greatest emphasis? What main idea holds the details together? If I had to summarize this material in one sentence, what would it be? If you can answer one or more of these questions, you can identify central issues.

Practicing the Skill

Read the passage about the *Book of Changes* and answer the questions that follow.

❝ The *Book of Changes—I Ching* in Chinese—is unquestionably one of the most important books in the world's literature…. Nearly all that is greatest and most significant in the three thousand years of Chinese cultural history has either taken its inspiration from this book, or has exerted an influence on the interpretation of its text…. Indeed, not only the philosophy of China but its science and statecraft as well have never ceased to draw from the spring of wisdom in the *I Ching*…. Even the

commonplaces of everyday life in China are saturated with its influence. In going through the streets of a Chinese city, one will find, here and there at a street corner, a fortune teller sitting behind a neatly covered table, brush and tablet at hand, ready to draw from the ancient book of wisdom pertinent counsel and information on life's minor perplexities…. ❞

1. What is the general subject of the passage?
2. Which idea has the greatest emphasis?
3. What are some details that support this idea?
4. Which sentence states the central issue of the passage?

Applying the Skill

Find a newspaper or magazine article that interests you. Identify the central issues in this article and summarize them in your own words.

For More Practice

Turn to the Skill Practice in the Chapter Review on page 235 for more practice in identifying central issues.

Historical Significance

Confucian ideas have had a major impact on China's development. On the negative side, some historians point to the Confucian denial of women's rights and its stress on total obedience to authority. On the positive side, others state that the Confucian emphasis on stability helped early China build a strong government and that Confucius's ideas about relationships resulted in a more compassionate society. Confucius also left a revolutionary legacy. He considered it a society's duty to overthrow an unjust ruler and to ensure a fair distribution of wealth.

Using Key Terms

Write the key term that completes each sentence.

a. acupuncture
b. civil service
c. extended family
d. hierarchy
e. ethics
f. mandarin
g. yin and yang
h. filial piety
i. cavalry
j. nuclear family

1. The Chinese emperor Wudi created a school that helped students prepare for examinations for positions in the _____, a system that allowed anyone with abilities to attain public office.
2. An _____ consists of parents, children, grandparents, and other relatives living together in one household.
3. Chinese doctors treated ailments and relieved pain with _____, a technique in which the skin is pierced with thin needles at vital points.
4. The administration of China's government came under the control of the _____, a class of well-educated officials.
5. The typical household in Han China was made up of a _____, which included only parents and children.
6. A Chinese theory related to Daoism was the concept of _____, the two opposing forces believed to be present in all of nature.
7. The Chinese family was a strict _____ in which members were ranked in order of importance under the father.
8. Confucius taught that individuals should live according to principles of _____.
9. During the Zhou period, the Chinese organized their military, forming a _____ of mounted warriors and horse-drawn chariots.
10. The Chinese cared especially about _____, or children's respect for their parents.

Using Your History Journal

Many of Confucius's sayings compiled by his students after his death are similar to proverbs, or wise sayings. Write a set of your own proverbs about everyday decisions and situations.

Reviewing Facts

1. **Identify** Confucius (Kongzi) and his principal ideas.
2. **State** the differences between Confucianism and Daoism.
3. **List** the five important relationships in Chinese society that were identified by Confucius.
4. **Describe** the *Book of Songs*, the *Spring and Autumn Annals*, and the *Historical Record*.
5. **Explain** why Qin Shihuangdi ordered the construction of the Great Wall of China.
6. **Identify** three main groups that made up Chinese society during the Han era.
7. **List** the characteristics of China's government and politics under the Zhou, Qin, and Han dynasties.
8. **Analyze** how Confucius applied the idea of filial piety to governments as well as families.
9. **Explain** why Qin rulers strongly opposed the teachings of Confucius, though Han rulers like Wudi promoted Confucianism.
10. **List** three inventions that were especially important to Chinese life.

Critical Thinking

1. **Evaluate** Do you think merchants deserved the

low status they held in Chinese society?

2. **Evaluate** Was a strong family structure a positive or a negative influence on Chinese society?

3. **Apply** How does your society make use of the Han concept of appointing officials by ability?

4. **Synthesize** How would you respond if your government adopted the social policies of the Qin dynasty?

5. **Contrast** How did the Zhou and Qin systems of government differ?

6. **Synthesize** Think about how merchants were viewed in Han society and why. How might the United States be different if we felt that way about merchants?

Geography in History

1. **Movement** Refer to the map below. Buddhism came to China from which area of the world?

2. **Location** What cities became major Buddhist sites in China?

3. **Region** What large area was a major stronghold of Daoism?

4. **Region** What Daoist concepts made it possible for much of China to accept the teachings of Confucius, Laozi, and the Buddha into a unified belief system?

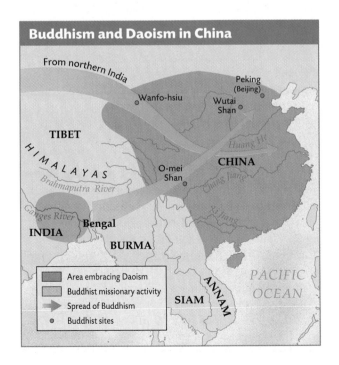

Buddhism and Daoism in China

From northern India

Peking (Beijing)
Wanfo-hsiu
Wutai Shan
TIBET
Huang He
CHINA
HIMALAYAS
O-mei Shan
Chang Jiang
Brahmaputra River
Xi Jiang
Ganges River
Bengal
INDIA
BURMA
ANNAM
PACIFIC OCEAN
SIAM

- Area embracing Daoism
- Buddhist missionary activity
- Spread of Buddhism
- Buddhist sites

Understanding Themes

1. **Uniformity** What methods did Qin Shihuangdi use to unify China?

2. **Innovation** How did the ethical philosophy of Confucius influence Chinese society?

3. **Cultural Diffusion** How did Buddhism reach China?

Linking Past and Present

1. The Qin tried to control people's ideas by limiting the books they could read. Provide an example of a modern government that limits the information its people receive.

2. The Han government forced peasants to work one month of each year on public projects. Was forced labor justified?

3. All candidates for China's civil service were required to master the Five Classics. Can you think of literature from our own culture that everyone should know? Why would it be difficult for Americans to agree on five classics?

Skill Practice

Read the passage below and answer the questions that follow.

❝Females should be strictly grave and sober, and yet adapted to the occasion. Whether in waiting on her parents, receiving or reverencing her husband, rising up or sitting down, when pregnant, in times of mourning, or when fleeing in war, she should be perfectly decorous. Rearing the silkworm and working cloth are the most important employments of the female; preparing food for the household and setting in order sacrifices follow next, each of which must be attended to. After that, study and learning can fill up the time. ❞

Book of Changes (I Ching)

1. What is the general topic of this passage?
2. What details are offered on this topic?
3. Which sentence, if any, states the central issue of this passage?
4. State the central issue in your own words.

*F*rom about 2000 B.C. to about A.D. 500, major civilizations arose throughout the world. Although each civilization had unique traits, they all had common features, such as a stable political system, one or more major religions, and an interest in the arts and sciences. These civilizations produced many achievements that still influence the world today.

Visualizing History **Chalices from the court of a wealthy Mycenaean king.** *Besides the Mycenaeans, what other peoples influenced the development of Greek civilization?*

Chapter 4
The Rise of Ancient Greece

Although Greece's mountains protected against invaders, they also limited travel and communication among the Greeks and prevented them from uniting under one government. Numerous harbors and closeness to the sea encouraged the Greeks to become traders, and eventually they founded colonies around the Mediterranean Sea.

Early Civilizations

Greek civilization had its origins in the Minoan civilization of Crete and the Mycenaean civilization brought in by Indo-Europeans. The Greeks immortalized their legends and early history in two epic poems, the *Iliad* and the *Odyssey*. These epics taught such values as courage, dignity, and love of beauty. The Greeks worshiped gods and goddesses—who were both humanlike and superpowerful—and imitated their deities by themselves striving for excellence.

The City-States

The polis—the Greek city-state—served as the center of Greek life. Each polis, especially Athens, encouraged participation by its citizens in government. Women, however, had no political rights, and slaves and foreign-born men were excluded from citizenship.

After years of rule by kings, aristocrats, and tyrants, most city-states became either oligarchies or democracies. The two major Greek democracies were Sparta and Athens. Sparta was a warlike society that used its army to control its noncitizens. Athens built a much freer society that introduced the Western concept of democracy.

During the 500s B.C., the Greeks defeated the Persians in a series of wars. A golden age of cultural achievement in Athens followed the Persian conflicts. Later, resentment against Athenian control led to the Peloponnesian War between Athens and an alliance of city-states led by Sparta. The war brought defeat for Athens and decline for the Greek city-state system.

SURVEYING CHAPTER 4

1. **Making Comparisons** How did the peoples of Sparta and Athens differ in their general attitudes toward life?
2. **Making Connections** How did Greece's geography affect the development of its political institutions?

Chapter 5
The Height of Greek Civilization

During the 400s B.C., Athens became the center of Greek civilization. Its classical style of art, architecture, and literature have endured in Western civilization. The Athenians expressed their love of beauty and harmony in such buildings as the Parthenon. They decorated their pottery with paintings and created masterpieces of sculpture. The Greeks were the first to write and perform plays—comedies and tragedies. They held the Olympic Games as a religious festival in honor of Zeus, the chief Greek god.

Thinkers and Writers

Greek thinkers believed in the power of reason to explain all things. Socrates constructed a way of teaching known as the Socratic method. His student Plato studied human behavior and wrote the first book on political science. Aristotle wrote on logic, rhetoric, poetry, and political science, among other topics. The Greeks also gave us the first true historians, Herodotus and Thucydides, and the father of medicine, Hippocrates.

Alexander the Great

By 330 B.C., Alexander of Macedonia had defeated the Persian Empire and conquered an area from Egypt to India. His goal was to combine the best of Greek and Persian cultures into one civilization. After Alexander's death, the empire was divided among three of his generals.

Although political unity vanished, Greek culture spread and mixed with Middle Eastern culture to form the Hellenistic civilization. This new civilization formed around newly built cities, such as Alexandria, Egypt. During the Hellenistic era, the Greeks excelled in the sciences.

SURVEYING CHAPTER 5

1. **Identifying Trends** In what ways did the ancient Greeks lay the foundation of the arts and sciences of the West?
2. **Analyzing Viewpoints** Do you think Alexander of Macedonia deserves to be called "the Great"? Explain your answer.

Chapter 6
Ancient Rome and Early Christianity

In 509 B.C. the Romans established a republic that lasted almost 500 years. The republic was ruled by upper-class patricians, although after a while representatives of the plebeians—the common people—also played a part in government.

The Roman Empire

Rome conquered the Italian Peninsula by 264 B.C. It then fought the Punic Wars against Carthage, finally defeating the North African city-state in 149 B.C. Rome's military conquests brought the Roman Republic wealth but also substituted slave labor on large estates for small, independent citizen-farmers. The latter crowded into Rome, where they voted for any leader who promised cheaper food and more public amusements. Rome's failure to reform brought Julius Caesar to power in 45 B.C. In 27 B.C. his grandnephew Octavian, or Augustus, became the first Roman emperor.

From 27 B.C. to A.D. 180, the Roman Empire enjoyed a time of peace and prosperity known as the *Pax Romana*. During this period the Romans developed their system of laws and built roads, aqueducts, and public buildings. Great literary figures include the poets Horace and Virgil and the historians Livy and Tacitus.

Christianity

Christianity, based on the life and teachings of Jesus, began as a sect of Judaism but quickly spread through the Roman world as a new religion. After great persecution, Christianity became the official religion of the empire in A.D. 392. During the A.D. 400s, the bishop of Rome began to claim authority over the Christian Church and eventually became known as pope. His claims, however, were rejected by the non-Latin speaking churches in the eastern part of the empire.

Visualizing History

Octavian, known as Augustus, preferred to be called "first citizen." *What was the period that began with his reign called?*

Roman Decline

During the A.D. 200s, political chaos, economic crisis, and Germanic invasions led to the decline of the Roman Empire. Reform efforts by Diocletian and Constantine preserved the eastern part of the empire but only delayed the downfall of the western part of the empire until the late A.D. 400s.

SURVEYING CHAPTER 6

1. **Relating Ideas** How did Christianity begin and later develop?
2. **Predicting Developments** What do you think might have happened if Diocletian and Constantine had lived about 100 years earlier than they did?

Chapter 7
Flowering of African Civilizations

Africa's diverse geography has influenced the development of civilizations. In a land of scarce rainfall, cultures arose near lakes or rivers, such as the Nile. Trading cultures, like Kush and Axum in eastern Africa, imported new ideas and religions along with goods. Movement of people, such as the Bantu migrations, spread culture to other parts of Africa. Family traditions and customs were built around religious beliefs in many African villages.

West Africa

Ghana was one of the wealthiest nations, trading gold for salt brought by Muslim traders. Mali, a nation that broke away from Ghana, also became a powerful kingdom. Its king, Mansa Musa, created a rich trading empire through his contacts with Muslims. Islamic culture spread throughout Africa. Songhai, the last of the great West African kingdoms, expanded its territory and developed a strong legal system based on Islam.

East, Central, and South Africa

Trade contacts also brought power and wealth to city-states along the coast of East Africa. There Arab traders brought cotton, silk, and Chinese porcelain from India and Southeast Asia to exchange for ivory and metals from Africa's interior.

Meanwhile, powerful Bantu kingdoms thrived in Central Africa and South Africa. These inland areas mined rich deposits of copper and gold.

Traders from the East African coast made their way to the Bantu kingdoms and began an active trade there.

SURVEYING CHAPTER 7

1. **Relating Ideas** How did the spread of new religions affect various cultures in Africa?
2. **Analyzing Trends** Why was trade so important to early African kingdoms and city-states?

Chapter 8
India's Great Civilization

About 1500 B.C. Aryan invaders conquered northern India, bringing with them the Sanskrit language and a social structure that divided people into *varnas*, four social classes. The *Rig-Veda*, dating from the Aryan period, is one of the oldest religious texts still in use. Between 900 B.C. and 500 B.C., two epic poems, the *Mahabharata* and the *Ramayana*, were recorded. These epics and later religious writings, the *Upanishads*, taught the principles of Hinduism, India's major religion. Hinduism includes belief in many deities and the concepts of an eternal spirit, reincarnation, and the obligation to perform the duties of one's caste.

Visualizing History
Gautama Buddha, a sculpture from Nepal. Buddhist statues are found throughout Asia. *What is the Eightfold Path?*

Rise of Buddhism

During the 500s B.C., Siddhartha Gautama founded Buddhism, which spread to India, East Asia, and Southeast Asia. Known as the Buddha, or Enlightened One, Gautama taught that people can escape the cycle of rebirth by eliminating desire and by following rules of behavior, the Eightfold Path. Buddhist artists created paintings and statues of the Buddha throughout Asia. Since Buddha's death, Buddhism has become one of the world's great religions.

Indian Empires

The Mauryas, who ruled from 322 B.C. to 184 B.C., founded an empire in northern India, and the Mauryan ruler Asoka helped spread Buddhism throughout India. About 500 years later, the Guptas reunited India, and their empire lasted from A.D. 320 to A.D. 600. Under the Guptas, scholars made numerous advances—including the invention of "Arabic numerals" and the concept of zero.

Visualizing History A treasure of 6,000 terra-cotta soldiers from the Qin dynasty was uncovered in Shensi Province. *What other large structure was built during this time?*

SURVEYING CHAPTER 8

1. **Making Comparisons** In what ways do ancient Greece and ancient India compare in their cultural achievements?
2. **Relating Ideas** What mathematical advances did early India pass on to other parts of the world?

Chapter 9
China's Flourishing Civilization

The Zhou, who replaced the Shang about 1000 B.C., ruled China until 256 B.C.—their dynasty lasting longer than any other Chinese dynasty. Under the Zhou, China made many technological advances and began to experience steady population growth.

Qin and Han Dynasties

The Qin and Han dynasties united China under powerful central governments that enacted strict laws, expanded China's borders, and increased Chinese contacts with the outside world. The Qin ruler Shihuangdi standardized weights and measures, built the Great Wall, and tried to control people's thinking by burning many books. Under the Han emperor Wudi, the government adopted a civil service system in which officials were appointed on the basis of examinations.

Chinese Beliefs

Two major philosophies appeared in early China: Confucianism and Daoism. Confucianism was developed by Confucius, or Kongzi. He stressed basic ethical relationships, especially those between ruler and ruled and between parent and child. Confucianism also emphasized the ideal of a courteous, knowledgeable individual. Daoism, another philosophy, emphasized living in harmony with nature. Toward the end of the Han dynasty, Buddhism entered China.

Society and Culture

The Chinese family of the Han era played an important role in Chinese society and was dominated by the oldest male. The family functioned as an economic unit to which all members gave their earnings and which supported the old, the young, and the sick. Chinese society was divided into three main groups—landowners, peasants, and merchants.

Producing numerous literary works, the Chinese also made great contributions in science and technology. These include the first printed book and the invention of paper, gunpowder, and acupuncture.

SURVEYING CHAPTER 9

1. **Making Comparisons** In what ways did the people of China differ from the people of India in their general attitudes toward life?
2. **Analyzing Viewpoints** How do you think Qin Shihuangdi's book burning would have been regarded by the ancient Greeks?

Regional Civilizations

Then & Now

As this period opened, advanced civilizations began to develop in many regions of the world. Although some cultures were cut off from other regions, trade and migrations spread ideas across continents and among several different peoples. Emerging centers of trade and commerce brought more highly organized social structures and governments. These regional civilizations contributed many ideas that influenced the development of the modern world. Christianity, Islam, Confucianism, and Buddhism spread over wide areas. Scientific discoveries crossed cultures. Some contact between cultures caused conflict that lasted for decades or centuries.

A Global Chronology

	A.D. 500	A.D. 700	A.D. 900
Political	A.D. 527 Justinian becomes Byzantine emperor.	A.D. 638 Arabs conquer Jerusalem.	
Scientific		A.D. 850 Arabs perfect the astrolabe.	A.D. 1000 Chinese invent gunpowder.
Social/Cultural		A.D. 622 Muhammad flees Makkah (Islamic Year 1).	

Mayan clay figurine of a man and a woman wrapped in a blanket, c. A.D. 700–1000. Campeche, Mexico

Portfolio Project

Americans share the benefits of foods, inventions, discoveries, and ideas from all over the world. Often we do not think about the cultures that contributed these things. Create a map on which you show some products or ideas that originated in each of the following areas: the Middle East, Asia, Africa, South America, or Europe.

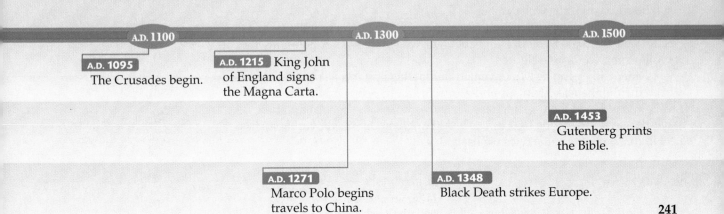

A.D. 1100

A.D. 1095
The Crusades begin.

A.D. 1215 King John of England signs the Magna Carta.

A.D. 1271
Marco Polo begins travels to China.

A.D. 1300

A.D. 1348
Black Death strikes Europe.

A.D. 1500

A.D. 1453
Gutenberg prints the Bible.

The Spread of Ideas

Mathematics

*T*he invention of mathematics changed the course of civilization. Astronomers used mathematics to account for the movements of the sun and moon so they could mark the seasons. Geometry enabled people to calculate the volume of a cylindrical granary. Mathematics supported travel, from the earliest sea travel to the development of the space program. It all began with the Sumerians.

Sumerian cuneiform tablet

Indus Valley
The Use of Numerals

The Sumerians devised one of the earliest numbering systems based on cuneiform. They used two wedge-like symbols for counting. One symbol stood for 1, the other for 10. But these symbols—and others to follow—basically came from the Sumerian alphabet. The wedges served double-duty for symbolizing words and figures.

Other early peoples who invented numbering systems also used letters from their alphabets. Then, around A.D. 500, Hindu people in the Indus River valley abandoned the use of letters. They created instead special number symbols to stand for the figures 1 to 9. Although modernized over time, these 9 Hindu symbols are the ones we use today.

Persian astronomer

The Middle East
The Rise of Algebra

Trade introduced people in the Middle East to the Hindu number system. About A.D. 825 an Arab mathematician, al-Khowarizmi of Baghdad, wrote a book recommending the new system to everyone. In a second book, al-Khowarizmi showed how the system could be used. He called the book *al-jabr w'al-muqabalah*, which roughly means "the art of bringing together unknowns to match a known quantity." The word *algebra* comes from the key word in the title—*al-jabr*, or "bringing together."

The wonder of the system caught Arab imaginations. Arabs especially liked the concept of zero—developed by the Hindus after they created the symbols for 1-9. In explaining this concept, one Arab mathematician wrote: "When [in subtraction] nothing is left over, then write the little circle so that the place does not remain empty." With the use of zero, mathematicians could build numbers of astronomical size using just 10 symbols.

Astrolabe

Europe
The Triumph of Arabic Numerals

Arab conquerors arrived in Spain in the A.D. 700s. Their presence opened the door for use of the new number system. At first, many Europeans rejected it. They clung instead to Roman numerals. The Italian city-state of Florence even passed a law banning the use of the Hindu-Arab system.

Later, however, "Arabic numerals," as they were called, proved a more powerful conqueror than Arab soldiers. European merchants embraced the new numbers first. They found it easier to do their tallies using the symbols for 1-10. European mathematicians soon learned the new arithmetic too. By the A.D. 1400s, the numbers could even be found in popular art.

As you will read in this unit, Europeans began to adopt other practices from the Middle East as well. The pace of change quickened as wars and trade brought more people in contact with each other.

Book of Hours *with Arabic numerals*

LINKING THE IDEAS

1. How did the Hindu system of numbers differ from earlier systems?
2. What was the importance of the invention of zero?

Critical Thinking

3. **Cause and Effect** What was the role of conquest and trade in spreading the use of the Hindu-Arab number system?

Byzantines and Slavs

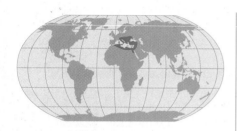

Chapter Themes

▶ **Conflict** Byzantines fight off invaders and struggle over use of icons. *Section 1*

▶ **Innovation** Byzantines develop Eastern Orthodox theology and distinctive art forms. *Section 2*

▶ **Cultural Diffusion** Trade routes and invasions spread beliefs and ideas. *Section 3*

The Storyteller

The awestruck visitor arriving in A.D. 600 in the city of Constantinople in southeastern Europe scarcely knew where to turn. Splendid public buildings as well as simple private homes lined the streets; the scent of rare spices perfumed the air; people dressed in fine silk thronged the church of Hagia Sophia. "One might imagine that one has chanced upon a meadow in full bloom," the Greek historian Procopius wrote about the newly built church. "For one would surely marvel at the purple hue of some [columns], the green of others, at those on which the crimson blooms, at those that flash with white, at those, too, which nature, like a painter, has varied with the most contrasting colors." The church's grandeur reflected that of Constantinople, "city of the world's desire," capital of a prosperous empire that controlled east-west trade and laid the basis for the Greek and Slavic cultures of modern Europe.

Historical Significance

What cultural achievements did the Byzantines pass on to western Europe? How did their civilization affect the development of the peoples of eastern Europe?

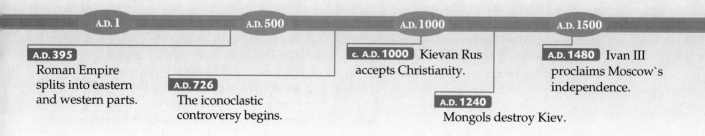

A.D. 1	A.D. 500	A.D. 1000	A.D. 1500

A.D. 395
Roman Empire splits into eastern and western parts.

A.D. 726
The iconoclastic controversy begins.

c. A.D. 1000 Kievan Rus accepts Christianity.

A.D. 1240
Mongols destroy Kiev.

A.D. 1480 Ivan III proclaims Moscow's independence.

The archangel Gabriel, an icon on wood, from the
Russian State Museum, St. Petersburg, Russia

Your History Journal

*Find out about a specific law in
Justinian's Code in an encyclopedia or a
book on the history of legal systems. Write
the law as an illuminated manuscript,
an art form described in this chapter.*

Section 1
....

The New Rome

Setting the Scene

▶ **Terms to Define**
    clergy, laity, icon, iconoclast, schism

▶ **People to Meet**
    Constantine, Justinian, Theodora, Leo III

▶ **Places to Locate**
    Byzantine Empire, Constantinople

 **Find Out** What made the Byzantine Empire rich and powerful?

The Storyteller

Byzantium [Constantinople] was in flames. A mob was screaming insults at Emperor Justinian and Empress Theodora. The emperor swiftly ordered the imperial treasury loaded onto ships to prepare for escape. Half crazed and without hope, Justinian held a final council of a few loyal friends; Theodora was present. After the military generals expressed their fears, Theodora suddenly rose and broke the silence. "I do not choose to flee," she said. "Never shall I see the day when I am not saluted as the empress.... You have the money, the ships are ready, the sea is open. As for me, I shall stay." Hearing her, the others took heart. That day, Theodora saved Justinian's throne.

—adapted from *Theodora, Empress of Byzantium,* Charles Diehl, 1972

Theodora, detail of mosaic

As you read in Chapter 6, after the Roman Empire was divided in A.D. 395, the eastern half became known as the **Byzantine Empire**. At its height in the A.D. 500s, the Byzantine Empire included most of the Balkan Peninsula, Asia Minor, Syria, and Egypt. Its major population group, the Greeks, lived mainly in the central part of the empire. Also included in the empire were Egyptians, Syrians, Arabs, Armenians, Jews, Persians, Slavs, and Turks. These varied peoples and cultures gave Byzantine civilization an international character.

Byzantine Foundations

The location of **Constantinople**, the Byzantine capital, reinforced this multicultural character. The city was located near the centers of early Christianity as well as on major trade routes.

A Strategic City

In A.D. 330 the Roman emperor **Constantine** built Constantinople at a strategic place where Europe and Asia meet. Located on a peninsula, Constantinople overlooked the Bosporus, the narrow strait between the Sea of Marmara and the Black Sea. A second strait, the Dardanelles, connects the Sea of Marmara and the Aegean Sea, which leads to the Mediterranean. These straits gave the occupiers of the peninsula control over movement between the Mediterranean and the Black Seas and, as a result, over the routes leading east to Asia and north to northern Europe. The site of Constantinople itself offered natural protection from attack at a time when Germanic invaders were assaulting Rome to the west. Water protected the city on three sides, and triple walls fortified the side open to attack by land. Eventually a huge chain was strung across the narrow mouth of the deep harbor on Constantinople's north side for still greater protection.

The straits also made the peninsula a natural crossroads for trade. By Constantine's time the Byzantine capital had become the wealthiest part of the Roman Empire, handling rich cargoes from Asia, Europe, and Africa.

Cultural Blend

After Rome's fall, the Byzantine Empire was regarded as heir to Roman power and traditions. Constantinople was known as the New Rome because its emperors were Romans who spoke Latin and many of its wealthy families came from Rome. Despite these ties, the Byzantine Empire was more than a continuation of the old Roman Empire.

Lands once part of the Greek world formed the heart of the Byzantine Empire. The Byzantine people not only spoke Greek but also stressed their Greek heritage. Eventually Byzantine emperors and officials also used Greek rather than Latin. Religious scholars expressed their ideas in Greek and developed a distinct form of Christianity known as Eastern Orthodoxy. In addition to the Byzantine Empire's classical Greek heritage and Christian religion came cultural influences from eastern civilizations such as Persia. This mixture of cultures created a distinct Byzantine civilization. Between A.D. 500 and A.D. 1200, this civilization was one of the most advanced in the world and had a higher standard of living than western Europe.

Justinian's Rule

At its height the Byzantine Empire was ruled by **Justinian**, the son of prosperous peasants from Macedonia in the western part of the empire. Justinian was called the Emperor Who Never Sleeps. While a young man in the court of his uncle, Emperor Justin I, he worked late into the night at his studies of law, music, religion, and architecture. His enthusiasm for knowledge and hard work continued after he became emperor in A.D. 527, at age 44.

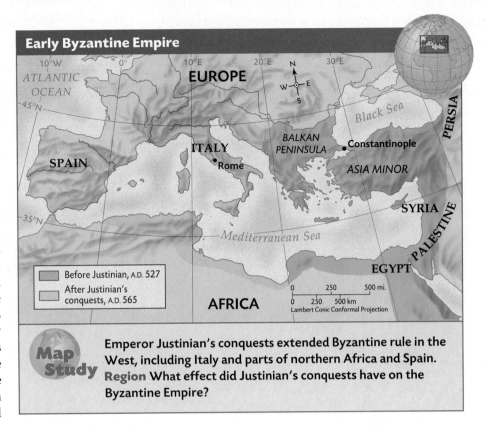

Early Byzantine Empire

Before Justinian, A.D. 527
After Justinian's conquests, A.D. 565

Map Study Emperor Justinian's conquests extended Byzantine rule in the West, including Italy and parts of northern Africa and Spain. **Region** What effect did Justinian's conquests have on the Byzantine Empire?

Theodora's Support

Justinian's wife, **Theodora**, was beautiful, intelligent, and ambitious. Justinian had married her in spite of court objections to her occupation as an actress—a profession held in low esteem in the empire. A capable empress, Theodora participated actively in government, rewarding friends with positions and using dismissals to punish enemies.

Theodora was especially concerned with improving the social standing of women. She persuaded Justinian to issue a decree giving a wife the right to own land equal in value to the wealth she brought with her at marriage. This land gave a widow the income she needed to support her children without the assistance of the government.

In A.D. 532 Theodora's political talents helped save Justinian's throne. When a revolt of taxpayers in Constantinople threatened the government, Justinian's advisers urged him to leave the city. As flames roared through Constantinople and the rebels battered at the palace gates, Justinian prepared to flee. Theodora, however, persuaded him to remain in control.

Inspired by his wife's determination, Justinian reasserted his power. His army crushed the rebels, killing 30,000 people. From that time until his death in A.D. 565, Justinian ruled without challenge.

MAXIMIANVS

The Emperor Justinian, a mosaic from the A.D. 500s from Ravenna, Italy.
Why was Justinian called the Emperor Who Never Sleeps?

Military Campaigns

During Justinian's reign, the Byzantines faced a serious military threat from the East. The Sassanian Empire of Persia, under Chosroes (kaz•ROH•eez) I, grew in strength and threatened to conquer the eastern provinces of the Byzantine Empire. The Byzantines rallied their forces and threw back the Persians. Justinian gained a brief period of security for the eastern borders by agreeing to pay tribute in return for peace.

Justinian dreamed of restoring the Roman Empire. In A.D. 533 he began the reconquest of Italy, North Africa, and Spain—Roman lands that had fallen to Germanic invaders. Under the general Belisarius, the Byzantine armies were strengthened and reorganized. Between A.D. 533 and A.D. 555, they fought a series of wars against the Vandals in North Africa, the Ostrogoths in Italy, and the Visigoths in southern Spain. The Byzantines conquered these Germanic groups and extended Byzantine rule in the west.

The successful reconquest, however, proved costly for the empire. The wars exhausted most of the Byzantine resources. Funds were low for defending the eastern borders, which faced attack by an expanding Persian Empire. Justinian's conquests did not last. Within a generation of his death, the empire lost many of its outlying territories.

Code of Laws

Justinian's legal reforms did last, affecting Western law even today. Shortly after becoming emperor, Justinian appointed a commission to codify, or classify, the empire's Roman laws. For centuries, these laws had accumulated without organization or classification.

The commission was made up of 10 scholars headed by a legal expert named Tribonian. For more than 6 years, the commission collected and organized vast numbers of laws. It threw out the ones that were outdated, simplified many, and put the remainder into categories. The commission's work was recorded in a collection of books known as the *Corpus of Civil Law,* or the Justinian Code. This massive work preserved Rome's legal heritage and later became the basis for most European legal systems.

The Arts

Under Justinian, Byzantine art and architecture

thrived and achieved their distinct character. The emperor ordered the construction of new roads, fortresses, aqueducts, monasteries, and other buildings. His most famous project was the church of Hagia Sophia, "Holy Wisdom," in Constantinople. The largest and most beautiful church in the empire, Hagia Sophia still stands today as one of the world's great architectural landmarks.

Byzantine Religion

Strong ties linked Byzantine emperors and the Church. The emperors were regarded as God's representatives on earth. Starting in the A.D. 400s, Byzantine emperors and empresses were crowned by the patriarch of Constantinople and took an oath to defend the Christian faith.

Church and State

Byzantine emperors frequently played a major role in church affairs. They appointed church officials, defined the style of worship, and used the wealth of the Church for government purposes.

Justinian strengthened this control over the Church by intervening in disputes over church beliefs. He also tried to unify the empire under one Christian faith, a practice that sometimes led to persecution of Jews and non-Greek Christians.

Religious Controversy

Both Byzantine clergy—church officials such as priests and bishops—and laity—church members who were not clergy—were intensely interested in religious matters. In their homes, markets, and shops, Byzantines often engaged in heated religious discussions. Visitors to Constantinople saw shoppers in the marketplaces having lively discussions about such topics as the exact relationship of Jesus the Son to God the Father. Such arguments often became political issues and led to fights and riots.

In the A.D. 700s, a dispute broke out over the use of icons (EYE•KAHNZ), or religious images, in worship. Although Christians had disagreed about this practice since the A.D. 400s, the use of icons in churches became a political issue by the A.D. 700s.

Those who objected to the use of icons in Christian worship argued that the Bible, in the Ten Commandments, prohibited such images. Defenders stressed that icons were symbols of

The Arts

Hagia Sophia

Hagia Sophia

Justinian ordered his architects to create the most spectacular building of all time. The construction of Constantinople's church of Hagia Sophia, or Holy Wisdom, began in A.D. 532. Workers completed the church in five years.

For Justinian, building this church was important for religious and political reasons. First, as the church of the imperial court, Hagia Sophia symbolized the importance of Orthodox Christianity in the Byzantine Empire. Second, by commissioning important buildings and art, Justinian asserted his authority as well as the Church's role in Byzantine society.

The design of Hagia Sophia was radically new. Its dome, supported by four arches, was larger and more prominent than any the world had ever known. Pierced by windows and covered with glimmering mosaics, the dome appeared to hover, weightless, above the vast church. Light streamed into the church from all directions and reflected off decorated surfaces.

To an extent, Justinian succeeded in his goal of creating the greatest religious monument of his time. It was centuries before a building of equal size and splendor was built in the Mediterranean world.

MAKING THE CONNECTION

1. What sort of effect did the interior of Hagia Sophia have on its viewers?
2. How did the splendor of the church of Hagia Sophia serve Justinian's goals?

not enough for them to squander the treasures of the Empire and to rob private individuals, whether great or small…. They have dared to lay their hands on the wealth of the churches. They have been seen tearing from the altars the silver adornments, breaking them in fragments, over which they quarrelled, violating the sanctuaries, carrying away the icons, crosses, and relics. **"**

The western Christians established "a Latin empire" in Constantinople. The Byzantine people resisted this rule successfully and reestablished their own culture in A.D. 1261.

Fall of Constantinople

The years of fighting had severely weakened the Byzantine Empire. Soon Serbs and Bulgars took over Balkan territory. New invaders from central Asia, **the Ottoman Turks**, attacked the eastern provinces. By the late A.D. 1300s, the Byzantine Empire consisted of only Constantinople and part of Greece.

About 100,000 people still lived in the capital; food was scarce, and wealth was gone. In A.D. 1453 the Ottomans laid siege to Constantinople. For six weeks their huge cannon blasted away at the city's walls. The Byzantines fought fiercely until their last emperor was killed.

For a thousand years, the Byzantine Empire had protected the Christian lands to its north. With the fall of Constantinople, central Europe lay open to attack by Islamic forces. Despite the empire's fall, the Byzantine heritage lived on in the civilization developed by the Eastern Slavs.

Neighboring Kingdoms

During the time of the Byzantine Empire, two neighboring kingdoms—**Armenia** and **Georgia**—went through periods of prosperity and decline. Both Armenia and Georgia lay south of the rugged, snow-capped Caucasus Mountains between the Black and Caspian Seas. Although the mountains made travel by land difficult, plains and valleys between the mountains allowed traders and invaders to pass between Europe and Asia. Over the centuries, the peoples of Armenia and Georgia faced a repeated pattern of conquest by larger neighboring powers that rivaled each other for control of the region.

Armenia

Historians believe that the first Armenians settled the area that is present-day Armenia in about the 700s B.C. Within 200 years, these settlers had intermarried with the local people, built walled towns, and prospered from the growing of wheat and other cereal crops. By about 400 B.C., the Persians who lived to the south absorbed Armenia into their empire and forced the Armenians to pay tribute to the Persian ruler.

When Alexander the Great conquered Persia in the 330s B.C., his armies also gained control of Armenia. The country, however, was allowed a degree of independence. King Tigran II, who came to power in 95 B.C., built an independent Armenian kingdom that reached from the Caspian Sea to the Mediterranean Sea. The Romans defeated Tigran in 55

Portrait of Sultan Mahmet II, who conquered Constantinople and renamed it Istanbul. *How long did the Byzantine city hold out against the sultan's siege?*

B.C., and Armenia became part of the Roman Empire.

In the early A.D. 300s, Armenia came under the influence of Christianity, which was spreading throughout the Roman Empire. One of the Christian missionaries working in Armenia was Gregory, an Armenian nobleman. Eventually known as Gregory the Illuminator, he converted the Armenian king **Tiridates** (TEER•uh•DAH•teez) **III** to Christianity. Most Armenians soon accepted the new faith, and Armenia became the first officially Christian country in the world.

Christianity gave Armenians a sense of national identity. Mesorb (MEH•zohrb), an Armenian monk and scholar, developed the Armenian alphabet in the early A.D. 400s. In A.D. 451, Armenians under Vartan Mamikonian (VAHR•tahn mah•mih•KOH•nee•uhn) defended their religion against the Persians in the battle of Avarair (ah•vah•RAHR). To gain peace, the Persians finally offered the Armenians religious and political freedom.

In the A.D. 600s another religion—Islam—arose among Arab peoples in the Middle East, which lay south of Armenia. Islam's followers, called Muslims, invaded Armenia, but failed to completely conquer the country. By the late A.D. 800s, an independent Armenian kingdom was thriving in the northern region. In the A.D. 1000s, peace was again interrupted when the Seljuk Turks, who had earlier conquered parts of the Byzantine Empire, won control of Armenia. The Seljuks were followed in the A.D. 1400s by other conquerors—the Ottoman Turks. Within 100 years, Armenia had become a battlefield between the Ottomans and their rivals, the Persians. Centuries later, in the A.D. 1800s, Armenia became a part of the Russian Empire to the north.

Georgia

People have lived in the area of present-day Georgia for thousands of years. By the 600s B.C., most of the present-day Black Sea coast of Georgia was part of a kingdom known as Colchis (KAHL•kuhs). Known for its riches, Colchis attracted the seafaring Greeks, who described the kingdom in their epic of the Golden Fleece. Another kingdom, Iberia, arose in the central part of present-day Georgia. In 65 B.C. Iberia and Colchis both came under the rule of the Romans.

The Roman conquerors built new roads and introduced their laws and customs to the region of Georgia. The Silk Road, which passed through the Caucasus Mountains, allowed the Georgians to prosper from trade between Europe and Asia. Caravans of silk cloth, spices, and other goods reached ports on Georgia's Black Sea coast and continued on to the Middle East and Europe.

Georgians accepted Christianity in the A.D. 300s. According to Georgian tradition, a Christian woman named Nino converted the people of Iberia to the new religion, which eventually spread to other parts of Georgia. Meanwhile, Georgia became a battleground between two opposing neighbors: the Persians and the Byzantines.

During the A.D. 1000s and A.D. 1100s, a series of Georgian rulers gradually freed Georgia of foreign influences and strengthened its government. These efforts eventually produced Georgia's golden age during the reign of Queen **Tamara** (tah•MAH•rah), who ruled from A.D. 1184 to A.D. 1212. During this time, the Georgians made great advances in culture, science, and the arts.

Beginning in the early A.D. 1200s, however, Georgia again suffered attacks from other nations. Mongol armies from central Asia raided Georgian lands from the A.D. 1220s to the early A.D. 1400s. These attacks sent Georgia into a period of decline. From the A.D. 1500s to the A.D. 1700s the Ottomans and the Persians fought over Georgian territory. In the late A.D. 1700s, the ruler of a small kingdom in eastern Georgia accepted partial control by the Russians to the north in return for military help. By the early A.D. 1800s, all of Georgia became part of the Russian Empire.

SECTION 2 REVIEW

Recall

1. **Define** theology, regent, mosaic, illuminated manuscript, monastery, missionary.

2. **Identify** Cyril, Methodius, the Seljuk Turks, Manzikert, the Ottoman Turks, Tiridates III, Tamara.

3. **Explain** why the Bosporus and the Dardanelles are strategic waterways.

Critical Thinking

4. **Analyzing Information** Examine how the doctrinal and cultural split between the Roman Catholic Church and the Eastern Orthodox Church contributed to the Byzantine Empire's decline.

Understanding Themes

5. **Innovation** How did Christianity affect culture in the Byzantine Empire, Armenia, and Georgia? What was the role of art and religion in these lands?

A.D. 980 Vladimir becomes
Grand Prince of Kiev.

A.D. 1240
Alexander Nevsky
defeats the Swedes.

A.D. 1380 Moscow
defeats Mongols at
the Battle of Kulikovo.

A.D. 1472
Ivan III of Moscow
takes title of czar.

Section 3

The Eastern Slavs

Setting the Scene

▶ **Terms to Define**
　steppe, principality, boyar, czar

▶ **People to Meet**
　the Slavs, Rurik, Olga, Vladimir, Yaroslav,
　the Mongols, Alexander Nevsky, Ivan III

▶ **Places to Locate**
　Dnieper River, Kiev, Novgorod, Moscow

Find Out How did the Eastern Slavs develop
separate cultures from those of western Europe?

The Storyteller

*As a pagan prince, Vladimir behaved kindly;
once he became a Christian, his generosity became
unlimited. Beggars assembled in his courtyard every*

*day for food, drink, cloth-
ing, and money. For the
sick and weak, supply wagons were loaded up and driven around the city of Kiev.
Once, when his friends
showed disgust at having to
eat with plain wooden
spoons, Vladimir laughed
and had silver ones cast for
them. He was also the first
Kiev prince to mint gold
and silver coins. The first
of these, made by inexperienced Russian crafts work-
ers, were slightly lumpy and uneven, but bore
Vladimir's picture and the inscription, "Here is
Vladimir on his throne. And this is his gold."*

Eastern Orthodox
church

—from *Vladimir the Russian Viking,*
Vladimir Volkoff, 1985

After the fall of Constantinople in A.D.
1453, the leadership of the Eastern
Orthodox world passed from the
Byzantines to **the Slavs**. The Slavs were among the
largest groups living in eastern Europe. Because of
their location, the Slavs had been in close contact
with the Byzantines since the A.D. 900s.

This relationship made a lasting mark on the
development of Slavic history. The Slavs, especially
those living in the areas that are today the Balkan
Peninsula, Ukraine, and Russia, borrowed much
from the Byzantines. On the foundation of
Byzantine religion, law, and culture, the Slavs built
a new civilization. They also borrowed heavily from
western European and Asian cultures. As a result of
these different influences, Russia—the farthest
north and east of the Slavic lands—never became a
completely European or completely Asian country.

The Setting

One of the Byzantine trade routes ran north
across the Black Sea and up the **Dnieper River**, then
overland to the Baltic Sea. From trading posts along
the river grew the roots of early Slavic civilization.

The Steppe

North of the Black Sea are vast plains, thick forests,
and mighty rivers. Much of the land is an immense
plain called the steppe. Ukrainian author Nikolay
Gogol vividly captures its spirit in his *Cossack Tales*:

❝ The farther the steppe went the grander it
became … one green uninhabited waste.
No plow ever furrowed its immense wavy
plains of wild plants; the wild horses,
which herded there, alone trampled them
down. The whole extent of the steppe was
nothing but a green-gold ocean, whose
surface seemed besprinkled with millions
of different colored flowers. ❞

Although the steppe has rich black soil, the harsh climate makes farming difficult and crop failures common. Too far inland to be reached by moist ocean breezes, the steppe often has scanty rainfall. In addition, most of the land lies in the same latitudes as Canada and has the same short growing season. During the long, hard winter, blasts of Arctic air roar across the land and bury it deep in snow.

Forests and Rivers

North of the steppe stretch seemingly endless forests of evergreens, birch, oak, and other hardwoods. North–south flowing rivers such as the Dnieper, Dniester, and Volga cross the steppe and penetrate the forests, providing the easiest means of transportation. Yet travel is difficult for much of the year. In winter, deep drifts of snow cover the ground, and in the spring thaw the land turns to knee-deep mud.

The People

Historians know little about the origin of the first Slavic peoples. Some believe the Slavs came from present-day eastern Poland. Others think they may have been farmers in the Black Sea region. It is known that by about A.D. 500 the Slavs had formed into three distinct groups and had settled in different parts of eastern Europe.

Slavic Groups

One group, known as the West Slavs, lived in the marshlands, plains, and mountains of east-central Europe. They successfully fought the Germans to the west and the Scandinavians to the north for control of territory. Today the descendants of the West Slavs are the peoples of Poland, the Czech Republic, and Slovakia. Their religious ties came to be with the Roman Catholic Church, and their cultural ties were with western Europe.

Another group, known as the South Slavs, settled in the Balkan Peninsula, and had frequent contacts with the Byzantines. Today, their descendants are the Serbs, Croats, and Slovenes, whose languages and cultures were shaped by both the Roman Catholic West and the Orthodox East. One group of South Slavs—the Bosnians—were influenced by the religion of Islam from the Middle East.

The third and largest Slavic group, the Eastern Slavs, includes those now known as Ukrainians, Russians, and Belarussians. They lived north of the Black Sea between the Dnieper and Dniester Rivers and traded with the Byzantine Empire and northern Europe. From A.D. 500 to A.D. 800, some Eastern Slavs moved eastward toward the Volga River.

East Slavic Lands A.D. 1100s

Map Study Trade with the Byzantine Empire helped build Kiev into a major city. **Movement** In what direction would traders have traveled from Kiev to Sweden?

Early Ways of Life

The early Eastern Slavs lived in villages made up of related families. They were farmers who hunted wild game and birds to supplement the wheat, rye, and oats they grew. In the forests they cleared land by cutting and burning trees and scattering the ash to enrich the soil. On the steppes they ignited a "sea of flame" to burn off the grass for planting.

Most farm homes were sturdy log houses called *izbas*. With knife, chisel, and ax the peasants skillfully shaped the logs, notching them so that they would fit together without nails. Many *izbas* had wooden gables and window frames decorated with painted carvings of flowers and animals. Skilled artisans also used wood to make furniture, cooking utensils, musical instruments, boats, and images of favorite deities.

The Eastern Slavs used the many rivers in their region for transportation and trade. They set up trading towns along the riverbanks. By the A.D. 800s, a trade route ran from the Baltic Sea in the north to the Black Sea in the south.

This *izba* in Russian Siberia's Lake Baikal region evidences the decorative style of Eastern Slav houses. *How did these people build without nails?*

Kievan Rus

The early Eastern Slavs were not warlike. During the late A.D. 800s, they relied on Vikings, a group of warriors and traders from Scandinavia, to protect their trade routes. The Vikings not only provided military aid, they also helped to lay the foundations of Slavic government.

The arrival of the Vikings is recorded in the *Primary Chronicle*, a collection of Eastern Slavic history, tales, and legends written around A.D. 1100. According to the *Chronicle*, in about A.D. 860 the Slavic people from the northern forest village of Novgorod asked Vikings from Scandinavia for aid: "Our land is great and rich, but there is no order in it. Come to rule and reign over us." The Viking leader **Rurik** accepted the invitation. The Slavs called the Vikings and the area they controlled *Rus*; the word *Russia* is probably derived from this name.

Rise of Kiev

In about A.D. 880, Rurik's successor, Prince Oleg, conquered the fortress-village of **Kiev** to the south. Built high on a bluff where the forest meets the steppe, Kiev prospered because it lay on the Dnieper River trade route. Some still call it the mother of Eastern Slavic cities.

Control of Kiev enabled Oleg to dominate the water trade route. Towns along the route were brought together under his leadership. Kiev soon became the major city of a region of Slavic territories known as Kievan Rus. The rulers of Kiev, known as Grand Princes, conducted raids against Constantinople. They were attracted by the wealth and civilization of the Byzantine capital. In A.D. 911 a treaty ended these raids and established trade between the Byzantines and the Eastern Slavs. During the summer months, Slavic merchants carried furs, honey, and other forest products by boat to Constantinople. There they traded their goods for cloth, wine, weapons, and jewelry.

Kievan Government

By A.D. 900, Kievan Rus had organized into a collection of city-states and principalities, or territories ruled by princes. Each region enjoyed local self-government; however, they all paid special respect to the Grand Prince of Kiev. The Grand Prince collected tribute from the local princes to support his court and army. The major duties of these princes were to administer justice and to defend the frontiers. The princes were assisted by councils of wealthy merchants and landed nobles, who were known as boyars. Assemblies represented all free adult male citizens. They handled daily affairs and had the power to accept or remove princes.

These three institutions—the princely office, the council, and the assembly—varied in power from region to region. In the northeastern territories, the prince wielded a great deal of political power. In the southeastern areas, the boyars had the greatest political influence. In Novgorod and a few northern trading towns and cities, the assemblies overshadowed both princes and boyars. In these areas, the assemblies came close to establishing a tradition of representative government in the Eastern Slavic lands. However, later princes limited the powers of the assemblies.

Jim Brandenburg

Rurik the Rus

This 19th-century statue of Russia's ancient ruler Rurik the Rus stands in the center of the city of Novgorod. The bronze Rurik, a mighty Prince, holds symbols of military might and political power: a shield and sword. His fur cape sweeps proudly over his shoulders. Founder of a nation, the Viking warrior proclaims a glorious past.

Rurik and his Viking warriors came from Scandinavia to what is now northern Russia in the A.D. 800s, perhaps invited there by native Slavic tribes constantly warring with each other. Russia during the A.D. 800s had no political stability, which made farming and commerce difficult. The Vikings changed that. Trading with the strong, plundering the weak, they moved south from Novgorod to Kiev, where they founded a political state, and from there they moved on to Odessa on the shores of the Black Sea. It took them two centuries. By then the Vikings had lost their Scandinavian ways and had become assimilated into the local cultures. ⊕

Arrival of Christianity

Before the late A.D. 900s, the Eastern Slavs honored nature spirits and ancestors, and worshiped many deities. The most popular gods were Perun, god of thunder and lightning, and the Great Mother, goddess of the land and harvest. Images of the deities were built on the highest ground outside the villages.

Vladimir's Conversion

Because of contact with the Byzantine Empire, many Eastern Slavs were influenced by Eastern Orthodoxy. **Olga**, a princess of Kiev, became the first member of the Kievan nobility to accept the faith. Her grandson, Prince **Vladimir** of Kiev, decided to abandon the old beliefs and to adopt a new religion that he thought would help the Eastern Slavs become a more powerful civilization. An old Slavic legend states that Vladimir sent observers abroad to examine Judaism, Roman Catholicism, Eastern Orthodoxy, and Islam. Only the beautiful ceremony in the splendid Byzantine church of Hagia Sophia impressed the observers. In A.D. 989, after his own conversion to Eastern Orthodoxy, Vladimir ordered a mass baptism in the Dnieper River for his people.

This ancient monastery stands as a symbol of the influence of Byzantine Christianity. *How was Eastern Orthodoxy introduced in Kievan Rus?*

Effects of Conversion

The conversion to Eastern Orthodoxy brought Byzantine culture to Kievan Rus. Byzantine priests and bishops introduced the Eastern Slavs to colorful rituals and taught them the art of painting icons. The Eastern Slavs also learned to write their language in the Cyrillic alphabet. Schools were established in the towns for the sons of boyars, priests, and merchants. Byzantine architects arrived in Kiev to build stone churches with onion-shaped domes. Monasteries also were founded in the towns and countryside, and attracted many of the new converts.

Acceptance of Eastern Orthodoxy, however, tended to isolate the Eastern Slavs from the outside world. Following the split between the Eastern and Western Churches, Kievan Rus was separated from western Europe. Its people lost contact with developments that took place in that area after A.D. 1200. At the same time, the Byzantine practice of translating the Bible and Orthodox church services into local languages had an important impact. Because Kievan scholars had translations of some classical and Christian writings in their own language, they did not learn Greek or Latin. As a result, they did not deepen their knowledge of the heritage of western European civilization. Instead, they turned for inspiration to the traditions of their own local culture.

Kiev's Golden Age

Vladimir, who ruled from A.D. 980 to A.D. 1015, was one of the most important grand princes of Kiev. Known for his skills as a warrior, he successfully defended Kievan Rus's eastern frontiers against nomadic invaders. He also expanded its western borders by capturing lands in Poland and near the Baltic Sea.

Yaroslav's Reign

After a time of dynastic conflict, Vladimir's son **Yaroslav** became Grand Prince in A.D. 1019. Under Yaroslav's rule, Kievan culture reached its height. Yaroslav encouraged the spread of learning by establishing the first library in Kiev. Yaroslav also organized the Kievan legal system, drawing from Justinian's Code. Written primarily for the princes and merchants, the code treated crimes against property as well as against persons.

A skilled diplomat, Yaroslav arranged for his daughters and sisters to marry kings in Norway, Hungary, France, and Poland. To the Europeans, who were just arising from the isolation and disorder of the early Middle Ages, Kiev was a glittering capital whose culture outshone that of any in western Europe.

Kiev's Decline

After Yaroslav's death, Kiev declined in power and wealth for several reasons. First, Yaroslav began the practice of dividing up his lands among all his sons instead of willing them to one heir. Since no law established a clear line of succession, the heirs battled one another over control of Kiev. Second, the Latin Christian state created in Constantinople disrupted trade with the Byzantines and weakened Kiev's economy. Finally, in A.D. 1240 Mongol invaders from central Asia captured Kiev and completely destroyed it.

Mongol Rule

The Mongols, or Tatars, as the Slavs called them, defeated the armies of the Russian princes and conquered most of the country except for Novgorod. They sacked towns and villages and killed thousands. Mongols sought to tax the peoples they conquered, rather than impose their culture. The Slavs were allowed to practice their Christian faith, but the Mongols required allegiance to the Mongol ruler and service in the Mongol army.

For two centuries, Mongol rule isolated most of the Eastern Slavs from European civilization. Although the occupation helped unify the Eastern Slavs, it also further distanced them from ideas and trends of the Western world.

Rise of Muscovy

As city life in the south declined after the fall of Kiev, many Eastern Slavs—led by monks, farmers, and artisans—moved into the remote northern forests in order to escape Mongol rule. By the late A.D. 1200s, the principalities of Vladimir–Suzdal and **Novgorod** were the strongest Eastern Slavic territories.

Alexander Nevsky

The Mongols had never advanced as far north as Novgorod because the spring thaw turned the land into a swamp they could not cross. Instead, the city faced attacks in the Baltic Sea area from Swedes and Germans who wanted to convert the Eastern Slavs to Roman Catholicism. In a ferocious battle on the Neva River in A.D. 1240, Alexander, prince of Novgorod, defeated the invading Swedes.

Visualizing History Alexander Nevsky, ruler of Novgorod, fought the German Teutonic Knights in A.D. 1242. *Why did the Germans and Swedes attack the Eastern Slavs?*

This victory earned him the nickname **Alexander Nevsky**, Alexander "of the Neva," and his victory established Novgorod as a strong, independent principality.

Moscow's Beginnings

Daniel, the youngest son of Alexander Nevsky, became ruler of **Moscow**, a small but prosperous town located near vital land and water routes. Using war and diplomatic marriages, the princes of Moscow, or Muscovy, gradually expanded their state's territory. Muscovy's importance grew in A.D. 1325 when the metropolitan, or leader of the Orthodox Church in the Eastern Slavic lands, was transferred there. By about A.D. 1350, Moscow had become the most powerful city. Cooperation with Mongol policies had kept it free from outside interference. Daniel's son, Prince Ivan I, became known as Money Bag because the Mongols even trusted him to collect taxes for them.

Muscovite forces defeated the Mongols at the Battle of Kulikovo in A.D. 1380. The tide had turned in favor of Muscovy. Over the next hundred years, the Eastern Slavs steadily drove out the Mongols. In A.D. 1480 during the rule of **Ivan III**, Moscow finally refused to pay taxes to the Mongols. The

**Gold-domed spires of the Church of
the Annunciation reach toward the
sky behind the Kremlin's walls.** *What was the original
purpose of the Kremlin?*

the last Byzantine emperor, he took the title czar, or "caesar," the title used by the Roman and Byzantine emperors. Ivan also made the two-headed Byzantine eagle the symbol of his rule.

In A.D. 1493 Ivan added the title Sovereign of All Russia. The lands he ruled, now known as Russia, were a hundred times as large as the original Muscovite state. The people spoke one language, and the princes served one czar. The Russian Orthodox Church, which identified its interests with those of the Muscovite ruler, proclaimed that Moscow was the Third Rome. The Church regarded Ivan as both the successor of the Byzantine emperor and protector of the Eastern Orthodox Church, a claim all succeeding Russian czars would also make.

Moscow's Culture

Eastern Orthodoxy shaped the development of Moscow's culture. Its leaders stressed the importance of obedience to the czar and the government. The Church taught the people that submission to authority was a Christian duty. Joseph Sanin, an influential church leader during Ivan III's reign, wrote that "although the [ruler] was like other men in his physical characteristics, in his power he was similar to God in heaven."

Although western European influences reached Russia, they were transformed by local Russian styles and tastes. Instead of using Greek, Latin, or other classical languages, the Church used the Russian language in its worship and writings. Russia's religious leaders and political rulers also encouraged the development of a unique national style of icon painting and building construction. Ivan III had western European and Russian architects rebuild the Moscow Kremlin, or fortress. In spite of Western influences on its construction, the Kremlin became known for the typically Russian splendor of its beautiful onion-domed churches and ornately decorated palaces. Today the Kremlin in Moscow is still a center of government, religion, and culture for Russia.

long submission to the Asian rulers was over. Today, Ivan is known as Ivan the Great because he was able to bring all the Russian principalities under his rule. His major gain was Novgorod, which controlled territory all the way east to the Ural Mountains, the traditional division between Europe and Asia.

The Third Rome

Other factors helped to strengthen the power of Moscow's rulers. After Constantinople fell to the Ottoman Turks in A.D. 1453, Muscovy stood alone as the center of the Eastern Orthodox Church. In A.D. 1472 when Ivan III married Sophia, niece of

---

SECTION 3 REVIEW

Recall
1. **Define** steppe, principality, boyar, czar.
2. **Identify** the Slavs, Rurik, Olga, Vladimir, Yaroslav, the Mongols, Alexander Nevsky, Ivan III.
3. **Locate** Kiev on the map on page

259. Why did Kiev prosper?

Critical Thinking
4. **Making Comparisons** Compare Kievan Rus with Muscovy. How was each dependent on geography? What role did the Orthodox Church play in each?

Understanding Themes
5. **Cultural Diffusion** What traditions that had originated with Rome became part of Russian culture? How did Russian culture differ from the civilization of western Europe? Why?

Distinguishing Between Fact and Opinion

Imagine that you are watching two candidates for President debate the merits of the college loan program. One candidate says, "In my view, the college loan program must be reformed. Sixty percent of students do not repay their loans on time."

The other candidate replies, "College costs are skyrocketing, but only 30% of students default on their loans for more than one year. I believe we should spend more money on this worthy program."

How can you tell who or what to believe? First, you must learn to distinguish between fact and opinion.

Learning the Skill

A fact is a statement that can be proved to be true or false. In the example above, the statement "Sixty percent of students do not repay their loans on time" is a fact. By reviewing statistics on the number of student loan recipients who repay their loans, we can determine whether it is true or false. To identify facts, look for words and phrases indicating specific people, places, events, dates, times.

An opinion, on the other hand, expresses a personal belief, viewpoint, or emotion. Because opinions are subjective, we cannot prove or disprove them. In the opening example, most statements by the candidates are opinions.

Opinions often include qualifying words and phrases such as *I think, I believe, probably, seems to me, may, might, could, ought, in my judgment*, or *in my view*. Also, look for expressions of approval or disapproval such as *good, bad, poor*, and *satisfactory*. Be aware of superlatives such as *greatest, worst, finest*, and *best*. Notice words with negative meanings and implications such as *squander, contemptible*, and *disgrace*. Also, identify generalizations such as *none, every, always*, and *never*.

Practicing the Skill

For each pair of statements below, determine which is fact and which is opinion. Give a reason for each choice.

1. (a) The Byzantine Empire came to a pitiful end at the hands of the savage Turks.
(b) The Byzantine Empire ended when Constantine XI died while defending Constantinople from invading Turks in A.D. 1453.
2. (a) The alliance with the Byzantine Empire made Kiev a major trading link between Europe and Asia and between Scandinavia and the Middle East.
(b) In the A.D. 900s Kiev was the most isolated, uncivilized place and possessed little in the way of culture.
3. (a) The Byzantine culture was more advanced than any other of its day.
(b) Vladimir's conversion to Eastern Orthodoxy brought Byzantine culture to Kievan Rus.

Applying the Skill

In a newspaper, find a news article and an editorial on the same topic or issue. Identify five facts and five opinions from these sources.

For More Practice

Turn to the Skill Practice in the Chapter Review on page 267 for more practice in distinguishing between fact and opinion.

Historical Significance

As a crossroads of trade, the Byzantine Empire was a center for cultural diffusion. Its scholars transmitted Roman law and classical and Christian learning to western Europe. The Byzantine Church spread Christianity by sending missionaries to convert the Slavs and other neighboring peoples.

In addition, the Byzantines were cultural innovators who made a lasting impact. Their icons and mosaics became part of the Christian artistic heritage of Europe, and their architecture inspired building styles in eastern Europe and the Middle East.

Using Key Terms

Write the key term that completes each sentence.

a. boyar
b. clergy
c. mosaic
d. iconoclasts
e. monasteries
f. illuminated manuscripts
g. missionary
h. regent
i. schism
j. laity
k. czar
l. steppe

1. Wanting to prevent superstition and idol worship, _____, or image breakers, supported the removal of all images from churches.
2. Church officials, such as bishops and priests, are referred to as members of the _____.
3. North of the Black Sea are thick forests, mighty rivers, and a vast plain known as the _____.
4. The Byzantines excelled in the art of _____, or pictures made of many tiny pieces of colored glass or flat stone set in plaster.
5. In A.D. 1054 doctrinal, political, and geographic differences led to a _____ between the Roman Catholic Church in the West and the Eastern Orthodox Church in the East.
6. The _____ Cyril and Methodius brought Eastern Orthodox Christianity and the Byzantine culture to the Slavs of eastern Europe.
7. In Kievan Rus, wealthy nobles and landowners who assisted the princes were called _____.
8. Religious scholars of the Byzantine Empire often preserved ancient writings in the form of _____.
9. In A.D. 1472 the Muscovite ruler Ivan III took the title _____, the title used by the Roman and Byzantine emperors.
10. _____ were communities of devout Christians set apart from the world.

Using Your History Journal

Write a short story describing a fictional case that may have come before an official of Justinian's court. Base the story on the law you described in Your History Journal at the beginning of this chapter.

Reviewing Facts

1. **Explain** the significance of the Justinian Code to later generations.
2. **Describe** how the use of religious art became the center of a controversy in the Eastern Orthodox Church.
3. **Analyze** how the Byzantine Empire promoted Christianity.
4. **Explain** the focus of Byzantine art as revealed in mosaics and icons.
5. **Explain** the contribution that Nino made to the development of the kingdom of Georgia.
6. **Identify** the three groups of Slavs and the part of modern Europe in which each is found.
7. **Explain** how the Russians became isolated from the rest of Europe.
8. **Describe** how Christianity affected the East Slavs.
9. **Explain** the role of the Vikings in Slavic and Byzantine history.

Critical Thinking

1. **Analyze** How was the title of New Rome both suitable and unsuitable for the city of Constantinople?
2. **Evaluate** Why was the preservation of Greek

and Roman learning a significant contribution of Byzantine civilization?

3. Analyze What do these Byzantine coins reveal about the level of development of Byzantine civilization?

4. Analyze What were the causes of the schism in the Christian Church? Could the split have been prevented? Explain.

5. Compare/Contrast How were the Byzantine Empire and the Roman Empire alike? How were they different?

6. Synthesize What were Constantine's reasons for his location of Constantinople? What other factors are of concern in the location of a city?

7. Analyze How did trade affect the Byzantine Empire?

8. Synthesize Imagine you are a Russian boyar under Ivan III. Would you resist calling him Czar? Explain.

Understanding Themes

1. Conflict How does conflict—such as the iconoclastic controversy in the Byzantine Empire—weaken a government?

2. Innovation Using Byzantine civilization as an example, explain how one civilization's ideas can be adapted to other societies.

3. Cultural Diffusion How can two societies be enriched by sharing cultural aspects? Give examples from the cases of Kievan Rus and Muscovy.

Linking Past and Present

1. Investigate the role the Bosporus played in World War I and World War II.

2. Explain the historical reasons why Russia has a continuing interest in the affairs of eastern European nations.

3. Investigate the historical roots of religious controversies in modern societies, such as Bosnia and Northern Ireland.

Skill Practice

Read the following statements. Determine which are facts and which are opinions. Give a reason for each choice.

1. The *Primary Chronicle* states that in A.D. 911 Grand Prince Oleg agreed on a peace treaty with the Byzantine emperors Leo and Alexander.

2. The Volga River is longer than the Danube River.

3. The Russian Orthodox Church is the most spiritually uplifting faith in the world.

4. Nomads wandered aimlessly throughout the steppes and lived in flimsy shelters.

Geography in History

1. Location Refer to the map below. By what year had the area around the Volga River been added to Moscow's holdings?

2. Place What enabled the princes of Muscovy to expand the city of Moscow?

3. Region By A.D. 1493 Moscow's ruler claimed to be "Sovereign of All Russia." About how far did Moscow's territory stretch from north to south in A.D. 1462?

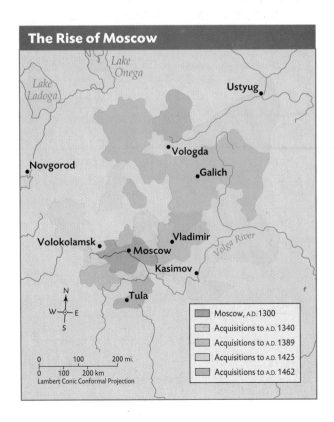

The Rise of Moscow

Lake Onega
Lake Ladoga
Ustyug
Novgorod
Vologda
Galich
Volokolamsk
Vladimir
Moscow
Volga River
Kasimov
Tula

N
W—E
S

0   100   200 mi.
0   100   200 km
Lambert Conic Conformal Projection

- Moscow, A.D. 1300
- Acquisitions to A.D. 1340
- Acquisitions to A.D. 1389
- Acquisitions to A.D. 1425
- Acquisitions to A.D. 1462

Chapter

11

Islamic Civilization

Chapter Themes

▶ **Innovation** The faith and principles of Islam become the basis of a new civilization. *Section 1*

▶ **Movement** Armies and merchants spread Islam through the Middle East and North Africa, and into Spain and Asia. *Section 2*

▶ **Cultural Diffusion** Contributions from many cultures and peoples enrich the Islamic state. *Section 3*

Storyteller

"I was in Makkah at last," writes a devout Muslim woman about her pilgrimage to Makkah, the holiest city of the religion of Islam. She continues, *"Before me was the Kaaba, a great black cube partly submerged in a torrent of white-robed pilgrims circling round and round. Around us, like a great dam containing the torrent, stood the massive walls and the seven slim minarets of the Sacred Mosque. High above, the muezzin began the evening call to prayer: 'Allahu Akbar! ... God is Most Great!'...*

"Around the Kaaba ... repeating the customary prayers, swirled men and women of every race and nation, from every corner of the earth...."

All believers of Islam hope to share in this event at least once in their lives. Since the A.D. 600s, it has been one of the unifying celebrations for all Muslims.

Historical Significance

What are the basic beliefs and principles of Islam? What contributions has Islamic civilization made to world knowledge and culture?

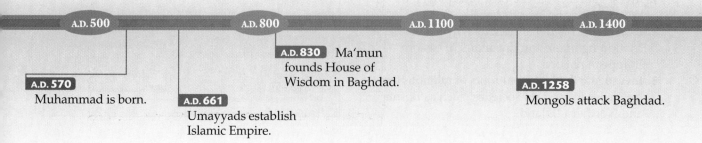

A.D. 500	A.D. 800	A.D. 1100	A.D. 1400

A.D. 830 Ma'mun founds House of Wisdom in Baghdad.

A.D. 570 Muhammad is born.

A.D. 661 Umayyads establish Islamic Empire.

A.D. 1258 Mongols attack Baghdad.

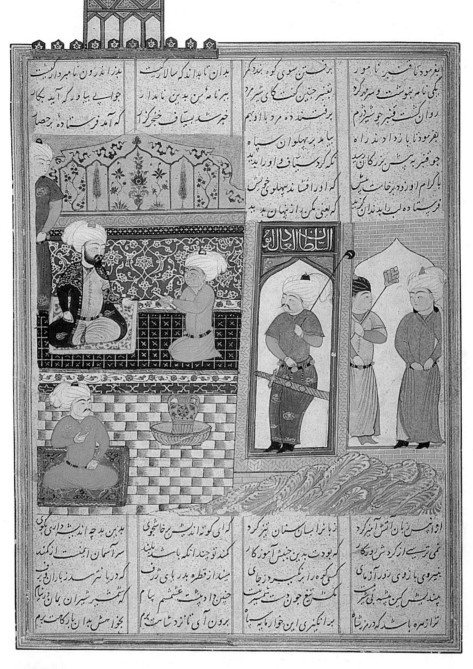

Apocryphal Life of Ali, from the *Kharar-nama*, late A.D. 1400s

Your History Journal

Choose a topic from the text headings on astronomy and geography, chemistry and medicine, or art and architecture in the Muslim world. Research the subject in a library and write a short report.

A.D. 600	A.D. 625	A.D. 650

A.D. 610	A.D. 622	A.D. 630	A.D. 632
Muhammad has his first revelation.	Muhammad and followers depart on the *Hijrah*.	The people of Makkah accept Islam.	Muhammad dies at Madinah.

Section 1

A New Faith

Setting the Scene

▶ **Terms to Define**
sheikh, revelation, *shari'ah*, mosque, imam, hajj

▶ **People to Meet**
Muhammad

▶ **Places to Locate**
Arabian Peninsula, Makkah

Find Out What are the basic beliefs and practices of Islam?

The Storyteller

Ubadah sat on the only chair in the crowded room and began to recite. The men sitting on the floor did not seem to pay much attention at first, but soon conversation died away. As imam, Ubadah described the rewards awaiting the pious after death. The Paradise he described was vastly different from the baked, dusty town where they sat. He spoke of a green garden with fruit trees of every kind and fountains of water, milk, wine, and honey. In Paradise everyone would rest on silken couches, have beautiful wives, and all his sins would be pardoned. "Which, therefore, of your Lord's benefits will you ungratefully deny?" Ubadah concluded.

—freely adapted from *The Short Koran*, George M. Lamsa, editor, reprinted in *Sources of World History*, Mark A. Kishlansky, 1995

A reading from the Quran

South of Asia Minor lies the **Arabian Peninsula**, home of the Arabs. This location placed the Arabs at the margins of the great Middle Eastern civilizations. Like the ancient Israelites, Phoenicians, and Chaldeans, the Arabs were descended from Semitic tribes. Archaeologists have traced Arab civilizations in the Arabian Peninsula to at least 3000 B.C.

Arab Life

The relative geographic remoteness of the Arabian Peninsula kept the empires in the northern part of the region from invading Arab lands. Their isolation allowed the Arabs to create their own civilization.

The Setting

The Arabian Peninsula is a wedge of land of about 1 million square miles (2.6 million sq. km) between the Red Sea and the Persian Gulf. It is made up of two distinct regions. The southwestern area, across from the northeast coast of Africa, has well-watered valleys nestled between mountains. The rest of the peninsula, however, consists of arid plains and deserts.

Yet the peninsula is not entirely forbidding. Grass grows quickly during the showers of the rainy season, and oases, the fertile areas around springs and water holes, provide a permanent source of water for farmers, herders, and travelers. For centuries, nomadic herders and caravans have crisscrossed the desert, traveling from oasis to oasis.

Lives of the Bedouin

In ancient times many of the Arabs were bedouin (BEH•duh•wuhn), nomads who herded sheep, camels, and goats and lived in tents made of felt from camel or goat hair. They ate mainly fresh or dried dates, and they drank milk from their herds; on special occasions they also ate mutton.

The bedouin lived in tribes, each made up of related families. Arabs valued family ties because they ensured protection and survival in the harsh desert environment. Leading each tribe was a sheikh (SHAYK), or chief, appointed by the heads of the families. A council of elders advised the sheikh, who ruled as long as he had the tribe's consent. Warfare was part of bedouin life. The Arab tribes went on raids to gain camels and horses and battled one another over pastures and water holes, the most precious resources in the desert. To protect their honor and their possessions, the bedouin believed in retaliation—"an eye for an eye, and a tooth for a tooth."

For entertainment the bedouin enjoyed many activities. Camel and horse races and other games sharpened the men's abilities as warriors, and then everyone enjoyed an evening of storytelling around the campfires. Poets composed and recited poems about battles, deserts, camels and horses, and love. In these lines an Arab sheikh states his view of war:

> From the cup of peace
> drink your fill;
> but from the cup of war
> a sip will suffice. 99

Growth of Towns

By the A.D. 500s, many tribes had settled around oases or in fertile valleys to pursue either farming or trade. Groups of merchants soon founded prosperous market towns. The most important of these towns was **Makkah**, a crossroads of commerce about 50 miles (80 km) inland from the Red Sea.

People from all over the Arabian Peninsula traveled to Makkah to trade animal products for weapons, dates, grain, spices, jewels, ivory, silk, and perfumes. Enormous caravans from the fertile southwest passed through Makkah en route to Syria, Iraq, and as far away as China. Arabs also visited Makkah to worship at the peninsula's holiest shrine, the Kaaba, which contained statues of the many Arab deities. The business the pilgrims brought to Makkah made its merchants wealthy.

Signs of Change

As business ties replaced tribal ties in the trading towns, the old tribal rules were no longer adequate. At the same time, the Byzantine and Persian Empires were threatening to take over Arab lands. The Arabs had a common language, but they lacked a sense of unity and had no central government to solve these new problems.

Religious ideas were also changing. Contacts with the Byzantines, the Persians, and the

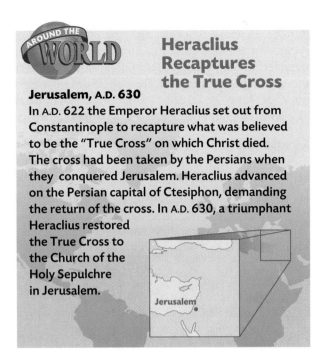

AROUND THE WORLD

Heraclius Recaptures the True Cross

Jerusalem, A.D. 630
In A.D. 622 the Emperor Heraclius set out from Constantinople to recapture what was believed to be the "True Cross" on which Christ died. The cross had been taken by the Persians when they conquered Jerusalem. Heraclius advanced on the Persian capital of Ctesiphon, demanding the return of the cross. In A.D. 630, a triumphant Heraclius restored the True Cross to the Church of the Holy Sepulchre in Jerusalem.

Jerusalem

Ethiopians introduced the teachings of the monotheistic religions of Judaism and Christianity. Moreover, a number of Christian and Jewish Arabs lived in the peninsula. Dissatisfied with their old beliefs, many idol-worshiping Arabs searched for a new religion. Holy men known as hanifs (hah•NEEFS) denounced the worship of idols and believed in one god. They rejected Judaism and Christianity, however, preferring to find a uniquely Arab form of monotheism.

This ferment in Arab religious life contributed to the emergence of the religion known as Islam, which means "submission to the will of Allah (God)." This faith would bring the Arabs into contact with other civilizations and change Arab history.

Muhammad and His Message

The prophet of Islam, **Muhammad**, was born in the bustling city of Makkah around A.D. 570. Muslim traditions state that Muhammad was orphaned at an early age and raised by an uncle.

Life of Muhammad

During his teens, Muhammad worked as a caravan leader on a trade route. His reputation as an exceptionally honest and able person prompted his employer, a wealthy widow of 40 named Khadija (kuh•DEE•juh), to put him in charge of her business affairs. When Muhammad was about 25 years old, Khadija proposed marriage to him.

Muhammad's marriage to Khadija relieved

him of financial worries and gave him time to reflect on the meaning of life. Muhammad was troubled by the greed of Makkah's wealthy citizens, the worship of idols, and the mistreatment of the poor. Seeking guidance, Muhammad spent time alone praying and fasting in a cave outside the city.

Revelation

Islamic tradition holds that, in A.D. 610, Muhammad experienced a revelation, or vision. He heard a voice calling him to be the apostle of the one true deity—Allah, the Arabic word for God. Three times the voice proclaimed, "Recite!" When Muhammad asked what he should recite, the voice replied:

> 66 Recite in the name of your Lord,
>   the Creator,
> Who created man from clots of blood.
> Recite! Your Lord is the most bountiful
>   One
> Who by the pen has taught mankind
>   things they did not know. 99

A second revelation commanded Muhammad to "rise and warn" the people about divine judgment. Although Muhammad had doubts about the revelations, he finally accepted his mission and returned to Makkah to preach.

In A.D. 613 Muhammad began sharing his revelations with his family and friends. He preached to the people of Makkah that there was only one God and that people everywhere must worship and obey him. He also declared that all who believed in God were equal. Therefore the rich should share their wealth with the poor. Muhammad also preached that God measured the worth of people by their devotion and good deeds. He told the people of Makkah to live their lives in preparation for the day of judgment, when God would punish evildoers and reward the just.

Muhammad made slow progress in winning converts. Khadija and members of Muhammad's family became the first Muslims, or followers of Islam. Many of the other converts came from Makkah's poor, who were attracted by Muhammad's call for social justice.

Opposition to Islam

Most Makkans rejected Muhammad's message. Wealthy merchants and religious leaders were upset by the prophet's attacks on the images at the Kaaba. They feared that monotheistic worship would end the pilgrimages to Makkah. Wealthy Makkans believed that this development would ruin the city's economy and lead to the loss of their prestige and wealth. Driven by these fears, the merchants persecuted Muhammad and the Muslims.

Muhammad persisted in his preaching until threats against his life forced him to seek help outside the city. He found it in Yathrib, a small town north of Makkah. In A.D. 622 Muhammad sent about 60 Muslim families from Makkah to Yathrib; soon after, he followed them in secret. His departure to Yathrib is known in Muslim history as the *Hijrah* (HIH•jruh), or emigration. The year in which the *Hijrah*

Visualizing History Nineteenth-century Turkish decorative tile with inscription "Allah is Great." The Ottoman Turks built an Islamic state that lasted until 1918. *What was the command Muhammad received in the second revelation?*

took place, A.D. 622, marks the beginning of the Islamic era and is recognized as the first year of the Muslim calendar.

The Islamic Community

Many of the people of Yathrib accepted Muhammad as the messenger of God and the ruler of their city. As the center of Islam, Yathrib became known as Madinat al-Nabi, "the city of the prophet," or Madinah (muh•DEE•nuh).

Origin of the Islamic State

Muhammad proved that he was a skilled political as well as religious leader. In the Madinah Compact of A.D. 624, Muhammad laid the foundation of an Islamic state. He decreed that all Muslims were to place loyalty to the Islamic community above loyalty to their tribe. Disputes were to be settled by Muhammad, who was declared the community's judge and commander in chief. All areas of life were placed under the divine law given to Muhammad and recorded in the Quran (kuh•RAHN), the holy scriptures of Islam. Muhammad also extended protection to Jews and Christians who accepted the political authority of the Islamic community.

Acceptance of Islam

Eventually the Makkans invaded Yathrib, forcing the Muslims to retaliate in self-defense. In the resulting battles, the Muslims defeated the Makkans, and the Muslims won the support of many Arab groups outside Madinah.

When Muhammad and his followers entered Makkah in A.D. 630, they faced little resistance. The Makkans accepted Islam and acknowledged Muhammad as God's prophet. The Muslims destroyed the idols in the Kaaba and turned the shrine into a place of worship for Muslim pilgrims. Makkah became the spiritual capital of Islam, and Madinah remained its political capital.

The Muslims also extended their control into other parts of Arabia. By A.D. 631 the Islamic state included the entire Arabian Peninsula and was supported by a strong army recruited from all of the Arab tribes.

After a brief illness, Muhammad died at Madinah in A.D. 632. He left behind two major achievements: the growth of a monotheistic religion that stood on an equal level with Judaism and Christianity, and a well-organized political-religious community that increased the Arabs' power and influence.

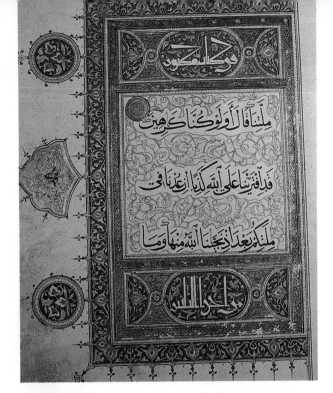

Visualizing History Because the Quran was written in Arabic, Muslims of many cultures adopted Arabic as a universal language. *What does the name "Quran" mean?*

Beliefs and Practices of Islam

Muhammad established beliefs and practices for his followers based on his revelations. In spite of social and political changes, these Islamic beliefs and practices have remained remarkably stable through the centuries.

The Quran

According to Muslim tradition, the angel Gabriel revealed divine messages to Muhammad over a 22-year period. Faithful Muslims wrote down or memorized these messages, but they were not compiled into one written collection until after Muhammad died. Then his successor, Abu Bakr, ordered Muslims to retrieve these messages from wherever they could be found, from the "ribs of palm-leaves and tablets of white stone and from the breasts of men." It took 20 years before the messages were compiled into the Quran, whose name means "recital." For all Muslims, the Quran is the final authority in matters of faith and life style.

Written in Arabic, the Quran is believed to contain God's message as revealed to Muhammad. This message is expressed in stories, legends, teachings, and exhortations. Some of the stories—such as

Islamic mosque lamp from the Sulmaniyeh Mosque in Istanbul, **Turkey** *What are the various uses that a mosque may serve in an Islamic community?*

touching one's forehead to the ground as a sign of submission to God.

Muslims can offer their daily prayers outside or inside, at work or at home. At noon on Fridays, many Muslims pray together in a mosque, a building that may serve as a place of worship, a school, a court of law, and a shelter.

An imam (ih•MAHM), or prayer leader, guides believers in prayer, and a sermon sometimes follows. Any male Muslim with the proper religious education can serve as an imam.

Alms

The third pillar of Islam is the giving of alms, or charity. It reflects the Islamic view that the wealthy should assist the poor and weak. Almsgiving is practiced privately through contributions to the needy and publicly through a state tax that supports schools and aids the poor.

Fasting

The fourth pillar of Islam, fasting, occurs in the month of Ramadan (RAH•muh•DAHN), the ninth month in the Muslim calendar. During Ramadan, Muhammad received the first revelation. From sunrise to sunset Muslims neither eat nor drink, although they work as usual. Children, pregnant women, travelers, and the sick are exempt from fasting. At sunset the call for prayer—and in large cities the sound of a cannon—announces the end of the fast. Muslims then sit down to eat their "evening breakfast." In the cool evening hours, people stream out into the streets to greet their friends. At the end of Ramadan, there is a three-day celebration for the end of the fast.

Pilgrimage

The fifth pillar of Islam is the annual pilgrimage, or hajj, to Makkah. Every able-bodied Muslim who can afford the trip is expected to make the pilgrimage at least once in his or her lifetime. Those who perform the hajj are especially honored in the community.

The hajj takes place two months and ten days after the Ramadan fast and involves three days of ceremony, prayer, and sacrifice. Today, hundreds of thousands of Muslims come together to worship at the Kaaba and other shrines of Islam in Makkah and Madinah. The hajj is more than a religious pilgrimage. A visible expression of Muslim unity, the hajj allows a continuing exchange of ideas among the peoples of Africa, Europe, Asia, and the Americas who follow Islam.

SECTION 1 REVIEW

Recall
1. **Define** sheikh, revelation, *shari'ah*, mosque, imam, hajj.
2. **Identify** Arabian Peninsula, Makkah, Muhammad, Muslims, *Hijrah*, Madinah Compact, Quran.
3. **Explain** What made life possible in the harsh environment of the Arabian Peninsula?

Critical Thinking
4. **Analyzing Information** In what ways was Islam a new religion? In what ways was it an extension or a continuation of other religions that were also founded in this region—Judaism and Christianity?

Understanding Themes
5. **Innovation** Describe the Five Pillars of Islam and the Madinah Compact, and tell how they changed life in the Arabian Peninsula.

A.D. 600		A.D. 800	A.D. 1000	A.D. 1200

c. A.D. 1050 The Abbasids enter period of decline.

A.D. 632
Abu Bakr becomes the first caliph.

A.D. 732
Muslims and Christians fight the Battle of Tours.

A.D. 750
The Abbasid dynasty comes to power.

Section 2

Spread of Islam

Setting the Scene

▶ **Terms to Define**
caliph, jihad

▶ **People to Meet**
Abu Bakr, Ali, Mu'awiyah, the Shiite, Husayn, the Sunni, Harun al-Rashid

▶ **Places to Locate**
Damascus, Baghdad

ind Out How did the Islamic state expand, and how did it decline?

The Storyteller

From the far reaches of the Mediterranean to the Indus River valley, the faithful approached the holy city. All had the same objective—to worship together at the holiest shrine of Islam, the Kaaba in Makkah. One such traveler was Mansa Musa, king of Mali in western Africa. Musa had prepared carefully for the long journey he and his attendants would take. He was determined to go, not only for his own religious fulfillment, but also for recruiting teachers and leaders, so that his land could learn more of the Prophet's teachings.

—adapted from *The Chronicle of the Seeker*, Mahmud Kati, reprinted in *The Human Record*, Alfred J. Andrea and James H. Overfield, 1990

Pilgrimage to Makkah

When Muhammad died in A.D. 632, he had left no clear instructions about who was to succeed him as the leader of Islam. Muslims knew that no one could take Muhammad's place as the messenger of God. They realized, however, that the Islamic community needed a strong leader who could preserve its unity and guide its daily affairs. A group of prominent Muslims met and chose a new type of leader, whom they called *khalifah* (kuh•LEE•fuh) or caliph (KAY•luhf), meaning "successor."

"The Rightly Guided Caliphs"

The first four caliphs were elected for life. All were close friends or relatives of Muhammad. The first caliph was Muhammad's father-in-law and close friend, **Abu Bakr** (uh•BOO BA•kuhr). The last, his son-in-law Ali, was married to Muhammad's daughter Fatimah (FAH•tuh•muh). The first four caliphs followed Muhammad's example, kept in close touch with the people, and asked the advice of other Muslim leaders. For these reasons, Muslims have called them "the Rightly Guided Caliphs."

Early Conquests

The Rightly Guided Caliphs sought to protect and spread Islam. Their military forces carried Islam beyond the Arabian Peninsula. In addition to religious motives, the Arabs were eager to acquire the agricultural wealth of the Byzantine and Persian Empires to meet the needs of their growing population.

Arab armies swept forth against the weakened Byzantine and Persian Empires. By A.D. 650, these armies had acquired Palestine, Syria, Iraq, Persia, and Egypt. The conquests reduced the Asian part of the Byzantine Empire to Asia Minor and the Constantinople area and brought the Persian Empire completely under Muslim control.

The Arab armies were successful for several reasons. Their faith united them in seeking a common goal—to carry Islam to other peoples. According to the Quran, Muslims had a duty to follow their faith and to struggle for its expansion. The Islamic state, therefore, viewed the conquests as a jihad (jih•HAHD), or struggle to introduce Islam to other lands. The Quran forbade the use of force in winning converts to Islam. Islamic teaching, however, promised that warriors who died in a jihad would immediately enter paradise. Furthermore, the Byzantine and Persian Empires had been weakened militarily and economically by the wars they had been fighting with each other for many years.

Division Within Islam

While Muslim armies were achieving military success, rival groups fought for the caliphate, or the office of the caliph. The struggle began when **Ali** was elected the fourth caliph in A.D. 656.

One of Ali's most powerful rivals was **Mu'awiyah** (moo•UH•wee•uh), governor of Syria and nephew of the third caliph, Uthman, who had been murdered. Mu'awiyah wanted revenge for that murder and accused Ali's supporters of encouraging it. When Ali tried to depose the Syrian governor, Mu'awiyah refused to step down.

In the battle that followed, Mu'awiyah's defeat seemed certain. Then the Syrian soldiers tied copies of pages from the Quran to the tips of their lances and charged, shouting, "Let Allah decide!" Unwilling to strike an enemy bearing the word of God, Ali was forced to negotiate with Mu'awiyah.

While Ali was trying to reassert his control as caliph, Mu'awiyah took over Egypt and raided Iraq. In A.D. 661 Ali was fatally stabbed by a disillusioned follower, and his older son renounced his claim to the caliphate. Mu'awiyah became the first caliph of the powerful Umayyad (oo•MY•uhd) dynasty.

Followers of Ali, known as **the Shiite** (SHEE•EYET), never accepted Mu'awiyah's rule. When he died in A.D. 680, they claimed the caliphate for Ali's son, **Husayn** (hoo•SAYN), then in Madinah. Husayn's followers in Iraq invited him

Images of the Times

Islamic Art and Architecture

Inspired by their faith, artists and architects of Islam created unequaled geometric designs, floral patterns, and calligraphy.

Carpets and other textiles were turned into fine art pieces by the skilled hands of Islamic weavers.

Shoes of the Faithful by Charles Robertson is a reminder of the centrality of religious belief in Muslim daily life.

to lead them as caliph. When he arrived in Iraq with his family and a small group of followers, Umayyad troops massacred all but the women and a young son in a battle at Karbala. The leader sent Husayn's head to Mu'awiyah's son, who had assumed the caliphate.

The murders of Ali and Husayn led to a permanent schism in the Islamic world. The majority of Muslims, known as **the Sunni** (SU•nee), or "followers of the way," follow the teachings of Muhammad, the tradition followed by the Rightly Guided Caliphs. In Sunni Islam, the caliph may be any devout Muslim who is accepted by the people.

The Shiite, the smaller group of Muslims, followed a series of leaders who aimed to destroy the existing caliphate and establish a new one in its place. Living mostly in Iraq and Iran, the Shiite believe the caliphate should be held only by descendants of Muhammad through his daughter Fatimah and her husband Ali. The Shiite stress the imam's power as a spiritual leader.

The Islamic State

The Umayyad dynasty, which was founded by Mu'awiyah, ruled from A.D. 661 to A.D. 750. The Umayyads moved the capital from Madinah to **Damascus**, Syria, which was more centrally located in the expanding state.

Umayyad Conquests

In the next century, Umayyad warriors carried Islam east, to the borders of India and China. In the west, they swept across North Africa and into Spain, the southernmost area of Christian western Europe.

By A.D. 716 the Muslims ruled almost all of Spain. They advanced halfway into France before the Frankish leader Charles Martel stopped them at the Battle of Tours in A.D. 732. This battle halted the spread of Islam into western Europe.

Life in the Umayyad State

The Umayyads built a powerful Islamic state that stressed the political, rather than the religious,

Court of the Myrtles, Alhambra, Granada, Spain remains as a striking example of intricate Islamic architectural design.

REFLECTING ON THE TIMES

1. What details characterize the interior walls of the Court of the Myrtles?
2. Why do you think the decorative arts flourished in the Islamic world during this period?

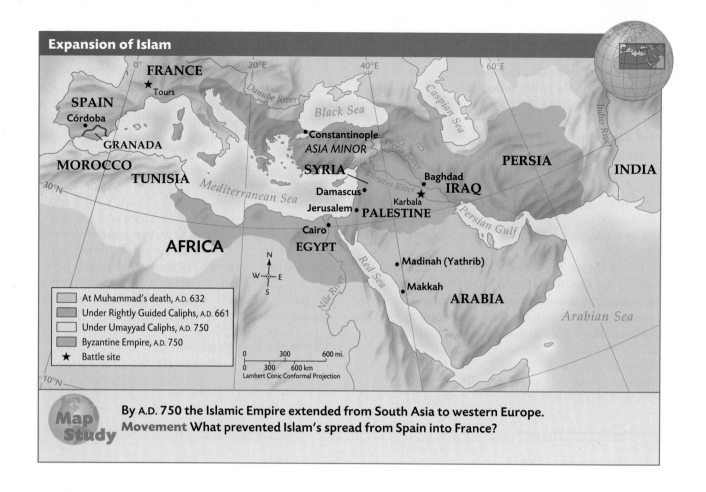

Expansion of Islam

Legend:
- At Muhammad's death, A.D. 632
- Under Rightly Guided Caliphs, A.D. 661
- Under Umayyad Caliphs, A.D. 750
- Byzantine Empire, A.D. 750
- ★ Battle site

0   300   600 mi.
0   300   600 km
Lambert Conic Conformal Projection

Map Study By A.D. 750 the Islamic Empire extended from South Asia to western Europe.
Movement What prevented Islam's spread from Spain into France?

aspect of their office. As time went by, they ruled more like kings and less like the earlier caliphs.

The Umayyads did, however, help to unite the lands they ruled. They made Arabic the official language, minted the first Arabic currency, built roads, and established postal routes. Their administration depended on a civil service made up of well-trained bureaucrats who had served as officials in the Byzantine and Persian Empires.

Umayyad rule also improved conditions for many, particularly Jews and non-Greek Christians, who had often suffered under Byzantine rule. They had to pay a special tax, but they were tolerated because they believed in one God. The great Arab commander Khalid ibn al-Walid, who had led the conquest of Syria and Persia, described Muslim policy:

66 In the name of Allah, the compassionate, the merciful, this is what Khalid ibn al-Walid would grant to the inhabitants of Damascus.... He promises to give them security for their lives, property and churches. Their city wall shall not be demolished, neither shall any Muslim be quartered in their houses. Thereunto we

give to them the pact of Allah and the protection of His Prophet, the Caliphs and the believers. So long as they pay the tax, nothing but good shall befall them. 99

Opposition to Umayyad Rule

Despite this enlightened outlook, Umayyad rule caused dissatisfaction among non-Arab Muslims. They paid higher taxes, received lower wages in the army and government, and were discriminated against socially. Discontent was particularly strong in Iraq and Persia, the center of the Shiite opposition to Umayyad rule.

The Abbasids

In the year A.D. 747, the anti-Umayyad Arabs and the non-Arab Muslims in Iraq and Persia joined forces, built an army, and, in three years of fighting, overwhelmed the Umayyads. The new caliph, Abu'l-'Abbas, was a descendant of one of Muhammad's uncles. He established the Abbasid (uh•BA•suhd) dynasty and had a new city, **Baghdad**, built on the banks of the Tigris River. By the A.D. 900s, about 1.5 million people lived in Baghdad.

Baghdad lay at the crossroads of the land and

Islamic Achievements

The use of Arabic not only promoted trade but also encouraged communication among the different peoples in the Islamic state. From these peoples the Islamic state built a rich storehouse of knowledge and scientific discovery.

Between the A.D. 800s and A.D. 1300s, Islamic scientists made important contributions in several scientific areas, such as mathematics, astronomy, chemistry, and medicine. They based their work on two main intellectual traditions. The first, and most important, was that of Greece. The second was that of India, which came to the Arabs by way of Persia.

The House of Wisdom

The Islamic world experienced a scientific awakening under the Abbasids. During the A.D. 800s, Baghdad became a leading intellectual center.

According to Muslim tradition, the Abbasid caliph **Ma'mun** (mah•MOON) founded the House of Wisdom at Baghdad in A.D. 830. This research center specialized in the translation into Arabic of Greek, Persian, and Indian scientific texts. Ma'mun staffed the institute with Christian, Jewish, and Muslim scholars who shared ideas from different intellectual traditions. They performed scientific experiments, made mathematical calculations, and built upon the ideas of the ancients. The House of Wisdom, therefore, sparked many of the mathematical and scientific achievements in the Islamic world.

Muslim science involved more than just theory; it was put to practical use. For example, mathematics was used to solve daily problems in business and agriculture. Astronomy was used to determine the hours of prayer and the time period of celebrations.

Mathematics

As you read in Chapter 7, Gupta mathematicians in India devised the numerals we know as Arabic numerals and the concept of zero. Muslim mathematicians adopted these numerals and used them in a place-value system. In this system, today used worldwide, a number's value is determined by the position of its digits. The place-value system made possible great achievements in mathematics.

Muslim mathematicians invented algebra and expressed equations to define curves and lines. Their work in geometry led to the development of trigonometry, which was used to calculate the distance to a star and the speed of a falling object. Mathematicians also were interested in practical applications, such as devising pumps and fountains and applying their skills to building and surveying.

Astronomy and Geography

At Ma'mun's observatory in Baghdad, astronomers checked the findings of the ancient Greeks, made observations of the skies, and produced physical and mathematical models of the universe. They accurately described solar eclipses and proved that the moon affects the oceans.

Muslim astronomers improved on a Greek device called the astrolabe, with which they determined the positions of stars, the movements of planets, and the time. The astrolabe made navigation easier and safer. It was also useful in religious practices, enabling Muslims to ascertain the direction of Makkah, the beginning of Ramadan, and the hours of prayer.

Using the astrolabe, Muslim geographers measured the size and circumference of the earth with accuracy unmatched until the 1900s. From such studies, geographers concluded that the earth was round, although most continued to accept the Greek theory that heavenly bodies revolve around the earth.

By the A.D. 1100s, Muslim geographers had determined the basic outlines of Asia, Europe, and North Africa and had produced the first accurate maps of the Eastern Hemisphere. They also traveled widely to gain firsthand knowledge of the earth's surface, its climates, and its peoples.

Chemistry and Medicine

Muslims developed alchemy, the branch of chemistry that attempted to change lead into gold. Although alchemists never succeeded in their goal, they did develop the equipment and methods that are still used in modern chemistry.

The renowned chemist and physician **al-Razi** (ahl•RAH•zee), who lived from A.D. 865 to A.D. 925, classified chemical substances as animal, mineral, or vegetable, a classification system that remains in use today. Al-Razi also made invaluable contributions to medicine. Among his nearly 200 works are a medical encyclopedia that describes the origin of disease and a handbook identifying the differences between smallpox and measles.

In the A.D. 900s, the doctor **Ibn Sina** (IH•buhn SEE•nuh) produced the *Canon of Medicine*, a monumental volume that attempted to summarize all the medical knowledge of that time. It described the circulation of the blood and the functions of the kidneys and the heart. It also offered diagnosis and treatment for many diseases.

Muslim physicians founded the science of optics, or the study of light and its effect on sight. Ibn al-Haytham, the founder of optics, discovered that the eye sees because it receives light from the object seen. Earlier physicians had believed the opposite: that the eye sees because it produces rays that give light to the object seen. Muslim medicine, in fact, was centuries ahead of the medicine practiced in the West.

Art and Architecture

Like mathematics and science, Islamic art and architecture benefited from the cultural diversity of the Islamic Empire. Muslim theologians, fearful of idol worship, did not allow artists to make images or pictures of living creatures. Instead, artists used the beautiful script of written Arabic in an art form known as calligraphy (kuh•LIH•gruh•fee), or the art of elegant handwriting, to decorate public walls with passages from the Quran. Often calligraphy was accompanied by geometric designs entwined with plant stems, leaves, flowers, and stars. These arabesques (AR•uh•BEHSKS) decorated books, carpets, swords, and entire walls.

Islamic architects and artists did their best work in architecture, particularly in building and decorating mosques. Gardens and water, both precious in the arid Islamic lands, became artistic objects. Sun-drenched courtyards in mosques, palaces, and wealthy homes had trees to provide cool shade and flowers to delight the eye and nose; splashing fountains and running water refreshed both eye and ear.

Literature

Until the A.D. 600s, Arabic literature consisted mostly of poetry passed orally from one generation to the next. After the rise of Islam, religion had much influence in the creation of Arabic literature. The Quran, the first and greatest work in Arabic prose, was familiar to every Muslim, and its style influenced Islamic writing.

During the A.D. 700s, nonreligious prose appeared that both taught and entertained. The most famous of these writings was *Kalila and Dimna*, a collection of animal fables that presented moral lessons.

During the Abbasid period, Islamic literature blossomed as a result of contact with Greek thought, Hindu legends, and Persian court epics.

Science and Technology

At the Doctor's

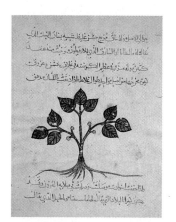

Medicinal herb from an Islamic manuscript

Today we take it for granted that the doctor can make us better when we get sick. In A.D. 765, however, the caliph Mansur was not so fortunate. His personal physicians—the best in Baghdad—could find no remedy for his chronic indigestion.

The caliph had heard that physicians in a Persian medical school based their practices on rational Greek methods of treatment. Traditional Arab medicine was based mainly on magic or superstition.

When the caliph asked the medical school for help, the chief physician, a Christian named Jurjis ibn Bakhtishu, cured Mansur. This encouraged other Muslim doctors to practice medicine based on the methods of the Greeks and Persians.

Muslim doctors were the first to discover the functions of internal organs and to diagnose illnesses such as meningitis. They also advanced surgery, carrying out head and stomach operations with the aid of anesthetics such as opium.

Believing that medicine required long training, Muslim doctors studied in hospitals and medical schools. Doctors based their treatments upon careful observation of their patients rather than superstition. They also diagnosed diseases such as measles and smallpox, prescribed treatments, and performed surgery. Such practices were unknown in the West until the A.D. 1100s and A.D. 1200s, when Islamic knowledge reached western Europe.

MAKING THE CONNECTION

1. Why was Islamic medicine far ahead of Western medicine during the Middle Ages?
2. What new methods of treatment have doctors developed in the past 50 years?

The upper classes valued elegant speech and the ability to handle words cleverly. Reading and appreciating literature became the sign of a good upbringing; every wealthy person took pride in having a well-stocked library. Córdoba, the Umayyad capital in Spain, had 70 libraries and more than half a million books. In contrast, the largest library in the Christian monasteries, at that time the center of European learning, held only a few hundred volumes.

In the A.D. 1000s, Persian became a second literary language in the Muslim world. Persian authors wrote epics about warrior-heroes, religious poetry, and verses about love. One of the best known works of this period is the *Rubaiyat* of **Omar Khayyám** (OH•MAHR KY•YAHM), a Persian mathematician and poet. You may also have heard some of the stories found in *A Thousand and One Nights*, also known as *The Arabian Nights*—stories such as "Sinbad the Sailor," "Aladdin and His Lamp," and "Ali Baba and the Forty Thieves." Originating in Arabia, India, Persia, Egypt, and other lands, the tales reflect the multinational character of the Islamic state.

Philosophy and History

Muslim philosophers tried to reconcile the teachings of the Quran with Greek philosophy. They believed that religious truths could be analyzed and defended using logic. Many of their works were translated into Latin and later brought a new understanding of philosophy to western Europe. Ibn Sina, known for his work in medicine, also wrote numerous books on logic and theology. Ibn-Rushd, a judge in Córdoba, was the most noted Islamic

philosopher, and Christian scholars in western Europe later used his commentaries on Aristotle.

Moses Maimonides (my•MAH•nuh•DEEZ), a Spanish Jew born in A.D. 1135, fled to Morocco and then Egypt to escape persecution. Maimonides became a leader in the Jewish community and a doctor to the Egyptian ruler. Like several Muslim scholars, Maimonides attempted to reconcile his faith with the teachings of Aristotle.

One of Maimonides' major contributions was the *Mishne Torah*, a 14-volume work on Jewish law

History & Art Turkish miniature depicting angels, from the *Ajac, ib Mahlukat* by Sururi, A.D. 1500s. British Museum, London, England
Why did Muslim theologians forbid images of living creatures in works of art?

Visualizing History A modern Islamic mosque in Isfahan, Iran, one of the most magnificent cities in the early Muslim world. *What kind of writings traced the early historical events of Islam?*

and tradition, written in Hebrew. His other major religious work, *The Guide of the Perplexed,* was written in Arabic and later translated into Hebrew and Latin. After his death in A.D. 1204, Maimonides was recognized as one of the world's great philosophers.

Like Judaism and Christianity, Islam traces its origins to historical events. Therefore, Islamic scholars were interested in writing history. At first they wrote chronicles, or accounts in which events are arranged in the order in which they occurred. The most famous of the Islamic chroniclers were al Tabari (al tah•BAH•ree), who in the early A.D. 900s wrote a multivolume history of the world, and Ibn

al-Athir (IH•buhn ahl•ah•THEER), who wrote an extensive history during the early A.D. 1200s.

Later, historians began to organize their accounts around events in the lives of rulers and others. The first Muslim historian to examine history scientifically was a North African diplomat named **Ibn Khaldun** (IH•buhn KAL•DOON). He looked for laws and cause-and-effect relationships to explain historical events. Ibn Khaldun believed that history was a process in which human affairs were shaped by geography, climate, and economics, as well as by moral and spiritual forces. His work later influenced European historical writing.

SECTION 3 REVIEW

Recall
1. **Define** *madrasa,* bazaar, calligraphy, arabesque, chronicle.
2. **Identify** Ma'mun, House of Wisdom, al-Razi, Ibn Sina, Omar Khayyám, Moses Maimonides, Ibn Khaldun.
3. **Locate** on the map on page

284 the major trade routes used by Muslim merchants. What features gave the Islamic state its multicultural character?

Critical Thinking
4. **Evaluating Information** Were Islamic theologians justified in their fear that people might worship paintings

or sculptures of people or animals? Explain your answer.

Understanding Themes
5. **Cultural Diffusion** What examples of cultural diffusion in the Islamic state can you find in these areas: (a) art, (b) mathematics, (c) commerce, and (d) literature?

Interpreting Demographic Data

Demographic data are statistics about a population, or group of people. Demographic data can tell us a great deal about where and how people live.

Learning the Skill

Demographers measure populations in different ways. Sometimes they simply count the number of people living in a country or region. By comparing these numbers, we can determine which countries have more people than others.

Suppose, however, that country A and country B each has five million people, but country A has five times more land area than country B. Country B would be more crowded, or more densely populated, than country A. Population density measures the number of people living within a certain area. Demographers also measure the population distribution, or the pattern of settlement within a country. For example, in Egypt most people live in the fertile Nile River valley and few people live in the desert.

Demographic data also describe population growth. Zero population growth occurs when births equal deaths. If births exceed deaths, the population is growing; if deaths exceed births, the population is shrinking. Population growth is expressed as a percentage rate. Demographers use growth rates to predict the future size of a population. A population pyramid is a graph showing the age distribution of a population. If the

pyramid is wider at the bottom than at the top, the population is growing. If a pyramid is smaller at the bottom, the population is shrinking.

Practicing the Skill

The graphs on this page show demographic data for seven countries in the modern Islamic world. Use the graphs to answer these questions.
1. What kind of demographic data appears in each graph?
2. Which three countries have the largest total populations?
3. Which three countries are growing fastest?
4. How is population size related to growth rates in the graphs of these countries?

Applying the Skill

At the library, find demographic data about your city or county and illustrate it in a table, graph, or map. You could show population increase or decrease, population distribution, population growth rates, or age distribution. Write a short paragraph interpreting your data.

For More Practice

Turn to the Skill Practice in the Chapter Review on page 291 for more practice in interpreting demographic data.

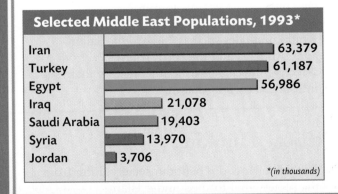

Selected Middle East Populations, 1993*

Country	Population
Iran	63,379
Turkey	61,187
Egypt	56,986
Iraq	21,078
Saudi Arabia	19,403
Syria	13,970
Jordan	3,706

*(in thousands)

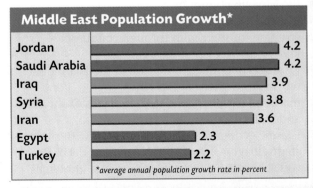

Middle East Population Growth*

Country	Growth Rate
Jordan	4.2
Saudi Arabia	4.2
Iraq	3.9
Syria	3.8
Iran	3.6
Egypt	2.3
Turkey	2.2

*average annual population growth rate in percent

Historical Significance

From Muhammad's revelations in the A.D. 600s grew the religion of Islam, which now includes more than a billion worshipers and ranks as one of the world's leading faiths. Today, Muslims predominate in the Middle East, North Africa, and parts of sub-Saharan Africa and Southeast Asia. Other areas of the world have significant numbers of Muslims.

During the Islamic Empire, Muslims preserved much ancient knowledge and made advances in the arts and sciences. Their achievements have enriched the cultures of the world.

Using Key Terms

Write the key term that completes each sentence.

a. arabesques
b. caliph
c. chronicle
d. hajj
e. imam
f. jihad
g. *madrasa*
h. bazaars
i. revelations
j. calligraphy
k. *shari'ah*
l. sheikh
m. mosque

1. Islamic scholars and theologians organized Islamic moral rules into the _____, or code of law.
2. Each Arab tribe was led by a _____, or chief, appointed by the heads of tribal families.
3. Islamic tradition holds that, in A.D. 610, Muhammad experienced the first of his _____.
4. At noon on Fridays, many Muslims pray together in a _____ .
5. Islamic artists used the beautiful script of Arabic in _____ , or the art of elegant handwriting.
6. The fifth pillar of Islam is the annual pilgrimage, or _____, to Makkah.
7. After Muhammad's death in A.D. 632, a group of prominent Muslims chose a _____ to head the Muslim community.
8. Muslims believed they had a religious duty to struggle for their faith through conquests known as _____.
9. Products obtained from trade in the Islamic world were often sold in city _____, or marketplaces that consisted of mazes of shops and stalls.
10. Islamic geometric designs entwined with plant stems, leaves, flowers, and stars that decorate walls, books, and various objects are known as _____.

Using Your History Journal

Calligraphy, an elegant form of handwriting, is still used as an art form. Look at samples of calligraphy in an encyclopedia. Then, in calligraphy, reproduce the beginning page of your short report on Muslim life.

Reviewing Facts

1. **Identify** the changes that took place in the Arabian Peninsula during the A.D. 600s.
2. **Explain** how the Madinah Compact formed the basis for the Islamic state.
3. **Outline** the events that led to the schism between Muslims.
4. **Explain** why some Muslims revolted against the Umayyads.
5. **Describe** the status of women in the Islamic Empire.
6. **List** some achievements of the Islamic Empire in science and the arts.
7. **Describe** the career of Moses Maimonides. In what ways did he reflect the multicultural character of the Islamic Empire?
8. **Name** the author and work in which a person would find tales such as "Sinbad the Sailor" and "Ali Baba and the Forty Thieves."
9. **Describe** the change in writing history that was introduced by Ibn Khaldun.

Critical Thinking

1. **Contrast** How did bedouin society differ from the society that formed under Islam?

CHAPTER 11 REVIEW

2. **Apply** Would there have been a struggle for the caliphate if Muhammad had named a successor before his death?
3. **Analyze** Why do you think Abu Bakr wanted to compile Muhammad's revelations into one written collection?
4. **Synthesize** If the hajj was not among the Five Pillars of Islam, how might its omission have affected the Islamic state?
5. **Evaluate** How did Muslim scholars contribute to the world's knowledge?
6. **Contrast** How did the Islamic Empire under the Abbasids differ from the early Islamic community under Muhammad?

Geography in History

1. **Movement** Refer to the map below. Identify how far the Abbasid Empire had spread by A.D. 800 by naming the areas that it encompassed.
2. **Place** What was the capital city of the Abbasid Empire, and where was it located?
3. **Location** How did the city of Baghdad fortify itself against invasion?

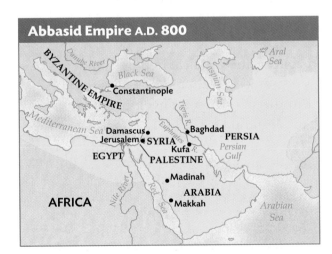

Understanding Themes

1. **Innovation** Why was Islam an innovation in the way the people of the Arabian Peninsula worshiped?
2. **Movement** How was the Umayyads' decision to move the nation's capital from Madinah to Damascus a result of Islamic expansion?

3. **Diversity** How did the failure of the Umayyad government to embrace non-Arab Muslims destroy Umayyad rule?

Linking Past and Present

1. What evidence can you find in today's world of the split between the Sunni and the Shiite?
2. How have students today benefited from the work done at the House of Wisdom?
3. What words in the English language have their origins in the Arabic language?

Skill Practice

Study the population pyramid below and then answer these questions.

1. What is the general shape of the graph?
2. What percentage of the female population is between 0 and 19 years old?
3. Are there equal numbers of males and females in this population? How can you tell?
4. What conclusion can you draw about the growth rate in this population? On what data do you base this conclusion?

Age Distribution in Jordan

Age	% of Pop'n	Male	Female	% of Pop'n	Age
70+	0.8%			0.8%	70+
60-69	1.2%			1.1%	60-69
50-59	2.4%			2.2%	50-59
40-49	3.8%			3.4%	40-49
30-39	4.5%			4.2%	30-39
20-29	8.1%			7.3%	20-29
10-19	13.9%			12.4%	10-19
0-9	17.6%			16.3%	0-9

640 320 0 320 640

Total Population: 3,413,000
Total Male Population: 1,785,000
Total Female Population: 1,628,000
Life Expectancy (Male): 70 years
Life Expectancy (Female): 73 years
Source: Broderbund Software, Inc.

Chapter 12

A.D. 500–1300

The Rise of Medieval Europe

Chapter Themes

▶ **Movement** Invasions by Vikings, Magyars, and Muslims influence medieval Europe. *Section 1*

▶ **Cooperation** Nobles, church officials, and peasants develop ties of loyalty and service to one another. *Section 2*

▶ **Uniformity** The Catholic Church affects every aspect of medieval life. *Section 3*

▶ **Conflict** European kings, feudal lords, and popes struggle for political dominance. *Section 4*

The Storyteller

It was tournament day. As trumpets flourished, the marshal shouted, "In the name of God and St. Michael, do your battle!" Knights on horseback thundered toward each other and met with a deafening clash. Lords and ladies cheered as their favorite unhorsed his opponents. The victor was awarded a prize from the lady whose colors he wore.

Such tournaments provided more than just entertainment. They also trained soldiers for combat. After the fall of Rome, wars were frequent. A professional warrior class—the knights—led the new, vigorous, competitive society that would reshape western Europe.

Historical Significance

How did Christianity, the classical heritage, and Germanic practices combine to form a new European civilization? How did this civilization develop and lay the foundation for modern European life?

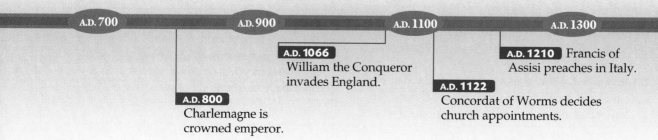

A.D. 700

A.D. 900

A.D. 1100

A.D. 1300

A.D. 1066 William the Conqueror invades England.

A.D. 1210 Francis of Assisi preaches in Italy.

A.D. 1122 Concordat of Worms decides church appointments.

A.D. 800 Charlemagne is crowned emperor.

The Effect of Good Government on a City by Ambrogio Lorenzetti.
Palazzo Pubblico, Siena, Italy

Your History Journal

Medieval life was governed by many mutual obligations. Build a diagram that shows the relationships among lords and ladies, knights, and vassals.

A.D. 496 Frankish King Clovis accepts Catholicism.

A.D. 768 Charlemagne becomes Frankish king.

A.D. 843 Treaty of Verdun divides Carolingian lands.

c. A.D. 850 Vikings begin explorations.

Section 1

Frankish Rulers

Setting the Scene

▶ **Terms to Define**
   mayor of the palace, count

▶ **People to Meet**
   Clovis, Charles Martel, Pepin the Short, Charlemagne, the Vikings

▶ **Places to Locate**
   Frankish Empire, Scandinavia

Find Out What made Frankish rulers, such as Charlemagne, exceptional rulers for their time?

The Storyteller

The men of medieval times, including Charlemagne, loved hunting. It was a cruel sport, but at least it provided meat for the royal tables.

Charlemagne

When Charlemagne sat down to dinner, the main course was usually a roast of game from the morning hunt. During the meal, one of the poets of the royal court might rise to read aloud a poem—to the dismay of the king's soldiers, who sometimes clapped their hands over their ears and glared at the poet until Charlemagne scolded them. With dinner, the king enjoyed "the wine of learning."

—freely adapted from *Charlemagne,* Richard Winston, 1968

By A.D. 500, Germanic invasions had all but destroyed the urban world of the Roman Empire. Trade declined. Cities, bridges, and roads fell into disrepair and disuse. Law and order vanished, and education almost disappeared. Money was no longer used. For most people, life did not extend beyond the tiny villages where they were born, lived, and died.

Western Europe was so backward because of this decline that the early part of this period was once called "the Dark Ages." Scholars later combined the Latin terms *medium* (middle) and *aevum* (age) to form the term *medieval*, recognizing that this period was an era of transition between ancient and modern times. Out of this violent medieval period, or Middle Ages, a dynamic civilization arose. It combined elements of classical and Germanic cultures with Christian beliefs.

Merovingian Rulers

During the A.D. 400s the Franks, who settled in what is now France and western Germany, emerged as the strongest Germanic group. Their early rulers, known as Merovingian (MEHR•uh•VIHN•jee•uhn) kings for the ruler Merowig, held power until the early A.D. 700s.

Clovis

In A.D. 481 a brutal and wily warrior named **Clovis** became king of the Franks. Fifteen years later, Clovis became the first Germanic ruler to accept Catholicism. Clovis's military victories and his religious conversion gave his throne stability.

A century later the Frankish kingdom began to decline. Frankish kings had followed the custom of dividing the kingdom among their heirs. Heirs became rivals and fought each other for land. By A.D. 700 political power had passed from kings to government officials known as **mayors of the palace.**

Charles Martel

In A.D. 714 **Charles Martel**, or "Charles the Hammer," became mayor of the palace. When Muslim forces threatened Europe in A.D. 732, Charles led the successful defense of Tours, in France. This victory won him great prestige. As you read in Chapter 11, the victory ensured that Christianity would remain the dominant religion of Europe.

Pepin the Short

In A.D. 752, with the backing of nobles and church officials, **Pepin the Short**, the son of Charles Martel, became king of the Franks. The pope anointed, or put holy oil on, Pepin, making him a divinely chosen ruler in the eyes of the people.

In return for the Church's blessing, Pepin was expected to help the pope against his enemies. In A.D. 754 Pepin forced the Lombards, a Germanic people, to withdraw from Rome. He then gave the pope a large strip of Lombard land in central Italy. In appreciation, the pope cut his political ties to the Byzantine Empire and looked to the Franks as his protector. As a result, the fortunes of western Europe and Catholicism were bound more closely together.

Charlemagne's Empire

In A.D. 771 Pepin's son, **Charlemagne**, became the Frankish king. Charlemagne, or Charles the Great, was one of Europe's great monarchs. In Latin his name is written *Carolus Magnus*, which gave the name Carolingian to his dynasty. The king cut an imposing figure. His biographer, a monk named Einhard, described him this way:

> ❝ Charles was large and strong, and of lofty stature, though not disproportionly tall … nose a little long, hair fair, and face laughing and merry…. He used to wear the national, that is to say, the Frankish, dress—next his skin a linen shirt and linen breeches, and above these a tunic fringed with silk; white hose fastened by bands covered his lower limbs and shoes his feet, and he protected his shoulders and chest in winter by a close-fitting coat of otter or marten skins. Over all he flung a blue cloak, and he always had a sword girt about him. ❞

Charlemagne nearly doubled the borders of his kingdom to include Germany, France, northern Spain, and most of Italy. His enlarged domain became known as the **Frankish Empire**. For the

Visualizing History Shown here, a decorated Merovingian buckle. Gregory, bishop of Tours, wrote the best source of the history of the Merovingian kings. *Why did the political power of these kings fade?*

first time since the fall of Rome, most western Europeans were ruled by one government.

Because few western Europeans could read and write, Charlemagne encouraged the formation of schools in churches and monasteries. He gathered scholars from all over Europe to teach in his palace school. These scholars helped preserve classical learning by making accurate Latin copies of ancient religious manuscripts and Roman classics. When knowledge spread from Charlemagne's court to other areas of Europe, western Europeans became united by a common set of ideas.

A Christian Realm

One of the ideas that united western Europeans was the creation of a Christian Roman Empire. Church leaders believed that Charlemagne could turn this idea into reality. In A.D. 800 Charlemagne came to Rome to militarily defend Pope Leo III against the Roman nobles. To show his gratitude, Leo crowned Charlemagne the new Roman emperor. As protector of the Church and ruler of much of western Europe, Charlemagne wanted the title, but he had misgivings about receiving it from the pope. By crowning a monarch, the pope seemed to be saying that church officials were superior to rulers.

In spite of his concern, Charlemagne accepted his duties as emperor and worked to strengthen the empire. Because the central bureaucracy was small, he relied on local officials called counts to assist him. Each count was carefully instructed in the duties of office. The counts solved local problems, stopped feuds, protected the weak, and raised

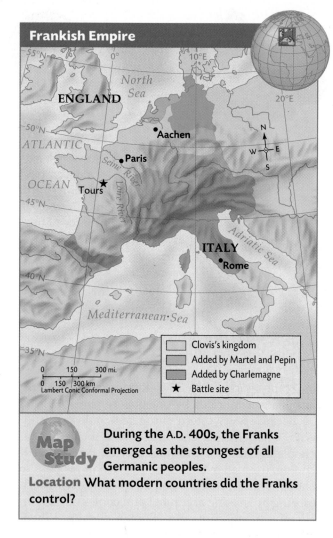

Map Study

During the A.D. 400s, the Franks emerged as the strongest of all Germanic peoples.

Location What modern countries did the Franks control?

Invasions Increase Disunity

While internal feuding weakened the Carolingian kingdoms, outside invasions nearly destroyed them. Muslims from North Africa seized parts of southern Italy and gained control of the western Mediterranean. The Slavs marched out of the east to invade central Europe. From Asia a new group of fierce nomads called Magyars galloped west, leaving a trail of destruction. The most threatening attacks, however, came from **the Vikings**, raiders from **Scandinavia** to the north.

Viking Invasions

In medieval Scandinavian, to go *a-viking* means to fight as a warrior. Viking warriors traveled in long, deckless ships with one sail that were designed to slide swiftly through the water propelled by long oars. These boats were sturdy enough to cross the Atlantic Ocean, shallow enough to navigate Europe's rivers, and light enough to be carried past fortified bridges. The Vikings became known for surprise attacks and speedy retreats. What they could not steal they burned. No place in Europe was safe from attack.

Boasting names like Eric Bloodax and Harald Bluetooth, the Vikings sought riches and adventure. In the A.D. 800s they left their overpopulated homeland, which later became the kingdoms of Norway, Denmark, and Sweden. Viking warriors fought ferociously and showed their victims no mercy.

Viking Trade

The Vikings, however, were more than just raiders. They were also explorers and settlers. Skilled in sailing and trading, they moved along the Atlantic and Mediterranean coasts of Europe. The Norwegians settled the North Atlantic islands of Greenland and Iceland, and even reached North America. The Danes temporarily held England and established the Viking state of Normandy in northwestern France. The Swedes settled in present-day Ukraine and Russia.

Viking Culture

In Scandinavia and their new homelands, the Vikings worshiped many deities. They were proud of their gods and told stories of the gods' great deeds. These stories became written poems called *Eddas*. The Vikings also made up sagas, or long tales. At first, storytellers recited them at special feasts. After A.D. 1100 the Vikings wrote down their sagas. By this time they had converted to Christianity. With their acceptance of the new religion, the Vikings began to write their languages with Roman letters.

armies for the emperor. Each year royal messengers, the *missi dominici*, went on inspections in which they informed Charlemagne about the performance of the counts and other local administrators. The emperor also traveled throughout the empire observing the work of his officials firsthand.

Collapse of Charlemagne's Empire

More than anything else, Charlemagne's forceful personality held his empire together. His death in A.D. 814 left a void that his only surviving son, Louis the Pious, could not fill. After Louis's death, Charlemagne's three grandsons fought one another for control of the empire.

In A.D. 843 the three brothers agreed in the Treaty of Verdun to divide the Carolingian lands. Charles the Bald took the western part, which covered most of present-day France. Louis the German acquired the eastern portion, which today is Germany. Lothair, who became the Holy Roman emperor, took a strip of land in the middle of the empire stretching from the North Sea southward to Italy.

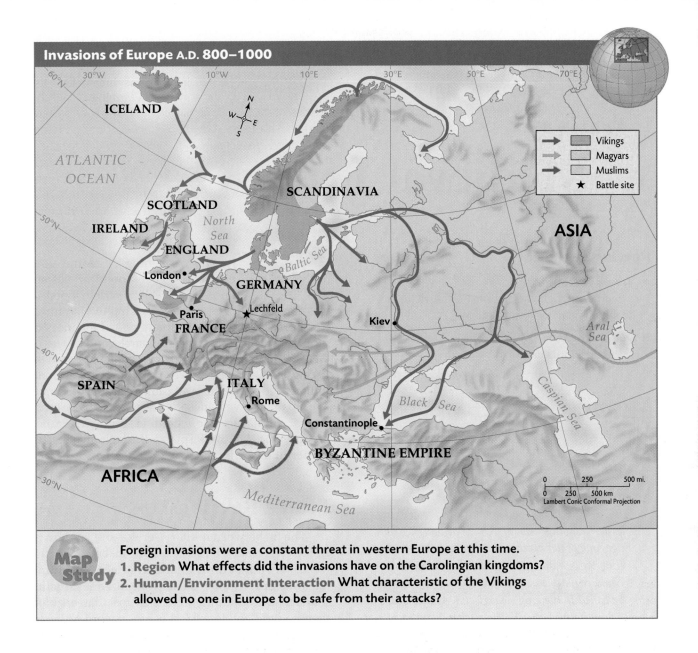

Invasions of Europe A.D. 800–1000

Legend:
- Vikings
- Magyars
- Muslims
- ★ Battle site

Map Study

Foreign invasions were a constant threat in western Europe at this time.
1. **Region** What effects did the invasions have on the Carolingian kingdoms?
2. **Human/Environment Interaction** What characteristic of the Vikings allowed no one in Europe to be safe from their attacks?

A New Europe

The people of western Europe suffered at the hands of Vikings and other invaders. These raids isolated communities and severely weakened the central authority of monarchs. Trade declined, and many areas faced economic collapse. As a result of royal weakness, nobles and local officials took over the local defense. Beginning in the A.D. 900s, a new political and social system brought more stability to western Europe.

SECTION 1 REVIEW

Recall
1. **Define** mayor of the palace, count.
2. **Identify** Clovis, Charles Martel, Pepin the Short, Charlemagne, Treaty of Verdun, the Vikings.
3. **Explain** what problem resulted when Charlemagne was crowned by the pope.

Critical Thinking
4. **Making Comparisons** Contrast Charlemagne with his weak successors. Why do you think Charlemagne was successful in enlarging and maintaining his empire?

Understanding Themes
5. **Movement** Why did the Vikings, the Magyars, and the Slavs leave their homelands and invade western Europe?

A.D. 700		A.D. 900		A.D. 1100

c. A.D. 750 Charles Martel grants warriors landed estates with peasants.

c. A.D. 900 Feudalism takes hold in northern France.

c. A.D. 1000 Peasants begin to use three-field system in farming.

Section 2

Medieval Life

Setting the Scene

▶ **Terms to Define**
   feudalism, fief, vassal, homage, tournament, chivalry, manorialism, serf

▶ **People to Meet**
   knights, lords, ladies, peasants

Find Out   How were loyalties maintained in a divided and often violent Europe?

The Storyteller

Medieval law laid down rules for marriage. When a young woman arrived at marriageable age, one of her brothers or male relatives had to find her a suitable husband. If he did not, she could register a complaint, and her relative could be called to the king's court and given a year and a day to find her one. The husband had to be suited to her social status and property. If the relative did not do this, the king would step in and assign the woman a part of the family inheritance. Then she could marry whomever she wished.

—from *Women's Lives in Medieval Europe, A Sourcebook*, edited by Emile Amt, 1993

Medieval tournament

With the weakening of central government, a new political system known as feudalism developed in western Europe. Feudalism was a highly decentralized form of government that stressed alliances of mutual protection between monarchs and nobles of varying degrees of power. The system was based on giving land to nobles in exchange for loyalty and military aid. With the land came peasants to farm it and many powers usually reserved for governments. Feudalism took hold in northern France around A.D. 900 and spread through the rest of western Europe by the A.D. mid-1000s.

Feudal Relationships

The tie between military service and land ownership that characterized feudalism began in the A.D. 700s. At that time, Charles Martel was fighting the Muslims. Unlike the Europeans, the Muslim soldiers used saddles with stirrups that enabled them to fight on horseback, using a sword or lance. Charles wanted to adopt the stirrup and develop a cavalry. However, the cost of keeping such a force required a new type of military system. To support the cavalry, Martel began granting warriors fiefs, or estates with peasants. From these fiefs, warriors got the income to buy horses and battle equipment.

Frankish kings later enlarged this system by giving fiefs to counts and local officials. In time, such nobles assumed many of the powers usually held by government: raising armies, dispensing justice, and in some cases even minting coins. In return, the nobles swore an oath of loyalty and pledged military support to the king.

By the A.D. 900s, such arrangements among nobles and monarchs emerged as feudalism. Lords who had been granted fiefs were allowed to pass their lands on to their heirs. In return, these nobles were to provide **knights**, or mounted warriors, for the royal army.

In theory, feudal relationships were like a pyramid. The king was at the top. In the middle were various ranks of lords. Each lord was a vassal—a noble who served a lord of the next higher rank. At the bottom were the knights. In practice, however, a noble might be both a lord and a vassal, since a noble could pledge his allegiance to more than one lord. In fact, one German warrior, Siboto of Falkenstein, was vassal to 20 different lords. Of course, conflicts of loyalty arose if one of a vassal's lords went to war with another.

Feudal Obligations

Ties between a lord and a vassal were made official in a solemn ceremony known as homage. In return for a fief, the vassal pledged to perform certain duties. The most important obligation was military service. The vassal agreed to provide his lord with a certain number of knights for battle during a period of 40 to 60 days each year. In addition, the vassal agreed to serve in the lord's court, to provide food and lodging when the lord came visiting, and to contribute funds when the lord's son became a knight or when his oldest daughter married. Vassals also pledged to pay ransom in the event of the lord's capture in battle.

Castles for Defense

Because of the lack of a strong central government, warfare occurred frequently in feudal society. As a result, every noble built a castle, or fortified manor house, for defense against enemies. The first castles were wooden buildings with high fences of logs or mounds of hard-packed earth around them. By the A.D. 1100s castles were built of stone, with thick walls and turrets, or small towers. Each castle was built on a hill or mound surrounded by a deep moat. Castles had a square tower called a keep. The keep, located in the strongest part of the castle, contained many rooms, a hall, and a dungeon. Surrounding the keep was a large open area called a bailey. Within the bailey were various buildings, including barracks, storerooms, workshops, and a chapel.

Life of the Nobility

Lords, ladies, and knights made up the nobility of the Middle Ages. Although the nobles lived much easier lives than the peasants who worked for them, their lives can hardly be called luxurious or glamorous. Castles were built for security, not comfort, and were largely cold, dingy, and damp places.

Within his fief, a lord, or nobleman, had almost total authority. He collected rents from peasants and

Visualizing History An illustration from the *Trés Riches Heures du Duc de Berry* shows peasants at work outside a castle. *Why did feudal lords need castles?*

administered justice in disputes between his vassals. Any outside attempt to seize the land or control the inhabitants of his fief was met with violent resistance.

In contrast, a **lady**, or noblewoman, had few, if any, rights. A noblewoman could be wed as early as her twelfth birthday to a man her father selected. Her primary duties lay in bringing up children and taking care of the household. Noblewomen took pride in their needlework, turning out cloth and fine embroidery. They also learned to make effective medicines from plants and herbs. Some women shared the supervision of the estate with the lord and took over their husband's duties while the men were away at war.

Entertainment

Nobles looked forward to tournaments—mock battles between knights—as a show of military

1–Moat; 2–Drawbridge; 3–Guardroom; 4–Latrine; 5–Armory; 6–Soldiers' quarters; 7–Kitchen garden;
8–Storerooms and servants' quarters; 9–Kitchen; 10–Great hall; 11–Chapel; 12–Lord and lady's quarters; 13–Inner ward

Harry Bliss

Life in the Castle

The medieval castle was both fortress and home. The first castles, raised in the A.D. 900s, were square towers encircled by wooden ramparts. By the A.D. 1100s, castles had become mighty stone fortresses. From the towers and walls archers took aim and soldiers dumped boiling liquids on attackers. The castle was surrounded by a moat—a body of water encircling the castle—that could be crossed when a drawbridge was let down.

Inside it was crowded, smelly, dirty, and damp. The animals ate and slept with the people, and the smell of animal and human waste was everywhere. The occupants of the castle had to contend with cold earthen or stone floors, drafty halls, smoky rooms, and windows without glass that let in cold and heat along with light. Not even the lord and lady had their own private room. Grand but never comfortable, the castle's main purpose was military security. 🌐

skills. They also loved to hunt, and both men and women learned the art of falconry and archery. A dinner featuring several dishes of game and fish might follow. In a castle's great hall, nobles and their guests ate while being entertained by minstrels, or singers.

Becoming a Knight

A nobleman's son began training for knighthood at age 7. Beginning as a page, or assistant, in the house of a lord, he learned manners and the use of weapons. At 15, the page became a squire who assisted a knight and practiced using weapons. Once he proved himself in battle, the squire was knighted in an elaborate ceremony.

The behavior of knights was governed by a code of chivalry. This code called for knights to be brave in battle, fight fairly, keep promises, defend the Church, and treat women of noble birth in a courteous manner. Chivalry eventually became the basis for the development of good manners in Western society.

The Manorial System

The wealth of a feudal lord came from the labor of the **peasants** who lived on and worked the lord's land. Since the last years of the Roman Empire, many peasants had worked for large landowners, in part because they could not afford their own land and in part for protection. By the Middle Ages, economic life across Europe centered around a system of agricultural production called manorialism. It provided lords and peasants with food, shelter, and protection.

Manors, or estates, varied in size from several hundred to several hundred thousand acres. Each manor included the lord's manor house, pastures for livestock, fields for crops, forest areas, and a

Visualizing History A suit of armor made of steel, brass, and leather belonging to an English knight, Master Jacobe. *What knightly code became the basis of good manners in Western society?*

village where the peasants lived. While feudalism describes the political relationships between nobles, manorialism concerns economic ties between nobles and peasants.

Work on a Manor

In return for the lord's protection, the peasants provided various services for the lord. Chief among the obligations were to farm the lord's land and to make various payments of goods. For example, each time a peasant ground grain at the lord's mill, he was obligated to leave a portion for the lord. If he baked in the lord's oven, he left a loaf behind for the lord. In addition, peasants were obligated to set aside a number of days each year to provide various types of labor, such as road or bridge repair.

Warfare and invasions made trade almost impossible, so the manor had to produce nearly everything its residents needed. Most of the peasants farmed or herded sheep. A few worked as skilled artisans, for each manor needed a blacksmith to make tools, a carpenter for building, a

Footnotes to History

Identifying a Knight
To identify themselves, knights had individual designs painted on their shields and tunics. His particular design became known as the knight's coat of arms. In noble families, coats of arms were passed down from one generation to the next. The flags of some modern countries are based on the system of designs that were developed by the knights.

shoemaker, a miller to grind grain, a vintner to make wine, and a brewer to make beer. Peasant women made candles, sheared sheep, spun wool, and sewed clothing.

Peasants rarely left the manor. Most were serfs, people who were bound to the manor and could not leave it without permission. But the serfs were not slaves—they could not be "sold" apart from the land they lived on.

Increased Production

The manorial system normally produced only enough food to support the peasants and the lord's household. However, a number of improvements gradually boosted productivity and eased the threat of famine.

The first improvement was the development of a new, heavier type of plow. The new plow made deeper cuts in the ground and had a device called a mould-board that pushed the soil sideways. The heavier plow meant less time in the fields for peasant farmers. As a result, farmers developed a better method of planting.

Instead of dividing plots of land into two fields, one of which lay fallow, or unsown, each year, farmers in the A.D. 1000s began to use a three-field system. One field might be planted with winter wheat, a second with spring wheat and vegetables, and a third left fallow. The next year, different crops were planted in the fallow field. One of the two remaining fields was planted, and the other one was left fallow until the next year. This system produced more crops than the old system and helped to preserve the soil.

Peasant Life

Poverty and hardship characterized peasant life, and few serfs lived beyond the age of 40. Famine and disease were constant dangers. In times of war, the peasants were the first and hardest hit. Invading knights trampled crops and burned villages, causing famine and loss of life. To support the war, their lord might require additional payments of crops or labor. A monk of Canterbury described an English serf's account of his day:

> ❝ I work very hard. I go out at dawn, driving the oxen to the field, and I yoke them to the plough; however hard the winter I dare not stay home for fear of my master; but, having yoked the oxen and made the ploughshare and coulter fast to the plough, every day I have to plough a whole acre or more. ❞
>
> —Aelfric, *Colloquy*, A.D. 1005

Serfs like this man lived in tiny, one-room houses with dirt floors, no chimney, and one or two crude pieces of furniture—perhaps a table and stools. People slept huddled together for warmth. Coarse bread, a few vegetables from their gardens, and grain for porridge made up their usual diet. Meat was a rarity.

In spite of hardships, peasants were able to relax on Sundays and holy days. They enjoyed dancing, singing, and such sports as wrestling and archery. In addition, there were other amusements, such as religious plays, pageants, and shows by minstrels.

Despite the obvious differences between serfs and nobles, the two groups did share a common interest in the land. Medieval Europeans believed that every person was equal in the "eyes of God." In practice, however, society was viewed as a hierarchy with ranked leaders from top to bottom. Each person—no matter what his or her place might be in the hierarchy—had certain duties that were attached to his or her position in life. In general, people did not question their standing or obligations. Although the manorial system seemed to lack freedom and opportunity for most of the people involved in it, it did create a very stable and secure way of life during a time that was generally violent and uncertain.

SECTION 2 REVIEW

Recall
1. **Define** feudalism, fief, vassal, homage, tournament, chivalry, manorialism, serf.
2. **Identify** knight, lord, lady, peasant.
3. **Explain** the stages that were necessary for a medieval nobleman to become a knight.

Critical Thinking
4. **Making Comparisons** Compare and contrast the feudal class structure in medieval Europe with the *varna* system in early India discussed in Chapter 8.

Understanding Themes
5. **Cooperation** Diagram the ways nobles, knights, and peasants cooperated during the medieval period.

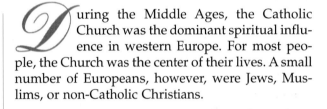

A.D. 500   A.D. 900   A.D. 1300

A.D. 520 Benedict introduces rule for monasteries.

c. A.D. 650 Irish missionaries win converts in western Europe.

A.D. 1073 The monk Hildebrand becomes Pope Gregory VII.

A.D. 1232 The Inquisition begins.

Section 3

The Medieval Church

Setting the Scene

▶ **Terms to Define**
sacrament, abbot, abbess, cardinal, lay investiture, heresy, excommunication, friar

▶ **People to Meet**
Benedict, Gregory I, Gregory VII, Innocent III, Francis of Assisi, Dominic

▶ **Places to Locate**
Monte Cassino, Cluny

 **ind Out** How did the Catholic Church shape the development of medieval Europe?

The Storyteller

Alcuin, a Benedictine monk, arose to begin his day. The day's work in a monastery depended on sunlight hours, for candles were expensive and no one in medieval times had access to cheap artificial light. Because it was winter, Alcuin had to get up at 2:30 A.M., and go to bed at 6:30 P.M. after sunset. Sometimes he was already tired by noon! His workday included reading, choir practice, bookbinding, sewing, gardening, and worship services—which were the only times during the day that he was permitted to break his vow of silence and speak.

—from *Monastic Life in Medieval England*, J.C. Dickinson, 1962

Ancient monastery in Glendalough, Ireland

uring the Middle Ages, the Catholic Church was the dominant spiritual influence in western Europe. For most people, the Church was the center of their lives. A small number of Europeans, however, were Jews, Muslims, or non-Catholic Christians.

The Medieval Church

Although the Church's primary mission was spiritual, the decline of Rome in the A.D. 400s led the Church to assume many political and social tasks. During this time, the bishop of Rome, now called the pope, became the strongest political leader in western Europe. The pope claimed spiritual authority over all Christians, basing this claim on the belief that Peter the Apostle, Rome's first bishop, had been chosen by Jesus to lead the Church.

Religious Role

The Catholic Church taught that all people were sinners and dependent on God's grace, or favor. The only way to receive grace was by taking part in the sacraments, or church rituals: baptism, penance, eucharist, confirmation, matrimony, anointing of the sick, and holy orders. One of the most important sacraments was the eucharist, or holy communion, which commemorated Christ's death. People shared in the eucharist at a mass, or worship service. At each mass, the priest blessed wheat wafers and a cup of wine that stood on an altar. According to Catholic teaching, the priests and the worshipers received Jesus' invisible presence in the forms of the bread and the wine.

During the Middle Ages, people generally had a limited understanding of church rituals. Masses were said in Latin, a language few people understood. Also, many priests were poorly educated

Chapter 12 *The Rise of Medieval Europe* **303**

and did not preach effectively. Moreover, few worshipers could read or write. What the average person learned about the Christian faith came from the statues, paintings, and later the stained glass windows that adorned most medieval churches.

Church Organization

The church hierarchy, which was described in Chapter 6, remained largely the same during the Middle Ages. The contact most people had with the Church was through parish priests, who conducted services and oversaw the spiritual life of the community. Occasionally bishops visited a parish to supervise the priests.

The pope, bishops, and priests formed what is called the secular clergy because they lived *in saeculo*, a Latin phrase that means "in the world." Other clergy, known as regular clergy, lived by a *regula*, or rule. Regular clergy included monks and nuns who lived apart from society. These Christians played an important role in strengthening the medieval Church.

Benedict's Rule

In A.D. 520 a Roman official named **Benedict** founded a monastery at **Monte Cassino** in Italy. His monastery became a model for monks in other communities. Benedict drew up a list of rules that provided for manual work, meditation, and prayer. According to the Benedictine rule, monks could not own goods, must never marry, and were bound to obey monastic laws. Their life was one of poverty, chastity, and obedience to the directives of an abbot, or monastery head.

Monastic Life

Monks dressed in simple, long robes made of coarse material and tied at the waist by a cord. They ate one or two plain meals each day. Most monasteries had a rule of silence; monks could not converse with one another except for a short time each day. In some monasteries total silence was the rule. During meals, one monk might read passages from

Images of the Times

Monastic Life

Although monasteries were closed religious communities, their members often worked in the outside world.

An illustrated page from a book copied by monks shows the careful, artistic writing that became the manuscript before printing was developed.

St. Benedict and his monks, like all those who lived at the monasteries, ate together in a refectory.

Mont St. Michel presents a view of the beautiful old monastery's lower ramparts.

the Bible while the others meditated.

Women took part in monastic life by living in a convent under the direction of an abbess. Known as nuns, they wore simple clothes and wrapped a white cloth called a wimple around their face and neck. They alternated prayer with spinning, weaving, and embroidering items such as tapestries and banners. They also taught needlework and the medicinal use of herbs to the daughters of nobles.

Influence of Monastics

Although monks and nuns lived apart from society, they were not completely isolated. Indeed, they played a crucial role in medieval intellectual and social life. Since few people could read or write, the regular clergy preserved ancient religious works and the classical writings. Scribes laboriously copied books by hand, working in a small drafty room with only a candle or small window for light. Illuminated manuscripts decorated with rich colors and intricate pictures indicate that, although the task was tedious, it was lovingly done.

Monasteries and convents provided schools for young people, hospitals for the sick, food for the needy, and guest houses for weary travelers. They taught peasants carpentry and weaving and made improvements in agriculture that they passed on to others. Some monks and nuns became missionaries who spread Christian teachings to non-Christians.

Missionary Efforts

Pope **Gregory I** was so impressed with the Benedictine Rule that he adopted it to spread Christianity in Europe. In A.D. 597 he sent monks to England, where they converted the Anglo-Saxons to Catholicism. From England, missionaries carried Christianity to northern Germany. During the A.D. 600s, monasteries in Ireland sent missionaries throughout the North Atlantic and western Europe. Although the Irish were isolated from the pope in Rome, their missionaries won many converts. By the A.D. mid-1000s, most western Europeans had become Catholics.

A father who has bought a place for his son in a monastery presents the youngster to an abbot.

Power of the Church

During the Middle Ages, the Catholic Church helped to govern western Europe. Bishops and abbots played an important part in the feudal system. Because many of them were nobles, they received land from kings in return for military service. Since they were religious leaders, however, these vassals could not fight. They fulfilled their military duty by giving some of their land to knights who would fight for them.

These feudal ties boosted the Church's wealth and political power. The Church also received donations of land and money from rich nobles who wanted to perform acts of piety. As a result, local lords began to control many church offices and lands, contrary to church tradition. They often appointed relatives as bishops or abbots, instead of awarding those offices to the most qualified people. Furthermore, as religious leaders and monasteries grew wealthier, many church officials became increasingly careless about carrying out their religious duties.

Visualizing History **A young boy, having obtained the office of bishop, carries sacred church relics.** *How did Pope Gregory try to stop the selection of church officials by secular rulers?*

Church Reform

By the A.D. 900s, many devout Christians were calling for reform. The reform movement began in the monasteries and spread throughout much of western Europe. Most famous was the monastery at **Cluny** in eastern France, whose monks won respect for leading lives of pious simplicity. The abbots of Cluny sent representatives to other monasteries to help them undertake similar reforms.

Other church leaders tried to free the Church from the control of feudal lords. They wanted the Church, not the state, to be the final authority in Western society. In A.D. 1059 a church council declared that political leaders could no longer choose the pope. Instead, the pope would be elected by a gathering of cardinals—high church officials in Rome ranking directly below the pope. In addition, the reformers insisted that the pope, not secular rulers such as lords and kings, should be the one to appoint bishops and other officials to church offices.

In A.D. 1073 the cardinals elected a reform-minded monk named Hildebrand as Pope **Gregory VII**. Gregory believed that the pope should have complete jurisdiction over all church officials. He especially criticized the practice of lay investiture, in which secular rulers gave the symbols of office, such as a ring and a staff, to the bishops they had appointed.

Fighting Heresy

Innocent III, one of the most powerful popes, also tried to reform the Catholic Church. In A.D. 1215 he convened a council that condemned drunkenness, feasting, and dancing among the clergy. The council also laid down strict rules for stopping the spread of heresy, or the denial of basic church teachings. Heresy had increased as corruption and scandal had rocked the Church. In the Middle Ages, heresy was regarded as seriously as the crime of treason is viewed today.

At first, the Catholic Church tried to convert heretics, or those who challenged its teachings. When that failed, however, heretics were threatened with excommunication, or expulsion from the Church. An excommunicated person was not allowed to take part in the sacraments and was also outlawed from any contact with Christian society. Since receiving the sacraments was considered to be essential for salvation, banishment was an especially severe penalty.

Early in the A.D. 1200s, for example, the Church became concerned about a group of heretics in France known as Albigensians (AL•buh•JEHN •shuhnz). The Albigensians believed that the material world was evil and rejected church sacraments. To end this heresy, Pope Innocent III sent French knights to crush the group.

The Inquisition

In order to seek out and punish people suspected of heresy, the Church set up a court in A.D. 1232 known as the Inquisition. Those brought before the court were urged to confess their heresy and to ask forgiveness. Often, however, Inquisition officials accused people without sufficient proof; sometimes they even used torture to obtain confessions. The Church welcomed back those who repented, but those who did not repent were punished. Punishment ranged from imprisonment to loss of property and even execution. According to church officials, these punishments were needed to save the souls of the heretics.

Friars Inspire Reform

Other reformers of the Church during the early A.D. 1200s were **friars**, or wandering preachers. At a time when church leaders were criticized for their love of wealth and power, the friars lived simply, owned no possessions, and depended on gifts of food and shelter to survive.

The friars followed monastic rules but did not isolate themselves from the rest of the Christian community. Instead, they lived in towns and preached Christianity to the people. The best-known friars were the Franciscans and the Dominicans. Because they were well known and liked, the friars kept many people loyal to the Catholic Church.

Francis of Assisi, the son of a wealthy Italian cloth merchant, founded the Franciscan friars about A.D. 1210. Francis and his followers sought to follow the simple life of Jesus and his disciples. They became known for their cheerful trust in God and their respect for nature as a divine gift.

A Spanish priest named **Dominic** organized the Dominican friars in A.D. 1215. Like the

 St. Dominic and Albigensians, c. 1450–1504. Museo Del Prado, Madrid, Spain
Here, St. Dominic tests books in the campaign against heresy. *How did the life of a friar differ from that of other clergy?*

Franciscans, the Dominicans lived a life of poverty, simplicity, and service. In addition, they were well-educated, persuasive preachers who could reply to the arguments of heretics.

Church councils, the Inquisition, and the efforts of the friars were all signs of the Church's power during the Middle Ages. By the A.D. 1000s, however, that power was increasingly being challenged by secular rulers.

SECTION 3 REVIEW

Recall
1. **Define** sacrament, abbot, abbess, cardinal, lay investiture, heresy, excommunication, friar.
2. **Identify** Benedict, Gregory I, Gregory VII, Innocent III, Francis of Assisi, Dominic.
3. **Explain** how the Catholic Church provided the link between the ancient world and the medieval world.

Critical Thinking
4. **Synthesizing Information** Imagine that you are a religious, but superstitious, peasant living during the Middle Ages. Invent an explanation for the famine that has struck your village.

Understanding Themes
5. **Uniformity** How effective were the actions of the Catholic Church in trying to make all western Europeans believe and practice one faith?

A.D. 700	A.D. 900	A.D. 1100	A.D. 1300

A.D. 871 Alfred the Great begins rule in England.

A.D. 955 German King Otto defeats the Magyars at Lechfeld.

A.D. 1180 Philip Augustus becomes king of France.

A.D. 1215 English King John and his barons sign the Magna Carta.

Section 4

Rise of European Monarchy

Setting the Scene

▶ **Terms to Define**
common law, grand jury, petit jury, middle class

▶ **People to Meet**
Alfred the Great, William the Conqueror, Henry II, Thomas à Becket, Philip Augustus, Otto the Great, Henry IV

▶ **Places to Locate**
England, France, Germany

Find Out What were the achievements of medieval European monarchs?

The Storyteller

The English throne was at stake as the Battle of Hastings approached. William decided to provoke Harold to fight in single combat and called on him to spare the blood of his followers. Under Norman law, personal combat decided difficult cases, looking for the judgment of God to settle the matter. Harold refused because he knew the cause was not personal, but national. It would take a full-scale invasion to decide who would wear the English crown.

—adapted from *William the Conqueror*, Edward A. Freeman, 1927

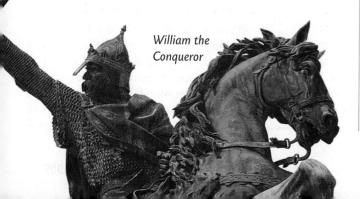
William the Conqueror

After the decline of the Roman Empire, central authority in western Europe disappeared. Except for Charlemagne's reign in the late A.D. 700s, kings were rulers in name only, their lands and power gradually lost to nobles. However, beginning in the A.D. 1100s, many European monarchs began to build strong states.

England

After the Romans abandoned Britain in the A.D. 400s, the island was invaded by Germanic Angles, Saxons, and Jutes. These groups took over much of Britain from the native Celts (KEHLTZ) and set up several kingdoms. In the late A.D. 800s, the Danish Vikings from Scandinavia posed another threat. King Alfred of Wessex, known as **Alfred the Great**, united the Anglo-Saxon kingdoms and defeated the Danes in A.D. 886. His united kingdom eventually became known as "Angleland," or **England**.

The Anglo-Saxons

Alfred ruled Anglo-Saxon England from A.D. 871 to A.D. 899. Like Charlemagne, he was interested in the revival of learning. The English king founded schools and hired scholars to translate many books from Latin to Anglo-Saxon. He also had the scholars write a history of England, known as the *Anglo-Saxon Chronicle*.

The kings who followed Alfred were weak rulers. When the last Anglo-Saxon king, Edward the Confessor, died in A.D. 1066, three rivals claimed the throne.

The Norman Conquest

One of the claimants to the throne was William, the Duke of Normandy. A cousin of the late English king and vassal of the king of France, William had a strong feudal organization in the area of northwestern France. Gathering a force of several hundred boats and some 6,000 soldiers, he invaded England in A.D. 1066. At the Battle of Hastings, William defeated Harold Godwinson, another rival for the throne. The victory won William the English crown and the name **William the Conqueror**.

To keep the loyalty of his Norman vassals, William gave them the lands of Anglo-Saxon church leaders and nobles. He also set up a Great Council of royal officials, bishops, and nobles to advise him and used local officials called sheriffs to collect taxes.

To find out how much money he could collect, William sent officials throughout the land to conduct the first census in western Europe since Roman times. Every person, every farm, every town and manor, every cow and pig, every horse and sheep became an entry in the *Domesday Book*.

Royal Power

William's son, Henry I, ruled from A.D. 1100 to A.D. 1135 and further strengthened the English monarchy. He set up the Exchequer, or department of royal finances, and a system of royal courts.

The court system developed under Henry's grandson, **Henry II**. In place of the old feudal rules, which differed from lord to lord, Henry II established a common law throughout the kingdom. In each community, judges began to meet with a grand jury, a group of men who submitted the names of people suspected of crimes. Soon a system of trial by jury was developed to establish the guilt or innocence of the accused. The kind of jury used in these cases was called a petit jury

The Magna Carta

Thomas à Becket, the Archbishop of Canterbury, however, opposed Henry's reform that brought priests under the jurisdiction of the royal courts. Becket's resistance surprised the king, who had counted on Becket as a friend. Their quarrel lasted many years until four of Henry's knights heard the king declare in a fit of rage that he wished Becket dead. The knights murdered the archbishop in his own cathedral during the Christmas season.

CONNECTIONS
The Arts

The Bayeux Tapestry

Bayeux Tapestry (detail)

The Bayeux Tapestry, made between A.D. 1073 and A.D. 1083, is a remarkable work of medieval art. In fact, the Bayeux Tapestry is not a tapestry at all. By definition, a tapestry is a textile woven of different-colored threads to produce a design or picture. The Bayeux Tapestry is really a work of embroidery, a band of linen upon which pictures and patterns are stitched in colored wool. Twenty inches high and 230 feet long, it probably once decorated the walls of an entire room.

The 72 scenes on the tapestry illustrate William the Conqueror's invasion of England in A.D. 1066. The story is shown in a series of individual scenes, much as a story is told in a comic book today. The tapestry even includes words to indicate what is happening in each scene. The images are lively and simple. No complicated settings are shown; only the people or objects necessary to the story appear. The figures themselves are outlined in a cartoonlike fashion, giving a sense of movement and vitality.

The Bayeux Tapestry was probably the work of Matilda (the wife of William the Conqueror) and the ladies of her court. Such textiles seem to have been common in the Middle Ages, and were often used to decorate castles and the homes of wealthy clerics. The Bayeux Tapestry is a part of this decorative tradition.

MAKING THE CONNECTION

1. What story is told by the Bayeux Tapestry?
2. How did the artists of the Bayeux Tapestry convey a sense of movement in the scenes depicted?

Historical Significance

Many of today's European nations, such as Great Britain and France, as well as many of the Western world's legal procedures and forms of government, trace their origins to the political struggles of medieval times.

The medieval Catholic Church wove Christianity into the fabric of Western culture and laid the basis for modern scholarship by preserving and transmitting the learning of the ancient world. Debates today concerning the relationship of Church and state have their echoes in the contest of medieval popes and monarchs for political supremacy.

Using Key Terms

Write the key term that completes each sentence.

a. counts
b. cardinals
c. chivalry
d. fief
e. feudalism
f. friars
g. heresy
h. manorialism
i. abbess
j. common law
k. excommunication
l. sacraments
m. serfs
n. vassal

1. The medieval Catholic Church threatened heretics with _____, or expulsion from the Church.
2. Popes were elected by a gathering of _____, or high church officials in Rome.
3. _____ are formal church rituals, such as baptism, eucharist, confirmation, marriage, anointing of the sick, and holy orders.
4. Charlemagne relied on local officals called ____ to help him rule his large empire.
5. During the Middle Ages, economic life in Europe centered around a system of agricultural production called _____.
6. Peasants in medieval Europe often were _____, people who were bound to the manor.
7. _____, such as the Franciscans and the Dominicans, followed monastic rules but did not isolate themselves from the rest of the Christian community.
8. In place of old feudal rules, Henry II of England established a _____ that applied throughout his kingdom.
9. The code of _____ called for knights to be brave in battle, fight fairly, keep promises, defend the Church, and treat noblewomen courteously.
10. Medieval women took part in monastic life by living in a convent under the supervision of an _____.

Using Your History Journal

The Church had a significant role in medieval life. Imagine living as a monk or a nun. Write a short diary entry called "Today at the Monastery" or "Today at the Convent," describing the life of a monk or a nun.

Reviewing Facts

1. **List** the invading groups that attacked the Carolingian Empire.
2. **Describe** how and when the tie between military service and landownership began.
3. **Explain** the role that church leaders played in the feudal system.
4. **Outline** briefly how missionaries carried Christianity across Europe.
5. **List** the factors that helped maintain religious uniformity during medieval times.
6. **Explain** the monks' rule of silence that was kept in many monasteries.
7. **List** several services that monasteries and convents provided for the community in medieval times.
8. **Name** the history of England that Alfred had scholars write.
9. **List** the various kinds of entries that were recorded in the *Domesday Book*.

Critical Thinking

1. **Apply** Until the 1970s, "good manners" required a man to help a woman with her coat, and push in her chair. How do these customs

relate to chivalry?

2. **Evaluate** Every society has to develop ways to deal with ignorance, ill health, hunger, and homelessness. How did feudal society handle these problems compared to the way modern society handles them?

3. **Synthesize** Use a diagram to describe what goods and services were exchanged among nobles, knights, and peasants.

Geography in History

1. **Place** Refer to the map below. Where did Leif Eriksson's journey lead him?

2. **Movement** What reasons did Vikings have for leaving Scandinavia and venturing out into the Atlantic?

3. **Human/Environment Interaction** Why did the Vikings sail across the far northern part of the Atlantic rather than through the warmer waters to the south?

4. **Location** After leaving Scandinavia, which landmasses did the Vikings explore?

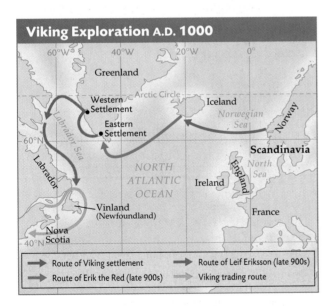

Viking Exploration A.D. 1000

→ Route of Viking settlement	→ Route of Leif Eriksson (late 900s)
→ Route of Erik the Red (late 900s)	⇢ Viking trading route

Understanding Themes

1. **Movement** How can the movement of people both have created and crippled Frankish society?

2. **Cooperation** How were lords and peasants mutually dependent?

3. **Uniformity** How is uniformity implied in the term *regular clergy*?

4. **Conflict** How did the conflict between King John and the nobles eventually have positive results for all English people?

Linking Past and Present

1. Great Britain, defended by its island location, has not been invaded since A.D. 1066. What structure has recently been built that will reduce Great Britain's physical isolation from the rest of Europe?

2. People often cherish a romantic view of medieval life: for example, medieval Europeans lived in elegant castles, wore beautiful clothes, and enjoyed festivals. Do you think such a view is justified by historical evidence?

3. Improvements changed farming in Europe around A.D. 1000. What improvements today will increase farm productivity? What far-reaching effects will they have?

Skill Practice

Read the passage about knights. Use stated facts and your knowledge to answer the questions that follow.

> A knight cannot distinguish himself in [war] if he has not trained for it in tourneys. He must have seen his blood flow, heard his teeth crack under fist blows, felt his opponent's weight bear down upon him as he lay on the ground and, after being twenty times unhorsed, have risen twenty times to fight.

1. From this passage, what can you infer about the physical appearance of many European knights?

2. What fact(s) or observations helped you make this inference?

3. What can you infer about the average length of a knight's career?

Chapter 13

A.D. 1050–1500
Medieval Europe at Its Height

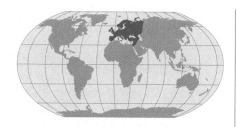

Chapter Themes

▶ **Cultural Diffusion** The Crusades increase European contact with other areas. *Section 1*
▶ **Innovation** Advances in commerce, learning, and the arts change Europe. *Section 2*
▶ **Conflict** England and France battle while their monarchs gain power. *Section 3*
▶ **Conflict** The Church faces a split from within and opposition from without. *Section 4*

The Storyteller

"Well-beloved father," wrote a medieval student, "I have not a penny, nor can I get any save through you, for all things at the University are so dear: nor can I study in my [law books], for they are all tattered. Moreover, I owe ten crowns in dues to the [university administrator], and can find no man to lend them to me.

"Well-beloved father, to ease my debts ... at the baker's, with the doctor ... and to pay ... the laundress and the barber, I send you word of greetings and of money."

This letter from a medieval student sounds very much like something a modern student might write. At that time, however, the university was something new. It was part of the cultural awakening that took place in the High Middle Ages.

Historical Significance

What features of modern Western civilization had their beginnings during the height of the Middle Ages in western Europe? What new developments changed European society during the High Middle Ages?

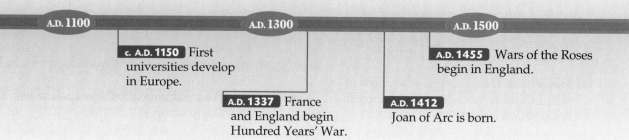

A.D. 1100 | A.D. 1300 | A.D. 1500

c. A.D. 1150 First universities develop in Europe.

A.D. 1337 France and England begin Hundred Years' War.

A.D. 1455 Wars of the Roses begin in England.

A.D. 1412 Joan of Arc is born.

316

The Church Militant and Triumphant, a fresco from the A.D. 1300s by Andrea de Bonaiuto. The Spanish Chapel in Santa Maria Novella, Florence, Italy

Your History Journal

Medieval literature contains epics that were put into writing for the first time. Read an excerpt from Beowulf, *the* Song of Roland, *or* The Canterbury Tales *and take notes about life in Europe at the time.*

Section 1

The Crusades

Setting the Scene

▶ **Terms to Define**
the Crusades

▶ **People to Meet**
the Seljuk Turks, Pope Urban II, Saladin, Richard I

▶ **Places to Locate**
Jerusalem, Constantinople

 **Find Out** How did the Crusades begin, and what were their results?

The Storyteller

Geoffrey de Renneville was footsore, thirsty, and covered with dust. He had joined the Crusade as an adventure. The Crusaders had traveled for weeks and were beset by flies, bandits, disease, poor food, and limited drink. The cavalcade stopped and the weary men dropped into an uneasy slumber. Suddenly, they were startled awake by the cry "Help for the Holy Sepulchre!" One by one the knights took up the cry. Shouting with the others, Geoffrey was reminded of the Crusade's purpose.

—adapted from *The Dream and the Tomb*, Robert Payne, 1984

Leaving for the Crusades

Life in the Early Middle Ages was characterized by decentralized and destabilized government, warfare and invasions, cultural isolation, famine, and wretched living conditions. Trade was sparse, and agricultural production—the mainstay of the European economy—was inefficient.

By A.D. 1100, however, conditions in Europe had begun to improve. Some European monarchs succeeded in building strong central governments. Better farming methods led to larger crop yields and a growth in population. Towns and trade began to reappear. The Church held a powerful sway over the emotions and energies of the people. Changes in religion, society, politics, and economics made the High Middle Ages—the period between A.D. 1050 and A.D. 1270—a springboard for a new and brilliant civilization in western Europe.

The transformation of medieval society began with a holy war over the city of **Jerusalem**. European Christians undertook a series of military expeditions—nine in all—to recover the Holy Land from the Muslims. These expeditions were called the Crusades, from the Latin word *crux*, meaning "cross." Those who fought were called Crusaders because they vowed to "take up the cross."

Call for a Crusade

Jerusalem was a holy city for people of three faiths. Jews treasured it as Zion, God's own city, and as the site of the ancient temple built by Solomon. To Christians, the city was holy because it was the place where Jesus was crucified and resurrected. Muslims regarded Jerusalem as their third holiest city, after Makkah and Madinah. According to Muslim tradition, Muhammad ascended to heaven from Jerusalem.

Jerusalem and the entire region of Palestine fell to Arab invaders in the A.D. 600s. Mostly Muslims, the Arabs tolerated other religions. Christians and

Jews were allowed to live in Jerusalem as long as they paid their taxes and followed certain regulations. European traders and religious pilgrims traveled to Palestine without interference.

In the late A.D. 1000s, however, **the Seljuk Turks**—a Muslim people from central Asia—took control of Jerusalem and closed the city to Jewish and Christian pilgrims. The Seljuks also threatened the Byzantine Empire, especially **Constantinople**. As a result of this threat, the Byzantine emperor wrote to the pope in A.D. 1095 requesting military assistance from the West. Reports of persecution against Christians in Palestine gave added urgency to the emperor's request.

First Crusade

On a cold November day in A.D. 1095, **Pope Urban II** mounted a platform outside the church at Clermont, France. His voice shaking with emotion, he addressed the assembled throng, asking for a volunteer army to take Jerusalem and Palestine from the Seljuks:

> ❝ I exhort you … to strive to expel that wicked race from our Christian lands…. Christ commands it. Remission of sins will be granted for those going thither…. Let those who are accustomed to wage private war wastefully even against believers go forth against the infidels…. Let those who have lived by plundering be soldiers of Christ; let those who formerly contended against brothers and relations rightly fight barbarians; let those who were recently hired for a few pieces of silver win their eternal reward. ❞

"Deus vult!" (God wills it!) shouted the crowd in response to the pope's plea. Knights and peasants alike vowed to join the expedition to the Holy Land. For knights, the Crusade was a welcome chance to employ their fighting skills. For peasants, the Crusade meant freedom from feudal bonds while on the Crusade. All were promised immediate salvation in heaven if they were killed freeing the Holy Land from non-Christians. Adventure and the possibility of wealth were other reasons to join the Crusade. In preparation for the holy war, red crosses of cloth were stitched on clothing as a symbol of service to God.

This First Crusade heightened already existing hatred of non-Christians and marked the onset of a long period of Christian persecution of the Jews. During the First Crusade, which began in A.D. 1096, three armies of Crusader knights and volunteers

Visualizing History **Pope Urban II arrives at the Council of Clermont.** *What did the pope ask the people to do?*

traveled separately from western Europe to the eastern Mediterranean. On the way, many of them killed Jews and sometimes massacred entire Jewish communities.

Led by French nobles, the three armies finally met in Constantinople in A.D. 1097. From there the Crusaders made their way to Jerusalem, enduring the hardships of desert travel as well as quarrels among their leaders. In June A.D. 1099, the Crusaders finally reached the city. After a siege of almost two months Jerusalem fell. Crusaders swarmed into the city and killed most of its Muslim and Jewish inhabitants.

The success of the First Crusade reinforced the authority of the Church and strengthened the self-confidence of western Europeans. The religious zeal of the Crusaders soon cooled, however, and many knights returned home. Those who stayed set up feudal states in Syria and Palestine. Contact between the Crusaders and the relatively more sophisticated civilizations of the Byzantines and the Muslims would continue for the next 100 years and become a major factor in ending the cultural isolation of western Europe.

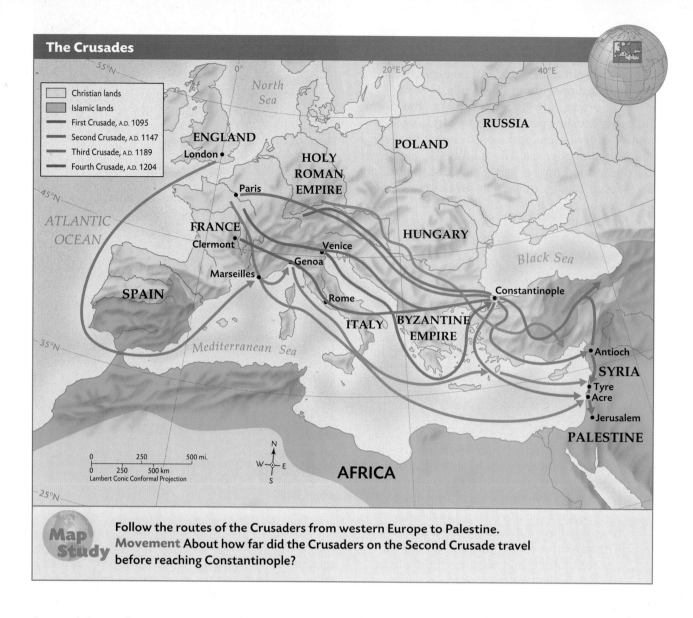

Legend:
- Christian lands
- Islamic lands
- First Crusade, A.D. 1095
- Second Crusade, A.D. 1147
- Third Crusade, A.D. 1189
- Fourth Crusade, A.D. 1204

Map Study

Follow the routes of the Crusaders from western Europe to Palestine. **Movement** About how far did the Crusaders on the Second Crusade travel before reaching Constantinople?

Second Crusade

Less than 50 years after the First Crusade, the Seljuks conquered part of the Crusader states in Palestine. Pope Eugenius IV called for a Second Crusade to regain the territory. Eloquent sermons by the monk Bernard of Clairvaux (KLAR•VOH) persuaded King Louis VII of France and Holy Roman Emperor Conrad III to lead armies to Palestine. The Second Crusade, which lasted from A.D. 1147 to A.D. 1149, was unsuccessful. Louis VII and Conrad III quarreled constantly and were ineffective militarily. They were easily defeated by the Seljuks.

Third Crusade

A diplomatic and forceful leader named **Saladin** (SA•luh•DEEN) united the Muslim forces and then captured Jerusalem in A.D. 1187. The people of western Europe were stunned and horrified. Holy Roman Emperor Frederick Barbarossa of

Germany, King Philip Augustus of France, and King **Richard I** of England assembled warriors for the Third Crusade. This "Crusade of Kings" lasted from A.D. 1189 to A.D. 1192 and was no more successful than the Second Crusade. Frederick Barbarossa died on the way to Palestine, and his army returned home. Philip Augustus returned to France before the army reached Jerusalem. Richard continued the struggle alone.

Although his army defeated the Muslims in several battles, Richard could not win a decisive victory over Saladin's well-trained and dedicated forces. After three years of fighting, Richard signed a truce with the Muslims and tried to persuade Saladin to return Jerusalem to the Christians. "Jerusalem," he wrote to the Muslim leader, "we are resolved not to renounce as long as we have a single man left." Saladin's reply to Richard showed his equal determination to keep the city:

> **"** To us Jerusalem is as precious, aye and more precious, than it is to you, in that it was the place whence our Prophet made his journey by night to heaven and is destined to be the gathering place of our nation at the last day. Do not dream that we shall give it up to you…. It belonged to us originally, and it is you who are the real aggressors. When you seized it, it was only because of the suddenness of your coming and the weakness of those [Muslims] who then held it. So long as the war shall last God will not suffer you to raise one stone upon another. **"**

Although Saladin refused to turn over Jerusalem, he allowed Christian pilgrims access.

Other Crusades

Other Crusades followed in the A.D. 1200s, but none succeeded in winning permanent Christian control of Palestine. In fact, the Muslims slowly conquered all the remaining Christian territories. In A.D. 1291 they captured Acre, the last Christian stronghold in Palestine. By this time, western Europeans had lost sight of the religious goal of the Crusades. They were now more concerned about political and economic gain. As a result, European rulers lost interest in regaining Palestine and shifted their attention to other matters.

Effects of the Crusades

The Crusades failed to free the Holy Land from the Muslims. Nonetheless, the Crusades had a major impact on the development of western Europe. In Europe, the Crusades helped break down feudalism and increase the authority of kings. Kings levied taxes and raised large armies of fighting forces. Some nobles died in battle without leaving heirs, and their lands passed to kings. To raise money for weapons and supplies, many lesser nobles sold their estates or

History & Art *Return from the Crusade* by Karl Friedrich Lessing. Rheinland Museum, Bonn, Germany *How did the Crusades help to break down feudalism?*

allowed their serfs to buy their freedom to become freeholders on the land or artisans in the towns.

European contact during the Crusades with the more advanced Byzantine and Muslim civilizations helped to bring classical texts back to the West. This knowledge fueled a renewed interest in literature and art that later swept across Europe.

In addition, European cities—especially Venice and Genoa in Italy—became more prosperous and powerful due to increased trading in the Mediterranean. Contact with the East spurred a new demand for luxury goods: spices, sugar, melons, tapestries, silk, and other items previously hard to come by.

Finally, the Crusades improved European technology. From the Muslims, the Crusaders learned how to build better ships and make more accurate maps. They began to use the magnetic compass to tell direction. The Crusaders also learned new military skills, especially in siege techniques. Weaponry significantly improved as well.

SECTION I REVIEW

Recall
1. **Define** the Crusades.
2. **Identify** the Seljuk Turks, Pope Urban II, Saladin, Richard I.
3. **Explain** why both Christians and Muslims of the A.D. 1000s and A.D. 1100s felt that Jerusalem should belong to them.

Critical Thinking
4. **Analyzing Information** In what ways were the Crusades a success? In what ways were they a failure?

Understanding Themes
5. **Cultural Diffusion** Describe how cultural diffusion in the Middle Ages occurred throughout Europe and the Mediterranean world as a result of the Crusades.

A.D. 1000	A.D. 1200	A.D. 1400

c. A.D. 1000 Europe's economy begins to revive.

c. A.D. 1150 French architects begin to build in the Gothic style.

c. A.D. 1348 The Black Death spreads throughout Europe.

c. A.D. 1386 Geoffrey Chaucer begins writing *The Canterbury Tales.*

Section 2

Economic and Cultural Revival

Setting the Scene

▶ **Terms to Define**

money economy, guild, master, apprentice, journeyman, charter, scholasticism, troubadour, vernacular

▶ **People to Meet**

Thomas Aquinas, Dante Alighieri, Geoffrey Chaucer

▶ **Places to Locate**

Venice, Flanders, Champagne, Bologna

Find Out How did the growth of towns affect the society of medieval Europe?

The Storyteller

To help rebuild the cathedral, people for miles around brought their goods. So that the church might rise swiftly, larger and more beautiful than any they had seen, peasants, skilled workers, and even nobles pulled heavy carts filled with wood and stone. Religious fervor motivated the people, and the reward was a renewed spirit in the community. Perfect harmony reigned. During the night, the workers formed a camp with their wagons, and by the light of candles, they sang canticles and psalms. Everyone was doing penance and forgiving their enemies.

—adapted from *Chronique*, Robert de Torigni, in *Chartres*, Emil Mâle, translated by Sarah Wilson, 1983

Cathedral at Reims, France

The Crusades accelerated the transformation of western Europe from a society that was crude, backward, and violent—showing little cultural and technological advancement—to a civilization that exhibited some early features of modern Western civilization. Towns grew, trade expanded, and learning and the arts thrived.

Economic Expansion

The economy of western Europe had begun to show vigor around A.D. 1000. Agricultural production increased. Expanding opportunities in trade encouraged the growth of towns, and the lively atmosphere of the towns in turn stimulated creative thought and innovations in art.

Agricultural Advances

Plows during the Early Middle Ages were light and did not cut much below the surface of the soil. The invention of a new, heavier plow made it possible to cut through the rich, damp soils of northwestern Europe. This plow enabled farmers to produce more and to cultivate new lands, increasing food production. Nobles and freeholders—peasants not bound to the land—migrated to new areas, clearing forests, draining swamps, and building villages. In one of the largest migrations of the time, the Germans moved to areas of eastern Europe, doubling the territory they controlled.

About the same time, the collar harness replaced the ox yoke. Horses were choked by the ox yoke, but the new harness shifted weight off the neck and onto the shoulders, allowing farmers to replace oxen with horses. Horses pulled the plow faster than oxen, allowing farmers to plant and plow more crops.

As you read in Chapter 12, the three-field system of planting also made the land more productive. As the land began to feed more people, the population naturally increased.

Expansion of Trade

The revival of towns caused a rapid expansion of trade. Soon the sea-lanes and roads were filled with traders carrying goods to market. Important sea and river routes connected western Europe with the Mediterranean, eastern Europe, and Scandinavia. The repaired and rebuilt Roman road system carried international traders to and from Europe.

Italian towns such as **Venice**, Pisa, and Genoa controlled the Mediterranean trade after A.D. 1200, bringing silks and spices from Asia to Europe. The town of **Flanders**, a region that includes present-day northern France and southern Belgium, became the center of trade on Europe's northern coast. The textiles produced by these towns were traded at Middle Eastern markets for porcelain, velvet and silk, and silver. Towns along the Baltic coast controlled trade between eastern Europe and the North Atlantic.

The merchandise for sale in a town was varied and seemingly endless. This was especially true during trade fairs. Each year hundreds of traders met at large trade fairs in places convenient to land and water routes. Feudal lords charged the merchants fees, charged taxes on goods, and offered protection to the merchants. The most famous fair was at **Champagne** in eastern France, located in almost the exact center of western Europe. For four to six weeks each year, Champagne was a distribution point for goods from around the world.

Banking

Early merchants used the barter system, trading goods without using money. Before long, however, merchants found this system impractical. Moreover, some of the merchants who supplied luxury goods such as silk would only accept money in payment. European merchants therefore needed a common medium of exchange.

The rise of a money economy, or an economy based on money, had far-reaching consequences. Initially, it led to the growth of banking. Since traders came from many countries, they carried different currencies with different values. Moneychangers—often Jews or Italians—determined the value of the various currencies and exchanged one currency for another. They also developed procedures for transferring funds from one place to another, received deposits, and arranged loans, thus becoming the first bankers

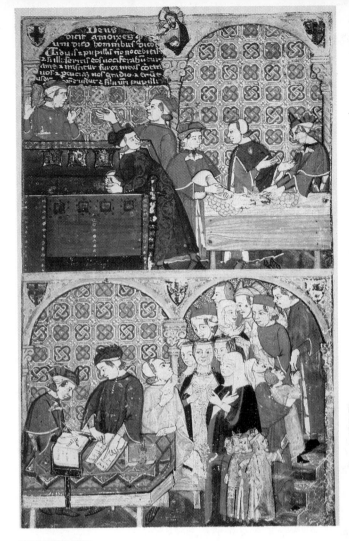

Visualizing History Italian bankers, from *Treatise on the Seven Vices: Avarice*. The Church viewed lending with the intent to charge interest as evil. *What is the origin of the term "bank"?*

in Europe. Indeed, the word *bank* comes from the *banca*, or bench, that the moneychangers set up at fairs.

As the money economy grew, it put the feudal classes in an economic squeeze. Kings, clergy, and nobles became dependent on money from banks to pay their expenses. To pay off their loans, they had to raise taxes, sell their lands, or demand money in place of traditional feudal services. As serfs became able to buy their freedom, the feudal system declined.

Growth of Towns

The number of towns in western Europe grew tremendously in the A.D. 1000s and A.D. 1100s. Many grew up beside well-traveled roads or near waterways. Although warfare had declined, settlements still faced bandits. To protect themselves, townspeople built walls around their towns. At first these enclosures were simple wooden fences. As the population grew, stone walls were built, with guard towers at the gates.

Inside the walls narrow, winding streets bustled with people, carts drawn by horses and oxen, and farm animals on the way to market. A din of noise and overpowering smells attacked the senses. Church bells chimed the hours; carts piled high with goods creaked and rumbled through streets that were little more than alleys. Shops lined the streets at ground level, and the shop owners often lived in quarters above. Most buildings were of wood and had thatch roofs, making fire a constant hazard.

Medieval towns had almost no sanitation, and a constant stench assailed the people from the garbage and sewage tossed into the streets. These conditions caused the rapid spread of diseases such as diphtheria, typhoid, influenza, and malaria. In crowded towns such diseases often turned into epidemics and took many lives. The worst of these epidemics—the bubonic plague—ravaged Europe between A.D. 1348 and 1350, killing one-third of the population and earning the name the Black Death.

Guilds

During the A.D. 1100s, merchants and artisans organized themselves into business associations called guilds. The primary function of the merchant guild was to maintain a monopoly of the local market for its members. To accomplish this end, merchant guilds severely restricted trading by foreigners in their city and enforced uniform pricing. The following regulations from Southampton, England, indicate the power of the merchant guilds:

❝ And no one shall buy honey, fat, salt herrings, or any kind of oil, or millstones, or fresh hides, or any kind of fresh skins, unless he is a guildsman; nor keep a tavern for wine, nor sell cloth at retail, except in market or fair days … ❞

Images *of the* Times

Medieval Life

The recovery of commerce and the beginnings of industries stimulated the growth of European towns.

Market scene in a medieval town is the subject of this fresco from Castello de Issogne, Val d' Aosta, Italy.

Craft guilds, by contrast, regulated the work of artisans: carpenters, shoemakers, blacksmiths, masons, tailors, and weavers. Women working as laundresses, seamstresses and embroiderers, and maidservants had their own trade associations.

Craft guilds established strict rules concerning prices, wages, and employment. A member of the shoemakers' guild could not charge more (or less) for a pair of shoes than other shoemakers, nor could he advertise or in any way induce people to buy his wares. Although the guilds prohibited competition, they set standards of quality to protect the public from shoddy goods.

Craft guilds were controlled by masters, or artisans who owned their own shops and tools and employed less-skilled artisans as helpers. To become a master at a particular craft, an artisan served an apprenticeship, the length of which varied according to the difficulty of the craft. Apprentices worked for a master without pay. An apprentice then became a journeyman and received pay. However, a journeyman could only work under a master. To become a master, a journeyman submitted a special sample of his work—a masterpiece—to the guild for approval. If the sample was approved, the journeyman became a master and could set up his own shop.

Aside from business activities, guilds provided benefits for their members such as medical help and unemployment relief. Guilds also organized social and religious life by sponsoring banquets, holy day processions, and outdoor plays.

Rise of the Middle Class

The medieval town, or burg, created the name for a new class of people. In Germany they were called *burghers*; in France, the *bourgeoisie* (BURZH•WAH•ZEE); and in England, *burgesses*. The name originally referred to anyone living in a town. Gradually it came to mean the people who made money through the developing money economy. They were a middle class made up of merchants, bankers, and artisans who no longer had to rely on the land to make a living.

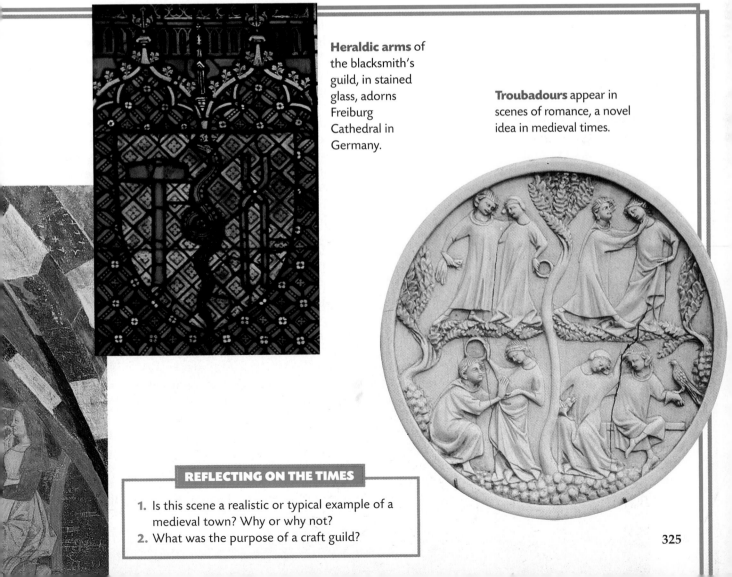

Heraldic arms of the blacksmith's guild, in stained glass, adorns Freiburg Cathedral in Germany.

Troubadours appear in scenes of romance, a novel idea in medieval times.

REFLECTING ON THE TIMES

1. Is this scene a realistic or typical example of a medieval town? Why or why not?
2. What was the purpose of a craft guild?

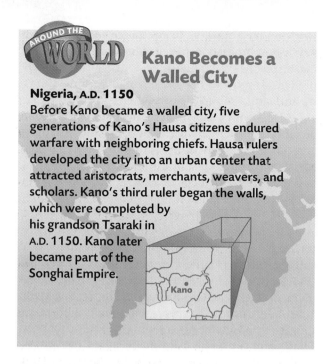

AROUND THE WORLD

Kano Becomes a Walled City

Nigeria, A.D. 1150
Before Kano became a walled city, five generations of Kano's Hausa citizens endured warfare with neighboring chiefs. Hausa rulers developed the city into an urban center that attracted aristocrats, merchants, weavers, and scholars. Kano's third ruler began the walls, which were completed by his grandson Tsaraki in A.D. 1150. Kano later became part of the Songhai Empire.

Kano

The middle class helped turn towns into organized municipalities. Businessmen created councils to administer town affairs and gained political power for themselves. As the money economy spread, kings began to depend on the middle class for loans and for income from the taxes they paid. The leading merchants and bankers became advisers to lords and kings.

Town Government

Conflict gradually developed between the feudal classes and the burghers. City dwellers did not fit into the feudal system; they resented owing taxes and services to lords. They wanted to run their own affairs and have their own courts and laws. At the same time, feudal lords feared the growing wealth and power of the middle class. To try to keep the burghers in line, the lords began to strictly enforce feudal laws.

The money economy gave the towns the income and power they needed to win the struggle against the lords. In the A.D. 1000s Italian towns formed groups called communes. Using the political power they gained from the growing money economy, the communes ended the power of feudal lords and made the Italian towns into independent city-states. In other areas of Europe, kings and nobles granted townspeople charters, documents that gave them the right to control their own affairs. At the same time, many towns remained a part of a kingdom or feudal territory.

Education

During the Early Middle Ages, most people were illiterate. Education was controlled by the clergy. In monastery and cathedral schools, students prepared for monastery life or for work as church officials. In addition to religious subjects, students learned grammar, rhetoric, logic, arithmetic, geometry, astronomy, and music.

As towns grew, the need for educated officials stimulated a new interest in learning. The growth of courts and other legal institutions created a need for lawyers. As a result, around A.D. 1150, students and teachers began meeting away from monastery and cathedral schools. They formed organizations that became known as universities.

Universities

At first the university was not so much a place as it was a group of scholars organized like a guild for the purpose of learning. Classes were held in rented rooms or churches or in the open air. Books were scarce. In most classes a teacher read the text and discussed it, while students took notes on slates or committed as much information as possible to memory. Classes did, however, meet on a regular schedule. University rules established the obligations of students and teachers toward each other. To qualify as a teacher, students had to pass an examination leading to a degree, or certificate of completion.

By the end of the A.D. 1200s, universities had spread throughout Europe. Most southern European universities were modeled after the law school at **Bologna** (buh•LOH•nyuh), Italy, and specialized in law and medicine. Universities in northern Europe, on the other hand, specialized in liberal arts and theology. These were generally modeled after the University of Paris.

New Learning

At medieval universities, scholars studied Latin classics and Roman law in depth. They also acquired knowledge from the works of the Greek philosopher Aristotle and from Islamic scholarship in the sciences. This interest in the physical world eventually led to the rise of Western science.

Many church leaders opposed the study of Aristotle's works, fearing that his ideas threatened Christian teachings. In contrast, some scholars thought the new knowledge could be used to support Christian ideas. They applied Aristotle's philosophy to theological questions and developed a system of thought called scholasticism. This new type of learning emphasized reason as well as faith in the interpretation of Christian doctrine. Scholastics sought to reconcile classical philosophy with the Church's teachings. They believed all knowledge could be integrated into a coherent whole.

One early scholastic teacher, Peter Abelard, taught theology in Paris during the early A.D. 1100s. In his book *Sic et Non* (Yes and No), he collected statements from the Bible and the writings of early Christian leaders that showed both sides of controversial questions. Abelard then had his students reconcile the differences through logic.

In the A.D. 1200s the most important scholastic thinker was **Thomas Aquinas** (uh•KWY•nuhs), a brilliant theologian and philosopher who taught philosophy in Paris and Naples. In his work *Summa Theologica* (a summary of religious thought), Aquinas claimed that reason was a gift from God that could provide answers to basic philosophical questions. The Catholic Church later accepted and promoted Aquinas's way of teaching and thinking.

Medieval Literature and Art

The spread of universities and the revival of intellectual endeavor stimulated advances in literature and the arts. Songs and epics of the Early Middle Ages were put in writing for the first time.

Epics and Romances

One of the earliest surviving literary works of the feudal world was the Anglo-Saxon epic *Beowulf*. A tale of grim battle and gloomy scenery, *Beowulf* reveals the harshness of life in northern Europe. Handed down by oral tradition for two centuries, it was finally written down in Old English (Anglo-Saxon) by an unknown poet in about A.D. 700. In colorful verses and exciting narrative, the epic describes how the Anglo-Saxon warrior Beowulf defeats a horrible monster named Grendel.

French epics called *chansons de geste*, or songs of high deeds, celebrated the courage of feudal warriors. The *Song of Roland*, written around A.D. 1100, gives an account of the chivalrous defense of Christianity by Charlemagne's knights.

Romances about knights and ladies were also popular. In southern France in the A.D. 1100s and A.D. 1200s, traveling poet-musicians called troubadours composed lyric poems and songs about love and the feats of knights. They helped define the ideal knight celebrated in the code of chivalry.

Geography

The Trail of the Black Death

The Black Death

Outbreaks of the Black Death—today known as the bubonic plague—erupted throughout Europe in the A.D. 1340s. It continued at 10-year intervals throughout the Middle Ages. The worst epidemic, which claimed nearly 25 million lives between A.D. 1348 and A.D. 1350, began in China and spread swiftly across Asia.

When ships from Asia reached the Mediterranean, the disease spread to Sicily, North Africa, and western Europe. People in crowded towns with poor sanitation—and rats—were at greater risk than those in the countryside. About one-third of Europe's population died in this single epidemic. It was not until A.D. 1906 that flea-infested rats were identified as the carrier of the Black Death.

The plague brought many changes to Europe. Wars stopped, and trade slowed. People were forbidden to gather in groups, religious services were suspended, and infected homes were sealed off. Businesses shut their doors, and many city people fled to the country. It would take two centuries for Europe to regain its pre-1348 level of population.

MAKING THE CONNECTION

1. How was the plague brought to western Europe?
2. How is the spread of disease still related to human movement?

Interior of a Gothic cathedral at Reims, France. *How did the Gothic style differ from the Romanesque?*

Vernacular Literature

Most medieval literature was written in the vernacular, or language of everyday speech, of the writer. Instead of using Latin as a common language, people spoke the language of their own country—English, German, French, Italian, or Spanish. These vernacular languages helped give each kingdom of Europe a separate identity. Use of vernacular languages in writing made literature accessible to more people.

Some outstanding works of literature were written in the vernacular in the A.D. 1300s. **Dante Alighieri** (DAHN•tay A•luh•GYEHR•ee) wrote *The Divine Comedy*, an epic poem in Italian. Written over a period of several years, the poem discusses medieval ideas of life after death by describing an imaginary journey from hell to heaven.

In England a government official named **Geoffrey Chaucer** started writing *The Canterbury Tales* in A.D. 1386, and continued the series of tales probably right up to his death in A.D. 1400. The narrative poems describe a group of pilgrims, representing people of various classes and occupations, who tell stories to amuse one another on their way to a shrine at Canterbury, England.

Medieval Art

Early medieval churches were built in a style called Romanesque, which combined features of Roman and Byzantine structures. Romanesque churches had thick walls, columns set close together, heavy curved arches, and small windows. About A.D. 1150, French architects began to build in a new style called Gothic. They replaced the Romanesque heavy walls and low arches with flying buttresses. These stone beams, extending out from the walls, took the weight of the building off the walls. This allowed the walls to be thinner, with space for stained-glass windows. The ceiling inside was supported by pointed arches made of narrow stone ribs reaching out from tall pillars. These supports allowed architects to build higher ceilings and more open interiors.

Medieval painters, by contrast, turned their attention to a much smaller art form, the illuminated manuscript. Adorned with brilliantly colored illustrations and often highlighted with gold leaf, these works were miniature masterpieces whose beauty has endured to the present day.

SECTION 2 REVIEW

Recall
1. **Define** money economy, guild, master, apprentice, journeyman, charter, scholasticism, troubadour, vernacular.
2. **Identify** Peter Abelard, Thomas Aquinas, Beowulf, Dante Alighieri, Geoffrey Chaucer.
3. **Explain** why membership in a guild was advantageous for a medieval artisan. Why was it disadvantageous?

Critical Thinking
4. **Synthesizing Information** Create an imaginary medieval town. Briefly explain its physical characteristics. Then describe what a typical day for an artisan working there would be like.

Understanding Themes
5. **Innovation** Choose one of the following and trace its effect on medieval society: three-field system, money economy, guilds.

Section 3

Strengthening of Monarchy

Setting the Scene

▶ **Terms to Define**
   cortes

▶ **People to Meet**
   Joan of Arc, Louis XI, Richard III,
   Henry VII, Ferdinand of Aragon, Isabella of
   Castile

▶ **Places to Locate**
   Crécy, Agincourt, Burgundy, Castile, Aragon

 **ind Out** How did European monarchs
strengthen their powers during the Middle Ages?

Storyteller

A popular legend in English history is the story of the first Prince of Wales. Edward, King of England, desired to make the proud chieftains of Wales acknowledge his power. He campaigned against them, soon controlling their lands. The Welsh chiefs refused to accept Edward as their prince. They agreed, however, to serve a prince

The Tower of London

whom Edward would choose— provided he was noble and spoke neither English nor French. Edward accepted these terms and showed them their prince, his newborn son, who was indeed of noble birth and could speak neither language. The chiefs accepted the baby as their lawful lord, the Prince of Wales.

—adapted from *The Three Edwards*, Thomas Costain, 1964

uring the Middle Ages, power rested in the hands of nobles who owned feudal estates. But as trade flourished and towns grew, feudalism weakened. Beginning in the A.D. 1100s, power in western Europe began to shift from nobles to kings or queens. Gradually the influence of the clergy and nobles diminished as educated common people and laymen became advisers to monarchs. At the outset, however, a period of violent warfare swept through western Europe.

The Hundred Years' War

During the A.D. 1300s, feudal disputes often led to wars among Europe's monarchs. The Hundred Years' War between England and France grew out of such a dispute. The war—actually a series of wars—lasted from A.D. 1337 to A.D. 1453, before the French claimed victory.

Causes

After William of Normandy conquered England in A.D. 1066, conflicting feudal claims caused great bitterness between the English and French kings. Because William had been duke of Normandy—an area in northwestern France—before becoming king of England, his successors in England saw themselves as rulers of Normandy and England. English control over French lands increased in A.D. 1152, when Henry II married Eleanor of Aquitaine, heir to lands in southwestern France. As a result of the marriage, Henry II controlled more land in France than did the French king.

The French monarch Philip II regained most of the northern lands held by England by defeating Eleanor's son, King John, in the early A.D. 1200s. The French kings, however, wanted all of the lands claimed by the English.

Chapter 13 *Medieval Europe at Its Height* **329**

History & Art *"La Pucelle!" Jeanne d' Arc Leads Her Army* by Franck Craig, 1907. Musée d' Orsay, Paris, France *What did the "Maid of Orléans" accomplish for the French?*

Matters between the English and the French worsened in A.D. 1328, when the French king died without leaving a direct heir. King Edward III of England, a grandson of the French king, declared himself king of France and announced that he would not recognize French sovereignty over his feudal lands in France. The successor to the French throne, Philip of Valois—himself only a nephew of the dead king—quietly began to prepare for war with England.

Major Battles

Despite being poorer and less populated than France, England won the early battles of the Hundred Years' War. English unity contributed to this success. English kings received popular support from the nation and financial support from Parliament. Superior military tactics also gave England an edge.

When French knights arrived at the small village of **Crécy** (kray•SEE) in A.D. 1346, they outnumbered the English two to one. They were surprised to see foot soldiers fighting alongside the English knights. These soldiers carried a new weapon, the Welsh longbow. As tall as a man, longbows could shoot arrows capable of piercing heavy armor at 300 yards (274 m). French swords and crossbows were useless at such a distance. French historian Jean Froissart described the battle:

❝ Then the English archers stept forth one pace and let fly their arrows so wholly [together] and so thick, that it seemed snow. When the [soldiers] felt the arrows piercing through heads, arms and breasts, many of them cast down their cross-bows and did cut their strings and [retreated]…. ❞

At Crécy the English forces also used the first portable firearm in European warfare: a long iron tube mounted on a pole. This cumbersome firearm led to the development of the cannon, which became a major weapon in later fighting.

By the late A.D. 1300s, France was in disarray. War and plague were ravaging the country. Although a peasant revolt was quickly put down, it added to the disorder. At the Battle of **Agincourt** (A•juhn•KORT) in A.D. 1415, the English army once more triumphed, though again outnumbered, this time by a margin of three to one. Just as French fortunes had sunk to their lowest, a young woman helped bring about a dramatic reversal.

Joan of Arc

Born just three years before the French defeat at Agincourt, **Joan of Arc** grew up in the small French village of Domremy. Like most peasants, she did not learn to read or write. Joan left home at the age of 17,

Adam Woolfitt

Cathedral of Chartres

The cathedral stands out against a lowering sky. The old town of Chartres, France, crowds the foreground, where artisans, merchants, bakers, and stonemasons once lived, clustered near the great church. At the center of the photograph, the rose window provides a perfect example of medieval stained glass. The two towers, one ornate, the other plain, were finished in different periods. They pierce the sky—giving form to the faith and spirit of Europe's Middle Ages.

The cathedral reflects the technology of the High Middle Ages. Built before A.D. 1300, Chartres Cathedral, located about 50 miles southwest of Paris, is one of many works of Gothic architecture expressing both the fervor of the medieval era and the revival of the European economy, beginning around A.D. 1000. The growth of towns such as Chartres was a result of such changes. The combination of new building techniques, financial resources, and professional skills enabled the construction of the great cathedrals of Europe. ⊕

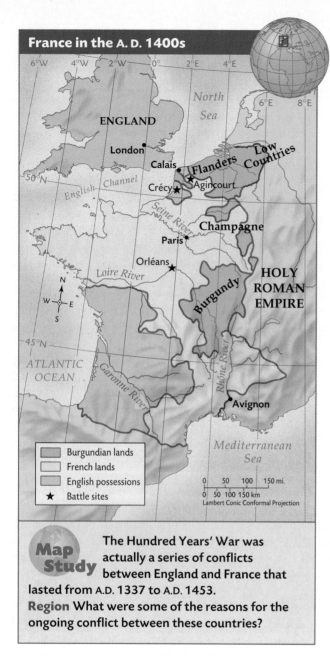

ENGLAND

London

North
Sea

Calais

Flanders

Low Countries

Crécy

Agincourt

English Channel

Seine River

Champagne

Paris

Orléans

Loire River

Burgundy

HOLY
ROMAN
EMPIRE

N
W · E
S

ATLANTIC
OCEAN

Garonne River

Rhône River

Avignon

Mediterranean
Sea

- Burgundian lands
- French lands
- English possessions
- ★ Battle sites

0 50 100 150 mi.
0 50 100 150 km
Lambert Conic Conformal Projection

Map Study The Hundred Years' War was actually a series of conflicts between England and France that lasted from A.D. 1337 to A.D. 1453.
Region What were some of the reasons for the ongoing conflict between these countries?

insisting that she had received messages from God telling her to help drive the English from France.

In A.D. 1429 Joan arrived at Chinon (shee•NAW) to persuade Charles, heir to the French throne, to give her command of his troops. After several tests of her unique powers, Charles gave her armor, a banner, and command of troops.

Joan then set off to Orléans (AWR•lay•AHN), a town in northern France that had been besieged by English troops for several months. Inspired by her piety and sincerity, French soldiers broke the siege of Orléans in only 10 days, and the English fled. Under the leadership of the Maid of Orléans, as Joan of Arc came to be known, French soldiers fought their way to Reims, where Charles was officially crowned King Charles VII.

In A.D. 1430 Joan was captured by rivals of the French king and sold to the English. After nearly a year in prison and a long trial in which she steadfastly insisted on the truth of her visions, Joan of Arc was condemned to be burned at the stake as a witch and a heretic. On a mild May day in A.D. 1431, onlookers wept as Joan calmly went to her fate. Twenty-four years after her death, a new trial proclaimed her innocence.

Joan's courage rallied the French around the king and drove the English out of France. When the war ended in A.D. 1453, the port of Calais was the only French territory still in English hands.

Effects of the War

During the Hundred Years' War, France suffered more severely than England, since all of the fighting occurred on French soil. Yet victory gave the French a new sense of unity that enabled them to rebuild their country.

Although England had been spared destruction, English nobles who had owned lands in France were bitter about the defeat. For the rest of the A.D. 1400s, England was torn by civil war. In the long run, however, the loss of French lands contributed to national unity for England and encouraged the English to concentrate on problems at home.

The Hundred Years' War also hastened the decline of feudalism. The use of the longbow and firearms made feudal methods of fighting based on castles and mounted knights obsolete. Monarchs replaced feudal soldiers with national armies made up of hired soldiers. Maintaining these armies, however, was expensive. Monarchs turned to townspeople and the lower nobility for new sources of revenue. These groups willingly paid taxes and made loans in return for security and good government.

France

By the end of the Hundred Years' War, the French monarchy had gained much power and prestige. Warfare emergencies allowed kings to collect national taxes and maintain standing, or permanent, armies. Therefore, after Charles VII defeated the English, he was able to renew the royal tradition of ruling the country assertively.

Louis XI, son of Charles VII, set out to unite France by taking back lands once part of the royal territory but now held by French nobles. Louis especially wanted **Burgundy,** one of the most prosperous regions of Europe. However, its ruler, Charles the Bold, wanted Burgundy to be an independent state.

Louis was a shrewd diplomat. Rather than fight Charles openly, he encouraged quarrels between Burgundy and the neighboring Swiss. After Charles was killed in a battle with the Swiss in A.D. 1477, Burgundy was divided into two parts: the northern half, Flanders, went to Charles's daughter Mary; the remainder became part of France.

Through a series of reforms, Louis strengthened the bureaucracy of government, kept the nobles under royal control, and promoted trade and agriculture. By the end of his reign, France was strong and unified, and its monarch ruled with increased power.

England

After the Hundred Years' War, England became mired in a struggle for the English throne. The 30-year conflict, known as the Wars of the Roses (because of the symbols of the rival royal families), began in A.D. 1455. The royal house of Lancaster bore the red rose; its rival, the house of York, a white rose.

During the Wars of the Roses, Edward, duke of York, overthrew the weak Lancaster dynasty and became King Edward IV. As king, Edward worked to strengthen royal government and to promote trade. Edward's death in A.D. 1483 brought uncertainty to England. The heirs to the throne were the late king's two sons. Edward's brother, Richard, however, proclaimed himself **Richard III** and locked his young nephews in the Tower of London. Not long after, the boys were found murdered. Many suspected Richard—who himself fell to the forces of Henry Tudor, a Lancaster noble, on Bosworth Field in A.D. 1485.

Henry became King **Henry VII**, the first Tudor king. Henry steadily eliminated rival claimants to the throne, avoided expensive foreign wars, and gradually reasserted royal power over the lords and nobles. As a result, the English monarchy emerged from the Wars of the Roses strengthened and with few challengers. The Tudor dynasty ruled England for more than 100 years until 1603.

Spain

During the late A.D. 1400s, Spain emerged from a period of turmoil and warfare to become an important European power. Even before Pope Urban called for the Crusades, the Christian kingdoms of northern Spain were engaged in the *Reconquista* (RAY•kohn•KEES•tuh), or reconquest, of the lands the Muslims had taken in the A.D. 700s. By A.D. 1250 the Iberian Peninsula consisted of three Christian kingdoms: Portugal in the west, **Castile** in the center, and **Aragon** on the Mediterranean coast. Only Granada in the south remained in the hands of the Moors, or Spanish Muslims.

In A.D. 1469 **Ferdinand of Aragon** and **Isabella of Castile** were married. The two kingdoms maintained separate governments, however, and the power of their monarchs was limited by local interests and large minority religious groups. The Christian settlers who had been moved into the reconquered territories and the large Jewish and Muslim communities in Castile and Aragon had their own laws and elected their own officials. Special royal charters allowed many towns to keep their own courts and local customs. Finally, assemblies known as *cortes* (KOR•tays), in which nobles were powerful, had the right to review the monarchs' policies.

The two monarchs strengthened the powers of the Crown in Castile. Royal officials governed the towns, and special courts enforced royal laws. In A.D. 1492 their armies forced the surrender of the last Moorish stronghold at Granada. Shortly afterward, Ferdinand and Isabella ended the traditional policy of toleration for minority groups. They believed that all Spaniards had to be Catholic if Spain was to become one nation. Spanish Jews and Muslims were given the choice to convert to Catholicism or leave Spain. Later the two monarchs set up the Spanish Inquisition, a court that enforced Catholic teachings. The fear caused by the Inquisition further strengthened the power and authority of the Spanish monarchs over their people. However, it limited Spanish contacts with other parts of Europe.

SECTION 3 REVIEW

Recall
1. **Define** *cortes*.
2. **Identify** Joan of Arc, Louis XI, Richard III, Henry VII, Ferdinand of Aragon, Isabella of Castile.

3. **Explain** the causes and results of the Hundred Years' War.

Critical Thinking
4. **Applying Information** Relate how one European monarchy

changed during the Middle Ages.

Understanding Themes
5. **Conflict** Explain the reasons for the struggles between the various European monarchies.

A.D. 1300	A.D. 1400	A.D. 1500

A.D. 1305 Pope's court moves to Avignon, France.

A.D. 1378 Great Schism in the Church occurs.

A.D. 1415 Church authorities burn Jan Hus as a heretic.

A.D. 1436 Compromise reached between the Church and Hussites.

Section 4

The Troubled Church

Setting the Scene

▶ **Terms to Define**
pilgrimage, simony

▶ **People to Meet**
Pope Clement V, John Wycliffe, the Lollards, Jan Hus

▶ **Places to Locate**
Avignon, Bohemia

ind Out ▶ Why was the Church under pressure to reform?

The Storyteller

The situation was intolerable, Nicholas of Clèmanges thought angrily. The Church was increasingly corrupt. Greed, pride, and love of luxury prevailed in place of humility and charity. Comparing the current priests and bishops with the holy leaders of antiquity, he reflected, was like comparing mud to gold. What would come of such ills? "So great a flood of evils must assuredly be crushed and utterly

destroyed by God's most righteous judgment. It does not seem possible in any other way to chasten it." Nicholas prayed that the Church might be spared from complete destruction—that a little seed might remain in the world.

—adapted from *On the Ruin and the Repair of the Church*, Nicholas Clèmanges, reprinted in *Readings in Western Civilization*, 1986

The Church besieged by evil forces

During the upheavals of the Late Middle Ages—caused by warfare, the plague, and religious controversy—many people turned to the Church for comfort and reassurance. Religious ceremonies multiplied, and thousands of people went on religious pilgrimages, or journeys to holy places. In spite of this increase in religious devotion, the temporal authority of the Church was weakening due to the influence of strong monarchs and national governments. A growing middle class of educated townspeople and a general questioning of the Church's teachings also contributed to this decline.

Babylonian Captivity

During the early A.D. 1300s, the papacy came under the influence of the French monarchy. In A.D. 1305 a French archbishop was elected **Pope Clement V.** Clement decided to move his court from Rome to **Avignon** (A•veen•YOHN), a small city in southern France, to escape the civil wars that were disrupting Italy. While in France, the pope appointed only French cardinals. Pope Clement V and his successors—all French—remained in Avignon until A.D. 1377.

This long period of the exile of the popes at Avignon came to be known as the Babylonian Captivity, after the period of the exile of the Jews in Babylon in the 500s B.C. For centuries, Rome had been the center of the western Church. With the pope in France, people feared that the papacy would be dominated by French monarchs. Others disliked the concern the Avignon popes showed for increasing church taxes and making church administration more efficient. They believed the popes had become corrupted by worldly power and were neglecting their spiritual duties. The Italian poet Petrarch complained:

❝ Here reign the successors of the poor fishermen of Galilee; they have strangely

forgotten their origin. I am astounded …
to see these men loaded with gold and
clad in purple, boasting of the spoils of
princes and nations. **"**

The Great Schism

Finally, in A.D. 1377, Pope Gregory XI left
Avignon and returned to Rome. After his death,
Roman mobs forced the College of Cardinals to
elect an Italian as pope. The cardinals later declared
the election invalid, insisting they had voted under
pressure. The cardinals then elected a second pope,
who settled in Avignon. When the Italian pope
refused to resign, the Church faced the dilemma of
being led by two popes.

This controversy became known as the Great
Schism because it caused serious divisions in the
Church. The Great Schism lasted from A.D. 1378 until
A.D. 1417 and seriously undermined the pope's
authority. People wondered how they could regard
the pope as the divinely chosen leader of Christianity
when there was more than one person claiming to be
the single, unquestioned head of the Church.

Calls for a Council

Many kings, princes, and church scholars
called for a reform of church government. The most
popular remedy was a general church council.
However, this solution posed many problems. First,
such councils were traditionally called by popes.
No pope was willing to call a council that would
limit his authority. However, the legality of a council would be questionable if it did not receive papal
approval. Second, different rulers in Europe supported particular popes for political reasons. Such
political divisions made it almost impossible to
reach agreement on even the site of a council, let
alone to reach agreement on the deeper and more
important issues involved.

By A.D. 1400 many western Europeans were
committed to the idea of a church council. In A.D.
1409 a council met at Pisa, Italy, to unite the Church
behind one pope. It resulted in the election of a
third pope, since neither the pope at Rome nor the
pope at Avignon would resign. Finally, in A.D. 1414,
another council met at Constance, Germany. It
forced the resignation of all three popes and then
elected Pope Martin V, ending the Great Schism.
The long period of disunity, however, had seriously weakened the political influence of the Church.
Moreover, many Europeans had come to feel a
greater sense of loyalty to their monarchs than to
the pope.

Calls for Reform

Church authority was also weakened by people's dislike of abuses within the Church. The clergy used many unpopular means to raise money.
Fees were charged for almost every type of service
the Church performed. Common people especially
disliked simony—the selling of church positions—
because the cost of buying these positions was
passed on to them. The princely lifestyles of the
clergy further eroded regard for the Church. Many
Europeans called for reform. Two of the clearest
voices belonged to an English scholar and a
Bohemian preacher.

John Wycliffe

John Wycliffe (WIH•KLIHF), a scholar at
England's Oxford University, criticized the
Church's wealth, corruption among the clergy, and
the pope's claim to absolute authority. He wanted
secular rulers to remove church officials who were
immoral or corrupt.

Wycliffe claimed that the Bible was the sole
authority for religious truth. He began to translate
the Bible from Latin into English so people could
read it themselves. Since church doctrine held that
only the clergy could interpret God's word in the
Bible, this act was regarded as revolutionary. Some
of Wycliffe's followers, known as **the Lollards**,
angrily criticized the Church. They destroyed
images of saints, ridiculed the Mass, and ate communion bread with onions to show that it was no
different from ordinary bread.

Widespread antipapal feelings made it difficult
for the English government to suppress Lollards.
Wycliffe was persuaded to moderate his views and
received only a mild punishment. He died peacefully in A.D. 1384, but his ideas spread.

Among those who supported the Lollards was
Bohemian-born Queen Anne, the wife of King

Silver Spoons
During the Middle Ages,
pewter spoons became
common utensils for eating. In the A.D. 1400s silver "apostle spoons," bearing the image of a
child's patron saint, were favored gifts for new-
borns in Italy. Only the wealthy could afford such
a luxury. From these apostle spoons came the saying that a privileged child is "born with a silver
spoon in his or her mouth."

John Wycliffe Reading His Translation of the Bible to John of Gaunt by Ford Madox Brown. *Why was Wycliffe's translation of the Bible revolutionary?*

Richard II. Anne sent copies of Wycliffe's writings to her homeland in the Holy Roman Empire, where they influenced another great religious reformer.

Jan Hus

During the late A.D. 1300s and A.D. 1400s, the Slavs of **Bohemia**, known as Czechs, became more aware of their own national identity. They wanted to end German control of their country and backed sweeping reforms in the Catholic Church in Bohemia, which had many German clergy. Their religious and political grievances combined to produce an explosive situation.

The Czechs produced religious pamphlets and copies of the Bible in Czech and criticized the corruption of leading church officials, many of whom were German. The leader of the Czech religious reform movement was **Jan Hus**, a popular preacher and professor at the University of Prague. When Hus and his works were condemned by the Church and political leaders, a violent wave of riots swept across Bohemia.

Faced with a possible full-scale rebellion against the Church, in A.D. 1415 the council at Constance demanded that Hus appear before them to defend his views. The Holy Roman emperor promised Hus safe conduct to Constance, Germany, but this guarantee was ignored. Hus was burned at the stake as a heretic, but his heroic death caused many Czechs to rally around their new martyr.

From A.D. 1420 to A.D. 1436, Hus's supporters, called Hussites, resisted the Church and the Holy Roman emperor, and the Church launched five crusades against the Hussites. All five failed. Using firearms and the tactic of forming movable walls with farm wagons, the Hussites defeated the crusading knights.

In A.D. 1436 representatives of the pope and the Holy Roman emperor reached a compromise with the Hussite leaders. They gave the Hussites certain religious liberties in return for their allegiance to the Church. The ideas of Jan Hus, however, continued to spread throughout Europe to influence later and more radical reformers. While this agreement gave the appearance that the Church had successfully met the challenges to its authority, the basic spiritual questions raised by Hus and others did not go away.

SECTION 4 REVIEW

Recall
1. **Define** pilgrimage, simony.
2. **Identify** Pope Clement V, Babylonian Captivity, Great Schism, John Wycliffe, the Lollards, Jan Hus, the Hussites.
3. **Explain** the effects of the Babylonian Captivity and the Great Schism on the Church.

Critical Thinking
4. **Synthesizing Information** Imagine you are a follower of Jan Hus just after his execution. How would you feel about carrying on his work?

Understanding Themes
5. **Conflict** Explain the rise of dissent among many devout Europeans. Why were they against the Church and its leadership?

Analyzing Historical Maps

When you walk through your town, you may see changes in progress. Perhaps a new restaurant has opened, or an old factory has been torn down. Change also takes place on a larger scale across nations and continents. Historical maps illustrate political, social, and cultural changes over time.

Learning the Skill

To analyze a historical map, first read the title to identify its theme. Then identify the chronology of events on the map. Many historical maps show changes in political boundaries over time. For example, the map below of the Frankish Empire uses colors to show land acquisitions under three different rulers. On the other map, however, colors represent areas controlled by different rulers at the same time. Read the map key, labels, and captions to determine what time periods and changes appear on the map.

To compare historical maps of the same region in different time periods, first identify the geographic location and time period of each map. Then look for similarities and differences. Which features have remained the same and which have changed? What groups control the area in each map? Has the country grown larger or smaller over time? Have other features changed?

After analyzing the information on historical maps, try to draw conclusions about the causes and effects of these changes.

Practicing the Skill

The two maps on this page show the same region in different time periods. Study both maps and answer these questions.
1. What is the time period of each map?
2. How did the Frankish Empire change from A.D. 500 to A.D. 800?
3. Did France grow larger or smaller between A.D. 800 and A.D. 1400?
4. What other changes appear on these maps?

Applying the Skill

Compare a map of Europe today with a map of Europe in 1985 or earlier. Identify at least five changes that have occurred since the early 1980s.

For More Practice

Turn to the Skill Practice in the Chapter Review on page 339 for more practice in analyzing historical maps.

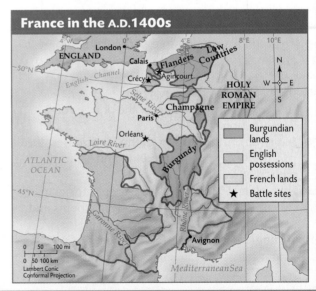

Frankish Empire A.D. 481–814

North Sea

ENGLAND

Clovis's kingdom
Added by Martel and Pepin
Added by Charlemagne
★ Battle site

Aachen

ATLANTIC

Paris

OCEAN   Tours ★

ITALY
Rome

N
W E
S

0   150   300 mi.
0 150 300 km
Lambert Conic Conformal Projection

Mediterranean Sea

France in the A.D.1400s

London
ENGLAND
Calais Flanders Low Countries
English Channel Crécy ★ Agincourt

HOLY
ROMAN
EMPIRE

Champagne

Seine River

Paris

Orléans

Loire River

Burgundy

ATLANTIC
OCEAN

Burgundian lands
English possessions
French lands
★ Battle sites

N
W E
S

Garonne River

Rhône River

Avignon

0   50   100 mi
0 50 100 km
Lambert Conic Conformal Projection

MediterraneanSea

Historical Significance

Many features of modern Western civilization arose during the Middle Ages. The medieval history of Europe's great cities can still be seen in great cathedrals. Modern labor unions and institutions of higher learning are related to medieval guilds and universities. Today's national languages in Europe first appeared during the Middle Ages. Finally, the middle class, which plays an important role in the world today, also had its beginnings during this period.

Using Key Terms

Write the key term that completes each sentence.

a. apprentice	g. vernacular
b. *cortes*	h. simony
c. charter	i. money economy
d. scholasticism	j. pilgrimages
e. Crusade	k. master
f. guilds	l. troubadours

1. A military expedition of Christian Europeans to free the Holy Land from the Muslims was known as a _____.
2. Church scholars developed a system of thought known as _____ that sought to reconcile faith and reason.
3. During the Late Middle Ages, many devout people demonstrated their faith by going on _____.
4. During the A.D. 1100s merchants and artisans organized themselves into business associations called _____.
5. The rise of a _____ led to the growth of banking and put the feudal classes in an economic squeeze.
6. To become an expert in a particular craft, an artisan served for a certain period of time as an _____ without pay.
7. In Spain, assemblies known as _____ at first had the right to review the policies of Spanish monarchs.
8. Many devout European Catholics opposed the practice of_____—the buying and selling of church offices.
9. In medieval France, traveling poet-musicians called _____ composed lyric poems and songs about love and the feats of knights.
10. During the Middle Ages, the rise of _____ languages gave each kingdom of Europe a separate identity.

Using Your History Journal

From your notes on **Beowulf,** *the* **Song of Roland,** *or* **The Canterbury Tales,** *write a short description of the manners, customs, and values of the Europeans described in the work.*

Reviewing Facts

1. **List** the various medieval Crusades and their results.
2. **Describe** several agricultural improvements in the Middle Ages.
3. **Outline** the steps taken by an apprentice to become a master.
4. **List** the key events in the Hundred Years' War.
5. **Identify** two church reformers and a major event in the life of each.
6. **Describe** what a typical medieval town was like.
7. **Identify** the bourgeoisie and state their role in late medieval Europe.
8. **Discuss** the impact of the Black Death on western Europe.
9. **Explain** why townspeople and the lower nobility supported the rise of strong monarchies in western Europe.
10. **List** the problems that the Catholic Church faced at the end of the Middle Ages.
11. **State** how Louis XI strengthened the French monarchy.
12. **Discuss** the major result of the Wars of the Roses.
13. **Identify** the *Reconquista*. How did it contribute to the unity of Spain?
14. **List** new business methods that developed in western Europe during the A.D. 1300s and A.D. 1400s. How did they change western European life?

Critical Thinking

1. **Apply** How did the medieval middle class change European society?
2. **Analyze** What various forces led to Europe's economic growth during the Middle Ages?
3. **Evaluate** How would Europe be different today if there had been no Crusades?
4. **Apply** How did European monarchies change during the Middle Ages? What were the effects of this change on culture, religion, and politics in Europe?

Geography in History

1. **Place** Refer to the map "Trade Routes A.D. 1400s." Name the major trading cities in western Europe during the 1400s.
2. **Human/Environment Interaction** Why did most European traders avoid overland routes whenever possible?
3. **Location** With which two areas to the east did the cities of Europe most want to trade?
4. **Movement** How did the desire for luxuries from the East lead to changes in transportation in the West?

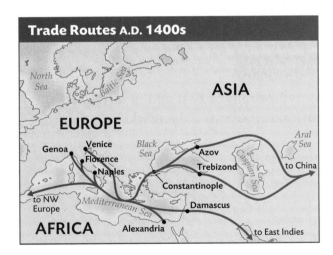

Understanding Themes

1. **Cultural Diffusion** How did a mix of cultures affect medieval Europe?
2. **Innovation** Choose one medieval innovation and describe its influence on medieval society.

Do the same for a modern innovation and modern society.
3. **Conflict** How did continual conflict between England and France strengthen the monarchies of those countries?
4. **Conflict** Why was there religious dissent in the Catholic Church of the Late Middle Ages?

Linking Past and Present

1. The Crusades were a series of "holy wars" conducted by Christians against Muslims. Can you find examples of holy wars in modern times?
2. Compare the rise of towns in medieval Europe with the rise of towns in America.
3. How do medieval European universities compare to today's higher educational institutions?

Skill Practice

Study the map "Spread of the Black Death" and answer the questions below.

1. What is the topic and time period of this map?
2. What does color represent?
3. When and where did the Black Death begin?
4. In which direction did the Black Death spread? How does the map show this?
5. What factor do you think caused this pattern of the epidemic?`

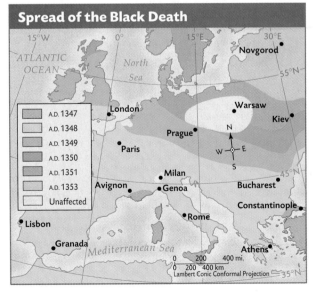

East and South Asia

Chapter Themes

▶ **Movement** The Mongols of central Asia conquer China and parts of Europe. *Section 1*
▶ **Uniformity** A centralized government, a state religion, and a common language maintain China's cultural continuity. *Section 2*
▶ **Cultural Diffusion** The civilizations of Southeast Asia reflect the influences of India and China. *Section 3*
▶ **Innovation** Japan and Korea produce innovations from a blend of Chinese and local traditions. *Section 4*

Storyteller

In China, in the year A.D. 1200, a lone student sat behind a desk in a room furnished only with a lamp, some paper, a writing brush, and an inkstone. He labored over a grueling government exam designed to test his knowledge of Confucian texts. He worried because examiners could fail a person for even a single misquotation. If he passed, he would be one of the Song emperor's officials. If he failed, he would have to hawk cheap goods in the streets.

Civil service examinations helped ancient China to maintain a consistent government no matter which dynasty was in power. Later, the neighboring countries of Korea and Japan adopted these civil service examinations as well as other aspects of Chinese culture.

Historical Significance

How did the civilizations of East and South Asia influence each other and the rest of the world?

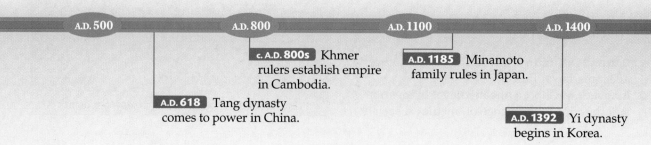

A.D. 500	A.D. 800	A.D. 1100	A.D. 1400

c. A.D. 800s Khmer rulers establish empire in Cambodia.

A.D. 618 Tang dynasty comes to power in China.

A.D. 1185 Minamoto family rules in Japan.

A.D. 1392 Yi dynasty begins in Korea.

A partial view of the summer palace constructed under
Emperor Ch'ien Lung. Bibliothèque Nationale, Paris, France

Your History Journal

Copy or obtain a blank map of East Asia. As you read the chapter, place 10 to 20 key events on your map in the countries or areas where they occurred. Include the dates of these events.

A.D. 1200

c. A.D. 1206 Genghis Khan becomes ruler of all Mongol tribes.

A.D. 1300

c. A.D. 1270 The Mongols establish rule in China.

A.D. 1400

A.D. 1398 Timur Lenk (Tamerlane) sacks Samarkand in central Asia.

Section 1

Central Asia

Setting the Scene

▶ **Terms to Define**
clan, yurt, *yasa*, khan

▶ **People to Meet**
the Seljuk Turks, the Mongols, Genghis Khan, Timur Lenk (Tamerlane)

▶ **Places to Locate**
Mongolia

**ind Out** How did the Mongols acquire the world's largest land empire?

The Storyteller

The caravan halted for the night. Chaghatai, the leader, before retiring posted a sign and fastened bells around the animals' necks. Maffeo, a young foreigner, wondered at these precautions. Chaghatai explained that strange things may happen in the Desert of Lop. "When a man is riding by night through this desert and something happens to make him ... lose touch with his companions ... he hears spirits talking.... Often these voices make him stray from the path.... For this reason bands of travellers make a point of keeping very close together.... And round the necks of all their beasts they fasten little bells, so that by listening to the sound they may prevent them from straying from the path."

—adapted from *The Travels of Marco Polo*, Marco Polo, translated by Ronald Latham, 1958

Porcelain figure on camel

From the A.D. 1000s to the A.D. 1400s, invaders from the steppe of central Asia conquered territories in eastern Asia, the Middle East, and eastern Europe. Originally nomads, the invaders settled in many of the conquered areas. They adapted to the local cultures, advanced trade, and encouraged the exchange of goods and ideas.

The Steppe Peoples

At the beginning of the A.D. 1000s, large numbers of nomadic groups roamed the steppe of central Asia. Loosely organized into clans, or groups based on family ties, they depended for their livelihood on the grazing of animals. To protect their pastures and provide for a growing population, they organized under powerful chiefs. The chiefs formed cavalry units of warriors armed with bows and arrows. The nomadic peoples became a military threat to neighboring territories that were more culturally developed. They carried out a series of invasions that transformed the cultures of eastern Asia, the Middle East, and eastern Europe.

The Seljuk Turks

The first people of the steppes to engage in conquest were the Turks. Around A.D. 800, weak Abbasid rulers centered in Baghdad hired Turkish warriors to fight in their armies. As a result, the Turks became powerful and soon controlled the Abbasid government. Later, about A.D. 1000, a group of Muslim Turks called **the Seljuk Turks** moved from central Asia into the Middle East. There they formed settlements and restored the Sunni caliphate. The Seljuks also gained control of the main trade routes between eastern Asia, the Middle East, and Europe. They benefited from this trade and used their wealth to build an empire.

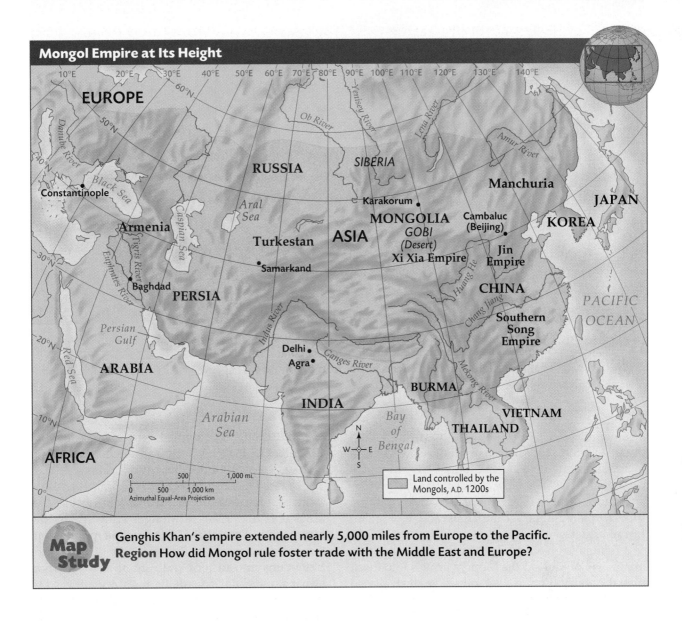

Mongol Empire at Its Height

EUROPE

RUSSIA

SIBERIA

Manchuria

JAPAN

Constantinople

Karakorum

MONGOLIA

Cambaluc
(Beijing)

KOREA

Armenia

Aral
Sea

Turkestan

ASIA

GOBI
(Desert)

Xi Xia Empire

Jin
Empire

Samarkand

Baghdad

PERSIA

CHINA

Persian
Gulf

Southern
Song
Empire

PACIFIC
OCEAN

ARABIA

Delhi

Agra

Ganges River

BURMA

INDIA

Bay
of
Bengal

VIETNAM

THAILAND

AFRICA

Arabian
Sea

0   500   1,000 mi.
0   500   1,000 km
Azimuthal Equal-Area Projection

Land controlled by the
Mongols, A.D. 1200s

Map Study Genghis Khan's empire extended nearly 5,000 miles from Europe to the Pacific.
Region How did Mongol rule foster trade with the Middle East and Europe?

Seljuk warriors also invaded the plains and highlands of Asia Minor. There they defeated the Byzantines at the Battle of Manzikert in A.D. 1071. The Byzantine emperor Alexius I Comnenus feared the loss of Byzantine territory to the Seljuks and appealed to the pope and the monarchs of western Europe for aid. About 20 years later, the Seljuk conquest of Palestine led to Pope Urban II's calling of the First Crusade.

Though the Seljuks were skilled warriors, they were unable to develop a well-organized government to rule their territories. Seljuk rulers lacked strong traditions of government administration and had difficulties holding the empire together. Local officials ignored the central government and acted like independent rulers. They began to fight each other for control of land. Weakened by internal upheavals, the Seljuks became prey to new nomadic invaders from central Asia.

The Mongols

During the late A.D. 1100s, **the Mongols** became the dominant nomadic group in central Asia. Their homeland was **Mongolia**, a region of forests and steppe northwest of China. In this wild and isolated area, they wandered from pasture to pasture with their herds of sheep, horses, and yaks, or long-haired oxen. Because of their nomadic life, the Mongols lived in movable tents called yurts. Their principal foods were meat and mare's milk. In a few fertile areas, Mongol farmers established small communities. There women raised grains while men herded animals.

Genghis Khan

Like other nomads, the Mongols at first were divided into clans. They were expert fighters on horseback, using bow and arrow. About A.D. 1206

Some people in Mongolia still live in yurts, circular domed tents of skins or felt stretched over a lattice frame. *Why did ancient Mongols choose this kind of housing?*

a Mongol leader named Temujin (teh•MOO•juhn) organized the scattered clans under one government. He brought together Mongol laws in a new code known as the *yasa*. Under Temujin's guidance, an assembly of tribal chiefs met for the first time to plan military campaigns and to appoint future leaders.

Temujin's greatest achievement was in military affairs. He organized the Mongol armies into disciplined cavalry units. These units were then placed under the command of officers chosen for their abilities and not for their family ties. These changes made the Mongols the most skilled fighting force in the world at that time. As a result of his efforts, Temujin was recognized as khan, or absolute ruler. Now called **Genghis Khan** (JEHN•guhs KAHN), he set out to create a large empire.

Mongol Conquests

The Mongol armies under Genghis Khan first conquered the other steppe peoples, most of whom were Turks. These victories brought tribute money to the Mongol state as well as new recruits for the Mongol armies. By A.D. 1211 the Mongols were strong enough to attack major civilizations. In that year, 100,000 Mongol horsemen invaded China. While fighting against the Chinese, the Mongols learned Chinese techniques of siege warfare. Using gunpowder, storming ladders, and battering rams, they won significant victories against their opponents. In spite of Genghis Khan's death in A.D.

1227, the Mongols continued their advance. By A.D. 1270 all of China's territory was in their hands, and a Mongol dynasty ruled the entire country.

Under Ogadai (OH•guh•DY) Khan, the other Mongol forces moved westward. During the A.D. 1230s and A.D. 1240s, a Mongol army led by the commander Batu (bah•TOO) conquered Russian territories and then crossed the Carpathian Mountains into eastern and central Europe. Upon hearing of Ogadai's death, Batu's army returned to Russia. There they awaited the selection of a new khan. Meanwhile, Ogadai's widow ruled the Mongols.

During the same period, another group of Mongols invaded the Middle East. Using terror to subdue the region, the Mongols destroyed cities and killed large numbers of people. In A.D. 1258 the commander Helagu (heh•lah•GOO) captured Baghdad, the old Abbasid capital, and enslaved its inhabitants. The destruction of Baghdad represented a major setback to Islamic civilization. However, the Mongol advance was finally halted by the Mamluks, a Muslim military group that ruled Egypt.

The Mongol Empire

The Mongols created the largest land empire in history. Their territories extended from China to the frontiers of western Europe. Many of the great trade routes between Europe and Asia passed through Mongol lands. During the A.D. 1200s

The Bodleian Library, Oxford, Ms·Bodl. 264, fol.219R

Kublai Khan and Marco Polo

This medieval English manuscript shows the Chinese emperor Kublai Khan presenting golden tablets to Marco Polo and his family to ensure their safe passage back to the West. In A.D. 1297 Marco Polo wrote an account of his 17 years in China, and his book eventually became popular with the small literate class in Europe. The painter who embellished this manuscript had never met Marco Polo nor had he ever seen a picture of an Asian. Maybe that's why the emperor looks European rather than Asian.

The Mongol rulers of China put the country in closer touch with the Middle East and Europe. The Mongolian khans were outsiders who distrusted, and were distrusted by, their Chinese subjects. The khans turned to outsiders to help them rule, especially after Kublai Khan moved the Chinese capital to Beijing. The Polos (Marco Polo's father and uncle accompanied him to China) were but three of hundreds of European and Muslim merchants and artisans who moved in and out of China. But Marco Polo became famous, both in his time and in ours, because he wrote a book about his adventures. The Polos brought Chinese noodles back to Europe, and other European and Muslim travelers brought Chinese inventions such as gunpowder and the compass back to the West. This transfer of technology had a major impact on the history of Europe. ⊕

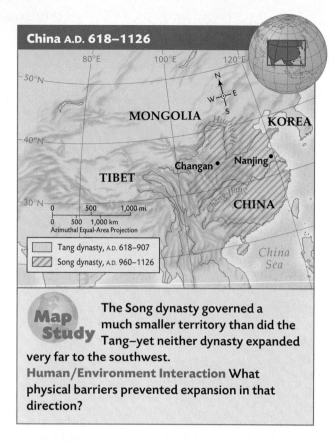

China A.D. 618–1126

Tang dynasty, A.D. 618–907
Song dynasty, A.D. 960–1126

Map Study The Song dynasty governed a much smaller territory than did the Tang—yet neither dynasty expanded very far to the southwest.
Human/Environment Interaction What physical barriers prevented expansion in that direction?

China's enemies, however, were eventually able to obtain the secrets of Song military technology. Thus, using the Song Empire's own technology against it, the Mongols were able to completely capture northern China in A.D. 1234 and bring about the fall of the Song dynasty in southern China in A.D. 1279.

The Yuan Dynasty

During the A.D. 1200s, the Mongols invaded China and overthrew the Jurchen and Song rulers. They established the Yuan (YOO•AHN), or Mongol, dynasty. They became the first conquerors to rule most of the country.

Kublai Khan

The first great Mongol emperor of China was **Kublai Khan** (KOO•BLUH KAHN). A grandson of Genghis Khan, Kublai ruled from A.D. 1260 to A.D. 1294. Kublai Khan extended Mongol rule beyond China's borders. He conquered Korea in the north and part of Southeast Asia. He made two attempts to invade Japan, using Chinese and Korean ships. Both efforts failed because the Mongols were not skilled in naval warfare.

Although Kublai complied with some Chinese traditions to better control the Chinese, he tried to maintain Mongol culture. Government documents were written first in Mongolian, then translated into Chinese. Moreover, the highest positions in the emperor's court were given to Mongols or foreigners.

The most famous of these foreigners appointed to government posts was a Venetian named **Marco Polo**. Polo arrived in China in A.D. 1271 and stayed 17 years, traveling through Mongol territory on the Khan's missions. After Polo returned to Italy, his tales of the splendor of Chinese civilization astounded Europeans.

Mongol Peace and Decline

Marco Polo was able to travel throughout China because the Mongols enforced a relatively stable order. Merchants could safely travel the roads built by the Mongols. Mongol rule thus fostered trade and connections with Europe.

Through contact with the Middle East, Russia, and Europe, the Chinese obtained enslaved people as well as products such as glass, hides, clothes, silver, cotton, and carpets. In return, Europeans got exotic products such as silk, porcelain, and tea.

After Kublai Khan died in A.D. 1294, a series of weak successors took over the throne. The Chinese, still resentful of foreign rule, began to stage rebellions against these rulers. Finally, in A.D. 1368, a young Buddhist monk named Zhu Yuanzhang (JOO YOO•AHN•JAHNG) led an army against the capital and overthrew the Yuan dynasty.

SECTION 2 REVIEW

Recall
1. **Define** meritocracy, mandarin.
2. **Identify** Tai Cong, Empress Wu, Xuanzang, Duo Fu, Li Bo, Zhao Kuangyin, Kublai Khan, Marco Polo.
3. **Locate** the city of Changan in central China on the map above. How was Changan restored years after the Han dynasty collapsed?

Critical Thinking
4. **Evaluating Information** Do you think the Tang and Song systems of government were true meritocracies? Explain.

Understanding Themes
5. **Uniformity** What methods did the rulers of the Tang, Song, and Yuan dynasties use to unite China?

A.D. 800   A.D. 1100   A.D. 1400

A.D. 802 The Khmer people establish capital at Angkor.

A.D. 938 The Vietnamese defeat the Chinese in the Battle of Bach Dang River.

c. A.D. 1200s The Mongols destroy Burman city of Pagan.

A.D. 1350 The Thai establish kingdom of Ayutthaya.

Section 3

Southeast Asia

Setting the Scene

▶ **Terms to Define**
archipelago, animism

▶ **People to Meet**
the Khmer, Suryavarman II, the Trung sisters, Ngo Quyen, Ramkhamhaeng

▶ **Places to Locate**
Angkor Wat, Pagan, Sukhothai, Ayutthaya, Melaka

Find Out How were Southeast Asians influenced by the cultures of China and India?

The Storyteller

The situation was a general's nightmare, T'u Sui thought despairingly. His lord, the Chinese emperor, was determined to subjugate the land of Yueh [Vietnam]. T'u Sui had gladly accepted the command of five hundred thousand men of ability to complete the task. However, when he attacked the Yueh fled into the mountains and forests where it was impossible to fight them or even to find them. Gradually, the troops grew weary of their duties. The Yueh would then attack, inflicting great losses upon the powerful Chinese army.

—from *Huai Nan Tzu*, reprinted in *Ancient Vietnam*, Keith W. Taylor

Mountains of Vietnam

Although China was the most culturally diverse and influential society in Asia from about A.D. 220 until A.D. 1400, other Asian civilizations were creating distinct and influential cultures of their own at the same time. Southeast Asian cultures were among these new societies.

Crossroads of Asia

South of China and east of India is the region known as Southeast Asia. Southeast Asia includes the present-day countries of Myanmar (Burma), Thailand, Vietnam, Laos, Cambodia, Malaysia, Singapore, Brunei, Indonesia, and the Philippines. Located in the tropics, many of these countries have fertile soils, warm climates, and abundant rainfall. Geographically, Southeast Asia is divided into mainland and maritime Southeast Asia. The latter includes more than 10,000 islands of the Philippine and Indonesian archipelagos, or chains of islands.

During the A.D. 100s, an exchange of goods and ideas began between India and Southeast Asia. This exchange led Southeast Asia to adopt many elements of Indian culture. For instance, at that time, traveling Indian traders and scholars introduced to Southeast Asia the Sanskrit language and the religions of Hinduism and Buddhism. Indian epics such as the *Ramayana* were interwoven with Southeast Asian stories and legends. Indian architecture, law codes, and political ideas also deeply influenced the cultures of the region. As contact with India increased, Indian culture gradually spread throughout Southeast Asia.

Southeast Asians nevertheless retained many of their own traditions. They continued to perform the art of shadow puppetry, to make intricately patterned cloth called batik, and to play their own unique instruments and music. They also believed in animism, the idea that spirits inhabit living and nonliving things.

The Khmer

In A.D. 802 **the Khmer** (kuh•MEHR) people of the mainland Southeast Asian country of Cambodia established a great Hindu-Buddhist empire with its capital at Angkor. The Khmer Empire reached its height during the A.D. 1100s, when it conquered much of the land that now includes Laos, Thailand, and Vietnam.

The empire's wealth came primarily from its rice production. Elaborate hydraulic engineering projects enabled the Khmer to irrigate and produce three crops of rice a year. With the wealth from this bountiful harvest, Khmer rulers subsidized mammoth construction projects. Adapting Indian building techniques to create their own distinctive architecture, the Khmer built hundreds of temples that glorified Hindu and Buddhist religious figures. They also constructed roads, reservoirs, irrigation canals, harbors, and hospitals. Khmer rulers were known for the splendor of their court. Borrowing from the Indian idea of kingship, Khmer rulers presented themselves as incarnations of the Hindu gods or as future Buddhas, which served to enhance their power. They bedecked themselves in elaborate finery and filled their palaces with ornate thrones and beautiful furnishings. A Chinese traveler named Zhou Dakuan (JOH DAH•KWON) described the splendor of a Khmer king in dress and manner:

66 His crown of gold is high and pointed like those on the heads of the mighty gods. When he does not wear his crown, he wreathes his chignon [hair gathered in a bun] in garlands of sweet-scented jasmine. His neck is hung with ropes of huge pearls (they weigh almost three pounds); his wrists and ankles are loaded with bracelets and on his fingers are rings of gold set with cats' eyes. He goes barefoot—the soles of his feet, like the palms of his hands, are rouged with a red stuff. When he appears in public he carries the Golden Sword. 99

Images of the Times

Angkor Wat

Angkor Wat (meaning "temple of the capital") was built in the A.D. 1100s by the Khmer ruler Suryavarman II. Suryavarman believed he was the incarnation of the Hindu god Vishnu.

The temple complex at Angkor Wat is encircled by a three-mile moat. The temples and monuments within the complex honored the god-king Suryavarman II and impressed visitors with their size and detailed ornamentation.

A bas–relief of the Bayon depicts a battle between the Khmer and the Chams.

Seen through a doorway, the pavilion and the central sanctuary reveal a five-headed Naga serpent.

During the A.D. 1100s, under the rule of King **Suryavarman** (soor•yah•VAHR•mahn) **II**, the Khmer kingdom reached the height of its power. Having expanded Cambodia by conquest to include parts of areas known today as Laos, Vietnam, and Thailand, the king decided to glorify both the Hindu god Vishnu and himself. He ordered the construction of **Angkor Wat**, a temple complex covering nearly a square mile. Carvings depicting the Hindu gods cover the walls of Angkor Wat, and, at the center of the complex, the sanctuary stands 130 feet (40 m) high. Angkor Wat also was used as an astronomical observatory.

The Khmer king poured so much of the empire's wealth into building Angkor Wat, however, that he severely weakened the kingdom. This excess, along with rebellions against Khmer rule and infighting between members of the royal family, further crippled the empire. In A.D. 1431 the Thai, a neighboring Southeast Asian people, captured the capital city of Angkor, bringing an end to Khmer rule there.

Vietnam

East of Cambodia and south of China lies the area of present-day Vietnam. Because of Vietnam's proximity to China and because the Chinese dominated Vietnam for more than 1,000 years, Vietnam's culture in some ways came to resemble that of China.

The Vietnamese absorbed elements of Chinese belief systems such as Confucianism, Daoism, and Buddhism. The Vietnamese also adopted Chinese forms of writing and government. Just as in China, Vietnamese officials were selected through civil service exams based on Confucian principles.

The Vietnamese retained many of their own traditions, however. They adopted Chinese religions and beliefs, but they continued to believe in animism. The Vietnamese built a *dinh*, or spirit house, in each village. This tiny house served as the home for the guardian spirit of a village. The Vietnamese wore their hair long and tattooed their skin. They wrote and spoke their own Vietnamese

A stone bas–relief of elephant and gods helps tell the story of the ancient Khmer civilization.

REFLECTING ON THE TIMES

1. What values of the Khmer are reflected in these images?
2. How did Suryavarman attempt to impress upon visitors that he was an incarnation of Vishnu?

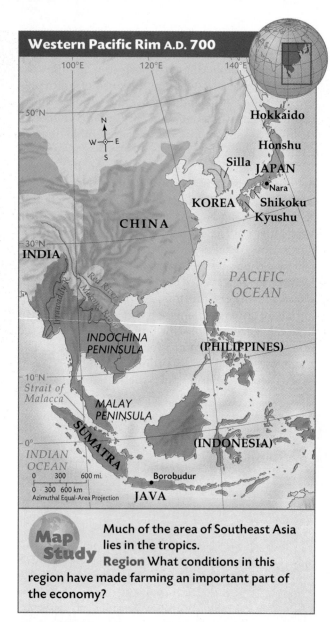

Western Pacific Rim A.D. 700

Map Study

Much of the area of Southeast Asia lies in the tropics.

Region What conditions in this region have made farming an important part of the economy?

In A.D. 39 two Vietnamese sisters called **the Trung**, clad in armor and riding atop elephants, led a successful revolt against the Chinese. For two years Vietnam was independent of China. Then the Chinese returned in greater numbers and defeated the Vietnamese. Rather than surrender to the Chinese, the Trung sisters are said to have drowned themselves in a river.

During the confusion after the overthrow of the Tang dynasty, the Vietnamese took advantage of China's disunity to revolt again. The Chinese sent a fleet of warships to Vietnam to try to subdue the rebels. In A.D. 938, however, under the leadership of **Ngo Quyen** (noo chu•YEHN), the Vietnamese defeated the warships in the Battle of the Bach Dang River. Although Emperor Tai Cong countered this defeat by launching an invasion of Vietnam, the Vietnamese date their independence from the battle, because Tai Cong's invasion failed.

After the Song dynasty gained control of China, the Song emperor threatened the Vietnamese with invasion. To keep peace with China, the Vietnamese agreed to send tribute—gifts—to the Chinese emperor. In return, China agreed not to invade Vietnam. From then on, the Vietnamese ruler called himself emperor at home, but in his messages to the Chinese court he referred to himself merely as a king.

Myanmar

The easternmost area of mainland Southeast Asia today includes the country of Myanmar (Burma). The first peoples to extensively settle most of present-day Myanmar were the Mons and the Tibeto-Burmans. From 200 B.C. to A.D. 100, these two groups gradually occupied different parts of the country. The Mons established villages in southern Burma, while the Tibeto-Burmans lived along the Irrawaddy (IHR•uh•WAH•dee) River in the northern part of the country. Although they developed their own traditions, the Mons and the Tibeto-Burmans accepted Buddhism and other aspects of Indian culture from visiting South Asian sailors and traders.

During the 500s B.C., the Tibeto-Burmans became the dominant group and pushed the Mons southward. In A.D. 849 they set up a capital city called **Pagan** (pah•GAHN), which eventually became a center of Buddhist learning and culture. By the A.D. 1200s, skilled architects had transformed Pagan from a small settlement into a city of elaborate Buddhist temples and monasteries.

During the A.D. 1200s, the Mongol armies of Kublai Khan captured Pagan and ended its glory. To escape Mongol rule, many Burmans moved into

language, although in writing it they used Chinese characters. Even though the Chinese controlled Vietnam almost continuously from about 200 B.C. to A.D. 939, the Vietnamese fought hard to retain—and then to regain—their independence.

> **"** The Viets [Vietnamese] were very difficult to defeat. They did not come out to fight, but hid in their familiar mountains and used the jungle like a weapon. As a result, neither side could win.... The Viets would raid suddenly, rob and get away fast, so that just as our army obtained its supplies from the home base, the Viets obtained theirs from our army. **"**
>
> —Chinese general, c. 200 B.C.

the southern part of Myanmar. There they founded fortified towns along the rivers between their ruined capital and the Andaman Sea. Although Burman culture was preserved, a united kingdom did not arise again in Myanmar until the A.D. 1500s.

The Thai

More than four out of every five people who live in the Southeast Asian country of Thailand today belong to the ethnic group called Thai. They are descendants of people who began migrating south from China about A.D. 700. About A.D. 1238 the Thai established their first kingdom at **Sukhothai** (SOO•kah•TY) in the north-central part of the country.

Sukhothai

The Sukhothai kingdom lasted only about 100 years, but it was known for its wise leaders. The kingdom's greatest monarch, King **Ramkhamhaeng** (rahm•KAHM•hong), ruled from A.D. 1275 to A.D. 1317. He made Sukhothai into a center of learning and the arts. During Ramkhamhaeng's reign, the Thai developed an alphabet and writing system based on the Khmer script. Artisans from China taught the making of porcelain, and Buddhist monks from South Asia won most of the Thai people to Buddhism. Beautiful Buddhist temples, with many levels of roofs, rose gracefully above the skyline of Sukhothai. Even during Ramkhamhaeng's lifetime, the Thai saw his reign as a golden age. A stone pillar erected in A.D. 1292 and still standing has the following words engraved on it:

" This Sukhothai is good. In the water there are fish. In the fields there is rice. The king does not levy a [tax] on his people.... Who wants to trade in elephants, trades. Who wants to trade in horses, trades. Who wants to trade in gold and silver, trades.... **"**

Ayutthaya

In A.D. 1350 a prince named Ramathibodi (rah•MAH•thee•BOH•dee) overthrew the last Sukhothai ruler and founded a new kingdom known as **Ayutthaya** (ah•YOO•thy•yuh). He set up his capital south of Sukhothai and up the Chao Phraya River (chow PRY•uh) from where Bangkok, the present Thai capital, is today.

Wat Mahathat, an ancient Buddhist temple now restored, is in Sukhothai Historic Park, which was opened to the public in 1980. *What was accomplished in Sukhothai's golden age?*

The Ayutthaya kingdom lasted for about 400 years, with a succession of 33 kings. At its height, it held control over large areas of Southeast Asia, including parts of Myanmar and the Malay Peninsula. Like Sukhothai, Ayutthaya was an important center of Buddhist learning and culture. Economically prosperous, Ayutthaya carried on trade in teak wood, salt, spices, and hides with China and neighboring Asian kingdoms.

Seafaring Kingdoms

Many kingdoms in early Southeast Asia developed around strategic ports. The Indonesian islands became a crossroads in the expanding international trade that stretched from the Arabian Peninsula to China. Merchants of many lands—Arabs, Chinese, Indians, and Persians—traded such products as porcelain, textiles, and silk for Southeast Asian spices and valuable woods.

The **Srivijaya** (SHREE•vih•JAY•uh) Empire arose on the islands of Java and Sumatra in present-day Indonesia. Lasting from about A.D. 600 to A.D. 1100, the Srivijaya Empire was one of the region's

The Hindu temple of Ulu Danua on Lake Bratan in the Central Mountains of Bali has a typical thatched roof. *How is Bali's religious heritage different from that of the rest of Indonesia?*

great seafaring powers. It controlled shipping along the Strait of Malacca that separates Sumatra from the Malay Peninsula. By the end of the A.D. 1100s, Srivijaya was reduced to a small kingdom, and the Majapahit (mah•jah•PAH•heet) kingdom began to dominate the Indonesian islands.

From the A.D. 400s to the A.D. 1400s, Buddhism and Hinduism were the dominant religious influences that affected maritime Southeast Asian life. During the early A.D. 1200s Muslim traders from the Arabian Peninsula and India brought Islam to the peoples of the Malay Peninsula and Indonesia.

The first major center of Islam in Southeast Asia was **Melaka**, a port kingdom on the southwestern coast of the Malay Peninsula.

From Melaka, Islam spread throughout the Indonesian islands. The only island to remain outside of Muslim influence was Bali, which has kept its Hindu religion and culture to the present day.

During the A.D. 1500s, a number of Muslim trading kingdoms competed for control of the Indonesian islands. European explorers, beginning with the Portuguese in A.D. 1511, gradually won control by setting local rulers against each other.

SECTION 3 REVIEW

Recall
1. **Define** archipelago, animism.
2. **Identify** the Khmer, Suryavarman II, the Trung sisters, Ngo Quyen, Ramkhamhaeng.
3. **Locate** mainland Southeast Asia on the map on page 354.

Why would the mainland, and not the Indonesian and Philippine archipelagos, be more likely to come under the influence of India and China?

Critical Thinking
4. **Synthesizing Information** How might Buddhism or

Confucianism complement a belief in animism?

Understanding Themes
5. **Cultural Diffusion** What were some of the ways in which the cultures of China and India influenced the peoples of Southeast Asia?

Critical Thinking SKILLS

Making Generalizations

Have you heard statements such as "Only tall people play basketball well" or "Dogs make better pets than cats"? Do you consider the validity of such statements? Or do you accept them at face value?

Learning the Skill

These statements, called generalizations, are broad statements about a topic. To be valid, a generalization must be based on accurate information. Let's examine the generalization "Only tall people play basketball well." Is this accurate? We can find many examples of tall basketball players. However, there are also many shorter players who excel at this sport.

In this case, we began with a generalization and looked for facts to support or disprove it. In other cases, you will make a generalization from a group of facts about a topic. To make a valid generalization, first collect information relevant to the topic. This information must be accurate facts, not opinions.

Suppose that you want to make a generalization about the relative danger of air and automobile travel. First, you would collect accident statistics involving airplanes and cars. Then classify the information into categories. Look for relationships between these categories. For example, you might put the airplane and automobile statistics in separate categories. You might also categorize the number of accidents and the number of fatalities. Finally, make a generalization that is consistent with most of the information.

Practicing the Skill

Read the passage about literature in the Tang dynasty and answer the questions that follow.

“ Xuanzang welcomed artists to his splendid court.... Two of China's greatest poets, Duo Fu and Li Bo, produced their works in Xuanzang's court. Scholars compiled encyclopedias, dictionaries, and official histories of China. Writers popularized stories about ghosts, crime, and love. And while European monks were still slowly and laboriously copying texts by hand, Chinese Buddhist monks invented the more efficient technique of block printing. ”

1. What facts about literature in the Tang dynasty are presented?
2. Organize these facts into categories.
3. How does the invention of block printing relate to the other facts?
4. What generalization can you make about literature during the Tang dynasty?

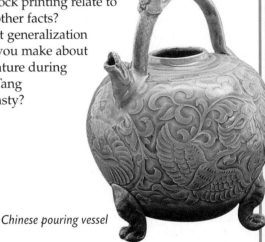

Chinese pouring vessel

Applying the Skill

Review the information in the chapter about religion in China, Cambodia, Vietnam, Korea, and Japan. Write a generalization about religion in East and Southeast Asia. Then support your generalization with at least five facts.

For More Practice

Turn to the Skill Practice in the Chapter Review on page 371 for more practice in making generalizations.

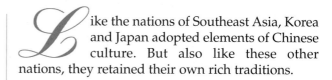

A.D. 400	A.D. 1000	A.D. 1600

c. A.D. 400 Yamato clan founds Japanese imperial dynasty.

A.D. 668 The Silla kingdom conquers all of Korea.

A.D. 1274 Mongols make first attempt to invade Japan.

A.D. 1336 The Ashikaga family rules in Japan.

Section 4

Korea and Japan

Setting the Scene

▶ **Terms to Define**
shamanism, shogun, shogunate, samurai, daimyo

▶ **People to Meet**
Sejong, Yi-Sun-shin, Prince Shotoku, Lady Shikibu Murasaki, Yoritomo Minamoto

▶ **Places to Locate**
Heian Kyo (Kyoto)

 **Find Out** How did the Koreans and the Japanese accept China's culture?

The Storyteller

Zeami Motokiyo was adamant as he lectured his students. "Actors are not thoughtless mimics incapable of intellectualism or philosophy. We seek excellence, as do courtiers and men of letters." Motokiyo had been developing a new form of drama, the Noh play, that had uplifting stories and moral lessons, aspects that appealed to the educated upper classes. "Actors must always bear in mind the correct balance between mental and physical actions. An actor, using his intelligence, will make his presentation seem beautiful." Motokiyo wanted his actors to think as well as to rehearse.

—adapted from *Sources of Japanese Tradition,* Ryusaku Tsunoda, reprinted in *Sources of World History,* Volume 1, edited by Mark A. Kishlansky, 1994

Noh theater mask

Like the nations of Southeast Asia, Korea and Japan adopted elements of Chinese culture. But also like these other nations, they retained their own rich traditions.

Korea

A glance at Korea on the map on page 354 will reveal why a Korean proverb describes the country as "a shrimp between whales." Korea forms a peninsula on the east coast of Asia, extending south toward the western tip of Japan. Thus, it acts as a bridge between its two neighbors, China and Japan.

Early History

By legend, the Koreans claim descent from Tangun, the son of a bear and a god who supposedly founded the first Korean kingdom 5,000 years ago. Historians believe that the first Korean people were immigrants from northern Asia. These settlers lived in villages, grew rice, and made tools and other implements of bronze. They were animists who practiced shamanism, a belief that good and evil spirits inhabit both living and nonliving things. Shamans, or priests, interceded between the spirit world and humans.

In 109 B.C. China first invaded Korea, putting Korea under the control of the Han dynasty. From 109 B.C. until the fall of the Han dynasty in A.D. 220, Korea was dominated by China. But after the fall of the Han dynasty, Koreans regained control of their peninsula and, by A.D. 313, eventually formed three kingdoms—Silla, Paekche (pah•EHK•chee), and Koguryo. During the Three Kingdoms period, from 57 B.C. to A.D. 668, the Koreans adopted many elements of Chinese culture. Among these were Confucianism, Buddhism, calligraphy, and ideas about government.

Koreans also used Chinese knowledge of arts and sciences to make their own unique creations. For example, in the A.D. 300s, Koguryo artists produced mammoth cave art murals. In Silla, Queen Sondok built an astronomical observatory that still stands today and is the oldest observatory in Asia.

In A.D. 668 the kingdom of Silla conquered all of Korea, ushering in a period of peace, prosperity, and creativity. Korean potters produced superb porcelain decorated with flower designs. Koreans also created a unique mask dance that expressed sentiments of shamanism and Buddhism, which had been adopted as the state religion in A.D. 528. Over a 16-year period, Korean scholars compiled the *Tripitaka Koreana*, the largest collection of Buddhist scriptures in the world today. The *Tripitaka* has 81,258 large wooden printing plates.

The Yi Dynasty

In A.D. 1392 a dynasty called the Yi came to power in Korea. The Yi called their kingdom Choson and built Hanyang—today the city of Seoul—as their capital. They opened schools to teach Chinese classics to civil service candidates and made neo-Confucianism the state doctrine.

The adoption of Korean neo-Confucianism deeply affected people's roles and relationships. According to Korean Confucian doctrine, the eldest son in each family was bound by duty to serve his parents until their death. Korean women—who had been accorded high status under shamanism and Buddhism—were given much lower standing under Korean Confucianism. In fact, women from the higher ranks of society had to stay indoors until nightfall, when a great bell signaled the closing of the city gates. Even then, to go out they had to obtain permission from their husbands.

One of the greatest Yi rulers, King **Sejong**, had two significant accomplishments. He ordered bronze instruments to be used in measuring rain. As a result, Korea now has the oldest record of rainfall in the world. He and his advisers made a greater contribution by creating simplified writing to spread literacy. Together they devised *hangul*, an alphabet that uses 14 consonants and 10 vowels to represent Korean sounds. Although scholars continued to write with Chinese characters after the invention of *hangul*, writers began using *hangul* to transcribe folk tales and popular literature.

Although the Japanese tried to capture Korea in A.D. 1592, the Yi dynasty managed to successfully rebuff the Japanese invaders, mainly because of an invention created by Korea's Admiral **Yi-Sun-shin**. The admiral's ironclad warships, or "turtle ships," devastated the Japanese fleet. The Koreans won the war. However, in the years that followed, they increasingly avoided contact with the outside world and isolated themselves so totally that Korea became known as the Hermit Kingdom.

Japan

Just 110 miles (204 km) east of Korea lies the Japanese archipelago. As the map on page 354 shows, Japan consists of four large islands—Honshu, Shikoku, Kyushu, and Hokkaido—and many smaller ones.

Visualizing History Shown here is the world's oldest astronomical observatory in Asia. It was built at Silla, Korea, from 365 stones. *How much territory did the kingdom of Silla hold by A.D. 668?*

Mount Fuji and Ashinto (lake) at Hayoke, Japan. *How did the physical beauty of the land affect Japanese art?*

Island Geography

Because of its island geography, Japanese culture formed mostly in isolation from mainland Asian cultures, except for that of China. Although the Japanese borrowed from Chinese civilization, their customs and traditions were different from those of most other Asian peoples.

The geography of these islands influenced the formation of Japanese culture in other ways as well. Because much of the land is mountainous—less than 20 percent of it is suitable for farming—the Japanese learned to get most of their food from the sea. They also learned to rely on the sea for protection from invaders—being a natural barrier to invasion from the mainland—and yet to regard it as a route of transport between the islands. The physical beauty of the land inspired deep reverence for nature in works by many Japanese painters and poets. Because these islands are located in an area where earthquakes, typhoons, floods, and volcanic eruptions are frequent, the Japanese long ago created a myth that helped to explain the stormy weather there.

Creation Myth

An ancient Japanese creation myth is the oldest explanation for the origins of Japan, its turbulent weather, and its first emperor. According to the myth, brother and sister gods Izanagi and Izanami dipped a spear into the churning sea. When they pulled it out, the drops of brine that fell upon the water's surface became the islands of Japan. The two gods then created the sun goddess Amaterasu, and because they loved her best of all their children, they sent her to heaven to rule over the world. Next they created Tsuki-yumi, the moon god, and Susanowo, the storm god, to be her companions.

Amaterasu gave life to everything around her. But Susanowo, who had a fierce temper, ruined his sister's rice crop and so frightened her that she hid in a cave. Without her in heaven, the world became dark. The other gods placed a jewel and a mirror on a tree outside the cave to coax Amaterasu back outside. When she came out and told them why she had hidden, the other gods banished Susanowo to the earth.

According to the myth, Susanowo's descendants were the first inhabitants of Japan. Amaterasu sent her grandson, Ninigi, to govern these descendants on the island of Honshu. So that all would acknowledge his divine power, she sent with him her mirror, her jewel, and a great sword. According to legend, Ninigi's grandson, Jimmu, conquered the rest of Susanowo's descendants in 660 B.C., becoming the first emperor of Japan.

By tradition, each successive emperor has received Amaterasu's three gifts: a mirror, a jewel, and a sword. Also by tradition, each emperor—until Hirohito—has claimed to be Amaterasu's descendant. In 1945, after the Japanese defeat in

World War II, Emperor Hirohito announced that he did not possess divine status.

Early Inhabitants

Among the first people to inhabit the Japanese islands were hunter-gatherers who came there from the mainland more than 10,000 years ago. These people had developed the technology to make pottery but not to make bronze or iron. When Koreans and others from mainland Asia invaded Japan during the 200s B.C. and 100s B.C., they were easily able to defeat the early inhabitants by using iron and bronze weapons.

The invaders introduced the islanders to agricultural methods, such as how to grow rice in flooded paddies. Heavy summer rains in Japan made it the ideal place to grow rice, which soon became Japan's most important crop.

Between A.D. 200 and A.D. 300, another influx of mainlanders came to Japan. According to scholars, these armor-clad warriors who fought on horseback were probably the ancestors of the aristocratic warriors and imperial family of Japan referred to in the creation myth.

In early Japan, though, even before there was an emperor or an imperial family, separate clans ruled their own regions. Clan members practiced a form of animism called Shinto, meaning "the way of the gods." Each clan included a group of families descended from a common ancestor, often said to have been an animal or a god. The clan worshiped this ancestor as its special *kami*, or spirit. Practitioners of Shinto believed that *kami* dwelled within people, animals, and even nonliving objects such as rocks and streams. To honor this *kami*—and the *kami* of their ancestors—they held festivals and rituals. Often these ceremonies were conducted by the chief of the clan, who acted as both military leader and priest.

The Yamato Clan

By about A.D. 400, the military skill and prestige of the Yamato clan, which claimed descent from Amaterasu, enabled it to extend a loose rule over most of Japan. Although other clans continued to rule their own lands, they owed their loyalty to the Yamato chief. In effect, he became the emperor.

Initially, the emperor had a great deal of political power. By the A.D. mid-500s, however, the emperor had become more of a ceremonial figure who carried out religious rituals. The real political power was held by the members of the Soga

---

CONNECTIONS

The Arts

The Art of Feudal Japan

Kiyomatsu, a samurai hero

In A.D. 1185 the rise of military rule in Japan ushered in a new style of art. Japan's shoguns, daimyo, and samurai wanted to see paintings that reflected and glorified their military values. Artists and writers responded by creating art forms highlighting the skill and bravery of soldiers.

Paintings from the Japanese feudal era often show warriors in richly patterned clothing, riding magnificent horses and wielding long swords. The expressions chosen for the rider and his horse often communicate wild, but disciplined, emotions aroused in the moment just before charging into battle. By posing the figures as if on the verge of battle—rather than at rest—artists give their paintings an active quality. The splendor of the soldier coupled with the dramatic intensity of the moment imparted a sense of glamor to doing battle. This artistic approach appealed greatly to a military patron of the arts.

MAKING THE CONNECTION

1. What things identify the subject of this painting as a samurai warrior?
2. Choose one military value reflected in this painting. Explain how the artist has managed to convey this value.

family. The emperors kept their position as heads of Japan because people believed that only they could intercede with the gods. But the Soga family controlled the country.

Chinese Influences

In A.D. 552 a Korean king sent a statue of the Buddha and some Buddhist texts to the Japanese court. The king wrote, "This religion is the most excellent of all teachings" and suggested that the emperor make Buddhism the national religion. Buddhism had come to Korea from China, and its introduction to Japan made the Japanese open to Chinese culture. This curiosity about China was especially strong among Japan's nobles and scholars.

Through a kind of cultural exchange program that lasted four centuries, the Japanese learned much from the Chinese. Not only did they learn about the teachings of the Buddha, they also learned a great deal about Chinese art, medicine, astronomy, and philosophy. They incorporated much of this knowledge into Japanese culture. For instance, the Japanese adopted the Chinese characters for writing to create their own writing system.

Prince Shotoku was responsible for much of this cultural exchange. When he became the leading court official in A.D. 593, he instituted programs that encouraged further learning from Chinese civilization. He ordered the construction of Buddhist monasteries and temples and sent officials and students to China to study. When Shotoku heard about the Chinese Confucian ideas of government, he wrote a constitution for Japan in which he set forth general principles that explained how government officials should act.

After Shotoku's death, the Fujiwara family seized power in the name of the emperor and began to urge him to pattern the government more closely on that of China. China had a strong central government at that time.

In A.D. 646 government officials instituted the Taika reforms, or "Great Change." These reforms attempted to do what the Fujiwara family had begun. They proclaimed that all the land was the property of the emperor rather than clan leaders. Clan leaders could oversee the peasants working the land, but they could no longer assign them land or collect taxes from them. Instead, government officials were to allocate plots to peasants and collect part of their harvest in taxes for the emperor.

Although these reforms were somewhat effective at increasing the central government's control over the clans, most clan leaders refused to give up their land. Even after the Taika reforms, Japan remained much divided under the control of regional clan leaders.

The Nara Period

Greater government centralization did not take place until A.D. 710, when Japan built its first permanent capital at Nara. A smaller version of China's Changan, Nara had an imperial palace, broad streets, large public squares, rows of Chinese-style homes, and Buddhist temples.

With the completion of the colossal Todaiji Temple at Nara in A.D. 752, Buddhist fervor in Japan reached its peak. Buddhism, however, did not replace Shinto, for each religion met different needs. Shinto linked the Japanese to nature and their homeland. Buddhism promised spiritual rewards to the good. Therefore, people practiced both.

During the Nara period, the Japanese also produced their first written literature. Scribes wrote histories of ancient Japan that combined the creation myths with actual events. Other writers compiled collections of Japanese poems.

The Heian Period

In A.D. 794 the Japanese established a new capital, **Heian Kyo**, "the City of Peace and Tranquillity," later called **Kyoto**. For more than 1,000 years, this city remained the capital of Japan.

A century after the city was founded, Japan stopped sending cultural missions to China. In the period that followed, a small group of about 3,000 Japanese aristocrats, calling themselves "dwellers among the clouds," created Heian culture.

The focus of Heian court life was the pursuit of

AROUND THE WORLD   Temple of Kailasa

India, A.D. 760
Emperor Krishna of the Rashtrakuta dynasty ordered construction of the Kailasa Temple at Ellora. The temple, completed in A.D. 760, was cut from a single outcropping of rock. It was 165 feet (50 m) long and 96 feet (29 m) high. Kailasa was dedicated to the Hindu god Siva. Its elaborate carvings featured Hindu gods and mythological figures in various poses.

INDIA

• Ellora

The Lady Fujitsubo Watching Prince Genji Departing in the Moonlight by A. Hiroshige and U. Toyokuni, A.D. 1853. *What author may have written the world's first novel,* The Tale of Genji?

beauty. It pervaded all of life's activities, from wrapping presents to mixing perfumes and colors. People devoted hours each day to writing letters in the form of poems. Calligraphy was as important as the poem itself, for a person's handwriting was taken to be an indication of his or her character. People were even said to fall in love upon seeing each other's handwriting.

During the Heian period, women were the creators of Japan's first great prose literature. **Lady Shikibu Murasaki** wrote *The Tale of Genji*, which some believe to be the world's first novel. The novelist chronicles the life and loves of a fictional prince named Genji. Filled with poems about the beauty of nature, *The Tale of Genji* quickly became very popular.

The Heian aristocrats were so deeply involved in their search for beauty, however, that they neglected tasks of government. Order began breaking down in the provinces. Warlike provincial leaders started running their estates as independent territories, ignoring the emperor's officials and refusing to pay taxes. Thus the Heian aristocrats eventually lost control of the empire completely.

The Way of the Warrior

As Heian power faded, two powerful court families, the Taira and the Minamoto, struggled for control. The families fought a decisive battle in A.D. 1185 in which the Taira were defeated. To **Yoritomo Minamoto**, head of the Minamoto family, the emperor then gave the title shogun, or "general," and delegated to him most of the real political and military power. While the emperor remained with his court in the capital of Kyoto carrying on ritual tasks, Yoritomo and his soldiers ran a shogunate, or military government, from Kamakura near present-day Tokyo.

The shogunate proved to be quite strong. Even though Kublai Khan tried twice to invade Japan— once in A.D. 1274 and again in A.D. 1281—he did not succeed. On the first occasion, Japanese warriors and the threat of a storm forced the Mongols to withdraw. On the second occasion, 150,000 Mongol warriors came by ship, but a typhoon arose and destroyed the fleet. The Japanese thought of the storm as the *kamikaze*, or "divine wind," and took it to be confirmation that their islands were indeed sacred.

In A.D. 1336 the Ashikaga family gained control of the shogunate. But the family failed to get control of regional warriors. Japan soon broke into individual warring states, leaving the shogun and the emperor as mere figureheads.

The powerful landowner-warriors in the countryside were called samurai. The most powerful samurai became daimyo (DY•mee•OH), or lords. Like the medieval knights of feudal Europe who pledged their loyalty to lords, samurai pledged their loyalty and military service to their daimyo. There were many samurai and many daimyo. Poor

Friends mourn the death of the Buddha in this Japanese painting.

How was Buddhism introduced to Japan?

rice farmers paid high taxes for the right to farm a daimyo's lands. In return, that daimyo provided the farmers with protection. The system in which large landholders give protection to people in exchange for their services is called feudalism. Japanese feudalism was similar to European feudalism as described in Chapter 12.

The samurai fought on horseback with bows, arrows, and steel swords. They dressed in loose-fitting armor. The samurai followed a strict code of honor called Bushido, meaning "the way of the warrior." Bushido stressed bravery, self-discipline, and loyalty. It demanded that the samurai endure suffering and defend his honor at all costs. If a samurai was dishonored or defeated, he was expected to commit suicide.

Japanese women too could be warriors. This passage from *The Tale of the Heike* describes a female Minamoto samurai:

“ Tomoe had long black hair and a fair complexion, and her face was very lovely; moreover she was a fearless rider whom neither the fiercest horse nor the roughest ground could dismay, and so dexterously did she handle sword and bow that she was a match for a thousand warriors and fit to meet either god or devil. Many times

had she ... won matchless renown in encounters with the bravest captains, and so in this last fight, when all the others had been slain or had fled, among the last seven there rode Tomoe. ”
—*The Tale of the Heike*, A.D. 1200s

Growth of a Merchant Class

Despite the political turmoil during its feudal period, Japan developed economically at this time. Workshops on daimyo estates produced arms, armor, and iron tools. Each region began to specialize in goods such as pottery, paper, textiles, and lacquerware. Trade increased between regions.

The increasing trade led to the growth of towns around the castles of the daimyos. Merchants and artisans formed guilds to promote their interests—just as they did in medieval Europe. These guilds, called *za* in Japan, benefited their members in many ways. A *za* might pay a fee to exempt its members from paying tolls for shipping their goods. Over a long period of time, this exemption would save the members quite a bit of money.

Japanese merchants began to trade with Chinese and Korean merchants. Chinese copper coins became the chief means of exchange. The Japanese exported raw materials such as lumber, pearls, and gold, as well as finished goods such as swords and painted fans. The Japanese imported items such as medicines, books, and pictures.

Religion and the Arts

By the A.D. 1200s Buddhism had spread from the nobles to the common people. The opening words of *The Tale of the Heike* describe the Buddhist sentiments that were prevalent in Japan during its feudal period:

“ In the sound of the bell of the Gion Temple echoes the impermanence of all things. The pale hue of the flowers of the teak tree show the truth that they who prosper must fall. The proud do not last long, but vanish like a spring-night's dream. And the mighty ones too will perish in the end, like dust before the wind. ”

During Japan's feudal age, Buddhist teachings were simplified and gave rise to many religious groups. The new varieties of Buddhism all taught about a personal afterlife in paradise. The way to paradise, they stated, was through simple trust in the Buddha. With salvation so easily available, the influence of priests, monks, and nuns declined. For

Zen Buddhist monks sit in a meditation garden at Ryoanji Temple in Kyoto, Japan. *To a Zen Buddhist, what is the purpose of meditation?*

the first time, the common people began to play an important role in Buddhist life. With widespread support, Japanese Buddhist groups linked religion with patriotism. Some believed that Japanese Buddhism was the only true Buddhism and that Japan was the center of the universe.

While the common people turned to new forms of Buddhism, the samurai followed a form of Buddhism called Zen. The Japanese scholar Eisai had brought Zen to Japan from China late in the A.D. 1100s. Zen taught that the individual had to live in harmony with nature and that this harmony could be achieved through a deep religious understanding called enlightenment. The followers of Zen rejected book learning and logical thought, embracing instead bodily discipline and meditation. They believed that by meditation a student could free his mind and arrive at enlightenment.

Zen was particularly useful for warriors because it taught them to act instinctively, and thinking was a hindrance to action. Samurai could improve skills such as archery by freeing their minds from distractions to better concentrate on the object or target.

Zen also perfected art forms and rituals such as ikebana, or flower arranging, meditation gardens, and the tea ceremony. Ikebana grew out of the religious custom of placing flowers before images of the Buddha. The Zen practice of meditation gave rise to meditation gardens, consisting of carefully placed rocks surrounded by neatly raked sand.

Meditation also sparked the tea ceremony, an elegant, studied ritual for serving tea. One tea master said of the ceremony that it was intended to "cleanse the senses … so that the mind itself is cleansed from defilements." These and other arts and rituals derived from Buddhism are still popular in Japan today.

SECTION 4 REVIEW

Recall

1. **Define** shamanism, shogun, shogunate, samurai, daimyo.

2. **Identify** Sejong, Yi-Sun-shin, Amaterasu, Jimmu, Shinto, Prince Shotoku, Taika reforms, Lady Shikibu Murasaki, Yoritomo Minamoto, Bushido.

3. **Explain** What is traditionally given to each new emperor of Japan? Why?

Critical Thinking

4. **Evaluating Information** Which would you prefer to follow, the ideals of the Heian court or the samurai code of Bushido? Why? What effects do you think each viewpoint might have had on the people of Japan?

Understanding Themes

5. **Innovation** Identify one Chinese innovation that the Koreans or Japanese borrowed, and describe how they made it their own.

Louis S. Glanzman

Serious Sport

In this illustration of an ancient Mayan game a rubber ball bounces off the leather pad on the player's chest. The object was to drive the ball through a stone ring, but players could not throw or bat the ball. They had to hit it off a leather pad on their elbow, wrist, torso, or hip. Making a goal was so rare that when a player scored, crowds rewarded the hero with all their clothing and jewelry—unless they could first flee.

Scholars believe that these games were played not only for sport but also on special holidays as ritual reenactments of Mayan raids. Large cities contained numerous walled courts lined with images of warfare and sacrificial victims. According to Mayan religious beliefs, ordinary humans could never outwit death, and so the Mayan ball court became a symbolic meeting ground—a kind of threshold between earth and the underworld. ●

Writings

The Maya were one of the first Native American peoples to develop a writing system. They wrote in accordion-folded books made of flattened bark covered with a thin layer of plaster. Four of these books have survived. They also carved inscriptions in clay, and on jade, bone, shells, and large stone monuments. Only within the past 25 years have linguists made major breakthroughs in translating Mayan writing. Linguists discovered that some inscriptions are phonetic syllables, while others represent full words. The Maya recorded the genealogy of their kings and royal families, mythology, history, ritual practices, and trade.

Collapse

By A.D. 900 the Maya in the lowlands showed signs of collapse. They stopped building and moved elsewhere. Why this happened is unclear. There is evidence of increasing conflict and warfare among Mayan royal and nonroyal families. Outsiders were also attacking. Agricultural breakdown, perhaps caused by warfare or by erosion and over-farming, may have produced rising malnutrition, sickness, and death rates.

Visualizing History The Teotihuacáno rain god Tlaloc is shown in an *incensario* (container for burning incense) from A.D. 400–700. *Where was the Teotihuacáno civilization located?*

Other Mesoamericans

In a high fertile valley 30 miles (48 km) northeast of present-day Mexico City, **the Teotihuacános** (TAY•oh•TEE•wuh•KAHN•ohs) flourished for about 750 years. By A.D. 100, they dominated the centrally located Mexican Plateau. At its height their main city, **Teotihuacán**, had an estimated 120,000 to 200,000 inhabitants.

Teotihuacán was laid out on a grid. The most important buildings were built along the north-south axis. Excavations of the ruins have revealed 600 pyramids, 2,000 apartment compounds, 500 workshop areas, and a huge marketplace. A valuable source of obsidian was found near Teotihuacán. Obsidian, a volcanic glass, was used for sharp-edged tools, arrow points, and other objects. It was easily traded, because Teotihuacán lay on the trade routes east to the Gulf of Mexico.

Teotihuacán declined about A.D. 750. Historians still are uncertain about the reasons for its decline. Drought may have been the cause, or invasion by **the Toltec**, a people from the north.

With a powerful army, the Toltec conquered land as far south as the Yucatán Peninsula. The Toltec capital of **Tula** was the center of a powerful mining and trading empire. Their gods Quetzalcoatl (ket•suhl•KWAH•tuhl), the "plumed serpent" god of the air, and Tezcatlipoca (tehz•KAHT•lee•POH•kuh), the god of war, would be adopted by the Aztec, a later Mesoamerican group. When invaders destroyed Tula in A.D. 1170, the Toltec Empire collapsed.

SECTION 2 REVIEW

Recall
1. **Define** jaguar, slash-and-burn farming, obsidian.
2. **Identify** the Olmec, the Maya, the Teotihuacános, the Toltec, Quetzalcoatl.
3. **Use** the map on page 390 to locate the area settled by the Maya. What large city did the Maya establish? On what landform was it located?

Critical Thinking
4. **Synthesizing Information** What common features linked the Mesoamerican civilizations?

Understanding Themes
5. **Innovation** What were some of the major achievements of the Mesoamerican civilizations?

The Maya

Some 2,000 years ago, the lowland Mayan civilization of what is now Central America flourished. A society dating to 1200 B.C., the Maya developed the most complex writing system in the Americas, built majestic temple-pyramids and palaces, and mastered astronomy and mathematics. Then suddenly, in the A.D. 800s, the record of life in the region fell silent: The people stopped erecting monuments, carving hieroglyphic texts, and making pottery. Their cities lay in ruins, their fields and villages were abandoned to the jungle, and the great civilization of the Maya vanished.

What happened to end the golden age of the Maya more than a thousand years ago? To answer that question, in 1989 an international team of archaeologists, sponsored in part by the National Geographic Society and Vanderbilt University, went to the Petexbatún rain forest of northern Guatemala. Amid the ruins of the ancient city of Dos Pilas, the team set to work on one of archaeology's greatest mysteries.

Enrico Ferorelli

Enrico Ferorelli

NGS Cartographic Division

After setting up a fully functioning camp complete with a computer lab and drafting workstations, scientists began their task. They studied thousands of potsherds, scores of monuments, bone fragments, spearheads, trash heaps, and miles of fortifications of Dos Pilas—built by renegades from the great Mayan center of Tikal—and nearby cities.

One spectacular find that told the fate of the Maya was a hieroglyphic stairway. Five limestone steps, about 20 feet wide, each with two rows of glyphs carved on the risers, climb to the base of the royal palace near the main plaza at Dos Pilas. Experts at deciphering glyphs were on hand to translate each glyph as it was uncovered. The story on the steps gives an account of the battles of the first ruler of the Petexbatún (referred to as Ruler 1) against his brother at Tikal, some 65 miles northeast of Dos Pilas.

One of the epigraphists summed up the inscription: "It begins by talking about the 60th birthday of

▨ *A Mayan warrior-king is portrayed on a stela carved in A.D. 731. Discoveries at Dos Pilas have led to new theories on the collapse of the Mayan civilization along the border of Guatemala and Mexico.*

▨ *A stairway of five long steps (top) came to light during excavations at the Dos Pilas site.*

Enrico Ferorelli

⬡ **As Vanderbilt graduate student Stacy Symonds excavated a defensive wall, she discovered the hieroglyphic stairway beneath it. Here she records information about the glyphs.**

Ruler 1, that he danced a ritual dance. As you read down the steps, the glyphs give a historical sequence to his reign. We think Ruler 1 left Tikal and started a splinter kingdom at Dos Pilas. There's an emblem glyph——which is like a political title ——for Tikal, and both brothers claimed it. Ruler 1 was defeated, but then there was another war. This time Dos Pilas won."

Although the glyphs told archaeologists about the origin of a dynasty, what was even more intriguing was a stone wall built on top of the stairs during the kingdom's fall. Less than a hundred years after memorializing their founder, the people of Dos Pilas threw a wall up over his monument in what must have been a desperate attempt to

protect themselves. Why did the people of Dos Pilas build defensive walls, which are rarely found at Mayan sites?

The second and third rulers of Dos Pilas changed traditional warfare when they set forth on campaigns of expansion. Digging a 30-foot shaft into the burial temple of Ruler 2, archaeologists discovered hieroglyphs on fine pottery that offered more clues. These glyphs suggest that Ruler 2, who reigned from A.D. 698 to A.D. 726, expanded the influence of Dos Pilas and gained control of other cities through marriage and political alliances.

Ruler 3 went on to wed a royal lady from the city of Cancuén and to dominate the entire region. He traveled to the cities of Tamarindito, Aguateca, Seibal, and others to perform ceremonies and quell unrest. After Ruler 3 died in A.D. 741, Ruler 4 took control, living mostly at Aguateca—by then a twin capital— which rests on a limestone bluff high above Lake Petexbatún.

In A.D. 761 something went wrong. According to hieroglyphs, the kings of the Petexbatún had overextended their domain. There had been hints of trouble for more than a decade: Ruler 4 had spent much of his 20-year reign racing from one end of the realm to the other, performing bloodletting rituals, leading battles, and contracting alliances. He used every technique to sustain the kingdom, but to no avail.

Then the city of Tamarindito threw off the yoke of Dos Pilas. Hieroglyphs at Tamarindito tell us that its warriors attacked the capital and killed Ruler 4.

About that time the citizens of Dos Pilas made a valiant last stand. In desperation they ripped stones from temples and monuments, including the tomb of Ruler 2 and the hieroglyphic stairway. They tore

down much of the royal palace to build two walls around the central palaces and temples.

The surviving nobles deserted their citizens and fled to Aguateca, proclaiming themselves the new rulers of the kingdom. They chose Aguateca as its final capital because of its defensive location. The people of Aguateca held out for about 50 years, but disappeared in the early A.D. 800s

IN A SPAN of only a few hundred years the kingdom rose, expanded, and collapsed as a succession of kings moved from limited conflict to widespread warfare. Scholars have argued that the Mayan civilization simply outgrew its environment, exhausting the soil and creating environmental and economic stress. But another possibility is that intensive warfare forced the Maya, at least in the Petexbatún area, to move close to fortresses such as Aguateca, where they would have soon run out of fertile land. Perhaps farmers were limited to fortified areas near cities that could provide protection, forcing them to forsake traditional agricultural practices that had sustained them for hundreds of years. The wars must have disrupted trade, upset population distribution, destroyed crops, and killed young farmer-warriors, exacting a huge price.

Scholars have added greatly to our view of Mayan society. Once regarded as a network of ceremonial centers ruled by peaceful priest-kings, Mayan civilization is no longer seen that way. Battle and human sacrifice were aspects of life. Perhaps siege warfare was ultimately too costly for the Maya. For years to come, scientists will study the ruins in the Petexbatún rain forest researching changes that may have contributed to the collapse of the lowland Mayan civilization.

Enrico Ferorelli

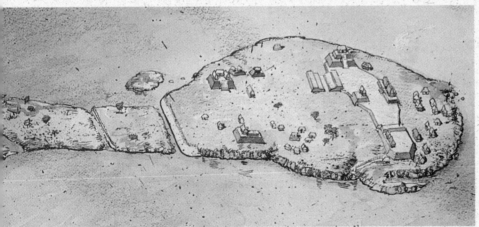

Enrico Ferorelli

■ *In proper Mayan style Dos Pilas's ceremonial precinct (above, top) featured palaces for rulers and temples to the gods. But an apparent golden age came to an abrupt end in A.D. 761 (above, bottom). After the killing of Ruler 4, warfare consumed the region. Residents tore down facades of temples and palaces to raise two walls. A cleared area between the walls likely served as a killing alley. Seeking refuge, farmers moved into the plaza and erected huts. Soon the city was abandoned.*

■ *A peninsula became an island (left, top and bottom) as defenders of the Lake Petexbatún port dug three moats across the neck of land. At the tip of the island, a walled wharf protected a canoe landing. Perhaps the enemy proved too strong or conditions too harsh, for the outpost was abandoned.*

Chapter 15 *The Americas* **387**

A.D. 1325 The Aztec found their capital, Tenochtitlán.

A.D. 1438 The Inca emperor Pachacuti comes to power.

c. A.D. 1500 The Aztec control all of central and southern Mexico.

Section 3

The Aztec and Inca Empires

Setting the Scene

▶ **Terms to Define**
 chinampas, hierarchy, quinoa

▶ **People to Meet**
 the Aztec, the Inca, the Moche, Pachacuti

▶ **Places to Locate**
 Tenochtitlán, Cuzco

 **Find Out** What factors led to the rise and decline of the Aztec and the Inca Empires?

The Storyteller

  Cortés captured many Aztec cities. This Aztec song remembers how it was:
 "Broken spears lie in the roads;
   we have torn our hair in our grief.
 The houses are roofless now, and their walls
   are red with blood....
 We have pounded our hands in despair against
   the adobe walls, for our inheritance, our
   city, is lost and dead.
     The shields of our warriors
       were its defense, but they
       could not save it.
     We have chewed dry twigs
       and salt grasses;
     We have filled our mouths
       with dust and bits of
       adobe; we have eaten
       lizards, rats and
       worms...."

Aztec Stone of the Sun calendar

—from *Sources of World History*, edited by Mark A. Kishlansky, 1995

oth **the Aztec** and **the Inca** were latecomers to power. In scarcely more than 200 years, they transformed themselves from little-known peoples to masters of vast empires. They borrowed from earlier civilizations to create their own distinctive cultures. They developed highly centralized governments and became productive farmers, master builders, artisans, and weavers. Although they held quite different religious beliefs, religion was important to both peoples and motivated their expansion. Both sophisticated civilizations came to sudden ends in the early A.D. 1500s, when they were overwhelmed and destroyed by Spanish invaders from Europe.

The Aztec Empire

The early Aztec were semi-nomadic hunters and warriors who migrated from the north into central Mexico in the A.D. 1200s. They founded what became the capital of their empire in A.D. 1325 on a small, uninhabited island near the western shore of Lake Texcoco. The Aztec named their capital **Tenochtitlán** (tay•NAWCH•teet•LAHN). Today it is the site of Mexico City.

Tenochtitlán

The Aztec turned Tenochtitlán into an agricultural center and marketplace. Since land for farming was scarce on the island, they built *chinampas*, or artificial islands, by piling mud from the bottom of the lake onto rafts secured by stakes. These became floating gardens where farmers grew a variety of crops, including corn and beans. With a plentiful food supply, the population grew and people moved outside the city to the mainland. A network of canals, bridges, and causeways was built to connect the mainland with the capital city.

Empire

Strengthened by early alliances with neighboring city-states, the Aztec then conquered more distant rivals. By A.D. 1500 their empire stretched from north-central Mexico to the border of Guatemala, and from the Atlantic Ocean to the Pacific Ocean. Conquered peoples had to pay heavy tribute in the form of food, clothing, raw materials, and prisoners for sacrifice.

As the Aztec Empire expanded, Tenochtitlán prospered. Estimates of the city's population by A.D. 1500 range from 120,000 to 200,000. Goods and tribute came to the city from all parts of the empire.

Government and Society

The Aztec civilization was organized as a hierarchy—divided into levels of authority, each level more powerful than the level below it. At the top was the emperor. His power came from his control of the army and was reinforced by religious beliefs.

The Aztec social order had four classes: nobility, commoners, serfs, and slaves. Land could be owned by noble families and commoners. Commoners included priests, merchants, artisans, and farmers. Serfs were farmworkers tied to noble lands. The lowest class included criminals and debtors, as well as female and children prisoners of war. Male prisoners of war were sacrificed to the Aztec gods.

Religion

Religion was the driving force behind the Aztec emphasis on war and sacrifice. Borrowing religious beliefs from the Maya and the Toltec, the Aztec believed that live human sacrifices were necessary to keep the gods pleased and to ensure abundant harvests.

Much of Aztec art reflected religious and military themes. The walls of temple-pyramids were decorated with scenes of gods or battles. Poets and writers glorified Aztec gods and the legendary history of the Aztec people. The empire, however, proved to be more fragile than the poets dreamed. Tenochtitlán faced rebellions from its outlying territories that weakened the empire. In A.D. 1521 these groups joined Spanish explorers in invading and destroying Aztec villages and cities.

Footnotes to History

Aztec Markets
The market was a very important economic and social institution for the Aztec. The market at Tlateloco was the largest in the Americas. About 60,000 people may have visited the market daily.

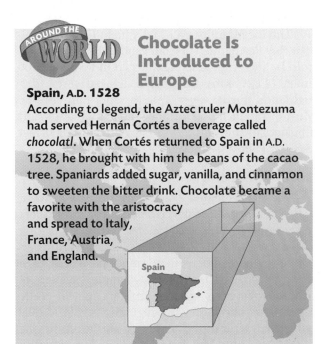

AROUND THE WORLD

Chocolate Is Introduced to Europe

Spain, A.D. 1528
According to legend, the Aztec ruler Montezuma had served Hernán Cortés a beverage called *chocolatl*. When Cortés returned to Spain in A.D. 1528, he brought with him the beans of the cacao tree. Spaniards added sugar, vanilla, and cinnamon to sweeten the bitter drink. Chocolate became a favorite with the aristocracy and spread to Italy, France, Austria, and England.

Spain

The Inca Empire

In South America, along the Pacific coast and in the mountain ranges of the Andes, other civilizations developed independently of those of Mesoamerica. In the late A.D. 1980s, archaeological finds revealed that complex societies first emerged in South America between 3000 B.C. and 2100 B.C., 2,000 years earlier than previously thought and 1,000 years earlier than in Mesoamerica.

One of the early peoples was **the Moche**, who flourished on the north coast of present-day Peru between A.D. 100 and A.D. 600. In A.D. 1987 the discovery of a noble's pyramid tomb proved that the Moche had a social order based on ranks, skilled artisans who produced ornaments of gold, silver, and copper, and religious beliefs that included a sacrifice ceremony.

Rise of the Inca

The Inca began as one of many small tribes competing for scarce fertile land in the highland valleys of the Andes. Around A.D. 1200 the Inca settled in **Cuzco** (KOOS•koh), which became their capital. They raided other tribes and slowly established a powerful empire.

The decisive period of Inca expansion began in A.D. 1438, when **Pachacuti**, the ninth Inca ruler, came to power. He and his son, Topa Inca Yupanqui, have been compared to Philip and Alexander the Great of Macedonia. By persuasion, threats, and force, they extended Inca boundaries far to the north and south.

The Inca Empire eventually included all of present-day Peru, much of Chile, and parts of Ecuador, Bolivia, and Argentina. It stretched more than 2,500 miles (4,020 km) through coastal deserts, dry highlands, fertile river valleys, and rain forests. Most of the Inca lived in the Andes highlands and adjusted to high altitudes. Cuzco was 11,600 feet (3,560 m) above sea level.

Government and Society

Pachacuti created a strong central government to control the vast realm. He permitted local rulers to continue governing conquered territories as long as they were loyal. Rebellious peoples were resettled elsewhere where they could pose less of a threat. Pachacuti instituted a complex system of tribute collections, courts, military posts, trade inspections, and local work regulations to bind outlying territories to the center. To further unite the diverse peoples, the Inca established a common imperial language—Quechua (KEH•chuh•wuh).

The Inca emperor and his officials closely regulated the lives of the common people. As a divine ruler, the emperor owned all land and carefully regulated the growing and distribution of foods, such as potatoes and quinoa (KEEN•WAH), a protein-rich grain. Under the emperor's direction, Inca officials supervised work crews in the building of a network of roads and woven fiber suspension bridges that linked the various parts of the empire.

As a divine ruler, the Inca emperor was believed to have contact with the deities. Like the Aztec, the Inca believed in many deities, including a creator god and a sun god, whom they worshiped in a variety of religious ceremonies. Food and animals were typical sacrificial offerings, but human sacrifices were also made for special events. In A.D. 1995 archaeologists working in the ice fields of the Peruvian Andes discovered the frozen, carefully preserved body of a teenage Inca girl. The food fragments and pottery shards in the girl's coffin seemed to indicate that she was a sacrificial victim

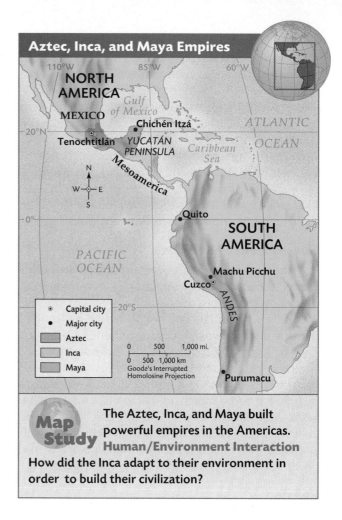

Aztec, Inca, and Maya Empires

Legend:
- Capital city
- Major city
- Aztec
- Inca
- Maya

0   500   1,000 mi.
0   500 1,000 km
Goode's Interrupted Homolosine Projection

Map Study The Aztec, Inca, and Maya built powerful empires in the Americas. **Human/Environment Interaction** How did the Inca adapt to their environment in order to build their civilization?

offered by Inca priests to appease the gods.

Inca Decline

The obedient, well-disciplined Inca would prove to be no match for the Spanish conquerors who arrived in South America in A.D. 1533. In spite of fierce resistance, the Inca Empire declined and eventually disappeared. Aspects of Inca culture, however, have survived among the Inca descendants living today in western areas of South America.

SECTION 3 REVIEW

Recall
1. **Define** chinampas, hierarchy, quinoa.
2. **Identify** the Aztec, the Inca, the Moche, Pachacuti.
3. **Use** the maps in the Atlas to describe the physical geography of Mexico and western

South America. How did geography affect the early civilizations that arose in each of these two areas?

Critical Thinking
4. **Synthesizing Information** What do modern nations take as tribute after a war? How is

this the same as or different from the tribute paid by Aztec people?

Understanding Themes
5. **Change** Contrast the methods used by the Aztec and the Inca to expand and administer their vast empires.

Critical Thinking SKILLS

Hypothesizing

Imagine that half your history class failed a chapter test. The rest of the students, with one exception, received a grade of D. Can you think of any explanations for this poor showing? Perhaps there was a big basketball game the night before the test, and students spent too little time reviewing. Perhaps the chapter contained a large amount of new information that was difficult to learn. Each possible explanation is called a *hypothesis*.

Learning the Skill

Hypothesizing, or developing possible explanations for events, is an important part of any research process. Each hypothesis forms the basis for further investigation to determine whether it is true or false. In the example above, you could test your hypotheses by interviewing other students to find out why they did so poorly on the test. Once you have more information, you can accept, reject, or revise your hypotheses.

To improve your skill at hypothesizing, first identify the event, trend, or condition you want to explain. Gather information that relates to causes of this event, trend, or condition. Brainstorm all possible hypotheses.

Once you have developed some hypotheses, you have to test each one. There are several ways to do this. First, see if the explanation fits all the known facts. Then, gather more information that can prove or disprove the hypothesis. In the example above, your survey reveals that most of the class attended school events on two evenings just prior to the test, leaving little time for study. This research enables you to revise your explanation.

Practicing the Skill

Read the statement below and answer the questions that follow it.

Despite their great accomplishments, around A.D. 800 the Mayan civilization declined.

1. What event, trend, or condition do you want to explain?
2. What facts do you have that relate to this situation?
3. What are two hypotheses that might explain it?
4. What information could help you prove or disprove each hypothesis?

Applying the Skill

Write a short story using one of the following ideas:

1) You are an archaeologist studying a culture. After finding some unusual artifacts, you hypothesize about the practices and beliefs of the culture.

2) You are a detective investigating a crime. You find some evidence and use it to hypothesize who committed the crime and how.

In either case, include details about the information you need to prove or disprove your hypotheses.

For More Practice

Turn to the Skill Practice in the Chapter Review on page 393 for more practice in hypothesizing.

Artifact— gold chalice

Historical Significance

Throughout the early history of the Americas, Native Americans established a variety of cultures and civilizations. The environment gave these peoples spiritual strength and economic support. Regarding the earth as sacred, they used the land's natural resources to develop agriculture, build ceremonial centers, and advance trade. Several Native American groups in Mesoamerica and South America formed vast empires that linked diverse peoples and spread new ideas and products.

The cultural aspects of these empires are still held by Native Americans living today in Mexico, Central America, and South America. In recent years, Native Americans in North America have reclaimed much of their heritage that had been suppressed with the advance of European civilization in the Americas.

Using Key Terms

Write the key term that completes each sentence.

a. *chinampas*	f. maize
b. weirs	g. obsidian
c. quinoa	h. potlatches
d. confederation	i. hierarchy
e. jaguar	j. slash-and-burn farming

1. Around A.D. 1500 the Cayuga, Mohawk, Oneida, Onondaga, and Seneca formed a _____, or loose union.
2. Aztec society was based on a _____, which consisted of the emperor, nobles, commoners, serfs, and slaves.
3. Because of the scarcity of land to farm, the Aztec devised a way of making _____, or artificial islands.
4. Among Native Americans of the Pacific Northwest, the wealth of each lineage group was given away at _____.
5. Many Olmec jade carvings show the features of a large spotted wild cat called a _____.
6. The early Olmec practiced a form of agriculture known as _____.
7. Groups in Mexico and Central America used _____, a volcanic glass, to make sharp-edged tools, arrow points, and other objects.
8. By about 5000 B.C., hunter-gatherers in the highland area of present-day Mexico had discovered that the seeds of _____ could be planted.
9. Native Americans in the Pacific Northwest developed ways to harvest salmon with elaborate wooden traps called _____.
10. Native Americans in the Andes mountain ranges grew _____, a protein-rich grain.

Using Your History Journal

Parallel to your time line of important dates in Native American civilizations, add a time line of significant civilizations and achievements in Africa, Asia, and Europe. Use dates from the Unit 3 Digest on pages 394–397.

Reviewing Facts

1. **Explain** how the food resources of Native Americans along the California coast differed from those of Native Americans living in the Great Basin.
2. **Discuss** how the people of southwestern North America adapted to the desert.
3. **Identify** the purposes or possible uses of the large earthen mounds left by the Mound Builders of the Eastern Woodlands.
4. **Name** the two principal sites where excavations have revealed an ancient Olmec culture.
5. **Describe** the four books that have survived from the Mayan civilization.
6. **Identify** the events in the early A.D. 1500s that were responsible for the sudden end to the Inca and the Aztec civilizations.
7. **Explain** the scientific fields in which the Maya excelled.
8. **State** what was unique about the location and geography of the Aztec city of Tenochtitlán.
9. **Discuss** how Inca emperors worked to unify their empire.

Critical Thinking

1. **Apply** How do climate and geography affect the development of a civilization?
2. **Analyze** How did the rise and decline of the Aztec and Inca Empires differ?
3. **Synthesize** What were some daily activities of the Eastern Woodlands peoples?
4. **Analyze** High in the Andes mountain ranges, the city of Machu Picchu was the last refuge of the Inca. Why did Inca rulers retreat to a city in such a remote location?

Ruins of Machu Picchu

Understanding Themes

1. **Relation to the Environment** How did Native Americans in the Eastern Woodlands differ from the Native Americans of the Great Plains? How were they similar?
2. **Innovation** What were some of the cultural achievements of the Mayan civilization?
3. **Change** How did the arrival of the Spaniards in the Americas affect the development of the Aztec and Inca civilizations?

Linking Past and Present

1. What impact do Native American traditions have on life in the Americas today? In what ways has modern civilization been affected by the early Native Americans?
2. Religion played an important role in early American and other ancient civilizations. What role does religion have in modern societies?
3. Why did ancient civilizations decline? Would the same factors lead to the weakening of civilization today?

Skill Practice

Stelae are vertical shafts of stone, about the height of a human being. They have been found among the ruins of several civilizations around the world. Many stelae found in Mayan ruins were sculpted with portraits and carved with hieroglyphics; archaeologists believe that each stela commemorates a ruler. The Mayan monuments were destroyed, leaving only fragments that archaeologists have put together. Suggest as many hypotheses as you can for this destruction. What evidence would help you prove or disprove your hypotheses?

Geography in History

1. **Movement** Refer to the map below. In the A.D. 1500s and A.D. 1600s Native American civilizations declined as the whole region came under the rule of powerful European nation-states. The triangular trade linked four continents between A.D. 1600 and A.D. 1760. How did trade change the population of the Caribbean Islands?
2. **Human/Environment Interaction** How did farming change when crops such as sugarcane began to be raised for trade?
3. **Movement** What positive and negative changes resulted from the cultural contact of peoples from four different continents?

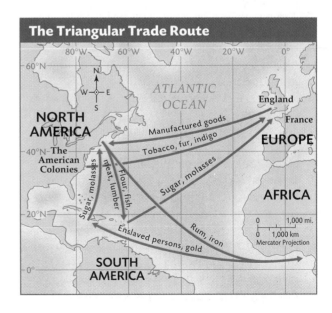

The Triangular Trade Route

The period from A.D. 500 to A.D. 1500 was one of growth in many areas of the world. Expanded trade routes and missionaries' journeys spread intellectual, cultural, and religious beliefs from one people to another. Such contact between cultures caused conflict that lasted for decades, even centuries; yet at other times, ideas and ideals were peacefully assimilated.

Chapter 10
Byzantines and Slavs

When the Roman Empire was divided in A.D. 395, the eastern half became known as the Byzantine Empire. One of the most advanced civilizations of its time, Byzantine culture blended Greek teachings, Christianity, and influences from Eastern cultures. Emperor Justinian, seeking to restore the Roman Empire, reconquered lands that had been taken by Germanic invaders. He also created great architectural masterpieces in the capital city of Constantinople. But his greatest contribution to posterity was his revision of Roman law known as the Justinian Code.

Following its founding, the Byzantine Empire was repeatedly attacked. In A.D. 1054 after centuries of conflict, the Church, divided over papal rule, split into two separate bodies: the Roman Catholic Church in the west and the Eastern Orthodox Church in the east. The empire, weakened by this schism, was further pressured in the west by Christian Crusaders who had conquered part of

Italy, and in the east by attacking Seljuk Turks.

Byzantine culture was spread north by traders and missionaries, who converted the Slavic peoples to Christianity. Schools, churches, and monasteries were constructed in towns and villages throughout the countryside, attracting many Christian converts. Kiev, a fortress-village on the Dnieper River, became the first center of Eastern Slavic civilization. In A.D. 911 Kiev made a trade agreement with the Byzantines, establishing the city as an important trade link between Europe and Asia. But in A.D. 1240, Kiev was destroyed by Mongol invaders in an invasion that isolated the Eastern Slavs from Western influence. The Mongols did, however, allow the Slavs to continue to practice their Christian religion and to govern themselves. Mongols allowed special privileges to the Russian state of Muscovy and its capital, Moscow. Muscovy declared itself the center of the Eastern Orthodox Church after Constantinople fell in A.D. 1453. The Russian czar Ivan III proclaimed Russia the "Third Rome," the protector of Eastern Christianity.

SURVEYING CHAPTER 10

1. **Relating Ideas** What cultural influences shaped the development of the Byzantine Empire?
2. **Identifying Trends** How was the Eastern Orthodox Church affected by the decline of the Byzantine Empire?

Chapter 11
Islamic Civilization

While the Byzantine influence was spreading Christianity, another religion was emerging on the Arabian Peninsula. In A.D. 610 Muhammad, a businessman in Makkah, experienced a revelation from Allah (the Arabic name for God), and spread the religion called Islam. Muhammad's religion called for devotion to one God and preparation for the judgment day. Suffering persecution, Muhammad and his followers, known as Muslims, fled Makkah and settled in the town of Madinah. Muhammad

Visualizing History These silver inlaid bronze weights were used by merchants in the **Byzantine Empire.** *What two cities were major centers of trade between the Byzantines and Slavs?*

created an Islamic state in Madinah, putting Islamic law above tribal law.

Muslims eventually won control of Makkah and extended their influence throughout the Arabian Peninsula. The holy book of Islam, the Quran, relates the revelation of God to Muhammad. It outlines moral values and guidelines for daily life and presents the five pillars of Islam: faith, prayer, almsgiving, fasting, and pilgrimage to Makkah.

Islam spread through the efforts of caliphs, the successors of Muhammad. Their military expeditions carried Islam throughout the weakened Byzantine and Persian Empires. While Islam's cultural influence widened abroad, it also suffered from internal strife. Following years of struggle, Islam split into two separate factions, the Sunni and the Shiite.

The Umayyad dynasty (A.D. 661–750) ruled the Muslim world during a period of tremendous change. Umayyad conquerors carried Islam eastward to India and China, as well as to North Africa and Europe. The Umayyads were later overthrown by the Abbasids, who established the capital city of Baghdad.

During Islam's early centuries, Muslim scholars preserved Greek philosophy and made advances in mathematics, astronomy, geometry, and medicine. Islamic art, architecture, and literature were also deeply influenced by religion. In later centuries western Europe would reflect all these advances.

Visualizing History Throughout the Islamic world, building complexes known as mosques serve as places of worship, centers of education, courts of law, and shelters. *What are the Five Pillars of Islam?*

SURVEYING CHAPTER 11

1. **Explain** What were the two major points of Muhammad's preaching?
2. **Relating Ideas** What were the major cultural contributions of the Islamic Empire?

Chapter 12
The Rise of Medieval Europe

Compared with the Byzantine and Islamic societies of this period, western European culture was relatively backward. This period in western European history has, in fact, been referred to as the Dark Ages. Yet many forces were combining to create a new civilization in Europe.

Charlemagne, king of the Franks (A.D. 768–814) and Holy Roman emperor (A.D. 800–814), united most of Europe for the first time since the fall of Rome. Charlemagne also strengthened the ties between the pope and the monarchy. However, within 50 years of his death, Charlemagne's empire was destroyed by internal strife and external invasion.

The feudal system evolved in Europe as a means of protection against such invaders as Muslims and Vikings. Feudalism joined loyalty between lord and vassals to ownership of land and military service. It provided for mutual protection in an age of conflict. Individual fiefs had their own political and legal rules but had no allegiance to and got no support from a central government. Because the fiefdoms and their knights spent much of their time warring among themselves, trade was limited. The manorial system, onto which feudalism was grafted, formed a self-sustaining unit. Each lord, in his castle on his manor, could in theory dispense with trade.

The Church exerted strong influence, both religious and political, over daily life in the Middle Ages. In A.D. 520 a monk named Benedict established a model monastery at Monte Cassino in Italy. Benedict's monks lived simply, prayed and meditated, and worked in the monastery. Although apart from society, they influenced it by preserving religious writings, establishing schools, and teaching various skills to peasants. Missionaries began spreading Christianity throughout Europe.

Although medieval kings were generally weak rulers, William the Conqueror and his successors began to strengthen the English monarchy. In A.D. 1215 the Magna Carta, the great charter of English

This illuminated manuscript depicts scenes from the life of Charlemagne, including his coronation. *How long after Charlemagne's death did his empire last?*

political and civil liberties, placed some limits on the king's growing power. A council called Parliament was formed to advise the monarch and pass laws. In France, too, the monarchy was strengthened under Philip II and his grandson, Louis IX. Louis's grandson, Philip IV, established the Estates-General.

While England and France were strengthening their monarchies, the Holy Roman Empire based in Germany continued to struggle with the papacy. A compromise was reached at Worms, but power struggles between popes and emperors continued.

SURVEYING CHAPTER 12

1. **Relating Ideas** What were the major features of feudalism as it developed in early medieval Europe?
2. **Making Comparisons** How did the development of monarchy in England and France differ from the development of monarchy in the Holy Roman Empire?

Chapter 13
Medieval Europe at Its Height

When the Seljuk Turks conquered Jerusalem, Christian pilgrimages were forbidden. The Byzantine emperor's call for help to Pope Urban II resulted in a series of Christian military expeditions to the Holy Land known as Crusades. In A.D. 1099 warriors of the First Crusade recaptured Jerusalem.

Other crusades followed, but the goal of making the Holy Land Christian did not succeed in the long run. The Crusades did, however, open Europe to new ways of life and stimulated trade.

Around A.D. 1000 Europe's economy began to revive. Innovations in agriculture increased food production. As trade expanded through annual fairs, banking and a money economy were established. Towns soon grew up along trade routes. Merchants and artisans founded guilds to regulate commerce and protect their interests. Merchants' guilds could buy materials cheaply and keep prices up. Craft guilds set standards for membership, training, quality, and prices.

The money economy created a new wealthy middle class, the bourgeoisie. This class gained political power that led to the decline of the feudal system. The rising middle class also influenced the growth of art, literature, and the universities. Intellectual movements such as scholasticism flourished.

The Hundred Years' War between England and France (A.D. 1337–1453) grew out of a feudal dispute between the English and French monarchies over control of lands in France. England won the major battles, including Crécy, Poitiers, and Agincourt, but in the end was driven out of France. After the long off-and-on war, the French monarchy was firmly established. King Louis XI strengthened the French bureaucracy and created a unified state in France. In Spain, Christians were engaged in reconquering lands taken earlier by the Muslims. Meanwhile, the Holy Roman Empire continued its struggle with the papacy, which was experiencing its own problems.

The Babylonian Captivity, as it was called,